Wisdom Teachings of the Mahāyāna

THE COMPLETE WORKS OF SANGHARAKSHITA include all his previously published work, as well as talks, seminars, and writings published here for the first time. The collection represents the definitive edition of his life's work as Buddhist writer and teacher. For further details, including the contents of each volume, please turn to the 'Guide' on pp. 797–805.

FOUNDATION

1 A Survey of Buddhism / The Buddha's Noble Eightfold Path
2 The Three Jewels I
3 The Three Jewels II
4 The Bodhisattva Ideal
5 The Purpose and Practice of Buddhist Meditation
6 The Essential Sangharakshita

INDIA

7 Crossing the Stream: India Writings I
8 Beating the Dharma Drum: India Writings II
9 Dr Ambedkar and the Revival of Buddhism I
10 Dr Ambedkar and the Revival of Buddhism II

THE WEST

11 A New Buddhist Movement I
12 A New Buddhist Movement II
13 Eastern and Western Traditions

COMMENTARY

14 The Eternal Legacy / Wisdom Beyond Words
15 Pāli Canon Teachings and Translations
16 Mahāyāna Myths and Stories
17 Wisdom Teachings of the Mahāyāna
18 Milarepa and the Art of Discipleship I
19 Milarepa and the Art of Discipleship II

MEMOIRS

20 The Rainbow Road from Tooting Broadway to Kalimpong
21 Facing Mount Kanchenjunga
22 In the Sign of the Golden Wheel
23 Moving Against the Stream
24 Through Buddhist Eyes

POETRY AND THE ARTS

25 Poems and Short Stories
26 Aphorisms, the Arts, and Late Writings

27 Concordance and Appendices

COMPLETE WORKS 17 **COMMENTARY**

Sangharakshita
Wisdom Teachings of the Mahāyāna

EDITED BY PABODHANA

Windhorse Publications
38 Newmarket Road
Cambridge CB5 8DT

info@windhorsepublications.com
www.windhorsepublications.com

First published in 2023.

Cover design by Dhammarati
Cover images: Front: *Buddhist deity: Gokei Monju (Manjushri)*, Freer Gallery of Art. Back flap: Sangharakshita leading a women's study seminar at Padmaloka, June 1980, Urgyen Sangharakshita Trust.

Typesetting and layout by Tarajyoti
Printed by Bell & Bain Ltd, Glasgow

British Library Cataloguing in Publication Data:
A catalogue record for this book is available from the British Library.

ISBN 978-1-915342-00-3 (paperback)
ISBN 978-1-911407-99-7 (hardback)

CONTENTS

List of Illustrations x
Editorial Note xi
Acknowledgements xv
Foreword, Vajradevi xvi
Editorial Note xxvi

OFFERING THE MANDALA 1

THE WAY TO WISDOM 3

Editorial Note 5
Introduction 10

1 Faith 17
2 Vigour 58
3 Mindfulness 79
4 Concentration 113
5 Wisdom 127

VERSES TO TĀRĀ 139

Editorial Note 141

Candragomin's Flower-Garland Hymn to the Goddess Tārā 143

LIVING ETHICALLY 149

Editorial Note 151
Introduction 153

1 Friendship 178
2 Generosity 198
3 Sexual Relationships 214
4 Skilful Speech 228
5 The Ethics of Views 241
6 Mental States 265
7 The Results of Actions 292

WRATHFUL DEITIES 311

Introductory Note 313
Editorial Note 315

Invocation to the Wrathful Deities 317

LIVING WISELY 319

Editorial Note 321
Introduction 323

1 The Relationship Between Wisdom and Faith 326
2 The Essence of the Matter 339
3 Images of Emptiness 346
4 Nothing Left at All? 362
5 Elements and Arguments 373
6 Truths and Illusions 382
7 An Adventure With no End in Sight 392
8 To End as we Began 414

TSONGKHAPA'S *THREE CHIEF PATHS* 419

Editorial Note 421
A Note on the Translation 422
Introduction 423

Je Tsongkhapa's Verses on *The Three Chief Paths* 426

KNOW YOUR MIND 429

Editorial Note 431
Introduction 433

1 The First Buddhist Analysts 439
2 Analysing the Path to Enlightenment 455
3 What's the Point? 467
4 The Nature of Mind 481
5 The Perceptual Situation 501
6 A Steady Focus 532
7 The Creative Mind at Work 549
8 Forces of Disintegration 591
9 Factors of Instability 643
10 Unclassifiable Mind 683

Conclusion: Making the Most of Analysis 691
Appendix 699
Further Reading 702

Notes and References 706
Index 779

A Guide to *The Complete Works of Sangharakshita* 797

LIST OF ILLUSTRATIONS

A Seminar at Padmaloka, 1979 xii
Acknowledgements from the 1984 edition of
The Way to Wisdom, by Nagabodhi xiii
Jinananda (1952–2018) xiv
The Bodhisattva Tārā, by Aloka 142
Botticelli (1445–1510), *The Birth of Venus* 223
The wrathful Vajrapāṇi, by Aloka 316
Je Tsongkhapa, by Aloka 425
The Tibetan wheel of life, by Aloka 477
The Mandala of the Five Buddhas, by Aloka 487

EDITORIAL NOTE

Most of the material in this volume of Sangharakshita's *Complete Works* is drawn from three study seminars: one conducted in 1976 and two in 1978. Sangharakshita led well over one hundred such seminars between 1973 and 1990, of which the majority were recorded on audio tape and later transcribed by teams of volunteers, who typed them up, duplicated them, and made the material more widely available for study across the growing Triratna community.

These teachings were conducted at Padmaloka, a large house in the Norfolk village of Surlingham which by the mid-1970s was becoming a training focus for the male wing of the growing Order. In each case, small groups of Order members and Mitras were invited for intensive study seminars of a few days' duration led by Sangharakshita. Vajragupta describes a typical scene:

> Each day they'd sit round in a circle, books in hand, he in robes and carpet slippers, an old reel-to-reel tape machine recording the proceedings, as he guided them carefully through the text, line by line.[1]

The books brought together in this volume provide a representative sample of the kinds of texts Sangharakshita chose to study. There were traditional Buddhist works such as the second-century *Precious Garland* of Nāgārjuna, the source of *Living Ethically* and *Living Wisely*; there were

A seminar at Padmaloka, 1979

commentaries on traditional texts, such as Yeshe Gyaltsen's eighteenth-century commentary on his own *Necklace of Clear Understanding*, the basis of *Know Your Mind*; and very occasionally there was the study of twentieth-century Buddhist scholarship, such as *The Way of Wisdom*, by Edward Conze, the first of the texts included here.

Whatever their focus, the seminars established a body of core teachings drawn from the Buddhist tradition that greatly enriched the fast-developing Triratna community, and did so in ways not limited to their subject matter. Each seminar offered a ground-breaking lesson in how to read a Buddhist text, how to think critically about the teachings, and how to use the exigencies of day-to-day living as a basis for further reflection.

Due to the scarcity of material resources, the seminar transcripts were for many years available only as duplicated copies in their unedited question-and-answer format. In the early 1980s, however, Windhorse Publications was able to publish four selected titles lightly edited by Sangharakshita himself, who freed the transcripts from the inevitable digressions, repetitions, and half-finished sentences of the originals. These comprised *Auspicious Signs*, *Salutation to the Three Jewels*, *The Threefold Refuge*, and *The Way to Wisdom*. These books were budget productions intended specifically for study purposes and each title was limited to a print run of, at most, two hundred copies. The text was produced on golf-ball electric typewriters in lieu of typesetting, and each volume was then professionally printed and bound. Nagabodhi's preface to *The Way to Wisdom*, which is included below, provides a flavour of the conditions under which these early books were produced. The three other edited seminars in the series appear in Sangharakshita's *Complete Works*, vol. 15.

From the mid-1990s, as Windhorse Publications steadily established its profile in the field of Buddhist publishing, a more soundly professional approach became possible. This was when the Spoken Word Project began its close collaboration with Sangharakshita in transforming certain key lectures and seminars into continuous prose targeted at a worldwide readership. The Spoken Word Project's principal editors were Vidyadevi and Jinananda, who between them produced an impressive series of books based on Sangharakshita's seminars and talks, three of which appear in this volume: *Living Ethically* (2009), *Living Wisely* (2013), and *Know Your Mind* (1998).

Acknowledgments

The publication of this seminar transcript comes about once again as a result of a team effort.

As with the seminar of The Threefold Refuge, we have been unable to track down the identity of the person or persons who transcribed the original tape recordings. But our thanks go out to them nevertheless.

The Venerable Sangharakshita edited the transcript, and a very big team of typists retyped his manuscript, mainly during the course of a typing 'marathon' held one weekend at the London Buddhist Centre. Around twenty people came in for a couple of hours, from dawn til dusk, so that the project could be moved forward.

Dharmachari Gunavajra tracked down the rather numerous errors, and Judy Child corrected them. Chris Bennet is responsible for marking up the lion's share of the square brackets.

Chris Kruyper designed the front cover, using an image provided by the British Museum.

And of course, the Venerable Sangharakshita is responsible for the seminar itself: he arranged it and led it, and made the major contribution to it. To him must go the major part of our gratitude.

At this time it is hard to know how popular these edited transcripts will be. For this reason the technology employed is simple, the print-run low, and the price therefore high. Perhaps we will discover that there is enough demand for such texts that we will be able to print bigger runs of properly typeset copy - and charge less. For now we hope that the material will be well appreciated and well-used by those who really want it, and that their enthusiasm will spread throughout the Movement - along with something of the wisdom contained within the pages before you.

Nagabodhi. August 1984

Acknowledgements from the 1984 edition of The Way to Wisdom

JINANANDA (1952–2018)

Jinananda is perhaps best known in the Triratna Buddhist Community for his editing of Sangharakshita's work, but he was also an accomplished author in his own right. His titles include *Warrior of Peace* (2002), a biography of the Buddha; and *Meditating: A Buddhist View* (2012), both published by Windhorse Publications. Under the name of Duncan Steen, Jinananda was also the translator of Sophocles' *Oedipus the King*, recorded on Naxos AudioBooks with Michael Sheen in the title role. His reading of Marcus Aurelius's *Meditations*, again for Naxos, was widely recognized and has sold in the tens of thousands. His first book, *The Essential Englishman*, was published in 1989.

Although Jinananda spent most of his time writing or teaching meditation and aspects of Buddhism, he was far from sedentary by nature. His name, after all, means 'Bliss of the Conqueror'. He was a judo black belt and from time to time wrote on judo for the *Guardian* newspaper. 'When he became ill with cancer', his friend Jinamitra recalls, 'Jinananda would cycle up to Highgate Ponds in north London and swim in winter, and he must be one of the few people to have cycled to his chemotherapy sessions.' In 2017 Jinananda married his partner of many years, Claudia de Campos, a psychotherapist whom he met at the West London Buddhist Centre.

ACKNOWLEDGEMENTS

Acknowledgements specific to the various items that make up this volume will be found in the editorial note accompanying each one. In relation to the volume as a whole, however, particular thanks are due to the following individuals: to Vajradevi for her excellent and very useful foreword; to Aloka for his generosity in offering his illustrations and to Padmajaya for making them so readily available; likewise to Mokshapriya in supplying the photograph of Sangharakshita in seminar and to Tarajyoti for her expertise and good humour in laying out the text; to Nagabodhi for insight into the early days of Windhorse Publications and to Jinamitra for information about his friend Jinananda; to Dhivan and Prasadacarin, whose contributions regarding Sangharakshita's Pāli sources were especially helpful; to Kamalashila for his advice on *Living Wisely*; to Vidyadevi for her skill in the discovery of new texts for inclusion in the volume; and to Shantavira for his steady hand and presence of mind in editing them. Finally, thanks are due to Dhammamegha, Michelle Bernard, Helen Lewis, Walter Monticelli, and the late lamented Lee Walford at Windhorse Publications, for their enduring commitment to making the teachings available in their present form.

FOREWORD

On a convention many years ago, surrounded by hundreds of members of the Triratna Buddhist Order, I listened to Sangharakshita say something that has stayed with me ever since. He reminded us very clearly that 'we should be watching our minds all the time'. If I could have pumped my fist in the air without embarrassing myself, I would have! I was so pleased with this one small sentence, not only because I had followed my nose into this way of working in meditation many years before, but also because, even though Sangharakshita had implicitly alluded to mind-watching in his lectures, seminars, and writings, I had never heard him refer to it so clearly and explicitly.

The books in this volume go a long way towards redressing that imbalance. In fact, one way you could describe Sangharakshita's writings on the mind and Buddhist psychology is that they are all about becoming more and more familiar with the workings of our own minds. And this familiarity seen through the eyes of the Dharma is a path to deepening our understanding of what the mind, and even life itself, are really all about. The teachings offer a path to wisdom and compassion accessible through study, reflection, and especially through the wholehearted practice of meditation.

AN ARRAY OF TEACHINGS

Living Ethically and *Living Wisely* are Sangharakshita's commentary on Nāgārjuna's *Ratnāvalī* (also known as the *Ratnamālā*) or *Precious*

Garland of Advice for a King and were drawn from a seminar given in 1976 and published in 2009 and 2013. *Know Your Mind*, based on *The Necklace of Clear Understanding*, an eighteenth-century Tibetan text translated by Dr Herbert Guenther, preceded them, being published in 1998. It maps the mind, sketching the continents of 'mind' before colouring in countries, towns, rivers, and mountains of 'mental events'. *The Way to Wisdom*, which explores the five spiritual faculties in depth, is something of a secret *terma*.[2] Based on an essay, *Way of Wisdom*, by Dr Edward Conze, this material was delivered on a weekend retreat in October 1978 and published in a very limited edition in 1984. It was then only accessible to the tenacious few who burrowed through the unedited seminar text, or tracked down the single copy tucked away in a corner of the Order Library.

Read together, these four volumes offer an extraordinarily rich and deep array of Dharma teachings and an immensely practical guide to living in line with one's ideals. The teachings progress through ethics, meditation, and wisdom and are as satisfying and stimulating as they are challenging to the intellect, offering much material for continued reflection. However, where the teachings have equal, if not more, value, is from the point of view of the meditator. The material in this volume can greatly contribute to the arising of wisdom and compassion when used in support of *śamatha*, or calming meditation, and *vipaśyanā*, or meditation that helps to bring about insight.

All this comes about through the practice of watching our minds. In being invited to 'watch the mind' we open up a universe within. By looking inwards at our mental functions and capacities such as memory, and even the capacity to think, we can come to know the mind and see what we are usually looking outwards from. This can be a fascinating experience.

WHAT CAN YOU SEE?

As children, my sisters and I were each given a kaleidoscope. By looking through a small hole at one end of a tubular column and twisting the other end slightly, bright shining fragments of colour were visible. Each twist at the base of the tube changed the patterning visible, transforming one complex formation into another, vividly unique. One moment tiny shapes of red, purple, and green predominated, the next, yellow, and orange flashes of colour with perhaps a background of blue or pink. It was a mesmerizing toy, endlessly fascinating, with shapes and forms that were never ever the same.

The mind is just like this, not static but ever-changing, consisting of many different factors. What we call 'mind' is simply different combinations of those mental factors coming together. This means that one aspect of the mind can observe another, or even observe itself. Through mindfulness we can know what's happening not only in the external physical senses, but also through the internal mind sense when we are aware of mental 'objects' such as thinking and remembering. This is what reflexive consciousness, which is essentially awareness, really is. We can use the mind to watch the mind. We can be aware of awareness; we can know that we know.

It's important not to hear this type of language and mistake mind-watching as being all in the head or the brain. After all, the brain is part of the body, and as we are learning through science,[3] we also have a 'gut brain' in the digestive system and many neurons within the heart. It appears that the brain is not just in the head! What is called for, with mindfulness or awareness, is a quality of 'knowing' that is free from a narrow idea of where consciousness rests and which encompasses all our experience – within or 'off' the body–mind system. Body and mind, or matter and mind as Sangharakshita elucidates in *Know Your Mind*, are ultimately not separate but 'symbols for the two poles of the one perceptual situation'.[4]

We need a particular quality of awareness to undertake this type of observation. This is traditionally termed *smṛti* or recollection. 'As a spiritual practice', says Sangharakshita, 'recollection may be said to be about remembering what is really important, what life is really about, and what one is really supposed to be doing. "Why am I here? What am I doing this for?".'[5] Recollecting ourselves right here and now and recollecting our purpose in life as spiritual beings are both essential. We're 'present' rather than off somewhere else in a dream, and we're in touch with an inner direction that is in line with our deepest values. Our usual consciousness is biased in the opposite direction, looking outwards to what I think of as the end of the perceptual process, at the objects of sight, for example, like trees and people and cars. Our usual type of consciousness is often pulled quickly from one thing to another and tends towards superficiality.

This is necessary in our daily life where we tend to come across the same type of objects and because perception easily does the job of recognizing what's in front of it. It simplifies our lives and cuts out a lot of complication. At breakfast, for example, there are the square dry crispy things we know as 'toast', and the hot, brown liquid we relish, called 'coffee' (or tea). As well as knowing what they are, we know quite well what to do with them. But when we are watching the mind, we pay less attention to the objects of the senses than to our subjective experience, and to the inner processes involved in seeing, hearing, or tasting. It's a subtle change but an important one.

RIGHT VIEW

In *Living Wisely*, Sangharakshita asks the rhetorical question, 'How much intellectual knowledge of the Dharma do we need?' His answer might surprise some: 'A lot less than we think,' he says.[6] But, he adds, we need to use the knowledge that we have well. We need to apply that Dharma knowledge to our experience to investigate our own physical and mental processes. But what is Dharma knowledge? One important understanding is that things do not stand alone. Things depend on other things and on causes for their existence. They are conditioned. Similarly, the way we look at things exerts a strong influence on how those things appear to us.

When we apply a Dharmic perspective (which we call right view) to whatever is happening through our senses, it will change the way we think about our experience. We can think of right view not so much as a view in itself but as a benign and open perspective infused with the Buddha's teachings. With awareness and right view, many habitual views and perspectives are seen more clearly. Eventually all our conditioned assumptions, ideas, and opinions come swimming into view and are seen from the standpoint of the Dharma. Then we can see if they hold up to scrutiny! We might notice quite familiar thoughts, feelings, and views such as 'I'm not good enough' or opinions such as 'of course I'm right' or 'it has to be done this way'. And recognizing thoughts as thoughts, or a view as a view, is a powerful tool to understanding how the mind creates its stories and with them a strong sense of self.

Right view allows us to see more clearly into the mind as it creates what Sangharakshita, following Dr Guenther, calls a 'perceptual situation'.[7] We start to see how we create a world through our thoughts and feelings, reinforcing our belief in a sense of self. When we identify in this way with experiences such as views, ideas, feelings, and bodily sensations, we take personally something that is an impersonal and conditioned process. By learning to recognize the processes of identification with experience, we use the conditioned to see through the conditioned. In Sangharakshita's words, we 'get rid of concepts with concepts, dualism by means of dualism'.[8]

ALL THE TIME

It is natural to talk of the mind as if it were a singular 'thing', yet we all know there are many aspects to the mind, and with just a little effort mind and mental events can be observed quite easily. What takes more practise is to make this observation continuous. Sangharakshita alluded to this aspect of mind watching when he said, 'We should be watching our minds all the time.' When a lamp connection is faulty and it flickers on and off, we don't see very much. We can see a lot more when the light is steady and continuously lighting the room. Likewise, when we have continuity of mindfulness it enables us to see more deeply and clearly the patterns and processes in the mind. When we are mindful only intermittently, we miss the connections between experience that allows us to see how one mind-moment of experience conditions another, leading to a deeper understanding of conditionality.

When we watch our minds with a degree of continuity, 'having analyzed well all deeds of body, speech, and mind', as Nāgārjuna's verse puts it,[9] we're able to glimpse the long tails of views and ideas casting their influences at the deepest level of the mind. Like a fascinating kaleidoscope, consciousness changes from moment to moment through conditioned mental states arising because of habits of mind we've repeated over and over again in the past. If an unskilful collection of mind states arises together and we are not aware of it, we are likely to ruminate on them, 'growing' negativity until, almost inevitably, we express them in some unhelpful speech or action. The converse is also true. Through continuous observation we are likely to have more skilful states of mind leading to happiness and freedom from suffering.

Simply being aware of all this is enough to bring about change, but not in the way we might expect. 'Higher spiritual experience',

Sangharakshita reminds us, 'is always going to be more than we can anticipate theoretically. It will always exceed our expectations'.[10] In fact, rather than changing things at a single stroke, awareness with a Dharma perspective can act more akin to a blood-thinning medicine. This type of drug doesn't actually make a blood clot go away but it stops more blood coalescing with it and making it larger. Over time the blood in the clot is naturally reabsorbed into the body. Similarly, each time a wrong view or unhelpful idea is seen for what it is in the present moment, with spaciousness and kindly awareness, simply as an idea in the mind, the view or idea is seen through. It is not augmented and solidified. Eventually (or sometimes suddenly) the idea simply dissolves into clear knowing, and the energy tied up in it is released into the whole body-mind system.

WHAT'S HAPPENING?

Two other qualities are important and work together to support awareness. The first is receptivity, which allows us to notice what's happening without directing our attention to any particular area of experience. And the second is a quality of energy or effort, which is akin to interest or curiosity rather than a strong 'trying' type of energy. Receptivity and curiosity allow us to ask, 'What's actually happening here in this body and mind?' and help us distinguish between our direct experience and the various thoughts and ideas we have about those experiences. We are usually much more familiar with 'thinking about' things, which is quite habitual and active, and so, initially, it can feel counter-intuitive to settle back and simply notice the various happenings within our experience.

In *Know Your Mind, Living Ethically*, and also in *Living Wisely*, we're encouraged to become aware of the narrowness of the 'thinking about' perspective and its interpretive role, especially thinking from a rational scientific frame. This 'band' (like a rainbow) of consciousness is where our sense of self hangs out and tends to dominate. Sangharakshita warns against this tendency of the rational mind to appropriate other bands of consciousness; he says a rainbow doesn't consist solely of orange but of a vivid range of beautiful colours.[11] Perhaps 'dream consciousness' is sunset pink, deep meditative experiences are the blue of lapis lazuli, with wisdom soft yellow or violet? Poetic and symbolic truth could form another band of the rainbow, with the archetypal bodhisattvas expressing a whole range of colour and consciousness.

Awareness itself is another colour in the rainbow that invites a different way of being, distinct from 'thinking about'. Regularly touching into these other realms undermines the deep-seated view that what the rational mind thinks is how things actually are. We learn through our own experience that the rational mind does not have a monopoly on truth. Being open to and inhabiting these other realms enriches and enlivens our practice and opens us to deeper realities.

This openness is by no means vague or aimless, however. When we are able to watch the mind with an unreactive quality of awareness and right view, we can become familiar with the different manifestations of craving, aversion, and delusion. The detailed accounts of skilful and unskilful mind states in this volume help us to recognize them as they arise. This is how we learn from our own experience; for example, how does slyness and concealment, or deceit, feel in the body? Is there contraction or tensing? Does your heart pound? What type of thoughts are present when those states (or others) are uppermost?

This type of practice can take us a long way. We recognize the states themselves – faith, greediness, arrogance, or the desire to conceal something, and many others – and we also notice how we are relating to those states. Do we add more aversion to a state of irritation, or craving, or are we able to be mindfully aware of the state in a way that doesn't whip it up further or try to squash it out of existence? Do we hold tightly to 'positive' states with unseen craving, squeezing the goodness and joy out of them, or are we able to simply hold them in light, open, awareness for as long as they last?

WORKING WITH KARMA

When we are aware not only of the experience, but also how we are with it, we allow the force of accumulated habit to play itself out. If we can meet whatever arises in our experience with a spacious, kindly awareness as well as clear recognition of the mind state and its ethical implications, this will affect future moments. And this is measurable and observable. Take the experience of boredom that Sangharakshita explores in *Living Wisely* for example.

> When you are really bored the best thing you can do is sit down and let yourself experience the boredom more fully. It may not be a deep or satisfying state, but at least you are not indulging in the things with which you usually cover up this kind of experience. Your real state of mind is more nakedly exposed, because for the time being there are no distractions. If you can stay with the experience of boredom, you can try to feel your way through into something deeper, truer, and more spontaneous within yourself.[12]

When we are able to bear with strong destructive emotions rather than act them out or suppress them we usually feel the mind calm down. There is even a certain pleasure and satisfaction in being able to ride the impulse to unskilfulness with a mind that is curious and open about what is happening within it. And while mindfulness can clearly recognize and help minimize unskilful states, awareness has a natural affinity to skilful states such as faith and wisdom that encourages them to flower further. It is as if mindfulness as a skilful state provides good soil for positive qualities to grow.

With a curious and open attitude, question marks start to form around very basic assumptions about what we think we are. Sangharakshita goes into this in his discussion of 'views', which involves not just 'wrong views' but all views in general. To suppose, for example, that 'the relation between body and life can be discussed in terms of their being either one thing or two',[13] becomes harder to justify, as does the view of a unified 'self' neatly divided into body and mind. Mind and body are in fact not separate, and science bears this out. In recent years a lot more has been understood about neuroscience, brain chemistry, and neuroplasticity. One area of confluence of the body and mind, that has had a light shone on it over the past twenty years or so, is trauma, especially 'developmental' or 'relational' trauma.[14] It is now known that human babies don't come into the world with a fully functioning nervous system. It needs to mature in relationship to caring, nurturing, and available adults (usually parents). When this doesn't happen – and there are many reasons for this including parental absence or illness as well as neglect and abuse – there are potentially life-long consequences affecting the complex interrelationship of mental, emotional, and physical conditioning.

This has a direct effect on our practice. To quote Sangharakshita,

> Yes, the ego is an illusion – as many neuroscientists and psychiatrists confirm today – but the question is not whether that can be accepted on a purely conceptual level, but whether the truth of the argument is experienced and absorbed emotionally.[15]

The ability to 'feel' those truths also has ethical implications, as seen, for example, in the need to be careful not to bring a judgemental attitude to our own or others' 'unskilfulness'. Whether another person's 'unskilful' behaviour is a result of an underdeveloped nervous system, or the karmic results of past actions, the best attitude we can bring to them is one of awareness imbued with loving-kindness and right view. Rather than the terms 'skilful' and 'unskilful' I prefer, at times, to talk instead of unhelpful actions of body, speech, and mind that conduce to suffering, or helpful attitudes that lead to greater freedom from suffering.

When we clearly recognize unhelpful thoughts and actions, we start to understand the suffering these mind states cause, and even more so when we identify with them as somehow belonging to 'me'. We need to take responsibility for these unskilful states so that at times we can know on a more experiential – and absolute – level, and with wisdom, that this quality, this mind, and these mind states, do not belong to us: they are 'empty'. There is simply a kaleidoscope – or a shimmering rainbow – of changing sensations, impulses, and feelings.

NEW DIRECTIONS

Among those with whom I have been practising over the years an increasing emphasis has been laid on the importance of connecting with our 'direct experience' in meditation, to be in touch with the live 'stuff' experienced as sensations, or feelings rather than our 'thoughts about' those same experiences. The material in this volume shows that Sangharakshita's emphasis never excluded this essential basis of spiritual practice, and moreover, shows us many ways to cultivate it.

In *The Way to Wisdom*, a whole path is outlined. The work (and joy) of practice spans an arc from a complete reliance on, and addiction to, our physical senses for satisfaction, gradually transitioning to a mind that consists more and more of spiritual faculties. We move from focusing on the pleasure gained from what we see, hear, touch, smell, taste, and think about, to a mind where the dominant and immeasurably more satisfying qualities are faith, energy, stability of mind, mindfulness, and wisdom.

When this happens the work of awareness and right view/wisdom is not done, but it does become a whole lot easier. What is known in each moment is less the back-and-forth of a cyclic path but, increasingly, the naturally conditioned outward-moving spiral.[16] The recognition of faith or energy conditions more moments of these qualities as they arise, and stability of mind allows a deepening and settling. When the conditions are such that it could no longer be otherwise, deeper wisdom unfolds, liberating the whole being from suffering.

At times this can seem like a very distant goal. It is not easy to sustain our motivation to practise, especially where that requires becoming aware – in Sangharakshita's words – of the 'bedrock of the mind'.[17] For all of us there are things about ourselves we would rather not see and it takes courage to face them in order to go beyond ourselves, even when we know it is the only quest that is really worthwhile. So this is an invitation to let Sangharakshita's words accompany you on the journey. He is an invaluable guide, full of wisdom, great depths, compassion, and humour. May you benefit from these texts as I have and enjoy the fruits in your practice and your life.

Vajradevi
Shrewsbury
15 February 2022

EDITORIAL NOTE

In the present volume, the longer books based on Sangharakshita's study seminars are complemented by four short pieces of writing dating from his time in Kalimpong, between 1957 and 1964. Each of the latter pieces has been translated by Sangharakshita from the Tibetan with the help of Dhardo Rimpoche, John Driver, and Mr Trethong. The first of these translations, a short verse on the offering of the mandala (opposite), begins the collection.

OFFERING THE MANDALA

Meru, the king of mountains, on a ground
Of incense, sun and moon, the continents four,
I offer up to the Enlightened One,
Together with the Pure Land's radiant store.
O may all sentient beings, freed from pain,
The bliss of Full Enlightenment obtain!

From '*The Stream of the Immortality-Conferring Nectar of the Esoteric Oral Tradition of the Lama's Bestowal of the White Tara Abhishekha*', rendered according to the explanations of Dhardo Rimpoche.[18]

THE WAY TO WISDOM

EDITORIAL NOTE

The Way to Wisdom is a lightly edited transcript of a study seminar held at Padmaloka on the weekend of 28–29 October 1978. The source text is Edward Conze's *The Way of Wisdom: the Five Spiritual Faculties* (Wheel publication no. 65/66), first published in 1964 by the Buddhist Publication Society, Kandy. Sangharakshita led the seminar and also edited the transcript for publication.

The quotations from Conze's text are followed by page numbers from the 1980 edition of *The Way of Wisdom* instead of the 1964 edition cited above. The endnotes contained in Conze's original text have been labelled (EC). Sangharakshita's own endnotes, added to the first Windhorse edition, have been labelled (S). All other endnotes are new additions for this volume of the *Complete Works*.

Sangharakshita's commentary covers themes that are not always apparent from the section titles in Conze's original, and to help the reader navigate the text, a number of supplementary subheadings have been added. Extra lines from the original transcript have also been reintroduced to mark the beginnings and endings of the weekend's study sessions and thus retain something of the seminar's original setting. Nagabodhi's acknowledgements from the first edition, and included here, provide a further sense of the early days of its publication.

Some quotations from Conze's original text, such as his lengthy discussion of Cervantes' *Don Quixote*, contain material to which Sangharakshita makes no reference. In the seminar transcript,

Sangharakshita himself acknowledges that these detract from the central focus of his commentary, and we have therefore moved them to endnotes as a means of making Sangharakshita's main arguments stand out more strongly.

The Way to Wisdom, published in 1984, retains its original 'transcript' format, but has nonetheless come a long way from the original seminar in its unrevised state. A comparison of its length reveals that Sangharakshita's lightly edited version of *The Way to Wisdom* is nearly 2,000 words longer than the unedited version. Other lightly edited seminars show a similar tendency. This literary intervention on the part of their author confirms these versions' worthiness of inclusion in the *Complete Works* series, unlike seminars in their unedited form, which fall outside that remit.

Apart from its question-and-answer format, and the early date of its publication when compared to the other books in this volume of the *Complete Works*, *The Way to Wisdom* is also unusual in that it is a critique of a modern interpretation of traditional Buddhist doctrine rather than a commentary on a traditional text. The shortcomings, as well as the strengths, of Conze's exposition are clearly apparent and a little more can also be learned about Conze himself, one of the 'great Buddhists of the twentieth century' as Sangharakshita affirms elsewhere.

Along with Sangharakshita, the seminar participants were as follows:

SURATA

Surata was ordained at Padmaloka earlier in 1976 while working on the construction of the London Buddhist Centre. The following year he spent a month in Pune practising yoga with B. K. S. Iyengar. This was the trip that led to Lokamitra's decision to return to Maharashtra the following year to initiate the TBMSG, the movement's Indian wing (see *Complete Works*, vol. 24). Surata took part in the Tuscany ordination retreat of 1982 as part of the Order team, and in 1988 he joined the ordination team at Padmaloka. In 1995 he became a private preceptor and was later a founding member of Triratna's College of Public Preceptors. He performed his first public ordinations at Guhyaloka in 2001. Surata still lives at Padmaloka and works in the men's ordination team.

JOHN WAKEMAN

John Wakeman joined the Triratna Buddhist Order in 1980 with the name Tejananda. Since then he has worked in a vegetarian café in Croydon, helped establish the Bristol Buddhist Centre, of which he was chair for six years, worked for the Karuna Trust, and taught meditation and Dharma in the UK, Europe and the USA. He has been part of the resident team at Vajraloka meditation centre since 1995 and became its chair in 2001. Tejananda is the author of *The Buddhist Path to Awakening*, published by Windhorse Publications in 1999.

SUVAJRA

Suvajra's public ordination took place at Padmaloka on the weekend directly preceding this seminar. He later became chair of the Manchester Buddhist Centre, moving to Padmaloka to join Subhuti and others to form the first men's ordination team in 1989. He was one of five senior Order members who formed the College of Public Preceptors in 1993, at Sangharakshita's request. From 1994 to 2010 he lived in India supporting ordination training for men, and from 2003 he was chair of Bhaja Retreat Centre. In 2014 he moved to Adhisthana, Triratna's rural retreat centre in Herefordshire, England, as one of the companions and helpers to Sangharakshita. Suvajra is the author of a biography of Dhardo Rimpoche: *The Wheel and the Diamond*, Windhorse Publications, Glasgow 1991.

ANDY SKILTON

Andy Skilton was ordained with the name of Sthiramati in 1979. A keen student of Sanskrit and Pāli, he moved to Oxford in 1991 where he went on to publish a translation and study of Śāntideva's *Bodhicaryāvatāra* (with co-translator Kate Crosby) and *A Concise History of Buddhism*, both published by Windhorse Publications. Sthiramati resigned from the Triratna Buddhist Order in 2010 and later became a Senior Research Fellow at King's College London. His numerous works on the history and texts of South and South-east Asian Buddhism include a translation of Harṣa's *Nāgānanda* (*How the Nāgas were Pleased*, New York University Press, New York 2008).

MAHAMATI

Mahamati was ordained in 1977 at the age of 22, after less than a year's contact at the newly-opened Norwich Buddhist Centre. Once ordained he helped Devamitra, the founder of the Norwich Centre, before moving to Padmaloka in Norfolk and then to Sukhavati community in London. Mahamati went on to become Director of the Karuna Trust and later relocated to India working for Karuna and other Dharma activities. Returning to England at the end of the millennium, Mahamati joined the community at Madhyamaloka, where Sangharakshita then lived. During this period he was an International Order Convenor. He remains active as a public preceptor. Latterly, Mahamati has lived in Malvern, a few miles from Adhisthana.

MARK BOWDEN

Mark Bowden was ordained in 1981 with the name Prajnananda. He went on to study theology and religion at university, trained as a teacher, and led classes and courses in hatha yoga, meditation, and Buddhism for many years at Buddhist centres in London and Bristol. Later, he trained in secular mindfulness-based approaches to health and well-being and continues to teach, supervise, and contribute to research.

SUSIDDHI

Like Suvajra, Susiddhi was ordained in the week immediately preceding the seminar on *The Way to Wisdom*. He went on to play a major role in the development of both Glasgow and Sheffield Buddhist Centres, donating his savings and earnings to help buy properties for them. As chair of the Glasgow Buddhist Centre in 1989, Susiddhi began the search for what eventually became Dhanakosa Retreat Centre. He lived in men's communities for many years and was involved in team-based right livelihood businesses including Ink Print and Design in Glasgow and the Rivelin Café and Evolution shop in Sheffield. Susiddhi has been described as an 'essential restraining voice' in the headstrong early days of the Triratna Buddhist Community in Glasgow and was renowned for being a caring and quietly generous man of great integrity. He died in 2018 at the age of 77.

JOS HINCKS

Jos (Josiah) Hincks, also from Glasgow, was a very active Mitra working in and around the newly-opened London Buddhist Centre. Jos attended one other seminar in 1980 but did not go on to join the Order. He eventually became a 'focusing' trainer, specializing in helping artists and performers to engage more effectively with their creative processes.

INTRODUCTION

Day 1: morning

SANGHARAKSHITA: *The Way of Wisdom*[19] is an essay by Dr Edward Conze on the five spiritual faculties. Though short, consisting of no more than twenty pages, the text is quite concentrated, and it will keep us well occupied for all the time that we have at our disposal.

> Spiritual progress depends on the emergence of five cardinal virtues – faith, vigour, mindfulness, concentration and wisdom. The conduct of the ordinary worldling is governed by his sense-based instincts and impulses. As we progress, new, spiritual forces gradually take over, until in the end the five cardinal virtues dominate and shape everything we do, feel and think. (p. 1)

SANGHARAKSHITA: This introductory paragraph really sums it all up very well: it tells us what spiritual progress depends on. Usually people have got a very vague, not to say wishy-washy, idea about spiritual progress and what it consists in, but here we are given a very clear criterion indeed. We are told it depends on the emergence of five cardinal virtues, five '*indriyas*',[20] as the footnote says, 'variously translated by faculties, controlling faculties, spiritual faculties.' Spiritual progress consists in the emergence of these five, that is to say, in the emergence of faith, vigour, mindfulness, concentration, and wisdom, which is very specific indeed. Dr Conze contrasts these five spiritual faculties, or five cardinal virtues, with the sense-based instincts and impulses. This is quite important. Spiritual progress takes place when, instead of being dominated, instead of being shaped, in everything that we do, feel, and think, by our sense-based instincts and impulses, we start depending more and more on the five spiritual faculties. In this way they become more and more emergent; they come more and more definitely into operation: they gradually take over.

So we should try to see what the present situation is, because we are not always very clear about it. We are not usually very clear what is *actually* dominating and shaping everything that we do, feel, and think; we are often unaware of our own motivations. According to what is said here in the text, 'The conduct of the ordinary worldling is governed by his sense-based instincts and impulses,' as a result of which he just goes round and round in the cycle of existence, or 'wheel of life'. (In speaking of 'the ordinary worldling' probably Dr Conze has at the back of his mind the *pṛthagjana*, that is to say, a person who is not an *ārya*. Anyone who falls short of Stream Entry[21] is called a 'worldling'.) We need to reflect upon this, and to realize the extent to which we are governed by these sense-based instincts and impulses. Take, for instance, one that is absolutely basic, the instinct, or the impulse if you like, to eat. Three times a day you eat. Your life is virtually shaped by that, i.e. by the fact that you have to eat. If you make an appointment with someone, at the back of your mind there is the thought, 'I have to leave time for lunch; I have to leave time for tea.' It is there all the time, isn't it? If you are going out somewhere you ask yourself, 'Will I have time to eat first, or shall I eat when I come back?' That thought of eating interweaves with every other thought. If you haven't had anything for a day, or even two or three days, the thought of food becomes absolutely paramount.

Nor is that all. One of the reasons you have to work is to earn so that you can eat. Maybe that's the main reason. If you didn't have to eat your life would be completely different. If you 'fed' on the air you inhale you probably wouldn't feel such a strong need to have a job and to earn money, because food is the basic thing you have to work and earn for. You wouldn't need things like kitchens and cooking utensils, and cups and saucers and plates, and you wouldn't need gas stoves or fuel. There would be no shopping to do. You can see, therefore, the extent to which everything we do, feel, and think is somehow linked with the fact that we have to eat, linked with that particular instinct. This is why fasting is considered quite an important spiritual practice. It just gives us a holiday from eating – even if it's only for a day. As I know from my own experience of fasting, especially in India, when I fasted for a week or ten days, you feel so free. There is so little you have to do. It's as though you have, if not infinite time, certainly an enormous amount of time on your hands if you are not having constantly to think about food, or about eating, or about meals, or even about cooking. These things do really take up a disproportionate amount of our time and energy.

THE X-FACTOR

SANGHARAKSHITA: This is just one simple, basic example – one that we usually overlook – of our sense-based instincts and impulses, and there are all sorts of others there is no need to go into in detail. There is, for instance, what I sometimes call the x-factor. Suppose you ask somebody to do something, and they say they are unable to do it for certain reasons which you know are not the real reason. At the back of their mind there is some factor which is influencing them deeply, but of which they are hardly aware, and it is this sort of factor that I call the x-factor. More often than not, the x-factor is the sex factor. Maybe they promised their girlfriend that they would go out with her that evening, but don't want to admit this to you. Instead, they say they are busy, or they are not feeling very well, or whatever. They will say anything rather than admit the truth. At the back of their mind, very often, there is that factor dominating everything that they do, feel, and think, just as food does.

There are so many things that can be x-factors, on so many different levels. Some people, for example, are very interested in books. If they happen to visit a new town or a new city, or even a new village, what is the first thing they look for? A bookshop! Maybe that factor is unconsciously influencing them the whole time, because that's what they're interested in. In this sort of way the ordinary worldling, as Conze calls him, is governed by his sense-based instincts and impulses, and we don't quite realize this. The ideals we profess usually have a quite minimal, a quite peripheral, effect on our conduct, on our life. What is really dominating – this is not too strong a word – and shaping everything we do, feel, and think are these sense-based instincts and impulses. Therefore we need to be very well aware of ourselves, and just see what is really happening. Otherwise we can so easily deceive ourselves and rationalize.

Thus our instincts and impulses are sense-based, and there are five physical senses. They are based, therefore, on these five physical senses, as well as on what Buddhists call the sixth sense, which is the ordinary mind. Corresponding to the five physical senses, and functioning as their spiritual counterparts, are the five 'spiritual faculties' of faith, vigour, mindfulness, concentration, and wisdom. It is not difficult to see in what sense there is an analogy between them. Normally we are under the domination of our five physical senses plus the mind; but, as we make spiritual progress, these five other faculties, or other senses if you like, come into operation, come into play, and gradually take over, so that our lives, instead of being governed by sense-based instincts and impulses, are increasingly governed by these five higher, spiritual faculties. This is the sign of spiritual progress. When we become aware that we are less and less swayed by the senses and the lower mind, and more and more influenced by the five spiritual faculties, then we can be sure that spiritual progress is actually occurring.

This way of putting it presents the whole situation very neatly and very clearly, and in a way that we can understand. So, 'As we progress, new, spiritual forces gradually take over, until in the end the five cardinal virtues dominate and shape everything we do, feel and think.' One can therefore think of spiritual life itself entirely in terms of the five cardinal virtues or the five spiritual faculties, and quite a lot of early Buddhist literature does just that. You may remember that in Conze's *Buddhist Texts Through the Ages*[22] the selections from the Pāli scriptures are arranged under the five headings of faith, vigour, mindfulness, concentration, and wisdom, because you've really got it all there.

BORN INTO A BODY

SUSIDDHI: I'm a wee bit worried about the word 'instincts'. It is obviously not what's called biological instincts you're speaking about. Do the biological instincts come before the senses?

SANGHARAKSHITA: Biological instincts seem to come before the senses because, though biologists don't agree about them, in a popular, nontechnical sense one can say that they are innate. When the baby is born it's as though even before it has any sense experience, those instincts are there. It cries for food before it has any experience of food. Not that it has a concept of 'food', of course. So the instincts are very deeply rooted indeed. The Buddhist would say that you've got those senses because you've got those instincts. I mean you have got them under the law of karma. Because you wanted that particular sort of experience, therefore you were born or reborn into a body equipped with those particular senses which could give you the sort of satisfaction that you wanted. That's why you are born into a body at all – and a gross physical body at that. If your desires had been more refined you would have been born into a more refined environment, with a more refined 'physical' body, i.e. in a heavenly world – or, in extreme cases, in the opposite case in an animal body, in the animal world. 'Instincts and impulses' cover everything that is blind and unconscious, and unaware of itself. They represent a sort of basic irresistible urge that you're hardly aware of.

SUSIDDHI: I get the feeling that what happens is that a baby starts with a few very strong instincts, but when it develops senses these have to spread out into very, very many, and different, desires and impulses.

SANGHARAKSHITA: Because basically the baby's only instinct or desire or whatever is for nourishment. Such things as food, comfort, warmth, something to support it, i.e. physical security, are very simple. Then, as you say, as it gets older and becomes more conscious of what is going on around it, its instincts, its desires, its needs, start diversifying and, therefore, multiplying. It's as though a more and more complicated net is spun, and you are there right at the centre of all that, as though in a sort of cocoon. Eventually you create your world around yourself in that way. This world is the network of your desires. If you look at it, you can see that your world is made up of the ways in which you satisfy your desires. When you feel at home somewhere, it is because it is a place where you are quite familiar with the ways of fulfilling your desires. You know where all the shops are, you know where the post office is. These are all representative of desires of one kind or another, more or less crudely instinctual. *That's* where you feel at home, i.e. where you know exactly where to lay your hands on anything you may happen to want, and *that's* why you may feel quite uncomfortable in a completely new situation.

MAKING A WORLD

SANGHARAKSHITA: For instance, suppose you are in some strange new centre or community, and don't know where they keep their bread. It will give you a sort of uneasy feeling, won't it? You won't feel quite settled. You will feel almost alienated in that situation. But if someone says, 'Make yourself at home. The bread's in that cupboard; you'll find the tea over there, and the jam....' Gradually, as you settle somewhere, you start making arrangements for the satisfaction of your own most basic needs, whatever they may be. If you are interested in books, you will quickly find the nearest bookshop. Thus all around you, within various distances, are various sources of satisfaction for your own needs, and these, for all effective purposes, make up your world. There are these pinpoints, as it were, with threads stretching between them, and they make a pattern according to the particular nature of your needs, and that's your world. In the case of some people, if they arrive in any new place, what's the first thing they look for? The pubs! They know where the pubs are; that's their world: those five or six, or seven or eight, or nine or ten, pubs in the locality. They feel at home when they've found them, and when they know what sort of beer is sold in each one and what sort of people go there, whether they can have a game of billiards, and so on. In any place, if there's a particular need which you haven't found the means of satisfying, then you don't feel quite easy, quite settled, quite at home. You're not completely in your world.

What happens when you die (just to carry this a stage further) is that your senses are no longer there. The instruments through which you were accustomed to fulfil your desires aren't there any more. The world is no longer there. That network, or framework, within which you were accustomed to satisfy your desires is no longer there, and if you haven't been prepared for this, by meditation and so on, you can feel completely disorientated. This is what the *Tibetan Book of the Dead*[23] and other sources tell us. You are in a sort of empty space with no signposts. You have got desires still, carried over from your previous life, but you have no senses through which to satisfy them. Thus you are in quite a confused sort of state, as you can very well understand.

MAHAMATI: Perhaps one gets a taste of that, on a much lesser level, when one goes away on solitary retreat. You haven't got the normal ways of satisfying your desires.

SANGHARAKSHITA: Yes. But even on solitary retreat you do provide for the most basic need of all, which is food. It's significant that you do this almost unconsciously, because obviously it isn't really a viable alternative, for any length of time, to do without food. At least you take a minimum of food with you, and you do make a few simple cooking arrangements. And of course there's shelter. So even on solitary retreat you are not completely free from needs, and the satisfaction of needs, but you certainly do cut them down very much. Especially you do cut down your need for people, because you are on your own, and that need for people is perhaps one of our biggest needs on different levels: instinctual, emotional and so on. Let's go on.

I
FAITH

FAITH AND FEELING

> Faith is called 'the seed',[24] and without it the plant of spiritual life cannot start at all. Without faith one can, as a matter of fact, do nothing worthwhile at all. This is true not only of Buddhism, but of all religions, and even the pseudo-religions of modern times, such as Communism. And this faith is much more than the mere acceptance of beliefs. It requires the combination of four factors – intellectual, volitional, emotional and social. (p. 1)

SANGHARAKSHITA: 'Faith is called the "seed"'. This is a reference to the *Sutta-Nipāta*. Without faith 'the plant of spiritual life cannot start at all'. Faith is the seed; faith is the starting point. 'Without faith one can, as a matter of fact, do nothing worthwhile at all.' I'm not going to go very much into the meaning of faith, but it is clear that 'Without faith one can do nothing worthwhile at all.' One could even say one can't do *anything* at all. He says, 'nothing worthwhile at all', but you can in fact have a bad faith[25] which can cause you to do a lot of harm. So why is faith so important? How is it that faith is the seed, and that without it one can't really do anything worthwhile?

SUSIDDHI: Without faith you're not emotionally involved, so there's no power.

SANGHARAKSHITA: Yes, it's because of the emotional nature of faith, really. He does mention four factors: intellectual, volitional, emotional, and social, but predominantly faith is an emotional thing. It is a matter of feeling. It is what keeps you moving, keeps you going, keeps you striving. 'This is true' he says, 'not only of Buddhism, but of all religions.' Would you agree with that? That it's true of all religions?

MAHAMATI: Is he thinking that faith gives one some ideal other than just blindly following the senses and one's instincts?

SANGHARAKSHITA: Faith not only gives you an ideal. It's a question of what we can only call faith *in* that ideal. You can entertain an ideal as an abstract intellectual conviction, but unless you have faith – unless you are emotionally moved by it – you won't really do anything about it. In general it seems as though faith is the capacity for being emotionally moved and stirred by something that transcends the senses and even the rational mind – at least for the time being. Certainly there is something of that in all religions. Maybe it isn't always skilful, or very illumined, at least from a Buddhist point of view, but something of that kind is there. And Dr Conze adds, 'even the pseudo-religions of modern times, such as Communism.' Why do you think he calls Communism a pseudo-religion?

SUVAJRA: Perhaps everybody is trying to aspire towards a greater ideal?

SANGHARAKSHITA: But is that pseudo? What makes it a pseudo-religion?

JOHN: There's no spiritual element.

SANGHARAKSHITA: There's no spiritual element. It's as though it stirs up something of an emotional nature very similar, in outward appearance, to religious faith, but it doesn't actually direct it to a definitely spiritual – something of a transcendental – goal. In that sense Communism is a pseudo-religion. You could also say there is something murky about the faith itself, because it can be mixed up with various negative factors, especially hatred, envy, and so on. But again, you could say that of Christian faith. *That* is often mixed up with negative emotional factors too, from a Buddhist point of view. So perhaps there isn't such a clear-cut distinction between the religious and the pseudo-religious as Dr Conze seems to suggest. Perhaps Buddhism would put Christianity, also, among the pseudo-religious, in this respect, if you want to be quite strict.

THE ONE TRUE FAITH

SUSIDDHI: Do you mean guilt is a more negative thing than hate?

SANGHARAKSHITA: In the case of Christianity it is not just a question of guilt or even hate. Christian faith, or faith in Christianity, usually involves a very negative attitude towards other beliefs, other religions. This is something I have experienced in India. If I met a Christian, and if I happened to say that I was a Buddhist, the usual reaction was not 'Oh that's interesting!' but rather one of suspicion, resentment, annoyance, and irritation. That was the standard reaction.

SUSIDDHI: Isn't that a cultural thing, that they were spreading themselves throughout the world, and taking Christianity with them, regarded themselves as a bit above everyone else?

SANGHARAKSHITA: Yes, because they regarded Christianity as above other religions, as the one true faith, and themselves as its representatives.

SUSIDDHI: I thought it was the other way round, actually: that they were the top men in the world, so their religion was the top faith. Christianity is not the only religion that regards itself as the one true faith.

SANGHARAKSHITA: No, it is not. The sort of thing the Christian missionaries used to tell people in India in the old days – it doesn't quite hold good now – was 'Look, who are the most powerful people in the world? It's the Europeans; and among the Europeans it's the British. And why is this? It's because God is pleased with them. God is pleased with them because they are Christians, and following the right path. Therefore God has blessed them. He has blessed them with wealth, blessed them with fine houses and motor cars. This is all God's blessing. But as for you, in India, what have you got? You've got nothing! Why? God is angry with you, because you worship idols!' For illiterate Indians this can be quite a powerful argument, because even in India people are not all that highly spiritual; they do have a tendency to associate religiosity with mundane well-being, just as the Jews did in the Old Testament.[26] They think that material prosperity is a sign of divine approval. So when they hear the Christian missionary preaching they think, 'There must be something in this. We are poor, wretched people; maybe God is angry with us. These European people have all these good things; maybe God is pleased with them.' When you have just this very simple kind of faith in God, what the missionaries say may seem very plausible. I don't know if the missionaries still think that God blesses only those who are Christians, but when I was there in India fourteen or fifteen years ago American missionaries were still saying, 'We are God's own country. God favours us above all other countries because we're the most religious, the most Christian, the most pious nation in the world.' This material prosperity is annexed to the *right faith*. They believe they are culturally and economically superior because they started off with the right religion, because they were religiously superior.

But of course, this superiority is beginning to be a bit doubtful now, because the Arabs are now becoming the really righteous people.[27] Perhaps some people will start thinking, 'Maybe there's something in that. Maybe Allah has blessed them in some special way. After all, God is the ruler of all. God knows what is going to happen. Why did God put the oil especially in the *Arab* countries, in all those countries which were going to become Muslim? He knew! It was all part of his grand design. For those countries which were Muslim, and which were so good and faithful, he would have a reward in store without them knowing it. They would discover oil, and become the richest and most powerful people, or at least among the richest and most powerful people, in the world.' To simple-minded people this sort of argument is quite appealing. If you start off with the idea of a God who is the creator and ruler of the universe it sounds quite plausible.

FRIENDLY PERSUASION

SANGHARAKSHITA: Anyway, we got onto that from the subject of pseudo-religion. Buddhism would perhaps even say that it's not just Communism that is a pseudo-religion, but even Christianity – to the extent that the Christian faith is not completely pure, and often contains very negative emotional elements, or negative emotional factors, where other religions are concerned. This is quite an important point. Buddhism itself does believe there is a difference between right and wrong view, and a Buddhist will certainly think that in holding right views he is better off than – or if you like even superior to – the person who is holding wrong views. He would certainly think that it is better to hold right views rather than wrong views. But on the other hand he wouldn't have a negative attitude toward the person holding the wrong views. He'd like to talk with him: to discuss, to persuade; but not get so angry and so furious as to want to send him to the stake, which is what the Christians did. *That's* the difference. Surely every religion will believe it's in the right. It cannot do other than that. So in a sense you could say there's nothing wrong in believing you are right, and even believing that others are wrong, because you can't both be right, if the propositions you respectively advance are contradictory. But the difference comes in that Buddhism is so deeply convinced of the value of the individual that it cannot contemplate any violation of that. It is so deeply convinced that the individual must understand and see things for himself, that it cannot contemplate any way of changing somebody's opinion, even when it is a wrong opinion, other than by plain and simple discussion in a friendly sort of way. There is no question of forcing him just to say, 'I believe in Buddhism.' That has no value whatever in the eyes of the Buddhist. A Buddhist may believe as strongly, in a way, as any Christian that what he teaches, or what he believes, is right and what others believe is wrong, but he will go about convincing others in a completely different way – which means, really, that even the way in which he believes he is right is different. It's as though the Christian's psychological security is bound up with his being right; but the Buddhist's, apparently, is not, because the Buddhist won't get upset and irritated if others disbelieve what he believes. He won't mind, because he gives first place to the individual. Even if somebody else rejects Buddhism, and disagrees with what he believes in as a Buddhist, he won't get alarmed or upset or irritated. He'll just see another individual trying to work things out in his own way, even though he, as a Buddhist, may think he's quite mistaken. He won't see a sinner, or someone who is deliberately flouting the Will of God, or rejecting God's revelation as the Christian does. He'll just see another individual, who is trying in his own way to get to the bottom of it all, and make sense of it all. He'll just feel like talking with him, and discussing things with him, and just trying to help him clarify his mind.

The Buddhist hopes that by clarifying it he will move in the direction of Buddhism; but if not, never mind: as a Buddhist you don't get upset and irritated. That's the difference.

EVIDENCE AND DOUBT

> 1. *Intellectually*, faith is an assent to doctrines which are not substantiated by immediately available direct factual evidence. To be a matter of faith, a belief must go beyond the available evidence and the believer must be willing and ready to fill up the gaps in the evidence with an attitude of patient and trusting acceptance. Faith, taken in this sense, has two opposites, i.e. a dull unawareness of the things which are worth believing in, and doubt or perplexity. In any kind of religion some assumptions are taken on trust and accepted on the authority of scriptures or teachers. Generally speaking, faith is, however, regarded as only a preliminary step, as a merely provisional state. In due course direct spiritual awareness will know that which faith took on trust, and longed to know. 'Now we see through a glass darkly, but then face to face.' Much time must usually elapse before the virtue of wisdom has become strong enough to support a vigorous insight into the true nature of reality. (pp. 1–2)

SANGHARAKSHITA: Let's go into that a little. 'Intellectually, faith is an assent to doctrines which are not substantiated by immediately available direct factual evidence.' He is making the matter very clear isn't he? 'Doctrines which are not substantiated by immediately available direct factual evidence.' Suppose, for instance, you had never seen an artichoke[28] before and refused to believe there was any such vegetable and I said there was and you asked me to prove it. I could go out into the garden and pick one, because we have some artichokes here, and I could bring it back and show it to you. That is what is meant by 'immediately available'. I don't say I will show you next week, or next year, or after you are dead. It is immediately available as well as being 'direct' – because you can see the artichoke for yourself, 'factual' – because an artichoke is a concrete thing, not something abstract and theoretical, and 'evidence' – because you can't refuse to accept it then. But the doctrines of religions are not like that. 'Faith is an assent to doctrines which are not substantiated by immediately available direct factual evidence.' You can't prove them, or demonstrate them, or show them to be true in the way that you did in the case of the artichoke. 'To be a matter of faith, a belief must go beyond the available evidence' – if there is sufficient evidence then it's no longer a matter of belief but of knowledge – 'and the believer must be willing and ready to fill up the gaps in the evidence with an attitude of patient and trusting acceptance'. That's quite important. The believer is 'patient', because he's prepared to maintain that attitude of faith indefinitely, 'trusting', because he has confidence in the credentials, and the good intentions, of those who are asking him to accept certain things on faith, and there is 'acceptance' on his part because there is a genuine opening of himself to those things which are the objects of faith.

'Faith, taken in this sense, has two opposites, i.e. a dull unawareness of the things which are worth believing in, and doubt or perplexity.' Do you see the difference between these two? First of all, 'dull unawareness of the things which are worth believing in.' One can actually see this state in people. Very often they say, 'There's nothing to believe in.' They adopt a cynical, so-called worldly-wise kind of attitude. They even go so far as to say, 'No one really believes in anything. It's all a matter of self-interest, self-concern. There is nothing beyond that.' In the case of 'doubt or perplexity' you might be confronted by a number of alternative beliefs, and not knowing which one to accept you might experience doubt and perplexity. Or you might have a definite reason, almost, for not believing in a particular doctrine which made it difficult for you to accept it. In this case too there would be doubt and perplexity – or doubt or perplexity.

NO ABSOLUTE KNOWLEDGE

SANGHARAKSHITA: 'In any kind of religion some assumptions are taken on trust and accepted on the authority of scriptures or teachers.' You can't start off knowing everything. You have to take some things on trust. This is not only a condition of religion: it is a condition of life. I think it is quite important to point this out. It is not as though religions are the only things that demand belief, or that require faith. Your life requires faith at every step. For example, you set out for this place, for this weekend. Maybe you caught a train. You had complete faith that the train would be running – a faith that is sometimes shown to be unjustified. You have faith that you will get here: that you are going to continue living; that you aren't going to have a heart attack on the way; that there isn't going to be a collision – even that a ticket will be available. This is all a matter of faith. You don't *know*. You may ring up from your home to enquire whether the trains are running, and the answer may be yes, but there's no guarantee that something won't happen to stop them running by the time you get to the station. There may be a strike. Anyone can call a strike in half an hour. That's plenty of time, nowadays, in which to hold a strike, or for things to go wrong in some other way. So our whole life is grounded on faith at every step; on a more or less reasonable faith: not on absolute knowledge. It's very rarely based on knowledge. This is something which needs to be borne in mind. It is not that only religions demand faith. Life itself demands faith. You can't live without faith. If you have too much of a sceptical, anxious, disbelieving attitude that wants to know the reasons for everything, and to be sure of everything in advance before you do it, you will cripple and inhibit yourself. There are some things which you just can't know in advance, can't be sure of. You have to take a chance. In other words, you have to have faith. So, 'In any kind of religion,' as in life in general, 'some assumptions are taken on trust and accepted on the authority of scriptures or teachers.' The difference, of course, is that what you take on trust in the case of religion pertains to a realm of experience other than that of this world. When you have faith within the context of ordinary life, it's faith with regard to other things on the same level, as it were; but when you have faith with regard to spiritual things it's faith with regard to things existing on a different level about which you are told by scriptures or teachers. But there is no real difference in principle.

'THROUGH A GLASS DARKLY'

SANGHARAKSHITA: 'Generally speaking, faith is, however, regarded as only a preliminary step, as a merely provisional state. In due course direct spiritual awareness will know that which faith took on trust, and longed to know. "Now we see through a glass darkly, but then face to face."' Where does that quotation come from?

JOHN: St Paul.[29]

SANGHARAKSHITA: Yes, St Paul. So when St Paul says, 'Now we see through a glass darkly, but then face to face' what does he mean by 'now'? When is 'now'?

JOHN: The time when you have faith.

SANGHARAKSHITA: No, he's not quite thinking that. When he says 'now' he's thinking of this life. So when is 'then'?

SEVERAL VOICES: After death.

SANGHARAKSHITA: After death. There's a bit of a difference here. In the case of Buddhism, because Buddhism doesn't teach that faith is provisional until such time that you're dead and stand in front of God. According to Buddhism it's provisional until such time that you have your own personal experience, which you can have in this life itself as a result of your own spiritual efforts. Thus there is some difference here.

MAHAMATI: It's quite sort of pessimistic, St Paul's point of view, that you can only see through a glass darkly.

SANGHARAKSHITA: Yes. According to Buddhism, too, there is a difference between seeing through a glass darkly and seeing face to face, but it's a distinction which does, or which can, obtain within this life itself. You don't have to wait until you die. If you have to wait until you die then the whole thing, i.e. the whole content of faith, becomes very uncertain, because there's no possibility of verification. Nobody apparently comes back to say, 'This is what happened.' Well there are one or two stories about people who did come back. There is a story, which has been shown to be legendary, of how St Bruno, the founder of the Carthusian order, became a monk.[30] This was in the eleventh century. Apparently a quite well known and very respectable ecclesiastic of Paris died. He was laid out in his coffin in the midst of the church to which he had been attached. Suddenly, to everybody's consternation, he sat up and said, 'I have been justly arraigned before the judgement of God.' Then he fell back. People were so terrified they just fled. Anyway, they eventually came back, and the funeral service continued. In the middle of the service the corpse sat up for the second time and said, 'I have been justly judged before the judgement seat of God.' Again everybody fled in consternation. When they came back yet again and tried to finish the funeral service the corpse sat up for the third time and said, 'I have been justly condemned before the judgement seat of God.' At this there was a general horror, and his body was thrown onto the dunghill, because he'd gone to hell.

There are a few stories like that, but they don't really amount to very much. If one has to rely on that sort of thing, one hasn't got very much to go by. But Buddhism makes the point that you can verify the content of faith in this life itself. Buddhism says, for instance, that hatred doesn't cease by hatred: it ceases only by love. Well, you can verify that in your own experience. There is nothing that is really a part of Buddhism that you can't verify in this way. One could even reverse that statement and say if you can't verify it, in this very life itself, it's not part of the essential teaching of Buddhism. This comes up with regard to things like karma and rebirth. In a way you can't verify that, in the course of this life, with regard to the whole expanse of successive lives – unless, of course, you had a recollection of previous lives that was completely convincing to you. But it would be very difficult for you to convince others. *You* would be convinced, because you had been able to see for yourself that your experience of recollection of previous lives was in principle exactly the same as, and continuous with, your recollection of previous years in this life itself. There would be no difference at all for you between the two, and you'd know it wasn't fantasy in the same way that you know your recollection of last week isn't fantasy. Thus there is a difference in this respect between Buddhism and Christianity. The Buddhist scriptures and Buddhist teachers ask you to have faith in a very provisional sense, i.e. until such time as you have your own experience, and you can have that in this life itself; whereas in the case of Christianity it seems you have to wait for verification until after death. 'Much time must usually elapse before the virtue of wisdom has become strong enough to support a vigorous insight into the true nature of reality.' And, of course, that wisdom becomes strong with the support of meditation: with the support of your whole spiritual practice and spiritual life.

> Until then quite a number of doctrinal points must be taken on faith. What then are in Buddhism the objects of faith? They are essentially four: (1) the belief in karma and rebirth; (2) the acceptance of the basic teachings about the nature of reality, such as conditioned co-production, emptiness, etc.; (3) confidence in the 'Three Refuges', the Buddha, the Dharma and the Order; and (4) a belief in the efficacy of the prescribed practices, and in Nirvāṇa as the final way out of our difficulties. (p. 2)

SANGHARAKSHITA: I'm not quite satisfied with this subdivision, actually; I think it distorts things a little. I would prefer to stick to the traditional classification and speak in terms of faith in the Three Jewels, beginning with the Buddha, and lump (1) and (2) and maybe (4) also under the Dharma. That gives importance to the Buddha. In Conze's classification the Buddha is simply included in the Three Jewels under (3). But in a way it is essentially the Buddha you have faith in. In other words you have faith in the possibility of Enlightenment. That means you have faith that the Buddha is Enlightened, and *that* faith is provisional. You believe that you too can gain Enlightenment if you follow the Buddha's instructions. Inasmuch as it is a question of Enlightenment *for yourself*, i.e. Enlightenment as a personal experience, *not* Enlightenment for yourself and not for others, which is what you are mainly concerned about as a Buddhist. Your faith is mainly in the Buddha as an Enlightened being of the kind which you too can become. Faith in this doctrine or that doctrine is quite secondary, because that's only the means to that goal of Enlightenment. I think here Dr Conze somewhat distorts the overall picture by relegating the Buddha, and faith in the Buddha, to this relatively unimportant position.

MAHAMATI: It seems to be quite a distance from the actual way that it seems to work. In a way the belief in karma and rebirth.

SANGHARAKSHITA: I don't know whether he intends to represent these four subdivisions for us as constituting a sort of logical sequence, but one doesn't actually start off like that. One might never believe in karma and rebirth. Sometimes people used to ask me, in the old days, whether it was necessary to believe in karma and rebirth in order to be a Buddhist. I would say, 'Yes and no. If you are prepared to make every effort to gain Enlightenment in this very life you don't need to believe in karma and rebirth: that can look after itself. Presumably, when you're Enlightened you'll know the truth of the matter yourself.' Maybe for some people it is helpful to think in terms of a whole series of lives, and of karma – your own karma – extending from life to life in accordance with your own deeds. Maybe it is quite encouraging to think of yourself as slowly following the Path, progressing little by little, over scores and hundreds and thousands of lives. For some people that's very convincing, very appealing, and very helpful. But suppose you can't believe that. Suppose you're of a doubting, enquiring, sceptical turn of mind. Suppose you can't accept, much as you might like to, this concept of a whole series of lives, of karma and rebirth – you can still gain Enlightenment in this life. The only thing that prevents you from being a Buddhist is if you don't believe that you can develop more and more as a human being in this life itself. That's the only thing that you have to believe as a Buddhist, i.e. that is the only thing that is indispensable. You must believe that you can grow. And if you want to be a Buddhist, and grow in that particular kind of way, obviously you believe in the Buddha as an example of that growth. The Buddha represents what a man can be, what a human being can be, and therefore what you can be. You have faith in him in that sense.

This faith is also something emotional: it's not just a doctrinal belief in the Buddha. You actually feel inspired by the Buddha. When you read the story of his life, especially maybe in poetic form, you feel very attracted by it.[31] There's a definite emotion that you have in response to that life, and that also is faith. You feel that there is something very beautiful about that life – something very attractive, appealing, inspiring, uplifting – and you feel some sort of kinship, even, distant though it may be, with that. You feel, 'Yes I could be like that – that's an ideal for me.' So this faith in the Buddha is your primary faith, and it's provisional until such time as you yourself actually become like that, or at least more like that, and then it won't be provisional any longer: then you won't see – won't be peering – through the glass darkly; you'll be seeing face to face. In fact, more than that. You will be not even seeing face to face. Yours will be the face, just like the face seen in the mirror. And see! – It's you!

So I think that Dr Conze here relegates the Buddha rather to a secondary, not to say tertiary, place. This is not quite in accordance with tradition, and gives, maybe, a little too much importance to the doctrinal side of things.

KARMA AND REBIRTH

SANGHARAKSHITA: So much for belief in karma and rebirth. Do you find karma and rebirth easy to believe in? Does it seem reasonable or not?

A VOICE: I don't find it easy at all.

SUSIDDHI: It's sensible; I wouldn't say it's easy to believe in it.

SANGHARAKSHITA: There is also the question: is it *really* all that much a question of belief?

SURATA: It all seems pretty logical to me. It's just like an extension of the principle that the things you do have consequences in the future.

SANGHARAKSHITA: What I meant was: is there not some evidence for karma and rebirth? Is it really so much a matter of belief? Because it does seem that there is some evidence, and therefore that one can believe it on rational grounds, at least tentatively.

SUVAJRA: What is the evidence?

SANGHARAKSHITA: There is evidence in the form of alleged recollections of previous lives which have been checked up on and apparently verified. There is a growing literature of this sort.[32] But what, perhaps, is interesting is that, although there is this literature, there are people who, even though they might be Buddhists, and quite 'into' their own growth and development, are not very interested in checking up on it. I mean, here is what purports to be evidence, so one might think such people would rush off to read it, to go through it, and to see whether there is anything in it; but apparently not. Apparently you are either interested in karma and rebirth and believe in it, or you are not interested in it and don't believe. In neither case do you particularly want to find out whether it's true or not. It's almost as though it's outside your sphere of interest. In a way, perhaps, it is. If you've got enough faith to keep you going in terms of personal development without that belief in karma and rebirth maybe you just don't need it. You've got your motivation; you don't need to look for a second one. Maybe it's something of that sort that causes people not to be interested in the evidence for karma and rebirth, even though they are Buddhists.

MAHAMATI: I find karma and rebirth completely rational, and when I come across a Muslim or a Christian who talks in terms of one life, and heaven and hell afterwards, I find it just completely absurd.

SANGHARAKSHITA: There's no complete *a priori* proof for karma and rebirth and all that, but certainly it's more rational than believing in just one life, with no before and no after. It might be difficult to explain karma and rebirth, but it's much more difficult to explain all those other theories. You have to fall back entirely on revelation and authority and believe that, for instance, your soul was created the instant your mother conceived you, especially, by God – which takes some swallowing. Or, if you don't believe in the Christian view, or the Buddhist view, or the Muslim view, you've got to believe that it all came about entirely by accident – which takes a bit of swallowing too. So there are those views, none of them from the logical point of view very satisfactory; but I think one could say, modestly, that the Buddhist point of view about karma and rebirth – which includes, to some extent, the Hindu point of view – is at least the least unsatisfactory. You may not be completely happy with it, but you couldn't possibly be happy with those other solutions or other explanations.

LIFE BEFORE LIFE

MAHAMATI: The general lack of interest in rebirth is almost a cultural thing: just complete blindness and complete disinterest.

SANGHARAKSHITA: Yes, it could be. But interest seems to be growing, judging by a few books that have been published lately. I've just received one from America: a very good anthology of extracts from the writings of people all over the world, in the West as well as in the East, on the subject of rebirth.[33] It is certainly surprising how many people have believed in it, even in the West – admittedly in an underground sort of way. There weren't many people during the Middle Ages who believed in it, you know, because the Church suppressed that belief as heresy. But since those days it seems to have been gradually and steadily growing. All sorts of prominent people seem to believe in it: writers, scientists, politicians, poets, and so on. Even military men.

JOHN: I think there tends to be an underlying feeling that there is something slightly cranky about it. It tends to merge into spiritualism and that sort of thing.

SANGHARAKSHITA: There could be that feeling, because so far as the modern West is concerned karma and rebirth came in with the theosophists and whatever good work the theosophists might have done, there are certain rather cranky and eccentric aspects of the theosophical movement.[34] So maybe for a lot of people belief in karma and 'reincarnation' have come to be associated with that sort of thing. I remember Christmas Humphreys telling me once that he'd known at least seven women who believed that they were reincarnations of Cleopatra! One doesn't feel like being associated with women of that sort, does one? Christmas Humphreys himself believes he lived in ancient Egypt and was an officer in Pharaoh's bodyguard, according to his autobiography![35] I don't know whether Mrs Humphreys believed that she was Cleopatra but she also believed that she was something pretty distinguished in Egyptian times. As far as I remember from reading the autobiography, at the time when Christmas Humphreys was an officer in Pharaoh's guard she was a virgin of Isis and they had an ill-starred relationship. When stories of this sort are dished up in connection with karma and rebirth you can imagine logical people shying away. Maybe that is one of the reasons for the feeling that there is something cranky about the belief in karma and rebirth. It's been the vehicle of so much personal fantasy that people just don't want to be associated with it, which is unfortunate. It's just like the case of religion. So much of a wrong nature has been associated with religion that people just don't like to use the word 'religion', or to think in those terms: quite understandably. Maybe it means putting this belief in karma and rebirth on a much more solid, sensible, practical sort of basis, and getting away from all these fantasies and wish-fulfilments, and what one can only describe as occult snobbery.

ANDY: The question very rarely seems to come up actually at classes and things like that.

SANGHARAKSHITA: Again this is something Christmas Humphreys mentioned to me. When he started the Buddhist Society[36] in 1925, he said, the majority of the people who came into it – and I think they must have had some association with theosophy – came into it because they were attracted by the teaching of karma and rebirth. 'But now', he said (this was about fifteen years ago), 'hardly anyone seems to come in for that sort of reason. People don't seem so interested in karma and rebirth.' He was rather regretful about that. But maybe it is because there are now other motivations for coming into Buddhism, which is not a bad thing in a way. Maybe in the case of people in the Friends, the motivation is the desire to grow.[37] Buddhism in any case means just that, and quite rightly means that: in this life; here and now. So karma and rebirth, regardless of whether you believe in it or don't believe in it, has become something peripheral. Your life as a Buddhist is not based on that. You don't believe in a little bit of effort in this life, a little bit in the next, and a little bit more in the one after that, as many Buddhists do in the East. You've got this life. As much as possible you aim even to gain Enlightenment in this life. You are not thinking in terms of future lives; you want to do as much as possible here and now. You believe – if you have any belief on the subject – that if you do the right thing here and now, the future will look after itself. So, in a way, you do believe in the law of karma then. You don't need to bother about the future if you look after the present. In a way, that is believing in the law of karma. But a lot of people, no doubt, don't even think about it to that extent. They might even go so far as to deny the teaching of karma and rebirth. But they'd still be getting on with their personal development here and now, which is the main thing.

MAHAMATI: But is believing in the law of karma, without thinking about rebirth, more than just understanding that through positive action one can change oneself?

SANGHARAKSHITA: Clearly one must believe in the psychological law of cause and effect – that if you undertake a certain spiritual practice it will have a certain effect on the mind. In other words, one must believe that there is a law in accordance with which those effects will accrue to one, and one can call that the law of karma, but it's the law of karma operating within the present lifetime – perhaps within the space of a few months, weeks, days, and even hours. In principle it is the same law that those people who believe in, who envisage it as extending to cover a whole series of lives. All right then, on to Dr Conze's second object of faith.

REASON AND EMOTION

> (2) The acceptance of the basic teachings about the nature of reality, such as conditioned co-production,[38] emptiness, etc. (p. 2)

SANGHARAKSHITA: If you believe that only the Enlightened person sees things as they really are, and if you are aware that you at present don't see things as they really are, because you aren't Enlightened, then it means that you have to take on trust whatever the Enlightened person says about the way things are, or about reality. If the person in whom you believe says reality is void, is *śūnyatā*, and says that there is such a thing as conditioned co-production, and that that's the way things really are, you accept that as your working basis until such time as you can verify, from your own personal spiritual vision and insight, that it is in fact so. But these are of course very basic things indeed, and there aren't many things of this order. There's conditioned co-production, there's voidness or emptiness, and there's also the three characteristics of conditioned existence. One believes in those teachings which pertain to ultimate reality because you believe that the fully Enlightened person, which is what you want to be, sees things in that way, and that you will see them in that way when you are Enlightened. Meanwhile, you accept on trust, or in good faith, that that is the way things are; and you proceed accordingly. Clearly there are a number of things that this short list of basic teachings to be accepted on faith does not include. It doesn't pertain to matters of mundane fact, which can be independently verified. The Buddha might have made a mistake about geography, just because he was misinformed, and that mistake might be in the scriptures; but you don't have to accept it, because it doesn't pertain to ultimate reality.

> (3) Confidence in the 'Three Refuges', the Buddha, the Dharma and the Order. (p. 2)

SANGHARAKSHITA: As I said, confidence or faith in the Buddha is the main one, then confidence or faith in the Dharma, and then in the Order, which presumably comes under Dr Conze's 'social' factor. At the beginning he says that faith 'requires the combination of four factors – intellectual, volitional, emotional and social.' He treats even the Three Jewels under this first heading of 'intellectual', as though it's a matter of an intellectual assent to the Three Jewels, rather than an emotional response to them. But that is in fact what one is primarily concerned with in the case of the Buddha. It's a matter of your emotional response to the actual concrete example of an Enlightened human being, not merely an intellectual assent to the fact that he is Enlightened. And then, item number four.

> (4) A belief in the efficacy of the prescribed practices, and in Nirvāṇa as the final way out of our difficulties. (p. 2)

SANGHARAKSHITA: This really comes under the heading of Dharma, doesn't it? 'I shall say more about them when I have dealt with the other aspects of faith.' Thus under the heading of 'intellectual' one is concerned with faith in, or assent to, doctrines about the nature of ultimate reality. The intellectual factor doesn't really cover, doesn't in a sense really apply to, your faith in the Buddha. It's much more than an intellectual thing.

SUSIDDHI: Isn't it an intellectual thing to accept that someone attained that state of perfection once: then what you are going to do about it goes into the emotional....

SANGHARAKSHITA: That's true, but you've also got to have some sort of emotional feeling for what has been attained before you really start doing anything about it.

SUSIDDHI: I think you've got to intellectually accept that it was possible to attain Enlightenment and that probably did happen, before you have even an emotional....

SANGHARAKSHITA: This probably depends on whether you're a doctrine-follower or a faith-follower.[39] A faith-follower will be inspired by the Buddha as an Enlightened human being, without even thinking whether it's possible or not to gain Enlightenment, whereas probably the doctrine-follower, as you say, is first of all convinced of the abstract possibility of someone becoming Enlightened and only then becomes convinced of, or at least develops faith in, the fact that the Buddha has actually gained that Enlightenment, and starts responding or warming to the figure of the Buddha as Enlightened.

MAHAMATI: Perhaps the doctrine-follower has some unconscious urge, some emotional response to the Buddha, for him to accept it even intellectually.

SANGHARAKSHITA: There is that possibility too. It can't really be accepted on purely abstract, theoretical grounds alone. You do both get there, but in the case of the doctrine-follower intellectual considerations predominate at least for the time being, whereas in the case of the faith-follower it's the emotional considerations that predominate.

FAITH, WILL, AND COURAGE

> 2. In this sceptical age we, anyway, dwell far too much on the intellectual side of faith. *Śraddhā* (Pāli *saddhā*), the word we render as 'faith', is etymologically akin to Latin *cor*, 'the heart', and faith is far more a matter of the heart than of the intellect. It is, as Prof. Radhakrishnan incisively puts it, the 'striving after self-realization by concentrating the powers of the mind on a given ideal'.[40] *Volitionally*, faith implies a resolute and courageous act of will. (p. 2)

SANGHARAKSHITA: That's very well put. He starts off by saying, 'In this sceptical age we, anyway, dwell far too much on the intellectual side of faith.' He seems quite aware, in a way, of his own shortcomings. '*Śraddhā* (Pāli *saddhā*), the word we render as "faith", is etymologically akin to Latin *cor*, "the heart,"' – one would never have thought so – 'and faith is far more a matter of the heart than of the intellect.' This just puts it in a nutshell, in a very simple way: 'Faith is far more a matter of the heart than of the intellect. It is, as Prof. Radhakrishnan' – another intellectual – 'incisively puts it, the "striving after self-realization by concentrating the powers of the mind on a given ideal."' That sounds more intellectual to me than a matter of the heart. It doesn't really help very much. It's very abstract. 'Striving after self-realization by concentrating the powers of the mind on a given ideal.' That won't really do in this context.

ANDY: It sounds like an act of the will.

SANGHARAKSHITA: Yes. 'Volitionally' – that is, in terms of will – 'faith implies a resolute and courageous act of will.' Where there's faith, there will be will in the true sense, not will in a forced sense.

> It combines the steadfast resolution that one *will* do a thing with the self-confidence that one *can* do it. Suppose that people living on the one side of a river are doomed to perish from many enemies, diseases and famine. Safety lies on the other shore. The man of faith is then likened to the person who swims across the river, braving its dangers, saving himself and inspiring others by his example. Those without faith will go on dithering along the hither bank. The opposites to this aspect of faith are timidity, cowardice, fear, wavering, and a shabby, mean and calculating mentality. (pp. 2–3)

SANGHARAKSHITA: This example of the man of faith, i.e. the person who swims across the river, is meant as an analogy with the spiritual person, but it can be taken quite literally too. As I said, faith is needed in the ordinary affairs of life. There's a great difference between the person with faith, and therefore with courage and will, in the ordinary affairs of life, and the person who doesn't possess these qualities. You can tell this, sometimes, when people give something as basic as money. Some people just give, because the faith – and therefore the will to give – is there. Others start calculating whether it's worthwhile, and whether the recipient is worthy, and whether they can afford it. People have these different attitudes in worldly affairs. You can easily distinguish the people with more faith and more will and, therefore, more courage, enterprise, initiative, and so on, as well as less timidity, cowardice, fear, and wavering. From this you can see what a creative and powerful thing faith is, and the way in which it is linked with volition. You *will*, and you *can*. Where there's faith there are these two attitudes 'I will' and 'I can'. This is, of course, one could say, faith in oneself. You could even say there's no faith without faith in oneself. Even when you have faith in the Buddha, you have faith in the Buddha as an Enlightened human being: but *you're* a human being, and so to have faith in the Buddha is to have faith in humanity; to have faith in humanity is to have faith in yourself. Thus to have faith that a human being has gained Enlightenment is to have faith that a human being *can* gain Enlightenment, and if *you're* a human being it means that you have faith that *you* can gain Enlightenment. Faith in the Buddha is really inseparable from faith in yourself. If you have faith in the Buddha, you have faith in yourself; if you don't have faith in yourself, you don't have faith in the Buddha. If you have faith in yourself without having faith in the Buddha, so to speak, that's just egotism, because you just accept yourself as what you are now: there's no question of any future higher potential.

MAHAMATI: Could you say it again? What's egotism: if you have faith in the Buddha but not faith in yourself?

SANGHARAKSHITA: No: faith in yourself but not faith in the Buddha, because then you don't have faith in something higher than yourself into which you can grow. That's what I meant. You just accept yourself as you are now, on your present relatively underdeveloped level. It's a horizontal faith, you might say, not a vertical faith. You have faith in what you can do on your present level of development, but you don't have faith that you can develop to a higher level.

On to paragraph three then.

FAITH IN THE IDEAL

> 3. *Emotionally*, faith is an attitude of serenity and lucidity. Its opposite here is worry, the state of being troubled by many things. It is said that someone who has faith loses the 'five terrors', i.e. he ceases to worry about the necessities of life, about loss of reputation, death, unhappy rebirth and the impression he may make on an audience. It is fairly obvious that the burden of life must be greatly lightened by belief in karma, emptiness, or not-self. Even an unpleasant fate can be accepted more easily when it is understood

> as a dispensation of justice, when vexations are explained as an inevitable retribution, when law seems to rule instead of blind chance, when even apparent loss is bound to turn into true gain. (p. 3)

SANGHARAKSHITA: There's a bit of mean calculation here, I think.

> And if there is no self, what and whom do we worry about? If there is only one vast emptiness, what is there to disturb our radiance? (p. 3)

That's all very well, but then, even though he's supposed to be talking about what faith is emotionally, he seems to have got very quickly onto this intellectual level.

MAHAMATI: I seem to get in quite a state myself when...

SANGHARAKSHITA: So where is faith in the Buddha? If, as I've said, Buddhist faith is primarily faith in the Buddha, then it's that which gives you your attitude of serenity and lucidity and freedom from worry about the necessities of life, loss of reputation, and so on – not reasonings about karma and emptiness and not-self. It's faith in the ideal which keeps you in that state of extreme emotional positivity, so that you don't worry about the things mentioned, and are free from intellectual worries too. Anyway, I agree with what he says here about faith being an attitude of serenity, and its opposite being worry; but I think this is true, above all, of faith in the Buddha, as faith in the ideal is from a Buddhist point of view, and also, therefore, faith in oneself. It's also interesting that if you have faith you cease to worry about the necessities of life. You're not bothered so much about them because you're happy and buoyant. Faith is an extremely emotionally positive state. You're not bothered about loss of reputation, or death, or unhappy rebirth. In a way you're not bothered about rebirth at all. You're not bothered about the impression you may make on an audience, because you're not thinking about yourself. You're imbued with the ideal: you're full of that. You're emotionally positive. You're not dependent on the applause of the audience, or on their approval. You're just talking to them – happily. Dr Conze ought to have gone on to write something like, 'It is fairly obvious that the burden of life must be greatly lightened by the recollection of the glorious figure of the Buddha', rather than 'by belief in karma, emptiness, or not-self.' If you have the Buddha you have all those things too, because they represent the way in which the Buddha sees things. All the things Dr Conze says here are quite true, but it's not faith in the sense of belief in those doctrines which is really operative here so much as faith in the Buddha. All right then, on to number four.

BEYOND THE GROUP

> 4. *Socially*, and that is more difficult to understand,...

SANGHARAKSHITA: That's odd, isn't it?

> ...faith involves trust and confidence in the Buddha and the Sangha. Its opposite here is the state of being submerged in cares about one's sensory social environment, cares which spring from either social pressure or social isolation....[41] By placing one's reliance on spiritual forces one gains the strength to disregard public opinion and social discouragement. Some measure of defiant contempt for the world and its ways is inseparable from a spiritual life. The spiritual man does not 'belong' to his visible environment, in which he is bound to feel rather a stranger. He belongs to the community of the saints, to the family of the Buddha. Buddhism substitutes a spiritual for the natural environment, with the Buddha for the father, the Prajñāpāramitā for the mother, the fellow seekers for brothers and sisters, relatives and friends. It is with these more invisible forces that one must learn to establish satisfactory social relations. In carrying out this task, faith requires a considerable capacity for renunciation. (pp. 3–4)

SANGHARAKSHITA: Yes, that's quite important. I thought, for a moment, that he wasn't really going to mention the Sangha; but anyway, it does come in towards the end of the paragraph. I wouldn't include the Buddha here, under 'socially', at all. I'd include the Buddha more under 'emotionally' and include only the Sangha here. There must be a break with the normal social environment and a transition to that spiritual environment which is constituted by the Sangha.

'The spiritual man does not "belong" to his visible environment, in which he is bound to feel rather a stranger. He belongs to the community of the saints,' – the Āryasaṅgha – 'to the family of the Buddha.[42] Buddhism substitutes a spiritual for the natural environment, with the Buddha for the father, the Prajñāpāramitā for the mother, the fellow seekers for brothers and sisters, relatives and friends.' I think we must be a bit careful about this mother and father imagery. There was a programme on the radio – in fact two programmes recently, called 'The God-mongers'. These programmes dealt with five religious sects; the Children of God, the Hare Krishna movement, Divine Light, Scientology, and the Moonies, i.e. the followers of the Reverend Sun Myung Moon.[43] Thus there were two that were Hindu, two that were Christian, and the Scientologists. I was rather pleased Buddhism wasn't included. In the first programme the compiler, or presenter, of the programmes analysed the five needs which these sects met. First of all, there was the need for a family, i.e. a group within which you could feel warm, cosy, accepted, loved. It was clearly a group that was needed, not what we would call a spiritual community.[44] Second, a need for an experience, in the sense in which I have used the term in the talk I gave on 'Enlightenment as Experience and as Non-Experience',[45] or at least the promise of an experience. Third, a complete set of answers to all the problems of existence. Fourth, a completely authoritative guidance as to how to live your life, even down to the last detail. (It wasn't put in this way, but that is what it amounted to.) Fifth and last, a loving father figure who was, of course, the great guru of the sect. The presenter of the programmes actually used the expression 'father figure'. Thus there is danger in using this sort of imagery. I know it has a spiritual meaning, but it can also be taken psychologically. We have to be quite careful about such expressions as the Buddha being your father, and Prajñāpāramitā being your mother. We even have to be quite careful about the brother and sister bit. What you want is a spiritual family, *not* a substitute social family, if you see what I mean.

BEYOND THE GROUP

SUSIDDHI: You want an idealized family.

SANGHARAKSHITA: Not even an idealized family. Not even a good, happy family in the ordinary sense. You want something more than that.

You want a spiritual community – which goes far beyond the healthy group. I'm not saying the group is bad: certainly the healthy group isn't. You could say there is a level on which you need the healthy, positive group. Even within a spiritual movement like the Friends[46] there is room for that. That is a definite, acknowledged, and accepted level. But you mustn't confuse it with the spiritual community. *That* goes even further. So, 'it is with these more invisible forces' – you notice he speaks of forces rather than persons – 'that one must learn to establish satisfactory social relations.' Well, they are more than social. Perhaps you should say socio-spiritual, or even just spiritual. 'In carrying out this task, faith requires a considerable capacity for renunciation.' Yes: renunciation of the existing biological family, renunciation of the group, *even* the positive group, if you want to make that transition to the spiritual community.

You must be quite clear on what level you are operating, or within what context. Enjoy the positive group by all means. You need to do that sometimes, just by way of a bit of refreshment and relaxation. But don't kid yourself that you're still immersed in the spiritual community, at that moment. You're not. It's just the healthy, happy, positive group that you are experiencing. The spiritual community is something other; they may be the same people, but at different times, and operating on different wavelengths. It's not necessarily that there is one set of people – I'm talking about the Friends now – that make up the positive group, and another completely different set that make up the spiritual community. It isn't quite so cut and dried as that. The same people may function in different ways at different times, or operate more in one way than in another. Sometimes it may be difficult to tell whether they're functioning as positive group or spiritual community. It may seem a bit borderline. Or, maybe, some people are taking the existing situation as a group situation, while others are taking it as a spiritual community situation. Renunciation is certainly required. You need actually to move from the one to the other, i.e. from the group to the spiritual community, at least in your own mind, and to be aware of what level you are operating on, and not mix up the two.

He also says, 'Some measure of defiant contempt for the world and its ways is inseparable from a spiritual life.' He's putting it a bit strongly, because he's been very much a loner. At the beginning of the paragraph it's almost as though he sees the alternatives as (a) the social group and (b) being on your own, though he does bring in the spiritual community towards the end. I think his personal experience is more of being on his own, *outside* the social group, rather than of being in the spiritual community, *away from* the social group. He has probably had hardly any experience of the spiritual community at all.

MAHAMATI: I thought initially that when he said 'invisible forces' it meant that one saw spiritual friends as quite visible and quite tangible.

SANGHARAKSHITA: On the other hand, you *can* think of the invisible aspect of spiritual friends – though not quite in his way – as forces. You can be very much in touch with other members of the spiritual community even when you're not in touch with them physically. If you are on solitary retreat and, if you are an Order member, do the Order *mettā bhāvanā* practice on the appropriate night, you can feel very much in touch with the rest of the Order, as though you really are there with them and they really are there with you, and that you're not separate.[47] Contact doesn't have to be physical, though even when it is not physical it is still, in a way, personal.

EVER-PRESENT FAITH

> Like other spiritual qualities, faith is somewhat paradoxical in that in one sense it is a *gift* which one cannot obtain by merely wanting to, and in another sense it is a *virtue* that can be cultivated. The capacity for faith varies with the constitution of the individual, and his social circumstances. It is usual to classify types of personality according to whether they are dominated by greed, hatred or confusion. Those who walk in greed are said to be more susceptible to faith than the other two, because of the kinship which exists between faith and greed. To quote Buddhaghosa (*Visuddhimagga*, III.75): 'As on the unwholesome plane greed clings and takes no offence, so faith on the wholesome plane. As greed searches for objects of sense-desire, so faith for the qualities of morality, etc. As greed does not let go that which is harmful, so faith does not let go that which is beneficial. (p. 4)[48]

SANGHARAKSHITA: 'Like other spiritual qualities, faith is somewhat paradoxical in that in one sense it is a *gift* which one cannot obtain by merely wanting to, and in another sense it is a *virtue* that can be cultivated.' It's a gift in respect of temperament – though I'd personally mention here not so much the personality type dominated by greed as the faith-follower. The faith-follower seems to be a person with a temperamental inclination to believe or to have faith. He starts off, in a way, with an advantage. But faith is an integral part of the spiritual life. According to the Abhidharma (e.g. *Mind in Buddhist Psychology*),[49] faith is present in all wholesome states of consciousness, because all wholesome or skilful states of consciousness are upward-striving states, and how can you strive upwards unless you have faith in something higher? Thus faith enters in all the time. But to look at it in ordinary terms, you're either a person who finds it easy to believe or a person who finds it difficult. In either case you need to cultivate faith.

One could, of course, question Buddhaghosa, if one can do anything as temerarious as question Buddhaghosa.[50] Because faith is not really a conditioned thing in the way that he seems to suggest. It's a matter of faith, ultimately, in the Transcendental, and there can hardly be a temperamental disposition to *that*. That is why I say that even if you have the *gift* of faith you still need to cultivate faith as a *virtue*. The gift of faith isn't enough. It *could* be not so much faith as credulity. You could even say that credulity is the near enemy of faith.

JOHN: When you say cultivate faith as a virtue, how do you mean in practical terms?

SANGHARAKSHITA: It is a question of the whole emotional side of the spiritual life. One cultivates faith by reading the life of the Buddha, by performing puja, etc. In this way one develops one's faith, one's *feeling* for the spiritual life as distinct from one's understanding of it.

AN AGE OF BELIEF

> As regards social conditions, there are ages of faith and ages of unbelief. The present age rather fosters unbelief. It puts a premium on intellectual smartness, so that faith is easily held to indicate nothing but a weak head or a lack of intellectual integrity....[51]
> The prestige of science, the concern with a high standard of living, and the disappearance of all institutions of uncontested authority are the chief foes of faith in our present-day society. It is largely

> a matter of temperament whether we believe that matters will improve in the near future. (p. 5)

SANGHARAKSHITA: I'm not so sure I believe that 'as regards social conditions, there are ages of faith and ages of unbelief'. He's probably thinking of the Christian Middle Ages. I don't think the present age is an age of unbelief: it's just that the objects of belief differ. Whether there can be an age of belief in the sense of belief in the Transcendental, is very, very doubtful, for the reason which I mentioned before, i.e. that belief or faith in the Transcendental by its very nature cannot be a conditioned thing, it can't be something you're born with, or just imbibe from the general atmosphere. The Middle Ages in Europe were ages of faith in the sense that you believed in God and believed in the pope, but what sort of real faith was that? At present you don't believe in those things unless you're still a Catholic. But you believe in lots of other things: in the power of science, for instance. You don't really know much about science, but you've unlimited faith in it. Maybe in *certain* respects this is not an age of faith, but in certain other respects it is. A hundred years ago everybody in Russia was an orthodox Christian: now they're mostly orthodox Marxists; but it's the same sort of passive, acquiescent belief which perhaps you can hardly dignify with the name of faith in the Buddhist sense. What he says about the present age multiplying 'the distractions from the sensory world' is all very true. As for it exposing 'the citizen to so great a variety of conflicting viewpoints', you found that in the Buddha's time too. There were those six different sectarian teachers going around.[52] Admittedly the variety of conflicting viewpoints is even greater now. I don't believe that 'institutions of uncontested authority' have disappeared. It's the scientific institutions which give us our faith now. They are of uncontested authority, by and large. He sounds a bit hopeless when he says, 'It is largely a matter of temperament whether we believe that matters will improve in the near future.' Well, perhaps it is; but again, perhaps that isn't the whole story.

> As a virtue, faith is strengthened and built up by self-discipline, and not by discussing opinions. (p. 5)

SANGHARAKSHITA: To what extent do you think that is true; that 'faith is strengthened and built up by self-discipline'?

MAHAMATI: I think it's very true. You go through with your practice, you get results, and that inspires you.

SURATA: You also get verifications through discussing opinions, don't you?

SANGHARAKSHITA: Do you get clarification?

SURATA: Yes.

SANGHARAKSHITA: Yes you do, if it's discussion of the right sort and with the right people.

ANDY: Just through contact with other members of the sangha.

SUSIDDHI: Is it not strengthened by awareness?

SANGHARAKSHITA: Yes, it's strengthened by awareness of the object of faith. It's strengthened if you see more clearly the virtues of the Buddha.

SUSIDDHI: I mean, at the beginning you have certain things which you have confidence in, and you try to build on them. You're aware of doing certain practices, or trying to do them. You are even being aware, and trying to be aware of the effect of being aware. And the other practices sort of build on what you had to begin with.

TAKING A RISK

> Intellectual difficulties are by no means the most powerful among the obstacles to faith. Doubts are inevitable, but how one deals with them depends on one's character. The first of our four 'articles of faith' well illustrates this situation. There are many sound reasons for accepting the rebirth doctrine. This is not the place to expound them, and I must be content to refer the reader to the very impressive 'East-West Anthology' on *Reincarnation* which J. Head and S. L. Cranston have published in 1961.[53] (p. 5)

SANGHARAKSHITA: The book I referred to a short while ago is the new enlarged edition of that, which has just come out and which I have just received.

> Yet, although belief in rebirth is perfectly rational and does not conflict with any known fact, the range of the average person's vision is so limited that he has no access to the decisive evidence, which is direct and immediate experience. The rebirth doctrine assumes at least two things, i.e.: (1) that behind the natural causality which links together events in the world of sense there are other, invisible, chains of a moral causality, which assures that all good acts are rewarded, all bad actions punished; and (2) that this chain of moral sequences is not interrupted by death, but continues from rebirth to rebirth. To the average person these two assumptions cannot be proved absolutely conclusively and beyond the possibility of a doubt. However plausible they may seem on rational grounds, Buddhism teaches that they become a matter of direct experience only after the 'superknowledges' (*abhijñā, abhiññā*) have been developed....[54]
>
> Until that time comes, we cannot claim that we *fully know* the doctrine of karma and rebirth to be true. We take it partly on faith. And this faith of ours is maintained less by our dialectical skill, as by the virtues of patience and courage. For we must be willing to wait patiently until we are spiritually ripe for the emergence of the super-knowledges, however far off that might seem to be. And secondly, we must be willing to take risks. Life nowhere offers a one-hundred-per-cent security, and for our convictions least of all. (pp. 5–7)

SANGHARAKSHITA: This is why I said that faith was necessary even in ordinary life. We can't have certainty; we can't have knowledge: we rely on faith all the time. He gives some examples of that.

> Employed in gaining wealth, a merchant must risk his property.

SANGHARAKSHITA: You risk because you have faith and not knowledge.

Employed in taking life, a soldier must risk his own life. Employed in saving his soul, the spiritual man must risk his own soul. The stake automatically increases with the prospect of gain. Of course, we may be mistaken. I sometimes wonder what I would think if, on dying, I would not, as I now fondly imagine, wake up on the Bardo plane, but find myself confronted with Acheron and the three-headed Cerberus, or, worse still, were ill-treated with fire and brimstone in a Christian hell.[55] The experience would, I admit, be rather disconcerting. All that I can say in the face of such uncertainty is that I am willing to take the consequences, and that I hope that my fund of boldness, audacity and good humour will not run out. (p. 7)

SUSIDDHI: Conze is shining through there, isn't he?

SANGHARAKSHITA: Thus there is this question of faith in all of it. You can't move a step without faith – and that implies risk. Someone reminded me the other day that he, many years ago, had asked me what was the antidote to *moha*, bewilderment or mental confusion, the third of the three unskilful roots. I said commitment. (I only vaguely remembered all this: it was quite a few years ago.) He had then asked, 'How can you be sure, when committing yourself, that you're not taking a risk?' and I said you can't; you've always got to take a risk. That is true, you know. The two things, the taking of the risk and the having faith, go hand in hand. It's because of faith that you take risks. You have to take risks, because you have faith and not knowledge. So you cannot go through life without taking risks. You mustn't go through life with credulity; then you'll just be the dupe of anybody you happen to encounter. You mustn't go through your life recklessly; then your life will soon come to an end. But certainly you must go through it with faith, and with a willingness to take risks. Otherwise you don't get anywhere. You won't grow: you won't even be willing to commit yourself. You'll be so anxious about making mistakes that you'll rule out the possibility of mistakes by not doing anything at all. You're so afraid of living that you'll virtually commit suicide. Or rather, you're so afraid of death that you commit suicide. Anyway, I think we'd better leave it there for this morning. We've done quite a chunk and there's some tea downstairs.

Day 1: afternoon

> One has the choice to magnify intellectual doubts, or to minimize them. It seems not unreasonable that one should blame the difficulties of the teaching on one's own distance from the truth, one's own intellectual and moral imperfections. How can one expect to remember one's past lives, if at present one cannot even recall hour by hour what one did during one single day a mere month ago! (p. 7)

SANGHARAKSHITA: What he says in the first sentence is interesting. 'One has the choice to magnify intellectual doubts, or to minimize them.' People don't usually realize this: that one does have a choice. Perhaps you don't have a choice as to whether you actually have intellectual doubts or not: they almost inevitably arise; but the question of your attitude towards them is a different thing. You can either leave them as they are, or make them bigger by dwelling on them, or minimize them by paying them as little attention as possible. It's really up to you. He also says, 'It seems not unreasonable that one should blame the difficulties of the teaching on one's own distance from the truth, one's own intellectual and moral imperfections.' If you say that a teaching is 'difficult', difficult is a subjective term: it doesn't tell you anything about the teaching. The teaching is neither easy nor difficult. 'Difficult' refers to your understanding of the teaching. So if you say the teaching is difficult that's not really quite correct. You should say the teaching is difficult to understand. Then the question arises: Difficult for whom? – Difficult for me. – Why is that? – I'm not particularly bright. Well, that is in fact the reason, because there are other people who seem to understand quite well, i.e. the sages of the past at least. It's just my own dullness and denseness and obtuseness that makes me unable to see very easily, or very clearly. One should have more of *that* sort of attitude rather than dismiss something out of hand merely because one can't understand it, or have difficulty in understanding it. Hence, 'It seems not unreasonable that one should blame the difficulties of the teaching on one's own distance from the truth, one's own intellectual and moral imperfections.'

Then he goes on to say, 'How can one expect to remember one's past lives, if at present one cannot even recall hour by hour what one did during a single day a mere month ago?' What were you doing on this day a month ago? Now it's Saturday. Four Saturdays ago what were you doing? If you had a regular weekly programme, and on Saturdays always went to a certain class, you would know that since it was a Saturday you must have gone to that class; but you may not actually remember going on that particular day. In any case, if you've been in the habit of a going to a class every Saturday your memory of all the different Saturdays is blurred. It becomes a memory of a single Saturday with, as it were, variations. You can't tell one Saturday from another, because they don't stand out distinctly enough. This is the case, I find, with seminars I have conducted. I have conducted so many of them that although I can remember saying something on a seminar I can't remember which one it was! I can't remember whether it was one held six months ago, or one held two years ago. It's as though there is just one great seminar which lasts for months and months, and on which one says all sorts of things, but one no longer remembers the distinct separate events of each particular seminar.

A lot of our life is like that. We don't remember things clearly and distinctly day by day, much less still hour by hour. We don't remember even month by month. As you get older you might look back and be not sure what you did in a particular year – whether, for instance, you went to a certain place in 1952, or 1953, or 1954. The recollection might be blurred to *that extent*. Is it any wonder that we don't remember our previous lives? We don't usually remember the first year or two of *this* life. We don't even remember our dreams. We may know that we had dreams. Friends who were awake at the time tell us that our eyeballs were moving, so we must have been having dreams. We might even have been talking in our sleep, quite audibly, and others might have heard, but *we* don't remember. Maybe when we woke up we remembered a whole series of dreams. Five minutes later we've forgotten them all. So is it surprising that we should have had past lives that we no longer remember? Is it really surprising that we don't remember? We're very forgetful creatures. When people object to the teaching of rebirth: 'Oh we don't remember our previous lives!' as though that means there *could* not have been any such lives, it's as though they assume that our memory is brilliant and pure and clear and that we remember every single event of every single day – but not our past lives, so we could not have had any. But it isn't like that at all. The greatest part of what we've experienced – ninety-nine per cent of it, if not more – we've forgotten. So is it surprising that we should have forgotten previous lives?

> If one hesitates to accept, as not immediately obvious, the doctrine that this world is the result of ignorance and of the craving of non-existent individuals for non-existent objects – is this not due perhaps to the very denseness of one's own ignorance, for which one can collect plenty of proofs all day long? (p. 7)

SANGHARAKSHITA: A typical Conzean statement!

> Doubts are effectively overcome when one purifies one's own life, so as to become more worthy of knowledge. (p. 7)

SANGHARAKSHITA: This is something that people often forget. We need, in a way, to become more worthy of knowledge; more receptive: more open to it.

> It is a condition of all learning that one accepts a great deal on trust, that one gives the teacher the benefit of the doubt. (pp. 7–8)

SANGHARAKSHITA: Sometimes people's attitude towards a teacher is that of the prosecution lawyer who has got the witness for the defence in the witness box.

> Otherwise one can learn nothing at all, and remains shut out from all truth. To have faith means to take a deep breath, to tear oneself away from the daily cares and concerns, and to turn resolutely to a wider and more abiding reality. At first we are, by ourselves, too stupid and inexperienced to see the tracks which lead to salvation. So we must put our trust in the Sages of the past, and listen intently to their words, dimmed by distance and the noise of the present day, but still just audible. (p. 8)

SANGHARAKSHITA: That's quite a good way of putting it. The words of the sages are still audible, but there's such a hullaballoo going on nowadays you have to listen carefully. If you listen carefully you can just catch the sound of those words.

TOLERANCE

> One last word about tolerance, without which faith remains raw and unsure of itself. It is a perpetual trial to our faith that we should constantly meet with people who believe differently. We are easily tempted to wish this irritant removed, to coerce others, if only by argument, and to annihilate them, if only by dubbing them fools. Intolerance for men of other faiths, though often mistaken for ardour, betrays nothing so much as doubts within oneself. We can, of course, always console ourselves by assuming that the others, in their own way, believe what we do, and that in the end it all comes to the same thing. But that does not always sound very convincing, and what we must, I am afraid, learn to do is to bear with their presence. (p. 8)

SANGHARAKSHITA: This is quite important. 'One last word about tolerance, without which faith remains raw and unsure of itself. It is a perpetual trial to our faith that we should constantly meet with people who believe differently.' This is true, though more true, one might say, within the Western, and specifically the Christian, context. Buddhists, and Hindus even, aren't bothered in that sort of way. If you go to a Buddhist country and say that you are a Christian or a Muslim, or something else other than Buddhist, they don't find that a trial to their faith at all. But I have certainly noticed myself, that if I say I'm a Buddhist to people who are Christian it seems to have quite an unsettling effect. So, 'We are easily tempted to wish this irritant removed,' – I'm afraid this applies to Christians and ex-Christians – 'to coerce others, if only by argument, and to annihilate them, if only by dubbing them fools. Intolerance for men of other faiths, though often mistaken for ardour, betrays nothing so much as doubts within oneself.' This is very true. So what religion, do you think, probably doubts itself the most: the one that is the most intolerant – and we all know which one that is.[56] Intolerance is almost a sort of yardstick. The ages of faith were the ages of great doubt. 'We can, of course, always console ourselves by assuming that the others, in their own way, believe what we do, and that in the end it all comes to the same thing.' This is, of course, what many Hindus do, and what many people do nowadays even in the West. This also avoids the issue. You're afraid of standing on your own feet; you're afraid of taking the risk of forming your own judgements, and possibly being wrong. There's safety in numbers. So you start saying, or thinking, 'I won't be different. It doesn't matter what one believes.' It's all the same thing under different clothes, under different names.'

This is what the Hindu usually says. In his case it seems that he says it more to preserve the social status quo in the form of the caste system. But in the West it's more that people won't take the risk of thinking for themselves and possibly being wrong. If you all really think alike, well, it seems incredible that you should all be wrong. Reasoning that way, you should all be right! One person might make a mistake, but could *everybody* be mistaken? And in this case everybody really believes the same thing: I believe what everybody else believes; so others can't possibly be mistaken, and I can't possibly be mistaken. There's a sort of comfort in that. Do you see how it works? This is the psychological basis of a great deal of what is called universalism, such as you saw exhibited in connection with the Mind Body Spirit Festival,[57] the official basis of which seems to be: we all believe the same thing, and so we all get together on this common platform. We're all manifestations of the New Age. Some of the Order members and Friends who were around the Festival remarked on the fact that many of the words we use in the Friends were used by these other groups, words like Enlightenment, development, creativity; but they seemed to use them, they said, in quite a different sort of way from the way in which *we* use them. The fact that there was this common terminology tended to obscure the difference between their teaching and ours and give other people outside the impression that we were all talking about the same thing whereas, though they were actually using the same words as we use, we were talking about quite different things, in at least some cases. This New Age universalism is a manifestation of group mentality. You're afraid of thinking for yourself; you're afraid of being wrong and, therefore, of being different. The more people who think as you do, the more likelihood there is that you are right. That is how people think: that is their group thinking – their group mentality.

SUSIDDHI: The group try to absorb elements which escape from it.

SANGHARAKSHITA: If it cannot suppress them it will try to absorb them. I used to say this in India, because there I came up against this tendency with Hindus. Hindus used to say to me: 'We are very tolerant. Hinduism is the most tolerant of all religions. We accept everything in other religions and philosophies as teaching basically the same thing that Hinduism teaches.' In reply I used to say, 'This is not tolerance; this is intolerance. Tolerance means *acceptance* of difference, and accepting the fact that other people have the right to think differently from you.' If you tell them, against their wish, as it were, 'No, you are mistaken in thinking you are thinking something different from me,' – that is a form of coercion. You're in fact coercing them. You're forcing *their* thought into *your* mould. Thus intolerance has got these two different forms. You can either crush the person who thinks differently from you, or you can deny that there is any difference between you. Both are forms of intolerance. Tolerance means that you recognize there is a difference which you haven't, as yet, been able to overcome, but that you accept that that other person has got the right to think differently, and that you've got the right to discuss and argue with him, and try to convince him and convert him, just as he's got the same right to do that with you. But you recognize his right to think for himself as an individual, even though he comes to different conclusions from what you've come to. You've no right either to suppress him by force, or to 'conscript' his thought saying it's the same as your thought. That is also, in effect, denying his right to think for himself.

That sort of attitude is really very invidious, because it also puts you – or you try to put yourself – into a superior position. You flatter yourself that you're so tolerant whereas he is so intolerant. He insists on thinking *differently*. He won't see the oneness of things: he's not universal. I've been told by Hindus, 'Buddhism is so narrow-minded! Why do Buddhists insist on difference all the time? Why can't they see the glorious unity of everything – that whether it's God and No-God, or Self and No-Self, it's all the same? Why can't Buddhists see this? Why are they so narrow-minded? Why do they insist that these things are different? We Hindus are very broad-minded, and very tolerant, and because we are very tolerant we are superior to you.' That's their attitude, which is very, very false. To tell someone that he doesn't know what he is thinking is as bad as to tell him he doesn't feel what he's feeling. Suppose somebody says, 'I'm feeling very angry,' and the other person says, 'Oh no, you're not feeling angry, you couldn't be angry. It's not anger – I'm sure it isn't. I just don't get that sort of vibe off you,' etc. They then deny your feeling. Similarly, suppose somebody says, 'I think differently from you. You believe in God, but I'm sorry, I don't,' and the other says, 'No, it's not any different. You really think exactly the same as me. Actually you do believe in God, but you call it No-God. It's just the same thing.' Really you are denying the other person, who doesn't believe in God. You're really denying him as an individual. You're not allowing him to think for himself, or to feel for himself. It's all very insidious, and very unpleasant, and a case of a vice pretending to be a sort of virtue. You get so much of this in India, though not so much of it in this country. Here you tend to get outright suppression and intolerance. But in India, among Hindus, you get this pseudo-tolerance which is, in fact, a very insidious form of intolerance. I'm therefore glad that Dr Conze mentions this: 'We can, of course, always console ourselves by assuming that the others, in their own way, believe what we do, and that in the end it all comes to the same thing. But that does not always sound very convincing, and what we must, I am afraid, learn to do is to bear with their presence.'

Let us accept the fact that others do think differently from what we do. If you accept them as individuals who are, in terms of the relative truth,[58] different from you, you will have to accept that they feel and think, perhaps, differently from what you do, and you must tolerate that. Not tolerate in the sense of regarding it as a regrettable necessity, but in a way be glad of it. Even if they're wrong, never mind: they're thinking for themselves as individuals – assuming that they *are* thinking, and not just accepting what they've been told by someone in a position merely of group authority.

Anyway, this is all under the heading of faith. Look back over this section and see whether there's any point that needs further clarification or discussion.

NATURAL CONSEQUENCES

SURATA: Are these four factors Conze's, or are they traditional Buddhist?

SANGHARAKSHITA: They seem to be Conze's.

SURATA: I don't find them personally very satisfactory.

SANGHARAKSHITA: As I said, I'd much rather we started with the Buddha, and then went on to the Dharma, and then the Sangha, in the traditional way. The emotional factor that enters into faith comes under Buddha, the intellectual factor under Dharma, and the social factor under Sangha.

A VOICE: What about the volitional factor?

SANGHARAKSHITA: The volitional factor comes under the emotional factor.

MAHAMATI: Conze says that the rebirth doctrine assumes two things, the first of which is 'that behind the natural causality which links together events in the world of sense there are other invisible chains of a moral causality, which assures that all good acts are rewarded, all bad actions punished.' I hadn't thought that there was a sort of difference between natural causality and the law of karma.

SANGHARAKSHITA: According to the Abhidharma there are five different trends of cause-effect relationship, or rather, five different trends of conditionality going on in the universe, one of which is karma. These are the five *niyamas*.[59] It isn't so much that behind natural causality there's another invisible type of causality which is karma. Rather, there is the general law of conditionality existing in five different forms or operating on five different levels, i.e. the physical inorganic, the physical organic, the mental or psychological, the karmic, and the Dharmic or, as one might call it, the spiritual.

MAHAMATI: It just made moral causality sound something rather mysterious, like under the control of God, or something like that.

SANGHARAKSHITA: Yes: right. One could also say that one mustn't look at the law of karma too mechanically. It is not that you do something and, in some almost arbitrary way, there is a certain effect which nature, or the law of karma, has attached to that action. It seems to me that the result grows quite naturally out of the cause itself: it's not something that accrues to it as it were from the outside. In the case of an ordinary crime, say against the civil law, you might indeed be punished, but the punishment might be quite arbitrary. It might even change from time to time, or from place to place. It doesn't grow out of the offence itself. In the case of offences against the moral law, so to speak, the results do grow out of the offence itself, and are inseparable from it. Suppose you become an alcoholic. Your sufferings, the sufferings which eventually befall you as a result of your alcoholism, aren't a punishment suddenly inflicted out of the blue upon you for the sin of being an alcoholic. They emerge from the offence itself, stage by stage, and are indistinguishable from it. I see it much more like that. In other words, not as anything very mysterious at all. It's not something hiding behind the natural sequence of causation on the level of which you actually lift up the drink, put it to your lips, and swallow it. There's not a 'law of karma' mysteriously lurking behind that simple action to make you suffer for it. What really happens is that there is the greed, this thirst, metaphorical as well as literal, on account of which you become addicted. And then, of course, the more you drink the less the euphoric effects, and the more you have to drink in order to get the same effects as before. Then you really do become addicted, and various physical and mental sufferings start taking place. Thus you can see the whole process. It's not that you complete a whole series of actions, and then – wham! – out of the blue, as I said, you get a consequence which is quite separate and distinct from what you have actually done. It is not like that at all. Or again, suppose during your lifetime you become very addicted to certain sense pleasures. Well, after death there are no physical senses present, so you can't enjoy those sense pleasures, and therefore you suffer. But the suffering is not a punishment inflicted on you because you've been naughty and have done something that you shouldn't have done. It's a natural consequence of your own mental state. No one is inflicting the suffering upon you from the outside – not even an impersonal law. In a way it's as misleading to think of the law of karma punishing you as it is to think of God punishing you. You are punishing yourself, and the offence and the punishment are really inseparable.

SUSIDDHI: It's a process of becoming different all the time just by what you do.

SANGHARAKSHITA: You have to live with the consequences in your own personality, of what you did in the past. Somebody once said that you are not forgiven your offences, or rather the results of your offences, simply because in the meantime you have repented. For instance, suppose as a result of your alcoholism you've completely destroyed your liver. Well, you might repent of your alcoholism, you might give up drink, but you're left with your bad liver. The fact that you've repented doesn't mean that your liver suddenly becomes all right. But it's not the law of karma punishing you with a bad liver. It's not even the result of what you've done: it *is* what you've done. I think we have to be careful not to personalize this so-called impersonal law of karma, regarding it as something acting upon us from outside, quite separate from our actions. In a way the effect is not separate from the cause, really: not in the extreme sort of way that is suggested sometimes.

SUVAJRA: He says, 'Emotionally, faith is an attitude of serenity and lucidity.' Why lucidity?

SANGHARAKSHITA: If you've got serenity you're not disturbed; you're balanced. You can see things much more clearly, because you see them more objectively: you're not swayed this way and that by your emotions. Therefore your whole vision becomes clearer and more lucid.

Anyway, this is all under the heading of faith. Let's go on to vigour.

2
VIGOUR

PSYCHO-SPIRITUAL ENERGY

> Next to faith, vigour (*vīrya*, Pāli *viriya*). Little need be said about the need for being energetic if one wants to achieve something. Without vigour, without strenuous effort, without perseverance, one can obviously not make much progress. Everybody knows what 'vigour' is, although a generation which made the fortune of the discoverers of 'night starvation' might wish that it had more of it. (pp. 8–9)

SANGHARAKSHITA: Are you old enough to remember what 'night starvation' was? It was an advertisement for Ovaltine! If you took Ovaltine before going to bed you wouldn't suffer from 'night starvation'. In every newspaper, a few years ago, one saw the slogan, 'Are you suffering from night starvation?' You must be, because you wake up tired in the morning; so take Ovaltine before you go to sleep. Anyway, be careful you don't suffer from spiritual night starvation.

'Next to faith, vigour (*vīrya*, Pāli *viriya*).' Etymologically, the word *vīra*, which is 'hero', is connected with this. A hero is someone with courageous energy and vigour. The English word virtue is also connected with *vīrya*. Virtue originally meant strength. We still speak of the virtue of herbs, for instance, meaning their particular strength, their special quality. Old English poetry speaks of the virtue of the stars, i.e. their power, their influence.[60] There is also 'virility', which is masculine energy, masculine vigour. These words are all interconnected.[61]

INTEGRATION

> The fact that faith and vigour are virtues does not, however, imply that they are good all through, and that, regardless of the consequences, they should be strengthened at all times. Excess is to be deprecated, even in virtues. All the five virtues must be regarded as one whole. Their balance and harmony is almost as important as the virtues themselves.[62] They support each other to some extent, but they also stand in each other's way. The one must sometimes be used to correct the excess of the other. In this way, concentration must come to the rescue of the latent faults of vigour. When vigour and energy have it all their own way, tranquillity is in danger. We all know people with a large dash of adrenaline in their blood, who are always busy, perhaps even 'madly efficient', but not particularly restful. Vigour by itself leads to excitement, and has to be controlled by a development of concentrated calm. (p. 9)

SANGHARAKSHITA: I think we're very familiar with that, aren't we? The key sentence here is, 'All the five virtues must be regarded as one whole.' That is quite important. Why do you think this is? Why, essentially, are the five virtues to be regarded as one whole?

SUSIDDHI: Because they balance out.

SUVAJRA: If you have one perfected fully, the others must be perfected fully also.

SANGHARAKSHITA: Let's take it a bit more 'psychologically' than that. Whose virtues are they?

ANDY: One's own.

SANGHARAKSHITA: One's own. So how many persons' virtues are there in that case? One person's. That means that inasmuch as they are all virtues of the same person they form a whole, because that person is a whole. If there is any imbalance in the virtues there is an imbalance *in you*. So, inasmuch as ideally you are a whole, the virtues must be regarded as a whole. I mean the virtues should not be allowed individual autonomy. There is no question of vigour being developed *regardless*; no question even of faith being developed regardless, and so on. They are *your* virtues; they are parts of a whole, which is *you*. It is not only a question of them hanging together with one another, but of hanging together with you, of being an integral part of *your* spiritual life. They're not ends in themselves. Essentially, the virtues must be regarded as one whole, because you and your spiritual life must be regarded as one whole. So, 'Their balance and harmony is almost as important as the virtues themselves.' If you were to have a runaway vigour, it would be almost better not to have any vigour at all. Almost: not quite.

BEING DRIVEN

SUSIDDHI: I think there's an exception to that. I seem to remember you saying that you can't have too much mindfulness.

SANGHARAKSHITA: Yes: that's right. That is to say, the *right* kind of mindfulness, not an alienated awareness but an integrated awareness. You can't have too much of that, by definition.

'They support each other to some extent, but they also stand in each other's way. The one must sometimes be used to correct the excess of the other. In this way, concentration must come to the rescue of the latent faults of vigour. When vigour and energy have it all their own way, tranquillity is in danger. We all know people with a large dash of adrenaline in their blood, who are always busy, perhaps even "madly efficient", but not particularly restful.' Do you think it always is just the adrenaline?

SUSIDDHI: A lot of people seem to feel the need to prove themselves all the time.

SANGHARAKSHITA: In other words, it's psychological and it's neurotic. This was something we thought about a bit in the early days of the Friends, because I noticed that in each of the different Buddhist groups you usually had one or two quite high-powered people who kept things moving and did all the work. It was pretty obvious that their basic motivation was quite neurotic. Such people would get into an organization, even into a Buddhist group, and at once rise to a leading position just because of the force of their neurotic energy and their willingness to do things which, maybe, other people weren't willing to do. I thought that this must be guarded against in the case of the Friends. This is why, in the case of the FWBO, all the office bearers and so on are Order members, so that you can't get anybody going as it were straight from the general public into the organization powered simply by his neurotic energy. Those sort of people hopefully get weeded out before they're ever ordained. Either they themselves are weeded out of the Movement[63] and go and offer their services elsewhere, or they themselves weed out their neurotic drive, and become more calm and less restless, and able to commit themselves to the Three Jewels and genuinely to work and put their energy into things in a positive, non-neurotic way. So the people who run the FWBO as office bearers, council members, and so on, are ideally all filtered through the Order, so that it isn't possible for someone with that kind of neurotic drive to get into any kind of position of influence within the FWBO.

This is one of the reasons why we've got the kind of set-up that we do have. It seemed to me that most organizations were run by most unsuitable people, whose style and personality, in the case of the religious groups, was quite incompatible with the professed objectives and aims of those groups. Of course, there is the difficulty in the case of an organization that seeks to run on non-neurotic energy that in the meantime a lot of work doesn't get done. These neurotically high-powered people really can work, in the sense of achieving output: they really can. So, if you refuse on principle to make use of that type of energy, well, it's sometimes quite difficult to get things done. But we accepted that in the case of the FWBO, and that's one of the reasons why we didn't really get off the ground for quite a long time. We had to wait, as it were, for people's natural healthy energy to emerge rather than exploit people's neurotic energy which we thought it wasn't right to do, either for them or for the Movement as a whole. Anyway, now we are beginning to reap the results of that policy, or that principle, and there is a lot of healthy non-neurotic energy in the Movement getting things done.

'Vigour by itself leads to excitement, and has to be controlled by a development of concentrated calm.' Has anyone ever seen this in oneself, i.e. vigour by itself leading to excitement? You've got so much energy you just get excited and restless and dissipate it all over the place. So what should you do then?

JOS: Sit down and meditate.

SANGHARAKSHITA: But is it easy to do that? Because you're in that excitable state that's the last thing you want to do, really. What other things do you think you could do?

ANDY: Hatha yoga.

SANGHARAKSHITA: Hatha yoga, yes. You can also just do nothing. That's probably the most effective, in a way. Just sit down and do nothing until you've calmed down.

SUVAJRA: It's been a way to sort of include the just sitting practice[64] along with your ordinary meditation.

SANGHARAKSHITA: Oh yes. But you wouldn't really be doing just sitting. You'd be sitting and not doing anything.

FANTASY

> Similarly, faith alone, without wisdom, can easily become mere credulity. Wisdom alone can teach what is worth believing. This can be illustrated by Don Quixote, who in literature is perhaps the purest embodiment of faith, and whose actions demonstrate that too much faith, by itself, is not necessarily a good thing....[65] His faith has conquered the senses, it transmutes the data of common-sense experience, and the barber's basin becomes Mambrino's helmet.[66] (pp. 9–10)

SANGHARAKSHITA: He wears the basin on his head thinking it Mambrino's magic helmet of invulnerability.

> And yet, when we consider the intellectual basis of his faith, we find that it consists in nothing more than a belief in the truth and

> veracity of the Romances which describe the fictitious and not particularly edifying doings of the knights-errant of the past. This is the reason why his adventures form a sorry sight, why he is a caricature even of a knight of the Middle Ages, why, shorn of all common-sense, faith in this case becomes slightly pathological. (p. 10)

SANGHARAKSHITA: What would be a corresponding case in this age? Nowadays people don't read these romances of knight-errantry and take them seriously, as Don Quixote did. What sort of thing might they read and take seriously in this sort of way, and even start acting out, or acting upon? Science fiction corresponds a bit, doesn't it? There was a case I read about in the newspaper of someone in America, who'd been reading too much science fiction, or watching too many science fiction films, and who thought he could fly like Superman. He jumped out of the window of a skyscraper from the fortieth floor or something like that, and of course he couldn't fly and crashed. Small boys sometimes have to act out things. In their case it's not too bad, just cowboys and Indians. It doesn't depart too far from fact. But, you know, you can easily see the borderline between reasonable faith and pathological faith, so faith needs to be corrected, if not by wisdom at least by common sense, or by a certain amount of reason.

Anyway, Don Quixote is a very good example. I don't think Conze's interpretation or faith is quite correct. I think there is more to it than that; but we can see what he is getting at in the case of Cervantes' novel. You can certainly see that it can be looked at like that. Don Quixote had been reading these romances of knight-errantry and his head was completely turned. He saw windmills as giants, and ragged village wenches as high-born damsels in distress – the barber's basin as the helmet of an ancient hero. You can find people who do have this slightly distorted vision of reality, even if it is in a more humdrum sort of way than Don Quixote – people who interpret things differently all the time, as in cases of paranoia. Faith tends to do that. There was a case I read about in the newspaper only a few weeks ago. I'm not sure if this was in Britain or in the States. An American, who was on tour with his wife and their baby child, pulled in somewhere for petrol. For some reason the baby's carrycot was put on the roof of the car while they were filling up and he drove off forgetting that it was there. The poor baby fell off and was very seriously injured. Anyway, the father, realizing what had happened, stopped and went back and found the child. Far from being distressed he was overjoyed that a miracle had happened, that God had intervened to save the life of his child and that the child wasn't actually dead. Isn't this extraordinary! Instead of interpreting what had happened in terms of 'Due to my foolishness my child has been seriously injured' he interpreted it in terms of 'God has performed a miracle and saved the life of my child.' Thus do some Christians see the hand of God in everything. God has intervened.

ANDY: It's fantasy rather than faith.

SANGHARAKSHITA: Yes, it's fantasy rather than faith. That's why faith needs the corrective of wisdom, or at least of common sense. Otherwise it can just become fantasy: wish-fulfilment. You get a lot of this sort of thing in 'theosophical' circles. For instance, walking down the street you happen to meet someone who looks a bit foreign; he gives you a passing glance, and you thereupon go and tell someone, 'You know, I think I met one of those oriental masters. I was walking down the road and he gave me such a look. He gazed into my eyes: I really felt something. I'm sure I must have met one of the *mahatmas* from the Himalayas.' They want to believe that sort of thing and, as Dr Conze says, 'faith in this case becomes slightly pathological.'

ALICE IN ZEN-LAND

> Mr Blyth claims that 'the Don Quixote of the First Part is Zen incarnate', that 'the man who surpasses Hakuin, Rinzai, Eno, Daruma and Shakyamuni himself is Don Quixote de la Mancha, Knight Errant.'[67] Zen, it seems, like all good things, can be abused. It is not very probable that, when the cloak of 'Zen' is thrown over them, all donkeys do become tigers, all absurdities profundities. Irrationalism is not without its attractions, but can be overdone. To suggest that one scripture, one conviction, one faith is as good as another, smacks rather more of the spiritual nihilism of our present age, than of the wisdom of Seng-t'san.[68] (p. 10)

SANGHARAKSHITA: Who is this Mr Blyth? Do you know? Reginald Blyth was an English gentleman who lived in Japan for many years, taught English literature, compiled a number of works on Zen and English literature, and who was always trying to find resemblances between the two.[69] Dr Conze is not very happy about this. 'Mr Blyth claims that "the Don Quixote of the First Part"' – the first part of the book – '"is Zen incarnate."' People have said all sorts of silly things about Zen in this connection. Mr Humphreys says, for instance, that *Alice in Wonderland* is pure Zen; but it seems more like pure rubbish to say such a thing.[70] Why do you think they say it? Why do they make statements like that?

MARK: Apparent irrationality, I suppose.

SANGHARAKSHITA: Apparent irrationality, yes. But why should people be attracted by irrationality? Why should they see Zen as irrationality – leaving aside the fact that Dr Suzuki misled them a bit, to begin with, by presenting Zen in terms of irrationality or at least non-rationality.[71] But why should people take Zen ...

ANDY: Lack of contact.

SANGHARAKSHITA: It does seem to be something like this. For instance, who was the author of *Alice in Wonderland*?

SUSIDDHI: Lewis Carroll.[72]

MARK: He was a mathematician.

SANGHARAKSHITA: Yes, Lewis Carroll. He was a mathematician. What could be more logical, in a way, than that? There is a story that Queen Victoria was so delighted with *Alice in Wonderland* that she asked for a complete set of his works to be sent to her, with the result that she received a pile of books on advanced mathematics and was most disappointed. But it's a bit like that, isn't it? In the case of Mr Humphreys he's a lawyer and a judge, and all that kind of thing. Reason, or rationality, is very strong in him. Hence there is that 'attraction to the opposite' though without his balancing the rational and the irrational or harmonizing them. There's simply a compensatory influence at work. It degrades Zen, really, to look on it as a manifestation of irrationality. It also dockets and classifies it neatly. You've disposed of it; you've dealt with it: you know what it's all about. We know *Alice in Wonderland* very well. We know Don Quixote very well. What is Zen? Just something of the same sort. Just a zany kind of irrationality which highly intellectual people amuse themselves with as with a sort of game.

MAHAMATI: Maybe nonsense has an attraction for people who don't want to stop to think, who don't want to think clearly at all, who don't want to face up to their own situation clearly and who therefore rationalize.

SANGHARAKSHITA: As with the solving of crossword puzzles, it's a form of intellectual exercise for people who've got very restless, active minds, but who don't want to use them in any fundamental way – who merely want to keep themselves occupied. Do you see the difference between these two things? You've got this very active, restless, quite powerful mind ticking over the whole time; but you don't want to use it to investigate such questions as: Who am I? What am I? Why am I in this world? What is the purpose of life? – You don't dare, as it were, to face all those issues. So you occupy yourself with more and more difficult crossword puzzles, with chess, or with the analysis of symbolism in English literature. You occupy yourself in all sorts of futile ways – maybe with the writing of detective stories with very complex plots. Detective stories are written by intellectuals, I believe. And who reads them? I'm told clergymen read them. There was also a bishop who wrote detective stories. That was George Birmingham, Bishop of Birmingham, who was well known as a writer of detective stories.

MAHAMATI: And Colin Wilson, who wrote *The Outsider*.[73]

SUSIDDHI: If *Alice in Wonderland* is pure Zen, that would mean that the chap who deliberately wrote it is a Zen master.

SANGHARAKSHITA: Blyth is almost saying that in the case of Don Quixote. 'The man who surpasses Hakuin, Rinzai, Eno, Daruma and Shakyamuni himself is Don Quixote de la Mancha, Knight Errant.' He should have said Cervantes, shouldn't he? It's so ridiculous! You wonder that people can make these sorts of statements – that Don Quixote surpasses the Buddhist sages, including Śākyamuni, and that *Alice in Wonderland* is pure Zen. What on earth does Zen mean to you if you talk in that way? And it's presented as a sort of broad-mindedness. You're so broad-minded, so liberal, you see Zen everywhere – in the classics of English literature, in ordinary life. It's all Zen! Again, you are negating the real Zen. Still, let's not go to the other extreme.

SOBER AND CALM

> Don Quixote's faith was a rather puerile one, because he had no judgement, and his vision was defective. Blyth himself admits in the end that Don Quixote 'lacks the Confucian virtue of Prudence, the balance of the powers of the mind.' (p. 11)

SANGHARAKSHITA: 'Don Quixote's faith was a rather puerile one' – fair enough – 'because he had no judgement' – definitely not – 'and his vision was defective.' Well, that's pretty clear. 'Blyth himself admits in the end that Don Quixote "lacks the Confucian virtue of Prudence, the balance of the powers of the mind."' No, prudence is not the balance of the powers of the mind. Prudence is usually defined as the capacity to select the means appropriate to the achievement of a certain end.

> I am not so sure about prudence, but the 'balance of the powers of the mind' is certainly not only a Confucian, but also a Buddhist virtue, and a very essential one. Buddhaghosa, whom I am expounding here, leaves us in no doubt on this matter.[74] What distinguishes a *bhikkhu* from a knight-errant is that he is essentially sober and calm, that his view of the world is sweetly rational, that he avoids violence in the pursuit of his aims, and that his estimate of his own role in the world does not greatly exceed his actual size in relation to the universe. (p. 11)

SANGHARAKSHITA: What do you think of that last sentence? Do you completely agree with it? Is the *bhikkhu* 'essentially sober and calm'? Do you think this could possibly be misunderstood?

JOHN: The 'sober' part could be.

SANGHARAKSHITA: The 'sober' part could be. It seems to suggest, almost, a denial of enthusiasm, and ardour, and joy; a denial of rapture, overflowing energy, compassion. Maybe it's because Conze is, as he says, following Buddhaghosa, who is, of course, a Theravāda writer. Some of the Tantric sages were certainly not sober and calm. They might have been essentially *very* calm, but they were hardly sober – at least, not in outward manifestation. 'Sweetly rational' sounds a bit too good to be true doesn't it? Rational, yes, but you can be incisively rational, as well as sweetly rational. 'Avoids violence in pursuit of his aims'? Well, certainly he does. 'And that his estimate of his own role in the world does not greatly exceed his actual size in relation to the universe.' Dr Conze says 'does not greatly exceed' as though you can hardly help exaggerating your place in the universe a little bit. That's inevitable even in the case of your essentially sober and calm *bhikkhu*.

SUSIDDHI: It's a wee bit of a denial of the bodhisattva ideal.

SANGHARAKSHITA: Yes, in a way.

SUSIDDHI: He just underestimates his own role.

SANGHARAKSHITA: Dr Conze hasn't really said very much about vigour. What more could be said about it? If you like, about energy?

MAHAMATI: At the beginning of this section he says, 'Without vigour, without strenuous effort, without perseverance.' Perhaps one could say that vigour even flows quite naturally. It's certainly not necessarily tied up with a forced effort.

SANGHARAKSHITA: Not necessarily?

MAHAMATI: Well, not mentally to do strenuous effort; not going to strain.

SANGHARAKSHITA: Yes. *Vīrya* is more like innate vigour. It's a natural thing. You're not necessarily having to show it all the time.

SUVAJRA: He mentions that you maybe have to keep vigour in control by developing calm, but how do you cultivate vigour?

SANGHARAKSHITA: Well, how do you *think* you do? Maybe you should first of all look and see why vigour is lacking. Is it that you haven't been taking your Ovaltine? Do you see what I mean? Suppose you *do* come to the conclusion that you don't have enough vigour, you can look at the whole question in two ways, because there is vigour in the ordinary sense of life-energy, and there is spiritual vigour or the same thing transported, as it were, to the spiritual plane. But first of all one has to see the situation. One has to ask oneself such questions as do I have vigour or do I not? It seems one can have spiritual vigour without having vigour in the ordinary sense. There are highly developed people who, even in the absence of physical energy, health, and strength, seem to have tremendous spiritual vigour nonetheless; but they are quite exceptional. For most people, I think, what one might call psychospiritual vigour is quite difficult to develop except on a basis of ordinary, even physical, vigour and physical health. So suppose one finds that, generally, one is lacking in vigour, including spiritual vigour, what should one look for to begin with? You should ask yourself whether there is something basically wrong with your physical health; ask yourself whether you are even eating enough. It might be as simple as that! Are you looking after yourself sufficiently well? Suppose you are. Suppose you've got sufficient physical health, strength, and vigour, are you lacking in *spiritual* vigour?

CULTIVATING VIGOUR

SANGHARAKSHITA: Before we go into that, though, let's look at a traditional definition of vigour that might be helpful in this connection. The *Akṣayamati Sūtra* says the bodhisattva's *vigour* 'consists of his bringing about (in himself) the *dharmas* in which he has faith.'[75] *Dharmas* here meaning mental states. Thus your vigour consists in your bringing about in yourself the *dharmas*, the mental states, qualities, or experiences, in which you have faith. So suppose you don't have that sort of vigour, what might be the reason?

A VOICE: Faith.

SANGHARAKSHITA: You don't have the faith. You don't actually have faith in those *dharmas*. But if you *have* faith in those *dharmas*, surely then you will make an effort to bring them into existence. There's another traditional definition of vigour. In the *Milindapañha* the king asks, 'And what is the mark of vigour? Vigour props up, and when propped up by vigour, all the wholesome *dharmas* do not dwindle away.' – 'Give me a simile!' – 'If a man's house were falling down, he would prop it up with a new piece of wood, and, so supported, that house would not collapse.'[76] In the first quotation vigour is necessary to keep them in existence and to prevent them from falling down, because, until such time as you gain real insight and become a Stream Entrant, all your wholesome *dharmas* may fall down; you may regress: so you've got to be making a constant effort. It's not so much like preventing the house from falling down; it's more the case of a juggler keeping a number of coloured balls in the air at the same time. If you relax your effort for a moment, an instant, they'll all just fall to the ground. You need to be handling them constantly – *that's* what it's like – because the gravitational pull is at work all the time. You throw that little ball up, but it comes down each time – but *you've* got to keep throwing. When you've developed insight, and have become a Stream Entrant, then the balls start staying up. You throw them up, and they stay there! Until you've reached that point of Stream Entry, therefore, vigour, in the ordinary sense, is always necessary: you can't afford to stop. It's vigour that brings into existence the wholesome *dharmas* in which you have faith, and it's vigour which continues them in existence – which props them up, as it were, and prevents them from falling, from coming to an end. Thus there is a need not only for continuous vigour but for continuous faith. If that faith isn't there neither will you have the energy to bring the wholesome *dharmas* into existence – the wholesome *dharmas* in which you have faith, nor will you have the energy to keep them in existence: to keep them in the air, as it were, without falling to the ground. Thus faith becomes very, very important. There is no vigour, you could say, without faith.

SUVAJRA: What about after the point of Stream Entry? If you don't then need this vigour to keep the balls in the air....

SANGHARAKSHITA: Well, you need it, of course, to develop the further stages beyond, but at least the stage of Stream Entry itself is now self-perpetuating. From that point onwards you don't fall back. But if you don't make that further effort you remain just a Stream Entrant, and that further effort requires further faith – faith in the further possibilities ahead. So if you don't have faith, what are you going to do? How are you going to get faith? Vigour depends on faith. All right: what does faith depend on?

MARK: Inspiration.

SANGHARAKSHITA: Inspiration, yes. Where are you going to get *that* from? Suppose you are flat, dull, dry, uninspired, uninterested, feeling that you couldn't care less, where is it going to come from?

SUSIDDHI: The Sangha.

SANGHARAKSHITA: The Sangha. That's really where it comes from, and that's why you can't really do without the Sangha, and why the Sangha is one of the Refuges. The Buddha, historically speaking, is dead and gone. The Dharma may be very difficult for you to understand. But at least there is the Sangha, at least there is the circle of spiritual friends. This is why recourse to the sangha, the circle of spiritual friends, is very, very important – because it will help keep alive your faith, in the sense of your emotional aliveness to spiritual ideals, when it is in danger of becoming a bit flat and dead, or even of drying up altogether.

A FOUR-LETTER WORD

SANGHARAKSHITA: What is another thing that energy depends upon, something very mundane, that stimulates energy? You all know it but you're probably not able to think of it at the moment because it's right under your nose. You've all done it, I hope.

MAHAMATI: Meditation?

SANGHARAKSHITA: No. it's something much simpler and easier than that.

A VOICE: Give us a clue.

SANGHARAKSHITA: Well, it's a four letter word.

SUVAJRA: Sex.

SANGHARAKSHITA: No; sex is a three letter word.

A VOICE: Work.

SANGHARAKSHITA: Work! I'll read you an extract from a letter which I received only today which illustrates this point and which, you could say, put me in mind of it. The letter is from New Zealand. 'Dear Bhante. Some really amazing things have been happening in Auckland over the last two months. At the beginning of September, Jim Sharples' – that's a Mitra (now Dharmachari Vipula)[77] – 'arranged for us as part of our centre fund-raising to undertake a job with an advertising agency making eight thousand jack-in-the-boxes.' – There's one on the shelf behind you. – 'Getting the job done in the required time has needed an all-out effort, but it really seems to have brought good things out of people. Sometimes we've had up to twenty people working at the Centre on the boxes, and most of our regulars have been remarkable in the amount of time and energy they've been willing to put into things. We've had several instances of almost completely new people who didn't know much about the FWBO or Buddhism but who have been willing to throw themselves into the work effort.' etc, etc. They've now done the job, and the writer concludes by saying, 'The centre and classes have been quite affected by the general raising of the level of energy as well and we've been getting excellent attendances'. Isn't that interesting? Making eight thousand of these wretched advertising gimmicks; but, you see, it gets people's energies moving – that is the main thing. Even if it's only making jack-in-the-boxes, at least it gets their energies going and they're all working together. There is some kind of fellowship in working together in this way even if not exactly spiritual fellowship. And the energy of the classes goes up: meditation classes, Dharma study groups, all improve. Doesn't it seem ridiculous?

There was somebody in the community, not so long ago, who had a few problems and was not feeling too good; but he discovered a simple cure: he started going for a bicycle ride every day. This did the trick. It got his energies going and he then felt much better. In a way it's so incredibly simple. One can so easily let oneself get into this energyless state and, therefore, vigourless and faithless state. We've really noticed, in England, the same thing as Purna has written about in the case of New Zealand: that if you get started on work, work does arouse energy.[78] If you don't have energy, either because you're deficient in energy, or for some other reason, you can get inspiration from the spiritual community but you can also go and do some work. That will get your energy flowing, and once you've got it well flowing you can skilfully direct it into spiritual channels. You need a certain amount of tact, as it were, in dealing with yourself. Sometimes you might have to engage in a skilful mundane activity in order to get even your spiritual energies moving, because you're not on the spiritual level to begin with; you can't do anything on that level: you're stuck. You therefore have to do something on the mundane level first, and then lead those newly awakened mundane energies onto the spiritual level.

In the course of the last two or three years, ever since Sukhavati was started up, and since other projects have been got going in other centres, people have appreciated the value of work.[79] It's not surprising that the old Zen master used to say, 'A day of no working is a day of no eating.'[80] I've seen the value of work myself in the Buddhist countries of South-east Asia. The fact that the monks, the *bhikkhus*, don't work, or even are not allowed to work, is most unfortunate. I've seen quite a few *bhikkhus* who would love to work, but the lay people won't let them. They do what they can, but there are certain things that they are just not allowed to do. This is a real pity, because they've got the energy and the willingness to work, but the laity think it's not right that they should do those practical things. They think that *they* should do them for the monks and that the monks shouldn't ever do anything for the laity apart from reciting the scriptures and preaching. A lot of monks have got their energy bottled up, which isn't very good for them.

ANDY: I've been working by myself for quite a few weeks, and I noticed that if I could get into the work I felt quite inspired.

SANGHARAKSHITA: If you're working without really being into it, you start feeling resentment; you start feeling that the work has been imposed on you from outside: that you're being made to work. That's a quite unfortunate sort of situation. In a way you have been made to work, but at the same time you're making yourself work.

MAHAMATI: What's the difference between the physical and the spiritual element, the mundane and the spiritual?

SANGHARAKSHITA: I think in the ultimate sense one can't really say there is any difference. It's one energy taking different 'turnings', or existing in different degrees of grossness or refinement. When one says that if you can't do anything on the spiritual level you have to start off on the material level, what it really means is that if your energy is fairly gross, in order to refine it to a higher degree you have to go through various intermediate stages of refinement. Suppose your energy is really quite gross. It's no use trying to make that a very refined energy all at once. There are a number of intermediate stages to be gone through. You have to refine it gradually. That is what one really means by speaking of leading mundane energy into spiritual channels. It really means giving oneself enough time and space to effect that process of gradual refinement – which might be quite a lengthy one. You can't bypass those intermediate stages, though maybe you can speed them up. But I don't think one can speak in terms of two irreducibly different kinds of energy.

ENERGY, MALE AND FEMALE

SANGHARAKSHITA: In the same way that one has heard about physical and spiritual energy one has heard about male and female energy. I regard this as just mythology, in a way. Have you heard anyone making references to this male and female energy? If so in what sort of way?

SURATA: It's just accentuating the difference between the sexes.

SANGHARAKSHITA: But do you think there is such a thing as 'male energy' and such a thing as 'female energy'? Did the people using these terms seem to think that there was?

ANDY: People using those terms ...

SANGHARAKSHITA: How did they seem to use them? How did they seem to understand them?

ANDY: It was something I just heard.

SANGHARAKSHITA: What do you think they meant?

SUSIDDHI: Sounds like the expression of energy: male attributes and female attributes; which is a bit misleading anyway.

SANGHARAKSHITA: For instance – I've mentioned this before – some months ago there was an Order Day at Aryatara.[81] For the earlier part of the proceedings there were only men Order members present and they had a session of meditation and a session of walking and chanting. While the walking and chanting was going on two female Order members arrived, and as they opened the door of the shrine (they afterwards reported) they were 'hit' by a blast of 'male energy'. They went on to develop this theme of 'male energy', and afterwards it was developed further by other people. Some women started saying they didn't want to operate with male energy but with female energy. That's how the discussion arose. I was going into this and trying to understand what this male energy was that was different from female energy, or this female energy that was different from male energy.

ANDY: Isn't it that there is basically energy, but that there are also other qualities in the people themselves which ...

SANGHARAKSHITA: One could say that. Take this question of the walking and chanting. When men do it it's different from when women do it, but can one speak of a different *energy* being used? Is that really accurate? Put it another way: if a man meditates and a woman meditates are they using different energies? Could one say that? I came to the conclusion that if there was any difference at all it was simply a difference in the quantity of the one energy itself. 'Male energy' meant a more powerful energy and 'female energy' a weaker energy. One couldn't really see anything more in it than that. One could see not a different kind of energy, but only a difference of degree. What 'hit' the two female Order members on that occasion was not 'male energy' but a more vigorous walking and chanting practice than they were accustomed to. As for some of the women saying they didn't want to work with male energy but only with female energy, that seemed really to mean that they couldn't keep up the same pace as the men – that they didn't have the same amount of energy. To speak of there being a *different* energy in the case of women seemed a bit of a rationalization. Actually they had less energy but rationalized it as a different kind of energy.

SUSIDDHI: I don't think you can claim there are two kinds of energy. The transformation of Amaravati,[82] the women's community in East London, wasn't really a female ...

SANGHARAKSHITA: No, it wasn't a case of 'female energy'. It is just that the project got up somewhat more energy, as applied to that sort of repair and decoration work, than women usually have. They got it done in the same way that men would have got it done. There was no difference in respect of the type of energy used. So I think one can say that essentially there is just this one energy, and that one can't really divide it up into physical and mental, or male and female. It is just energy. This energy can take various forms. It has different levels, different degrees, different manifestations, and of course different qualities may be associated with it. But it is in fact just one energy.

SURATA: If one is feeling at rather a low ebb, and one comes in contact with someone who has got a lot of energy, you tend to really react, don't you? You get very defensive.

SANGHARAKSHITA: Yes. So instead of saying 'I am weaker' you say 'I am different.'

SUSIDDHI: 'I feel gentle.'

SANGHARAKSHITA: We used to have a lot of this in the Order generally, though not with regard to men and women. People who were weak and lacking in energy would accuse those who had a lot of energy of being very rough and crude and clumsy and insensitive and unaware. But this was clearly defensiveness on their part. This is now relatively a thing of the past, but we had a lot of it three or four years ago at Pundarika.[83]

RECEPTIVE ENERGY: A CONTRADICTION IN TERMS?

MAHAMATI: Can one explain the difference between a receptive energy and an active energy? If one can talk in those terms. Like, for instance, receptive is often associated with females.

SANGHARAKSHITA: I'm afraid I must scotch another heresy here. I don't think women are particularly receptive. One has to beware of slogans and catchwords. Because the female is physiologically receptive it does not mean that the female, the human female, is necessarily psychologically or spiritually receptive. She may be – but not simply because she is a female.

MAHAMATI: I know one does talk of a feminine and a masculine side of, say, the same process, but you can't really look at that in terms of energy.

A VOICE: Can one look at it in terms of attitude?

SANGHARAKSHITA: Yes, but I think the association of the terms 'masculine' and 'feminine' with certain attitudes tends to be a bit arbitrary and not necessarily gender-linked. What I've said about receptivity is a case in point. It's almost a cliché that women are more receptive than men. I don't think this at all. I think this is a sort of metaphorical extension from the fact of their physiological receptivity. For instance, are women more receptive to ideas than men? I doubt it very much. You could argue the opposite. But certainly they are not more receptive. Therefore you cannot associate receptivity with gender-linked femininity. Certainly a particular woman may be more receptive than a particular man, not because she is a woman but because she is receptive as an individual.

ANDY: It becomes a form of projection, doesn't it?

SANGHARAKSHITA: Yes, it does. I think one has to be quite careful about this business of receptive energy and – what should one call it? – creative energy, or active energy. 'Receptive energy' is almost a contradiction in terms. One can just speak of receptivity. Sometimes energy is an unnecessary extra word. We could say, 'he's very receptive,' or 'she's very receptive.' You don't have to say, 'they've got a lot of receptive energy'. But there does seem to be a tendency for people to translate things into terms of energy. It's like this idiom they've got nowadays of 'situation'. Instead of saying people are starving they say there is a situation of extreme food shortage, or even there is an extreme food shortage situation. So why bring in the word energy? Why not say 'he's very receptive' or 'she's very receptive', rather than saying 'they've got a lot of receptive energy' which adds nothing to the statement?

Why do you think the word 'energy' is brought in sometimes unnecessarily? It seems that people are quite preoccupied with the question of energy. Why should they be preoccupied with it? Well, it's obvious, isn't it?

SEVERAL VOICES: They haven't got any.

SANGHARAKSHITA: They haven't got any. So it's normal, in a way, that they should be preoccupied with it. People even come and see me at the end of a retreat and say, 'After this retreat I'm feeling really full of energy.' So what does this tell you about them? That they normally *don't* have energy; that they're certainly not full of it. Sometimes – this is another favourite – people come and say, 'After this retreat I'm feeling really strong.' But what does that tell you about them? Or else they say, 'I'm feeling really together.' These are the three things usually mentioned: energy, strength, and togetherness. So that tells you at once that normally they don't feel like that. We tend to be preoccupied with energy just because much of the time, unfortunately, we are deficient in energy. Perhaps Dr Conze hasn't got much to say about energy because he's quite an energetic person. Judging by the amount of material he produces, he's certainly a very hard worker. So perhaps energy is not a problem for him. Perhaps he's not all that interested in vigour because he's got plenty of it.

Anyway, I think we've dealt with that section, more or less. Is there any further or final point about vigour or energy? It's interesting that faith and vigour are enumerated in that order. Arranging them in this way you have faith leading to vigour or energy, and vigour helping to bring into existence within your own psychophysical continuum – to use the Buddhist expression – those *dharmas*, those skilful mental states and experiences, in which you have faith.

You have faith in them having seen them, as it were, fully exhibited in the person of the Buddha, and realizing that they can be developed – or can emerge within yourself. That about sums it up.

We might have gone over time just a little bit. I'm wondering when the meditation is starting. Ah, it was four o'clock. I think we should stop.

3
MINDFULNESS

Day 2: morning

> A Buddhist owes his soberness to the cultivation of the third virtue of *mindfulness* (*smriti*, Pāli *sati*). Whereas faith and vigour, when driven to excess, must be restrained by their counterparts, i.e. wisdom and tranquil concentration, the virtue of mindfulness does not share this disability. 'Mindfulness should be strong everywhere. For it protects the mind from excitedness, into which it might fall since faith, vigour and wisdom may excite us[84] and from indolence, into which it might fall since concentration favours indolence. Therefore, mindfulness is desirable everywhere, like a seasoning of salt in all sauces, like the prime minister in all state functions. (pp. 11–12)

SANGHARAKSHITA: There are quite a few points to be commented on here. First of all, this question of soberness. We did touch upon it a little yesterday. 'A Buddhist owes his soberness to the cultivation of the third virtue of mindfulness (*smriti*, Pāli *sati*)'.[85] What about this soberness of the Buddhist? Do you think that's really an adequate description? Doesn't it need to be supplemented or complemented by something? 'Soberness' is all right: it suggests continued mindfulness and awareness; but what is a bit lacking, a bit missing, as it were?

SUSIDDHI: Joy.

SANGHARAKSHITA: Yes, joy. There must be, not exhilaration exactly, but a sort of radiant joy. This is one of the things we started noticing on retreats quite a long time ago: that it was very difficult to strike a balance as between mindfulness, which tended to go a bit stiff and rigid, and joyfulness, which tended to become a bit hysterical. In those days, of course, people used to come on retreat straight from work, and since nearly everybody had a full-time job of a conventional nature they'd need a bit of time for loosening up. So you'd let them loosen up for a day or two, and they'd be happy; but then they'd start getting a bit skittish, and playful, and unmindful. So you'd remind them about the need for mindfulness and awareness, and maybe have a short period of silence. But then they'd start going a bit stiff, and rigid, and blocked. If that went too far you'd ease up, maybe have some communication exercises,[86] and that would restore the balance a little. And then they might get carried away again by *that*, so you'd have to have a little more silence. In this way one would try to bring people back to a middle path where they did have mindfulness and awareness, but also joy, and energy, and liveliness at the same time. It's very difficult to have these two not just side by side, not even just alternately, but fused, or interfused, or blended together. 'Soberness' seems a bit too much weighted on the side of mindfulness. Not that mindfulness shouldn't be there: not that soberness itself shouldn't be there; but that element of joy, and lightness, and radiance is also needed.

SUVAJRA: Is this Conze himself coming out here? Is he a very sober sort of person because he's not in contact with the sangha?

SANGHARAKSHITA: Not really. He's quite a jovial old chap, actually. I'm sure he's been carried away more than once in his life – judging by his autobiography, anyway. I think he's forming his picture of the Buddhist simply from the texts, some of which are a bit one sided. A Buddhist does owe 'his soberness to the cultivation of the third virtue of mindfulness', but we mustn't allow that to give us the impression that a Buddhist is simply all soberness – that a Buddhist is the embodiment of soberness and nothing more. There's more to the spiritual life than that.

SANGHARAKSHITA: 'Whereas faith and vigour, when driven to excess' – I don't like that expression – 'must be restrained by their counterparts.... the virtue of mindfulness does not share this disability. "Mindfulness should be strong everywhere. For it protects the mind from excitedness, into which it might fall since faith, vigour and wisdom may excite us; and from indolence into which it might fall since concentration favours indolence."' This is a quite interesting thought – that faith, vigour, and wisdom may excite us. There is a footnote here: 'Faith lends itself to emotional excitement; vigour to the excitement of doing things and wanting to do more; wisdom to the excitement of discovery.' Do you agree that faith lends itself to emotional excitement? Can you think of any rather extreme examples, possibly outside Buddhism, of faith lending itself to emotional excitement?

MAHAMATI: And fanaticism.

SANGHARAKSHITA: Yes, fanaticism, such as you get at a revivalist meeting, with the preacher whipping up people's feelings, or such as you get in the Hindu *kirtan*, or congregational singing and chanting, where everybody gets really carried away, as I've described in my memoirs.[87] This is the faith which 'lends itself to emotional excitement.' Then vigour lends itself 'to the excitement of doing things and wanting to do more' – I think most people are familiar with that, aren't they? No need to say very much about it. 'And wisdom to the excitement of discovery.' Maybe not everybody has experienced that. You get a new idea: you are very excited, very interested. You look it up here, you look it up there, in this reference book and in that. There are new vistas unfolding before you all the time. You get very excited. Thus wisdom leads to excitement, to the excitement of discovery. It's quite interesting that that excitement needs to be toned down by the interposition of mindfulness; but all the same you don't want to carry the mindfulness so far that it becomes a very one-sided sort of soberness, so that you not only get rid of faith itself – not only get rid of the excitement of vigour but get rid of vigour itself. Again, you must be really careful to follow the Middle Way.

Mindfulness protects the mind not only from excitedness but 'from indolence into which it might fall since concentration favours indolence.' Do you think this is true?

A VOICE: I didn't understand that.

SUSIDDHI: Introversion.

SANGHARAKSHITA: I think it's maybe Buddhaghosa being a little 'symmetrical'. I can see what he's getting at, but I wouldn't really call that state that 'favours indolence' *samādhi* in the true sense.[88] You can, of course, fall into a dreamy sort of pseudo-meditation in which you are just thinking beautiful thoughts and getting into beautiful states and floating away on a little rose-coloured cloud. You might want just to indulge in that, and not do anything. You might want just to be quiet and peaceful and beautiful and not soil your hands with any dirty work. I assume Buddhaghosa is thinking of that sort of thing. But that is not real *samādhi*, of course, because *samādhi* consists in the constant, uninterrupted production of highly skilful, or highly positive, mental states. That means really hard work. Even if things have come to the point where it's no longer hard work and there's a spontaneous flow of these skilful mental states on a relatively high level, you're certainly not in a state of indolence. So the *samādhi* that might fall into indolence, I would say, is not true *samādhi* at all. It's true that mindfulness can protect you against that, but what it's protecting you against is not really *samādhi* as a spiritual faculty or a cardinal virtue but something much, much inferior to that. Mindfulness is useful because it helps you to balance the four remaining spiritual faculties, and because it protects you against the excitedness into which three of them might fall and the indolence into which one of them might fall when wrongly understood or wrongly experienced. Therefore mindfulness is always useful. If you wanted to be a little pernickety you might object that if faith can go to extremes, and vigour, and wisdom, and even concentration, why not mindfulness? In that case it would be a sort of pseudo-mindfulness that you could regard as mindfulness gone to the extreme.

MARK: Over self-consciousness.

SANGHARAKSHITA: Yes, if you were self-conscious in such a way as to inhibit yourself all the time that could be regarded as mindfulness gone to the extreme. It might be objected that that isn't real mindfulness, but then you could retort that the *samādhi* that might fall into indolence is not the real *samādhi*. Perhaps we shouldn't make so much of an exception in the case of mindfulness as perhaps tradition does, and as we ourselves, following tradition, have been in the habit of doing. In the sense in which *samādhi*, at least, can go to extremes, mindfulness too, perhaps, can go to extremes. You can have too much mindfulness of the wrong sort, but then again, the faith of which you might have too much is by definition of the wrong sort. Certainly that holds good in the case of *samādhi* and indolence. Even the right sort of faith needs to be balanced by wisdom. Similarly, even the right kind of mindfulness needs to be 'balanced', you might say, by joy and spontaneity.

STEP BY STEP

JOHN: Does that mean that the five have to be developed simultaneously, or in a particular order? Because you have faith and not wisdom, which means …

SANGHARAKSHITA: An order seems to be followed in this exposition. First you develop faith, and it's because of your faith, of the fact that you have faith, that you develop vigour. Sometimes it's explained in this way. 'His vigour consists of his bringing about (in himself) the *dharmas* in which he has faith.' Mindfulness and awareness consists in guarding the skilful mental states that you've brought into existence and preventing them falling away, as well as in weeding out any unskilful mental states that might spring up amongst them. When those skilful mental states become established in you uninterruptedly, so that your mind is nothing but a pure continuous flow of highly positive mental states, that is *samādhi*. When your *samādhi* is sufficiently strong, and when on the basis of that *samādhi* you have an insight into reality itself, that is wisdom. In this way the five spiritual faculties are developed in sequence. At the same time they need, all of them, to be fully developed, because if you develop your faith to the full then your vigour can be developed to the full; if you develop your vigour to the full your mindfulness can be developed to the full, and so on. You could say that here there is a possibility of a path of regular steps and a path of irregular steps.[89] You could start off by developing wisdom without much in the way of faith or much in the way of vigour. You wouldn't get very far, though. You'd have to come back and strengthen and consolidate your base in the form of the other spiritual faculties. But this is what most people do. They work a little on this faculty then a little on that. But you can't *perfect* vigour, say, before you've perfected faith. You can't *perfect* mindfulness before you've perfected vigour. This is where the path of regular steps comes in.

THE DEWAN OF SIKKIM

SANGHARAKSHITA: 'Mindfulness is desirable everywhere' – let's take that for granted and not question it too much – 'like a seasoning of salt in all sauces, like the prime minister in all state functions.' The ancient Indian prime minister or *dewan*, as he was called at a later date, was a sort of administrative maid-of-all work. I remember a little story in this connection. You know that when I lived in Kalimpong I used to go up to the state of Sikkim, which at that time was a protectorate of India. Now India has annexed it, unfortunately. Anyway I used to go up to Gangtok, the 'village capital' as it was called, where the toy government of the state was located, and the toy court. At that time there were less than 150,000 people in Sikkim, but they had their own government, complete with an Indian representative, and of course they had their maharaja, their king, with his court and all.[90] In the days when I was going up there everything was in process of democratization. A secretariat was built, and two hundred people were employed there – a miniature bureaucracy. There was a prime minister, or *dewan*, and a number of ministers. Altogether between two and three hundred people were administering this tiny state. One day I was talking to an old friend of mine there who was at that time chief secretary to the government. He was a Tibetan Buddhist, Sikkimese-born; an aristocrat of the old school; a very, very devout Buddhist; connected by marriage with the Sakyapa lamas, and completely and openly contemptuous of anything democratic. We were talking in his office in the secretariat building, and he said, 'Look at this secretariat! Look at all these ministers, and these clerks! In the old days, when I was private secretary to His Highness, I ran the whole state single-handed, with the help of *one* clerk.' Moreover, he ran the state in his spare time. Being private secretary his main task was to look after the maharaja's private affairs. He had to get his children admitted to school in Darjeeling, order his wines and spirits from Calcutta – these were the important things. When he had time he saw to the administration of the state with the help of his one clerk. He held all the different portfolios, and according to his own account at least, he ran the state perfectly satisfactorily. This is what the old-style Indian prime minister or *dewan* was like. Therefore, mindfulness is desirable everywhere, 'like the prime minister in all state functions'. The prime minister was present everywhere!

THE CENTRALITY OF MINDFULNESS

> Hence it is said, 'The Lord has declared mindfulness to be useful everywhere, for the mind finds refuge in mindfulness and mindfulness is its protector. Without mindfulness there can be no exertion or restraint of the mind.'[91] (p. 12)

SANGHARAKSHITA: This is quite interesting, that 'without mindfulness there can be no exertion or restraint of the mind', as though you might forget to exert yourself, or forget the reason why you should exert yourself, or exercise restraint.

> Although traces of it are not altogether absent in other religious and philosophical disciplines, in Buddhism alone mindfulness occupies a central position. If one were asked what distinguishes Buddhism from all other systems of thought, one would have to answer that it is the *dharma*-theory and the stress laid on mindfulness. Mindfulness is not only the seventh of the steps of the holy eightfold path, the third of the five virtues, and the first of the seven limbs of enlightenment. On occasions it is almost equated with Buddhism itself. So we read at the beginning of the *Satipaṭṭhāna Sutta* that 'the four applications of mindfulness are the one and only way (*ekāyano maggo*) that leads beings to purity, to the transcending of sorrow and lamentation, to the appeasement of pain and sadness, to entrance upon the right method and to the realization of Nirvāṇa'.[92] (p. 12)

SANGHARAKSHITA: 'Although traces of it are not altogether absent in other religious and philosophical disciplines, in Buddhism alone mindfulness occupies a central position.' You notice he says a central position and not *the* central position, as though to say *the* central position would be to give mindfulness just a little too much importance. 'If one were asked what distinguishes Buddhism from all other systems of thought, one would have to answer that it is the *dharma*-theory and the stress laid on mindfulness.' The *dharma*-theory is the theory – or doctrine, or teaching – that the whole of our experience, in fact the whole of existence, can be analysed into ultimate, irreducible, mental and physical events called *dharmas* and that these *dharmas* are not entities, as sometimes is thought, but processes.[93] As for 'the stress laid on mindfulness', it's certainly true that no other religion lays stress on mindfulness in the way that Buddhism does. Do you think any equivalent of mindfulness is ever taught in Christianity? Do you ever hear of a Christian preacher speaking about mindfulness from the pulpit? Are you *likely* to hear? In Christian monastic circles there is what they call 'recollection', which to some extent resembles mindfulness, but it's a distinctively monastic virtue: it's not a general Christian virtue. The ordinary Christian is certainly not advised to practise recollection; but monks are sometimes, or used to be – I don't know about now. There's also the term 'consideration'. There's a work by St Bernard called *On Consideration*.[94] This is addressed to a pope who had been a monk, and of course St Bernard himself was a monk, so this again was very much a monastic teaching. It's as though the whole conception of mindfulness, or recollection, or consideration, has significance only within the context of a comparatively intense spiritual life – of an actual effort to develop. It's virtually useless to the masses. You can't imagine an ethnic religion teaching mindfulness. Buddhism being so concerned with the development of the individual, it's not surprising there should be this stress on mindfulness. The fact that there is this stress on mindfulness in Buddhism, in a way that you don't get in any other religion, is simply a reflection of the fact that no other religion or religious teaching is concerned with the development of the individual in such an intensive and central way that Buddhism is.

SATIPAṬṬHĀNA

SANGHARAKSHITA: 'Mindfulness is not only the seventh of the steps of the holy eightfold path, the third of the five virtues, and the first of the seven limbs of enlightenment. On occasions it is almost equated with Buddhism itself.' The Eightfold Path is pretty central in Buddhism, as are the five virtues and the seven limbs of Enlightenment (*bodhyaṅga*, Pāli *bojjhaṅga*), and in all of them mindfulness figures.[95] Thus one can correctly speak of a stress laid on mindfulness by Buddhism, in that all the most important formulations of the teaching include mindfulness – certainly all the most important formulations of primitive Buddhism, as we might call it. 'On occasions it is almost equated with Buddhism itself.' To be a Buddhist is to be mindful; to be mindful is to be a Buddhist, practically.

'So we read at the beginning of the *Satipaṭṭhāna Sutta* that "the four applications of mindfulness are the one and only way (*ekāyano maggo*) that leads beings to purity, to the transcending of sorrow and lamentation, to the appeasement of pain and sadness, to entrance upon the right method and to the realization of Nirvāṇa."' I take it you know what these four applications of mindfulness are. You ought to know. These are quite basic things.

MARK: Is this the qualities of the emotions?

SUSIDDHI: States of mind, consciousness.

SANGHARAKSHITA: The four applications of mindfulness are to the body and bodily movements, to feelings, to thoughts, and to *dhammas* which means something like 'realities' or 'formulations of the teaching.'[96] Thus there is a constant awareness of (1) the state of your physical body, as well as of its position and its movements – if in fact you are moving; of (2) your emotional state, i.e. whether you are happy, or sad, and so on; of (3) your thoughts, whether these concern your lunch, the *dharma*-theory, or an absent friend; and of (4) the truth of universal impermanence, or the five *skandhas* or 'aggregates' of conditioned existence, or even Nirvāṇa.[97] These are the four applications – sometimes called the four foundations of mindfulness. I've also spoken in lectures in terms of the four dimensions of awareness, that is to say: (1) awareness of oneself (one's own body, feelings, and thoughts); (2) awareness of other people; (3) awareness of nature, the whole natural environment (you could speak of ecological awareness – or even of eco-awareness – if you wanted to be very 'with it'!); and (4) awareness of Reality.[98]

This classification is, perhaps, more comprehensive. But again I think there is some danger in speaking of the spiritual life, or of

Buddhism, exclusively – or almost exclusively – in terms of mindfulness and awareness. It does tend to become a bit dry, just a little bit too one-sidedly sober. This sort of teaching was fine for ancient Indians who were, so far as we can make out, very exuberant people, full of the joy of living – both in the Buddha's day and before that. There was no danger of them becoming emotionally dried up, or emotionally blocked. They came into the Buddha's teaching in a very healthy, lively, exuberant sort of state, and just needed to be calmed down with this teaching of mindfulness. But if you come into Buddhism already emotionally blocked, and already overly self-conscious, then perhaps the teaching of mindfulness is not going to help you quite so much. It needs to be supplemented by something else: it isn't then an all-sufficing teaching. You may need a different sort of approach – maybe one with more emphasis on faith, or more emphasis on vigour, and not so much emphasis on mindfulness. You might have, already, too much of the wrong sort of mindfulness. For instance there are one or two quite good books on these four foundations of mindfulness, but though excellent, and really very worthy, they do strike one as rather dry and even almost dull at times.[99]

MAHAMATI: Perhaps mindfulness itself can be talked about in another way. You know, really experiencing it.

SANGHARAKSHITA: Yes, or perhaps one could speak of it in terms of awareness rather than mindfulness, because the so-called *vipassanā* teaching (I say 'so-called' because it bears that label without having much resemblance to the original *vipassanā* teaching of the Buddha) includes a strong element of 'mindfulness'. In fact, it is exclusively a teaching of mindfulness. When I came back to England in 1964 and found people practising this kind of 'mindfulness' I was quite shocked. They were just making themselves into zombies. It was really terrible to see. Some of them ought to have been in a mental hospital – in fact some of them did go into a mental hospital later on. They had been taught this kind of 'mindfulness' practice by some Thai *vipassanā* teachers and by a Canadian monk who had been in a meditation centre in Rangoon for three weeks and had come back full of theory and technique which he had started applying vigorously and getting people to do.[100] As a result they became acutely alienated from themselves in a way that in the

Friends I've seen nobody even approaching. They were really just like zombies. When I went to a meditation centre where they were doing this so-called *vipassanā* I found them walking around in that alienated state. This is what the wrong practice of mindfulness can do to you.

BUDDHĀNUSMṚTI

> What then is 'mindfulness'? The Abhidharma, guided by the etymology of the Sanskrit term (*smriti* from *smri*, 'to remember'), defines it as an act of remembering which prevents ideas from 'floating away', and which fights forgetfulness, carelessness and distraction. This definition by itself, though correct, does not really make the function of this virtue very clear to us today. The theoretical assumptions which underlie the various practices summed up in the word 'mindfulness', are too much taken for granted. (pp. 12–13)

SANGHARAKSHITA: So it 'prevents ideas from floating away.' Do you remember functioning in this sort of way? What is this tendency of ideas to 'float away'? Why do they float away? Why don't they stay?

JOHN: Because you get other ideas which just kind of ....

SANGHARAKSHITA: You get other ideas: you get interested in other things.[101]

SUVAJRA: You haven't really paid attention to them in the first place.

SANGHARAKSHITA: Yes, that also. They float away because they haven't made a sufficiently strong impression on the mind. Suppose you have the idea of the Buddha. Presumably you shouldn't allow that idea to float away, should you? Presumably that idea should be there all the time. But does that idea tend to float away? Unfortunately it does. One could therefore say, in this case, that mindfulness is the act of remembering which prevents the idea of the Buddha from floating away – as when you practise *buddhānusmṛti*, recollection or mindfulness of the Buddha.[102] You try to keep that idea of the Buddha in your mind because you are convinced that is an idea which you ought to be entertaining all the time, thus making it a permanent part of your mental make-up. Thus mindfulness can be defined as an act of remembering which prevents those ideas which ought to be a permanent part of your mental make-up from floating away; which fights forgetfulness of such ideas, as well as carelessness about them, and distraction from them brought about by the intervention of other, opposite, or inimical ideas. This is quite a useful way of looking at mindfulness – as this sort of act of remembering. Because we get all sorts of good ideas, in the sense of positive ideas, which we ought to be thinking about all the time, but they float away. What is going to prevent them floating away? It is this act of remembering them, in a sense hanging on to them, not letting them float away – and this is mindfulness. One could even say never allow the idea of development, the idea of yourself as a developing person, to float away! Hang on to that idea. There should be an act of remembering with regard to it, so that it doesn't float away.

MAHAMATI: The idea of the Buddha would remain with one because one felt ... I don't quite see how mindfulness would ...

SANGHARAKSHITA: Then what about the traditional practice of recollection of the Buddha? Recollection of the Buddha is not just the thought, or the abstract idea, of the Buddha, but the recollection of the qualities of the Buddha, that is to say, the bringing of those qualities powerfully before the mind in an imaginative sort of way, which means that faith would then automatically be present. Suppose you have forgotten the Buddha because you are without faith. How are you going to bring the Buddha back? You bring the Buddha back by an act of recollection. You call to mind his qualities, and start vividly realizing and imagining them; and then, of course, faith arises. As long as that faith lasts you've no difficulty in recollecting the Buddha. It seems, then, that mindfulness does play its part here, i.e. in the absence of faith. If faith in the Buddha is present you don't need mindfulness in the sense of 'formal' recollection of the Buddha, but if faith fades away, and even disappears altogether, you then need mindfulness in the sense of recollection of the Buddha to bring back the 'image' of the Buddha, which will then stimulate faith in the Buddha.

'The Abhidharma, guided by the etymology of the Sanskrit term (*smriti* from *smri*, "to remember"), defines it as an act of remembering which prevents ideas from "floating away", and which fights forgetfulness, carelessness and distraction.' What do you think 'carelessness' would be? How would carelessness come about with respect to those ideas that you ought to be bearing in mind?

SUSIDDHI: By just letting them be displaced by other things.

SANGHARAKSHITA: That is covered by 'distraction'. What does carelessness really convey?

A VOICE: Lack of reverence.

SANGHARAKSHITA: Lack of reverence, or maybe something a little more general than that. It suggests you don't value those ideas as you ought to. When you treat something carelessly, it means you don't really value it. If you possess a really valuable painting you look after it very carefully. If you look after it carelessly it means you don't value it. Similarly, if you are careless with regard to those highly positive ideas that you ought to be making a permanent part of your mental make-up it means you don't really value them: that's why you're careless about them. Mindfulness helps you to remember how valuable they are, and how useful, and therefore it fights carelessness. In the same way mindfulness fights distraction, it fights those less positive, less skilful ideas which get in the way of the more highly positive ideas and of your spiritual development in general. Mindfulness makes you work at the fact that if you allow the less positive ideas in, you thereby sacrifice the more valuable ideas. These less positive ideas are, therefore, dangerous, and should be kept out.

As an act of remembering, mindfulness therefore has a threefold function. It prevents us from forgetting ideas that we ought to remember, prevents us from undervaluing them, and prevents us from allowing them to be interrupted by ideas which are less valuable, less helpful to us.

Anyway, Dr Conze isn't very satisfied. He says, 'This definition by itself, though correct, does not really make the function of this virtue very clear to us today.' I'm not so sure that I agree with that, but anyway, 'The theoretical assumptions which underlie the various practices summed up in the word "mindfulness", are too much taken for granted.' What are those theoretical assumptions?

> What one assumes is that the mind consists of two disparate parts, – a depth which is calm and quiet, and a surface which is disturbed. The surface layer is in perpetual agitation and turmoil. The centre, at the bottom of the mind, beyond both the conscious and the unconscious mind as modern psychologists understand it, is quite still. The depth is, however, usually overlaid to such an extent that people remain incredulous when told of a submerged spot of stillness in their inmost hearts. In most cases the surface is so turbulent that the calm of the depth can be realized only in rare intervals. (p. 13)

SANGHARAKSHITA: So according to Dr Conze the Abhidharma definition, though correct, 'does not really make the function of this virtue' – mindfulness – 'very clear to us today.' This is because 'The theoretical assumptions which underlie the various practices summed up in the word "mindfulness", are too much taken for granted.' Now is that really so? Do these theoretical assumptions, as he describes them, i.e. about there being these two levels of the mind, really underline these practices, and does one have to understand these assumptions in order to have a clear understanding of what mindfulness is?

A VOICE: No.

SUVAJRA: I can't remember coming across it, apart from TM.[103]

SANGHARAKSHITA: It seems rather odd, doesn't it? It doesn't really make things any clearer: it only introduces a sort of quasi-metaphysical explanation. It seems to me a bit like what I talked about on the *Sūtra of Wei Lang* seminar several years ago, i.e. what I think I called the metaphysics of potentiality.[104] For instance, we say that if you make an effort you can become Enlightened; you can become a Buddha, or realize Buddhahood. That is all that the original Pāli or, if you like, the Theravāda teaching, or the original teaching, of Buddhism actually says. But you can interpret that 'metaphysically'. You can say that if you are able to gain Enlightenment, or gain Buddhahood, that means you are potentially Enlightened, that you are potentially Buddha. *That* means you are Buddha, in fact, here and now, even though you don't realize it. Thus there are two levels: the level of your unenlightened, un-Buddha-like nature, and the level of your Enlightened, Buddha-like nature. The truth is that here and now, in the depths of your being, you *are* Buddha. All you have to do is contact that deeper level, which is your real nature. That is the more metaphysical way of putting it, which to some extent the Mahāyāna adopted later on.[105] But the Buddha himself seems quite clearly not to have used that sort of language. Do you see the difference? The Buddha only said if you make the effort, you can become Enlightened. He did not speak of the state of Enlightenment which you were potentially capable of realizing in the future as actually existing here and now in some hidden depth within you.

One can understand that the use of such language as 'you are potentially Buddha, in fact *are* a Buddha even now,' is all right to encourage people, but it can lead to intellectual difficulties. For instance, there is the question: if you are a Buddha, how did you come to think you were anything else? How did this horrible mistake – that you were Mahamati or whoever – arise? How can a Buddha forget that he is a Buddha? – assuming that he is really a Buddha to start with. Thus this metaphysics of potentiality, as I call it, is fraught with difficulties. I therefore think it's much better, and safer and sounder, and no less helpful, just to speak in the same sort of terms as the Buddha used, and to say that if you make the effort you can develop a specific mental state, including the state of Enlightenment. There is no need to have recourse to a metaphysics of potentiality, in the way that Dr Conze seems to be doing. Instead of being satisfied with the simple statement that through mindfulness you can develop a calmer and clearer state of mind than you have at present he talks about 'the theoretical assumptions which underlie the various practices summed up in the word "mindfulness"' in terms of these two disparate parts – the calm, quiet depth, and the agitated surface. Such assumptions seem quite unnecessary, and were in any case not made by the Buddha when he gave this teaching of mindfulness.

So it's not surprising that 'people remain incredulous when told of a submerged spot of stillness in their inmost hearts'. It's not surprising at all. It's a sort of metaphysical fiction. It's much better to say, look, you are in a terrible state now, your mind is very disturbed, it's in a state of turmoil. But if you go about it in the right way, if you practise correctly, if you follow the right methods, you can develop at least a measure of calm. That will seem much more convincing to them than saying, no, you're not really in a state of turmoil; deep down you're just still, calm, quiet. – You see? We are taking the analogy of the ocean which is ruffled on the surface but still in the depths much too literally. We don't need to do that sort of thing. We don't need these pseudo-metaphysical, or pseudo-Jungian, assumptions or whatever. I'd say, if anything, from what I'd seen of people, that their minds are in a state of turmoil from the surface right down into the depths! So speak in terms of calming that tumult on all levels, which can be done.

SUSIDDHI: It's not assumptions you need, it's just a wee bit of experience of it. Sometimes you're calm, other times not, and ...

SANGHARAKSHITA: You don't need any assumptions of this 'metaphysical' order.

SUVAJRA: It's like telling an acorn that it really is an oak tree – that it should be fully grown.

SANGHARAKSHITA: It's like saying that if you dig deep enough into the acorn you will find a tiny oak tree there. This is what it was like in the case of the homunculus. In medieval times, I think it was, people used to believe that each spermatozoon contained a tiny man – complete, of course with genitals containing spermatozoa containing tiny men to infinity.[106] The metaphysics of potentiality is rather like that. In other words, it's a negation of the concept of growth. And then you present yourself with the problem of *how*, in this world of static levels, growth is possible. If you say that you are already Buddha, in a sense you are negating growth; you are regarding the growth which takes place when you pass from one level to another as something illusory, if you see what I mean, because there's no real growth: you already are that; you just have to uncover the fact, reveal yourself to yourself, as you really are. There's no question of growth or development. So, if growth or development becomes a sort of metaphysical fiction you can hardly expect people to put energy into it.

The whole of the Buddha's teaching, so far as one can see, is based on the reality of change, the reality of development, the reality of the progress of the individual – based on the fact that change is real. The situation is not complicated by any metaphysical assumptions: these, I am sure, would have been dismissed by the Buddha as *diṭṭhis*, mere views, which were not at all helpful. There's only one passage in the whole Pāli canon which speaks in terms of an essentially pure mind which is defiled by adventitious defilements.[107] So it might, on occasion, be all right to encourage people who were riddled with strong feelings of guilt and unworthiness, and who were convinced that they were thoroughly evil, by saying no, you are not evil; you are potentially Enlightened. That immaculate Buddha-nature is there underneath. That could be a skilful thing to do in those circumstances, but not as a general approach. It just isn't necessary for ordinary, healthy people. They feel themselves alive and growing: they don't feel themselves uncovering some metaphysical Buddha-nature stage by stage. I think here it's a case of the strongly metaphysically-inclined Indian mind getting to work on Buddhism, on the Buddha's teaching, and trying to metaphysicalize it, when that's quite unnecessary. It is really a form of substantialism, really a form of *ātmavāda*, this thinking in terms of the final stage of development as being already present, actually existing within you, as it were, potentially. It negates the reality of process, and therefore of *śūnyatā*.[108]

SUSIDDHI: It negates the *dhamma* theory as well.

MAHAMATI: Why therefore is it a negation of *śūnyatā*?

SANGHARAKSHITA: Because *śūnyatā* isn't a sort of metaphysical absolute. It represents, as it were, the possibility of complete change, complete transformation. It represents the fact that nothing is limited to being what it is. *Śūnyatā* is the 'guarantor' of the possibility of unrestricted change and development. *Śūnyatā* is what prevents anything from being what it is.[109]

NATURE AND CULTURE

> Mindfulness and concentration are the two virtues which are concerned with the development of inward calm. The principal enemies of spiritual quietude are: (1) the senses; (2) the

movements of the body; (3) the passions, wants and desires; and (4) discursive thinking. They have the power to be enemies when: (1) they are not subjected to any discipline; and (2) when the ego identifies itself with what takes place on the surface of the mind, participating heartily in it, and the illusion arises that these activities are 'my' doings, 'my' concerns and the sphere in which 'I' live and have my being. (p. 13)

SANGHARAKSHITA: Is it necessary to think of these 'enemies of spiritual quietude' as occurring on the surface of the mind? Can't one just think of them as occurring at one's present level of development? That's quite sufficient, really.

When thus busy with worldly things, we have neither strength nor freedom. In order to conquer these enemies of spiritual quietude we must: (1) withdraw the senses from their objects, as the tortoise draws in its limbs; (2) keep watch on our muscular movements; (3) cease wanting anything, and dissociate all wants from the ego; and (4) cut off discursive thinking.

By an effort of the imagination one must try to see oneself at rest, floating freely, with no force exerted on one's spiritual self. The practice of mindfulness then is a series of efforts which aim at maintaining this isolation. Mindfulness is the name given to the measures which we take to protect the patch of inner calm, which may at first not seem very large. One, as it were, draws a line round this domain and at its boundaries keeps watch on trespassers.[110] (pp. 13–14)

SANGHARAKSHITA: That's all right, provided one thinks of that calm as something one is actually developing and keeping in existence, rather than as something already existing in the depths of one's heart.

Now Dr Conze gives one or two traditional methods of practising mindfulness.

First, as regards the *sensory stimuli*, there is the 'restraint of the senses', also called the 'guarding of the doors of the senses'. For two reasons sense stimulation may disturb inner calm: (1) because it gives an occasion for undesirable states, like greed, hate,

> etc., to invade and flood the mind; (2) because attention to the sensory world, however necessary and apparently innocuous, distracts from the object of wisdom, which is the emptiness of *dharmas*. One cannot grasp what is meant by 'restraint of the sense dominants', if one regards it as quite a natural thing that the mind should dwell on sense-linked objects. This is, indeed, most unnatural. In its natural purity thought abides in the calm contemplation of emptiness. The mind which sees, hears, etc., is a fallen mind. (p. 14)

SANGHARAKSHITA: He's getting a bit away from Buddhism, in a way, isn't he? This 'fallen mind' sounds almost like Adam and Eve in the Garden of Eden. 'One regards it as quite a natural thing that the mind should dwell on sense-linked objects. This is, indeed, most unnatural. In its natural purity thought abides in the calm contemplation of emptiness.' Well, why on earth doesn't thought do what is natural to it? What makes it do anything else? On that basis why should it be 'a fallen mind'? This raises the question of the inherent difficulty of this 'metaphysics of potentiality'. There's really no need to speak of it in terms of natural or unnatural. If anything, it's natural for the mind to wander. If the natural is the already existing, then what your mind usually does – what everybody's mind usually does, and always has done – would seem to be the natural. It would be better to take that as the basis, and if anything think of the spiritual life itself as unnatural. Certainly in biological terms, in the same way that culture is unnatural, houses are unnatural, art is unnatural, philosophy is unnatural, so spiritual life is unnatural. It is unnatural because it goes right against nature. Turning the other cheek is unnatural; practising *mettā bhāvanā* is unnatural. Goethe once said, 'Whatever is against nature is to be cultivated.'

Looking at things in that way, i.e. naturalistically rather than metaphysically, seems to make more sense. Otherwise you have to explain why this pure, clear, free, Enlightened mind fell. The Christians have enough difficulty understanding how Adam fell. True, there was Eve; there was also the serpent; there was even an apple; and they were, of course, created with free will – so the Christians say. Thus they could either follow the right path or not; it was up to them: they chose to fall. But can an Enlightened mind fall? How can an Enlightened mind, a pure mind, do anything that isn't Enlightened and pure? – In this manner,

I'm afraid, Dr Conze gets himself into difficulties. Surely it is natural for the mind to 'dwell on sense-linked objects', despite what Dr Conze says. 'In its natural purity thought abides in the calm contemplation of emptiness.' No, despite the Mahāyāna and the Vajrayāna there's no such thing as natural purity of thought – not as something actually experienced, or real in experiential terms. It's only what Dr Guenther would call an operational concept.[III] It might be useful, in certain circumstances, to speak in that way; but one shouldn't take it at all literally. What you really mean when you say that you are fundamentally pure is that you can jolly well become so if you only pull your socks up and make the effort! This is what it really amounts to. Otherwise you can dwell on the thought of how pure you really are, deep down, without making any real, actual effort to realize that. You are satisfied with the fact – as you believe it to be – that deep down you are pure. So you just go along in your usual grubby way, making no effort to purify yourself, because you're convinced, or have *been* convinced, that deep down you are pure and so have no need to make any such effort. Now here's Dr Conze's second reason why inner calm may be disturbed by sense stimulation.

TAKING RESPONSIBILITY

SANGHARAKSHITA: 'For two reasons sense stimulation may disturb inner calm: (1) because it gives an occasion for undesirable states, like greed, hate, etc., to invade and flood the mind; (2) because attention to the sensory world, however necessary and apparently innocuous, distracts from the object of wisdom, which is the emptiness of *dharmas*.' What Dr Conze says on this level is perfectly all right. Sense stimulation may indeed disturb inner calm because it's the occasion for the arising of unskilful mental states, and because it represents a distraction from what we really ought to be occupying ourselves with, which is reality. But there's a bit more than that, even, to be said on these topics. 'Sense stimulation may disturb inner calm: (1) because it gives an occasion for undesirable states…' Do you realize the significance of this word 'occasion'? He is using 'occasion' quite deliberately, and quite correctly, and not 'caused'. He doesn't say sense stimulation may disturb inner calm because it is the cause of undesirable states arising: it's the occasion. Now what is the point of the distinction?

MAHAMATI: It doesn't *have* to arise.

SANGHARAKSHITA: It doesn't *have* to arise: yes. It's only an occasion.

SUVAJRA: It's like an opportunity.

SANGHARAKSHITA: It's more than an opportunity, but it's not a cause. It's very important to make this distinction. Sometimes we say of another person: 'He made me angry. It was *his* fault I became angry; he *made* me angry.' – But no, he didn't make you angry: he only gave you the occasion for anger. The anger came from within *you*; *You* were responsible for your becoming angry. The fact that one uses this word 'occasion' suggests that withdrawal from sense stimuli is not in itself a solution, because you will still have to deal with the unskilful mental states within yourself. The sense contact has only been the occasion of their arising: it hasn't caused them. Even if you were to go off into a solitary retreat with the minimum of sense stimuli, you'd still be confronted by these unskilful mental states. They may arise in the entire absence of appropriate sense stimuli, and you may therefore still have to deal with them. You *could* deal with them without an actual physical withdrawal – if you were of a strong, heroic, determined, spiritual character. But most people need periods of respite and withdrawal from the sense stimuli, so that they can 'study' the unskilful mental states independently of the actual occasions of their arising in the external world. They need a more laboratory-like situation.

'Because attention to the sensory world, however necessary and apparently innocuous, distracts from the object of wisdom, which is the emptiness of *dharmas*.' That is not completely true, i.e. that attention to the sensory distracts from the object of wisdom. What is the object of wisdom? To give a very simple example from early Buddhism, from the Buddha's own teaching (leaving aside the emptiness of *dharmas*), it is impermanence. But when you contemplate impermanence do you simply contemplate the *abstract* notion of impermanence, apart from concrete things that are impermanent? No. So isn't it, in a sense, a little bit absurd to speak of withdrawing yourself from sense objects in order to contemplate the impermanence of those sense objects? Maybe you need to withdraw a little just to strengthen the general idea of impermanence, but ultimately it's to those very things that you've got to apply the concept of impermanence. You've got to realize that *this* is impermanent and *that* is impermanent, not just review a general conception of impermanence. Wisdom is not the contemplation of an abstract idea of impermanence. That's letting you get away with it too easily. It's letting you off too lightly. You've got to realize that this food that you are eating is impermanent, that this person that you are attached to is impermanent, that these books you read so lovingly every day are impermanent. It is not that you just withdraw from all these things and contemplate an abstract idea of impermanence. Therefore what he says here, though correct so far as it goes, has to be qualified somewhat. You may well have to withdraw for a time, but withdrawal from sense objects, from sense stimulation, is not the last word.

MAHAMATI: I've been thinking of mindfulness, and you're really in touch with things around you.

SANGHARAKSHITA: There are some experiences which are incompatible with mindfulness. In order to preserve the mindfulness you've got to separate from the experience. If you insist on having the experience *along* with the mindfulness, either the mindfulness will disintegrate, or the experience. You can't have the two together, just as you can't have love and hate together – or rather, *mettā* and hate.

MAHAMATI: That's only in certain circumstances.

SANGHARAKSHITA: For instance, suppose you go to a party. Well, a party is usually a situation that excites unmindfulness. You can either preserve your mindfulness by leaving the party, or you can stay at the party and lose your mindfulness. Suppose ten people at the party wanted to preserve their mindfulness and *not* leave the party; what would happen? The party would disintegrate. You'd have ten mindful people there, and they certainly wouldn't have a party. They'd do something else. Thus the state of excitability associated with the party is incompatible with mindfulness, so that if you stayed with the situation but remained mindful your mindfulness would have the effect of disintegrating the situation – if your mindfulness was sufficiently strong. You couldn't have both excitableness and mindfulness. Either your mindfulness would disintegrate the excitableness of the situation, so that the situation itself was transformed, or the excitableness of the situation would disintegrate your mindfulness. What I am getting at is that there are some mental states, and some sense experiences, that you can't have and be mindful at the same time. The mindfulness modifies the incompatible experience, and even disintegrates it completely, as may happen in some cases, only if it is strong enough.

MAHAMATI: If one is, say, mindful of another person, one really experiences them.

SANGHARAKSHITA: Oh yes, you don't necessarily have to go away and think about them to be mindful and aware of them. You can be mindful and aware of them in that actual situation in which you encounter them. Sometimes you can be with them in such a way that mindfulness is completely destroyed, but in that case the chances are that you are not really 'with' them any longer. Something else has taken over – as when you go off with a friend and get drunk with him. Well, you are together in a sense, but not really in any meaningful sense. You're not mindful any more; neither are you really aware of each other – and to that extent you are not really together any longer. In that sort of state you are not even aware of yourself, not to speak of the other person.

BEING DECISIVE

> The capacity of sense-experience to compel the mind to act in a certain way is greatly diminished if each sensory stimulus is examined at the point where it passes the threshold of consciousness. Attention, normally passive, involuntary and compulsive, is subjected to voluntary control. In the process of imposing some control on the senses one will be surprised to find how keen they are to function, how eager to find suitable objects with which to feed one's impulses and instincts, one's hopes and fears, one's interests and appetites, satisfactions and grievances. It is not so bad that one should see things, hear sounds, etc., but it is a threat to spiritual health when one gets interested and entranced, when one takes up what is seen and heard and seizes on it as a sign of what matters.[112] (p. 15)

SANGHARAKSHITA: This is all very true, but I think the crucial sentence, or the crucial point, is this: 'Attention, normally passive, involuntary and compulsive, is subjected to voluntary control.' This is really the point of this restraint of the senses and guarding the doors of the senses. From being passive you become active, or from being reactive you become creative. Usually we respond to sense stimuli automatically. We are quite passive; we respond mechanically, therefore reactively. What we have to do is slow the whole thing down, to be more aware of what is happening and select more, not simply allow ourselves to be played upon and influenced – not allow ourselves to remain simply passive but to become more active, more selective even, and therefore more creative. In order to do this it may be necessary to limit the sensory intake, at least for a while. Therefore Dr Conze quite rightly says, 'In the process of imposing some control on the senses one will be surprised to find how keen they are to function, how eager to find suitable objects with which to feed one's impulses and instincts, one's hopes and fears, one's interests and appetites, satisfactions and grievances.'

One really notices this. The senses, or the mind through the senses, is constantly reaching out towards various objects and is deflected from them with difficulty – feels angry and frustrated if it is so deflected, sometimes.[113] One has to observe this whole process, and not allow oneself to be simply played upon by these multitudinous external sense stimuli, but instead be more assertive, more in control, more creative.

Compare the two states of mind. Suppose you are walking along the street with nothing particular in mind. Looking to this side and that, you see something attractive in a shop window; you go and have a look at it, wonder whether to buy it, maybe go in and have a look at it and decide not to but because it's too expensive. Coming out, you see a pretty girl pass by; you follow her with your eyes up the road, until something else captures your attention. Maybe you see a café. You go and look at the menu in the window and decide to have this dish or that. So in you go. You are simply responding to sense stimuli. Here it's a case of your being mechanical, automatic, reactive all the time. But suppose you are walking down that same street with a definite idea in mind: that you have to buy such-and-such a book. You just go straight to the bookshop, buy the book, and go away. That's a quite different situation, because you're much more in control, or much more in charge; you're being much more creative – and that experience will not have the dissipating sort of effect upon you that the first one will. If you've spent an hour or so wandering down a street in the first kind of way, by the end of the hour you'll feel a bit dissipated, a bit tired, a bit exhausted, even a bit dirty; but you won't feel like that if you go about things in the second way, where you're being much more decisive, determined, selective, in charge, and creative – provided, of course, it's not just a case of one particular powerful, unskilful desire temporarily outweighing all the others. I don't mean *that*. Let's assume the book you're in search of is a book on Buddhism!

EXPERIENCING

> Secondly, as regards the *muscular movements of the body* – an unquiet body is a concomitant of a disturbed mind, both its cause and symptom. It is important to mindfulness that one should consciously notice the position and movement of the body when walking, eating, speaking, etc., and suppress and correct those movements which are uncontrolled, hasty and uncoordinated. This practice can, it is true, not be carried out at all times. In London traffic, for instance, the unhurried and unflurried demeanour of the mindful has little survival value. Where, however, it can be applied, we come to cherish this exercise which pulls us together, sometimes to an amazing extent in an amazingly short time. Insignificant as it may seem, compared with the splendours of Buddhist art and metaphysics, this training is their indispensable foundation stone. It is by his dignified and self-possessed deportment that the *bhikkhu* is recognized. And, of course, we should not forget that the mindful attention to muscular movements includes the breathing practices, which are a most fruitful source of insight. (pp. 15–16)

SANGHARAKSHITA: Awareness of 'the muscular movements of the body'. Again this is all very true, but again there is a sort of qualification. You can do this in the wrong sort of way: you can have a sort of alienated awareness here. You can just be watching yourself as though you were another person. Sometimes, I am afraid, one is even advised to do this, but that is quite wrong. What should one really be doing?

SUSIDDHI: Experiencing.

SANGHARAKSHITA: Experiencing oneself, physically, all the time, I think that is a much better way of putting it: not 'watching one's bodily movements'. *That* can certainly lead to alienation, at least in the case of Western people.

SUVAJRA: What about this word 'suppress' in 'suppress and correct those movements'?

SANGHARAKSHITA: He does say suppress and not repress, but perhaps one shouldn't take that word too literally. If you're truly mindful of any unskilful bodily movements that will have the effect of – perhaps one shouldn't say suppressing but of – *smoothing out* those movements. Also, there seems to be the suggestion here that if you're mindful you cannot do anything quickly. This is not necessarily correct. 'In London traffic, for instance, the unhurried and unflurried demeanour of the mindful has little survival value.' Well, you can be very mindful in crossing the road and very quick at the same time. You don't *have* to slow down in order to be more mindful, though you *may* have to do that in certain circumstances. You know from your own experience that there are some practical things that you can do very quickly and very mindfully at the same time. Or can you indeed do some things in this way?

SUVAJRA: Crossing the road quickly in London is one of them. If you didn't cross the road quickly in London with mindfulness, you wouldn't survive.

ANDY: Some things, I've found, I can only do quickly if I am mindful about what I am doing.

SANGHARAKSHITA: I was thinking of the case of a musician. He may have to play very rapidly indeed, but he is completely mindful. He doesn't have to slow down in order to play mindfully.

MAHAMATI: I quite often find that if I spend a long time doing things, and then get very mixed up, I'm not in all that good a state. In a good state I get more done much quicker.

SANGHARAKSHITA: Yes one can, if the 'good' includes the being more mindful.

SURATA: That's where discipline comes in. If you've been disciplined in your meditation practice you can do it quickly and mindfully.

SANGHARAKSHITA: Which is, of course, quite a different thing from trying to get it done quickly. Sometimes trying to get a thing done quickly will just get in the way and cause more hold-ups. Especially if one is skilled and experienced in practice, one *can* do things very quickly and very mindfully. In fact, in some cases you can't do them quickly without doing them mindfully.

MAHAMATI: What does he refer to by 'the breathing practices'?

SANGHARAKSHITA: Simply mindfulness of breathing.[114]

> Where we have to face the disturbance of the *passions* and of *stray thoughts* in general, the defence of our inward calm becomes more difficult. Mindfulness itself turns into incipient concentration. (p. 16)

SANGHARAKSHITA: Here he's thinking of calm as something already existing, and to be defended, rather than something to be developed.

TO KEEP ON GOING BACK

> At this point one may ask whether the practice of the five cardinal virtues, from faith to wisdom, is at all likely to be furthered by writing articles about them. It is, of course, not an entirely useless undertaking to guard the traditional teaching from current misunderstandings ... (p. 16)

SANGHARAKSHITA: Including those of Dr Conze.

> ... quite apart from the pleasure of putting fleas into people's ears, and fomenting discussions about the importance of faith, or the value of erudition. But what about the virtues themselves? Thomas

> à Kempis once said that he would rather feel compunction than know the definition of it. What matters to a Buddhist is that he should be strong in faith, vigour, mindfulness, concentration and wisdom, and what use to him is the knowledge of how they are defined? Detailed advice on how these virtues should be practised can, it is true, never be given in articles written for the general reader. Such advice must always be addressed to one person at a time, must take their individual constitution into account, and can, therefore, be given only by word of mouth. (pp. 16–17)

SANGHARAKSHITA: In other words, such advice must be given in the form of what the Tibetans call a precept, which is a teaching meant specifically for a certain person. A lot of the scriptures are really precepts, and you can read them (it's like overhearing a conversation between two people) and know that part of what is said applies to you too, because you're in the same situation as the person who is being addressed, i.e. the person to whom the precept originally applied. Sometimes, of course, as you 'listen in', you may feel that it just doesn't apply to you at all, and that it's got nothing to do with you. It might be all right, but it just isn't relevant so far as you're concerned. You might feel this even with regard to the 'greatest' scriptures. Also, of course, your experience may vary from time to time. You might have a certain experience yourself and then find a certain precept, a certain scripture, very applicable indeed, whereas before you hadn't found it applicable. For this reason you have to keep going back to the scriptures, and not consider you've dealt with them once and for all.

One could even say, in a way, that there shouldn't be any articles on Buddhism 'written for the general reader' – well, not for the general non-Buddhist reader anyway. What have *they* got to do with Buddhism? Buddhism is essentially practical. *They're* not going to practise it. Let them read something else more interesting, or more useful. It's a sort of voyeurism almost for them to read articles on Buddhism. Why do you bother about other religions? Go and practise your own! The chances are that if you're bothered about other religions, and are studying them too much, you're not devoting all that time to the practice of your own. I'm sure this is why some clergymen, for instance, go into the study of comparative religion, even go into the teaching of comparative religion. It's as an escape from the fact that they don't really have, any longer, any faith in Christianity, and are, in fact, no longer practising it.

SUSIDDHI: We've got to get recruits from the group, though. I mean, if we're not getting recruits, we're not ...

SANGHARAKSHITA: That's true. By writing articles on Buddhism for the general reader you hope to reach potential Buddhists.

MAP-READING

> On the other hand, if mindfulness be a virtue, then the ability to recollect one's own virtues is also a feature of the Buddhist life. And how can one attend in oneself to the presence or absence of mental states if one is unable to recognize them for what they are? The *Satipaṭṭhāna Sutta* recommends systematic meditation on the wholesome and unwholesome mental states which arise in the mind. To quote the *sutta*, one knows, for instance: (1) when there is vigour that there is vigour; (2) when there is no vigour that there is no vigour; (3) how the vigour which did not exist came to be produced; and (4) how and under what conditions it will grow to greater perfection. Psychology is so vital to Buddhist instruction because one cannot know anything definite about the furniture of one's mind unless one is acquainted with the categories into which mental conditions can be analysed. A mindful man is well-informed about his own mental condition. His capacity for introspection is highly developed. And his interest in his own mind will not really make him self-centred as long as he remembers that he has to deal with the rise and fall of impersonal processes. In addition, in the case of the higher mental states rational clarity is imperative if constant self-deception and wasteful groping in the dark are to be avoided. In a new country a map is helpful so that one may know where one is. The manuals of mystical theology written by the practising contemplatives of the Catholic Church are also rich in descriptions of the sublimer virtues. (p. 17)

SANGHARAKSHITA: What is Dr Conze really saying here, do you think? Do you think one can know one's own mind without external help, as it were, in the form of a systematic treatise on psychology, or religious psychology? Do you think these things really do help?

A VOICE: No, I don't think so.

SURATA: Yes, I think they do help. Otherwise you can waste a hell of a lot of time. Like he said, if you've got a map you don't take wrong turnings.

SANGHARAKSHITA: Is it necessarily as simple as that, though?

SURATA: You've got to be careful. Maybe it's more important to have a guide than a map.

SANGHARAKSHITA: Take *Mind in Buddhist Psychology*,[115] for instance. In that work there's a list of positive mental states or mental events. Would you say that list was helpful and useful, in terms of enabling one to recognize those states within oneself and thus to give one an idea of what had to be cultivated and developed?

SURATA: No, not on my own. I did look at that book on my own and thought it was rubbish; but I've been through it with Manjuvajra and going through it in that way it comes alive.

SANGHARAKSHITA: So perhaps it does come back to the teacher rather than the text. I must say that, in going through Buddhist texts, it does seem that very little *really* applies to, or seems relevant to, one's own experience. For instance, the descriptions of the *dhyānas*. Not only within the Friends, but in other Buddhist circles too, people seem to have a great deal of difficulty in squaring the descriptions of the *dhyānas* in the scriptures with their own experience of meditation. This suggests, perhaps, that those descriptions might have been 'edited' in the course of centuries, whether orally or in some other way, by monks who perhaps hadn't had overmuch experience of meditation themselves and who were just redacting accounts of somebody else's experiences. In that way they got rather remote from actual first-hand descriptions of meditation experiences. I think one has to be very careful. Make use of the maps, preferably with the help of the map-maker, or at least of a skilled map-reader; but one has to realize that human experience is much richer than any 'map', and that there might be quite a few prominent features of your own experience, even, which seem not to be found on any map. Sometimes things are introduced into these 'maps' which are just personal idiosyncrasies, almost.

Dr Conze mentions the practising contemplatives of the Catholic Church. There were practising contemplatives in the Catholic Church for many hundreds of years, but it was only in the seventeenth century that St John of the Cross produced his teaching about the 'Dark Night of the Soul' which is a very important mystical teaching.[116] Nobody had heard of it before. No one had even experienced the Dark Night of the Soul, apparently, before he wrote about it; but after he wrote about it, all sorts of people started experiencing the Dark Night of the Soul. This means you have to be careful about what is your own true, natural, spontaneous experience. You can 'condition' your own experience – perhaps in a quite healthy way – in accordance with these manuals, in order to make them fit the manuals – especially if you're Catholic. If you're a Catholic you want to be on the right, orthodox path; you don't want to go straying off into heresy. It's not quite like that with the Buddhists, but even so there might be a tendency to make your experience fit the maps rather than just read them to help you find your way around in your own experience.

SURATA: Certain things are more immediate than others, though.

SANGHARAKSHITA: Yes, but if one is thinking in terms of a detailed description of the path, and the experiences you have at each stage of the path, your own experience won't always tally, because usually the path is laid down in regular steps and you hardly ever follow the path of regular steps. The path described in the Buddhist scriptures is not a path that anybody actually follows exactly in that order. Not even the Buddha followed it in that order. What did he start off with? He started off with something wrong, i.e. first of all with self-indulgence, then with one-sided asceticism. Only afterwards did he get onto the right path, the Middle Way.[117] Though the Buddha has laid down the path correctly, as a path of regular steps, it can be followed in that way only by completely and utterly healthy persons, such as we don't, in fact, encounter. We follow the path in all sorts of irregular, weird, indirect, contradictory ways of our own, and though we do manage to make, hopefully, overall spiritual progress, it will be very difficult actually to plot the steps and stages of our progress as we look back. It will be very difficult to look back and see how there came first this stage, then that, and then something else. Manjuvajra managed to do something like that in his recent talk. That was probably relatively exceptional; or perhaps he simplified his experience very much indeed. Certainly there was one quite important stage or state he went through, on a retreat I took, which he didn't mention at all in his talk. On that retreat he was in a quite extraordinary state, so much so that everybody thought he was tripping. But he afterwards assured us that he hadn't been. It was a natural state; something that just happened. Well, he left it out of his little map. All that one really needs to bother about is whether one is actually growing, you know, looking at the picture as a whole. But even if you are quite sure that you are actually growing – or have grown since you last took a look at yourself – it might be very difficult to reduce that to a definite series of stages which you could advise another person to go through if they also wanted to grow. It seems to be a much more individual thing than that. That's one of the reasons why it's a mistake to regard the Eightfold Path as a path of eight *steps* which you take one after the other. It's a path of eight limbs, or factors, all of which must be developed, in some way, sooner or later. That's what it really stands for, what it really means.

CIRCUMSTANCES THAT HELP

> But this is not all. Where the Buddhist virtues are described for a lay audience one must not omit to mention the all-important fact that the upper ranges of these virtues demand a reformation of the conduct of life which is greater than almost any layman is willing to undertake. The higher mindfulness, and nearly the whole range of concentration and wisdom, presuppose a degree of withdrawal from the world which is incompatible with the life of an ordinary citizen. Those who are unwilling to achieve a radical seclusion from the world can practise these virtues only in a very rudimentary form. It is quite idle to pretend that they do not involve a complete break with the established habits of life and thought. Unless we make the sacrifices involved in withdrawing from the world, we are bound to remain strangers to the fullness of mindfulness, concentration and wisdom.[118] (p. 18)

SANGHARAKSHITA: What Dr Conze says about the need for 'a complete break with the established habits of life and thought' again is very correct, as well as what he says about our having to make 'the sacrifices involved in withdrawing from the world' (provided one understands the word 'sacrifice' correctly) – though it's not so much a question of withdrawal from the world as of a transition to a different kind of world. Do you see what I mean? It's a question of a transition from the world to the world within the world – from the world to the spiritual community. You make the spiritual community your world, your environment, because that makes it easier, so to speak, for you to practise the spiritual life and to develop yourself. It's not just a question of 'going forth', in the sense of 'leaving the world' and just being out in a void – though you might be for a while. It really means leaving the world and finding a spiritual community, i.e. *leaving* those conditions that *hamper* your development as an individual all the time and *finding* a set of conditions in the form of that other world, or that spiritual community, which *help* and which *further* your development. Suppose you had 'dropped out', i.e. given up your job, left your wife and family (those that had them), but there wasn't any spiritual community for you to be involved with; where would you be? You'd really be out on a limb. Well, maybe that would be better than going on in the old way, in the old rut; but it's infinitely better that you should have found your way into a spiritual community and be able to enjoy conditions which actually *help* you instead of conditions which hinder – or *even* conditions which are merely neutral.

It isn't so much a question of 'the higher ranges of mindfulness' being meant for the monk rather than for the layman in the old-fashioned sense. It isn't really as simple and as clear-cut as that. You can only practise the higher levels of mindfulness if circumstances help you rather than hinder you all the time. That means being in a spiritual community, being within the sangha, at least much of the time – if not most of the time, or even all the time. It's not a question of being a monk in any formal sense, because in the Buddhist countries lots of those ordained as monks remain *firmly* within the world in the fullest sense of the term. 'Monk' becomes a sort of vocation, a sort of profession, just like 'clergyman' in the West. You have your *place* in society; you don't go outside society any more, as you did in the Buddha's day. In newspapers and Buddhist magazines you can see pictures of Thai *bhikkhus* blessing guns and tanks. They have their place very much within the world.

Dr Conze also talks in terms of achieving 'a radical seclusion from the world'. *That* can be misunderstood. It doesn't necessarily mean that you are away in some remote hermitage. It really means, or should mean, that you're in the bosom of the spiritual community, where everything and everyone is helping you to develop instead of hindering you. Of course, periods of literal, physical seclusion – what we call solitary retreat – may also be necessary.

SUSIDDHI: Did Dr Conze write this booklet for Theravāda consumption, or from the Theravāda point of view?

SANGHARAKSHITA: It was first published in the *Middle Way* and has now been republished as a Wheel publication by the Buddhist Publication Society, Kandy. I think he follows mainly the *Visuddhimagga*,[119] which is why his 'slant' is a little Theravādin. Philosophically speaking he is of course very much the Mahāyānist, at least the Mādhyamika Mahāyānist.

Let's leave it there for the moment. I believe tea is ready.

4
CONCENTRATION

Day 2: afternoon

SANGHARAKSHITA: This afternoon we have to deal with concentration and wisdom.

> Concentration (*samādhi*) continues the work of mindfulness. It deepens our capacity to regain the peaceful calm of our inner nature. But here we are at once faced with the difficulty that in Buddhist psychology 'concentration' occurs twice: (1) as a factor essential to all thought; and (2) as a special, and rather rare, virtue.
>
> 1. In its simplest form, concentration is the narrowing of the field of attention in a manner and for a time determined by the will. The mind is made one-pointed, does not waver, does not scatter itself, and it becomes steady like the flame of a lamp in the absence of wind. Without a certain degree of one-pointedness no mental activity at all can take place. Each mental act lasts, strictly speaking, for one moment only, and is at once followed by another. The function of concentration is to provide some stability in this perpetual flux, by enabling the mind to stand in, or on, the same object, without distraction, for more than one moment. In addition it is a synthetic quality (*sam-ā-dhi* = syn-thesis), that binds together a number of mental states which arise at the same time, 'as water binds the lather of soap'. (p. 19)

SANGHARAKSHITA: There are two points here, really: that 'concentration continues the work of mindfulness', and that concentration is 'a factor essential to all thought'. Do you see how concentration continues the work of mindfulness? Mindfulness, we saw, is 'an act of remembering which prevents ideas from "floating away".' It keeps hold of the ideas, as it were; it keeps them together. Here you can see how the connection with concentration comes in, because if you keep those ideas in your mind for any length of time, and especially if you reduce the number of ideas and keep just one idea in your mind, then you're said to be concentrated. In this way there's an easy or natural transition from mindfulness to concentration. In a sense, therefore, mindfulness and concentration are mutually exclusive, in that concentration tends to involve fewer and fewer objects as it becomes more heightened. That's the reason why Newton could not attend to his landlady's egg at the same time as he attended to his own intellectual problems. If he had been more mindful he *would* have done; but he would therefore have been less concentrated. Thus there is a certain incompatibility between mindfulness and concentration, even though mindfulness does lead to concentration. Being spread out over a number of objects is incompatible with being spread out over just a few objects. Nonetheless, mindfulness and concentration are a movement in the same general direction. Concentration is a more intensified form of mindfulness. You increase the intensity by reducing the field.

SUSIDDHI: If you are doing a concentration practice, should you deliberately lay aside mindfulness at the start of it?

SANGHARAKSHITA: As one gets more and more mindful, the mindfulness will tend to narrow its field, and in that way the concentration will emerge. Suppose you are doing the mindfulness of breathing. At the beginning you'll be aware of sounds outside; you'll be aware of your own breathing, your own body, other people in the room, etc. But as you get more and more into the mindfulness of the breathing these things will recede to the periphery of consciousness and you may become completely oblivious to them.

SUSIDDHI: You narrow the mindfulness.

SANGHARAKSHITA: Yes, you narrow the mindfulness; or it narrows itself, as it were, as you just do the practice.

A UNIFYING ACTIVITY

SANGHARAKSHITA: That brings in another point. Dr Conze says, 'In its simplest form, concentration is the narrowing of the field of attention in a manner and for a time determined by the will.' It's not really quite like that in terms of practice. You don't say to yourself: I shall now proceed to progressively narrow my field of attention so that I can become concentrated. All that you aim at is doing the actual practice. If you do it faithfully, e.g. the mindfulness of breathing, the field of attention will automatically narrow. You don't have to exert a special separate act of will to make it narrow. *That* would in fact be a distraction. It would get in the way, and prevent you narrowing the field of attention in that particular manner. But perhaps we shouldn't take him up too literally on this point, because you have an *overall* intention to do that, to narrow the field of attention. It's just that a specific act of will at that particular time, at that particular moment, is not the way of bringing about that result.

> Buddhaghosa stresses the fact that intellectual concentration is also found in unwholesome thoughts. The mind must be undistracted so that the murderer's knife does not miss, the theft does not miscarry. A mind of single intent is capable of doing what it does more effectively, be it good or bad. The higher degrees of this kind of concentration owe much to the presence of the 'hunting instinct', and can best be observed in a stoat following a rabbit. Intellectual concentration is a quality that is ethically and spiritually neutral. Many scientific workers have an unusually high capacity for concentrated thought. Anyone acquainted with the 'scientific humanists' who inhabit our big cities will, however, agree that their intellectual achievements are not conducive to either peace of mind or spiritual progress. When Sir Isaac Newton boiled his watch instead of the egg his landlady had given him, he thereby showed the intensity with which he focused his mind on his intellectual task. But the result of his intellectual labours has been to cast a dark shadow over the spiritual radiance of the

universe, and ever since, the celestial harmonies have become nearly inaudible. As H. W. Longfellow, in his poem on 'The Arsenal at Springfield', has put it:

Is it, O man, with such discordant noises,
With such accursed instruments as these,
Thou drownest Nature's sweet and kindly voices,
And jarrest the celestial harmonies? (pp. 19–20)

SANGHARAKSHITA: Then, concentration 'as a factor essential to all thought'. This draws attention to the fact that all concentration, both concentration in general and concentration in the more specifically mental sense, is a sort of unifying, synthesizing activity.[120] You become more integrated, therefore more of an individual. So meditation or concentration (*samādhi*) in the more specific sense is only a much more specialized and wholesome form of something that is going on all the time. You could say that usually your thoughts are concentrated, but that they're only concentrated, in the ordinary way, for a certain purpose and for a certain length of time, and usually in accordance with one's instincts and desires, skilful and unskilful, and so on. The aim of meditation or concentration (*samādhi*) in the higher, more specialized sense, is to unify you as an individual: to bring everything together into harmony; to bring everything as it were to a head, to a point, instead of it being scattered and loose and disconnected and disjointed, as it usually is. Its aim is to make a whole out of floating bits and pieces.

Thus concentration is very important. Most of the time we're not concentrated. We're able to concentrate on this, or concentrate on that, for a certain length of time; but we, ourselves, as a whole, as a totality, are not concentrated, not unified, not synthesized. The aim of concentration, or meditation, in the more specialized sense, is to help bring that about. It's not just a question of being able to concentrate for a particular purpose – even the purpose of so-called concentration and meditation – but of ourselves being concentrated, if you like even meditating, *beings*. The *devas* in higher heavenly worlds are in that state all the time. They're not just concentrating by an act of will, with the rest of their being remaining as it were outside the concentration and remaining unconcentrated and ununified. No, they are totally integrated and unified on that higher level. That's why they're born there, or why they live on that level. So this should be the aim of concentration. It is not to enable us to concentrate simply while we're doing a certain exercise, but to concentrate the whole being, to unify all the energies, – if you like, bring them together, – and get them all going in the same direction. *That's* what *samādhi* really means.

Thus there is this tendency, or this capacity, present all the time, but we use it only in certain specific situations, for certain limited purposes, for certain limited lengths of time, in accordance with quite mundane and transitory desires and inclinations and wishes; but we ourselves, as a whole, as a total being, a total individual, remain unconcentrated and, to that extent, all the less an individual.

SUSIDDHI: Sorry, I've forgotten what that story of Newton boiling his watch was about.

SANGHARAKSHITA: Apparently he was sitting in front of the fire and his landlady gave him an egg and asked him to put it in the pot when the water boiled. But he was so deeply absorbed in some problem of mathematics or astronomy that when the time came he put his watch in instead. In those days pocket watches were almost spherical in shape, and you can imagine Newton sitting there, with his watch in one hand and the egg in the other, deeply absorbed in his problem, and only vaguely aware that he had put something in a pot. So he put his watch in. Concentration led to unmindfulness.

SUSIDDHI: Why is he being castigated? 'But the result of his intellectual labours has been to cast a dark shadow'. I'm not sure about that.

SANGHARAKSHITA: That is very much by the way; it doesn't really logically follow from what he's been talking about. It's an additional point. Conze seems to be following Blake here, knowingly or unknowingly. According to Blake, Newton emphasized rational understanding at the expense of imaginative insight, or spiritual vision, and presented a picture or model of the universe which was purely mechanical. Thus he banished all the elements of poetry, and beauty, and truth in the higher spiritual sense, and in that way 'cast a dark shadow over the spiritual radiance of the universe'. One could look at it like that; no doubt there are things to be said on the other side of the question. But as I said that is just an aside of

Dr Conze's. It doesn't really follow from the subject he's talking about. Even though 'many scientific workers have an unusually high capacity for concentrated thought', and even though the intellectual achievements of 'the "scientific humanists" who inhabit our big cities' are not conducive to either peace of mind or spiritual progress' meditation would disclose to you, presumably, 'the spiritual radiance of the universe'. When you as a Buddhist cultivate the five spiritual faculties, especially, you're not cultivating intellect or reason or rationality in a one-sided sort of way; therefore you're not seeing a mechanical universe: you're not seeing the universe as a gigantic machine, as Newton is alleged to have seen it. The poetry of the stanza by Longfellow is not very good, but one gets the general idea. The rhymes are pretty awful: 'noises' and 'voices', 'these' and 'harmonies'.

> How then does concentration as a spiritual virtue differ from concentration as a condition of the intellect? Spiritual or transic concentration results less from intellectual effort than from a rebirth of the whole personality, including the body, the emotions, and the will. It cannot possibly be achieved without some discipline over the body, since we must be able to endure the prescribed posture, practise the prescribed breathing exercises, and so on. It is further built on a change of outlook which we can well describe as 'ethical'. Tradition is quite unambiguous on this point. Before spiritual concentration can be even approached, we must have stilled or suppressed five vices, which are known as the 'five hindrances', i.e., sense-desire, ill will, sloth and torpor, excitedness and sense of guilt, and doubt. (p. 20)

SANGHARAKSHITA: There is a difference, of course, between 'concentration as a spiritual virtue' and 'concentration as a condition of the intellect'. I don't really like this expression 'condition of the intellect'. It's really more like concentration as a general psychical factor. 'Transic concentration' is Dr Conze's expression for concentration amounting to the experience of *dhyāna* or *jhāna* states. (He usually translates *dhyāna* or *jhāna* as 'trance'.)[121] So, 'Spiritual or transic concentration results less from intellectual effort than from a rebirth of the whole personality, including the body, the emotions, and the will'. That's fair enough, but in what does that 'rebirth of the whole personality' consist?

What is one really talking about when one says that 'Spiritual or transic concentration results less from intellectual effort than from a rebirth of the whole personality'?

ANDY: Integration.

SANGHARAKSHITA: Integration. In this connection one is talking about a much higher degree of overall unification and this 'cannot possibly be achieved without some discipline over the body, since we must be able to endure the prescribed posture, practise the prescribed breathing exercises, and so on.' There are various practices here which can assist concentration. Conze has presented them in a rather yogic, disciplinary sort of way, but things like mantra recitation, visualization, and even chanting can also be made use of. 'It is further built on a change of outlook which we can well describe as "ethical". Tradition is quite unambiguous on this point. Before spiritual concentration' – or what I would call vertical integration – 'can be even approached, we must have stilled or suppressed five vices' – I'm not very happy about this word 'vices', but anyway – 'which are known as the "five hindrances", i.e., sense desire, ill will, sloth and torpor, excitedness and sense of guilt, and doubt.'[122] This is very important indeed. Unless, at the time that one is meditating, or concentrating, there is present in the mind no sense desire, no ill will, no sloth and torpor, no excitedness and sense of guilt – to follow that translation for the moment – and no doubt, you will not be able to make the transition to that state or stage of vertical integration, or transic or spiritual concentration.

FORCES OF DISUNITY

SANGHARAKSHITA: That suppression of the five vices is absolutely essential. The usual procedure is that you sit down and concentrate. Maybe you do the mindfulness of breathing practice. As you do it, your mind becomes a little calmer, a little more concentrated. Even though you are aware of sense objects to some extent (you are at least aware of your immediate physical surroundings), for higher concentration to be possible there must be no sense desire.[123] There must be a total suppression of sense desire, at least for the time being. If the thought floats into your mind, 'Wouldn't it be nice to have an ice cream,' then you know that sense desire is present. Thus in order to be able to effect that transition to transic concentration there cannot be any sense desire. It may be that there is sense *awareness*, but it is, of course, suggested that one 'plays safe' and isn't even *aware* of sense objects. That's one of the reasons you close your eyes. After all, there might be a pretty girl meditating next to you! If you close your eyes you can't even see her; you can't even see the pretty flowers on the shrine: so there's no sense distraction through the organ of sight. You might hear sounds, and they might even be a bit disturbing, but they're unlikely to act as actual occasions of sense desire – unless you hear the sound of the ice cream van. Do you get the point? So long as sense desire connected with any of the senses is actually present in your mind that is an obstacle, or a hindrance, to the achievement of transic concentration, that is to say, the *dhyāna* states: vertical integration. The same applies to ill will.[124] If, at the time when you are trying to concentrate, there is any ill will rankling in your mind towards anybody, any sense of disgruntlement or dissatisfaction with anybody, even any annoyance or irritation (as when someone annoys you by not closing the door quietly), that is a hindrance, immediately. If as a result of your contact with people during the day you're left in a somewhat irritated frame of mind, just displeased with people in general, that is a hindrance too. Thus it is possible for you to make that transition to transic concentration only if there's no ill will whatsoever in your mind at the time when you are concentrating and meditating.

Also, there must be no sloth and torpor.[125] You mustn't be in a dull, sleepy, stupid, tired sort of state. You must be very alert, light, aware, bright, with your energy functioning – your energy flowing. There must be no excitedness and sense of guilt, as Conze translates it. *Uddhacca-kukkucca* really means something more like excitedness and worry-and-anxiety. Perhaps this latter does include a sense of guilt, but that is more like Conze's own paraphrase. You mustn't be agitated, or worried, or disturbed in any way about anything, since that too will be a hindrance to your achievement of those states of transic concentration. Moreover, there must be no doubt, no such reflections as: ought I really to be meditating at all? Is this really the way? Would not some other kind of practice suit me better? Am I wasting my time with Buddhism? Am I really making progress? – All this is doubt. If these five hindrances are present, or even any one of them, it is sufficient to inhibit your attainment of the higher states or stages of concentration. Therefore great importance is attached, in meditation practice, to what is called the suppression of these five hindrances – suppression, not eradication. It's only insight that can permanently and finally eradicate them. So long as one has not achieved insight, so long as one is not a Stream Entrant, the hindrances will always come and go. You may be able to hold them at bay for a short while, but not indefinitely, or not for any great length of time, without the help of insight. The idea is to suppress the hindrances for a sufficient length of time and then, when the hindrances are suppressed – *because* they are suppressed – to rise to the different levels of transic concentration. Then, firmly basing yourself on transic concentration, you develop insight, which will eventually cut the root of the five hindrances and render it impossible for them to arise again.

> Where these hindrances are present, where concentrated thought is fused with greed, the desire to excel, to get a good job, etc., there concentration as a spiritual virtue is not found. (p. 20)

SANGHARAKSHITA: So, 'Where these hindrances are present' – and they're almost always present – 'where concentrated thought is fused with greed, the desire to excel, to get a good job, etc., there concentration as a spiritual virtue is not found.' This is the great criterion: the presence or absence of the five hindrances. Concentration associated with the five hindrances, or with the five hindrances present, will not carry you into the *dhyāna* states.

CONCENTRATION GROWS

> In this sense physical ease, and self-purification, are the first two distinctive features of spiritual concentration. The third is the shift in attention from the sensory world to another subtler realm. The methods by which this shift is effected are traditionally known as the four trances (*jhāna*) and the four formless attainments. They are essentially a training in increasing introversion, achieved by progressively diminishing the impact of the outer stimuli. As a result of their successful withdrawal and renunciation the spiritually concentrated release the inward calm which dwells in their hearts. This concentration cannot be won, however, unless

> no attention is given to sensory data, and everything sensory is viewed as equally unimportant. Subjectively it is marked by a soft, tranquil and pacified passivity, objectively by the abstraction into an unearthly world of experience which lifts one above the world, and bestows a certainty greater than anything the senses may teach. The experience is so satisfying that it burns up the world, and only its cold ashes are found when one returns to it. (p. 21)

SANGHARAKSHITA: I'm not so sure about that!

SURATA: 'Pacified passivity'?

SANGHARAKSHITA: We'll deal with that in a minute. 'In this sense physical ease, and self-purification, are the first two distinctive features of spiritual concentration.' He seems to be paraphrasing, here, the five psychological factors present in the first *dhyāna*.[126] First of all there is *sukha*. This is more than just 'physical ease'. Though it includes the body, it's more like a sense of total well-being. You notice that when you get really concentrated – as you begin to approach the first *dhyāna* – and you can do *that* fairly easily if you meditate regularly. You notice that sitting is no longer uncomfortable. You notice that even if you've been feeling a bit stiff, or your leg has been aching, when you get really concentrated, then suddenly, almost miraculously, your body feels all right: it feels quite comfortable. So this psychophysical feeling of total ease and comfort is a sign that the first *dhyāna* is being entered upon or entered into. Conze speaks of 'physical ease', but it isn't just physical; it's not just a comfortable posture: it's more than that. It's a mental feeling of ease which communicates itself even to the physical body. 'And purification'. Well, since you're away from the five hindrances you feel, at least for a few moments, sort of pure, fresh, clean, clear. These, then, are the first two distinctive features of spiritual concentration: you feel buoyant, and at ease both physically and mentally; and you feel free and pure, there being no hindrances present. You have then entered upon the fringes, at least, of the first *dhyāna* state.

'The third is the shift in attention from the sensory world to another, subtler realm.' Yes and no. You're no longer paying attention to the sensory world: you're as it were enjoying your own state of concentration. You may not have any particular concentration object in view by that time, or, of course, you may be continuing to focus on your original object, whether the breath or anything else. 'The methods by which this shift is effected are traditionally known as the four trances (*jhāna*) and the four formless attainments.' This isn't really correct. The four trances are not methods of attaining anything; they are the actual states you experience as a result of your progressive vertical integration. 'They are essentially a training in increasing introversion' – introversion in a sense only – 'achieved by progressively diminishing the impact of the outer stimuli.' You can be aware of the outer stimuli. Suppose you open your eyes when you're in a concentrated state: you can be perfectly aware of everything around you; but no sense desire arises. Usually, in actual practice, we need to eliminate sense stimuli just so that we can concentrate; but it is possible to concentrate, or to enjoy the concentrated state, even in the presence of sense stimuli.

'As a result of their successful withdrawal and renunciation the spiritually concentrated release the inward calm which dwells in their hearts.' Well we've dealt with this before. It may be more helpful – as well as more correct – to say that you develop a state of calm, not that you sort of dig your way through to something that is already there. 'This concentration cannot be won, however, unless no attention is given to sensory data, and everything sensory is viewed as equally unimportant.' There's 'no attention' in the sense of active attention: there's no interest given. If you start giving active attention, and taking interest, of course your concentration will be lost. But if you've just a pure, mirror-like awareness of things around you that is quite compatible with concentration. 'Subjectively it is marked by a soft, tranquil and pacified passivity.' Do you agree with this? Not really; or at least it's really one-sided. The mind, then, can be in a very vibrant state. For instance, if you reach the fourth *dhyāna*, which I've described as the stage of radiation, it certainly couldn't be described as passive. On the other hand, paradoxically, passivity is not excluded. 'This concentration' is soft, but at the same time it is very vibrant. So one shouldn't describe it merely as soft, merely as tranquil, merely as passive. That is definitely one-sided.

SUSIDDHI: It is more balanced.

SANGHARAKSHITA: Yes, more balanced. In a way, you've gone beyond the distinction between active and passive. It would be equally true to say of your mind in that state that it was very, very active and also that it was completely still. It is intensely alive, but there are no separate thoughts, no discursive mental activity.

'The experience is so satisfying that it burns up the world, and only its cold ashes are found when one returns to it.' Well, not everybody says that. Quite a lot of people say that when you open your eyes after a really good meditation the world doesn't seem like 'cold ashes'; it seems all bright and lit up and radiant and clear – because you see it undistorted by your subjective preferences and likes and dislikes and so on. Anyway, are there any further points about concentration?

MARK: I've not come across this word 'transic' before.

SANGHARAKSHITA: It's a word of Dr Conze's. It's the adjective from 'trance'. If he wants to speak of concentration which is equivalent to the *dhyānas* he calls it 'transic concentration', or 'trance-level concentration'.

MARK: You could say 'dhyānic'.

SANGHARAKSHITA: Yes, you could. I don't like that word 'trance' at all, especially not as an equivalent to *dhyāna*. Most of his translations are very good, but I just don't feel happy about this particular one.

MAKING OUR ASCENT

MAHAMATI: There was something we were discussing in our study group a few weeks ago, about the *dhyānas*. It's whether there are levels within, say, the first, second, and third *dhyānas*, or whether it's just an experience of the particular *dhyāna*.

SANGHARAKSHITA: I think each *dhyāna* represents a whole range of psychical territory, as it were. It's not just one dead level. Looked at from a distance, in very broad, general terms, it's as though the *dhyāna* is one step; but looked at more closely that step is made up of a number of little steps. In fact, you could even say it was an inclined plane – or even that the four, or the eight, *dhyānas* represent one absolutely continuous inclined plane. In a sense you can't too literally mark them off from one another.

MAHAMATI: We were discussing whether one could experience the second *dhyāna* without fully experiencing the first *dhyāna*.

SANGHARAKSHITA: No, this would not be possible. For instance, take the difference between the first *dhyāna* and the second. In the first *dhyāna* you get *vitarka* and *vicāra*, usually translated as applied and discursive thought, whereas in the second *dhyāna* there is no *vitarka* and no *vicāra*. (Normally one experiences applied and discursive thought on the ordinary, non-dhyānic level of consciousness.) It would be self-contradictory to speak of attaining a state free from *vitarka* and *vicāra* before you had attained a state of *dhyāna* with *vitarka* and *vicāra*.

MAHAMATI: People may have had experience of the second *dhyāna* on a seminar and I was trying to work out how that can be.

SANGHARAKSHITA: It is possible, of course, to go very quickly through the *dhyānas* and then 'remain' in the one you eventually reach. You may have a prolonged experience of a certain higher *dhyāna* before you've had a prolonged experience of a lower *dhyāna*: that is not impossible. But in order to reach that higher *dhyāna* you would still go through the lower *dhyānas*. That is essential. Suppose there were different degrees of mental activity in the different *dhyānas*. Suppose in a higher state you've got, say, five thoughts, and in a lower one, ten. As you proceed from the lower state to the higher you reduce the thoughts from ten to five. You could go from one state to the other quickly, 'knocking off' five thoughts out of ten quickly, one after the other, and thus reach the state where there were only five thoughts; but you'd still be going through the same process as you would if you 'knocked off' the thoughts slowly.

The further the resultant experience is from your 'main base', the less likely you are to be able to prolong the experience. You could, of course, have a quite extraordinary experience which so impressed you that it precipitated you right into the third *dhyāna*; but if the general trend of your being was not in keeping with that, you would fall back relatively quickly. But even though you could be precipitated into the third *dhyāna* in this way you would pass, however rapidly, through the lower *dhyānas* before arriving at the final one, which you experienced in a more prolonged manner.

MAHAMATI: But would it be, maybe, that one wouldn't experience that, say, second or third *dhyāna* fully, because one hadn't integrated oneself fully at a lower level?

SANGHARAKSHITA: Yes, I would say that. You could compare it to falling in love – just to make it clear. There are certain recognized stages, aren't there? Correct me if I am mistaken. First of all you see somebody; then you get to the stage of wanting to see them every now and then; then you want to see them often; then you want to be with them all the time, and then you're violently infatuated. Thus you end up in the stage of infatuation, which corresponds, let us say, to the *dhyāna* you end up in. Sometimes people even think it's a sort of *dhyāna*-like experience. They find out their mistake later! You can go through the whole sequence of stages over a period of about a year, and end up infatuated; but you can also go through them in the course of a few days, even a few hours, and likewise end up infatuated. In the same way, you can go through the preliminary experiences and the *dhyāna* stages either very slowly or very rapidly, in both cases ending up wherever you do end up eventually. But again, we can't generalize too much. Suppose by some extraordinary fluke, some extraordinary experience, emotional or spiritual, you get into the third *dhyāna*, and are in it sufficiently long to develop transcendental insight. Well, then you really have achieved something and there is no question of your falling back. Somebody else might have been slogging away at their meditation and never got anywhere near insight. But then, one could also say: why did *you* have that extraordinary experience at all? – You were susceptible to it: it was *possible* for you to have it. Some kind of potential was there in you all the time. It's not just a free gift from heaven; in a way, you were prepared and ready. But, as a broad general principle, a prolonged experience of a higher state of being and consciousness, including dhyānic experience, depends on a fairly considerable experience of the lower levels.

5
WISDOM

THE THREE WISDOMS

And so we come to wisdom (*prajñā*, Pāli *paññā*), the highest virtue of all. 'Wisdom is based on concentration, because of the saying that "he who is concentrated knows, sees what really is".'[127] Is concentration then an indispensable precondition of wisdom? The answer lies in distinguishing three stages of wisdom, according to whether it operates on the level of: (1) *learning* about what tradition has to say concerning the psychological and ontological categories which form the subject-matter of wisdom; (2) *discursive reflection* on the basic facts of life; and (3) *meditational development*.[128] The third alone requires the aid of transic concentration,[129] whereas without it there can be proficiency in the first two. And the wisdom which consists of learning and reflection should not be despised.

The main stream of Buddhist tradition has always greatly esteemed *learning*. Our attitude to the apple of knowledge differs from that of many Christians. On the whole, we regard it as rather more nourishing than baneful. The wisdom, which is the fifth and crowning virtue, is not the wisdom that can be found in the untutored child of nature, the corny sage of the backwoods, or the self-made philosopher of the suburbs. It can operate only after a great deal of traditional information has been absorbed, a great

> deal of sound learning acquired. The required skill in metaphysical and psychological analysis would be impossible without a good knowledge of the material on which this skill ought to be exercised. From this point of view learning is perhaps less to be regretted than its absence.
>
> The second stage, after learning, is *reflection*, which is an operation of the intellect. Even the relative beginner can greatly increase his wisdom by discursive meditations on the basic facts of life. Finally, it is on the level of '*mental development*' (*bhāvanā*) that this meditational technique reaches its maturity, and then it does, indeed, require the aid of mindfulness and concentration. (pp. 21–2)

SANGHARAKSHITA: Are you familiar with this distinction between the three kinds of wisdom? It's a very basic one indeed.[130] Learning is *śruta-mayī-prajñā*, the wisdom or understanding that comes by 'hearing', where you simply take in information, where you simply learn. Then comes reflection or *cintā-mayī-prajñā*. I don't think Conze has brought out the sense, or the significance, of this kind of wisdom sufficiently. It's not just reflection, or discursive meditation. It's more like appropriating what you've 'heard', what you've learned, and making it your own. I have also distinguished between them by saying that in *śruta-mayī-prajñā* you understand the meaning of the words: you understand what is said; but in *cintā-mayī-prajñā* you understand the meaning of the meaning – or, you could even say, you understand why it is said, what its ramifications are, especially for you in your own life. You could also say that *cintā-mayī-prajñā* represents creative thought. You start off mulling over what you have learnt, what you have 'heard': that is your raw material. But then you appropriate it to yourself; you understand it in the light of your own experience of life, or in the light of wider, more general principles. It becomes something more than a matter of merely superficial understanding.

You can always tell when a book is written by someone whose understanding is of the *śruta-mayī-prajñā* type. You can get, you know, a book on Buddhism written by someone who has read other books on Buddhism, and translations of Buddhist scriptures: so he compiles something of his own. He understands the meaning of what he is writing: he understands the meaning of the words that he is drawing upon; but he doesn't understand the meaning of the meaning. He's not able to 'recreate' Buddhism for you out of his own creative thinking. A book which is based merely on *śruta-mayī-prajñā* is very flat and uninteresting, whereas one that is the product of *cintā-mayī-prajñā* is much more interesting and stimulating – even when you disagree with it. Even when it's written by a non-Buddhist, it's much more interesting than a factual compilation put together by someone who calls himself a Buddhist but who hasn't started thinking for himself about Buddhism.

'Hearing' is all right: 'learning' is all right; but you ought to be able to appropriate and transform that by your own original creative thinking. You can't think creatively in a void, in a vacuum. At least, most people can't. They need material. This is one of the reasons I appreciated the three talks that were given by the three speakers last night. They've all certainly 'listened': they know their four of this and five of that and eight of something else, and they've read their *Survey* and listened to a lot of tapes – you can tell that; but they've also *thought* about it themselves quite creatively. So they've at least reached the level, as it were, of *cintā mayī-prajñā*. They're not just parroting things that they've heard. They understand the meaning of what they have heard, and they've appropriated it for themselves. There are no undigested lumps of lectures given by me, as there used to be. It was amazing: sometimes a lecture would be simply an extended quotation.

COMPLETE TRANSFORMATION

SANGHARAKSHITA: In the case of *bhāvanā-mayī-prajñā*, '*bhāvanā*' means, as you know, development, making to become, causing to become, cultivation. So what happens there, do you think?

MARK: Is that insight?

SANGHARAKSHITA: That is insight. There the transcendental object about which you've heard, which you've mulled over, and about which you've thought creatively, has now been transformed into your being – or your being has been transformed into it. You've become one, as it were, with the object of your creative thinking. In other words, you *realize* it. In the case of the teaching about impermanence, for instance, you first of all hear what Buddhism has to say about impermanence.

You understand it, you can even explain it to others, but maybe you've not really started thinking about it yourself at all, much less still basing your life upon it. In the second stage, you really do have some original thoughts about impermanence. You really do see it; you really do understand the meaning of it: you think creatively about it. But in the third stage you just realize that truth. You've imbibed it, and you're so deeply imbued with it that whatever you do you are aware and mindful of the fact of impermanence, so that you never get attached anywhere. Your understanding of the teaching of impermanence has then become a form of *bhāvanā-mayī-prajñā*. To penetrate this far you require a high degree of vertical integration, and that is where 'the aid of transic concentration', as Conze calls it, comes in. But you must be careful not to think in terms of first having a theoretical understanding and then bringing in concentration (*samādhi*) as an aid in a technical sort of way, i.e. as though it was a kind of technique that you now needed. It's not really like that.

You could, in fact, say that these three kinds of wisdom are continuous. It's very difficult, sometimes, to see where one ends and the other begins. You 'hear', and because you 'hear' you can't help starting to think and trying to understand the meaning of what you have 'heard'. Then your thought becomes more and more creative; you take the idea that has been communicated to you more and more into your own mind – into your own being – and gradually you are transformed into it, it is transformed into you: you become one with it: you realize it – and that is wisdom or understanding in the highest sense. You don't just bring in a sort of technical aid to help you develop that third kind of wisdom.

> 'Wisdom' is, of course, only a very approximate equivalent of *prajñā*. To the average person nowadays 'wisdom' seems to denote a compound made up of such qualities as sagacity, prudence, a well-developed sense of values, serenity, and sovereignty over the world won by the understanding of the mode of its operation. The Buddhist conception of 'wisdom' is not unlike this, but more precise. It is best clarified by first giving its connotations, and then its actual definition.
>
> As for the connotations, we read in the *Dhammasaṅgaṇī*;[131] 'On that occasion the dominant[132] of wisdom is wisdom,

understanding,[133] search, research, search for *dharma*;[134] discernment, discrimination, differentiation, erudition, expert skill, subtlety, clarity,[135] reflection, investigation,[136] amplitude,[137] sagacity,[138] a guide (to true welfare and to the marks as they truly are), insight, comprehension, a goad (which urges the mind to move back on the right track); wisdom, wisdom as virtue, wisdom as strength (because ignorance cannot dislodge it), the sword of wisdom (which cuts through the defilements), the lofty (and overtowering) height of wisdom, the light,[139] lustre and splendour of wisdom, the treasure[140] of wisdom, absence of delusion, search for *dharmas*, right views'. From mere cleverness wisdom is distinguished by its spiritual purpose, and we are told expressly that it is designed 'to cut off the defilements.'[141] (pp. 22–4)

SANGHARAKSHITA: These 'connotations' are really verbal equivalents of wisdom, as well as functions and symbols of wisdom. No doubt one gets an idea of the general nature of wisdom from this rather miscellaneous array of terms. Is there anything that isn't immediately obvious?

SUVAJRA: What about 'goad'? I'm not quite sure about that.

SANGHARAKSHITA: Wisdom is a goad because it spurs you on. A goad is a sharp, pointed stick which you apply to the hindquarters of the bullocks drawing a cart to make them gallop a bit faster. Thus wisdom spurs you on, goads you on, in your spiritual life. It is a goad in the sense of being that 'which urges the mind to move back on the right track'.

You notice at the end of the paragraph that Conze says 'From mere cleverness wisdom is distinguished by its spiritual purpose, and we are told expressly that it is designed "to cut off the defilements."' That is to say, it is designed to cut off the *kleśas*,[142] all the unskilful mental states, because when those unskilful states are permanently vanquished, either wholly or in part, one is at least a Stream Entrant.

Now to the actual definition: 'Wisdom penetrates[143] into *dharmas* as they are in themselves. It disperses the darkness of delusion, which covers up the own-being of *dharmas*.'[144] (p. 24)

SANGHARAKSHITA: Ignorance causes us to see things *not* as they really are, but through wisdom we see things as they really are – or, if you like, we penetrate into the *dharmas* as they are in themselves. Wisdom frees us from delusion.

THE DOORS OF PERCEPTION

MAHAMATI: Is it possible to get a glimpse of them as they are, without developing wisdom?

SANGHARAKSHITA: How could you possibly do that without wisdom? If you have a glimpse of them at all, there is wisdom.

MAHAMATI: I'm thinking of some people saying that they are trying to do that on drug experiences.

SANGHARAKSHITA: Well, what would be the criterion? They would have eliminated the *kleśas*, or at least some of them. If you couldn't see that they'd eliminated any *kleśas* then you wouldn't be justified in agreeing that they had, in fact, some experience of wisdom.

MAHAMATI: Would they have eliminated some of them?

SANGHARAKSHITA: It depends, of course, on the degree of insight. There are, of course, a number of *kleśas*, some of them more gross, some of them more refined. But certainly the grosser ones at least would have been eliminated if one had had any tangible experience of insight and wisdom. For instance, you could not become so violently angry that you might kill somebody. That kind of gross *kleśa* you would have eliminated through even a moderate experience of insight or wisdom. So if someone was to exhibit a murderous impulse after claiming to have developed insight then one could hardly accept that.

MAHAMATI: So seeing things as they are is equivalent to wisdom.

SANGHARAKSHITA: Yes. The word *prajñā* is from the verbal root *jñā*, 'to know', *pra* being a prefix indicative of strength or abundance. *Prajñā* (Pāli *paññā*) is thus superlative knowledge or, if you like, insight. The *kleśas* on the contrary are associated with ignorance. Therefore, if you really have insight into things as they are – insight into reality, – if you have really developed wisdom, at least some of the *kleśas* will be eliminated, or, at the very least, seriously weakened – and that should be quite perceptible, quite noticeable, to other people. One of the things about the drug experience is that, very often, none of its effects are at all lasting. People might have quite extraordinary experiences, just as you might have quite an extraordinary dream, but a few days or a few weeks later it's as though you just hadn't had it. You might even forget all about it, or at least find it very difficult to remember, and your life would not have changed. Perhaps it's difficult to generalize too much. It may be that some people, in connection with the drug experience, do have a glimpse of reality and that does change them in a permanent way: that is not impossible. But that doesn't mean that each and every person who's had a rather colourful drug experience has had a glimpse of reality. That kind of experience is not an ultimate reality. Anyway, that's another matter. But one shouldn't be dogmatic and say that you can't possibly have any experience of reality in connection with drugs. I don't think one can be as positive as that about it. One does know people who might not have experienced wisdom as a result of drugs, but who have certainly had a change of outlook, which eventually led them onto the spiritual path, after a drugs experience. There are people like that even within the Friends.

THE VISION OF THE SAGE

> What then does wisdom meditate about? Wisdom may be held to concern itself with three possible topics: (1) true reality; (2) the meaning of life; (3) the conduct of life. Buddhist tradition assumes that the second and third depend on the first. In its essence wisdom is the strength of mind which permits contact with the true reality, which is also called the realm of *dharmas*. (p. 24)

SANGHARAKSHITA: Not all Buddhist traditions call it 'the realm of *dharmas*'. The Abhidharma calls it that; the Mahāyāna generally and the Madhyamaka might call it the realm of *śūnyatā*; the Yogācāra might call it the realm of the One Mind. And the Tantrics might call it the realm of the *ḍākas* and the *ḍākinīs*.[145]

> Delusion, folly, confusion, ignorance and self-deception are the opposites of wisdom. It is because ignorance, and not sin, is the root evil that wisdom is regarded as the highest virtue. (p. 24)

SANGHARAKSHITA: That is quite important. 'It is because ignorance, and not sin,' – as in Christianity – 'is the root evil that wisdom is regarded as the highest virtue' – or, one could say, not wisdom but Enlightenment, *bodhi*.

> A holiness which is devoid of wisdom is not considered impossible, but it cannot be gained by the path of knowledge, to which alone these descriptions apply. The paths of faith, of love, of works, etc., have each their own several laws. (p. 24)

SANGHARAKSHITA: I don't know that I'd agree with that: 'A holiness which is devoid of wisdom is not considered impossible'? I wouldn't say that at all. I don't think I've ever encountered, in any Buddhist scripture, or in any account of any Buddhist teacher, 'a holiness which is devoid of wisdom'. I think that's meaningless within the Buddhist context, 'but it cannot be gained by the path of knowledge, to which alone these descriptions apply. The paths of faith, of love, of works, etc., have each their own several laws.' I don't think that's really the Buddhist view: it seems more like the Hindu view. It's a bit reminiscent of the Hindu *jñānayoga* – all of them separate paths to God, as it were.[146] Whereas the Buddhist approach, as exemplified by the five spiritual faculties themselves, is a more balanced one. In Buddhism you've got to develop faith and wisdom, concentration and vigour, plus mindfulness – not choose one of them and then develop that only in the hope that it will, by itself, lead you straight to the goal. You can't really bypass wisdom. It may not necessarily take conceptual forms: I think the confusion arises here. You may not be able to present the content of your wisdom experience systematically, in terms of 'philosophy' as it were; but it is wisdom nonetheless. Can you imagine a holy person, in Buddhism, behaving in a truly foolish manner? You can imagine in Christianity a foolish saint. Most of the Christian saints seem to have been very foolish. But can you really imagine a foolish *arhant*?[147] All right, an *arhant* has wisdom by definition, so it isn't a very good example ; but what about a foolish bodhisattva, let's say a bodhisattva who has so much compassion that he becomes a fool? Well, no, there can't be a foolish bodhisattva, because if wisdom wasn't there, there wouldn't be any compassion either. So what is this holiness that can be dissociated from wisdom (as distinct from the conceptual expressions of wisdom)? In a Buddhist context I just fail to see it. But the substance of wisdom will certainly be there even in the absence of the conceptual expressions; the vision of the *dharmas* as they are will certainly be there: otherwise what holiness can there be in a Buddhist context? You might be a yogi, and have experience of the *dhyānas* without insight into reality, but that is not holiness – unless you use the word holiness in a very ambiguous sense indeed. You could be a great yogi without having any insight, but to be a great yogi is not to be holy. I don't like the use of the word 'holy' here at all. It isn't really a very Buddhistic term, especially when you think of Otto's *The Idea of the Holy* – i.e. think of the holy as something numinous, awe-inspiring, terrifying.[148] *That* sort of holiness isn't in Buddhism, really. So there's no path of faith, or of love, that can bypass wisdom substantially, i.e. bypass the 'substance' of wisdom as distinct from its conceptual expressions. There may not be much familiarity with conceptual formulations, but that does not mean that wisdom – essentially – is not there. You can have wisdom without being an intellectual, without even knowing much about Buddhist philosophy: you don't need to know much about it. You might not know the difference between the Mādhyamikas and the Yogācārins; but you could have wisdom: you could be Enlightened. You could answer questions from your own direct experience, even though you might not be able to explain the writings of Buddhist philosophers.

THE REAL VALUE OF THE FIVE SPIRITUAL FACULTIES

> As the unfaltering penetration into the true nature of objects, wisdom is the capacity to meditate in certain ways about the dharmic constituents of the universe. The rules of that meditation have been laid down in the scriptures, particularly in the Abhidharma, and a superb description can be found in the latter part of Buddhaghosa's *Path of Purity*. Mindfulness and concentration were, as we saw, based on the assumption of a duality in the mind – between its calm depth and its excited surface. Wisdom similarly assumes a duality between the surface and the depth of all things. Objects are not what they appear

> to be. Their true reality, in which they stand out as *dharmas*, is opposed to their appearance to commonsense, and much strength of wisdom is required to go beyond the deceptive appearance and to penetrate to the reality of *dharmas* themselves. (p. 24–5)

SANGHARAKSHITA: 'As the unfaltering penetration into the true nature of objects, wisdom is the capacity to meditate in certain ways about the dharmic constituents of the universe.' Surely, once again, he's got it the wrong way round. Just as the *dhyānas* are not methods of concentrating, but just states which you achieve as a result of concentration, in the same way, wisdom is not the capacity to do certain meditation exercises about the dharmic constituents of the universe but what you develop, hopefully, as a result of doing them. Then again, 'Mindfulness and concentration were, as we saw, based on the assumption of a duality in the mind – between its calm depth and its excited surface. Wisdom similarly assumes a duality between the surface and the depth of all things.' In a way that's true; but not altogether. For instance, what about the truth of impermanence? Is that not visible to common sense? Of course it is. You know perfectly well that trees, human beings, houses, your own body, your own life, are impermanent. You know that. Nonetheless, you remain attached to them, as though they were permanent. So it is something other that is missing. You need a deeper sort of recognition, a firmer sort of understanding. On the other hand, it's not immediately obvious to common sense that a table is a congeries of dancing atoms and that each atom is a dance of protons and neutrons and electrons. But I nonetheless think the fact of impermanence is sufficiently obvious, even to common sense. The only thing is, we don't follow that up: we don't act upon it. For *that* we need concentration. We need a higher degree of personal integration on all levels. We have to be wary of this talk of 'the surface' and 'the depth of all things'. It's all right to speak like that poetically, but we can't take it too seriously, too literally.

CONCLUSION

SANGHARAKSHITA: Are there any further points about wisdom? Or any further points about anything you've done these two days? Do you get a sense of the faculties as sequential, i.e. faith leading on to vigour, vigour to mindfulness, mindfulness to concentration, concentration to wisdom?

SUSIDDHI: You can't overdo that sequential way of looking at them; otherwise you don't balance out concentration and energy, and so on.

SANGHARAKSHITA: There is also the point, though, that when you go from faith to vigour, vigour to mindfulness, and so on, you don't literally go from the one to the other in the sense of leaving behind the earlier one. You go on *collecting* them. It's like walking on a strip of carpet, and as you walk along the carpet you roll it up behind you and take it along with you. When you go from faith to vigour, you go *with* faith to vigour, and then with faith and vigour you go on to mindfulness. The fact that you go from the one to the other doesn't mean that you're not balancing them. Of course, you don't proceed *quite* regularly: you have *some* faith, then *some* vigour; then maybe you have to go back to faith and strengthen that before you can strengthen your vigour. But you *perfect* faith before you perfect vigour; you *perfect* vigour before you perfect mindfulness. But you have to have quite a lot of all of them before you can get very far with any of them.

SUSIDDHI: *The Way of Wisdom* is a good text for a weekend's study.

SANGHARAKSHITA: Yes, I'm glad I selected it. One needs something short enough to be dealt with over a weekend, but on the other hand with sufficient substance in it, and it isn't easy to find a text like that. *The Way of Wisdom* certainly provides good study material for Mitras and non-Mitras alike. We've not gone into all the topics that we might have done, because I was keen to cover the whole ground. There are many points which one could discuss at much greater length; but I think I've indicated the main lines along which discussion needs to proceed, and also pointed out where we don't quite see eye to eye with Dr Conze (which I think is important), or where he seems to have left something out, even though his overall attitude is very traditional and very satisfactory indeed.

VERSES TO TĀRĀ

EDITORIAL NOTE

During his time in Kalimpong, from 1957 to 1964, Sangharakshita received initiations from various eminent Tibetan lamas. A number of these initiations centred in different ways upon the female bodhisattva Tārā, and Sangharakshita devoted a considerable amount of time to the associated practices. It was in this connection that, in collaboration with John Driver,[149] he produced for his own personal use an English rendering of the Tibetan version of the 'Flower-Garland Hymn to the Goddess Tārā', by the seventh-century Indian lay poet and bodhisattva Candragomin.[150] Some years later he presented a typescript copy of this rendering to his friend C. M. Chen,[151] the Buddhist hermit of Kalimpong, who rearranged the order of the verses and brought it out in booklet form. In this edition, the verses have been arranged in their original order.

The Bodhisattva Tārā

CANDRAGOMIN'S FLOWER-GARLAND HYMN TO THE GODDESS TĀRĀ

To Avalokiteśvara, Protector (*nātha*) endowed with Great Compassion, I make obeisance.

Bowing at the lotus-feet
Of that One Who with the Eye of Compassion looks upon beings,
In order to perfect my two stocks (of *puṇya* and of *jñāna*)[152]
I shall extol my Presiding Deity.

Obeisance, Tārā! God of gods, Thou
Art the source of all *siddhis* without exception;[153]
E'en as the precious Wish-Fulfilling Gem,
Donatrix of the fruit desired.

Obeisance: in a Body where all
Wondrous and pre-eminent virtues are perfected,
Emitter in the ten directions of Compassion's light-rays –
Extended self-luminance of the five *jñānas*.[154]

Obeisance: well dwelling beyond the four floods,
Released from deeds, affects and becoming (*karma-kleśa-bhāva-vimukta*),
She Who the remainderless end has reached, of the *bhūmis*[155] and paths
Of Buddha-virtues irreversible.

Obeisance: conquering the net of existence
Thou who fill'st the sky with the light of Works, Thy operations –
Pacifying, Expanding, Empowering and Enchanting –
From the Ten Letters, quintessence of (Thy) Heart (*cittagarbha/ hṛdaya*).

Obeisance, best refuge of beings Tārā,
Taming beings with a woman's form:
Daughter of glorious *Lokeśvara*,[156]
From the Holy One's tear(s) born.

Obeisance, (Thou) the lotus-feet of Whose
Unrivalled most excellent Body – seated
On a full-moon mat in outflowless bliss (*anāśravasukha*) –
Gods and anti-gods (*asuras*) touch with their crowns.

Obeisance, most great amongst the great,
Conquering the throng of vile ghouls (*bhūta*) and revenants (*vetāla*),[157]
Great in fierce skills, by others unmatchable,
Mighty, suppressor of the Other Side.

Obeisance, Tārā, releaser from the Round,
Bhagavatī – at Thy Feet
He who (seeks) refuge gains Nirvāṇa –
(Thou) Who accomplishes the highest great purposes.

Obeisance, Tārā, of the Acacia (*khadira*) grove,
Who, with the ship of Great Compassion
Of Thy Kind Heart that takes the six (classes of) beings as children,
Releasest from the sea of the three worlds (*tribhuvana-saṃsāra*).

Obeisance, defender from all misfortune (*vipanna*)
Who, when one tormented by living, lips and throat dried up, and
Starving, made prayer to Thee,
Let'st fall of goods (*bhoga*) an inexhaustible shower.

Obeisance! Heroine (*vīrā*), Vajratārā,
Of the colour of gold from the Jambu river:[158]
Accomplisher of beings' purposes through the Operations
Of Thy eight characteristic Implements, the vajra and so on.

Obeisance! Governing all beings,
Treader with the soles of Thy Feet
On the crowns of those drunk with Pride
Of being in the three worlds (*triloka*) possessed of power.

Obeisance! Released from the bonds of existence,
(Thou who hast) gained possession of the highest Means and
Wisdom (*prajñā*),
Unimpeded *ṛddhi*,[159] in (Thy) *jñāna*-Body:
(Thou) Who purifies the defilements of pain and the Round.

Obeisance! (Thou) Who, when the Quintessence of (Thee), the
Mistress of (magical) power
With its ten letters, is fastened to the top of one's head, and
He has gone amongst the four-armed host,
Repulses the warfare of the hostile army.

Obeisance! Embodiment of Wisdom and Kindness
Into the *svastika* (*śrīvatsa*),[160] treasury adorned
With many *dhyānas*, *samādhis*, *vimokṣas*,[161]
Ever inserting the centre and circumference of wisdom
(*prajñā*).

Obeisance! (Thou) with a lake of sun's lustre,
Thou Who by great *prajñā*'s blazing light-rays
Clearest away the gloom of unknowing's egg
In the minds of animate beings on the three planes (*tridhātu*).

Obeisance! Embodiment of the five *jñānas*: (Thou Who),
On Thy glorious and immaculate Body,
With the thirty-two excellent signs adorned,
Dost exhibit the eighty good characteristics.

Obeisance! Subjugator of the three planes:
Thou at whose Feet profoundly bow
The diademed heads of the great gods,
Brahmā, Viṣṇu, Mahādeva.[162]

Obeisance! Defendress from all dangers:
Of fire and water and the King's punishments,
Tigers, lions, snakes and ogres (*rākṣasas*),
Elephants – their terrors eliminating.

Obeisance! Thou of marvellous blessing (*adhiṣṭhāna*):
Remover of woes when Thou art prayed to –
Every kind of life-robbing illness
Engendered by disorder, humours and malign planets.

Obeisance! Queen in bejewelled dress:
Light of the 'treasure-hairs' from between (Thy) brows blazing,
The smiling expression of thy long eyes like lotus-leaves,
Thou looker upon beings with compassion and love.

Obeisance! (Thou Who) from the mire of the Round
With the hook of Compassion and Void drawest beings:
Thou taking us with compassion when (we) meet wrong ways,
Into the path of escape (*muktimārga*) dost guide us.

Obeisance! Conqueror of the four Māras:
All Buddhas in person, *bhaṭṭārakī*,[163] Thou
Rid of the five *skandhas*, (art) possessor of the five (*kāyas*),[164]
Perfecter of the five *jñānas* and ridder of the (five) *kleśas*.[165]

Obeisance! Great in righteousness and splendour:
Increaser of understanding and *prajñā*'s glory
In the mind of living beings by the light
Of Thy excellent youthful (lit. sixteen-year old) face like the full
moon.

Obeisance! Illusion of woman, Thou Whom
Māmakī, Locanā, Pāṇḍaravāsinī,[166]

Praise, and the greatest of the great among
Gods and serpent-deities (*nāgas* and *yakṣas*).

Obeisance! Having the acquirement of *hūṃ*:
Since that at Thy three centres is place,
Thou hast from Thy potent *ṛddhis* spread
To (all) extremes (i.e. everywhere), the power of the Four Operations.

Obeisance! Thou Who increasest merit (*kuśala*):
Who makest whoever has meditated on Thee
Rid himself of veilings – as the sun's disk
Purges darkness the moment it rises.

Obeisance! Mistress of many workings:
Thy Bodies various, in essence like a glass (i.e. reflecting many forms) –
Not definite in one colour and set of implements,
(But) arising differently (in accordance with) whom Thou art near.

Obeisance! (Though) from the Absolute (*paramārtha*), Jina's realm,
Not moving, having the form of a Relative (*saṃvṛtti*) goddess:
Of greenish blue colour, with the dances' nine graces
Posturing in non-ratiocinating bliss-illumination.

Obeisance! Repulser of the Round's warfare
Slayer of the warriors (*vīra*, *śūra*) of 'object-subject' error,
Having stabbed with the sword of *prapañca*-free *jñāna*[167]
The heart of egoism that longs for 'substantiae'.

Obeisance! Thy hair (symbolic) of the two stocks (*jñāna* and *puṇya*) perfected:
Thou, the light-rays of Whose Compassion emerge
In ten directions from Amitābha, the Perfect Buddha,
Amidst the coiled sapphire 'willow-leaves' (of Thy headdress seated).

LIVING ETHICALLY

Advice From Nāgārjuna's *Precious Garland*

EDITORIAL NOTE

Living Ethically is based on material from a seminar on Nāgārjuna's *Ratnāvāli*, the 'Precious Garland', an early text from the Mahāyāna Buddhist tradition, led by Sangharakshita in the summer of 1976. Due to the large amount of material in the original seminar, far too much for one book, it was decided to publish the work in two stages rather than making drastic cuts to the content. The decision as to how to divide the seminar was made on a thematic basis. That is to say, the first part, published as *Living Ethically*, focuses on what the text has to say about ethics; the second, published later as *Living Wisely*, focuses on Nāgārjuna's teachings on emptiness in the same work.

The separation of the two themes was by no means ideal, although for teaching purposes, ethics and wisdom are typically addressed separately. The editors of the first edition make this clear in their preface:

> A discussion which includes the observation that 'people will take pride in almost anything that might bring them a little attention, even if that attention is far from flattering' is very different in nature from a discussion around the point that 'if the existence of something necessarily involves the existence of its opposite, then that thing cannot be said to be absolutely real'.

The editing of the original seminar transcript was carried out by the Spoken Word team. Once the draft was complete, Sangharakshita was able to review the text, but with some limitations owing to his failing eyesight. In the event, he and Samacitta spent many hours together working through the edited text, she reading the text aloud and he listening to its effect. In the process, new insights emerged which were incorporated into the book. In this sense *Living Ethically* can be regarded as Sangharakshita's more developed thinking on the subject of Buddhist ethics.

For this edition, no significant changes have been made apart from the addition of new subheadings, introduced as an aid to understanding. For similar reasons, the fifty-seven mental events, which are the subject of chapter 6 of *Living Ethically*, have in some instances been cross-referenced to *Know Your Mind*, also included in this volume, which addresses similar topics from the standpoint of the Abhidharma.

Living Ethically owes its existence to the editorial work of Tim Weston, Pabodhana, Jinananda, and Vidyadevi, as well as to Shantavira, who edited and polished the text, and to Tarajyoti who typeset it. We are grateful also to Dhivan for his scholarly advice, especially with regard to the fourteen inexpressibles.

The numbers at the end of each quotation indicate verse numbers in Jeffrey Hopkins' translation of *Nāgārjuna's Precious Garland*. We are indebted to Snow Lion Publications for their permission to publish excerpts from the above work.

INTRODUCTION

The Buddhist monk Nāgārjuna lived some 600 years after the *parinirvāṇa* of the Buddha, in the second or third century CE. For many Buddhists, he is the greatest of the Indian Mahayāna teachers. An original thinker, he was the author of the *Madhyamakakārikā* or 'Verses on the Middle',[168] the foundational text of the Madhyamaka school, besides being the popularizer of the Prajñāpāramitā or 'Perfection of Wisdom' scriptures.[169] The work on which this book is based, the *Rāja-parikathā-Ratnamālā* or 'Precious Garland of Advice for a King',[170] is one of Nāgārjuna's less well known works. Succinct, comprehensive, and inspiring, it is a masterpiece of Mahāyāna expository literature. It deals with the two definitive, inseparable aspects of the bodhisattva's life, the bodhisattva being the ideal Buddhist of the Mahāyāna. These two aspects are the profound wisdom which realizes the truth of emptiness,[171] and the extensive compassion which engages in activities for the benefit of others. The *Ratnāvāli* is, in fact, a Mahāyāna manual, a handbook of the Mahāyāna tradition, and a guide to living in accordance with Mahāyāna principles. The work is addressed to an unnamed king, supposedly one belonging to the South Indian Sātavāhana dynasty.[172]

The *Precious Garland*'s theme is the relationship between the practice of ethics and the attainment of wisdom, and in the course of the work Nāgārjuna explores this relationship from a number of different angles, chiefly in relation to various traditional formulations such as the ten ethical precepts, the six perfections, and the fifty-seven faults to be abandoned.[173] In the course of this exploration he gives the king advice on a whole range of ethical matters, and it is this aspect of his advice to the king on which this book is based. Mahāyāna texts are not perhaps the first works of reference to which a Buddhist seeking advice on ethical matters will naturally turn; among the range of scriptures and commentaries available to us, it may seem more obvious to look to the scriptures of early Buddhism, many of which spell out clearly and uncompromisingly the ethical conduct that supports the seeking of Enlightenment. However, the Mahāyāna has plenty to say on the subject, and although it may seem strange that advice given by a monk to a king nearly two thousand years ago has relevance for modern life, Nāgārjuna's words are in fact extremely useful for anyone seeking to live a Buddhist life today.

The basic principle of ethics, according to the Mahāyāna, is to help others, whereas the view of the Hīnayāna (as Mahāyānists called the earlier form of Buddhism) is that the practice of ethics is undertaken largely as an exercise in cultivating and preserving positive mental states. The Mahāyāna does not contradict this viewpoint, but simply regards a wholehearted concern for others as a more positive motivation than a concern for one's own mental states. Another Mahāyāna certainty is that ethical behaviour is grounded in Perfect Wisdom, and at the same time that the development of wisdom is only possible on the basis of an ethical life. That reciprocal relationship is the context, Mahāyānists would say, in which the practice of ethics should be considered. It is entirely natural, therefore, that in the *Precious Garland*, Nāgārjuna, that famed exponent of the Perfection of Wisdom, returns again and again to reconsider the basics of ethical life and practice. But before we look at what he has to say on the subject, we could usefully ask how we *know* what he said. Where did these verses come from, and how have they reached us?

ORAL TRANSMISSION AND MODERN SCHOLARSHIP

Whereas the Buddha taught purely by word of mouth, and his teachings were preserved as an oral tradition for 400 years before they were written down in what we now know as the Pāli canon, by Nāgārjuna's time writing was in common use, and Nāgārjuna's work was composed as a literary text, a short work addressed to a particular individual in the form of a letter. Nāgārjuna wrote in Sanskrit, but the text on which this commentary is based is a translation from the Tibetan. This calls for a word of explanation.

Tibetan Buddhism, which also spread into Mongolia, Sikkim, Bhutan, and Ladakh, is one of three major historical forms of Buddhism that still flourish today, the others being south-east Asian Buddhism (found in Sri Lanka, Burma, Thailand, Cambodia, and Laos) and Sino-Japanese Buddhism (found in Korea and Vietnam as well as China and Japan). Each of these forms is a continuation of Indian Buddhism from a certain point in the history of its development, which continued until it was wiped out in the land of its birth by Muslim invaders in the twelfth century.[174] Indeed, the prominent position Nāgārjuna's works assume in Tibetan literature is evidence of the continuity between Tibetan Buddhism and its Indian antecedents.

Tibetan Buddhism is essentially the brilliant and complex Buddhism of the Pala dynasty in north-east India, supplemented by influences from central Asia.[175] The transmission of Buddhism from one country to another was not like taking an artefact from one place to another. Indian Buddhists, moving from the subtropical plains and forests of Bengal and Bihar across the huge barrier of the Himalayas into the icy, windswept tablelands of Tibet, were transporting not an object but their practice and teaching. It was like the migration of a living species which faithfully continues to pass on its defining features from one generation to the next while slowly adapting itself to its new environment, eventually to produce a distinct variant of the original species.

Through its various schools, and through the outstanding personalities of teachers such as Milarepa and Tsongkhapa,[176] Tibetan Buddhism has made original contributions of great value throughout its history, while retaining the essential features of the Indian Mahāyāna. In its monastic organization and teaching, Tibetan Buddhism perpetuates the Sarvāstivāda school of ancient Buddhist India. As regards Tantric practice, it keeps alive the symbolic rituals and esoteric meditations of a hundred different lineages of Indian yogis and adepts, and in the texts it uses, Tibetan Buddhism preserves the scriptures imported from India with a high degree of accuracy. Sanskrit Buddhist manuscripts, where they exist at all, tend to be very corrupt, but Tibetan translations are very faithful to the originals.

There is a further reason to trust the Tibetan translation. Although the text is a literary work, the translation we will be using here is based on an oral transmission, involving not just the passing on of the text but an explanation of it as well. If you read a text just by yourself, it might not yield much meaning, whereas if you are fortunate enough to be introduced to it by a competent teacher, you are likely to gain a deeper insight into what it is about. It is thus customary in Tibetan Buddhism to approach a text by going to a guru or teacher who is able to explain and interpret it in the light of what he knows about your own Buddhist practice. Eventually you may in turn explain the text to your own students, and it is in this way that the essential meaning of the work is passed down the lineage.

If the continuity of the lineage is interrupted, as sometimes happens, the correct interpretation might even be lost and have to be discovered afresh. In the case of some quite elementary works this is perhaps not so important, but if the work is an abstruse or difficult one, as the present work undoubtedly is in parts, then the correct interpretation of the text becomes very important. In all Buddhist traditions, it is understood that reading a work by oneself does not really count. Prior to my own monastic ordination, for instance, I was asked exactly which texts I had read and studied in conjunction with a teacher, and these were the only texts I was credited with having read in any proper sense. This attitude is inherited from the earliest times, and the *Precious Garland* itself was composed to be studied in this way. It is not written for the uninitiated reader. It is a pithy presentation of the ideas of the Mahāyāna, suitable for oral explanation by a teacher such as Nāgārjuna himself.

But if it is best to depend upon the interpretation of a teacher, what is the role of the scholar in aiding our understanding of a text like this? In any discussion of the development of Buddhist ideas there are, at the very least, two very different viewpoints: that of modern scholarship on the one hand and that of traditional Buddhism on the other. The traditional Indo-Tibetan point of view is that the Mahāyāna teaching was delivered in its fullness, exactly as expressed in the Mahāyāna *sūtras*, by the Buddha, but that by the time of Nāgārjuna, approximately 700 years after the Buddha's death, it had disappeared from view, and had to be revived, and in some cases rediscovered, by the Madhyamaka and Yogācāra masters. From the point of view of modern scholarship, however, the Buddha could not have taught the Mahāyāna *sūtras*, certainly not in the form in which they have come down to us.[177] Perhaps certain things he said and certain teachings he gave contained the seeds that later developed into the Mahāyāna, but the modern scholar would regard Nāgārjuna as having cultivated those seeds and produced from them something that was not previously envisaged. They would not accept the claim of the Mahāyāna that Nāgārjuna was simply the reviver of teachings that had already blossomed in the original dispensation of a Buddha.

These two views are obviously in conflict, but that is not to say that one is right and the other is wrong. The middle way is to give appropriate weight to each view. Clearly it is not possible to accept that the Mahāyāna *sūtras* were taught by the Buddha exactly as they have come down to us. At the same time, it is important to affirm that they do fully reflect the spirit of the Buddha's original teaching, albeit recast in another form at a later time. We can certainly see in the Pāli texts not only seeds but quite definite statements of teachings that come out more fully later on in the Mahāyāna tradition.

This difficulty arises when one is studying any Buddhist text, even the *suttas* of the Pāli canon, which Theravādin Buddhists traditionally claim to be literally the word of the Buddha. It is seldom easy to tell, even with these, to what extent they can be regarded as the actual words of the Buddha and to what extent they are later reshapings of his original message. In all likelihood, texts like the *Udāna* or the *Sutta-Nipāta* come as close as anything in the Buddhist canon to telling us what the Buddha said and how he said it,[178] but works whose literary forms reveal that they originated later may reflect the spirit of the Buddha's teaching just as faithfully. There is a very fine line to be drawn between the spirit of the teaching and the letter, and while scholarship is very helpful in any examination of the 'letter' of the text as a text, the guidance of a teacher will bring us closer to the spiritual meaning of that text. This is a process that takes place whenever someone who has realized the spirit of the teaching is engaged in trying to pass on that teaching. Thus in his *Precious Garland* we could say that Nāgārjuna is cultivating seeds that are already present in the Perfection of Wisdom (*Prajñāpāramitā*) *sūtras* and the *Sūtra on the Ten Stages* (*Daśabhūmika*)[179] for the benefit of his audience, the king, and giving a new form to the essential spirit of these teachings. In studying classics of Tibetan Buddhist literature such as Nāgārjuna's *Precious Garland*, we therefore come a good deal closer to the mainstream of Indian Mahāyāna doctrine and practice than we might at first have thought.

We can take it that the words ascribed to Nāgārjuna are indeed his, and that the *Precious Garland* gives us an authentic account of the communication between teacher and royal student. Needless to say, there is no royal road to perfect wisdom; the text soon makes it clear that, like anyone else, the king will need to pay attention to his ethical life if he is to become truly wise. Living ethically is essentially about developing compassion, and compassion, in the eyes of Mahāyāna Buddhism, is coordinate with wisdom, wisdom and compassion being the two wings by means of which the bird of Enlightenment can fly. As well as giving the king a great deal of specific advice about *how* to live ethically, Nāgārjuna makes various suggestions as to why one should do so. These are scattered throughout the *Precious Garland*, as though at various points the king needs to be encouraged or provoked into greater efforts. Nāgārjuna uses a combination of carrots and sticks: on the one hand, he points out that ethical behaviour is the basis of wisdom and that skilful action leads to happiness, whether in this life or the next; on the other hand, he issues sober warnings about the impermanence of life and about the serious consequences of unskilful actions. Skilful behaviour is thus shown to be the road to a wise and happy life and also the way to avoid pain and misery. What follows is a brief survey of Nāgārjuna's reflections on the necessity of ethical living, and the nature of its rewards.

ETHICS AS THE BASIS OF WISDOM

> O King, I will explain practices solely virtuous
> To generate in you the doctrine,
> For the practices will be established
> In a vessel of the excellent doctrine. (2)

The central idea expressed here is that ethical practice is the basis upon which wisdom may be developed. Nāgārjuna lays out his aims, which are not to impart doctrinal information but to plant seeds of the Dharma, the Buddha's teaching. The word 'doctrine' perhaps suggests something that is understood intellectually, but the Dharma is to be realized in every fibre of one's being. Nāgārjuna's organic metaphor – 'generate' – reflects this deeper meaning. It suggests that what he is going to say is intended to spark off something that will become the king's own realization, something that will be brought to birth within him, something that will live and thrive.

In other words, Nāgārjuna proposes to generate in the king not merely an understanding of the Dharma, but the Dharma itself, just as the Buddha did not speak *about* the Dharma, but simply spoke Dharma. Nāgārjuna doesn't want merely to talk *about* the truth. He wants to *awaken* the king to the truth. He is reminding the king of his inherent potential to attain Enlightenment, to establish the practices and to become thereby a vessel of the Dharma.

When Nāgārjuna speaks of the 'excellent doctrine' in the fourth line, the addition of an adjective is not just to fill up the verse line. In ancient Buddhist literature, especially verse, every word or syllable contributes to the meaning. He therefore refers to something slightly different from just 'doctrine' on its own, which appears in the second line. In the second line the Dharma is the fruit of solely – or simply – virtuous practices. This Dharma is real enough, it is a living spiritual principle, a practical realization of what is skilful and what is unskilful, but it can be practised even by a beginner. We can assume that the king did not know very much Dharma, if any at all. As a result, Nāgārjuna begins by speaking about morality. He wants to inspire the king, to spark off a more positive state of mind. The term translated as 'excellent doctrine', however, is *saddharma*, which means the true or real Dharma, the ultimate Dharma, the Dharma that is directly concerned with reality. Nāgārjuna foresees that as the king becomes established in the moral practices he takes up, he will become receptive to the Dharma at a significantly higher level.

When people first become interested in the spiritual life, they are not necessarily looking for profound philosophical teachings, or, even if they are, these may not be what it is most useful for them to hear. To begin with, they need something that will give them a feeling for states of mind more positive than the ones they usually experience. They don't need facts and figures about the history of Buddhism. They don't need requests for donations. Nāgārjuna therefore does not burden the king with a discussion of the finer points of the Abhidharma[180] or of Mahāyāna philosophy – at least not yet – nor does he bother his wealthy and influential student with requests for funds with which to build monasteries. If he cannot inspire the king from the start, he might as well save himself the trouble of trying to teach him anything, let alone the 'excellent doctrine'.

Nāgārjuna's 'vessel of the excellent doctrine' is a description of a practitioner of the Dharma. Another teacher compares the four different kinds of disciple to four kinds of pot. The first kind is like a pot that is turned upside down; he or she is completely unreceptive. The second is like a pot with holes in the bottom. Just as whatever you pour into the pot leaks away, likewise, whatever is communicated to this sort of disciple goes in one ear and out the other. They might seem to understand at the time, but nothing is retained long enough to make any real impression. The next kind of disciple is like a pot containing poison, full of negative mental states like resentment, craving, and cynicism. Such a disciple will corrupt and distort the teaching in such a way as to make it harmful to themselves and to others. Finally, there is the disciple who is like a pot that is clean, intact, and empty, ready to receive the Dharma. This sort of disciple is ready to receive the Dharma. He or she is the 'vessel of the excellent doctrine' of which Nāgārjuna speaks. The king's task is to become such a vessel.

> In one who first practices high status
> Definite goodness arises later,
> For having attained high status
> One comes gradually to definite goodness. (3)

High status and definite goodness are important terms within the *Ratnāvalī*. 'High status' means a happy, positive, and even prominent situation within conditioned existence. In the context of the Tibetan wheel of life,[181] the term means a good rebirth in the human realm or among the gods. It is a goal that tradition often assigns to the laity, especially in Theravāda countries. By observing the precepts, worshipping at stupas, and giving alms and donations to monks, one generates good karma, and thus earns the positive but still mundane fruits of that karma, without necessarily concerning oneself with the ultimate goal of Buddhism. 'Definite goodness', on the other hand, refers to those qualities that make for insight, for liberation from conditioned existence, for Nirvāṇa.

According to Nāgārjuna, one who seeks to lead a spiritual life first improves their position within *saṃsāra* (the round of mundane existence) and then goes on to cultivate 'definite goodness', the urge for liberation. Put like that, what he is saying is obviously true. But does everyone who attains 'high status' necessarily start thinking in terms of 'definite goodness', in the sense of trying to realize the inherently insubstantial and impermanent nature of conditioned existence? No, certainly not. We cannot assume that this higher aspiration will arise automatically as the result of a mere accumulation of *puṇya*, or merit, and the attainment of 'high status'. It will arise only if you start thinking seriously about the unsatisfactory nature of conditioned existence itself – despite your enjoyment of 'high status' within it.

Like many traditional teachings, the *Ratnāvalī* is meant for a particular audience. Everyone needs the Dharma to be presented to them in a way that will harness their personal predispositions and energies. Here, Nāgārjuna is addressing a king. The traditional Indian belief was that if you were born into a royal family, it was on account of previous good karma. Nāgārjuna is in effect saying that since, as a result of his previous virtuous deeds, the king has attained 'high status', he should now think of achieving or developing 'definite goodness'. He is presenting this as the next natural step, the only real option for a sensible person. The king's merits having gained for him the highest status it is possible to achieve in life, he seems to be saying, there is really only one further step for him to take.

Once you assume that a certain course of events will naturally follow from what you are doing now, it will often be those very events that take place. If you have made up your mind about the course before you, there can be a sense of inevitability about it, even though you have to continue to make an effort in that direction. Nāgārjuna is perhaps trying to encourage the king, and to persuade him that his achievement of 'high status' is just the foundation for this decisive step on the spiritual path.

This example of skilful means should not blind us to the fact that in reality there is no summit to human felicity. There is no point at which you will be sure to say to yourself, 'Well, I've come as far as one can get in this world. Now for something of an entirely different nature.' There is, that is to say, no end to human craving. One never feels that one has enough. Even a man who has contrived to bring a whole nation under his control might well want to extend his power still further. If they are to make spiritual progress, it would seem that people need to experience a few unpleasant shocks, just to make them think seriously.

If things are going along smoothly you might start taking everything for granted and become unmindful of the impermanence and fragility of human existence, in which case your 'high status' would not have helped you progress towards the goal at all.

This is a subject to which Nāgārjuna turns later in the text:

Always considering that impermanence
Of life, health, and dominion,
You thereby will make intense effort
Solely at the practices.

Seeing that death is certain
And that, having died, you suffer from ill deeds,
You should not commit ill deeds
Though there might be temporary pleasure.

Sometimes no horror is seen
And sometimes it is.
If there is comfort in one,
Why do you have no fear for the other? (143–5)

If the promise of happiness is not incentive enough to practise, consider, says Nāgārjuna, how precarious is our hold upon life. We assume that we will live out our allotted span of years, but this is by no means certain. Even in the conditions of modern life, the possible causes of death are legion, while the factors keeping us alive are comparatively few, and even they can become causes of death. Food, for example, keeps us alive, but there are so many cases, including that of the Buddha himself, in which it has brought a swift end instead.

The fact of impermanence manifests in a thousand different ways. If we look at life dispassionately and in detail, we can see the changes almost as they occur. Though these changes may be quite small, as we get older they add up to a process of increasing physical and mental decline. We are likely to acknowledge this decline sadly and reluctantly, even anxiously, but it is possible to see it as something from which we can draw strength and determination. It is even possible to draw inspiration from events that jolt us into greater awareness such as some sudden change in health or fortunes, or perhaps a brush with death. In fact we have every reason to take such reminders of impermanence as a spur to spiritual practice. It is obvious that we don't have much time, and that we may lose the faculties that we now possess. Life will become more difficult as we get older. In many ways, we who live in advanced democracies live like kings, but the privileges we enjoy, especially the freedom and opportunity to practise the Dharma, may not always be available to us.

As the fact of impermanence reminds us, life is a brief and precious opportunity, an opportunity to be seized with enthusiasm. Don't wait until you have more time. Just do it now, in the midst of everything else that you have to do. The message of impermanence is the message of the Dharma itself. Impermanence is a death sentence, but it is also our hope of freedom from death, if only we can accept its message at the deepest level of our being, and heed its warning. For Nāgārjuna, impermanence does not imply nihilism, the belief that death is the end. In the West, we tend to regard a belief in a future life or lives as reassuring, but such a prospect is not reassuring for Nāgārjuna or for any true Buddhist. The translation 'ill deeds' is perhaps not the happiest, but the message is clear; what Nāgārjuna is saying is: How can you take comfort from the fact that, despite your misdeeds, you appear to enjoy a good life now? You may relax when you see nothing threatening coming upon you in this life, but when you *do* experience the operation of karma, why do you not take it as a warning that you should mend your ways? Here is the paradoxical nature of human self-delusion. We take comfort when we don't see the karmic results of our unskilful actions, but we don't heed the warning when we do.

This, at least, is the traditional message. I would not put it that way myself, however. I would prefer to say that unskilful actions hinder our development as human beings, and therefore undermine our happiness. They certainly undermine the happiness that results from a good conscience. Why sacrifice real happiness for the sake of some transitory pleasure?

An aspect of 'high status' that it is easy to assume is spiritually advantageous, but which is not necessarily so, is the possession of physical and mental health. It might be assumed that if you are physically healthy and active, mentally robust and socially adept, you will necessarily be more receptive to the Dharma. However, being healthy sometimes comes with a sort of beefy and unreflecting insensitivity, while people who are unwell or unsuccessful in worldly terms – even people who are emotionally disturbed – are sometimes more spiritually sensitive and receptive. In other words, 'skilful' in its Buddhist sense is not equivalent to 'healthy'. That is, the criteria of psychological health espoused by psychotherapeutic or psychoanalytic theory do not quite correspond with Buddhist ideas of what constitutes a mentally healthy human being.

For example, a common rule of thumb used to estimate reasonable mental health is the ability to hold down a job, but the possession of spiritually skilful mental states can go with an inability to conform to worldly expectations that can render a person virtually unemployable. It is as if a little insight sets you going against the grain of the world; you might perhaps become a little eccentric, even unstable. Someone who is healthy in the worldly sense might appear to be a likely vessel for the Dharma, but a rather more battered specimen of humanity, even someone straight out of mental hospital or jail, might prove to be much the more successful Dharma practitioner. To be skilful in the Buddhist sense means to act, speak, and think in a way that takes one away from what are traditionally known as the three poisons: craving, hatred, and bewilderment or mental confusion. You may be healthy in the worldly sense, may function very well in society, and be successful and even happy, but unless you have sufficient insight to perceive the ways in which you are affected by the three poisons, you are not healthy in the Buddhist sense.

> High status is considered to be happiness,
> Definite goodness as liberation,
> The quintessence of their means
> Are briefly faith and wisdom. (4)

Here Nāgārjuna distinguishes between two ways of thinking. You can think in terms of gaining happiness, in which case you are still concerned with the world, or you can think in terms of gaining liberation. The difference is quite significant. The worldly-minded person asks, usually unconsciously, 'What will make me happy?' The spiritually-minded person on the other hand asks, consciously, 'How can I become free?'

If you are a healthy person in the ordinary sense of the word, you are likely to judge how well you are doing in terms of how happy you feel. This translates, objectively speaking, into what Nāgārjuna terms 'high status'. However, happiness is not a very reliable guideline. If you do something because you think it will make you happy, the chances are that you will be disappointed, and in all likelihood your search for ways to be happy will continue indefinitely. There will never be an object that can give you the happiness you seek; you will just go from one thing to another, becoming more and more frustrated, bored, disappointed, dissatisfied, and unhappy. On the other hand, if you are thinking in terms of 'definite goodness', you will not worry too much about immediate happiness, which means, strangely enough, that you are much more likely to find it. Happiness is a by-product of the quest for freedom.

> Having analyzed well
> All deeds of body, speech, and mind,
> Those who realize what benefits self and others
> And always perform these are wise. (7)

Nāgārjuna's conception of wisdom as including the realization of 'what benefits self and others' is thoroughly Mahāyānist in that it accepts the bodhisattva ideal with its aim of Enlightenment for oneself and others. The traditional phrase is not to be taken too literally, because to an Enlightened one there is ultimately no distinction between self and others, but it is meaningful for the non-Enlightened mind, and helps to break down that distinction on an emotional level. It also makes it absolutely clear that we are not being asked to put our own happiness to one side altogether in our concern for the happiness of others.

One might say that Nāgārjuna's aim in writing this letter to the king is to direct him towards true happiness, as distinct from the transitory happiness of worldly success. But if the quest for happiness is subsequently to be put aside in the transition from seeking 'high status' to seeking 'definite goodness', this does not mean there is anything wrong with wanting to be happy. It is a natural and healthy human impulse. How can we wish for the happiness of others if we are alienated from our own desire for happiness?

Unfortunately, many of us in the West were given to understand when we were young that it is selfish to want happiness for oneself, and we therefore feel unnecessarily guilty about wanting it. As a result, we can feel guilty even about *being* happy. 'After all,' the perverse logic goes, 'with all my selfish desires for my own happiness, how could I possibly deserve to be happy?' This further produces the still more perverse belief that if we are to make spiritual progress, we will necessarily have to subject ourselves to great suffering. Such a deep-down belief that you are undeserving, even basically wicked, will inhibit your practice of the Dharma from the very beginning.

This unfortunate state of affairs arises partly from our failure to distinguish between happiness and the good on the one hand and what is pleasant on the other. If we are to lead a spiritual life, it is imperative that we distinguish between happiness and pleasure. We have to realize that doing what is good for us is not the same thing as doing what we like or what we enjoy. However, it can sometimes be so difficult to disentangle the two that it is tempting to assume that the good cannot be pleasant, and that the pleasant is bound to do us harm. To avoid following one's blind desires, one may even make it a rule always to follow the advice of others and do what they think is best for one. From this it is only a short step to thinking that one's natural desire to benefit oneself and to be happy is reprehensible.

If you find yourself in this sort of dilemma, it might be best just to do what you enjoy doing, regardless of people's approval or disapproval, and in this way re-establish contact with your feelings. Ideally, we should act spontaneously, with ease and flexibility, rather than acting out of a sense of being hedged in on every side by self-recrimination or out of fear of transgressing some immutable moral law. Having said that, our wider aim should be to reach out beyond our personal happiness towards what is of profounder concern to us, namely, benefiting others. If you succeed in doing this, you are being a true friend to yourself.

HAPPINESS IS BENEFICIAL

Always observe the discipline
Of actions just as it has been explained,
In that way, O glorious one, you will become
The best of authoritative beings upon the earth.

You should always analyse well
Everything before you act,
And through seeing things correctly as they are
Do not put full reliance on others.

Through these practices your realm will be happy,
A broad canopy of fame
Will rise in all directions,
And your officials will respect you fully.

The causes of death are many,
Those of staying alive are few,
These too can become the causes of death,
Therefore always perform the practices.

If you always perform thus the practices,
The mental happiness which arises
In the world and in yourself
Is most favourable.

Through the practices you will sleep happily
And will awaken happily.
Because your inner nature will be without defect,
Even your dreams will be happy.

Intent on serving your parents,
Respectful to the principals of your lineage,
Using your resources well, patient, generous,
With kindly speech, without divisiveness, and truthful.

Through performing such discipline for one lifetime
You will become a monarch of gods
Whereupon even more so you will be a monarch of gods.
Therefore observe such practices. (275–82)

Here, Nāgārjuna is suggesting to the king that having obtained the acme of worldly power, prosperity, and happiness (through having performed virtuous deeds in previous lives), his next step is to become king of the gods, through further virtuous deeds in this life. As king of the gods he will be in a position of still greater influence, of course. One has only to think of Brahmā Sahampati[182] urging the Buddha to teach the Dharma to get some idea of what kind of influence that might be.

One of the fruits of spiritual practice is clarity: seeing things just as they are. Less coloured by self-interest and personal predicaments, one's views are more objective and one has less need to rely on the views of others for a kind of second-hand objectivity. The other major fruit is happiness. Nāgārjuna's reminder that happiness is beneficial may seem an obvious point, but it is one that is little regarded. Happiness is not only good in itself, but produces further positive results. If you can make people a little happier, cheer them up a bit, there is that much more positive energy moving around. To say, 'Even your dreams will be happy,' seems to be a common way, in Indian literature, of talking about exceptional good fortune.

> Through faith you will not be without leisure,
> Through good ethics you will move in good transmigrations,
> Through becoming familiar with emptiness
> You will attain detachment from all phenomena. (287)

The results to be looked for are not necessarily experienced in this life. If in this life you have faith, you will have leisure – presumably for hearing the Dharma – in the next. So why does Nāgārjuna make a connection between faith and having leisure? The point is that if you have faith in the Dharma you will make the best use of whatever opportunities you have to practise it here and now, as you are aware how precious those opportunities are. In fact you will do whatever you can to increase them. The word 'leisure' should not be taken too literally. Among the traditional list of eight conditions of non-leisure, along with various more obviously unsatisfactory rebirths, is rebirth as a long-lived god.[183] The holding of wrong views is also mentioned.

The next consequence of skilful behaviour mentioned by Nāgārjuna relates to an important Buddhist teaching. The practice of ethics is the key to a healthy human existence, whether in this life or the next. The connection he goes on to make is in a sense equally obvious. Insight leads to non-attachment. But the idea of being *familiar* with emptiness suggests more than the occasional flash of insight.[184] It suggests something that has sunk in so deep that it has become the way one normally sees things. The question is whether we have to achieve this first, or whether breaking down our attachments in other ways will by itself give us an appreciation of emptiness.

It seems to be a question of freedom versus discipline. Suppose, for instance, that you are very attached to chocolate. You can either gorge on it until you become sick of chocolate, or you can discipline yourself to give up the indulgence little by little. Both methods work. The insight can arrive either way. But neither method produces insight automatically. Even if you don't give up chocolate, you will in any case need to keep up your practice of reflection and meditation in order to see through the craving. If you give up chocolate as a matter of discipline, on the other hand, you can cut down the craving for it enough to allow you to start to see your habits more clearly. Reducing the craving leaves you freer to examine it. Discipline tends to simplify your life, it gives you more energy, and it helps to maintain morale and momentum. If a number of individuals undertake the same discipline and support one another in it, that also strengthens the sangha, as the Buddhist community is called. However, while discipline certainly makes insight more likely through its attenuating of craving, no amount of discipline is a substitute for seeing into the true nature of your craving, which is that it is the cause of suffering.

Crucially, discipline enables you to see the workings of your mind and get a sense of how you would get on if you didn't indulge that particular desire. If you were to fast for three days, say, you would see how your mind works without the physical and emotional support of food. You would see how you feel about food, what it means to you. It's like a laboratory experiment. You take away a certain factor in your life so that you can see what happens when that factor is not present. You don't have to guess. You actually see and feel the result, and as a consequence you know yourself better.

You might then want to make a vow. A vow is very simply a statement – usually a public statement – to the effect that you will do, or not do, something either for a certain period of time, or for ever. Not that you'll try to, not that you promise to: you *will*. When you make the vow it is already accomplished, and there is no question of your breaking it. To make the vow is to keep it. Even if you don't say it in front of other people, you say it in front of the Buddhas and Bodhisattvas, and you call upon them to witness your vow. Having done that, there is no going back, so that when you make a vow you need to know what you are doing and why. For example, you should know yourself well enough not to make a vow out of self-hatred, just as a way of making life difficult for yourself, although even if you did this, you would still have to keep the vow. Should you break a vow, it means you didn't really make it in the first place, and this will show that you are not an emotionally integrated person.

To make a vow presupposes a certain degree of integration. But if you haven't got that when you make the vow, one of the purposes of the vow is to make you become integrated in the course of its fulfilment. In fact, you become more integrated even as you bring yourself to the point of making it. Without being integrated you won't be able to observe the vow, and as there is no question of your not observing it, you just have to become integrated. There's no other way.

THE FOLLY OF UNSKILFUL ACTION

> Desisting from all non-virtues
> And always engaging in virtues
> With body, speech, and mind –
> These are called the three forms of practice.
>
> Through these practices one is freed from becoming
> A hell-being, hungry ghost, or animal.
> Reborn as a human or god one gains
> Extensive happiness, fortune, and dominion. (22–3)

The states of being of the denizens of hell, of hungry ghosts (*pretas*), and of animals are usually designated the 'three downward paths'. It is axiomatic not only for traditional Buddhism but for Indian culture generally that the performance of virtuous actions raises one in the scale of conditioned existence and increases one's happiness and well-being. In other words, virtue pays, in the form of what the translation calls 'high status'. It is very much the Indian belief that a life of virtue will not only raise the level of your consciousness but also produce mundane rewards in the form of a rebirth in which you will have a pleasant and happy time, in which you will be rich, good-looking, and so on. In most Buddhist countries, lay people observe the precepts largely for this reason.

I personally doubt whether karma operates quite so straightforwardly as that. In any case, the attitude of measuring the morality of actions by how far they are going to advance you in this world or the next is hardly a spiritual one. It is no more spiritual to think in terms of being reborn in a heaven realm than it is to want to be rich and successful in the present life. Both are inadequate solutions to the problem of human suffering. A utilitarian belief in karma is, at best, an incentive to moral action for people who are only able to think in very materialistic terms. No doubt this is an important consideration: if people are encouraged to behave well out of concern for their own well-being in a future life, it's a good beginning. But we need to be weaned off any dependency on that kind of incentive, for it inevitably compromises the purity of the intention behind moral action, and thus also compromises the spiritual effectiveness of that action.

Taken too literally or carried too far, this attitude towards the practice of ethics becomes what Swami Vivekananda once called a shopkeepers' religion[185] – a trading of good deeds for future worldly benefits. You might even find yourself calculating, for example, that having built up a nice surplus of moral credit you could well afford to backslide in a certain area of your ethical practice. Such naive spiritual materialism is unlikely to attract many people these days. The only people who would be motivated by it would probably be those involved in religious movements that interpret worldly prosperity as a sign of God's approval, or which promise the joys of heaven to the virtuous believer.

The only truly spiritual measure of moral actions is whether or not they lead to Nirvāṇa, or at least contribute to the basis upon which Nirvāṇa is attained: that is, whether or not they are performed out of a conscious concern for others as well as for oneself. Another way of putting this is simply to say that a truly virtuous action is its own reward. What better incentive for cultivating a generous, open state of mind than knowing it will lead to even more positive states, and ultimately to Enlightenment? If your skilful states of mind result in wealth and prosperity, there is no harm done, but such material rewards can only be a by-product of truly skilful behaviour, not its *raison d'être*.

How could those with senseless, deviant minds
On a path to bad transmigrations,
Wretched, intent on deceiving others,
Have understood what is meaningful?

How could those intent on deceiving others
Be persons of policy?
Through it they themselves will be cheated
In many thousands of births.

Even if you seek to harm an enemy,
You should remove your own defects and cultivate good qualities.
Through that you will help yourself,
And the enemy will be displeased. (130–2)

These verses expose the sheer pointlessness of unskilful activities of body, speech, and mind. Such activities cut us off from any possibility of mental clarity. Not only do we create suffering for ourselves; we lose our way, we lose sight of the path away from suffering. We lose any clear sense of our own good, of what is truly meaningful. In cheating others, one cheats oneself in a way that outweighs any possible advantage that may be derived from deceit.[186] Again, of course, it is very difficult to see this when one is dominated by a deceitful mindset. What is worse, it means that one is a stranger to the highly positive experience of unlimited and universal loving-kindness, known in the Buddhist tradition as *maitrī* (Sanskrit) or *mettā* (Pāli).

The advice in the third of these verses seems quite cynical, coming as it does from a great Buddhist philosopher, but we have to remember that it is given with the king's royal responsibilities in mind. A king may have enemies in the sense of enemies of the state, without anything really personal being involved, and he will have to deal with such political foes effectively, even have to prevail over them, without doing them more harm than was necessary. The principle seems straightforward: even if your motivation is impure and you want to get the better of someone, you are still obliged to be considerate. It will benefit you, karmically speaking, as well as influencing the way others view you, and it will discomfort your opponents if they have to revise their opinion of you. St Paul says something similar: by being kind to your enemy you 'heap coals of fire on his head'.[187]

From non-virtues come all sufferings
And likewise all bad transmigrations,
From virtues, all happy transmigrations
And the pleasures of all lives. (21)

Some Buddhists believe that all our sufferings are due to misdeeds committed in previous lives, so we have to be quite careful about how we understand Nāgārjuna's assertions here. It is not that all our sufferings are the direct result of unskilful actions on our part. Certainly an unskilful action will sooner or later be followed by suffering for the person who performs it, but this is not to say that if something unpleasant befalls us, it must be because of our previous unskilful actions. The fact is that sometimes we do feel that we suffer quite undeservedly, and the Buddhist view is that this feeling may be justified. Some of our experience is the result of karma, but some of it is the result of conditions of another kind.

What we *can* say is that all our suffering is *indirectly* the result of our past unskilful volitions. If we take the long view, we find that it is our own thoughts, words, and deeds that have brought us rebirth in the human realm. It is our own mental attitudes that have brought us into conditioned existence, and conditioned existence means suffering. The misfortunes we experience, often through no fault of our own, are an integral part of the mode of being within which our consciousness arose. The way Śāntideva puts it in the *Bodhicaryāvatāra* is that if someone beats you, they must bear the responsibility for taking up the stick, but you must bear the responsibility for having taken up the body that is beaten.[188] It is your own deluded consciousness that has brought about rebirth in the human realm where such things as this may well happen.

YOU AND THE WORLD

Thus observe the practices incessantly
And abandon those counter to them.
If you and the world wish to attain
Unparalleled enlightenment,

Its roots are the altruistic aspiration to enlightenment
Firm like the monarch of mountains,
Compassion reaching to all quarters,
And wisdom not relying on duality. (174–5)

As we have seen, there are all kinds of traditional incentives and warnings relating to the connection between ethical conduct and one's own happiness and well-being, but of course it is just as important – especially for the Mahāyāna – to consider the welfare of others. Nāgārjuna now puts before the king the Mahāyāna ideal, that is, the bodhisattva ideal. This ideal is the attainment of 'unparalleled enlightenment', and its 'roots' are the three factors that will help bring this about. The first of these is 'the altruistic aspiration', which is the *bodhicitta*, the wish to attain Enlightenment for the benefit of all beings.[189] This sublime aspiration is so imbued with a sense of the transcendental, and at the same time so deeply interwoven with one's everyday life, that it is unshakeable. The second root is compassion that is without boundaries, that does not falter under any circumstances, whatever the provocation. The third is wisdom that is ungraspable, that gives the ego no foothold.

> You should cause the assembling
> Of the religious and the worldly
> Through giving, speaking pleasantly,
> Purposeful behavior, and concordant behaviour. (133)

Much of Nāgārjuna's advice to the king is offered in terms of the traditional ethical formula of the ten precepts, and that is the basis of the following sections of this book. However, Nāgārjuna also refers briefly to another traditional list, the *saṃgraha-vastus*, the four 'means of unification' by which the bodhisattva brings people together to work for the common enterprise of creating, mythically speaking, a Pure Land.

Firstly, giving or generosity is the way in which we connect, in the most practical manner, with others. We let go of our tight grip on what belongs to us, whether material goods, money, time, or energy. That which expresses our possessiveness is transformed into a means of expressing its complete opposite. No doubt the recipient is pleased to receive what we give, but more important is the sense of care and concern that any such gesture communicates. Above all, we give the Dharma. We don't distinguish between our personal practice of the Dharma and our communication of it to others.

The second of the *saṃgraha-vastus* is affectionate speech. As we shall later see in greater detail, right speech is greatly emphasized in Buddhism. It is not just a matter of the content of our communication; much of our communication is conveyed in our tone of voice, which often reflects our true feelings much more accurately than what we are actually saying. At the same time, it is more difficult to monitor this feature of our speech, because it is much closer to a true communication of ourselves. By the same token, however, if we consciously cultivate affectionate speech, this can change us at quite a deep level.

The third means of unification is beneficial activity. This is not just a matter of helping others; it is also a matter of knowing what would be of most benefit to them, as well as understanding how best to employ one's energy. After all, there is a lot to be done, and one's energy is limited. What would benefit people most of all, at the deepest level, is helping them to access their own energy, by sparking them off, getting them going, inspiring them in some way.

The fourth *saṃgraha-vastu* is exemplification, or practising what one preaches. The Dharma is a teaching that has to be realized in daily life, and it is in this way that it is truly communicated. Do we exemplify the qualities that we are asking others to develop? If not, and if there is a discrepancy between the way we are and the way we aspire to be, clearly something is lacking. What is lacking is not so much the ability to be other than we are at present but the courage to be honest about where we really stand. If we can do this, even though it is quite difficult or humiliating to admit our deficiencies – to ourselves, let alone to others – then we are already making great progress. After all, reality is not a comfortable experience for the ego.

In the *Precious Garland*, the *saṃgraha-vastus* are part of Nāgārjuna's guidance to a king, not a bodhisattva, and in fact these practices are relevant at every stage of one's spiritual development. They embody the fundamental virtues of generosity, gentleness, helpfulness, and authenticity, and they can be cultivated in all sorts of ordinary ways.

THE TEN PRECEPTS

> Not killing, not stealing,
> Forsaking the mates of others,
> Refraining completely from false,
> Divisive, harsh, and senseless speech,
>
> Thoroughly forsaking covetousness, harmful intent,
> And the views of Nihilists –
> These are the ten gleaming paths of action;
> Their opposites are dark. (8–9)

In these two verses, Nāgārjuna introduces the precepts on which his advice to the king is mainly based. Seeking to make the point that the basis of wisdom is ethics, he spells out, in the clearest terms, what an ethical life involves. These verses refer to the ten traditional vows or precepts, the *daśa-kuśala-karma-pathas* or 'ten ways of skilful action'.[190] A precept is a training principle, a guideline to ethical behaviour in a certain area of life. The importance of observing the precepts consists not in 'obeying the rules' or in 'being good', but in cultivating skilful ways of being and behaving for their own sake. In that respect, there is always more to do. You throw yourself wholeheartedly into your ethical practice but you are aware at the same time that you may sometimes backslide, at least to a degree. If that happens, you have to begin again from where you left off and try not to indulge in guilty self-recrimination.

These precepts make up a path of practice rather than being a list of fixed rules or rigid prohibitions. An ethical precept isn't an absolute in the sense of being something you are either observing or not observing. As long as one is living with the precepts in mind, one's practice could always be worse and always be better. There is always further to fall, and always further to go. The precepts are therefore weightier than our limited experience of them usually allows us to realize. A potential problem is that the notion of precepts as 'training principles' might cause us to feel, consciously or unconsciously, that we are being 'let off the hook' a little. One might say to oneself, 'Well, perhaps I'm a bit lax in my attempts to be a vegetarian, but one of these days I'm going to do something about it....' 'Speech? Well, I'm afraid little white lies are a necessary part of doing business, and it's obvious that a little fruity language helps to get your point across. But perhaps when I get into a management position....' 'Yes, of course I could be more scrupulous in the way I administer the petty cash – if only I could get away with paying a little less tax....' 'I'm only getting drunk twice a week now that I'm no longer working behind the bar, so I'm in a much better state of mind most of the time....'

Of course, this is a caricature, but perhaps not much of one. Although we should be careful not to be too legalistic about observing the precepts, they call for more than a vague intention to behave better in future. We can try, for example, to be more imaginative in the way we approach them, especially by cultivating their positive counterparts: being kinder, more generous, more faithful (in thought and speech as well as in deed), more truthful, more mindful. We can look for new ways in which to express these positive, expansive qualities. As we shall see in the following chapters, the ten precepts deserve considerable thought and reflection; they go far beyond our usual conceptions of ethics.

I

FRIENDSHIP

'NOT KILLING'

In his advice to the king, Nāgārjuna speaks of this precept simply as 'not killing'. But the first precept as usually formulated, 'I undertake to abstain from taking life,' entails much more than that. In Pāli (in which ancient language it is still chanted by many Buddhists), the precept is *pāṇātipātā veramaṇī sikkhāpadaṃ samādiyāmi*. *Pāṇa* means a living (literally a breathing) being, *atipāta* means 'harming', 'assaulting' or 'attacking', *veramaṇī*, means 'abstain from', *sikkhāpadaṃ* is literally 'step in training', and *samādiyāmi* may be rendered as 'I undertake'. The whole precept is thus 'I undertake the step in training of abstaining from harming living beings.'

The most harmful thing one can do to living beings is to deprive them of life, and in the case of animals this is our main area of concern. When it comes to human beings, however, undertaking simply to refrain from killing them presents a rather perfunctory nod in the direction of the precept. Harming human beings is not only a matter of depriving them of life, or of inflicting pain and suffering. It includes preventing them from realizing their potential, preventing them from evolving and developing as true individuals. (How far animals are able to develop it is hard to say, but it is certainly possible to rob them of the continued enjoyment of their existence.)

The precept is phrased negatively because it is very difficult actively to help another person to grow. If you are able to do so, well and good, but the least one can do is not hinder their efforts to raise and expand their consciousness. The precept could thus be construed as saying: respect the individuality of others; don't get in the way of their positive development.

Some people it is impossible to hinder in this way. They might be prevented from meditating, or even be shut up in prison, but nothing that was done to them would be able to hinder their development as an individual. However, the development of the vast majority of people is much less definite and assured, and it is easily blocked or derailed by the actions, well-meaning or otherwise, of others. It is easy to assume we know what is best for others, but we very rarely do know. The most we can do for others is to provide them with the best possible conditions in which to find their own way, and allow them to make, if necessary, their own mistakes. People need freedom if they are to grow. If we can contribute to that, we certainly should. Apart from that, we should, generally speaking, leave well alone.

FEAR AND POWER

> To hunt game is a horrible
> Cause of a short life,
> Fear, suffering, and hell,
> Therefore always steadfastly keep from killing.
>
> Those who frighten embodied beings
> When they encounter them are malevolent
> Like a snake spitting poison,
> Its body completely stained with impurity. (171–2)

In these verses Nāgārjuna warns the king against hunting, which in most cultures has been regarded as a royal pursuit. It was a pursuit that required control over a large tract of territory, provided quasi-military recreation, and enabled the king to display his horsemanship and his tactical skills. At the same time, hunting represented a throwback to the day-to-day conflict with other species in which our Paleolithic ancestors were involved before the introduction of agriculture and animal husbandry. Besides being an aristocratic training for war, it enabled men to experience their primitive instinctual nature, with its craving for excitement and violence. There was also the desire to eat the vanquished creature, thus ingesting its power. Above all, it was probably hunting that originally determined the power structure within Paleolithic tribes, at least so far as the males were concerned. It might have been quite difficult for an ancient Indian king to give up the pursuit without jeopardizing his authority.

Nāgārjuna is no doubt aware of all this, but he still considers it necessary to warn his patron of the spiritual dangers of succumbing to the lure of the hunt. It was necessary for our ancestors to hunt for food, and it is still necessary for some tribal peoples to do so today. But when there is no need to hunt for food, then hunting, however much one rationalizes, is chasing and killing for pleasure, to satisfy bloodlust, and that is a thoroughly unskilful breach of the first precept.[191]

Frightening others is one of the ways in which people make themselves feel powerful, and unlike hunting it is an exercise of power to which almost anyone can be tempted. It is notable in this regard that one of the forms of giving practised by the bodhisattva, along with the giving of the Dharma, is the giving of fearlessness. To inspire terror in others could be considered as unskilful as the giving of fearlessness is skilful.

In ancient times, fear was perhaps a more common emotional reaction than it is today. There were then many immediate threats to be faced from which people are nowadays protected. We are therefore less inclined to regard giving way to fear as being reprehensible than were those who lived in more heroic ages. As a society we have less need for the kind of physical courage which in the past provided the community with protection. Nonetheless, extreme fear can still lead to a disintegration of our sense of self, and even cause us to abandon cherished personal values in the face of a threat to one's life. To instil fear in others is therefore highly unskilful.

Like desire, fear can be a positive thing. Just as we should have a healthy desire to change ourselves for the better, so we should also have a healthy fear of anything that holds us back from following the path of spiritual development and self-transcendence. Many of us are lulled by our day-to-day routine into a false sense of security, but human existence is uncertain. We are going to die and it is not morbid to be mindful of the fact. We should be 'afraid' of conditioned existence itself.

But fear on behalf of the ego is an unskilful mental state. It is a contraction, even a petrification of energy, and it is therefore unskilful to induce such fear in others. Nāgārjuna himself evokes a deliberately frightful image to make his point. Be frightened of being frightening, he seems to be saying. The result of trying to terrify others will be truly terrifying.

Fear is a primitive animal emotion, like lust and hatred, and it is noticeable how much of popular culture is designed to feed these emotions. Three genres of popular films, for example, cater for our need to titillate ourselves with these emotions: pornographic films, violent films, and horror films. Even the act of inducing a pleasurable thrill of horror, while not as unskilful as inducing hatred or lust, is mildly unskilful for the same reason.

In public life, political and journalistic doom-mongers continually warn us about weapons of mass destruction, terrorism, environmental pollution, over-population, global warming, the effects of passive smoking, the dangers of not wearing a cycle helmet, and so on. Many of their warnings relate to real dangers and reflect a genuine concern for people, and it is certainly a good thing to awaken a concern for the welfare of others, including the welfare of generations to come, jolting us out of any tendency to live for today in a narrow, deluded, and self-indulgent way. However, the motivation of those who deliberately seek to disturb people must be examined. People can be terrorized by violence or the threat of it, but they can be frightened in much more subtle ways too. It is even possible to relish frightening others under an appearance of concern, and some people do have a taste for this, just as some people have a taste for violence. The bearer of bad news may secretly enjoy having the power to influence others, and may get a kick from seeing the effect of their words. Similarly, there is a sort of dark glee to be derived from making people feel really frightened. Not everyone who comes with dire warnings has at heart the welfare of those they fill with dread. During the Second World War, 'spreading alarm and despondency' was popularly known as being a 'Dismal Jimmy' and it was frowned upon for very good reasons, it being a time of very real danger. Any assessment of a threat should be realistic but positive.

Unfortunately, even those who warn of spiritual perils are not always disinterested. Like some old-time hellfire preachers, they may do so in order to gratify their desire for power. If one puts the fear of God into people not out of concern for their spiritual welfare, but simply to reduce them to abject terror, the better to dominate and control them, such hypocritical behaviour is highly reprehensible. The bodhisattva, by contrast, spreads confidence and happiness, as in the following verse.

> Just as farmers are gladdened
> When a great rain-cloud gathers,
> So those who gladden embodied beings
> When encountering them are beneficent. (173)

Here Nāgārjuna is referring to the beginning of the monsoon. Today, farmers in India still scan the skies anxiously for the first monsoon clouds, because if the rains are even a few days late, the harvest will be poor. When the monsoon does arrive on time the farmers are glad indeed. The aspiration to gladden beings, which is central to Buddhism, especially to the Mahāyāna, is an important one. To make people happy, to stimulate positive emotion in them, is one of the principal activities of the bodhisattva (the bodhisattva being Mahāyāna Buddhism's ideal Buddhist). This does not mean merely being entertaining. Gladdening all beings does not involve anything frivolous; it means arousing genuine joy, in the sense of helping people overcome their deepest fears and anxieties, and awakening them to the truth of the Dharma.

This is the opposite of making oneself feel more powerful. It is not about trying to control others for your own purposes.

You are like the rain cloud, giving people what they want and need in order to be truly happy. Like the rain cloud, you open up and give yourself. A significant implication of this is that the aspiring bodhisattva has a duty to be joyful. You can't gladden others if you are not glad yourself. If you want others to be happy, in more than a theoretical sense, if you want to *do* something about making them happy, then you need to be emotionally positive yourself. If you're a wet blanket, if you're a prophet of doom and disaster, if you're a Dismal Jimmy, then you're hardly en route to becoming a bodhisattva.

So, if you are looking for Buddhist teaching, follow the joy. A Buddhist centre or community should have a happy, friendly, and peaceful atmosphere. The most important qualities for a bodhisattva, and for anyone whose life involves teaching or leading fellow Buddhists, are inspiration and *mettā*. If you cannot name the seven *bodhyaṅgas*, for example, that does not matter so much. But you cannot do without inspiration and *mettā*, and these need to be cultivated. Inspiration can be developed through the performance of puja (worship) and through the cultivation of spiritual friendship. *Mettā* is generated through the *mettā bhāvanā*, in which you develop a heartfelt desire for the welfare first of yourself, then of a dear friend, next of someone about whom you feel neutral, and fourthly of someone you dislike, before finally developing an equal concern for all four people and eventually for all beings everywhere. No practice is more supportive of the observance of the first precept, or of the aspiration to live in accordance with the bodhisattva ideal.

PRACTISING THE *METTĀ BHĀVANĀ*

The *mettā bhāvanā* is a key Buddhist practice. *Mettā* means responding positively and with warmth to people regardless of their attitude towards oneself. You don't need to practise the other *brahma vihāras*, *karuṇā* (compassion), *muditā* (sympathetic joy) and *upekṣā* (equanimity) separately, in order to respond in this way, though you might sometimes want to explore them within the context of your own meditation. However, you need to understand that the other three *brahma vihāras* are all based on a foundation of *mettā*. If you are unable to practise the *mettā bhāvanā*, and you don't feel kindly disposed, either to yourself or to others, practising any of the other *brahma vihāras* is out of the question. Should you try to generate compassion on its own, for example, without a solid basis of *mettā*, you will squeeze out only a kind of sentimental pity or a horrified anxiety. Or take *upekṣā*. Without *mettā* it is just indifference. As one of the *brahma vihāras*, *upekṣā* arises when you develop the same feeling of *mettā* towards all living beings, as in the last stage of the *mettā bhāvanā*.

Should you feel disinclined to engage in a session of the *mettā bhāvanā*, this will probably be because you are feeling slightly irritable, and want, consciously or unconsciously, to indulge the feeling. So you say to yourself, 'I can't get anywhere with the *mettā* today – I'll do the mindfulness of breathing instead.'[192] But it should be the other way round. The fact that you feel irritated is a very good reason for you to practise the *mettā bhāvanā*, for irritation can often be dispelled by this means. Even if you generally have difficulty with the practice, it is likely that you will still feel the benefit of it – even if the benefit is delayed.

You might not be able to generate any *mettā* during the practice itself, or even immediately afterwards, but a shift in your attitude will have occurred.

If you find the first stage of the *mettā bhāvanā* difficult, it is sometimes helpful to start with a stage that you can engage with more easily. I would also suggest spending less time on the first four stages and getting on to the fifth stage more quickly, if you can get your *mettā* flowing more strongly that way. Alternatively, if, as is often the case, you find the second stage the easiest, you can always move from it to cultivating goodwill towards yourself. For example, having found some feeling of goodwill towards a friend, you can imagine yourself in a happy situation with that person, in which each of you is feeling goodwill towards the other. This is how we can kickstart *mettā* towards ourselves. Even if we find it difficult to love ourselves, we usually have to acknowledge that at least somebody loves us.

This experience of being accepted and loved is deeply important to us, and the group exerts control over us by means of the fundamental human need for acceptance. It is terrible to feel rejected by the group to which one belongs, and most people would do anything to get back into a positive relationship with it. We will accept the group's evaluation of us, and reform ourselves accordingly, just in order to be welcomed back into its embrace. Interrogation works in the same kind of way. The person being interrogated is anxious to please someone, anyone: 'Yes, I am a heretic,' 'Yes, I am a spy.' What they are really saying is, 'I will go along with anything you say in order to please you and be accepted.' Only a very strong-minded person can hold out against such extreme pressure.

Even within the sangha or spiritual community we need to be careful not to bring pressure to bear upon anyone by treating them, or labelling them, in an unfavourable way. It is often the psychologically weaker person who gets picked on, and I'm afraid this can happen even within the spiritual community. The pressure may not be perceived as such, and most people would be appalled to think that they were picking on someone, but it is all too easy to find ourselves quietly pushing out of the nest the kind of person who does not appear to be a lot of use, who takes up the community's resources, or who is just different in some way. Mobilizing the united disapproval of the group against any one member can do the latter a lot of damage.

Most of us instinctively feel that we could not survive exclusion from the group to which we belong, and in tribal societies this would have been literally the case. Shakespeare expresses the horror of banishment in his play *Richard II*, in which the king exiles two noblemen. Thomas Mowbray, banished for life, leaves England, as he puts it, 'To dwell in solemn shades of endless night'. Henry Bolingbroke announces that, as an exile, he will be able to 'boast of nothing else but that I was a journeyman to grief'.[193] To roam the world as an outsider is bondage; freedom is to belong.

The challenge here is that of not banishing anyone from our concern, not giving up on a person we find difficult. More positively, we all need to offer to other members of the community, especially to those who are not so popular, whatever support and encouragement they need, and express our appreciation and gratitude whenever we can. Many of us experience a degree of self-hatred or self-contempt that makes it difficult for us to receive appreciation at all easily, and an important function of the spiritual community is letting us know that there are people who care for us. This makes it much easier for us to recognize our own good qualities. Some individuals can accept and love themselves regardless of what anybody else thinks and feels about them, but most of us need the approbation of others.

THE FRUITS OF KINDNESS

Even three times a day to offer
Three hundred cooking pots of food
Does not match a portion of the merit
In one instant of love.

Though (through love) you are not liberated
You will attain the eight good qualities of love –
Gods and humans will be friendly,
Even (non-humans) will protect you.

You will have mental pleasures and many (physical) pleasures,
Poison and weapons will not harm you,
Without striving will you attain your aims,
And be reborn in the world of Brahmā. (283–5)

This is reminiscent of certain verses in chapter 8 of the *Dhammapada*, one of which reads, 'Better than a thousand meaningless verses collected together is one line of verse on hearing which one becomes tranquil.'[194] He is not suggesting that giving (*dāna*) is meaningless, however. He believes it to be extremely meaningful, as we shall see. What he is saying here is that love or *mettā* is even more important – more important in the sense of its being primary. *Mettā* comes first. If there is love, *dāna* will naturally follow. But you could, conceivably, offer three hundred cooking pots of food three times daily without feeling much *mettā*. Your motivation might be a desire for merit, or for the praise of others, or for the satisfaction of feeling that you were a particularly generous person.

This verse emphasizes the importance of the mental state over the external action. It is the internal, mental, or spiritual state that really matters and which ultimately determines the ethical status of the external action. Again this brings us back to the *Dhammapada*: 'Experiences are preceded by mind, led by mind, and produced by mind.'[195] Of course, if you act positively, this will affect your state of mind for the better, but unless you make the maintenance of positive mental states your priority, your actions can easily become less ethical.

Mettā is the fundamental positive emotion and the foundation for the development of the *bodhicitta* or 'will to Enlightenment'. Without *mettā* between the members of the spiritual community, there is no possibility of the *bodhicitta* arising in their midst. Ultimately, *mettā* is impersonal, and is without an object, but to begin with it has to be developed in relation to people, and if there are no people around, it is going to be very difficult to develop it. In short, the arising of the *bodhicitta* depends upon there being, within the spiritual community, a palpable sense of *mettā*.

So can one be liberated through love? The short answer is: not on its own. Although it is not emphasized much in present day Theravāda Buddhism, 'the liberation of the heart through love (*mettā*)', as it is usually translated, appears in the Pāli scriptures in connection with one of two forms or aspects of liberation: *ceto vimutti*, liberation of the mind or heart, and *paññā vimutti*, liberation by wisdom.[196] *Ceto vimutti* is the development of consciousness, of positive mental and emotional states – to the highest possible degree – and this is achieved through *śamatha* or 'pacification' practices like the *mettā bhāvanā* and the mindfulness of breathing. *Śamatha* (Pāli *samatha*) literally means 'calming down', and it refers to the calming down, the pacification, of all unskilful mental states, and the consequent attainment of the *dhyānas*, states of higher consciousness in which only skilful mental states are present. *Ceto vimutti* represents the complete purification of one's emotional nature; it is a state of intense clarity and positivity. It does not, however, on its own constitute full liberation, for this must include *prajñā* (Pāli *paññā*), or wisdom, sometimes referred to as *vipaśyanā*, a term which is especially used to describe the initial flashes of insight. To be liberated by wisdom means to be free from all wrong views, and to have complete insight into the true nature of existence.

Ceto vimutti and *paññā vimutti* are often mentioned together. One who gains Enlightenment is said to be liberated in mind and liberated in wisdom, and thus to have attained Nirvāṇa. It might be said that the combination of *ceto vimutti* and *paññā vimutti* in the Pāli scriptures corresponds to the combination of *puṇya-sambhāra* and *jñāna-sambhāra* found in the Sanskrit texts of the Mahāyāna.[197] Both pairs of terms refer to the necessity of combining total emotional positivity with complete clarity of vision, and within their respective contexts they both point to the same spiritual fact: that while it is possible to develop these two aspects of the spiritual life separately to a degree, in the end one does need both. One needs both 'collections', that of merit and that of wisdom.

In the case of the bodhisattva, this balance of qualities becomes *karuṇā* and *prajñā*, compassion and wisdom, and the fact that here it is *karuṇā* that is the complement of wisdom, not *śamatha*, gives us an idea of what *śamatha* really means for the Mahāyāna. It isn't just a calming down of unskilful mental states. It is not quietude. When only skilful mental states are present, they are very strongly and actively present. Consequently, one's mind is much more powerful than when it is weighed down by conflicting emotions.

Nāgārjuna is not saying that you cannot be liberated through love. You can be, provided you develop love to such a degree of selflessness that it becomes coordinate with wisdom. What he is saying is that even if your practice of *mettā* does not amount to liberation by love, you will still attain the eight virtues of love. These are: gods will be friendly, humans will be friendly, non-humans will protect you, you will enjoy pleasures of mind, you will have mental and physical pleasures, poison and weapons won't harm you, you will effortlessly attain your aims, and you will be reborn in the world of Brahmā.

The first three of these benefits of practising *mettā* are obvious enough. If you are friendly towards others, others – even non-humans – will be friendly towards you. But does this mean that you will have no enemies? In the case of the Buddha, for example, a mad elephant was sent against him. The Buddha was able to pacify the elephant by virtue of his *mettā*. But who sent the elephant against him? It was his jealous disciple, Devadatta.[198] While even a mad elephant could be affected by the Buddha's *mettā*, a human being who was jealous of him and had resolved to kill him, remained quite impervious to that same *mettā*.

From this we conclude that *mettā* is not an irresistible force such that when we direct it at someone, they have no alternative but to like us. *Mettā* allows people the freedom to reject the *mettā* that is offered. Otherwise it would be an assertion of our will against theirs. *Mettā* is a genuine concern for the well-being of people, whether they like us or not. If we try to use *mettā* to make them like us, this shows a misunderstanding of the nature of *mettā* and we will not succeed. We may start getting irritated and even angry with people because they persist in spurning our so-called *mettā*.

The threat of violence can be extremely frightening, and to respond to it with genuine *mettā*, as the Buddha did on more than one occasion, constitutes a real victory. If you are able to respond in this way, it could have a beneficial effect on the situation. On the other hand, one does occasionally meet people who deliberately behave badly, who have made up their minds to harm one, and who know what they're doing. Such people will not be touched by your friendliness or love. If anything, your warmth will intensify their cold-blooded resolve to hurt you as much as possible. That said, the traditional Buddhist belief is that you can literally deflect weapons and counteract the effects of poison by the sheer force of your own emotional positivity, and perhaps that is so. If you are full of *mettā*, at least you will not draw active hostility upon yourself.

'Without striving will you attain your aims.' In other words, you will attain your aims effortlessly. Things will go more smoothly, more freely, more spontaneously, without the strain of your having to make a willed effort. *Mettā* cannot be forced. If you are powerfully generating *mettā*, you are already in an effortless, positive, and spontaneous state.

In this context, the fact that you experience 'mental pleasures and many (physical) pleasures' can probably be ascribed simply to your being in a positive state of mind. A healthy instinct for pleasure does not need much in the way of external stimuli. Finally, Nāgārjuna says that you will 'be reborn in the world of Brahmā'. The implication is that the practitioner will be reborn in a realm corresponding to the mental or spiritual level attained and stabilized through the experience of *mettā*.

There is a similar list in the *Mettānisaṃsa Sutta*:[199] good sleep, the friendliness of others, protection from violence, ease of concentration, good looks, a lucid death, and a good rebirth. The *Dhammapada* also has such a list.[200] An important theme of all these lists is that *mettā* protects one from arbitrary violence and even from simple accidents. People who are full of hatred are often rather accident-prone. Things seem to go wrong for them, for no apparent reason, and not necessarily as the direct result of their own actions. It is as though they had enemies who were secretly working against them. The root cause of their predicament seems to be self-hatred, even an unconscious need to suffer some kind of punishment. It is difficult to love others if one has no love for oneself, and in that case one will instinctively seek out situations in which one is likely to come to harm or get otherwise into trouble.

People who are positive and cheerful, on the other hand, often seem to lead a charmed existence. They attain their aims easily. It is as though they had friends who were secretly working on their behalf. The root cause of such good fortune seems to be a genuine liking of, and concern for, oneself. It is difficult to hate others if you truly love yourself. And if you feel positively about yourself you are instinctively going to look after yourself and seek out situations in which you will not come to harm.

'BEGET THE PERSON YOU NEED'

> If you cause sentient beings to generate
> The altruistic aspiration to enlightenment and make it firm,
> You will always attain an altruistic aspiration to enlightenment
> Firm like the monarch of mountains. (286)

The more you encourage and inspire others to be positive, the more positive you will be yourself, for you are encouraging and inspiring yourself at the same time that you are inspiring them. But you yourself have to be inspired in the first place, at least to an extent, since, otherwise, whatever encouragement you give will only be a matter of words. Your words must express your own genuinely positive feelings if they are to generate feelings in others. Conversely, the response others give you should be inspiring too. This is how communication within the sangha works. It is how the *bodhicitta* may come to arise, and how, having arisen within the sangha, it can be strengthened.

There is an anecdote about a Sufi master and his disciple. The disciple had come from far away, and eventually the time came for him to return home. Of course he was sad to go, but not just because he had to leave his old master. He was sad because he would be going back to his own rather uncultivated people. He said to the master, 'Here I have enjoyed communication of the highest kind, but where I'm going, there won't be anyone I can talk with in this way. I don't know how I'm going to survive. What should I do?' The master replied in his usual laconic way: 'Beget the man you need.' He did not of course mean beget in the literal sense. What he meant was that the disciple should sow seeds of inspiration in the hearts of people and that at least some of them would eventually be able to provide him with the kind of communication he needed.

There is no point in complaining about being surrounded by unsympathetic, negative people. You must produce the 'man' you need. It may look selfish, but it is, at the same time, highly altruistic. It is enlightened self-interest in the true sense, because the man you 'beget' will exist not only for you but also for himself. In fact, he cannot exist for you unless he exists for himself. There is no need to worry about your motivation, for here the whole distinction between selfishness and altruism breaks down. Doing good for yourself, you do good for others. Doing good for others, you do good for yourself.

THE IMPOSSIBILITY OF SACRIFICING YOURSELF FOR OTHERS

> Those who despise the Great Vehicle,
> Source of all good qualities in that (it teaches) taking delight
> Solely in the aims of others due to not looking to one's own,
> Consequently burn themselves (in bad transmigrations). (370)

This verse addresses a practical ethical issue. If you express negative opinions, you must take responsibility for the possibility that some people will take what you are saying sufficiently seriously not to get involved with the object of your criticism. This can have a profound effect upon their lives, especially if you have criticized a spiritual tradition.[201] Nāgārjuna goes even further than this. He suggests that because the Mahāyāna is concerned exclusively with the needs of others, criticizing it means that you are in effect preventing others from concerning themselves with *your* needs. On the one hand he appeals to one's narrow self-interest; on the other he presents the Mahāyāna ideal as one of pure altruism, utterly free from self-interest. The latter is the common view of the Mahāyāna, and is not to be taken too literally. It would be more true, if less dramatic, to say that in doing good to others, one is doing good to oneself as well, spiritually speaking. How can you separate the two? When you genuinely sacrifice yourself for others, it is as if something in you at a very deep level of your being, or something outside you with which you feel a deep connection, is being nourished. Conversely, if you sacrifice yourself simply out of self-hatred, or to be 'holier than thou', it is not really for the sake of others at all.

Perhaps this kind of exhortation to ignore or neglect our own needs entirely is to help us overcome our natural selfishness and egocentricity. One may find it more helpful, however, to think in terms of regarding oneself as just one person among many. If you are going to devote yourself to the good of all, that 'all' must surely include you. Otherwise, you are giving yourself a special status. You should include yourself in the same way that you include everybody else, rather than regarding yourself as a special individual whose needs must be sacrificed for the good of humanity.

The Buddhist ideal is often regarded as a selfish one. This can't be because of the concern of the Theravāda to attain individual Enlightenment, for in Christianity there is a similar concern for personal salvation (i.e. for saving one's soul). I think the Western impression of Buddhism as being selfish probably springs much more from the emphasis of Buddhism, as a whole, and of the Theravāda in particular, on monasticism, and therefore on the necessity of leaving one's home, one's job, and even one's family. One goes forth in search of one's own Enlightenment, leaving others to manage as best they can.

But if you are married, especially if you have children, do you not have a clear duty to stay with them? How can you justify leaving them? Some people are deeply shocked to hear that the Buddha-to-be left his palace, his beautiful wife, and his infant son, and went off into the forest in search of truth. It is not as if he knew for sure that he was going to become Enlightened and pass on his discovery to countless others down the ages. It was just that he found life deeply unsatisfactory. Well so do a lot of people, but does this mean that they can disregard their responsibilities? On the face of it, the future Buddha's action would seem to be thoroughly selfish.

There is no point in our trying to make excuses for what the young Siddhārtha did in the course of his progress towards Buddhahood. If we argue that he made up for his leaving home by teaching the Dharma to so many people afterwards, we are implying that his leaving was an unskilful action, the unskilfulness of which was subsequently outweighed by his skilful actions. All we really can say in this connection is that in life there are certain situations in which we have apparently only one choice. It is as if you are irresistibly impelled to embark on a certain course of action. You just do what you must do and nobody and nothing can stop you. It is not something you work out, weighing up the pros and cons: you cannot possibly do otherwise. That was clearly the situation in the case of the Buddha-to-be. He just could not stay at home any more, so he didn't.

In reality, however, there is nothing wrong with healthy self-interest. It is undoubtedly true that to be a decent human being one has to consider and act for the welfare of others as well as for one's own welfare. At the same time, it is necessary that one should have a positive attitude towards oneself and one's real needs. Such an attitude is an essential basis for the leading of an effective spiritual life. There is often a degree of cant in the way people speak of the selfishness of those who have chosen a lifestyle that is outside social norms. They are saying, in effect, 'If you do what you want to do, you are being selfish. If I do what I want to do, I am not being selfish.' Siddhārtha wanted to grow and develop, as we might say nowadays, and he felt he couldn't do that at home. It may be that some Buddhists have managed to lead a genuinely spiritual life without leaving home, but in the Buddha's time this would have been difficult. If he was to fulfil his potential as a human being there was only one option before him: to leave home.

The problem is resolved with the arising of the *bodhicitta*. It abolishes the tension between self and not-self. You no longer have to choose between them; there is no more having to balance and adjust the rival claims of self and others. What you do, quite spontaneously, is good for what used to be 'you' and good for what used to be 'others'. When the *bodhicitta* has arisen, you see that in reality there is no self, no other. In a manner of speaking, yes, there is 'me', in which case I must speak as well of 'you', but those distinctions are not to be taken too seriously, as though they were absolutely real, and as though there existed two mutually exclusive entities. Without pressing the analogy too far, or taking it too literally, the bodhisattva's relationship with all beings is like that of a mother with her baby. The mother doesn't distinguish between her own interests and those of her child. For her, they amount to the same thing. She doesn't think that she needs a rest or a holiday from her baby. On its own instinctual level of attachment, there is the same self-forgetting intensity of love. The difference is that in the case of the mother, her love is an extension of her ego, whereas in the case of the bodhisattva, it is an extension of his or her non-ego. The mother's love owes its strength to its exclusivity, but the strength of the bodhisattva's *mettā* and compassion springs from its inclusivity, its universality.

A Tibetan Buddhist story tells how a man once saw a crowd of people and realized that something was happening in their midst. Someone was being given a good beating, he was told, and he could not help feeling sorry for the unknown person. On his pushing his way through the crowd, however, he saw that the person who was being beaten was none other than his own mother, and the sorrow he had previously felt changed at once to a feeling of extreme distress. Almost everyone is like that man. We feel for a few individuals a strong concern that we do not feel for the rest of humanity. The bodhisattva, however, feels the same wholehearted concern for the welfare of all beings.

RIGHT LIVELIHOOD

The next topic I want to consider is work. Work, or what Nāgārjuna speaks of as 'good livelihood', is a hugely important factor in human life on account of the amount of time we have to devote to it. To this one might add the considerable investment of ego-identity in our work and in how much we earn. The way we spend those eight hours a day, forty-eight weeks a year, for over forty years, will be for most of us the single most significant activity of our lives in terms of its effect on our mental states. Generally, our primary concern is with what we earn from our economic activity and the particular status it confers. However, in the Buddhist context a 'good livelihood' is in many respects the opposite of what the world would see as desirable. A good livelihood is one that does not oblige us to violate the precepts in any way.

It has to be admitted that, according to this criterion, there are not many jobs that count as 'good' – or right – livelihood. One rule of thumb is that the simpler the work, the easier it will be to do it while observing the precepts. At the very least our work should not harm anybody. Building work, or cleaning, or some other straightforward physical labour might serve our spiritual needs best, especially in the earlier stages of the spiritual life when we may need to engage with, and integrate, our grosser energies. The early spiritual career of the great Tibetan yogi Milarepa, who was made to build towers and then knock them down over and over again, is an extreme example of this kind of approach, which does seem to work.

On the other hand, if our work holds no real interest for us, this may adversely affect our ability to do it mindfully.

The work to avoid is the kind that is repetitive and boring, that does not engage even your physical energies, and that offers no incentive to improve your performance. Such work drains energy; or rather, you have to use energy to suppress energy while doing this kind of work. To receive a wage is no compensation for the impoverishing effect of such work on one's mental state. Life is too precious to be wasted in this way. As well as doing no harm, our livelihood should ideally benefit ourselves and others. Work that calls for a refined sensibility like gardening or decorating, or work that gives people innocent pleasure, like catering, would do very well, as would the kind of vocational service that involves the direct relief of suffering, like nursing, caring for old people, or some forms of therapy. Work should not violate the first precept, which enjoins non-harming. Nor should one employ another person to do soul-destroying work that one does not want to do oneself, a practice which unfortunately is deeply ingrained in our culture.

Wrong livelihood frequently involves deception of some kind, as when a trader uses false weights and measures. Just as untruthful speech deceives another person, so dishonesty in any business transaction is an abuse of the trust of the other party. But all forms of wrong livelihood involve deception in a deeper sense than that of breaking the precepts.

Right livelihood is work that is conducive to the realization of our spiritual potential, but in deceiving others we do harm to ourselves as well as to them.

Some forms of wrong livelihood have unfortunate consequences for society at large. Helping to produce weapons of war, for example, is unskilful in the sense that one is enabling others to engage in killing and violence. But besides this it is unskilful in the further sense that one is directly subscribing to the fundamentally wrong view that wars can bring about peace, that killing is sometimes justified, that, in the words of Robespierre's infamous declaration, an omelette cannot be made without breaking eggs. In other words, you have to delude yourself. In order to engage in that kind of livelihood, you have to ignore the fact that a nation is driven to go to war by fear and hatred, however carefully masked by rational arguments those passions may be.

Working as a butcher involves the acceptance of another fundamentally wrong view. In order to pursue this means of livelihood, you must convince yourself that the slaughter of animals and birds is necessary, or at least justifiable. This wrong view finds expression in various ways. First, there is the scientific argument. As omnivores, human beings are natural consumers of animal flesh, so that not to eat meat goes against nature and is probably bad for our health. Asking people to abstain from eating meat is therefore unreasonable. Second, there is the fact that some religions sanction meat-eating, the sanction being based on their belief that the rest of creation exists to provide for the needs of human beings. Third, there is the butcher's own argument: that if he didn't do the work, and in this way support his family, someone else would do it.

These arguments are advanced in support of views that spring from ignorance, fear, and greed. The fact is that if one was not paid to work as a butcher, it is highly unlikely that one would care to be one, and if one was not attached to the taste of meat and to the supposed benefits of a meat diet, one would probably not want to be a meat-eater. If one really looked at what it means to eat meat, one would not be able to consume one's beef and mutton with a good conscience, much less still enjoy them. It would be felt to run counter to all that was truly human in one's nature. Like working for the arms trade, working as a butcher helps create an environment which is not conducive to the well-being of either society or the individual.

Wrong views affect all aspects of life. I once saw an advertisement that read, 'Pregnant? Why not deal with it the sensible way?' and these chilling words were followed simply by a telephone number. But if a woman is planning to have an abortion, she will have to hide from herself the reality of what she is doing, just as those who are engaged in wrong livelihood do. This may well be the only way she will be able to undergo the procedure.

Whatever our livelihood, the way we view it may involve a degree of deception. Work is not always fun. People need money and they don't know how else to get it. If they could, many would like to have the money without having to do the work. Work may indeed be seen as the best way of utilizing human energy, but here too there can be deception. One might even say that any form of wage slavery must involve an element of deception and even self-deception. Can you honestly say you are working if you do not really care about the work? You will be just 'going through the motions'. Things will no doubt get done, but if you are not giving yourself to what you are doing, there will be an element of make-believe involved. If they did not have to work for money, many people would not know what to do with themselves all day. But this in itself reveals the alienating effect of a narrowly utilitarian approach to work, as a result of which it becomes difficult to break out of this attitude in order to do things for their own sake.

We can also see an element of deception in the way that wages are set. The connection between the tasks performed and the reward obtained is really quite arbitrary. Why is one hour's work in the fields worth the price of a pound of rice? Why one pound of rice and not two? On what basis is one hour's work in an office equivalent to ten pounds of rice? The value of work in terms of wages received is largely determined by the vagaries of market forces and the calculations of accountants, even when different people are doing the same work. In any case, what is money? It is essentially a means of exchange, which in former times meant gold and silver coins and which now means banknotes, which have no intrinsic value. Our economic system is based on our all agreeing to treat these objects as if they had value. The situation becomes even more obscure when banknotes are replaced by numbers held in computer systems. Of course, quite often the things on which we spend our money have no intrinsic value either. Advertisers and fashion gurus persuade us to purchase articles which are supposed to change our appearance or our home life for the better but which often signally fail to do so.

The solution is to do work that is intrinsically worthwhile. Even work that is difficult, dirty, or unpleasant is nonetheless worth doing to the extent that it contributes to the well-being of oneself and others. Right livelihood is work that you would do regardless of how much, or how little, you were paid to do it. Unfortunately, few people are in a position to enjoy this kind of work.

2
GENEROSITY

Nāgārjuna renders the second precept as 'not stealing'. In Pāli this is *adinnādāna veramaṇī* – 'to abstain from taking the not-given'. It is usually assumed that following this precept means no more than not stealing, not pilfering, not surreptitiously taking what has not been given. Someone might say, 'I've never stolen anything in my life. Well, maybe a fountain pen when I was a kid. Oh, and there was a five pound note I borrowed in a pub. I always meant to give it back the next time I was in there. Apart from that I've never broken the second precept.' But this sort of self-satisfied moral accounting is not the way to practise the precept of giving in its full sense. Like the first precept, the second precept means far more than it appears to mean at first sight. It can also be seen as not hindering a person's development or violating their individuality. You might not take their money or their belongings, but it is very easy to waste someone's time or to rob them of their energy. It is easy to take from someone something other than material possessions that they may be no less sorry to lose. You have not asked, you have simply taken it, and time and energy are things that are not easily given back.

Practising the second precept implies generosity, of course, but it also involves another positive quality: the faith that one way or another you will receive what you need, so that you don't have to take from others against their will or without their permission. Sometimes others will disappoint you; they may forget to look after you in your old age, but your faith has to be a broader confidence in the spiritual and even the psychological rewards of skilful action. Feeling the need to grab your share, to pocket what you feel is yours by right, suggests a neurotic insecurity, as does trying to manipulate events to your own advantage. Any kind of possessiveness, and even the simple tendency to see things and people as commodities, goes against the spirit of this precept. The whole attitude of bargaining, trying to get the best deal for oneself, runs counter to it. The ability to be generous with your skills, your time, and your possessions, without calculating what you are going to get in return, can come only from a state of deep psychological security. You might not get the outcome you envisaged; you might be surprised, whether pleasantly or unpleasantly, at how things turn out; but you will be confident that ultimately there will be a positive outcome for you. The ideal society should function in this way: you give what you can and you take what you need. In the real world the situation is more complex, because there are people who will exploit you if you let them and you may need to drive hard bargains with them. Most people are pretty determined to hang on to what they have, however they may have acquired it, and in seeking to persuade them to let go one must be careful not to resort to methods which break this precept, either in the letter or the spirit.

One way is to appeal to people's natural – if sometimes rather deeply hidden – generosity. This method was pursued with some success in India by Acharya Vinoba Bhave, in his *bhūdān* or land donation programme (*bhū* meaning 'land' and *dān* 'giving').[202] In India, one of the great social, economic, and political problems is that of the landless labourer. At the same time, there are landowners who have far more land than they really need. The question was how to redistribute this surplus land without having recourse to coercion. Vinoba Bhave, as a follower of Gandhi, was totally committed to the principle of non-violence. His solution was to organize meetings of the big landowners and make the following appeal. He would ask them how many sons they had, between whom they would be dividing their land. They might say five. He would reply, 'So if you had a sixth son, each of the others would have to make do with a little less land,' and they would agree. He would then say, 'Well, take me as your sixth son, and let me have that share.' He didn't get the millions of acres that he had hoped for, but many of the landowners were deeply touched by his appeal and he was able to distribute tens of thousands of acres to landless labourers and their families. This direct approach, with its simple moral appeal, can sometimes work wonders. The beauty of it is that everyone benefits, including the donors. In a politically sensitive situation, motives will often be mixed, and no doubt some owners of land gave out of fear of the consequences of not giving, throwing a sop to the landless in order to reduce popular support for the Communist party. But some experienced a genuine change of heart and gave far more than they were asked to give. In this way, Vinoba Bhave's scheme helped to correct an imbalance in the ownership of land in many parts of India without recourse to violence. It goes to show that encouraging people to be generous doesn't necessarily mean taking advantage of their feelings of guilt. People do sometimes respond positively to a positive appeal. The precepts are not only about ceasing to do evil; they also inspire us to act positively towards others and to encourage them to act likewise.

GIVING AND EARNING

Giving is the fundamental Buddhist virtue. Before taking up any other practice, one should learn to be generous. Many of the *Jātakas*,[203] the stories of the Buddha's previous lives, depict the Buddha-to-be as practising *dāna* or generosity to a superlative degree. As a result, when he is reborn, he has only to open his hands to find them full of jewels – or so the legends relate.

But is the importance of giving reflected in our own experience of life? What is the real relationship between giving and getting? According to Nāgārjuna, and the Buddhist tradition in general, to be slow to give will result in one being poor, whether in this life or another, while giving freely will lead to wealth. But how are we to interpret this teaching? The first thing to remember is the importance of intention in the creation of karma. It is the spirit in which one gives that counts. But although giving without thought of benefit to oneself will, paradoxically, bring one the greater benefit, most people cannot help opting for the lesser benefit. We can't help thinking of what we will be getting in return, even with regard to such intangibles as esteem, gratitude, and so on. Having a preconceived idea of some sort of quid pro quo means that the gift isn't *really* a gift, and often the recipient will be subtly aware of this. It is usually not difficult to see that much of what we are given comes with various little strings attached. Past experience might make us a bit suspicious of almost any gift, seeing it as 'a sprat to catch a mackerel', as the old saying has it. When one is given something, it doesn't always feel like it, and one might even feel a little disappointed, as though something was missing.

Much of our discontent comes from a sense that life is not fair and that we don't get treated as we deserve; and this in turn may make us unwilling to give. According to the Buddhist view, meanness makes one poor, but meanness itself arises, it could be said, from the fact that one feels poor or has a 'poverty mentality'. True generosity involves the opposite: one not only gives all the time; one is also aware of receiving all the time. Part of the practice of generosity therefore consists in becoming aware of how much one is being given. That is, generosity is connected to the ability to experience gratitude, as well as to express it. It consists in the ability to feel wealthy even in the humblest circumstances.

At the most basic level we have sunlight, air, water, earth. All these are free. We might squander and pollute the elements that we need to live in the world, but they continue to be available to us. Moreover, any advanced society provides all sorts of astonishing services at little or no cost to the consumer. In Britain we have access to so many resources: healthcare and education, libraries, the BBC, all kinds of entertainment, even Buddhist centres. Besides all this, there is the support we are given by those around us. Many people, especially if they are young, are unaware that someone is shopping, cooking, and cleaning for them day after day. There is, for example, the story of the long-suffering housewife who has been cooking for her husband and sons day in, day out, for a quarter of a century with never a word of thanks. One day they lift the lid of the vegetable dish to reveal a pair of old boots. 'Well,' she explains in response to their expressions of shock and dismay, 'You've never said anything that would make me think you'd notice the difference.'

Many people find it difficult to give or receive thanks gracefully. Perhaps they were never introduced to the traditional courtesies, or perhaps they have discarded them as the hypocritical niceties of conventional middle-class life – or perhaps they just feel embarrassed. If one is a bit clumsy in this respect, there is no harm in working on one's social skills. It is always better to err on the side of excess in expressing gratitude. Practice, after all, makes perfect. On the other hand, there are situations where thanks in the formal sense would be out of place. Often, a little look of gratitude will suffice.

If we take things for granted we are depriving ourselves of a rich source of satisfaction. This in turn may deprive us of the capacity to give freely, as well as of the further rewards that follow in the form of happiness and free-flowing energy. If we are looking for a return from our generosity, we can find it in the freedom of letting go of possessions, in the natural pleasure we feel in helping someone, in the flow of energy out from us as well as the flow of energy towards us. A psychologically healthy person has energy, and energy naturally flows outwards, so that if you have energy you will feel like giving. Energy flows in different ways, depending upon one's temperament. You might feel like doing something practical for someone, like giving money or time, or you might want to give attention or affection. On the other hand, advice – which most of us are only too willing to offer – is often the one gift that is best withheld.

A friend of mine used to say, 'The greatest virtue is availability.' To be available to others is – quite simply – to be ready to give yourself. You don't insist that you will only help in a particular way. You're not concerned about 'doing your own thing' or 'expressing yourself' or exercising your own talents. You are not too grand for little humdrum jobs. You are simply there for someone or for a certain situation, and you don't mind what you do. This is the ideal of what one might call the 'non-specialized human being'. You are willing to turn your hand to practically anything, and you have no personal investment in the task you happen to be doing. You can see that there is a job to be done and you're happy to do it.

Giving is a kind of communication. In giving, you are opening the channels of communication, and this allows an exchange of energy to take place. Giving, affection, and energy can all flow in either direction. If you are able to give, you are able to receive, and in that sense giving and receiving are two sides of the same coin. A one-way communication can be genuine, but it is necessarily limited. Any interaction between people involves both giving and receiving. Of course, the more intense and the more true the communication, the less it is possible to speak in terms of either giving or receiving. The giving becomes the receiving, the receiving becomes the giving. Who is receiving from whom, and who is giving to whom, it becomes impossible to say.[204]

Just as you are intent on thinking
Of what could be done to help yourself,
So you should be intent on thinking
Of what could be done to help others.

If only for a moment make yourself
Available for the use of others
Just as earth, water, fire, wind, medicine,
And forests (are available to all).

Even during their seventh step
Merit measureless as the sky
Is generated in Bodhisattvas
Whose attitude is to give all wealth away.

If you give to those so seeking
Girls of beauty well adorned,
You will thereby attain
Thorough retention of the excellent doctrine.

Formerly the Subduer provided
Along with every need and so forth
Eighty thousand girls
With all adornments.

Lovingly give to beggars
Various and glittering
Clothes, adornments, perfumes,
Garlands, and enjoyments.

If you provide (facilities)
For those most deprived who lack
The means (to study) the doctrine,
There is no greater gift than that.

Even give poison
To those whom it will help,
But do not give even the best food
To those whom it will not help.

Just as it is said that it will help
To cut off a finger bitten by a snake,
So the Subduer says that if it helps others,
One should even bring (temporary) discomfort. (256–64)

We all think about our own needs very carefully. But we tend not to think with equal care about what will help others. Even when we are trying to help others, we are only too often self-referential. We would like others to be happy in a way that suits us, or at least matches our ideas of what one should do with one's life. I'm not sure if many people *love* to think about the needs of others, as Nāgārjuna tells the king he should do. We might be able to help others out of a sense of duty, but our aim should be to do so out of love. The first of these verses thus gives us something quite simple and straightforward – and at the same time quite challenging – to aim for in our spiritual life. If we can feel real concern for the needs of others, we will really have made some progress, spiritually speaking.

How should we go about this? Nāgārjuna gives us a clue in the next verse. He says, 'If only for a moment'. We don't necessarily have to commit ourselves permanently to this way of being. He reminds us that we can apply ourselves simply to meeting the demands of the present moment. Make yourself available to others – now, rather than when you feel like doing so. This suggests that it might not be so difficult after all. In a sense, 'making yourself useful' probably covers it. More deeply, it is a matter of radically changing the way we think of ourselves. Instead of looking out at a world made up of resources that could meet our own needs, we can think of ourselves as being a resource for the world.

Many of these verses could have come from the *Bodhicaryāvatāra,* whose author, Śāntideva, lived 500 years after Nāgārjuna and belonged to his spiritual lineage. 'Just as earth, water, fire, wind, medicine, and forests are available to all' inevitably reminds us of the verse from the *Bodhicaryāvatāra* that is recited in the final section of our sevenfold puja.

Just as the earth and other elements
Are serviceable in many ways
To the infinite number of beings
Inhabiting limitless space;
So may I become
That which maintains all beings
Situated throughout space,
So long as all have not attained
To peace.[205]

Nāgārjuna's suggestions as to suitable gifts, like providing beggars with garlands and perfume, and giving girls in marriage to those who seek them, might seem a little odd to us. However, at the time he gave this advice, if you were unable to afford a wife – and therefore were unable to produce children – you would have had no one to support you in your old age. And treating a beggar as you would your dearest friend, giving lovingly rather than with condescension, is a good example of true generosity.

Finally, Nāgārjuna mentions appropriate giving, or giving with a real awareness of the recipient's needs. Sometimes what one gives may even be temporarily unwelcome. Sometimes what someone really wants and needs may be a quite ordinary thing. Sometimes they may even need 'poison' in the form of powerful drugs because they are seriously ill or in pain.

GIVING THE DHARMA

Through making the hearing and the giving
Of the doctrine be unobstructed
You will [keep] company with Buddhas,
And will quickly attain your wishes.

Through non-attachment you will achieve the meaning (of
doctrines),
Through not being miserly your resources will increase,
Through not being proud you will become chief (of those
respected),
Through enduring the doctrine you will attain retention. (289–90)

There are two ways in which we can help the communication of the Dharma (that is, the Buddha's teaching): we can help people to teach it, and we can also help people to hear it. Even if we don't give the gift of the Dharma ourselves, we will keep company with the Buddhas if only we do everything we can to enable those who can teach the Dharma to do so, and if we enable those who might be receptive to the Dharma to hear it. This teaching is central to the Mahāyāna approach. To make an effort to help others to benefit from the Dharma is in effect to practise the Dharma yourself. The more you give, the more you receive. I would go so far as to say that you haven't really started practising the Dharma until you have started giving – above all, until you have started giving the Dharma. The principle of karma applies very directly to our giving of the Dharma: 'through not being miserly your resources will increase'; by being generous with your understanding of the Dharma, you are increasing your own understanding of it.

Until you concern yourself with the needs of others and start giving, you don't realize how attached you are to your own concerns and needs; and until you start teaching it, you don't realize how inadequate is your understanding of the Dharma. When you start teaching, then you really start learning. Teaching opens you up to an entirely different dimension of understanding. While it is inadvisable to start giving people the benefit of your wisdom prematurely – especially if it is mere book-learning – there does come a point beyond which you are going to learn more from teaching than you are from being taught. It is not therefore a question of being 'ready to teach'. You may be less than brilliant as a teacher in the beginning, but by being brought up against the limits of your knowledge, you are forced to grow beyond those limits, both as a teacher and as a student.

You may, for example, be asked about issues that you have shied away from addressing on your own account. Most people have areas about which they feel confident and others that they don't want to look at or are not interested in. Maybe it's some aspect of ethics, or a meditation practice that you have so far neglected. You then have to think about it for yourself, look up texts on the subject, ask your friends about it, and come back with something to discuss with your students. What you come back with may well have a deeper, more significant effect upon you than upon your students. In this way, not only do gaps in your knowledge get filled in, but you may be inspired to investigate further. You may even find you know more than you thought you did.

Of course, you need to have a small stock of Dharma knowledge before you start teaching. It's like going into business. You need a bit of capital to start with, and some people can make a success of a business with a comparatively small sum. If you think you need a really big sum before you can start, you may not take the plunge at all. In the same way, some people have the ability to start teaching on the basis of quite a small stock of Dharma knowledge, and through teaching they may increase this stock quite rapidly.

The necessary proviso is that you should be honest about what you know and what you don't know, rather than trying to bluff your students by guessing an answer or brushing off difficult questions. You should admit you don't know, or can't remember offhand, and you should look forward to investigating the matter. 'Through not being proud you will become chief (of those respected).' The converse of this is that if you try to impress people you may not be respected by them. Nobody can know everything about Buddhism. If you're asked a question that had never occurred to you before, you could say, 'That's interesting. I've never thought about that. What do you think?'

The other thing you need if you are going to teach the Dharma is a certain depth of spiritual practice. People don't want to be given information that they could just as easily find out for themselves. They want live contact with the Dharma, a feeling of how the Dharma is actually lived. They might not be ready to encounter a Buddha, and they are unlikely to find one teaching at a Buddhist centre, but so long as you have assimilated what knowledge you have acquired and have some experience to fall back on, you will be able to communicate something of value. The Dharma can be truly communicated only in the light of a solid practice of it over a period of some years. It isn't an abstract thing. It is not really to be encountered apart from the people who, at least to some extent, actually embody it in their lives. As a Buddhist, you should be turning aspects of the Dharma over in your mind whenever you can, so that if you are asked to teach you already have something to say, perhaps on a subject you have thought about for years. Thus you will always be ready to give a talk or lead a class.

I think we can interpret the second verse quoted here as a continuation of the theme of the first, namely, as being about learning and teaching the Dharma. If you are full of yourself, how can you be receptive? There is a Zen story that illustrates this point. A master called Nan-in once received a visit from a learned professor and poured him tea – and kept pouring until the cup overflowed. When the professor protested, Nan-in replied, 'You are like this cup. How can I give you the teaching when you are so full of your own views?'[206] Learning about the Dharma means learning to listen, not being so attached to one's own views that one is closed to what might be disturbing. This is why the disciple is called a *śrāvaka*, or 'one who hears'.

The self-defeating nature of selfishness is a constant theme of the Mahāyāna. If you are too attached to what is yours, and too full of yourself, you will end up ignorant, poor, and despised. This teaching is traditionally understood in terms of karma and rebirth, viewed as administering as a kind of poetic justice: if you are generous you will be reborn rich, if you are modest you will be reborn into a highly respected position in life. In fact, this is not necessarily the case; as well as karma, there are other factors that determine the nature of our lot in life. Nonetheless, a miser will always feel poor, and those who demand respect will never feel that they are getting enough of it. By contrast, if you are truly generous you are likely to feel that you are living in the midst of abundance, and if you are modest, you will at least enjoy the respect of the few who appreciate modesty.

Karma and rebirth are never a straightforward matter. Selfless actions are one thing, but selfless motivation, especially if you have future lives in mind, is another thing entirely. True selflessness is in the end not separable from insight. For the sake of the greater reward you have to forget all about rewards and just give for the sake of giving. That's the paradox. It's like trying to be happy or trying to love: the more you try to be happy, the less likely you are to be so, and the more you insist on how much you love people, the less likely they are to believe you. But forget all about being happy and loving and you will have a good chance of *being* happy and loving and even perhaps of being loved.

'Enduring the doctrine' is an odd expression, suggesting that the Dharma is a kind of burden, something to be put up with. But that is not what is meant. The term Nāgārjuna uses here is *dharmadhara*, one who bears or carries the Dharma by virtue of their practice of it. Such a person will retain it, that is, they will keep it in mind.[207]

THE BUSINESSMAN'S GUIDE TO PRUDENT GIVING

If you do not make contributions of the wealth
Obtained from former giving to the needy,
Through your ingratitude and attachment
You will not obtain wealth in the future.

Here in the world workers do not carry
Provisions for a journey unpaid,
But lowly beggars, without payment, carry to your future life
(What you give them) multiplied a hundred times.

Always be of exalted mind
And take delight in exalted deeds.
From exalted actions arise
All effects that are exalted.

Create foundations of doctrine, abodes
Of the Three Jewels – fraught with glory and fame –
That lowly kings have not even
Conceived in their minds.

O King, it is preferable not to create
Foundations of doctrine that do not stir
The hairs of wealthy kings
Because (those centers) will not become famous even after your death.

Through your great exaltation, use even all your wealth
Such that the exalted become free from pride,
(The equal) become delighted,
And the inclinations of the lowly are reversed.

Having let go of all possessions,
(At death) powerless you must go elsewhere,
But all that has been used for the doctrine
Precedes you (as good karma).

When all the possessions of a previous monarch
Come under the control of the successor
Of what use are they then to the former monarch
For practice, happiness, or fame?

Through using wealth there is happiness here in this life,
Through giving there is happiness in the future,
From wasting it without using or giving it away,
There is only misery. How could there be happiness?

Because of lack of power while dying,
You will be unable to make donations by way of your ministers
Who will shamelessly lose affection for you
And will seek to please the new monarch.

Hence while in good health create foundations of doctrine
Immediately with all your wealth,
For you are living amidst the causes of death
Like a lamp standing in a breeze. (307–17)

This series of arguments in favour of generosity is pitched, it has to be said, at a rather low level. Nāgārjuna clearly thinks that the important thing is to get the stream of generosity flowing. It doesn't matter too much how you go about persuading people to give, just so long as they do give. Giving is a virtue in itself; it frees up energy, it loosens the bonds of some basic unskilful attitudes, and the rest of the spiritual life can be based upon it.

'Here' means in the present life. If you enjoy wealth now, it comes to you as a result of the generosity you have practised in previous lives. If, therefore, you want to gain wealth in future lives, you must give from your present possessions. To most modern Buddhists, at least in the West, this attitude is at best meaningless and at worst ignoble. But if we are to understand how Buddhism has developed over the centuries, we have to take this traditional way of thinking into account. We have to appreciate that in the past this sort of argument was a real incentive for people. One reason for this must be that life then was much more precarious than it is now. Life was apt to be 'nasty, brutish, and short' for anyone without means. It is therefore hardly surprising that happiness should be so closely allied to the possession of wealth or – as is insisted here – to its profitable expenditure as well. No doubt mundane motivations sometimes fuel our own practice of the Dharma. Are we not often seeking happiness, success, and security for ourselves through such spiritual practice rather than Enlightenment for the benefit of all beings? So perhaps we should not be too censorious of the spiritual materialism of the past. However, to say, 'Lowly beggars, without payment, carry to your future life (what you give them) multiplied a hundred times' provides an almost grotesque reflection of this traditional, robustly mercenary way of thinking about generosity and its advantages. It envisages a situation in which, in effect, you employ beggars to transport your wealth from your present life to the next.

It may be hard for us to imagine a truly religious-minded person being quite as self-centred as this, but plenty of evidence of such attitudes is to be found in all religions. In India I came across a certain old-fashioned type of devotee belonging to the rich merchant community who would be very pious and very generous, but who would bring his commercial acumen into his religious life. Such a man might make big charitable donations, but he would blatantly attach conditions to them. He would quite shamelessly offer so many *lakhs* of rupees to open a charitable dispensary, a hospital, or a school, on condition that it should be named after his father, that he himself should be guest of honour at the opening ceremony, and that he should be introduced to the prime minister after he had opened the institution.

This combination of materialism and piety may seem strange to us, but it is ultimately based on traditional religious values. It is bound up with the idea that power and wealth come from one's good deeds in a previous life. It reinforces the notion that the wealthy man is the good man, and with it the notion that the poor man is morally suspect. This is not in fact the Buddhist view, but a rather literal presentation of the teaching of karma and rebirth can unfortunately lend itself to this sort of interpretation. It is, however, the generally accepted Hindu understanding of the teaching, and one that causes the pious and wealthy to feel very satisfied with themselves. I have met many people in India with a firm conviction of their own virtue, born out of little more than their fortunate and prosperous circumstances. And, sadly, I have met many poor people who assumed that they must have deserved their fate. This unpleasant twist, which is sometimes given to the teaching of karma and rebirth, even by some Buddhists, is institutionalized within Hinduism in the form of the caste system and is used to reinforce the social status quo.

Christianity has been put to much the same use in the past. The church regularly taught that it was one's duty to accept one's station in life since it been allotted one by God. There is a hymn in which there appears the following verse:

> The rich man in his castle,
> The poor man at his gate,
> God made them high and lowly
> And ordered their estate.[208]

It is as if organized religion tends to sanctify the status quo, and to be on the side of the rich against the poor. As St Paul said, 'The powers that be are ordained of God.'[209] Regardless of how those in power behave, they have God's authority behind them.

In India, I found that rich people often thought of themselves not as exploiters of the poor, but as providers of employment for those who hadn't the brains to create job opportunities for themselves. They genuinely believed that they were performing a public service and amassing wealth quite disinterestedly. It was their way of serving God, they would sometimes say. Such statements used to leave me speechless, but one did come across Buddhist monks who were only too happy to countenance such attitudes.

Throughout his career, the Buddha dealt with the rich and powerful without being in the least deferential. Yet in some Buddhist countries there are monks who will adopt a subservient attitude to those in positions of authority. This is due to a failure to grasp the central principle of the spiritual life, namely, that we are free to choose how to be, here and now, regardless of social and group constraints. We are free to be more or less aware, more or less creative, and more or less of an individual. Never mind karma and rebirth, or past and future; what is important is how we shape ourselves in the present moment. This is the Buddha's own emphasis, that is, the emphasis is on gaining Enlightenment here and now, in this very life. He didn't deny the truth of karma, but he never suggested that a good rebirth was the most worthy goal for a human being. In presenting any Buddhist teaching you have to relate it to that central principle, since otherwise you may be understood as appealing to a lower self-referential motivation.

In justice to Nāgārjuna, one has to bear in mind that in his day a king possessed unlimited power and was capable of doing so much harm that it was worth restraining him by virtually any means. Usually there was no other power within the state by which he might be constrained. If he was not highly intelligent, or religiously minded, one might have to put aside one's scruples in order to encourage some kind of ethical behaviour, however crudely motivated that behaviour might be. One might have to promise him a future life in which he would have more of whatever he had now, if this was the only way of inspiring him to rule ethically.

3
SEXUAL RELATIONSHIPS

The third precept – *kāmesu micchācārā veramaṇī* – is 'to abstain from sexual misconduct'. Forsaking the wives of others (which is how Nāgārjuna refers to this precept) is therefore the very least that a male practitioner of the Dharma should expect from himself. The masculine perspective is here taken as for granted because the text is addressed to a king. Furthermore, in ancient India a man's wife was considered to be his property, and the traditional interpretation of the precept reflects this belief. The precept was also seen as covering abstention from the violation or abduction of any woman, married or unmarried, and this was again in large part a matter of respecting the property of other men, inasmuch as a daughter or sister, however mature, literally 'belonged' to her family until she joined another family through marriage. Until then, she was under the protection of her father and her brothers.

Moving from history to modern practicalities, it is clear how the third precept is to be applied today, whether by women or by men. Two main principles seem to be involved. First, one should not violate another person's individuality by using them for one's sexual gratification against their wishes. Second, inasmuch as someone is regarded as 'belonging' to their sexual partner, knowingly breaking up a marriage or other sexual partnership is a form of 'taking the not-given', as well as being a case of violating the individuality of the person whose partner one has 'stolen'.

But if we limit our sexual activity to what is socially acceptable, can we leave it at that? Is this simple criterion enough? It is, if a rule is all that you want. It isn't, though, if you want to make the observance of the precept a real ethical practice. I once saw the precepts written up on a board in a vihara (Buddhist monastery) in London, and the third one was 'not to indulge in wicked love'. The monks obviously wanted people to think about this precept a bit more deeply. But how does someone practise the third precept if they are married and simply don't have the time or the inclination to indulge in 'wicked love' in any case?

Not to misbehave with other people's partners does not exhaust the implications of this precept. For a start, we should clear away a lot of the rationalizing and romanticizing that serves to idealize, even spiritualize, sexual activity. We like to imagine that sex is all about giving and sharing, but is this really the case? If we are honest with ourselves, can we say that the tremendous attraction we feel towards another person is really just an urge to give? I suspect that in the great majority of cases, sexual relationships are nicely judged reciprocal arrangements, balanced exchanges of services, physical and emotional – healthy enough on their own level, but not to be elevated above that level. Should one try to elevate them in this way, one is inevitably going to be disappointed, or even resentful, when those services are no longer being offered quite so freely, or when they are withdrawn altogether.

Then there is the question of mindfulness. What is the real effect of sexual activity upon one's state of mind? It is worth taking the trouble to notice this if one is attempting to combine a spiritual life with sexual activity. No doubt Tantric adepts and advanced bodhisattva yogis can incorporate sexual activity into their spiritual practice, but we have to ask ourselves if we are really anywhere near that level.[210] It is not as if an occasional lapse of mindfulness is going to put a stop to our spiritual life. Lapses are inevitable. Even after years of practice, instinctual urges and old tendencies may emerge from time to time and result in a temporary setback in our overall spiritual progress and there is no point in getting caught up in self-recrimination. What is spiritually incapacitating is self-deception.

Furthermore, making allowance for natural drives is not to be confused with the view that a healthy person *needs* sex, and that we are repressed or deprived if we do not get it. Unfortunately the assumption that sexual innocence or purity somehow blocks the healthy functioning of the individual is widely accepted. From this comes the curious idea that one needs to accumulate a lot of worldly experience in the form of personal difficulties and messy sexual relationships to be 'mature' enough to embark upon the spiritual life. There is almost a stigma attached to having to admit that one hasn't had sex for months or years at a time, as though that made one unattractive, a failure, even not quite a real man or a real woman. This is a very pervasive *micchā-diṭṭhi* (wrong view) these days. But it is certainly not the traditional view, either in the West or in the East. The mistaken assumption underpinning it is that the same rules can be applied to everyone. But people are different. There are many things that are important to one person but are of no consequence to another. Some people can't live without sex, while others get by quite happily without it, at least so long as they are not constantly being told that they must surely be unhappy. People who are temperamentally inclined to chastity, perhaps as a result of very positive karma, may come to the spiritual life innocent and pure and make considerable progress. Perhaps they have a 'gift' for chastity; if so, they should be allowed to enjoy that gift, not be pushed against the healthy and refined grain of their nature into seeking the kind of experience that most of us feel we cannot live without. Those of us who are not so gifted should allow ourselves an outlet for our sexual urges, without undermining the confidence of those who can practise the Dharma happily without the need for sex. Why not rejoice in purity and innocence as a virtue and a blessing, even if the rest of society takes a completely different view?

The third precept is concerned with what we do with our sexuality in the broadest sense. It is not just about sexual relationships; it is also concerned with how we use our sexuality in order to achieve other objects, as when we charm people in order to get what we want. There is an unpleasant mixture of mutual exploitation and deception in much of what we accept as normal social intercourse between the sexes. This precept is therefore also about being aware of a certain kind of power or energy that is available to us and of the part it plays in the half-conscious flirtation that creeps into so much of our communication. We should respond to people with real friendliness and *mettā*, but not get caught up in the kind of exchange that stirs up sexual feelings in a thoughtless way.

Along with this unconscious misuse of sexuality, there often goes a fear of experiencing sexual feelings, particularly when those feelings have for their object a person of the same sex as oneself. This is not to say that such feelings have to be acted upon, but sexual feelings cannot be kept in a sealed box apart from all one's other emotions. Our sexuality, for good or ill, seeps into all sorts of situations in which we would nevertheless not want to express it, and the danger is that we become afraid even to acknowledge the presence of this element in our experience. An unconscious fear of experiencing supposedly unacceptable sexual feelings sometimes prevents people from acknowledging and expressing normal feelings of attraction or affection. Being emotionally drawn to someone is automatically identified as a sexual feeling when it might not be anything of the kind. In this way, quite positive feelings can be replaced by emotional unease, by inhibition and, consequently, by loss of energy.

We need to be able to feel strong, warm emotions in connection with our sexuality, but we need also to be able to experience strong, warm emotions without sexual feelings being involved at all. If it is difficult for you to separate such emotions from sex, this doesn't mean that it's a good idea to repress the sexual feelings and take up a life of strict celibacy. Should you do so, those feelings will almost certainly emerge later in life and then be more difficult to handle. Conversely, the more freely we are able to express positive emotion, the better we will be able to deal with our biological or instinctual urges.

THE UGLINESS OF THE CONDITIONED

Lust for a woman mostly comes
From thinking that her body is clean,
But there is nothing clean
In a woman's body in fact.

The abdomen and chest is a vessel
Of feces, urine, lungs, liver, and so forth.
Those who through obscuration do not see
A woman this way, lust for her body.

There is pleasure when a sore is scratched,
But to be without sores is more pleasurable still.
Just so, there are pleasures in worldly desires,
But to be without desires is more pleasurable still.

> If you analyse thus, even though
> You do not achieve freedom from desire,
> Because your desire has lessened
> You will not lust for women. (148, 150, 169–70)

In his advice to the king, Nāgārjuna finds it necessary to devote over twenty verses (only four of which are quoted here) to curbing the male reader's sexual appetite. Why? Let us first look at the argument.

These verses have to be seen as pertaining to method rather than to doctrine, the method in this case being that of a means to help men overcome their sexual craving.

We are used to washing off all the various secretions and excretions of our own body, and yet we go into paroxysms of desire over the unclean body of another. There is something absurd, Nāgārjuna is suggesting, about such a situation. Similarly, there is a certain intense satisfaction to be gained from scratching an itching sore, yet no one who knew what it was like to be free of that terrible itch would willingly have it back.

The majority of teachings of this sort are addressed to men, but similar views about the body are found in the *Therīgāthā*, the Enlightenment verses of the early Buddhist nuns.[211] The corresponding reflections recommended for the nuns, to help wean them from their attachment to men, are less concerned with the repulsiveness of the body. At that time at least, they seem to have been attracted less by men's physical attributes and more by their apparent trustworthiness, so those verses make much of how treacherous and faithless, how disloyal and deceitful, men can be; how you cannot trust their sweet words, how they say one thing and mean another, and how they will betray your trust even as they gaze lovingly into your eyes. Their verses focus on the fact that it is the nature of men to be unfaithful and to lust after other women.

This harsh view of the male sex is probably quite acceptable to many people today. But the attitude towards woman's body that we find in the present verses runs right against the grain of modern sensibilities. Probably most people would consider the systematic cultivation of this way of thinking about the female body as morbid, unpleasant, and negative. Looked at superficially, these verses and other Buddhist texts like them may seem to represent a powerfully misogynistic strain running through the Buddhist tradition. They seem to put women down. But they are in fact not intended as an objective assessment of women; they have to be seen as pertaining to method rather than to doctrine, the method in this case being that of a means to help men overcome their sexual craving.

The problems that people have with verses like these stem, I would say, from the quite different nature of the major obstacles faced in the spiritual life by men and by women. These obstacles are more to do with identity than with sex itself. Nowadays men seem to find giving up sex a real problem, representing as this does a loss of an important part of their masculine identity. However, this identity is forged largely by male competitiveness in the workplace, and men probably start to make more real spiritual progress when they wholeheartedly give up worldly ambition rather than when they give up sex.

It would seem that a woman's difficulty with celibacy is also less to do with sex itself and more to do with her identity as a woman. In her case it seems to be more to do with losing the emotional intimacy that goes with sex, and with losing, ultimately, the possibility of her being a wife and mother. The adoption of a celibate lifestyle thus represents for her a tremendous step in itself. The question of children in particular, while it may have become less important for most men than it was in the past, remains comparatively important for women.

CONTEMPLATION OF BODILY IMPURITY

The Sanskrit term to which Nāgārjuna is making reference in these verses is *śubha*, which is here translated as 'clean', while the negative form *aśubha* is translated as 'filthy', although these terms can also be translated as meaning 'pure' and 'impure', or 'lovely' and 'unlovely'.

Aśubha is often associated with the three *lakṣaṇas* or characteristics of conditioned existence. According to Buddhist teaching, conditioned existence is *duḥkha* (unsatisfactory), *anitya* (impermanent), and *anātman* (without a substantial, unchanging, self). Sometimes *aśubha* is added to this list. When this is done and the four are seen in the opposite way, they become the four *vipariyāsas*, the 'mental perversities' or 'topsy-turvy views'. Being ourselves conditioned, we cannot help ascribing what are in fact the characteristics of the Unconditioned to conditioned existence. We see the world not as unsatisfactory but as *sukha* or pleasant. When we possess things we think we will always have them, that is, we see conditioned existence not as impermanent but as *nitya* or permanent. We also see it not as devoid of permanent unchanging selfhood, but as possessed of such selfhood, or *ātman*. Finally we see the objects of our craving not as *aśubha* but as being attractive and lovely.

In these verses, Nāgārjuna focuses on that aspect of conditioned existence to which we most easily and regularly ascribe the qualities of loveliness and purity that really belong to the Unconditioned: the body of a person with whom we are infatuated. After all, we don't fall in love with trees, for example, beautiful as they may be. We don't get so attached to a particular tree that we want to spend all our time with it and eventually move in with it. Our craving casts a sort of glamour over the bodies of certain people, a glamour that does not gather around any other object, however beautiful.

Therefore, serious Buddhist practitioners have always been advised to practise the *aśubha bhāvanā,* the contemplation of the less pleasant aspects of the human body. Just as we meditate on the impermanence and insubstantiality of conditioned existence, and on the lack of real satisfaction to be found in it, so we can also meditate on the unattractiveness (*aśubha*) of conditioned existence. In this practice, we focus on certain aspects of the human body, aspects which we would normally find unpleasant but whose unpleasantness we disregard when we are in the grip of sexual passion. The *aśubha bhāvanā* helps to expose how lust can override our natural repugnance for the secretions and excretions of other people's bodies. One tries to see the human body as it really is: impermanent, unsatisfactory, without fixed selfhood, and in truth unlovely.

Buddhist practice involves the cultivation of awareness, but sexual craving, on account of its blind instinctual nature, takes us in the opposite direction. To prevent this from happening, drastic action is needed, and this is what we get in these verses. Nāgārjuna is not necessarily hoping to free the king from sexual desire altogether; he may just be trying to help him to arrive at a degree of awareness. It's as if he is saying, 'Wake up! Take a closer look at this object of your craving. What is it really like?'

His invitation to examine the charms of the flesh with a critical eye perhaps also reflects a thought that at least occasionally crosses the minds of most people when they are engaged in pursuit of someone, or even when they finally achieve an intimate embrace with him or her. Perhaps the first few times you really are exploring the world of pleasurable human experience, but after that you might not be able to help thinking, 'Well, here we go again.' You know more or less what is going to happen, and you wonder, 'Is it really worth doing? What is the point? What am I getting out of this? How much am I even enjoying it?' Yet despite such misgivings, you feel somehow driven to it, as if by compulsion.

In order to counteract such compulsion, there is an emphasis on celibacy in most forms of Buddhism, celibacy being an indication that the sex drive is under control. The Pāli scriptures make it clear that the Buddha was completely celibate, while those who had attained Stream Entry (the point at which progress towards Enlightenment is assured),[212] while not necessarily celibate, were certainly not dominated by their sexual desires. However, in at least one place, the Buddha allows the possibility that someone might enjoy the pleasures of the senses and remain unattached. In the *Ariyapariyesanā Sutta* he classifies practitioners into three types.[213] He uses the image of a deer being hunted, but I'm going to use the image of a mouse as I think this makes the point more clearly. There are three kinds of mice. There are those who go after the cheese in the trap unwisely and who are caught, those who go after the cheese more carefully and who are not caught, and those who stay away from both cheese and trap and who, of course, are not caught. It is interesting that the Buddha did not deny the second possibility, that if you were very mindful you could 'nibble at' the pleasures of the senses without necessarily being overcome by craving. But this is dangerous. Most people are in fact overcome and suffer the consequences. It's much safer to stay away from the cheese. What Nāgārjuna is recommending in the king's case is in principle the second option, which in practice will mean restricting himself to a modest sex life, this being quite compatible with the aim of attaining Stream Entry.

CONTEMPLATION OF BEAUTY

Like celibacy, the *aśubha bhāvanā* is not an end in itself. Disgust or revulsion towards the body cannot be counted as a positive mental state unless it clears the way, as it is meant to do, for something better. In a sense, its purpose is to help us to distinguish between biological attractiveness and aesthetic beauty. One person might have conventional good looks and yet lack any real beauty, while another might be without any obvious attractions, and yet be truly beautiful. *Śubha*, the term used in this context, means pure as well as beautiful. It denotes a kind of spiritual beauty in the Neoplatonic sense.[214] The same kind of beauty is being referred to at the very beginning of the *Precious Garland* when Nāgārjuna extols the Buddha as 'adorned with all good qualities'.

The challenge for artists down the centuries has been to paint works that would appeal to their public's taste for sensuous beauty while aiming at the same time to achieve a more innocent vision – an impression of pure beauty – for those who were capable of enjoying it. Even the greatest artists may not always be appreciated for this higher achievement. It is said that at the end of the Second World War, two British soldiers were going round the Uffizi gallery in Florence and came upon Botticelli's *Birth of Venus*. 'Oi, come and look at this, Bill', said one, 'There's a girl here with no clothes on and two blokes spitting at her.'

Clearly, beauty isn't necessarily inherent in the object of our perception. It also depends on our looking at it in a certain way. If we look at it with greed or lust, then what we see is something sensuously attractive. If we look at it contemplatively, with *mettā*, then we see something rather different, something possessing beauty. The Buddha remarks more than once in the Pāli scriptures that a sign or characteristic of *mettā* is that you see things as beautiful, *śubha*. This is because the key element in both *śubha* and *mettā*, which raises them above ordinary human emotion, is disinterested awareness.

Schopenhauer emphasized this characteristic of aesthetic appreciation: that it is a pure delight in the object for its own sake, without any desire to make use of it. What he calls the will, 'a striving yearning force', is temporarily suspended.[215] If you find what you see sensuously attractive, you will probably want to grab it for the sake of your own pleasure, but if you find it aesthetically beautiful, you will just want to stand back and contemplate it, surrender to it, absorb yourself in it. Aesthetic contemplation is therefore not only disinterested but in a way impersonal. You lose yourself in the object, forgetting your personal concerns. Thus it is equivalent to the experience of the first *dhyāna*, the first level of meditative absorption.

This is the kind of vision for which the *aśubha bhāvanā* prepares us. Once we have established some initial control over our unskilful

Botticelli (1445–1510), The Birth of Venus

reactions to conditioned things, we can begin to reflect on the beauty of the Unconditioned. The *aśubha bhāvanā* helps us to stand back from the object of sensuous desire, to inhibit the impulse to reach out and grasp it, whether literally or mentally. To the extent that we can do this, to that extent we will be able to see things as purely beautiful. Seeing the unloveliness of conditioned existence prepares us to see the beauty that lies beyond it. Conversely, it is difficult to redirect one's desire towards the Unconditioned so long as one imagines that one has found perfect beauty in a particular human form. The positive approach to craving, raising one's gaze from grosser to more refined objects of desire, will be helpful at some point, but a vigorously negative approach is usually necessary to begin with.

Whether everyone could benefit from this approach is another matter. Whereas the Indians of Nāgārjuna's time apparently had a full-blooded and guilt-free relish for worldly pleasures, many in the post-Christian West are still burdened with a vague sense of the sinfulness of sexual pleasure. For us, sex is not quite such a straightforward matter as it seems to have been in ancient India. Someone might therefore take up the *aśubha bhāvanā* with an enthusiasm that came from a rather unhealthy, inhibited, or otherwise negative attitude to their body and their sexuality. In their case, the practice might serve only to reinforce their unhealthy attitude.

I would therefore not prescribe the *aśubha bhāvanā* for very many people in our culture today. Nāgārjuna's advice was offered at a specific time and to a particular person. If he were alive today, he would no doubt express himself in a way that addressed modern problems and preoccupations. For example, he might have thought that a 'romantic' emotional attachment to a particular person in some ways laid deeper snares for the practitioner than sexual desire itself. The processes that underlie such attachments have been investigated by modern psychology. According to Buddhism, we have within us various positive potentials. We are not always conscious of them, however, and we therefore tend to project them – as the psychologists would say – onto objects outside ourselves. We project our spiritual potential, for example, onto a guru figure; and, if we lack confidence, we may project that quality onto someone who appears to possess it. Of course, it is not easy to tell whether one is projecting a positive quality or whether one is simply appreciating its presence in another person in a healthy way. We can be reasonably certain that we will tend to project certain qualities onto those to whom we are sexually attracted. It is as though we were conscious of being somehow incomplete, and that instead of trying to develop what was lacking, we look for it in another person – usually someone of the opposite sex. Married people often refer to their spouse as their 'better half'. This is why people sometimes experience panic and terror when a relationship breaks up. It is as though you were losing far more than just another person; it can feel as though half of you was being torn away. But this is an illusion. The other person is not our other half, as we soon discover if we happen to come into conflict with them. And if a relationship becomes a way of avoiding the task of developing the qualities we believe are possessed by the other person, then it is clearly an unhelpful one.

WORKING WITH ROMANTIC PROJECTION[216]

Having said all this, projection may be initially useful in that it enables one to have, through contact with another person, some experience of one's unintegrated qualities. In the case of men, it is their unrealized 'feminine' qualities that tend to get projected onto their partner in a romantic relationship – their potential gentleness, sympathy, and receptivity. Because one does not experience certain qualities in oneself, in the sense of not having integrated them into one's conscious being, one is unconsciously drawn to finding them outside oneself.

Most people seem to go through this stage of romantic projection, usually in adolescence, and some go on repeating the experience again and again. But if you are relatively healthy, psychologically speaking, and fairly aware, you can learn to withdraw such projections without too much difficulty, and without disrupting your relationship with the other person. All this can be a normal part of growing up. As a result of falling out of love and possibly breaking up with your partner, you will develop, almost naturally, a more mature character.

It is possible to work with our projections even within a close relationship. We just need to ask ourselves, 'What do I really see in this person?' Once we recognize what it is, we know what we need to look for within ourselves. We can also ask ourselves how we feel in the loved person's absence. This is usually a good indication of how far the projection has progressed. When they are not there, do we feel that we ourselves are not really or fully there either, or that we are somehow lost, or helpless? If so, clearly something is missing. It is not just the other person that is missing, but a quality that we have got used to having available to us through them, a quality we experience as being outside rather than within us. Such projection is quite different from appreciating in someone else qualities that we know we ourselves do not possess. We will be pleased to have that person around, and when they are not there we might miss them, but we won't feel that we are being deprived of our very soul.

It is painful when a partner walks out on us, but this is a moment that provides an opportunity to see something about ourselves that perhaps we could not have seen in any other way. Now, at last, we are forced to face the inner lack that this person's presence in our life prevented us from seeing before. Even though we might look around for a substitute to fill the gap, the period of painful awareness into which we have been plunged may enable us to look with more open eyes at the unconscious processes that had been going on.

To conclude, the contemplation of the ugliness of the conditioned needs to be balanced by the contemplation of the purely beautiful. We need the stick *and* the carrot. I would suggest only that the carrot should be carefully chosen. In some circles it seems to be regarded as old-fashioned to look for beauty in the arts, but perhaps this is due to a confusion between true beauty and the merely pretty and decorative. Though one might react against the Victorian weakness for the picturesque and the sentimental, this is not a reason for turning one's back on what is truly beautiful, whether in art or in nature.

Many years ago I got to know a film producer in Bombay who, despite his busy and glamorous life, was quite thoughtful. He once visited the Ajanta caves to look for a film location, and on his return he had a question for me.[217] He had been impressed, he said, by the beauty of the cave paintings, but one thing puzzled him. He had noticed there were not only paintings of Buddhas and Bodhisattvas, and of animals and plants, but also of half-naked women. Why, he asked, had the monks who lived there, whose lives were dedicated to the practice of renunciation, depicted such images on the walls of their dwelling? I had not considered this question before, but the answer that immediately came to me was that the monks must have regarded the bodies of women as being simply part of the natural world, and that they were, as such, to be appreciated like other beautiful objects. They saw them aesthetically, not with desire, just as they saw fruit and flowers. One Buddhist approach is to reject these objects of craving altogether, and to persuade oneself that they aren't really quite so attractive after all. But perhaps aesthetic appreciation provides a middle way between complete rejection of craving and complete abandonment of oneself to it. This, it seems to me, is the ideal solution to the problem of sexual craving, and one that is well within the capacity of the serious Buddhist.

The implication here is that we need to derive pleasure from life, even – indeed especially – from a life of renunciation. There is not much point in steering clear of sexual involvements if you are unable to find pleasure anywhere else. If you find your spiritual practice a difficult, painful struggle, and your only enjoyments are crude, sensual ones, you have a problem. A simple solution is to find enjoyment in meditation. Don't take pride in undertaking marathon sessions for their own sake. A twenty-minute meditation that you enjoy is better than an hour's meditation that you do only because it is supposed to be good for you. Look for a natural momentum to take you deeper, beyond the imposed discipline that may have been necessary at the beginning. Broaden the scope of your interests to include innocent recreations that you can share with friends, especially spiritual friends. Let at least some of the skilful things you do be enjoyable. A Buddhist should be a walking paradox in the eyes of the world: he or she should be obviously happy, even in the absence of financial security, social status, luxury consumer goods, or a sexual relationship – all of which are commonly regarded as being essential to human happiness. The sight of such a person would make people wonder, 'How can this be? Perhaps my ideas about life are not the whole story.' It is what a Buddhist is that speaks to people, far more than clever presentations of Buddhist doctrine. It is where you look for your happiness and satisfaction, much more than what you talk about, that tells people who you really are and what you stand for.

Try bringing an aesthetically appreciative, rather than a utilitarian, attitude to your experience. Obviously we shouldn't just make use of others. We should try to shake off the attitude that sees attractive people, for example, as being simply objects of desire, underlying which is a view of people and the world around us as having value only as they contribute to our own enjoyment or advantage. The aesthetic attitude is one that sees everything, including other people, with a warm and clear awareness, and appreciates things just as they are, without thinking how they could be improved or put to some use. It is akin to the contemplative attitude of resting in pure awareness, without experiencing either desire or aversion. This certainly requires mindfulness, but it is a practice that will reduce the pressure of craving, and leave you feeling more at ease.

4
SKILFUL SPEECH

> Refraining completely from false,
> Divisive, harsh, and senseless speech. (8)

Abstention from false speech is the only speech precept in the traditional list of five precepts, the *pañcaśīla*. In the list of ten precepts, however, one of the *pañcaśīla* – abstaining from intoxicants – is left out, and replaced with three further speech precepts and three 'mind-training' precepts whose practice requires an additional level of awareness. These are ethical guidelines for Buddhists who wish to undertake a serious, 'full-time' practice of the Dharma. The emphasis on speech is very significant. In the West, the traditional division of our nature is mind and body, or body, soul, and spirit. In Buddhism the division is into body, speech, and mind, according to which analysis our capacity to communicate ourselves is accorded an equal place with our physical being and our inner experience.

As Buddhists, when we bow before a Buddha image, we do so by joining our hands and touching our forehead, throat, and chest in succession, in this way connecting with the psychophysical energy centres or chakras at those points which, according to the Tantric tradition, are associated with, respectively, body, speech, and mind. In doing this, we are symbolically offering the whole of ourselves to the ideal of Enlightenment, as represented by the Buddha, without holding anything back. Speech brings together head and heart, intellect and emotion, body and mind, and, of course, self and other.

The speech precepts are not just about being truthful. One's speech should also be kindly and helpful and it should bring about harmony rather than being harsh, senseless, or divisive. These four speech precepts reflect four progressive levels of human communication. First, there is the level of simple truthfulness, of abstention from false speech, *musāvāda*. Next, there is the level of kindly or affectionate speech, of abstention from harsh speech, *pharusavācā*. This involves being aware to whom one is speaking and being aware of their response. It should, after all, be possible to express oneself freely and cogently while at the same time considering the feelings of whoever one is addressing.

As a baby, one knows one's mother only as a wonderful sensation of warmth and comfort, security and well-being; one is not aware of her as a person. When grown up, one often knows people in much the same way, but refined and rationalized. This is one of the reasons why there are so many misunderstandings between people. Much 'communication' is pseudo-communication – communication between mutual projections. But speaking with affection is an attempt to communicate with a genuine awareness of the other person, quite apart from what they might be able to do for one physically, materially, or emotionally. Abstaining from harsh speech in the course of a debate requires extra mindfulness because it is very easy to get carried away, especially if one is very articulate. Some people get more and more heated about increasingly remote aspects of the original issue, until, in the end, they are just sounding off, having entirely lost sight of the existence of the other participants and forgotten the context of the discussion.

The third level of communication is that of meaningful and helpful speech, which is the positive counterpart of the precept of abstention from senseless speech, *samphappalāpavācā*. Most people think that senseless or frivolous speech is relatively harmless. Those with no desire to become more aware will probably be quite happy talking trivialities for the rest of their lives. If you become more mindful, though, you will notice that while a little small talk oils the wheels of communication, a whole session of it can be quite draining. This is because, while part of you is caught up in the banter, the more serious part of you is frustrated. You feel that you have betrayed your better self, and the resulting sense of conflict will be draining. This is not to say that you need to be talking about the Dharma morning, noon, and night, but that at the very least, you should abstain from spending too much time on small talk. Aim to make sure that whatever you say is meaningful and helpful.

The fourth level of communication is that of bringing about harmony between people, the positive counterpart of abstention from divisive speech, known as *pisuṇavāca*. This does not mean avoiding disagreement at all costs. It means speech that transcends selfhood, speech that leaves behind self-interest and helps to bring about a happier and more peaceful community. Between two or more people, the harmonious communication may culminate, eventually, in silence – a rich and living silence in which there is a common experience of self-transcendence. To develop this level of communication one can begin by cultivating an awareness of a deeper and more authentic level of being in the other person, particularly in a spiritual friend, and most importantly in one's spiritual teacher. Try to contact the real person behind the physical form, behind the words, and relate to what is deepest – or highest – in them. The fullest experience of harmonious speech takes place only between Enlightened human beings, between whom there is no barrier of selfhood.

THE PATH OF TRUTH

> Just as by themselves the true words
> Of kings generate firm trust,
> So their false words are the best means
> To create distrust.
>
> What is not deceitful is the truth;
> It is not an intentional fabrication.
> What is solely helpful to others is the truth.
> The opposite is falsehood since it does not help. (134–5)

Ideally, a democratic government would tell the electorate the truth, but there are a number of reasons why this does not always happen. First of all, in a complex political or economic situation the truth is rarely obvious. Even if all the facts are known, they do not necessarily tell you what is really going on. What you take to be the truth of the matter will differ from what others take to be the truth, and you will need to bear in mind the limitations of your own point of view.

Secondly, people do not necessarily want to be told the truth, and politicians often have to tell the public what it likes to hear in order to win popularity. For example, people prefer a politician who claims to be in control of events rather than one who admits to being at a loss – which is perhaps understandable.

Thirdly, in a democracy politicians band together to win elections and then stay in power. They therefore have to put their party first, sometimes at the expense of their own conscience. They are obliged to toe the party line, to subordinate their own view of the truth of a situation to the collective interest of the party to which they belong. What politicians probably tell themselves is that paltering with the truth is the price that has to be paid if they are to do all the good things they have promised to do in their manifesto. It is a grubby expedience for the sake of achieving worthy ends.

But such rationalizations are not convincing. The first aim of a politician should be to deserve people's trust, for once trust has been lost it is irretrievable. What the public does not realize is that it asks, in effect, for untrustworthy politicians. It votes for people who are plausible, and who will tell it reassuring untruths. It is only when there is a crisis that the general public insists on knowing the truth, and by then it is often too late. If you begin by telling the truth and go on telling it, you might have to spend a long time in the wilderness and not be believed in your own lifetime. But at least people will trust you to speak the truth as you see it, however unpalatable they might find it.

The choice between truth and reassurance is often a hard one to make, but it is one that the spiritual life, at bottom, is all about. The spiritual life is a matter of seeking the truth and learning to live by it, whatever the cost. It is much easier to criticize others, especially politicians, than it is to conduct our own affairs in accordance with our professed Buddhist values. Speaking the truth begins at home. As Buddhists, our first duty, in our capacity as citizens, is to be straightforward and honest in all our dealings. Preaching comes a long way after that.

In saying that the truth is that which is helpful, Nāgārjuna is suggesting that truth is something more than simple facts. Truth is not a thing to be dumped on people. It is a truthful *communication*. Truth is non-deception in action. Facts can be known in a coldly objective way, but knowing the truth involves appreciating what those facts mean for people, and how they connect with them. The time has to be right, the other person has to be receptive, and we ourselves have to be in a positive, kindly frame of mind. If the other person misunderstands what we have said or takes unreasonable offence, then we cannot really be said to have 'spoken the truth' in the full sense.

But even when speaking the truth causes pain, we have at some point to work our way round to it. We cannot indefinitely put off the day we actually speak the truth, the day we say what we really think. Let us be gentle and sensitive, certainly, and tactful if we can be so, but in the long run it is only the truth that is going to help people, not a pleasant falsehood.

The way to cultivate truthful speech varies from one person to another. The person who is liable to blurt out the truth without thinking, who talks first and thinks later, will have to learn to turn things over in their mind, while someone who is inhibited and tends to keep things back will need to be less fearful, less self-censoring.

The idea that speech should be helpful implies that truth may be subordinate to the principle of 'skilful means'. The classic example of this is the parable of the burning house in the *Lotus Sūtra*.[218] A father wants to get all his numerous children out of the house when it is engulfed by flames, so he tells them he has various toy carts for them, and that these are waiting outside. The children run out of the house in wild excitement to find they have been deceived. The carts they hoped for are not there. But their father goes on to give each of them a far bigger and better cart than they could have imagined in their wildest dreams. The father represents the Buddha, of course, and the burning house represents *saṃsāra*, the world wherein human beings are engrossed in their various 'games'. The question is, how far should we take this story as a model for the communication of the Dharma?

First of all, the story should not be taken literally. It is a parable. It is not an account of how a teacher gets people practising the Dharma by telling them tall stories; it is about a father doing whatever was necessary in a life-or-death situation. We should be careful to be as open and direct as we can in our communication of the Dharma and not induce people to practise it by promising them worldly benefits of one kind or another as a result of their efforts. Even if they are expected subsequently to discover for themselves the limitations of those benefits as compared with the spiritual rewards of practising the Dharma, the fact is that they will have been deceived. The deception does not relate to the material benefits, which may well follow, but concerns the nature of the transformation brought about by the practice of the Dharma, which is essentially a transformation of the mind, not one's material fortunes. Though we may indeed gain a measure of worldly happiness through our practice of the Dharma, that happiness should be less important to us than growth in our understanding of the Dharma.

Thus the parable of the burning house needs to be interpreted carefully.[219] Higher spiritual experience is always going to be more than we can anticipate theoretically. It will always exceed our expectations. Reality is always infinitely greater than any description of it, and any description will, to that extent, be misleading. When you attain Nirvāṇa, is it going to be what you thought it would be? Of course not. But has the Buddha deceived you? No. It is just that you needed to be told something about it, even if what you were told was so utterly inadequate to the reality as to be, from the point of view of Nirvāṇa itself, a complete misrepresentation. When the father promises toys to his children, he is being as truthful as he can. One could say that the cart he finally gives each of them is the same as the little carts he promised, but on an infinitely grander scale.

Much the same thing happens in the course of ordinary life. When you grow up, when you marry and have a child, are these events anything like what you originally envisaged? Almost certainly not. The same goes for when you receive Buddhist ordination, or when you yourself ordain someone. But were you deceived when you were told what to expect? No. All these events represent a breakthrough that could not be understood in terms of any previous experience. On its own much higher level, Nirvāṇa resembles such breakthroughs. In the end, you can speak the truth in abstract conceptual terms only to someone who knows it already – which means that it is not really a communication. We might therefore say that the truth is that which produces positive results, or which leads one in a positive direction.

Returning to the first of the four speech precepts, abstention from false speech, we may say that it requires, as do the other precepts, that we pay attention to the subtle ways in which we evade their spirit. For example, we sometimes confuse objective facts with our subjective interpretation of those facts without being aware that in so doing we are misrepresenting them. Underlying this tendency is the assumption that our view of things is the correct one, an assumption that simply reinforces our confusion. If we are unable to accept that our perceptions are conditioned by our confused views and by our assumptions generally, we preclude the possibility of our ever changing our view.

False speech often hides behind jargon. Instead of saying, for example, 'He's not being open with me,' or 'I'm afraid she isn't very receptive,' it might be more honest for one to say, 'He (or she) does not agree with me.' A failure to accept one's point of view *might* be because of a lack of openness or receptivity, but on the other hand it might be due to a genuine disagreement, to the fact that the other person thinks differently. We must be careful not to evaluate when we should simply be describing. To assert that somebody is not being open can be a dishonest way of winning the argument and shows a lack of understanding of what openness really means. Being open does not necessarily mean agreeing. Someone can be very receptive to what you say and sincerely try to understand your point of view but, in the end, disagree with you. Conversely, someone might not really be open to you at all, but might agree with you out of politeness.

Obviously you want the other person to agree with you, but if they refuse to do so, it simply means that you have been unable to convince them. To misrepresent them by saying – to take another example – 'I got a very negative response,' amounts to false speech. Did the other person fly into a temper and hit you over the head with a chair, or did they simply disagree with you? The danger of using psycho-spiritual jargon, like 'openness', 'receptivity', 'commitment', is that while our intention may be to use it to evaluate our mental states and cultivate positive ones, it can also be used in such a way as to put in the wrong someone who really does aspire to be open, receptive, and so on. As well as manipulating language, such jargon manipulates other people. It can be a kind of emotional blackmail, as if one was to say, 'You want to be committed, open, and receptive. So why not agree with me?' Such jargon represents an extra layer of false speech for us to deal with. When someone says, 'I'm sorry, I can't help you on this occasion,' do you find yourself saying they are unwilling to cooperate? Or do you report what they actually said, even though you might feel disappointed with their attitude and suspect they are being deliberately uncooperative? Other examples of psycho-spiritual jargon include 'rationalization' and 'projection'. We know that these complex self-deluding processes do take place, and that they sometimes need to be taken into consideration, and this is what gives words of this kind their edge when they are used in an accusatory manner. The golden rule is to point out the possibly unconscious basis of what another person says or does only privately and tentatively. Say, 'It may be my imagination, and I may be completely wrong, but this is what I think. At least give it some thought.' Motives can indeed be questioned, but one should not try to rebut someone's argument simply by questioning their motives, and certainly not by questioning allegedly unconscious ones. If someone disagrees with you, it does not necessarily mean that there is something psychologically wrong with them.

At the root of the whole issue is the insistence that one's feelings about something should be accorded the kind of objective validity that one would not claim for one's thinking. Rather than say 'I think' or 'this is my impression', one says, 'I feel'. Someone might say, 'I feel that so-and-so is not very committed to the Dharma,' and another person might point out that he meditates for three hours a day, lives in a single-sex Buddhist community, works in a team-based right livelihood business, studies the Dharma regularly, and helps out around the local Buddhist centre. But then the first person looks very thoughtful and replies, 'That's true, but still my feeling is that he's not very committed.' Apparently, one is expected to give to that feeling the status of an objective, evidential fact about the person being discussed.

The confusion arises when it is assumed that another person's feelings cannot be questioned, because they are, *ipso facto*, only verifiable by them, whereas rational arguments can be challenged by anyone. If for an argument you substitute a feeling – especially an *intuitive* feeling – you thereby preclude the possibility of any rational discussion. For example, if you feel that someone's attitude towards you is very negative, the next question to arise is often not 'Where does this feeling of mine come from?' but 'Why does he have a negative attitude towards me?' If you go ahead and ask, 'Why do you have a negative attitude towards me?' and the poor fellow replies, 'Actually, I don't feel negative towards you,' you can then point out, helpfully, 'Your trouble is that you're not really in touch with your feelings.'

Arguing in an emotional way can be a variation on this kind of obfuscation of the truth. It usually has the virtue of being artless, though there is a classic example that is by no means artless: that of the clergyman who wrote in the margin of his sermon, 'Shout here – argument weak.' The emotional emphasis with which a person says something tells us nothing about the truth of that statement. It tells us only about the strength of the conviction with which it was made.

All this is part of the larger issue of false speech by default or *suppressio veri, suggestio falsi*: suppression of the truth, suggestion of falsehood. It might be appropriate to speculate about someone's motives, but subjective views should not be confused with objective facts. If you don't know the reason for someone's absence from an important meeting, for example, it would be false speech to remark, 'So-and-so is failing in his commitment tonight.' Underneath the layer of assumptions there will always be a layer of fact, and that layer of fact is what you must get down to, however uncertain it might leave you as to how to judge a person or a situation.

THE CONSEQUENCES OF UNSKILFUL SPEECH

> From lying arises slander.
> From divisiveness, a parting of friends.
> From harshness, hearing the unpleasant.
> From senselessness, one's speech is not respected. (15)

Speech is the area of activity in which much of our ethical practice takes place. It is the first – and often the only – outlet through which our thoughts and feelings find expression. Nāgārjuna's theme here is that when we speak unskilfully we do not, in fact, get what we hoped for. He is pointing out that when we try to secure some kind of advantage at someone else's expense by telling lies, we get a poor return.[220] The more calculating we are, the more we find that our sums just don't add up. So why then do we lie, for example? Lying often seems to be an easy way of getting the better of someone. But Nāgārjuna reminds us that the advantage will be short-lived. If we tell lies, we are relying on people taking our given word for the truth, and that kind of trust is a priceless asset. But sooner or later we will be found out, and our word will then be worth nothing, at least in some quarters. Moreover, telling lies creates an atmosphere of mistrust in which others may be afraid to speak the truth. When lies become the accepted currency of communication, truth becomes worthless. If, for example, we pass the blame for something we have done onto someone else, that person might feel they have the right to do the same in their turn. It is likely, therefore, that at some point we will be made to bear the blame for someone else's misdeeds. We don't have to wait for another life in order to experience the consequences of our own unskilful speech.

The same goes for the other forms of unskilful speech. They, too, seem to produce consequences (*karma vipāka*) quite promptly. By divisive speech is meant tittle-tattle, backbiting, malicious gossip, creating dissension and disharmony between people: basically, causing your friends and acquaintances to think worse of one another than they did before you opened your mouth. Maybe you repeat to one person what another person said about them, or you tell someone an amusing story that reveals something discreditable about a friend of theirs. In this way, you undermine trust and respect between people, and the result is that the dissension and disharmony you have created eventually engulfs you. If we have a criticism to make about someone, it is far better to make it to them directly. If we criticize others behind their backs, we might be surprised to find how often our criticism reaches the person criticized. We might not hear anything about the matter for a long time, but we can never be sure that we won't, and one day we might get a nasty shock, especially if the person in question turns out to have a perfectly good explanation for the conduct with which we have found fault. This can happen quite easily between friends, if they have the kind of relationship that skirts around difficult issues. If they air those issues with other people instead of the person concerned, the result is likely to be a falling out and even a parting.

In the case of harsh speech we often find our unskilfulness reflected back to us quite quickly. Its painful effect is felt immediately and we can therefore expect a swift reaction. We will at least create around us an unpleasant atmosphere, one that may even flare up into violence and that will not easily be calmed down. If we engage in harsh speech, it is as though we expect others to bear it patiently, and they will not always do this. People might do our bidding when we speak harshly, but they will give us a wide berth if they can.

The result of idle and useless talk is that what we say is not respected. If someone is in the habit of talking nonsense, perhaps to entertain or just to be noticed, in the end no one will take them seriously. Consequently, when they do talk seriously, they may not get the kind of attention they want. Other people will think, 'It's only so-and-so babbling away as usual', and turn a deaf ear. But we should, in fact, make a point of trying to take seriously even people who are in the habit of talking frivolously. We don't know whether someone is chattering foolishly to avoid meaningful talk or to compensate for not being listened to in the first place. Moreover, a licensed fool is rarely a complete fool, and like King Lear's fool, they might have things to say that no one else is prepared to point out.[221]

One of the results of breaking precepts, particularly ones we break frequently, like the speech precepts, is that people start giving us labels. Acquiring labels and labelling others can be useful from a practical point of view. If someone is habitually late for appointments, or is forgetful, or indeed is punctual or conscientious, it is useful to know this. But we have to be careful with labels, especially negative ones. Once they are applied they can be difficult to remove, even when they are no longer appropriate, as in the case of someone who turns over a new leaf. Labels should be provisional, and it is important both to challenge the labels we ourselves are given and to question those we bestow on others. Otherwise we are likely to have a closed attitude to the people we meet, and thus to block both our own development and theirs. Parents are particularly prone to see their grown-up offspring in this fixed way, wanting to see them just as they were when young. As a result, the offspring can find themselves reverting to their teenage selves whenever they go home on a visit.

But we all have a tendency to burden others with our judgements, even to the extent of labelling them for life. Our fixed view of ourselves and of the world is based largely on our habit of stereotyping. For example, if someone is known for their rough tongue and bad temper, even if they are making a determined effort to be patient, we may not let go of our view of them. 'Maybe he's not showing it,' we might concede, sceptically, 'but he's clearly still very angry underneath.' If someone's efforts to change are not appreciated because of such cynicism, they might decide that it isn't worth trying, and revert to type. The same goes for the idle chatterer, or someone seen as lazy or irresponsible. Once they have a label, they may be stuck with it for life, unless they move somewhere else and make a fresh start. However, once you are determined to change, some labels can quite easily be removed. If you have a reputation for meanness, say, you can quite easily change people's perception of you by being so generous that they are sure to notice. If you tend to be late you can make a point of always being punctual, and people will get the message sooner or later. Some labels of course are much harder to remove.

One of the functions of the spiritual community is to encourage people to change. That is, we should try to see other people as individuals. An individual, a true individual, cannot easily be labelled or categorized. Ultimately, such an individual becomes free of labels altogether: people may try to label him or her, but their labels will not stick. This possibility has to be nurtured by a culture that does not feed our human tendency to label people. When we meet them, especially members of the spiritual community, it should be as though we met them for the first time, rather than seeing them on the basis of how we saw them in the past. Usually we don't know what conditions brought about our impressions of them, whether our own prejudices or the context in which we first met them. If we have only met them once before, we might have caught them at an uncharacteristic moment. Ideally, even in the case of an old friend, we should feel that we do not really know who we are now meeting. That attitude of openness in itself can make it possible for them to change.

HEARING THE TRUTH

> Wisdom and practice always grow
> For one who keeps company
> With those who speak advisedly,
> Who are pure, and who have unstained wisdom and compassion.
>
> Rare are helpful speakers,
> Listeners are very rare,
> But rarer still are those who act at once
> On words that though unpleasant are beneficial.
>
> Therefore having realized that though unpleasant
> It is helpful, act on it quickly,
> Just as to cure an illness one drinks
> Dreadful medicine from one who cares. (140–2)

Truth is relational: it depends partly (although only partly) upon who is hearing it. It follows that being able to hear the truth is just as important as being able to tell it. In a sense, they are different aspects of the same ethical practice. Nāgārjuna points out that people who can listen to beneficial speech are rarer than those who are able to speak it. This is obvious, really, because it is easier to see the truth about other people than it is to see the truth about oneself, even if another is very ready to tell us about it. We tend to resist the truth about ourselves, even pleasant truth sometimes. As for helpful but unpleasant 'home truths', it is certainly easier for most people to give someone else such bitter medicine than to swallow it themselves.

If an attempt to communicate was not a success and we find ourselves saying, 'I was only trying to be helpful,' it may be that the other person was not receptive, but alternatively it may be that we simply misunderstood them. It is difficult both to see the truth about someone and to communicate it to them in such a way that they can receive it. Above all, we need to be sure that we have their true welfare at heart, and that we are not simply speaking out of frustration or irritation. We can easily deceive ourselves in this regard. It is important that we communicate love and kindness, and affectionate concern for the other person's well-being, as well as communicating the helpful truth. If you have, or can develop, the ability to hear truths that are difficult to accept, this is a great quality, especially in a leader. If you are able to put aside your immediate emotional reactions and rationalizations, you should take the medicine quickly – that is, accept the unpleasant truth and act upon it at once. It is easier to respond positively when you have known the person giving you the unwelcome information for some time. When they have demonstrated their affection for you time and time again over a number of years, you know that they can be trusted to have your welfare at heart, even if they speak rather bluntly

5
THE ETHICS OF VIEWS

> Thoroughly forsaking covetousness, harmful intent,
> And the views of Nihilists – (9)

This is Nāgārjuna's succinct reference to the three 'mind precepts': undertaking to abstain from covetousness, animosity, and false views. Covetousness and animosity in their various forms are discussed in the next chapter, so here we will concentrate for the most part on what it means to abstain from false views.

ETERNALISM AND NIHILISM

It might seem that 'the views of Nihilists' belong to a completely different category of mental experience from covetousness and harmful intent, but for Buddhism there is a crucial connection between emotions and views, between negative emotions and spiritual ignorance. We feel the way we do because of the way we see things, and we see things the way we do because of the way we feel about them. Nihilism, for example, is ultimately connected with hatred, while its opposite, eternalism, is connected with craving.

Nihilism translates the Sanskrit term *ucchedavāda*, which literally means the 'ism' of 'cutting off'. This is the view that at death one is cut off completely, that there is no psychic or mental element that survives the dissolution of the body. One could call it annihilationism.

The opposite view, that of eternalism, maintains that one possesses an unchanging psychic essence, a permanent self or soul that exists independently of the body and continues to exist after death. Buddhism does not take either of these positions, but understands consciousness to be a stream, a flow of ever-changing mental events that continues from life to life, linking with one body after another, though not as a *thing* or entity that could be said to transmigrate or reincarnate. This is why Buddhism speaks of 'rebirth' or 'rebecoming' rather than of 'reincarnation'.

These two views seem to be intrinsic to the way the unenlightened mind sees things. Take, for example, Nirvāṇa, the ultimate goal of the Buddhist spiritual life. Because the term literally means 'blowing out (as of a flame)', it is easy to take a nihilistic view of it, to think of it as a 'state' of non-existence into which one disappears upon gaining Enlightenment. On the other hand, if Nirvāṇa is thought of as a kind of heaven in which one continues to exist after achieving Enlightenment, albeit in a subtle and sublimated form, one is labouring under a delusion of the eternalist kind. The truth is that Enlightenment transcends both these views. It is indescribable in terms of being or non-being, existence or non-existence, life or death. It is unclassifiable, belonging to no category of thought whatsoever. One can say neither that the self is annihilated, nor that it continues to exist. Nirvāṇa does not exist as we understand existence; neither does it not exist; nor is it anything in between.

An ancient eternalist wrong view, put forward in the Buddha's day by a teacher called Makkhali Gosāla, is that there are just 1,406,600 different kinds of life to be lived, and that after passing through all of these and thus exhausting all the possibilities of existence, one automatically attains Nirvāṇa.[222] Certain 'New Age' views are similar to this. One is here on Earth to learn certain lessons from one's present existence before progressing to the next life and the next lesson. There is also the view that the 'Age of Aquarius', a sort of collective raising of human consciousness, is upon us. According to this view, we are to be carried away by a great wave of spiritual regeneration into the 'New Age', whether we like it or not.[223] The general idea is that spiritual evolution happens automatically, and that it is, in fact, inevitable.

The mistake that is common to these wrong views is their conflating of biological evolution and spiritual development. They all leave out the crucial element of individual decision. The increasingly complex development of life-forms over millions of years has brought us a long way, from single-celled amoeba right up to the human organism, but from now on, our development depends upon our own initiative, our own individual effort. If we sit back and wait for the Age of Aquarius to dawn, we shall have to wait a very long time. Buddhism itself may seem to promote this kind of eternalistic wrong view in its doctrine of the Pure Land.[224] However, the Pure Land comes into being as the result of a bodhisattva's determination to help 'the infinite number of beings inhabiting limitless space' by creating for them a situation in which the Dharma is more easily *practised*. There is never going to be a kind of spiritual welfare state. The goal for everyone is to be oneself a creator of a Pure Land, not an endless consumer of spiritual goodies.

Of these two evasions of reality, the Buddha singled out nihilism as representing the worst tendencies of spiritual ignorance. He was of the view that if you *had* to choose between eternalism, the belief that things have an unchanging essence, and nihilism, the belief that there is no such thing as karma and that death means extinction, eternalism would be the better option.[225] Eternalists at least have an affirmative attitude to life. They believe in something positive. For example, the eternalist view that there is an afterlife that lasts for ever may be unfounded, but it does at least provide a basis for consistent and constructive courses of action aimed at definite goals, besides instilling a sense of responsibility towards other people.

Nihilism runs very deep, and it is the underlying source of innumerable superficially plausible wrong views. The way in which one sees through it will depend upon what sort of nihilist you are, and how the nihilism has managed to get so firmly rooted in your mind. According to the Pāli scriptures, the Buddha linked eternalism with craving for existence and nihilism with craving for non-existence, or the longing for oblivion.[226] The eternalist position seems natural enough: if you are an eternalist your attachment to your own being is such that you will see yourself as continuing to exist after Enlightenment, more or less unchanged, but free from suffering. But what causes a person to crave for non-existence? The Buddha seems to have seen nihilism as a rationalization of self-hatred. Perhaps fearing what might happen after death, perhaps on 'Judgement Day', you prefer to live your life in the belief that it is all going to come to a full stop, that you won't have to put up with yourself for ever. Alternatively, it may be that you are simply weary of life and would not willingly undergo more of it under the painful terms that appear to be the only ones on offer. It may seem that existence consists of nothing but suffering and that there is no positive exit. Unfortunately, a negative experience of life tends to translate into a negative view of death and of anything that might come after it. If all you can imagine is a great reckoning and (perhaps literally) hell to pay in the next life, or more of the same dreadful experience that you have had already, you may well be drawn to embrace the idea that there is nothing after death. According to Buddhism, belief in nihilism leads to an unhappy rebirth, and it would certainly seem that a consciousness imbued with despair and a loathing for life would have this kind of result.

However, even if you do have a generally unhappy experience of life, there is no need to make it the basis for the kind of nihilistic outlook that will have a bad outcome in terms of *karma vipāka*. It is possible to separate a painful experience from an unskilful reaction. Indeed, much Buddhist practice consists in doing just this. For example, why should you not, instead, view death as a great 'wiping the slate clean' in which you can forget everything and start afresh? It may be that in the experience of death you will be able to forget the sufferings of your previous existence, in which case your natural desire for life and its enjoyments should emerge once more. On the strength of this great forgetting you will be able to start all over again. Previous lives, after all, must have brought you a fair share of suffering, but how much of it have you remembered? For most people, even the suffering endured long ago in their present life eventually loses its sting. Many things that seemed desperately important at the time are virtually forgotten in a few months or years, and surely this will be even more so in the case of a future existence. We will carry into it our karmic propensities, but not the circumstances in which they were originally formed.

These matters of life and death are not easy for any of us to deal with, regardless of whether we are eternalist or nihilist by temperament or by conviction. But we need to find a middle way, and here, the middle way is to appreciate life as much as we can but not hang on to it, and to appreciate death when it comes but neither long for it nor fear it.

In brief the view of nihilism
Is that effects of actions do not exist.
Without merit and leading to a bad state,
It is regarded as a 'wrong view'.

In brief the view of existence
Is that effects of actions exist.
Meritorious and conducive to happy transmigrations
It is regarded as a 'right view'.

Because existence and non-existence are extinguished by wisdom,
There is a passage beyond meritorious and ill deeds.
This, say the excellent, is liberation from
Bad transmigrations and happy transmigrations. (43–5)

Nihilism is the view that after death nothing of you remains, that the mind perishes with the body, that there is no rebirth, and that there is, therefore, no future karmic fruit of one's actions committed in the present life. This is of course a prevalent modern view, even among those who call themselves Buddhists. Nāgārjuna says here that wrong view, in this case nihilism, leads to low status, whereas right view, which as described here is a form of eternalism, which may include an eternalist view of Nirvāṇa, leads to high status. If you hold such an eternalist view, you are at least on the right track to an extent. But any position within the wheel of becoming – depicted symbolically by the Tibetan wheel of life – falls short of Enlightenment. *Nirvāṇa* is beyond both low and high status. It is freedom from the whole cycle, liberation from 'good' as well as 'bad' rebirth. So long as you remain within the wheel of becoming, you are a prisoner. Simply to be reclassified as a prisoner with special privileges is no answer to your basic problem. Right view leads to good rebirths; wrong view leads to bad rebirths; 'no view' leads to Nirvāṇa. Wisdom is a dynamic understanding of experience that sees things as process or flux. It is this wisdom that destroys the static view of 'is' and 'is not', and that provides us with a way beyond the ups as well as the downs of the wheel of becoming, beyond high status as well as low status.

Seeing production as caused
One passes beyond non-existence,
Seeing cessation as caused
One also does not assert existence. (46)

This is the basic Buddhist view that the things we experience in ourselves and the world around us exist in dependence upon conditions and cease when those conditions cease. The nature of the conditioned mind is such that we treat things as though they were absolutely real when in fact they consist in a temporary coming together of factors, both objective and subjective, that are themselves conditioned by other factors.

Seeing the coming into being of conditioned things, one is aware that they are produced by causes or conditions. In doing so, one sees through the nihilistic view that they arise without cause – that is, 'one passes beyond non-existence'. Seeing also the cessation of conditioned things, and understanding that this too is the product of causes or conditions, one no longer asserts their prior existence independent of causes.

Previously produced and simultaneously produced (causes)
Are non-causes; (thus) there are no causes in fact,
Because (such) production is not confirmed at all
As (existing) conventionally or in reality.

When this is, that arises,
Like short when there is long.
Due to the production of this, that is produced,
Like light from the production of a flame.

When there is long, there is short.
They do not exist through their own nature,
Just as due to the non-production
Of a flame, light also does not arise.

Having thus seen that effects arise
From causes, one asserts what appears
In the conventions of the world
And does not accept nihilism.

One who asserts, just as it is, cessation
That does not arise from conventions
Does not pass into (a view of) existence.
Thereby one not relying on duality is liberated. (47–51)

So here, while we are still in the realm of ethical practice, we are plunged deeper and deeper into the 'Perfection of Wisdom' of which Nāgārjuna was such a master. Here he is saying that if a cause appears before the effect, it cannot be a cause in itself – it becomes a cause only with the arrival of the effect. If, on the other hand, cause and effect arise at one and the same time, their relationship cannot be causal, because by definition causes must precede effects. A cause is essentially an idea, a way of connecting up what we insist on seeing as separate items and entities. The idea of a cause is dependent on the idea of an effect. A cause cannot exist as a cause before the effect that has made it a cause has itself come into existence. If the cause exists before the effect has come into existence, it is not yet a cause, only something that happens. On the other hand, when the effect has happened, the 'cause' cannot be a cause either. The effect has already taken place, so does not need a cause to bring it into being.[227]

In other words, once you start thinking of cause and effect as entities having real existence, you find yourself involved in all sorts of logical contradictions. But this is more than just a clever trick of logic. It repays serious reflection. Our ideas of cause and effect subtly determine the way in which we interpret experience even while we are experiencing it. The relations between things, and even the things themselves, are not by any means always what we assume them to be. By understanding cause as cause only in relation to effect, we start seeing through the view of things as entities having real existence and consequently become less attached to them. In this way we gradually let go of 'a view of existence', that is, the idea of something or someone actually existing. In terms of ultimate reality, there is not even any coming into being or any ceasing to be. These ideas also are the result of limited ways of thinking. There is not some pre-existing 'thing' that is produced, nor any 'thing' that ceases to exist. Nāgārjuna rejects that entire static and rigid way of thinking, turning it upon itself to expose its invalidity.

In getting rid of the idea of a world of fixed entities, we enlist the help of the ideas of process, conditionality, even cause and effect. If, however, we come to regard these ideas as representing actual entities, we are simply repeating the same mistake on another level. Nāgārjuna is saying that cause and effect are relative terms: you cannot think of cause without effect, or effect without cause, just as you cannot think of long without short or short without long. Long is only long in comparison with short.

This warning against the mind's tendency to reify, to refer to processes as if they were things, parallels the Mahāyāna critique of a certain Hīnayāna interpretation of the Abhidharma. The Abhidharma took the idea of the *pudgala* or 'person' and broke it down into smaller elements known as *dharmas*. These *dharmas* were really a way of naming constituent processes within the overall 'being' of the person, but some of the Abhidharma scholastics tended to invest *dharmas* themselves with the same sort of reality that, in the case of the *pudgala*, they had used the *dharmas* to deny.[228] There is little use in exorcising the idea of a person or a thing with the concept of process if that process is itself thought of as consisting of a succession of self-existent things. More than this, it is potentially harmful. To deny the existence of a 'self' while offering a world of self-existent entities is simply alienating, without that denial having any effect upon the deep-seated delusion of selfhood.

Nāgārjuna's tactic throughout this section is to chip away at the idea of the self as something that really exists. He is giving the ego a hammering while at the same time denying that the object of his attack really exists. However, there is an inherent difficulty with this approach. The issue is one of the nature of concepts and how one employs them. In speaking of something whose existence one is endeavouring to disprove, one can end up strengthening, at a deeper, unconscious level, the sense of that thing as really existing.

Reification, or making things of processes, runs deep in the way we see ourselves and the world. We talk about someone having 'a problem with anger' or 'concentration difficulties' when in fact that person is just habitually angry or habitually inattentive. One who needs to change how they behave does not have something actually there to deal with called 'anger' or 'selfishness'. These are just words for ways in which energy is deployed. Anger occurs when energy is used in an unskilful way, whereas compassion or *mettā* occurs when energy is able to arise in skilful ways. Buddhism encourages us to think in terms of process or action, not in terms of things, objects, or entities. A person is not a living entity, a person is just living. Any word used as a noun apparently refers to a thing. Words check the flow of experience, chopping it up into a series of material objects and mental states. This in turn places limits on what we are able to experience: language conditions experience. No doubt in its earliest, primitive phase, language subserved practical needs: 'Let's go and hunt,' 'Throw your spear,' 'Bring me that stone.' But when it comes to the communication of spiritual truths, the language of particular terms, attached to particular things, is simply unequal to the task. We have to learn to use language against the grain of its original purpose, which was to tie things down. We have to use words to release the world of our named experience from the bonds that words themselves have forged. As T. S. Eliot says, in 'East Coker',

> Because one has only learnt to get the better of words
> For the thing one no longer has to say,... [229]

However, once we have realized that the terms we use refer to relative, conditioned processes, they can be put to effective use in helping us deal with the world, for useful they undoubtedly are, as Nagarjuna goes on to point out. Notwithstanding the fact that 'cause' and 'effect' are provisional terms, and inadequate to describe what is really going on, we should nonetheless assert the conventional truth that they represent. Only if we take our stand upon this provisional truth and reject nihilism can we realize the absolute truth, asserting as true what 'does not arise from conventions'.

Nāgārjuna goes on to reinforce his central point with additional arguments, apparently deployed in order to meet various objections and referring, at least by implication, to various contemporary schools of thought, both Buddhist and non-Buddhist. The modern reader does not need to get bogged down in the details of these debates, as long as he or she bears in mind the central point: that the idea of a self is a fiction obscuring awareness of reality.

EMPTINESS AS TRANSCENDING NIHILISM AND ETERNALISM

> One who conceives of the mirage-like world
> That it does or does not exist
> Is consequently ignorant.
> When there is ignorance, one is not liberated.

A follower of non-existence goes to bad transmigrations,
And a follower of existence goes to happy transmigrations.
Through correct and true knowledge
One does not rely on dualism and becomes liberated. (56–7)

For Nāgārjuna, a nihilist is one who believes that the mirage-like world does not really exist. He or she operates from a profoundly negative standpoint, refusing to accept that things are causally connected, arising in dependence upon definite conditions, and disappearing when those conditions are removed. Without this kind of connection the world has no sense or meaning, and spiritual practice becomes pointless. Nihilism is the philosophical expression of an attitude of aversion to the world. Aversion does, however, rely upon the existence of the thing that is disliked. If one hates the world so utterly as to deny its very existence, in the sense of regarding its operations as morally meaningless and life as ultimately futile, one is in fact asserting its existence quite strongly.

It is this negative attitude that will lead to bad transmigrations, in other words to rebirth in unhappy realms. At root there is an unwillingness to engage with the world on its own terms. Denying its very existence leaves us free to do whatever we like. A nihilist does not believe that unskilful actions result in suffering, and it is this that makes nihilism so dangerous both to the individual and to society. The problem with nihilism is that, like other forms of negativity, it can present itself in pseudo-spiritual guise – like the view that 'all is one' and that, morally speaking, there is no difference between right and wrong. A person who is by temperament nihilistic may even be attracted to Buddhism by the idea of destroying the self or ego. But self-hatred or self-denial, far from helping one to overcome or see through the self, may actually reinforce one's deluded emotional investment in it.

The 'follower of existence', on the other hand, is an eternalist. Such a person believes that the world is no less real than it appears to be, that life has a meaning, and that other worlds, like heaven and hell, are also real. In consequence of this view, that person takes the way he or she lives in this world seriously, and tends to be ethically scrupulous. If the mental attitude of the nihilist is characterized by hatred, that of the eternalist is marked by attachment.

Attachment is by no means a positive mental state, but it is a step up from nihilism. You will not find liberation as an eternalist; you will continue to experience further rebirths, but the belief that the world really does exist, and that you can grasp things, and even keep hold of them, will tend to make those rebirths happy ones. It is better to be a relatively well-adjusted, forward-looking, ethical person, albeit with strong worldly attachments, than to be a critical, carping, sour, disillusioned, and world-rejecting cynical one. From the spiritual point of view, a healthy acceptance of the mundane is a more promising foundation for future spiritual development than is a complete rejection of life as it presents itself, even if that rejection comes armed with 'Buddhist' credentials.

Liberation, however, is something different from those two views. Enlightenment is an awakening from the view either that the mirage-like world is existent or that it is non-existent. One cannot say of a mirage that it exists in the sense of being absolutely real, nor can one say that it does not exist at all, since it is perceived. The same is true of the world. In this way, one goes beyond dualism.

SELF-MORTIFICATION AND ASCETIC TRAINING

> Practice is not done by just
> Mortifying the body,
> For one has not forsaken injuring others
> And is not helping others.
>
> Those not esteeming the great path of excellent doctrine
> Bright with giving, ethics, and patience,
> Afflict their bodies, taking
> An aberrant path like a cow path (deceiving oneself and those following).
>
> Their bodies embraced by the vicious snakes
> Of the afflictive emotions, they enter for a long time
> The dreadful jungle of cyclic existence
> Among the trees of endless beings. (11–13)

Mortifying the body is an expression of the wrong view of nihilism. It arises from the association of the spiritual life with suffering, from the idea that pain does one good, and that suffering is the great purifier. The rationale underpinning this practice is that by mortifying the flesh one is able to bring bodily desires and instincts under control, and that by treating the body with aversion one distances oneself from it and ceases to identify with it. In reality, however, self-mortification succeeds only in placing the body as much at the centre of attention as does extreme sensual self-indulgence.

This mistaken rationale is understandable, given the central importance in Buddhism of the concept of *duḥkha*, suffering or unsatisfactoriness. But another way of looking at the Buddha's teaching about *duḥkha* is to reflect that he is simply reminding us that there is no point in imagining that discomfort and suffering can be avoided altogether. When they are unavoidable, one will best endure them if one does so with cheerful equanimity, rather than by trying to deny their existence, or seeking to distract oneself. The Buddha made it clear that the spiritual life is not necessarily a painful one. One type of disciple, he says, does indeed struggle all through their career: they never have an easy time. Another type has trouble to begin with but finds their practice more enjoyable as they go on. A third type begins practising with ease but runs into difficulties later. And there is a final type whose spiritual life starts off pleasantly and continues to be pleasant all the way through.[230]

The issue is not quite so clear cut as it appears. For one thing, there is a disparity between the pleasant conditions that the ordinary person needs in order to enjoy a pleasant existence, and the often spartan conditions within which the spiritual practitioner is able to feel happy and joyful. One's experience of the spiritual life might be happy and inspired while appearing difficult and painful to people who have no wish to live that kind of life. Looking at those conditions from the outside, the ordinary person naturally imagines that the spiritual life must be tough and pretty joyless, and that any rewards were being paid for in advance with suffering. But the practitioner might well be experiencing inner contentment and joy, regardless of the external conditions.

The fact is that at certain key points in one's spiritual life there will probably be a degree of discomfort, not least because having to undo long-established habits of body, speech, and mind goes against the grain of human nature. But as one goes on, one's experience should become ever more joyful, whatever discomfort or difficult circumstances might be encountered. In any case, the experience of discomfort and suffering does not in itself signify that anything of a truly spiritual nature is happening. In my early days in England, after my return from India, I found this misapprehension rife among certain practitioners of Zen and so-called '*vipassanā*' meditation. Basically, they were punishing themselves and calling it Buddhism. The chief benchmark they used to determine their progress was the degree of mental and physical suffering they had experienced in connection with meditation. To judge by his oddly gloating manner, the monk who had instructed them in '*vipassanā*' before my arrival seemed to relish their sufferings as much as they did themselves. When one of his disciples told me that I was not at all like him, I felt the remark was not really meant as a compliment. It was with a certain wistful admiration that she went on, 'He was a real sadist.'[231]

It is understandable that people should go awry in this way, because many in the West tend to confuse an unhealthy desire for self-mortification, based on feelings of guilt, self-hatred, and self-contempt, with a healthy appreciation of the need for self-discipline. The word asceticism comes from the Greek word *askesis* which means simply 'training'. Just as the athlete trains the body, so the spiritual practitioner trains the mind. This is quite different from self-mortification, though it must be admitted that much of what passes for self-discipline is in fact neurotic self-mortification. It seems that we often find it easier to punish ourselves than to apply true self-discipline. We are happy to indulge ourselves, and we are happy to punish ourselves, but the middle way of self-discipline and spiritual training we find almost impossible to follow. This is partly because much of what is really simple self-discipline we tend to think of as a form of self-mortification. A person who eats meat, for example, is likely to regard giving it up as an act of self-denial rather than as a part of training. The situation is further confused by the way occasional pleasures so easily turn into regular indulgences and even become indispensable in the end. Accustomed as we are to our comfortable beds, we would find making do with a mattress on the floor a real hardship. But for many people in the world who are used to sleeping on a mat on the ground, a mattress would be the height of luxury. The truth is that almost everyone in the West today enjoys a level of luxury and comfort that would not have been within the reach of even the wealthiest a few hundred years ago.

Training is therefore a question of loosening the ties that bind us to whatever comforts we have got used to, doing without them from time to time, and, most important of all, doing so cheerfully. A footballer is happy to train for six hours a day, a concert pianist to practise for eight hours a day. They are not punishing themselves. They are doing the training in order to achieve their particular objective. That is all. For the spiritual ascetic it is no different. If you want to help your team score goals – in the spiritual life as much as on the football pitch – you have to put in the training.

Nāgārjuna puts his finger on the nub of the matter when he points out that self-mortification is useless as regards the broad aims of the spiritual life. In putting energy into afflicting the body we are signalling our lack of interest in any real spiritual endeavour, and Nāgārjuna goes on to specify what it is that, at the most basic level of Mahāyāna endeavour, we are choosing not to practise: the first three perfections – giving, ethics, and patience. It is our failure to appreciate the positive nature of the spiritual path that allows us to adopt this harmful and useless approach. Far from leading to liberation, self-mortification only binds us more tightly to conditioned existence. By punishing yourself for your indulgences, you become more deeply attached to them. I should add that tormenting oneself mentally is a modern variation of this. If in your attempts to live a spiritual life you become anxious, make yourself wretched, and insist on working yourself into a state of exhaustion, something has clearly gone wrong. It is unfortunately not uncommon for people to use their idea of the spiritual life, unconsciously and compulsively, as a means of giving themselves or others a hard time. You don't really know you're doing it, or why you're doing it, but you can't help looking for suffering of some kind, even from the Dharma, which is the means of putting an end to anguish. If you do this, if you deliberately invite suffering in the context of your spiritual life in one way or another, then your spiritual life isn't really functioning as a means of liberation.

Self-hatred can be difficult to dislodge if it stems from childhood experiences. Those from whom we learn about ourselves and the world in our early years pass on to us, knowingly or unknowingly, attitudes that we imbibe with our mother's milk, so to speak. At that early stage in our development, we do not question those attitudes, and consequently we take them in deeply, so deeply that they sometimes stay with us for the rest of our lives. If we were given the message that we were inadequate or bad, in any situation later in life where things do not turn out as we would have liked, we naturally assume that this is owing to our inadequacy or our wickedness, because that was how we were taught to interpret any unpleasant experience.

If you are a person with this kind of mentality, you might imagine that you were leading a balanced spiritual life even though, at the same time, you were rejecting such practices as the *mettā bhāvanā* as being 'too positive'. Presented with the sort of practice that would do you the most good, you will object that you just can't get on with it, it doesn't suit your particular needs. This is where you need spiritual friends, because it is inevitable that your deepest compulsions are going to resist the change which, consciously, you are trying to make. That resistance will cunningly co-opt your spiritual efforts for its own purposes and use them to establish itself even more firmly if friends are not on hand to support a more helpful pattern of practice.

MINDFULNESS AND INTOXICATION

> Not drinking intoxicants ... (10)

There is of course a much more down-to-earth aspect of ethical practice in relation to the mind. In the *Precious Garland*, having listed the ten precepts, Nāgārjuna raises an issue that has become a major social problem these days, at least in some countries: drink. To which we can add the closely related issue of drugs. There is a clear analogy here with sex, in that sex, like drink and drugs, can be addictive, though one form of intoxication is purely psychological whereas the other is both psychological and chemical.

The Buddhist tradition rules out indulgence in intoxicating substances altogether. The last of the five ethical precepts taken by Buddhists refers to this. However, the fact that in the list of the ten precepts this fifth precept is replaced by extra speech and mind-training precepts suggests that the latter is meant more as a safeguard against any loss of mindfulness and awareness. It may be that we can take a slightly more liberal attitude towards intoxicants, so long as we can see some real benefit in doing so. The question is basically one of mindfulness, and mindfulness involves above all being aware of one's thoughts and emotions.

A rather deliberate, cool, and formal manner is sometimes taken as a sign of mindfulness, whereas in fact true mindfulness is relaxed and emotionally warm, even expansive. As it is difficult to be truly mindful when one is tense or self-conscious, there may be situations in which a glass of wine will promote relaxation. I found this to be the case in the early days of the Friends of the Western Buddhist Order, when from time to time I invited a few people round for a meal. A bottle of wine would loosen up the painfully stiff, inhibited atmosphere that sometimes prevailed on these occasions. Clearly such tactics are only a means to an end, and they should not be allowed to become a habit, and although a glass of wine may help, it does not follow that three or four glasses will help even more.

Drinking alcohol eventually leads to mental confusion, so one can only conclude that people who drink regularly *desire* such confusion. They fear clarity and some even long for oblivion. They drink to forget, at least to forget themselves, to take the sharp edge off painful feelings, to relieve pressure. And it works up to a point, at least temporarily. Thus begins the downward spiral of addiction. We therefore have to address our emotional needs somewhere other than at the bottom of a glass, because once drink takes hold, clarity – including moral clarity – slips away. Once you are addicted you will do pretty well anything to satisfy your craving.

> Intoxicants lead to worldly scorn,
> Your affairs are ruined, wealth is wasted,
> The unsuitable is done from delusion,
> Therefore always avoid intoxicants.
>
> Gambling causes avarice,
> Unpleasantness, hatred, deception, cheating,
> Wildness, lying, senseless talk, and harsh speech,
> Therefore always avoid gambling. (146–7)

More worldly advice: no one respects a drunkard or a drug addict. Such a person neglects their worldly affairs, since their time is spent either indulging their habit or recovering from the effects of the indulgence. Even in Nāgārjuna's day, getting drunk seems to have been an expensive business. Moreover, a drunkard does stupid things; he loses his inhibitions, and all sense of what is appropriate and seemly. The 'unsuitable' is indeed done. In these and many other ways intoxicants lay waste one's life.

There is quite a lot of advice of this sort in ancient Buddhist texts, suggesting that the people of India used to be rather more given to drink than they are today. These days, at least among unwesternized Indians, drinking alcohol is regarded as being utterly disreputable, especially in the case of religious practitioners.

As for gambling, a host of evils is said to follow in its wake. You become obsessed with money (or its equivalent), regardless of whether you are winning or losing. Money is, after all, the centre of interest in gambling. You also crave the feeling of elation that comes from winning, elation being a kind of drug, but more often than not there is the deflation that comes when you lose your money, together with the resentment you feel towards those to whom you have lost it. You will do anything in order to win: you will cheat and deceive. You lose control of yourself in your rage to win and your fury at losing. And you lie to your family about where the money has gone.

There is also an element of self-deception in the way we justify our addictions, whether it is to drink or drugs or gambling. We believe that we are in control. Similarly, we try to justify the addictions of others. For example, some defend bingo halls, bars, and pubs on the grounds that they are places of harmless enjoyment that promote social interaction, and no one, they say, has the right to object to the perfectly legal pleasures and amusements of other people. However, the fact is that bingo is gambling, while pubs and bars tend to encourage alcoholism. Drinking and gambling do indeed have the kind of effects that Nāgārjuna itemizes. If they are the only 'social' activities in which many people engage, that is sad, but why this should be so is another matter entirely.

CRAVING, HATRED, AND DELUSION

> Covetousness destroys one's wishes,
> Harmful intent yields fright,
> Wrong views lead to bad views,
> And drink to confusion of the mind. (16)

As ever, Nāgārjuna doesn't beat about the bush. He spells out for the king the consequences of not observing the three mind precepts. The result of covetousness, he says, is not that you get what you want, but rather that you get what you don't want, the nature of craving being such that once the desired object is obtained, it often ceases to be desired. As Oscar Wilde famously put it, 'In this world there are only two tragedies. One is not getting what one wants, and the other is getting it.'[232] Especially when we have set our heart on some very special object, we may well find, on finally getting possession of it, that we have invested it with qualities it does not really have. Whether it is an experience, an article, or a person – success, a car, a lover – we find, when we've got it, that it is not after all what we wanted. By that time, though, it is probably too late to change our mind; we've got it – or we've married it – and have to deal with the responsibilities and demands that such possession brings. And we are no more contented than we were before.

We have been warned that killing brings a short life, and that harming brings suffering. Now we are told that the intent to harm brings fear. These are all variations on the same theme, one that is of particular relevance to a ruler or, in fact, to anyone with power over others. For such people, 'harmful intent' is often associated with consolidating their position and neutralizing those who might threaten them. Nāgārjuna reminds his royal disciple that the fruit of such an intent is not security but its opposite: fear. If your days and nights are spent scheming to harm others, you will be living in a fearful, dangerous world. Putting it more psychologically, we may say that hatred produces paranoia, which is our own projected hatred reflected back to us. With paranoia, the fear is largely unfounded, and the hatred largely unconscious. The experience of paranoia tells us less about the real attitude of other people towards us than it does about our own unacknowledged emotions. Similarly, the feeling of victimization, the sense that others are out to get one, often comes from our unacknowledged ill will towards those who, we imagine, dislike us and wish to harm us.

This is paranoia as projection.[233] In a way, it arises naturally out of the fact that people tend to hate those who hate them. Thus if you hate someone, you are likely to think that they hate you. You interpret everything they do or say as a sign that they are plotting against you. Absolute rulers can easily slip into this way of perceiving the world around them. Victims of paranoia weave complex webs of 'evidence' to support their fantasies, while those of whom they are so crazily suspicious are guilty only of wondering why someone is looking at them in such a strange manner.

To say that wrong views lead to wrong views (presumably what is meant by 'bad views') is tantamount to saying that there is nothing worse than wrong views. No other affliction can match the bane of wrong views. Hell itself is not so much the deserved consequence of wrong views as is falling into further wrong views. Wrong views lead inexorably to more wrong views. Their nature is to breed. Once you embrace a wrong view, you sink more and more deeply into the morass of mere opinions and speculations.[234]

Nor should we hold too tightly even to right views. The Buddha regarded all views, even those that were practically helpful and therefore 'right', as having only a limited value as compared with the experience of Enlightenment. Once you regard a particular view not just as a provisionally held position, or as something to reflect on, but as being unconditionally true, it ceases to function as right view. A right view to which you cling, a right view you turn into a totem, becomes to that extent a wrong view.

> Afraid of the fearless abode,
> Ruined, they ruin others.
> O King, act in such a way
> That the ruined do not ruin you. (77)

'Ruined' might seem a strong word to use in this connection, but it reminds us of just what is at stake when we embark on the spiritual life. We face ruin if we 'back' the wrong view and views, moreover, can be contagious. Our own particular view of the world has been 'caught' from our experience of the world, especially the society in which we live. Those with whom we associate will constantly give off, with everything they say and do, a view of themselves and of others and of the world around them. We should therefore be careful about our choice of associates, as well as careful about how we ourselves affect others. In view of the fact that we are very rarely aware of being 'ruined' ourselves when such is the case, what Nāgārjuna is saying suggests that a certain watchfulness, a certain modesty and reticence, is always appropriate in our dealings with others lest they be 'ruined' through their association with us.

> Through not wavering you will attain mindfulness,
> Through thinking you will attain intelligence.
> Through respect you will be endowed with realization of meaning,
> Through guarding the doctrine you will become wise. (288)

Through overcoming mental distraction, you clearly will become more aware. When you are distracted, different parts of you are pulling in different directions, so to speak, and the communication between them breaks down, so that at that time you have very little overall awareness. If you can stabilize your thoughts, more of you will be present in what you say and do.

Next we come to how we apply this awareness, once it has been established. By thinking is meant creative thinking – specifically, the investigation of mental states. For most of us, thinking often involves anxiety, as when we worry about what is going to happen to us when we are old. For Nāgārjuna, intelligence consists in developing a clearer understanding of the true nature of our situation. It means bringing awareness into our thinking. It is directed thought, mindful thought, especially the mindful observation of our own mental processes.

If the mind is not used, the faculty of intelligence tends to atrophy. And we often use our minds more creatively when we ask questions, rather than when we assume we know the answers. Asking questions can take many forms: intelligent reading, for example, can be a matter of asking questions. When you open a book, perhaps out of curiosity, as when you are intrigued by the title, this too can be indicative of a questioning attitude. You are approaching the book with a mind of your own rather than just absorbing its contents like a piece of blotting paper.

The kind of questions you ask makes a difference. If you use your intelligence to ask only about mundane things, you are, in effect, excluding the possibility of any spiritual understanding. However cleverly your questions may be put, they will lead you gradually into a state of delusion in which there is no awareness of anything beyond what the senses convey. It is a matter of where your real interests lie. The spiritual life itself is a kind of interrogation of reality. This does not mean cross-examining the wise, or calling into question or impugning the wise. Nor is it a matter of asking questions without first thinking for oneself. Questioning the wise should be an extension of questioning ourselves. I would also say that we should not question the wise just in order to sound off, or to gain confirmation of our own opinions. That said, there are people who are not very assertive and who do not have many opportunities to say what they think and feel. When they find themselves with someone who is prepared to listen, they might feel they have at last been given permission to express themselves, and that is no bad thing, even if what they have to say is not very relevant. Questioning the wise does indeed mean being open to the wise, but there are people who need to experience someone who is prepared to be open to them before they can be open in their turn.

Even a sharp intelligence is not enough, however. By 'respect' is meant something more like 'reverence', and this positive quality, too, is needed. One needs, that is, a certain receptivity to higher things as well as the kind of attitude that comes with reverence. I would go so far as to say that without a measure of receptivity, and even of sympathy, you will not really understand anything, even intellectually, over and above mere facts. Such forms of emotional resistance as prejudice and defensiveness prevent us from being open to even ordinary knowledge, let alone open to higher spiritual truths. Respect or reverence involves an attitude of interest and openness and a warm, engaged curiosity. It is a readiness to learn. Without it we will distort or misrepresent whatever we engage with intellectually, whether the Dharma or anything else.

This attitude is to be cultivated not just towards the Dharma, but also towards members of the Sangha or spiritual community. We should always approach another individual with respect, whatever their level of spiritual development. There should always be sympathy between members of the spiritual community – that is, a real desire to understand what another person is saying or is endeavouring to express. One does not have to agree, but we should try to see other people objectively, and do our best to imagine what it might be like to be in their shoes. Without receptivity we cannot understand another person, however shrewd and sharp we may be. Respect for others involves an appreciation of the fact that our understanding of them is a limited one.

Having taken in the meaning of the Dharma, we have to retain it if we are to 'become wise'. In other words, we do not become wise simply by understanding the Dharma; we become wise by bearing it in mind, pondering it, not allowing ourselves to forget it. When we understand something or even get a flash of insight, it might seem at the time that we've got it for good. Yet we lose it. We lose it because we do or think or talk about other things, and fail to allow the time necessary for assimilation. The deeper the insight, the more time we may need to devote to its contemplation.

For anyone who leads a busy life, making notes is an essential element in this process. When you come back to them months or years later, you will often realize how little you have remembered. You find that points which made a deep impression on you at the time have left no trace in your mind. You might find it useful to make notes on your meditation, your reading, group study, or even on a serious talk with a friend. Sometimes just a few words will be enough to allow you to go back to an earlier insight and turn it over in your mind at your leisure. Coming back to your notes, you might also notice that you now understand them better. If you do not write things down, you will certainly lose the insight, especially in the earliest stages of its development. The phone rings, and when the call is over you might not even remember that you had been thinking at all. Personally, I wish that in my earlier days I had written down much more than I did.

A meditation notebook is useful in that it enables you to follow the ups and downs of your practice from week to week and month to month. You will notice perhaps that you have not done the *mettā bhāvanā* for a month, or that you have your best meditations around the time of the full moon. And when you hit a difficult patch, and start thinking you were not cut out for meditation, you can go through your notebook and find evidence to the contrary. Your mood, or even a passing negative attitude, might have deleted your more positive experiences from your memory. A notebook acts like an observant intimate friend who remembers everything you tell them.

> Through the concentrations, immeasurables, and formlessnesses
> One experiences the bliss of Brahmā and so forth.
> Thus in brief are the practices
> For high status and their fruits. (24)

The immeasurables are four meditation practices that involve the cultivation of positive emotion. They are also known, more poetically, as the four *brahma vihāras*, the 'divine abidings'. These are loving-kindness or *maitrī* (*mettā*), compassion or *karuṇā*, sympathetic joy or *muditā*, and equanimity or *upekṣā* (*upekkhā*). The rather cumbersome 'formlessnesses' refers to the four formless absorptions, the *arūpa dhyānas*: the experience or knowledge of the spheres of infinite space, infinite consciousness, no-thing-ness, and neither perception nor non-perception. Nāgārjuna is speaking of the successively higher superconscious states brought about by the practice of meditation, states which take one to the corresponding heavenly or *deva* realms of traditional Buddhist cosmology. These higher states can be experienced not only during this life, when one practises meditation; they can also be experienced after death when one is reborn in the heavenly realm corresponding to one's meditative attainment during one's lifetime. The heavenly realms into which one might be reborn are not eternal; even there one is still on the wheel of becoming. This is also true when one enters these realms in meditation. One may enter a heavenly realm, in the sense of having an experience of peace and bliss and spiritual renewal, but one will still be within conditioned existence unless one has the determination to pass beyond it into the still higher, transcendental realm of Enlightenment.

Of course, there is a clear difference between the idea that meditation leads to states of bliss and the idea that skilful actions lead to worldly prosperity, the former being verifiable in experience whereas with the latter this is not the case. Meditative absorption, once achieved, offers a direct experience of relaxation and tranquillity, whereas the karmic fruits of a virtuous life have to be taken on trust as something we can look forward to in the future, whether in this life or in a future existence. After all, honesty does not always pay. As the Bible says, the wicked man does sometimes 'flourish like the bay tree'.[235] His victims seem only too often to experience the sufferings which under the law of karma are rightly his. It might be comforting to think that the rich are miserable and unable to enjoy their ill-gotten gains. But is this true? Does the swindler really lie awake at night worrying about losing the money that he has obtained fraudulently, or is this just a consoling fantasy on the part of those of us who tread a more honest path? Whatever the truth of this – and we cannot really know – connecting the spiritual life with worldly gains, whether those gains are real or imagined, whether they constitute psychological well-being or a better life in the future, inevitably distracts us from the real purpose of spiritual practice. This fleeting reference to meditation in the context of skilful actions and their consequences reminds us that meditation is a form of action. All thoughts are actions. Positive thought is skilful action. It is easy to imagine that in practising meditation you are not really doing anything, but the truth is that meditation is a powerful thing, in that it is productive of important consequences for the meditator. An action will always produce some kind of result. (If no result is produced, it means that nothing has been done.) A thought, inasmuch as it constitutes an intention, produces a karmic result even if it is not acted upon immediately. It changes us to some degree, or at least begins to take us in a certain direction. The result, in the case of meditation, is more than simply a shift of emphasis among existing mental and emotional elements. When one meditates with conviction something quite new is generated and this contributes to one's spiritual development.

6

MENTAL STATES

> Having analysed well
> All deeds of body, speech, and mind,
> Those who realize what benefit self and others
> And always perform these are wise. (7)

This verse makes it clear that the full realization of what benefits oneself and others comes from cultivating mindfulness, from 'having analysed well all deeds of body, speech, and mind' – that is, from being keenly aware at any given moment of whether what you are doing is beneficial or harmful. This aspect of mindfulness is sometimes called *dharma-vicaya*, the investigation of mental states (*dharma* here meaning a mental state), and it is an important part of Buddhist practice. In it, one constantly examines oneself, scrutinizing one's deeds of body, speech, and mind, and judging as far as one can whether they are skilful or unskilful, whether they have been prompted by kindness and wisdom or by craving, hatred, and delusion. In more general terms, the skilful is whatever pertains to the path and to the goal, whether directly or indirectly; while the unskilful is that which takes one off the path and out of sight of the goal.

Here we are presented with another way of viewing ethical practice. But will such constant evaluation of our mental states not detract from our spontaneity? If you are forever stopping and analysing what you are thinking, doing, and saying, are you not adopting a rather mechanical and even alienating attitude to your experience? Will it not make you too self-conscious to be able to live authentically? There is another question, which needs to be dealt with first: is it, in fact, true spontaneity that we value, or do we simply want to indulge instinctive and reactive behaviour? After all, our negative instincts and destructive habits are no less spontaneous than our creative impulses. If we just want to give free rein to all our different energies, we might as well forget about practising mindfulness.

This granted, it is nonetheless essential to stay in contact with the springs of one's creativity. Somehow you have to strike a balance between giving so much free rein to your instincts and energies that you lose all hope of being able to bring mindfulness to bear on them and being so self-analytical that you simply inhibit and stultify yourself. Here, the challenge is to be active and spontaneous and, at the same time, aware and mindful, so that there is a single mental and spiritual process in which awareness and spontaneity are indistinguishable. This is what happens when you are absorbed in work, for example: all your energy is going into the work, yet at the same time you are very aware of what you are doing. With artistic or creative work, especially, is this the case. A unification of spontaneity and awareness can also take place in the course of human communication, when a real exchange of thoughts and feelings starts to flow between two people. It can happen in a crisis, or in a moment of danger, when all your energies are mobilized to meet an overwhelming challenge.

Mindfulness demands the ability to immerse oneself in one's experience whilst at the same time being conscious of the nature of that experience. It is not a cold, objective, intellectual process, not a question of somehow standing outside one's experience and observing it. The awareness should infuse and inform the action, or the speech, or even the thought. It should do so, moreover, with a strong element of positive feeling, even joy.

Mindfulness means that one is better able to decide whether or not to do something. If you are naturally a cautious, inhibited, self-controlled kind of person, you might try seeing what would happen if you were just to let rip. For some people mindfulness might mean unbuttoning a little, taking a risk and following a spontaneous impulse as a way of weakening their inhibitions. If, on the other hand, you are rather wild by nature, and tend to be spontaneous in a purely instinctual and reactive way, mindfulness would involve restraining yourself and learning to curb your reactivity.

Dharma-vicaya does not mean breaking the flow of life by stopping at every turn in order to assess yourself according to some abstract notion of spiritual progress. It is simply a general awareness of how *relatively* skilful or unskilful any given action, thought, or utterance is, a sense of the extent to which you are moving towards a positive goal. You do not need to tear yourself up by the roots every few minutes to see if you have grown a little. Rather you can make a start with *dharma-vicaya* by taking stock of yourself from time to time, in order to ascertain the general direction of your actions of body, speech, and mind. Are they expressive of greed, hatred, and mental confusion, or expressive of generosity, kindness, and understanding? Then at some point you need to embark upon the systematic development of moment-by-moment mindfulness, and become more aware of your mental states as they arise, as well as aware of the direction in which any given mental state is heading. In this way you will ensure that your confidence in what you are doing is sustained and that all the things you think and do and say contribute to the attainment of your goal.

With practice, the analysis can become more searching. It is *dharma-vicaya* that leads to wisdom, not theoretical knowledge. Generally speaking we understand intellectually far more than we are capable of putting into practice. After all, it is not so very difficult to take stock of one's actions of body, speech, and mind and judge whether or not they benefit oneself and others. But this is not enough. One has to live by the light of that knowledge. When it comes to putting what we know into practice, all sorts of conditions other than intellectual understanding, particularly habits, come into play. It is only by studying our actions and thoughts in detail, moment by moment, and seeing their effect upon us directly, that we will start to break down our habitual ways of responding to the world.

FIRST, FORSAKE ANGER

> Then having become a monastic
> You should first be intent on the training (in ethics).
> You should endeavor at the discipline of individual liberation,
> At hearing frequently, and delineating their meaning.

Then, you should forsake
These which are called assorted faults.
With vigor you should definitely realize
Those renowned as the fifty-seven.

Belligerence is a disturbance of mind.
Enmity is a (tight) hanging onto that.
Concealment is a hiding of ill-deeds (when confronted).
Malevolence is to cling to ill-deeds. (401–3)

Here Nāgārjuna recommends that the new monk should follow what I call the path of regular steps.[236] However lofty and altruistic your goal, at the beginning of your spiritual career you have to start by working on yourself, devoting yourself to your own 'individual liberation'. No doubt by getting on with your personal practice you will have a positive effect upon others, but unless you gain a degree of insight, you will not be able to help them more radically. It might seem selfish just to persist with your own practice of meditation rather than teaching others, but in the long run it is the depth of your meditative experience that is going to help you communicate the Dharma most effectively. Note that Nāgārjuna is recommending taking up not the *ideal* of individual liberation (i.e. the *arhant* ideal), but simply the *discipline* of individual liberation (i.e. the *prāṭimokṣa*). The ideal remains that of the Mahāyāna, not of the Hīnayāna, but for the time being at least your discipline is that of individual liberation. In the same way, while true spontaneity may be your ideal, your present discipline might have to be quite strict, even narrow, if you are to achieve that ideal in the long run.

There follows a touch of the Abhidharma, with a list of fifty-seven unskilful mental states.[237] It is not enough just to recognize the existence of these states in us; we have to bring mindfulness to bear on them. The purpose of our taking this long hard look at the unskilful tendencies of our own mind is so that we may take steps to eradicate them and thus become, eventually, free from them. Anger comes first, because it is from anger that resentment, hatred, and enmity all arise. Being the direct opposite of the bodhisattva's compassionate vow, these states are the most unskilful that we can experience. Anger is of a momentary and explosive nature, often being the result of a build-up of frustrated energy. You want something but you cannot get it, or you want to say something but you cannot say it. Eventually you explode. Resentment or hatred is a more settled anger, the result of brooding over one's wrongs, real or imagined, so that one's mind is slowly poisoned. Enmity goes even further, being the persistent desire to harm another person. While hatred is a mental attitude, enmity consists in attempting actually to harm the object of your aversion, even over a period of years.[238]

It has been said that hatred is the experience of pain, accompanied by the idea of an external cause.[239] Hatred arises from the natural impulse to remove or counteract the person you have identified as the cause of your suffering, though they might not be responsible for it, or even aware of the fact that you think them responsible. But some hatred is gratuitous. Such hatred is termed malice, the delight in inflicting suffering on others for its own sake, regardless of whether they have done you any harm. Thus there is a hierarchy of negative emotions consisting of anger, hatred, enmity, and malice.

Surprisingly enough, the greatest hatred often occurs between people who are supposedly very close to one another, between children and parents, between husband and wife, between people of the same religious tradition, and even between members of the same spiritual community. But these are the very people from whom we normally receive the most, emotionally speaking, and from whom we therefore expect the most. Bitter disappointment is thus more than likely. Another example is that of the welfare state, which was set up in Britain after the Second World War, and which has given rise to a great deal of resentment. People have been gradually conditioned into thinking that everything should be provided for them. When it is not, or when what is provided is not to their liking, they feel they have been cheated of what was due to them and become correspondingly angry.

A lot of resentment and unfocused anger comes from having everything you really need and yet still feeling deprived. This frustration and disappointment with a quite comfortable life is perhaps largely to do with spiritual deprivation. With no pressing material or physical needs, people are very quickly brought up against the basic question of what life itself is for, but without their having any real guidance on the subject. Our society has given us everything, without telling us how to make the best use of it. The innumerable petty regulations imposed by the government irritate people and breed resentment. Mundane freedom may in the end feel like bondage, just as material wealth may feel like poverty. No wonder people feel angry and hard done by. The trouble is that Utopia, which used to be in the future, has arrived now. If before the Second World War you had told the average working-class man or woman – especially the men in the long dole queues I saw in the 1930s – that in the future they would have a house of their own, a car, a television, new clothes every six months, a refrigerator and a washing machine, exotic ready-made meals and foreign holidays, and all for only five days' work each week, they would have said, 'That will be heaven. What more could you want?' But it has not worked out like that. People feel cheated of the happiness that should have been theirs. They feel cheated because they have got what they were promised without the happiness they assumed would accompany it.

The opposite of anger is patience, the capacity to endure difficulties or unpleasant situations without falling into, or expressing, negative emotions. Expressions like 'My patience snapped,' which ought to be a confession of weakness, are more often meant to be self-exculpatory, as if no one could be expected to be patient beyond a certain point. Initially, one who takes the practice of ethics seriously will feel disappointed, even frustrated, when hatred, or craving, or jealousy arises. You now know the harm these emotions can do, and yet they keep on arising. Rather than allowing yourself to be discouraged by this, you should remind yourself that the fact that you can recognize them for what they are means that you are on the way to overcoming them. If you indulge them, living with them easily, and if you ignore their malign influence, you are inviting them to arise again in the future. But if you can see them for what they are, you should also be able to see that simply berating yourself on their account only makes things worse. Gradually, you will learn how to deal with these negative emotions as soon as they arise.

For example, an angry thought, or even a spontaneous outburst of anger, is not necessarily a breach of your promise to generate compassion in place of ill will. In all likelihood you did not deliberately make yourself angry; the anger simply erupted owing to a long-standing lack of attention to your mental condition, possibly allied to a fiery temper. The promise is broken when you indulge anger and make no effort to eradicate it. If you take no positive steps to overcome it when it arises, you are in effect encouraging it to do so again. At bottom, anger is the product of frustrated desire, so a simpler lifestyle, if it is embraced happily, should have the effect of making anger and hatred less likely to arise.

Because hatred is intimately linked with craving or covetousness, it is always worth looking for its roots in frustrated desire. To take an obvious example, the nagging, restless itch of sexual craving can disturb our emotional balance, rob us of our peace of mind, and leave us discontented at best, and at worst full of jealous fury. Unfortunately, contemporary popular culture offers a constant invitation to indulge our many cravings, including sexual craving, and a spiritual practitioner has therefore all the more need to observe the ethical precepts. But if we are genuinely to observe them, we have to be able to find interest and pleasure and beauty elsewhere than in the objects of craving.

Bringing an element of friendliness and concern into our personal relationships can provide a degree of genuine emotional sustenance, the lack of which often lies at the root of our frustration and bitterness. Much of the time, what we are really looking for is this kind of sustenance. Another approach is the aesthetic one: the more our emotions are engaged with, and refined by, poetry and the fine arts or by devotional practices, the less likely it is that we will be troubled by the grosser forms of craving and hatred. The key is to broaden and deepen our interests, to cultivate contentment, and to adopt a more aesthetic attitude to life. Admire the 'flower in the crannied wall' by all means, but be aware of your desire to pluck it out of the crannies, and without ceasing to appreciate its beauty, relax and relinquish your desire to possess it.[240]

THE MANY FACES OF PRIDE

> Arrogance is haughtiness (due to wealth, and so forth).
> Non-conscientiousness is non-application at virtues.
> Pride has seven forms
> Each of which I will explain.
>
> Fancying that one is lower than the lowly,
> Or equal with the equal,
> Or greater than or equal to the lowly –
> All are called the pride of selfhood.

Boasting that one is equal to those
Who by some good quality are superior to oneself
Is called exceeding pride. Fancying that one is superior to the superior,

Thinking that one is higher than the very high,
Is pride beyond pride;
Like sores on an abscess
It is very vicious.

Conceiving an I through obscuration
In the five empty (aggregates)
Which are called the appropriation
Is said to be the pride of thinking I.

Thinking one has won fruits (of the spiritual path)
Not yet attained is pride of conceit.
Praising oneself for faulty deeds
Is known by the wise as erroneous pride.

Deriding oneself, thinking
'I am useless,' is called
The pride of inferiority.
Such is a brief description of the seven prides. (406–12)

Success is always dangerous. From a spiritual point of view, failure has its rewards, but worldly success tends to produce what the ancient Greeks called hubris, the pride that comes before a fall. Thoughtless or unmindful pride brings inflation, the sense that you can do nothing wrong. You become careless; you think nothing can stand in your way. When this happens you will either have your inflated ego abruptly punctured, or it will suffer a slow, gradual deflation. Either way, you will be brought down to earth, and this will make you angry. You will think you were brought down by people who were jealous of you and your success, who could not bear their own comparative mediocrity. In this way you become more and more blind to what is really going on, and even when you have achieved something worthwhile, this blindness can detract from the positive nature of the achievement.

Haughtiness is thinking a lot of oneself and adopting a posture of superiority towards others, whereas arrogance goes further, and involves trying to force people to recognize that superiority. In some societies, for example in the old Tibet, arrogance and haughtiness seem to have been considered positive qualities. When some of my Tibetan friends in Kalimpong wanted to speak well of an aristocratic lady, for example, they would say in tones of admiration, 'She's really haughty!' as if haughtiness was her crowning virtue.

When pride includes self-denigration we have to broaden the meaning of the term. Insisting on being equal to others is pride. Even humility, if it is at all self-conscious, is pride. According to Nāgārjuna, belief in a separate unchanging self is pride. Any way in which we fix or inflate our sense of self, or separate ourselves from others by thinking that we are someone special, is pride.[241]

You can be proud of a quality you have, you can be proud of a quality you do not have but think you have, and you can be proud of a quality you pretend you have. You might be genuinely learned, or enjoy an effective meditation practice, or even experience a degree of insight – all these can be accompanied by arrogance or inflation. You might, on the other hand, genuinely believe yourself to be Enlightened, say, or that you were a great painter, when in fact you were nothing of the kind. You might even allow people to believe you possessed certain spiritual attainments when you knew you did not really have them. All this is pride.

People will take pride in almost anything that might bring them a little attention, even if that attention is far from flattering. Some are proud of being good liars or successful cheats, or of how drunk they can get. Others are proud of being useless, at least in certain respects. The latter may be dressed up as self-deprecation. Such people will say, 'I'm afraid I'm absolutely hopeless at anything technical,' with a rather boastful air, as if to say, 'My mind is on higher things.' Pride is about measuring ourselves against others, and it might seem that, ideally, we should not compare ourselves with others at all. However, we can hardly avoid doing so; we need to compare our abilities with those of other people from time to time, for various purposes. But comparisons can be made skilfully or unskilfully. An unskilful comparison consists in being neurotically concerned to find a place for oneself in relation to others in order to feel secure. You are anxious to know where you stand, whether you are equal, inferior, or superior to others. You might insist on being equal because really you feel insecure and in fact are constantly comparing yourself with others to your own detriment. A more positive form of comparison would be to ascertain where you stood in relation to others for the purpose of mutual growth and communication and to achieve common objectives. Regarding someone as inferior to you does not necessarily mean that you look down on them. It could mean that you recognize that you can do more for them than they can do for you. Conversely, looking up to someone need not mean that you grovel.

Boasting consists in overemphasizing one's own abilities in relation to those of others. Usually it is simply a case of saying, 'He may be a better carpenter than I am, but *I'm* better at public speaking,' and a little awareness should prevent us from making too much of such relative advantages. Sometimes one person might be obviously superior to another in a general way, but given a change in circumstances the situation can be swiftly reversed. In J. M. Barrie's play *The Admirable Crichton*, a group of aristocrats are shipwrecked on a desert island, and the eponymous manservant shows himself to be vastly superior to everyone else in the party.

It is obvious that the Buddha was superior to the notorious bandit Aṅgulimāla, for example.[242] Even so, it needs to be made clear that banditry is not the point of comparison between them, for this would make Aṅgulimāla better than the Buddha! That aside, we can say with confidence that the Buddha was a better man than Aṅgulimāla. However, as soon as Aṅgulimāla becomes Enlightened the difference between them immediately becomes much less. Comparisons of this kind are thus, if not odious, at least otiose. At one time you might be in a position to help a particular person; at another time, it might be you who needs the help and they who give it. There are always inequalities between people, and these need to be acknowledged if there is to be mutual helpfulness, but in the end they are not what matters most.

Nowadays the general attitude towards the comparison of one person with another is rather strange. On the one hand, a professional has his or her performance judged and measured against that of other professionals; on the other, there is widespread resistance to the idea that one person might be better than another in a more general way. The truth is that we should go down on our knees in gratitude to the Buddhas and Bodhisattvas for the fact that we are *not* superior to all others, and that there are some people who are far better than we are at the vital business of being human. If there are those to whom we can look up, there is hope for us in our own future development, as well as help. Pride can also be collective. It can take the form of nationalism, for example, which is an extension of the pride of the individual, the pride that says 'I'.[243] Pride is a versatile, many-sided 'fault', and it is hardly to be expected that one will altogether escape it this side of Enlightenment.

Pride is not always negative. As a positive quality it comes under the heading of *apatrāpya* (*ottappa* in Pāli): conscience or self-respect. This kind of pride, radically transformed, is an important element in the Vajrayāna. There the practitioner is recommended to think, 'How can I, being in my essential nature a Buddha, behave unskilfully? Is it in accordance with my Buddha-nature? Could a *Buddha* behave in this way? Is it *possible*?' This 'Buddha-pride', as it is called, is a rather dangerous attitude for one to adopt. You could tell yourself, more modestly, not that you were a Buddha, but that you belong to the Buddha's spiritual family. You might say, 'How could I think of doing anything unskilful when I have been adopted into the family of the Buddha?' or even, 'I am a child of the Buddha; how could I disgrace my own father by behaving badly?'

Hand in hand with this kind of positive pride goes respect for the good qualities of others. In an earlier passage, Nāgārjuna has spoken of 'honouring the honourable', an expression which brings us up against a peculiarly modern wrong view. Today, the idea that one should reverence that which is worthy of reverence is rather foreign to us. People tend to be suspicious of anything which to them smacks of elitism. Since Freud, we have become very mistrustful of those who seem too good to be true, and we are only too aware that greatness may well conceal great weakness. Great achievements are often seen as compensations for the failure to address a deep emotional need. Along with this perception goes an urge to cut down to size anyone who succeeds in rising above the common herd. In the past, people were accustomed to look up to those in positions of social or political authority, in much the same way that they looked up to God. Now all that has gone. God is not worshipped as widely as before, and most people have completely lost the habit of looking up. Yet William Blake very truly observed that 'Worship of God is, Honouring his gifts in other men each according to his genius, and loving the greatest men best.'[244] The same should go for us: if we really worship the Buddha, we will worship the spirit of his teaching wherever it manifests.

We are quick to expose hypocrisy, to ridicule solemnity, and to bring pomposity down to earth. We like to insist that our own opinions are no less valid than anyone else's. We pride ourselves on not toeing the party line, on sticking to our own point of view. It is difficult for us to appreciate how great a shift this represents from the attitude that prevailed until the middle of the twentieth century. People were then more prepared to set aside their own personal – and thus necessarily limited and partial – views and interests out of respect for the supposedly better informed judgements of those in authority. They took pride in 'doing their duty'. Nāgārjuna's 'honouring the honourable' could be rendered as 'respecting the respectable', and this shows us how alien such deference is to contemporary thinking.

But what are we left with if we refuse to look up to anyone, and if we are so satisfied with our present level of understanding that we cannot imagine anything surpassing it? In fact, human beings have a deep-seated need to worship, so that we will inevitably look for someone or something to meet that need. But sometimes we set up idols only to cast them down and trample upon them. Moreover, we remain in thrall to group evaluations, except that nowadays those evaluations are often devaluations. Our cynical assumption is that the more we know about people, the less we will find to respect. We assume that what we do not know must be discreditable. In fact, while some of what we do not know may indeed be discreditable, there is much that is good which, being beyond our ken, we are simply unable to appreciate. As Coleridge said, we can reverence only what we do not understand.[245]

One would have thought that people would prefer to look up, rather than to look down. But in cynicism there is more satisfaction for the ego, for we then feel that we know everything worth knowing about people and ideas and can reassure ourselves that no one is better than we are. We are capable of acknowledging someone's mastery in certain areas so long as we can shake our heads over their failings in others. Probably, it is the fear of seeming naive and gullible, as much as anything, that prevents us from looking up to anyone. The Buddhist approach is always to examine the mental state behind any attitude, and from this point of view, a knowing cynicism is no better than starry-eyed idolization.

To take the most obvious example of human greatness, that of the Buddha himself, do we revere him as a Buddha or do we see him as just one of us, as human and therefore flawed? Of course, he was a human being, but not just a human being. His being human does not make him less of a Buddha. Indeed, his humanity is part of his Buddhahood. It is not easy for us to see his humanity *and* his Enlightenment at the same time, but if we are able to do so, we will see him more truly and therefore reverence him more deeply. Likewise, while it does a disservice to the memory of any great individual to ignore the weaknesses that testify to their humanity, we do ourselves a disservice if we allow our knowledge of those weaknesses to blind us to the fact that their qualities are vastly superior to our own.

For a Buddhist, 'the honourable' means, primarily, the Three Jewels: the Buddha, the Dharma, and the Sangha. We honour the Enlightened human source of the Dharma, the Dharma or teaching itself, and those who communicate and exemplify the Dharma, that is, the noble *arhants* and the glorious bodhisattvas as well as those more developed individuals with whom we are in personal contact. Foremost among the latter is our own teacher. In Tibetan Buddhism, one's teacher is revered as the manifestation, within the mandala of the disciple's spiritual life, of the Buddha himself. This shows how far Tibetan Buddhists are prepared to go in their concern to protect people from the grave fault of failure to 'honour the honourable'.

IGNOBLE MOTIVES

Hypocrisy is to control the senses
For the sake of goods and respect.
Flattery is to speak pleasant phrases
For the sake of goods and respect.

Indirect acquisition is to praise
Another's wealth in order to acquire it.
Pressured acquisition is manifest derision
Of others in order to acquire goods.

Desiring profit from profit
Is to praise previous acquisitions.
Repeating faults is to recite again and again
The mistakes made by others. (413–5)

Here we have the opposite of failure to 'honour the honourable'. Hypocrisy and flattery are closely connected with concealment and dissimulation.[246] An example of hypocrisy would be the adoption of the Buddhist lifestyle, whether as a monk in the East or as a Buddhist teacher in the West, for the sake of mundane rewards: an easy, pleasant life, respect, even quite a good living in some cases.

We flatter others not only 'for the sake of goods and respect', or to win their approval, but also out of fear. We are trying to placate them, to put them in a good frame of mind so as to render them less threatening. In India, flattery is often gross and open. People flatter you to your face in the most outrageous fashion, without the least hesitation or shame. I have been the object of embarrassing effusions of this kind myself when being introduced before delivering a talk. Some recipients of such flattery happily swallow it all, beaming down on the audience and nodding agreement and satisfaction with what is being said about them. This comes from their living in a hierarchical society in which flattery of superiors is regarded as right and proper. Here flattery is taken not so much as a statement of objective fact but rather as a clear indication of the recipient's importance and power and of the flatterer's dependence on that person's favour. In general, the Indian assumption seems to be that if you flatter someone sufficiently they can't refuse you anything that you ask.

A different kind of flattery comes into play when you cast your eye on a picture or some knick-knack, and say, 'I really do like that,' in such a way that the owner feels obliged to give it to you. Then there is the no less ignoble ploy of deprecating something for the same end: 'Oh, that doesn't really go with the rest of the decor, does it? It seems hardly worth keeping – it can't have cost you very much. I could find a home for it, though.' Another rather sordid tack Nāgārjuna warns us against is to tell someone how pleased you were with an object they gave you on some previous occasion, how useful it was, and how you could really do with another one just like it, in such a way that they too feel obliged to meet your wish. People have not changed much since Nāgārjuna's time.

An important Buddhist practice is to rejoice in the virtues of others, but unfortunately many of us prefer to dwell on their faults. ('Repeating faults is to recite again and again the mistakes made by others,' Nāgārjuna says.) But what are we really trying to achieve by doing that? Clearly we are looking down on the objects of our fault-finding in order to seem or feel superior by comparison. We try to distance ourselves from certain faults by criticizing them in others. A lot of humour works like this. The suggestion is that because we can see the folly or frailty of the person who is the butt of the joke and laugh at them, we are free from that folly ourselves. Laughter is sometimes accompanied by a feeling of relief – the relief that comes with recognizing a problem and knowing that one is not caught up in it oneself. The wide appeal of certain Zen stories, in which a stupid monk is shown up – and sometimes woken up – by a wise Zen master, is no doubt related to this human tendency to laugh at the stupidity of others.[247] In a story, we inevitably identify at some level with one of the characters, and I rather suspect that in the case of such Zen stories most people will identify with the wise master rather than with the ignorant disciple.

PRIDE

> Through arrogance, a bad lineage,
> Through jealousy, little beauty.
>
> A bad color comes through anger,
> Stupidity, from not questioning the wise. (17–18)

If you are arrogant you will eventually be looked down upon. This is the traditional Buddhist view. If you take pride in the eminence of your family or clan – or in modern terms, in your status as a professional – the result under the law of karma and rebirth is that you will be reborn in a low-class family and with low prospects. Jockeying for position is a natural and quite healthy feature of any human – indeed any animal – group. It is the way in which those who are stronger, cleverer, or more capable are enabled to influence the group as a whole. Within a healthy society, those who lack natural abilities at least understand the advantage of their relying for leadership on those who are better qualified. The ego exploits this kind of situation. When someone identifies with the status attached to a position of influence, that ego-identification will often find expression in arrogance, in which case they are probably less clever and capable than they think, because arrogance in the long run limits a person's ability to influence others. Arrogance is a presumption of higher status that depends upon treating others as inferior. But if you try to lord it over others, they will resent it and try to turn the tables on you. They might even succeed.

Sometimes, what appears to be arrogance is not really such, but is a wrong impression due to a misunderstanding or a clash of personalities. For example, within institutions there is often conflict between those individuals who are more highly organized and those who are less so. The first type will accuse the second of being lazy and unmotivated, while the latter will complain that the more highly organized are forever telling them what to do. This lack of understanding between the two types often manifests as the less organized perceiving the more organized as arrogant. But if you are truly cleverer or more capable you will try to appreciate ordinary people for what they are able to contribute, rather than looking down on them in a spirit of superiority.

JEALOUSY

Emotions like anger and jealousy also have consequences in terms of our outward appearance.[248] If we are habitually jealous we begin to look sour, bitter, and resentful. Shakespeare makes Nāgārjuna's point better than anyone, when in *Othello* he has Iago express his jealousy of Cassio:

> He hath a daily beauty in his life
> That makes me ugly;[249]

Jealousy is, in a way, the opposite of arrogance. One is the ego looking down, the other is the ego looking up. It is jealousy that makes us unwilling to rejoice in or even to acknowledge the success, the beauty, or the goodness of other people. We resent others for possessing qualities which, we feel, we do not possess. In fact it is jealousy that, by its very nature, makes it difficult for us to cultivate those qualities ourselves. In the *Bodhicaryāvatāra,* Śāntideva brings out the sheer irrationality of jealousy. Addressing the would-be bodhisattva, he says,

> You desire Buddhahood ... expressly for living beings.
> Why do you burn inside on seeing them have some slight
> honour?[250]

ANGER

Traditionally, one of the karmic consequences of anger, as of jealousy, is ugliness. Anger tends to distort the features, as one sees in many Renaissance drawings of grotesque faces. Ageing, also, allows our character to find its way into our appearance; our predominant emotions leave their imprint on the face more and more deeply as we grow older. Oscar Wilde's story, *The Picture of Dorian Gray*, turns on this fact. A handsome young man keeps a portrait of himself in a locked room, and in a sinister and eerie reversal of the natural order of things, his portrait takes on the effects of ageing while he himself continues to look as young as when it was painted. Though he leads a thoroughly disreputable life, he does not appear to age at all. It is the portrait that slowly, day by day and year by year, shows the terrible consequences of his depravity in its painted features.

THE MANY FACES OF ATTACHMENT

Non-collectedness is inconsiderate irritation
Arisen from illness.
Clinging is the attachment
Of the lazy to their bad possessions.

Discrimination of differences is discrimination
Impeded by desire, hatred, or obscuration.
Not looking into the mind is explained
As not applying it to anything.

Degeneration of respect and reverence for deeds
Concordant with the practices occurs through laziness.
A bad person is regarded as being a spiritual guide
(Pretending) to have the ways of the Supramundane Victor.

Yearning is a small entanglement
Arising from lustful desire.
Obsession, a great entanglement
Arising from desire.

Avarice is an attitude
Of clinging to one's own property,
Inopportune avarice is attachment
To the property of others.

Irreligious lust is the desirous praise
Of women who ought to be avoided.
Hypocrisy is to pretend that one possesses
Good qualities that one lacks, while desiring ill deeds.

Great desire is extreme greed
Gone beyond the fortune of knowing satisfaction.
Desire for advantage is to want to be known
By whatever way as having superior good qualities. (416–22)

'Discrimination of differences' suggests that discrimination is of two kinds. Discrimination can be a positive thing, but seeing differences on the basis of desire, hatred, or obscuration is not. We interpret almost all of our perceptions through conditioned emotional responses that make distinctions where none really exist. It isn't wrong to discriminate, but that discrimination must be, as it were, objective. It must be a seeing of things as they really are. Objective discrimination is in fact a very positive quality. At the highest level it is one of the five wisdoms of the five-Buddha mandala: the discriminating wisdom of Amitābha, the *pratyavekṣaṇā jñāna*, which sees the uniqueness of things, and discriminates them from one another accordingly.[251]

'Non-collectedness' in the first verse here means unmindfulness, and this is a fault that gives rise to a multitude of further faults. Becoming irritable when you are ill is one of them. Non-collectedness also means being scattered and prone to a mindless inconsiderate hilarity. One aspect of mindfulness is 'looking into the mind', which is achieved at least partly through applying the mind to a single object, and in this way unifying or integrating one's mental energies. This concentration or harmonization of the mind is the result of a process of weeding out unskilful mental states and developing skilful ones. By looking into the mind we make it still and calm, and by making it still and calm we are enabled to look more deeply into it. Thus the process goes on.

The first thing that most of us notice when we look into the mind is 'attachment' or 'entanglement', and on looking more deeply we find that this comes from simple human desires, desires arising out of the perception of certain objects. Attachment arises when we become emotionally dependent on the enjoyment of such objects. Thus desire comes first, leading to a smaller or a greater degree of entanglement, as the case may be. One becomes habituated to the enjoyment of a particular thing, and attachment therefore follows.[252]

Really addictive or obsessive entanglements are obviously a problem, even from the mundane point of view, but they are not always spiritually the most dangerous. For a practising Buddhist, there is real danger in small entanglements. It is when we say, 'This little fault is not really important in the larger context of my practice,' that we need to be on our guard. It is like when one is weeding the garden and it seems too much trouble to dig out a bramble root. It looks harmless when there is only a small shoot, but before one knows it the garden is overgrown with brambles. In a way there is no such thing as a small fault, particularly if we do not deal with it straight away, any more than there is any such thing as a small weed. Dismissing 'small entanglements' amounts to not acknowledging the truly enormous obstacle standing between you and what is supposedly your goal. This obstacle is your unwillingness to clear away even quite small entanglements. The *Dhammapada* puts this well:

> Do not underestimate evil, thinking, 'It will not approach me.' A water-pot becomes full by the constant falling of drops of water. Similarly, the spiritually immature person little by little fills himself with evil.[253]

The opposite attitude is considering as important things that really do not matter very much. Minor regulations become a substitute for spiritual principles. I have known Sri Lankan monks who were notorious for their strict observance of rules that most monks considered relatively unimportant, and who made a nuisance of themselves by insisting on following them to the letter. I remember a lunch held in the library of the Maha Bodhi Society headquarters in Calcutta in 1956, for which perhaps thirty or forty monks, mostly from Ceylon (as it was then), but also from Burma, Thailand, and other countries, had turned up. The food did not arrive until 11:40, so there was time to finish by twelve if you ate rather quickly.[254] One of the monks present was known for his punctilious observance of the Vinaya, one of whose minor rules was not to take solid food after midday. He was shovelling food into his mouth as fast as he could, all the time watching the clock on the library wall as its hand crept towards the hour. The moment it struck twelve he dropped his spoon as though it was red hot, and looked round as though expecting everyone else to do likewise. But the rest of the monks took no notice of the clock and went on steadily eating, while he surveyed the scene with a very virtuous expression. As he left the room some of the senior monks just looked at each other and smiled, before returning to their meal.

Our most obvious attachments are to material things. What Nāgārjuna calls avarice is attachment to our own property – a particular shirt, say, or a special chair, or even a house.[255] Similarly, inopportune avarice is attachment to the property of others. We all have a tendency to hang on to things, whether it is a book we have borrowed, or a book of our own that we are never going to read but which we keep anyway. It might seem that these attachments have little to do with our capacity to see into the nature of things, but in fact they represent our basic resistance to the truth. We cannot see things as they really are so long as we are attached to them.

Nāgārjuna has spoken of sexual attachment more than once. Here he warns against 'desirous praise of women who ought to be avoided'. We all know what this means. Such praise is often a topic of masculine conversation, as well as being the staple of much commercial advertising. It comes from not seeing women as they really are, either in the more metaphysical sense, or even in simply human terms. 'Avoiding' women might seem an extreme measure but what it really means is just leaving them alone. I have talked to women about their experience of women's retreats, and they have often said that they found it a great relief to be 'left alone' in this way. They said that normally they did rather enjoy having men around, who gave them attention, and who perhaps even competed with one another for them. But in same-sex situations they nevertheless felt a sense of relief, as though a weight had been lifted from them.

Attachments occur in every connection, and we can be hypocritical when they clash. For example, we are attached to our faults, but we are also attached to our reputation, as Nāgārjuna has already pointed out. In Sanskrit and Tibetan there are several words that have to be rendered by the one English word 'hypocrisy', but here hypocrisy is the precise equivalent that is needed. It means being a 'whited sepulchre', pretending to be pure and holy while your heart is set on worldly things. The archetypal hypocrite is Tartuffe, the eponymous hero of Molière's famous comedy, from whom derives the word 'Tartuffery' (rarely used these days) for consummate hypocrisy in general.[256]

The kind of attachment that can never be satisfied is represented by the *pretas* or hungry ghosts. Their neurotic craving is so intense that it is beyond even the possibility of satisfaction. This is the world of drug addiction or intense emotional dependency. Then there is the attachment we have to our own image or wanting 'to be known by whatever way as having superior good qualities'. The words 'by whatever way' make it clear why this kind of attachment involves such hard work. We want to be permanently identified with our own ideal image of ourselves, an image which we feel obliged to protect at all costs. Adulation can be a problem for the practising Buddhist, because the good qualities he or she has developed may end up becoming a cause for complacency and pride on their part.

Moral crusaders are like this. They are the holier-than-thou castigators of people's moral shortcomings. In some cases, no doubt, their sense of outrage is justified, but one suspects that many of them are just trying to attract attention to themselves and to make others feel uncomfortable. Some vegetarians, for example, do this to the unfortunate meat-eater. However worthy their work may be, it is the vehemence with which single-issue activists insist on the unique importance of their particular cause that often makes their position suspect. In India I once met a man, to take another example, who thought that everybody with a social conscience should be helping the lepers, just as he was doing. If you were not doing that, you were morally bankrupt. By identifying strongly with one worthwhile cause, you put yourself in a superior moral position. You create a situation in which you are one of the few who are in the right, which enables you to look down on everyone else. The more importance you give to your cause, the more importance you give to yourself.

Attachment to objects is to relate
Their good qualities in order to acquire them.
Fancying immortality is to be
Unaffected by concern over death.

Conceptuality concerned with approbation
Is the thought that – no matter what –
Others will take one as a spiritual guide
Due to possessing good qualities.

Conceptuality concerned with attachment to others
Is an intention to help or not help others
Due to being affected by desire
Or an intent to harm. (425–7)

Here Nāgārjuna exposes quite a varied collection of human vanities and attachments. 'Fancying immortality' is falsely believing that you will go marching on after death just as you are, that you will survive death more or less intact. This is a form of eternalism, or the over-literal view of rebirth: the idea that you will just wake up on the other side almost exactly as you are on this side, either to be reborn straightaway or to select a rebirth at your leisure, or else to spend a few hundred years in some pleasant heavenly realm.

This is a deluded view, to put it mildly. No doubt we ought to be concerned about death, which can be a traumatic experience. Most of us are very attached to the things of this world, whether we like to admit it or not, and we are going to suffer when we are torn away from them. So we should be concerned about death, and about what will happen to us afterwards. We certainly should not imagine that death will necessarily be simply a smooth transition to some other state.

The second verse quoted here refers to the way we casually let drop hints as to our social status when we meet people. There might not be any conscious intention to establish ourselves as superior; we drop such hints almost automatically. In India people often ask one's caste (or at least they used to), in order to find out where they stand in relation to you. In the West it is often our job that is the key indicator of our social status. Either way, we feel we need to know these things and we feel the need to communicate the more favourable indicators of our own status in order to secure as high a place in the social pecking order as we can. Some people do this to a ridiculous degree: 'My neighbour in Cannes was so late getting from his estate to the film studios that he had to borrow my helicopter.' Or, more subtly, 'Of course, my last book didn't do all that well, you know.' This tendency can easily find its way into the religious sphere, even into the sangha, which is presumably the context Nāgārjuna has in mind. People say, 'You wouldn't believe how damp my cave in the Himalayas was,' or 'A funny thing happened on my second three-year meditation retreat,' or even, 'As the Dalai Lama said to me, the last time we met,...' The hidden intention here is to assert one's spiritual prestige and status. In saying such things we are not necessarily laying claim to any actual spiritual attainment. We are not openly claiming anything at all. But hints of this kind are worse, in a way, than open bragging.

The next verse uncovers more hidden motives. However, being aware of these is no reason for us to condemn ourselves on their account. Our good intentions are often not entirely pure. We may even get a kick out of being altruistic. We are not in it just to help others; we enjoy being in the position of being the helper, the one others look up to. This is only natural. It is very difficult to be entirely disinterested in one's efforts to help others. There is almost always something in it for us, even if it is only that we accumulate merit or go to heaven when we die.

The fact is that we cannot delay embarking on compassionate action until such time as our motive is completely pure. We have to work on our motivation at the same time that we are engaged in such action. The real danger is that we might be getting out of our altruism some satisfaction that we do not acknowledge. But if we bring mindfulness to bear on our motives it will help purify them. In the early days of the Western Buddhist Order, people sometimes told me that they did not want to ask for ordination until they could be sure that their motive was perfectly pure. I used to say, 'In that case, you'll wait for ever. Your motives will never be completely pure. Your motives for committing yourself to the Buddhist path will always be tainted with self-interest. It's enough if on balance you feel that your motive is predominately pure.' Our Going for Refuge becomes complete only with Enlightenment, but in the meantime the very fact that we go for Refuge has the effect of helping to purify the motive with which we go for Refuge.

It is the same with meditation. You do not learn all about meditation before you start meditating. You learn a little, and then later, in the light of some practical experience, you correct or modify the ideas that led you to take it up. And so the process goes on. The reasons for which people stay with something, whether it is meditation, Buddhism, or a particular spiritual community (or even a marriage) are sometimes quite different from those with which they began. We are adjusting our direction, or our vision, or our motive, all the time.

MENTAL STATES HAVE CONSEQUENCES

Dislike is a mind that is unsteady,
Desiring union is a dirtied mind.
Indifference is a laziness with a sense of inadequacy
Coming from a listless body.

Distortion is for the afflictive emotions
To influence body and color.
Not wishing for food is explained
As physical sluggishness due to over-eating.

A very dejected mind is taught
To be fearful faintheartedness.
Longing for desires is to desire
And to seek after the five attributes.[257]

Harmful intent arises from nine causes
Of intending to injure others –
Having senseless qualms concerning oneself, friends, and foes
In the past, present, and future.

Sluggishness is non-activity
Due to heaviness of mind and body.
Drowsiness is sleepiness.
Excitement is strong disquiet of body and mind.

Contrition is regret for bad deeds
Which arises afterwards from grief about them.
Doubt is to be of two minds
About the (four) truths, the Three Jewels, and so forth.

(Householder) Bodhisattvas abandon those.
Those diligent in (monastic) vows abandon more.
Freed from these defects
Good qualities are easily observed.

Briefly the good qualities
Observed by Bodhisattvas are
Giving, ethics, patience, effort,
Concentration, wisdom, compassion, and so forth.

Giving is to give away one's wealth.
Ethics is to help others.
Patience is to have forsaken anger.
Effort is enthusiasm for virtues.

Concentration is unafflicted one-pointedness.
Wisdom is ascertainment of the meaning of the truths.
Compassion is a mind having one savour
Of mercy for all sentient beings.

From giving there arises wealth, from ethics happiness,
From patience a good appearance, from (effort in) virtue
brilliance,
From concentration peace, from wisdom liberation,
From compassion all aims are achieved.

From the simultaneous perfection
Of all those seven is attained
The sphere of inconceivable wisdom,
The protectorship of the world. (428–39)

Negative mental states do not simply pass through the mind leaving no trace behind; they have an effect on us. The mind becomes sullied or stirred up or dull and inert, and this unsatisfactory state of affairs tends to produce further negative mental states. Timidity saps our energy, our confidence, our strength. Eating too much makes us physically and mentally sluggish. All these negative states can also affect the health and general appearance of the body. They are felt in the body, and if they are habitual the body begins to register them in terms of posture or facial expression, and even in terms of the blood pressure.

Note that Nāgārjuna recommends that we should never eat so much that our appetite is fully satisfied. Healthy desire, such as the desire for food or for exercise, is positive; the energy in it is necessary for developing a powerful aspiration towards Enlightenment. Desire is unhelpful only to the extent that it is caught up in sense-objects. Aversion, too, can be useful, especially when it is directed towards *saṃsāra*. But generally our aversion takes the form of hatred or 'harmful intent', which arises from 'senseless qualms', i.e. from baseless fears, anxieties, and insecurities which in some cases may amount to paranoia.

Contrition is usually reckoned as a positive quality, but here it means the regret that is experienced when one's bad deeds produce unpleasant consequences one had not foreseen. You are not sorry that you have behaved unskilfully; you feel sorry because your bad deeds have not proved successful or have got you into trouble, leaving you with a bad reputation.

If you are 'of two minds' about such things as the four noble truths or the Three Jewels,[258] this is because you are unintegrated. The idiom 'to be of two minds' is revealing. It acknowledges that you can have, as it were, two minds that operate at one and the same time, or at least that jostle each other for control of your life. Faith, by contrast, implies that you are integrated, that you are of the same mind about such things as the four noble truths and the Three Jewels from one moment to the next. You retain a clear and conscious belief in the values they represent, and it is these values that give you your identity as a Buddhist.

Faith is to be distinguished from blind faith. Faith does not exclude honest doubt in the sense of openness of mind or suspension of belief until such time as one has sufficient grounds for making up one's mind. But doubt as a fault does not consist in just being of two minds. It is not really wanting to know what one thinks, and therefore not making a genuine effort to find out. The reason we are so loath to pursue the truth is simple. It is because once we have ascertained it, we might have to take up a definite attitude towards it, or do something about it, or even commit ourselves to its realization.[259]

The faults enumerated by Nāgārjuna are to be abandoned by both monk and householder. As far as the bodhisattva path is concerned, the Buddhist householder is expected to work on the elimination of all these negative tendencies in the same way that the monk is, though the monk has other precepts to observe in addition. Nāgārjuna is on safe ground when he assures the king that if he takes care of these defects, the corresponding virtues will take care of themselves. The virtues are the opposite of the faults. Once again, though, we must question the practical usefulness of presenting the spiritual life in predominantly negative terms. We have to assume that while the faults themselves are negative, the ancient Indians had the capacity to engage with them in a positive manner. For us, it is surely better to think in terms of cultivating fifty-seven virtues than correcting fifty-seven faults.

7
THE RESULTS OF ACTIONS

Throughout the *Precious Garland*, Nāgārjuna takes it for granted, as does the whole of the Buddhist tradition, that the law of karma operates not just within our lifetime, but over a series of lives. The advantage of this belief is that it helps to make sense of our observation that some people seem to 'get away with' committing unskilful actions. However, it may be more useful to consider the very real consequences of our actions in this life, regardless of whatever retribution may or may not be waiting for us in our next. What we do and what we experience as a result are directly connected here and now, not just that actions are matched with 'just deserts', but that the results of actions are part and parcel of the actions themselves. There is no cosmic policeman handing out speeding tickets. It is our own actions that help create our character.

Buddhist ethics are bound up with motivation. It is the intention behind your actions that constitutes karma, rather than the actions as such. Of course, if the intention expresses itself in action, the karma will be much more powerful than it would be if you simply imagined yourself doing something skilful or unskilful. At the same time, if you happen to do something accidentally, the relevant karma will pertain to the lack of mindfulness – or perhaps the intoxication – that was responsible for the accident, and this lack of mindfulness is bound up with motivation.

A short life comes through killing.
Much suffering comes through harming.
Poor resources, through stealing.
Enemies, through adultery. (14)

Here Nāgārjuna speaks about the consequences of specific actions, i.e. those relating to the breaking of the first three of the ten precepts. But how does the act of intentional killing shorten one's life? If you create around yourself an atmosphere of anger, hatred, and fear, you are likely to attract those people for whom that kind of atmosphere is natural, and who are at home in it. Acts of extreme violence require a very powerful charge of ill will. When you kill, you are 'tuning in' to a particular wavelength or to a particular realm of being. You will then tend to find yourself in the same world as other people who are inclined to kill, and of course it is quite likely that you will be the victim of one of them at some point. Alternatively, it may be guilt on account of what you have done that draws you into situations in which you, in your turn, may be harmed and thus punished.

This kind of approach, though not the traditional one, has the advantage of reflecting the complexity of the karmic process. One could easily jump to the conclusion that if someone dies young, for example, it is because they killed someone in a previous life. But this does not necessarily follow. There are a number of reasons, other than karma, for a person's early demise. The fact that actions have consequences does not mean that everything that happens to one is the karmic result of actions one has committed in this or in previous lives. This applies to all the examples of unskilful actions and their consequences given by Nāgārjuna.

Generally speaking, those who harm living beings will suffer. But do they always suffer in this life? Obviously not, it has to be said. Certainly they suffer no more than do many who are clearly innocent. Likewise, many who steal acquire considerable wealth, especially those who steal by devious means, like crooked financiers. But harming others is always dangerous. You will inevitably create animosity in those you harm, and sooner or later that animosity will be directed against you. It is significant that fierce competition is sometimes referred to as 'cut-throat' competition, and if you cut the throat of your competitor, you must expect that he will try to cut yours.

To identify the kind of suffering that must follow an unskilful action, one has only to look at the mentality behind the action. One has to imagine the mental state of one who is bent on harming others to know the kind of suffering they will eventually have to experience. As for stealing, this is the expression of a mind that is never satisfied with what it has. If killing is natural to the beings in hell, stealing is natural to the *pretas*, or 'hungry ghosts'. *Preta*-like people are always on the lookout for what they can appropriate. This is no less true of petty thieves than it is of crooked multimillionaires. So driven are they by acquisitiveness that they lose the capacity to appreciate and enjoy what they possess, as well as losing their ability to appreciate people. Human relationships are trampled underfoot in the pursuit of profit.

According to Nāgārjuna, the result of adultery is that one makes enemies. Adultery is not just a matter of stealing another person's spouse; one is seriously disrupting that person's whole life. It may be one thing to break up a casual sexual relationship, particularly when one is young, but it is quite another to break up a long-standing marriage, especially when there are children. You will probably deeply offend two entire families. In ancient times an adulterous affair could set off a feud that lasted for generations. If we are to believe Homer, the adultery of Paris with Helen of Troy led to a ten-year war that resulted in the destruction of an ancient city and the loss of thousands of lives.[260]

> These are effects for humans,
> But prior to all is a bad transmigration. (18)

We have been discussing all these faults with respect to the impact they have in the present life, and it is clear that within the span of one lifetime their consequences can be disastrous. But it is worth bearing in mind that for Nāgārjuna, as for most Buddhists throughout history, their *principal* 'fruit' is a bad rebirth.

THE FRUITS OF VIRTUE

> Opposite to the well-known
> Fruits of these non-virtues
> Is the arising of effects
> Caused by all the virtues.

Desire, hatred, ignorance, and
The actions they generate are non-virtues.
Non-desire, non-hatred, non-ignorance,
And the actions they generate are virtues. (19–20)

It might seem odd that the beneficial fruits of skilful actions should be couched in negative terms in certain respects. It is almost as though the moral virtues had no character of their own but consisted simply in not acting unskilfully. The implication is that the negative is, as it were, the original position and the positive merely the negation of the negative. But these negative terms are not really as negative as they seem. In Sanskrit, the words *alobha*, *adveṣa*, and *amoha* are formed by adding the negative prefix a- to the terms *lobha* (desire), *dveṣa* (hatred), and *moha* (ignorance), but in each case the connotation is not negative but positive. We find the same thing in the case of English. Terms like 'immortal', 'infinite', and 'immaculate' have a much more positive meaning than their negative form might suggest. Though formally they are negations of other terms, they stand as positive terms in their own right. Many Sanskrit and Pāli negative terms work in a similar way. They may be grammatically negative, but the impression they convey is often more positive than a literal English translation is able to communicate. That language appears to falter before these positive qualities, or these ideas, suggests that they are really beyond conceptual understanding.

However, does the fact that language is inadequate mean that we have to start from our experience of the morally negative? It is true that most people are caught up in all sorts of negative mental states and unskilful habits which, to begin with, have to be given up. But what is going to inspire us to give them up? It will surely be something positive. And how can that positive quality inspire us if it is simply the negation of something negative? There is nothing particularly Dharmic about expressing positive qualities by giving negative prefixes to negative terms. It is purely a matter of Indian linguistic and literary convention. Indeed, a positive term such as the Sanskrit *maitrī* (*mettā* in Pāli) is more truly positive than any of its negatively-formed equivalents.

Nāgārjuna spells out the negative consequences of various unskilful actions of body, speech, and mind and then adds, almost as an afterthought, that the corresponding skilful actions will have correspondingly positive results. He could have presented things in the opposite way, spelling out the positive results of skilful actions and leaving us to work out the negative consequences of unskilful actions for ourselves. That he does not do so is just a matter of Indian linguistic convention; it has nothing to do with the Dharma as such. Putting things negatively may have worked in the past, but in the modern context it is probably better to think of the moral virtues in more positive and inspiring terms, and to dwell on the positive results of skilful actions, rather than on the negative consequences of unskilful ones. Otherwise, we may give people the impression that the Dharma is just the taking away of something, and its goal a mere absence.

This is a common misconception of Buddhism, especially in the West. In the popular imagination, Nirvāṇa is often a literal snuffing out, and *śūnyatā* literally a yawning void, a blank emptiness.[261] It is as though one disappeared over the edge of Enlightenment into complete nothingness. In view of this understandable but utterly mistaken reading of the Dharma, we should be careful that we do not, as a matter of course, couch its supremely positive ideals in negative terms. Certainly in English at least, negative terms do not do justice to the sublime union of wisdom and compassion, which is the ultimate goal of the spiritual life. If, in teaching the Dharma, we have occasion to tell people what it is *not* good for them to do, we should make sure that we also tell them, in the same breath if possible, what it *is* good for them to do.

DEVELOPING A NEW WORLD

> Through multitudes of pure wishes
> Your Buddha Land will be purified.
> Through offering gems to the King of Subduers
> You will emit infinite light.
>
> Therefore knowing the concordance
> Of actions and their effects,
> Always help beings in fact.
> Just that will help yourself. (299–300)

The advice here is simple: we should make sure our actions accord with the effects we want to produce. We know that the best way of helping ourselves is to help others. Of course we often forget and revert to acting as if it were otherwise. So how do we remind ourselves? The easiest way, perhaps, is to rely on regular contact with spiritual friends, whose advice and example will jog our memory.

The Sanskrit term for Buddha Land is *buddhakṣetra*, and the idea of such a realm is based on the principle that thoughts can give rise to things, and that spiritual aspiration can be a creative force. For instance, if you practise generosity, if you have a generous heart, then, under the law of karma, you will be well provided for materially in the future. That is, we live in a certain kind of world, a world with certain general characteristics that give us a certain kind of experience. This world, this particular realm of experience, has been created by our actions. Our 'collective karma' produces the world in which we collectively live.

By changing your karma, however – that is, changing your mental state, your volitions or aspirations – you can modify your future environment. From this simple law can be extrapolated the further possibility that if your volitions or aspirations are sufficiently powerful, you will be able to create a whole world of your own, a world better and purer than worlds usually are.

Pure Buddha Lands feature prominently in the Mahāyāna scriptures.[262] They are depicted as the ideal environment in which to practise the Dharma and are often described in lavish detail. Each one is produced by a particular Buddha, not with a view to his living in it in solitary splendour, but so that others might be reborn in it and practise the Dharma under his guidance more easily than they could in an ordinary, impure world. His Pure Land is the product of his intense and sustained aspiration, as a bodhisattva, to bring such a world into existence. It is pure in the sense that it is inhabited only by human beings and gods. In it there are no animals, no *asuras*, no *pretas*, and no hell-beings. Moreover, there is no distinction of gender, one does not need to work, food and clothing appear spontaneously, and one is free to listen to the Dharma day and night.

The idea of the Buddha Land or Buddha-field need not be taken literally. It is myth, especially when named Buddhas are represented as creating their individual Buddha-fields. The principle underlying the myth is that of the power of positive thinking, as it used to be called. If you think positively, if you radiate positive emotion, especially the more refined spiritual emotions, you will have a subtle but perceptible effect on your surroundings; you will create a positive atmosphere, almost like an aura or a magnetic field, that influences everyone within its compass.

Any powerful personality tends to create around them a world that reflects their character and values. Some people set up an inharmonious world; others, one that is intensely fearful or suspicious. Politicians tend to create *asura*-like worlds of ruthless ambition, while artists tend to create worlds dedicated to beauty and other aesthetic values. In the case of a Buddha, his wisdom and compassion create a 'gravitational field' so strong that it affects all who come within its range. This is his world, his Buddha-field.

In certain Mahāyāna *sūtras*, this kind of phenomenon is vastly extended and amplified. They hold that a Buddha can, by sheer power of thought, create a whole ideal realm within which other living beings may be reborn. And there is more than a simple difference of degree between a Pure Buddha-field and an ordinary, impure Buddha-field, because the former is a separate, ideal environment, distinct from our own world. It has been brought into existence by an individual bodhisattva's unaided efforts, by means of his or her own entirely pure thoughts, aspirations, and vows. An impure Buddha-field, by contrast, overlaps with the ordinary world. The Buddha shares it with other beings who have brought that world into existence by virtue of their impure karma.

It is like the difference between trying to practise the Dharma in the midst of ordinary city life, with all its distractions and difficulties, and doing so in a rural retreat centre. Such a centre is a small temporary Pure Land, where spiritually positive external conditions have been deliberately created. Its sole purpose is to enable retreatants to hear and practise the Dharma.

According to the Mahāyāna, the way to ensure rebirth in a Pure Land is to make a solemn aspiration to be reborn in one, and then to engage in the appropriate spiritual practice. The best known of these Pure Lands or Pure Buddha-fields is Sukhāvatī, or 'abounding in bliss', the Pure Land of Amitābha, the Buddha of Infinite Light. This Pure Land figures prominently in Far Eastern Buddhism, where it is a central feature of the various Pure Land schools of China and Japan. These schools emphasize the importance of paying homage to Amitābha or chanting his name.

This Pure Land form of Buddhism seems to have arisen out of a widespread sense of spiritual despair. People felt it was no longer possible for them to attain Enlightenment in this world, where conditions were so unfavourable to the practice of the Dharma. They therefore aspired to be reborn not in this impure world but in a completely different world where conditions for practice were ideal. The Vajrayāna saw things differently. This world itself is the Pure Land, could we only see it as such. As you become pure yourself, the world too becomes pure or, rather, you experience it as pure. You are living in the midst of a divine mandala, not just in this defiled old world. You hear all sounds as mantras, see all forms as those of Buddhas and Bodhisattvas. Thus the Vajrayāna comes back to the general principle underlying the myth of the Pure Land, namely that we create our own worlds, whether now or in the future.

You can change the realm in which you live by setting up the conditions that will support a positive change in your mental states. In fact you are creating a world of your own around you all the time. The question is, what sort of world are you creating? And how are you going about creating it? A lot depends upon the kind of people with whom you associate, who will either draw you up to their own level of existence or drag you down. A Buddhist centre, for example, should be a little world, or at least an oasis, of awareness and kindness, quite different from other social environments. When one enters, it should look different, feel different, and be different, otherwise it isn't really a Buddhist centre at all. One should feel drawn into a lighter, purer, deeper realm of being.

> Just as it is explained in medicine
> That poison can be removed by poison,
> What contradiction is there in saying
> That what is injurious (in the future) can be removed by suffering?
>
> It is renowned (in Great Vehicle scriptures) that motivation
> determines practices
> And that the mind is most important.
> Hence how could even suffering not be helpful
> For one who gives help with an altruistic motivation?
>
> If even (in ordinary life) pain can bring future benefit,
> What need is there to say that (accepting suffering)
> Beneficial for one's own and others' happiness will help!
> This practice is known as the policy of the ancients.

If through relinquishing small pleasures
There is extensive happiness later,
Seeing the greater happiness
The resolute should relinquish small pleasures.

If such things cannot be borne,
Then doctors giving distasteful medicines
Would disappear. It is not (reasonable)
To forsake (great pleasure for the small).

Sometimes what is thought harmful
Is regarded as helpful by the wise.
General rules and their exceptions
Are commended in all treatises. (372–7)

We are all prepared, in certain circumstances, to endure a little pain in order to avoid a greater suffering later on. Yet for the sake of our little mundane pleasures we deny ourselves the far deeper pleasure, happiness, and fulfilment of the spiritual life. If someone in whom you have absolute trust were to say, 'Give me ten pounds today and I'll give you a hundred pounds tomorrow,' and you were to refuse the offer, you would in fact be refusing to give up ten pounds while being perfectly willing to give up a hundred pounds. It just makes no sense! Similarly, it makes no sense if one would rather forfeit the bliss of Nirvāṇa than give up the pleasures of worldly life.

All this sounds very logical, but whether we act in accordance with it depends upon our having faith. We need to be deeply convinced of the rewards ultimately in store for us before giving up those right under our nose. A bird in the hand, as they say, is worth two in the bush. Most people's attitude will be, 'Give me a clear and compelling *experience* of the rewards of the spiritual life, and no doubt my interest in mundane pleasures will drop away quite naturally.' But in order to enjoy spiritual pleasures you have to give up worldly pleasures at least to some extent, and to do this you need to be resolute and determined. People find it difficult to give up habits like smoking, despite the clear health benefits of doing so. It is going to be much more difficult to give things up for the sake of less tangible benefits.

Moreover, the spiritual rewards in store are not really to be compared with mundane rewards. We might have heard of spiritual pleasures, but I suspect that if one was to ask practitioners which were the greatest pleasures they had ever enjoyed, few would mention spiritual ones. They would probably come up with things like sex, drink, food, films, or perhaps music. The pleasures of meditation and the Dharma will seem to most of them rather anaemic in comparison. Spiritual pleasures may sometimes be very intense, but they are by nature a lot more subtle than are the pleasures of the senses. The idea of giving up worldly enjoyments for a few moments of meditative rapture every once in a while will seem to most people a poor bargain. Spiritual rewards are subtle and complex, being more a matter of fulfilment, peace, contentment, and freedom than simply a question of pleasure, however rarefied.

The argument suggests that pain or discomfort or deprivation is a safe investment, and I am not convinced that this is really the case. Nor does it express the true bodhisattva spirit. We are being invited to practise the Dharma not because doing so is intrinsically attractive and inspiring but because it is a safer investment of our time and energy than any mundane option. It will pay better dividends and you will get a better return for your money, so to speak. There is something less than elevating, even something ignoble, about such an argument.

Whatever the situation might have been in Nāgārjuna's time, today it is probably unwise glibly to advise people to give up the trivial, trashy pleasures of the world for the sake of the great spiritual pleasures to come, or to assure them that any sacrifice they make now will eventually prove to have been well worth it. To give up small pleasures in the hope of enjoying greater pleasures later on is something of a gamble. In any case, human beings need pleasure just to keep going. If life is devoid of pleasure of any kind, a reaction will surely kick in sooner or later; the denied need will make itself felt and in the end one is likely to resort to the grosser worldly pleasures rather than to the more refined ones in order to satisfy it.

Pleasure is an essential part of human life. Without it, the spiritual life itself becomes so joyless, dull, and arid that the practitioner may eventually lose interest in it altogether. The secret is to make sure that such pleasure is not incompatible with the spiritual life. Pleasurable experience that is skilful – and mundane pleasures *can* be skilful – has a tonic effect on the system. It is a mistake to imagine that by forcing ourselves to give up all our little pleasures now, we automatically move closer to the day when we will experience the pleasures of the spiritual life in all their glory.

This is not necessarily so. It would be like setting off on a week's journey thinking that if you do not weigh yourself down with food you will get to your destination more quickly. Travelling light might serve your purpose for the first day or two, but after that you will slow right down, and may give up altogether due to lack of nourishment. Small pleasures should be enjoyed quite consciously, for the sake of one's overall spiritual progress, not indulged in or snatched at furtively or guiltily.

Worldly pleasures, being ultimately unreal and ultimately unsatisfying, are not to be relied on and may even be harmful. But engaging with your friends in innocent recreation that leaves you with more positive energy than you had before, can only be beneficial. Milarepa, the eleventh-century Tibetan poet and hermit, may have given up all worldly pleasures, but his songs are full of the joys of the spiritual life. We have to be honest about how much spiritual joy we actually experience, and must be careful to make up for what may be lacking in that respect with the help of relatively skilful mundane enjoyments. Otherwise we may experience a strong reaction against the spiritual life itself. On the other hand, we must be quite honest about the importance we give to pleasure, whether we 'go for Refuge' to it, or are simply making room for it within the larger context of our lives as Buddhists.

The human attitude to pleasure and pain is a complex one. It may well be that those who are really struggling with difficulties will come out better and stronger in the end – but not necessarily. Nobody, however philosophical they may be, wants to lose all their money or to have their house burn down, and such calamities may even plunge some people into a prolonged depression. This important caveat aside, Nāgārjuna's point is crucial for the spiritual life. The wise person will always be able to turn a very real difficulty into an opportunity. Some people do not need to experience a hard time and may be very inspired, and fully committed to the spiritual life, without ever experiencing one. But for others, a hard time might be just what they need to bring about a radical change for the better in their life.

There are people who object to spiritual practice on the grounds that though it is supposed to free us from suffering, it nonetheless brings us varying degrees of discomfort, both physical and mental. Buddhist lifestyles seem to be all about the giving up of ordinary pleasures and comforts. However, any suffering experienced in the course of spiritual practice is only incidental. It is not the only result, nor even the necessary result of such practice. Solitary confinement is regarded by most people as a punishment. Naturally, therefore, they imagine that there is little joy to be had from a solitary retreat. 'Wouldn't you go mad with boredom?' they will say, 'Surely it's just masochism.' But the wise see solitude, when undertaken voluntarily, as a highly beneficial spiritual challenge. It may be difficult, even painful at times; one might experience boredom and even moments of despair, but if one persists, one will access inner resources that will be experienced as deeply enriching and pleasurable. Though sometimes painful, the process will eventually lead to blissful mental states and even to the bliss of liberation.

If your basic motivation is to help others, any pain that you experience in the course of making good this aspiration is going to enable you to be helpful in the long run. This can be quite a fruitful way of regarding any difficulties you may experience, especially when you are trying to follow the bodhisattva path. Suffering is also helpful in a more direct way, in that it helps you to understand the suffering of others. If you haven't suffered much, you are less likely to be able to empathize with those who have. Again, this is not an absolute rule. If you have sufficient imagination, you need little pain of your own in order to empathize deeply with the pain of others. But if you have always enjoyed good health, for example, you might tend to think that people who are often ill and physically frail are making a lot of fuss about nothing, and should pull themselves together and stop complaining. Or, if you have never smoked, you can be quite unsympathetic towards those who feel the need for a cigarette twenty or thirty times a day: 'What do you mean, you can't give it up?' you say, 'All you need is a little will-power.'

This lack of sympathy, based on having too easy a life oneself, can extend into quite diverse areas. If you are full of faith, for example, you may be less than understanding towards someone who is racked by spiritual doubts. Or, if you are quite content with a celibate life, it can be hard for you to appreciate the difficulties and responsibilities of someone who is married and has a family. But those who have experienced problems in their personal life, or who have discovered their own human weakness, often become more sympathetic to others. Those who can remember their own early difficulties with meditation are often the best teachers of the subject. They certainly will not insist on long sessions of meditation for beginners, sessions that can only result in discomfort and boredom.

It is very difficult to enter into another person's experience. It is difficult for a law-abiding citizen to feel sympathy for the convicted criminal, or for the criminal to feel sympathy for the law-abiding citizen who helps to send him to jail. The person who wears the shoe knows where it pinches, as the proverb goes. When it comes to defining compassion, I fall back on Tennyson's phrase, 'some painless sympathy with pain'.[263] But the way to that state is generally found through a personal experience of pain, whether in the form of chronic illness, sudden bereavement, or crushing humiliation.

(The limitlessness of the merit of) wishing to help limitless realms
Of sentient beings is like (the limitlessness of those beings).

These practices that I have explained
Briefly to you in this way
Should be as dear to you
As your body always is.

Those who feel a dearness for the practices
Have in fact a dearness for their body.
If dearness (for the body) helps it,
The practices will do just that.

Therefore pay heed to the practices as you do to yourself.
Pay heed to achievement as you do to the practices.
Pay heed to wisdom as you do to achievement.
Pay heed to the wise as you do to wisdom.

Those who have qualms that it would be bad for themselves
(If they relied) on one who has purity, love, and intelligence
As well as helpful and appropriate speech,
Cause their own interests to be destroyed.

You should know in brief
The qualifications of spiritual guides.
If you are taught by those knowing contentment
And having compassion and ethics,

As well as wisdom that can drive out your afflictive emotions,
You should realize (what they teach) and respect them.
You will attain the supreme achievement
By following this excellent system:

Speak the truth, speak gently to sentient beings.
Be of pleasant nature, compelling.
Be politic, do not wish to defame,
Be independent, and speak well.

Be well-disciplined, contained, generous,
Magnificent, of peaceful mind,
Not excitable, not procrastinating,
Not deceitful, but amiable.

Be gentle like a full moon.
Be lustrous like the sun in autumn.
Be deep like the ocean.
Be firm like Mount Meru.

Freed from all defects
And adorned with all good qualities,
Become a sustenance for all sentient beings
And become omniscient.

These doctrines were not just taught
Only for monarchs,
But were taught with a wish to help
Other sentient beings as befits them.

O King, it would be right for you
Each day to think about this advice
So that you and others may achieve
Complete and perfect enlightenment.

For the sake of enlightenment aspirants should always apply
themselves

To ethics, supreme respect for teachers, patience, non-jealousy, non-miserliness,
Endowment with the wealth of altruism without hope for reward, helping the destitute,
Remaining with supreme people, leaving the non-supreme, and thoroughly maintaining the doctrine. (487–500)

If the number of beings is limitless, then the merit accruing from wishing to help that limitless number of beings in limitless worlds is itself limitless. The practices that support this wish should therefore be valued accordingly. In the Indian idiom, they should be as dear to you as your own body or, as it is also said, your own eyes. The argument here is that one should look after one's spiritual practice with the same healthy attachment and daily attention to detail as one looks after one's body. You should feed, nourish, and cherish your practice as you do your body, to keep it alive and thriving. It is not something you can pick up and let drop when you feel like it. It has a life of its own, and it can die of neglect if one allows it to do so.

Just as the body finds its highest purpose in acting as a support for spiritual practice, so the spiritual practice itself must have some higher purpose of its own. We should take care of our practice just as we do of our empirical self, especially the physical body. But it is not enough to practise mechanically. We should ask ourselves, 'Am I making any progress? What difference are the practices making? Am I eliminating the unskilful and developing the skilful?' It seems that for Nāgārjuna, 'achievement' means achievement in meditation, though even this is not enough in itself. You may be radiating friendliness, compassion, sympathetic joy, and equanimity, but wisdom ultimately lies beyond these. Meditational achievement is for the sake of attaining wisdom.

Surely, once one has attained to wisdom, there can be nothing further to which one needs to pay attention. Why, then, does Nāgārjuna go on to advise us to 'pay heed to the wise as you do to wisdom'? If you have wisdom yourself, surely there can be no need to pay heed to the wise? Nāgārjuna's point is that in a sense there is no such thing as wisdom. There are only wise individuals. 'Wisdom' is just an abstract term, but if you meet a wise person you do in fact encounter wisdom. You may fancy that you have developed wisdom, but you can know if you have really done so only by coming into contact with a wise person, and through the existential exchange that takes place between you and that particular human embodiment of wisdom. It is folly, as Nāgārjuna observes, to have reservations about one's reliance on such a teacher.

Wisdom is not an abstraction. It can exist only in living men and women. It has to be embodied. In fact, it is of the nature of wisdom to distinguish between concepts and lived experience. You may think you have it, but the real test is how you fare when you meet a wise teacher, and are seen for what you are. No book will ask quite the questions that he or she will ask. No book will see beyond the words you speak. Thus it is clear why we might want to convince ourselves that we are better off not relying on a wise teacher. We are afraid that we shall be seen, and that the fixed view that we hold of ourselves will be questioned.

It is possible to start developing a more 'embodied' wisdom by teaching. That will give you a much clearer view of how deep your understanding of the Dharma really goes, especially if those you are teaching are intelligent and self-confident. Ordinary human contact with other members of the spiritual community also has the useful function of challenging us to live out what we know conceptually. It has also the more important function of bringing into consciousness a level of understanding that we had not, perhaps, known we possessed. More important than realizing you do not know what you thought you knew, is realizing that you knew what you did not know you knew.

The qualities that Nāgārjuna says we should look for in a teacher are relatively modest. They should be contented in the sense of being well centred. They should be compassionate in the sense of having a disinterested desire to help others. They should be ethically aware, of course. They should have 'wisdom that can drive out your afflictive emotions,' i.e. not necessarily perfect wisdom. We do not need to sit at the feet of a fully realized master; we need human contact with enough 'embodied' wisdom to enable us to overcome our negative mental states. If we were so fortunate as to spend time with someone who was fully Enlightened, that would indeed be marvellous, but sustained spiritual friendship of the more ordinary kind will really give us everything we need.

Many Westerners have reservations about committing themselves to any cause or any person of a religious nature. There are good reasons for this caution as well as bad ones. One good reason is that a person who is emotionally vulnerable or gullible may be exploited or abused by a charlatan. A bad reason is imagining that by avoiding any kind of commitment we can preserve our spiritual independence. The reliance that Nāgārjuna suggests we place on a teacher should not be understood as dependence in the sense of a passive clinging to the teacher for some kind of emotional security. Reliance on a teacher means taking their advice seriously and trusting their wisdom, but in the end we have to take responsibility for our actions, and not expect the teacher to do everything for us.

Nāgārjuna concludes with a simple, straightforward, and comparatively easy teaching. Wanting to leave the king with something inspiring and, at the same time, well within his capacity to practise, he comes right down to earth. His 'excellent system' begins with speech, for if you are an aspiring bodhisattva, it is probably through speech that you will make your first contact with the beings you want to help. We should say what is truly pleasant – that is, what is actually useful – and not necessarily say what people are going to find agreeable. We should speak with a kindly awareness of the hearer and of how they might feel. We should be aware of what we are saying and whether it is really worth saying. Without being glib, we should try to speak convincingly. We should speak methodically and with discretion, not simply at random. And of course we should not run others down or defame them. Finally, we should not simply parrot the words of others, but base what we say on personal experience.

Next comes a series of basic qualities which are mainly concerned with the stabilization of a positive mental state, with the containment of one's energies, and with keeping one's emotions under control. When you are excited and 'bubbly', it can feel quite positive, but in fact at such times your energy is loose and unintegrated. Moreover, if your energy is easily aroused, it is more likely to be reactive, so that excitability is not such a positive state as it may seem. Deceitfulness and procrastination make it difficult for others to like us.

The final precept offered to the king is that he should have contact with spiritually-minded people ('supreme people' in this translation). Nāgārjuna says we should associate only with those who are going to support our practice of the Dharma, and avoid those who might undermine it in any way. For someone who is living in the world, that is obviously a counsel of perfection. But we should maintain contact with spiritual friends, and keep these friendships in good repair. When all else fails, it is spiritual friendship that keeps us going through any difficulties, doubts, or disappointments we may encounter on the path to unexcelled Enlightenment.

WRATHFUL DEITIES

INTRODUCTORY NOTE

by Sangharakshita

The black or dark blue or brown figures are sometimes referred to by Western writers as demons or devils. Laurence Waddell, an early writer on Tibetan Buddhism, who was very well informed but didn't have much understanding, often used this sort of nomenclature, referring to the 'Buddha fiendesses' and 'Buddha demonesses', but this gives quite the wrong impression. These figures are not demons or fiends or anything like that. They in fact belong to the highest level of all, the Buddha level, but as seen under the aspect of the destruction of spiritual ignorance. Sometimes they are very fierce indeed. Often they have thick dark strong bodies, wear garlands of skulls and elephant hides and tiger skins, and have long teeth or tusks and three or more eyes. They are very wrathful, they trample upon enemies, and have an aureole of flames. Though they look very fearsome, they are not demons and have nothing to do with hell in the Western sense. They symbolize those aspects of Enlightenment which burn up, overcome, and destroy ignorance in all its forms.

The point is that ignorance is so strong, so powerful, that the beautiful peaceful figures are unable to cope with it. They have to assume these terrible, wrathful forms in order to make some impression, at least, on the forces of ignorance, which otherwise don't take any notice of them. There are many legends to this effect, describing how a Buddha or bodhisattva closed his eyes in meditation and out of his forehead emerged a great beam of light at the end of which appeared a terrifying monster, a wrathful figure brandishing a club and roaring 'I want your blood.' Apparently this is sometimes the only way in which the Enlightened mind can operate in this deluded world. When one confronts and surveys the world, one can feel every sympathy with this sort of approach. Perhaps it isn't the peaceful, meek and mild Buddhas and bodhisattvas who are going to get anything done, but the more wrathful and terrifying ones.

However, one must always remember that this is not ordinary anger but what the Tantric tradition calls 'the Great Anger' or 'the Great Wrath'. Great, *mahā*, here means 'purified by *śūnyatā*', because it has passed through the fires of the Absolute. It is not an anger based on ignorance or on the ego; on the contrary, it is based on pure compassion, pure love. When ignorance and hatred encounter that love, they can experience it only as wrath or anger. This is the basis of this sort of symbolism in Tibetan Buddhism, especially in the Tantra.

Sangharakshita, *Tibetan Buddhism, Complete Works*, vol. 13, pp. 68–9.

EDITORIAL NOTE

Like the mandala offering verse that opens this volume, the *Invocation to the Wrathful Deities* (p. 317) was translated from a traditional text with the help of Dhardo Rimpoche.

The wrathful Vajrapāṇi

INVOCATION TO THE WRATHFUL DEITIES

HŪṂ

Burst forth, O *Jñāna* blazing like fire at end of aeon!
Consume the blind darkness of delusion and craving,
And destroy all fear of the *Yamarāja*[264] of hatred.
Great Heroes, recognizable by the tiger-skins (you are wearing),
Tramplers upon the hosts of *Rākṣasas*[265] and evil spirits, slayers of foes,
O *Vidyārājas*,[266] O Wrathful Ones, be seated.
You are being summoned here to annihilate the evil spirits.
Puja is being performed for the benefit of all sentient beings:
Hence you must come.

HŪṂ

Appearing from the non-duality of the Voidness and appearance,
You are ever devoted to the welfare of the world;
(You) having manifested yourselves with awe-inspiring body,
To you, O Greatly Wrathful Ones, I make obeisance.

Within, abiding in the peaceful *Jñāna*,
Yet without of fearsome (foe-)devouring aspect,
Terribly roaring like a thousand claps of thunder,
And with these twain overcoming *Rākṣasas* and demons,
To you, O Greatly Wrathful Ones, I make obeisance.

You whose essence is the highest Knowledge,
(Who) wielding in your hands all sorts of weapons
Have rooted out the *kleśas* and (deadly) poisons,
To you, O Snake-Adorned Ones, I make obeisance.

By fire like that at aeon's end encircled,
Hero-like you stand with flexed legs (wide) apart,
Angrily glaring with sun-and-moon-like eyeballs,
To you, O Consumer of the *Yakṣas*,[267] I make obeisance.

Greatly Fierce, like fire at end of aeon,
Splendid (white) tusks gleaming like a thousand lightning flashes,
And shout like thousand thunderclaps forth sending,
To you, O *Yakṣa*-killer, Wrathful King, I make obeisance.

HŪṂ
Roaring HŪṂ and fear inspiring,
Yakṣas destroying without exception,
Ye Gods, bestowers of all *Siddhis* whatsoever,
To you, Foes of the *Yakṣa*s, I make obeisance.

From '*The Stream of the Immortality-Conferring Nectar of the Esoteric Oral Tradition of the Lama's Bestowal of the White Tārā Abhiṣekha*', rendered according to the explanations of Dhardo Rimpoche. (Words in brackets represent explanatory additions by the translator.)

LIVING WISELY

Further advice from Nāgārjuna's *Precious Garland*

EDITORIAL NOTE

Living Wisely is the second instalment of Sangharakshita's two-part commentary on Nāgārjuna's *Precious Garland*. Like *Living Ethically*, it is based on a study seminar led by Sangharakshita in 1976.

In her preface to the first edition of *Living Ethically,* Vidyadevi sheds light on the relationship between the two books. 'Beneath the question of how best to help others, and how to develop the altruistic spirit that wants to', she writes, 'are questions of another kind: what is "self", what are "others", and how does a world in which that distinction exists come into being?' Such questions are the subject matter of *Living Wisely*.

Nāgārjuna's original teaching in *The Precious Garland* moves continually between the ethical view and the view – or even no-view – of emptiness. In consequence, to seek a clear separation between the two themes would be to miss the subtle balance of Nāgārjuna's teaching. *Living Wisely* might therefore best be considered as a return to the themes already visited in *Living Ethically*, now viewed from the perspective of the Perfection of Wisdom.

The philosophy of the Madhyamaka can be challenging terrain. For further insights into Sangharakshita's explanations in *Living Wisely*, readers are directed to Nāgārjuna's monumental work, the *Mūlamadhyamakakārikā*, and especially to the translation and commentary by Jay Garfield available as *The Fundamental Wisdom of the Middle Way*, Oxford University Press, Oxford 1995. At various points in *Living Wisely*, endnotes refer the reader to corresponding passages in the *Mūlamadhyamakakārikā*. For additional support, an audiobook of Garfield's translation and commentary on the *Mūlamadhyamakakārikā* is available online from audible.com. Its use in conjunction with the print edition is highly recommended, as is an especially wholehearted reading of Śāntideva's *Bodhicaryāvatāra*, to which Sangharakshita makes occasional textual reference, also available from audible.com.

The text of *Living Wisely* was edited by Tim Weston, Pabodhana, and particularly Jinananda. It was then reviewed and revised by Sangharakshita with the help of his secretary Vidyaruchi and can therefore be regarded as Sangharakshita's more recent teaching on the subject.

The numbers at the end of each quotation indicate verse numbers in Jeffrey Hopkins' translation of *Nāgārjuna's Precious Garland*. We are indebted to Snow Lion Publications for their permission to publish excerpts from the above work.

INTRODUCTION

> The doctrines of definite goodness
> Are said by the Conquerors
> To be deep, subtle, and frightening
> To the childish who are not learned. (25)

The *Ratnāvalī* or *Precious Garland* is a long sequence of verses in which the second-century Buddhist monk Nāgārjuna explains to an unknown king how to make progress on the spiritual path. In the first set of verses, 'High Status and Definite Goodness', Nāgārjuna outlines the practices that produce what he calls 'high status', by which he means rebirth in a state of happiness within *saṃsāra* as a human being or a god. Following this is a longer and more detailed account of the wisdom by means of which one achieves 'definite goodness'. By 'definite goodness' Nāgārjuna means liberation and omniscience, and by wisdom he means the cognition of emptiness, as described in the Perfection of Wisdom *sūtras*. Then, in the second section, 'An Interwoven Explanation of Definite Goodness and High Status', he explores at length the doctrinal basis for the attainment of spiritual insight, and discusses the nature of emptiness. Insight being so difficult to achieve, however, Nāgārjuna recommends to the king that he should apply himself to the wholehearted practice of ethics, which eventually is sure to lead him to wisdom.

Nāgārjuna's advice to the king on ethical matters was the theme of the first volume of this commentary, published as *Living Ethically*.

This second volume goes on to consider the verses of the *Ratnāvalī* that deal with teachings on wisdom and emptiness, which Nāgārjuna calls doctrines of 'definite goodness'. This shifts the emphasis away from high status within *saṃsāra* towards liberation from *saṃsāra* altogether. In this endeavour we need guidance from those who are themselves liberated: the Buddhas, or to use an equivalent term, Jinas or 'Conquerors'.

The Buddha remarked more than once in the course of his teaching life that the doctrines he was attempting to communicate were deep and subtle. Indeed, according to the Pāli scriptures, this was on his mind immediately after his Enlightenment, when he was considering whether to teach at all. He reflected that 'this Dharma, this truth, this reality which I have realized is deep, profound,'[268] meaning that it could not be understood on a purely rational level; indeed, that it could not be fully comprehended at any level by anyone who was not Enlightened. He was thinking in that context about the doctrine of conditioned co-production, but the same reservations could apply to teachings about liberation in general. However deeply you may go into them, absorbing them at ever more profound levels of your being, there are always more things to learn, deeper and broader ramifications to consider.

When the Buddha was wondering how to communicate the Dharma, he thought at first that it was too 'subtle' (*nipuṇa* in Pāli) to be made known to people whose minds were caught up in mere reasoning. Not that it is subtle in the intellectual sense; it is more that it is elusive. Eventually, of course, he saw that it could be communicated to those 'with little dust on their eyes'.[269] The Dharma is not only subtle and profound. It is also frightening, though not – as the translation of this verse rather clumsily has it – simply to 'children who are not learned'. There is an antithesis here, as in the *Dhammapada*, between 'the fool' (*bāla*) and 'the wise' (*paṇḍita*). It is not lack of learning that renders the doctrines of definite goodness frightening, but immaturity – more precisely, spiritual immaturity. Likewise, if a 'pandit' is wise, it is not because he is learned. Where you are on the spectrum of spiritual maturity has nothing to do with intellectual acuity or learning or even how mature you are in the ordinary sense. Even the most learned adults are likely to be frightened by these doctrines. Why they might be so fearful, or even terrible, we shall be in a better position to understand when we look more closely at them.

Nāgārjuna sees this subtle wisdom as a middle way between extremes, for which reason the school he founded is known as the Madhyamaka, one of the two main schools of Mahāyāna philosophy. The other school is that of the Yogācāra. Nāgārjuna based his teachings on the Perfection of Wisdom *sūtras*, which he is said to have obtained from the *nāgas*, the wise serpent kings, and brought back from their palace in the depths of the ocean.[270] This mythic origin reflects the fact that they come from the very depths of human understanding, and in the Indo-Tibetan tradition, the Madhyamaka is always described as the 'profound Madhyamaka'. The Yogācāra on the other hand is described as the 'sublime Yogācāra', and again, the description is appropriate to the myth of its provenance, because the inspiration for the teaching is said to have come from above. Asaṅga, the founder of the school, is supposed to have ascended in meditation to the Tuṣita *devaloka*, the heaven of content. There he received his inspiration from the bodhisattva Maitreya, who waits in the Tuṣita heaven for the time to come when he will be reborn on earth for the last time and become a Buddha. As the teachings of the Yogācāra are said to have been brought back 'from on high' in this way, they are described as sublime.[271] The terms 'sublime' and 'profound' refer respectively to the heights and the depths of our experience; but these outer limits in either direction bring us to essentially the same realm of experience: one that is as far from our everyday understanding as it is possible to get. The teachings they describe come from another dimension; they are unimaginable to the mundane mind.

1

THE RELATIONSHIP BETWEEN WISDOM AND FAITH

I bow down to the Omniscient,
Freed from all defects,
Adorned with all virtues,
The sole friend of all beings. (1)

The Madhyamaka tradition is renowned for the relentlessness of its logic and for the subtlety with which it is able, from the perspective of *śūnyatā* (emptiness),[272] to undermine all concepts, all notions of a stable or concrete reality. It may come as a surprise, therefore, to find that Nāgārjuna begins his treatise with an expression of heartfelt devotion to the Buddha. There is nothing intellectual about this opening verse at all. In hailing the Buddha as an exemplar of virtue and of wisdom, and a friend to all beings, Nāgārjuna is establishing a devotional, emotional rapport between himself and the Buddha. The word 'adorned' is particularly significant, emphasizing as it does that the Buddha's virtues are beautiful and attractive. For many people the word 'virtue' may suggest something rather grim and forbidding, but Nāgārjuna reminds us that true virtue is not like that at all. Seen as adorned with virtues, the Buddha becomes beautiful and fascinating, and this vision is the beginning of faith, in the sense of a heartfelt response to the spiritually attractive.

As he contemplates the Buddha, Nāgārjuna feels a joy that gathers in emotional intensity as the verse progresses. Beginning with the purely 'intellectual' category of 'Omniscient', and then praising the apparently negative characteristic that the Buddha is free from defects of character, Nāgārjuna goes on to see the Buddha as manifestly adorned with positive spiritual qualities, and as 'the sole friend of all beings'.

Of all the superlatives in the verse, the final claim is perhaps the most surprising, suggesting as it does that only the Buddha can give us the help we truly need, so that he is the only real friend that any of us have. In other words, there is a link between virtue and friendship. Western philosophers would agree: Aristotle, for example, maintains that there can be no real friendship between those who are wicked. According to him, friendship is a virtue, and therefore only the virtuous can be true friends.[273]

How is this? What moral virtue and friendship have in common is an element of consistency and constancy. There may sometimes be a camaraderie amongst the wicked, but rarely is there true 'honour among thieves', and rarely therefore any real friendship between them. Without a high level of moral integrity, a person is always at the mercy of his or her own weaknesses and is therefore not dependable. In the normal run of things, most of us come to realize that there are certain people upon whom we can depend for most things and in most circumstances, while other people are likely to let us down when we are in trouble. It can be a distressing experience to learn that some of your 'friends' were only there for the good times; but it is comforting, on the other hand, to find out who your real friends are.

Ultimately, however, you can place complete trust only in someone whose virtues are solid enough to survive any change in circumstances whatsoever. The Buddha has this rock-like quality, but one who is full of kindness and concern as the result, say, of some temporary success in meditation may become rather less friendly when their meditation practice is less rewarding. Expressions of friendliness based upon positivity gained from meditation are certainly more reliable than protestations of eternal friendship made while in a state of alcoholic intoxication, say, but they are conditioned, nevertheless. The friendship of the unconditioned mind, on the other hand, can be trusted absolutely. A Buddha may express himself in ways that are not what you expect or may not even welcome, but you can nonetheless entrust your ultimate welfare to him and his teaching. Likewise, the spiritual community, by virtue of its connection with transcendental ideals, can be broadly trusted to provide you with what you need, even if it is not always what you want.

It might even be said that one can be a true friend only to the extent that one has a spiritual life, in the broadest sense, in which case one's commitment is primarily to the ideal, and secondarily to one's friend. This order of priorities might seem to be a restriction of friendship, making it dependent on something that is outside it. But this would be to misunderstand the nature of the spiritual ideal, which is essentially about freedom and spontaneity. Only on the basis of that ideal of freedom and spontaneity can you commit yourself to a friendship in a truly positive way. You do not commit yourself to your friend in the sense of committing yourself to the various imperfections of their character. The basis of the relationship and what makes that mutual commitment possible is your shared commitment to your ideals.

Of course, many people haven't even heard of the Buddha. How, then, can he be a friend to all beings? He can be in the sense that he is potentially, or in principle, the friend of all beings inasmuch as through his teaching he gives them the greatest of all gifts, the gift of the Dharma.

When Nāgārjuna calls the Buddha the 'Omniscient', can we take him literally, or does he simply mean that he is completely Enlightened? The Sanskrit term being translated is not *samyak-sambuddha*, 'completely enlightened', but *sarvajñā*, 'all-knowing', so it would seem that Nāgārjuna does indeed mean 'Omniscient'. In the time of the Buddha there were teachers who claimed to know literally everything; or at least their disciples made this claim on their behalf. One such teacher was Mahāvīra, the founder of Jainism, who in the Pāli scriptures is called Nāṭaputta. His omniscience was said to be of a kind that would know, for example, the exact number of leaves on a particular tree.[274] Some people of the Buddha's time seem to have thought of Enlightenment in this way, as being a complete factual knowledge about everything that exists. However, the Buddha said quite clearly that he did not possess this kind of knowledge. He was not all-knowing in the sense that he literally knew everything. All he claimed was that he knew Nirvāṇa and the path leading to Nirvāṇa, and he knew what helped and what hindered as one sought to follow that path. In other words, the Buddha's was a spiritual omniscience, and this is what Nāgārjuna means when he salutes him as *sarvajñā*.

After his Enlightenment the Buddha declares that he has seen the 'builder of the house'.[275] He has seen, in other words, that the world as we experience it, with its problems and disappointments, is the illusory creation of an illusory idea of a fixed self. It is in *this* sense that the Buddha knows everything there is to be known. He knows the *true nature* of all things. He also knows how illusory any kind of knowledge – except this direct cognizance of reality – really is. The Buddha's all-seeing knowledge is not concerned with the objects of ego-consciousness so much as with knowledge of what that ego-consciousness really amounts to.

Some Buddhist texts, particularly those of the Mahāyāna, out of devotion ascribe to the Buddha much more knowledge than he claimed to possess.[276] Indeed, in some quarters the idea that a spiritual teacher should be all-knowing still persists. In India, for example, people sometimes go to their spiritual teacher with a stomach ache expecting him to know precisely what is wrong and what they should do about it; and some Indian teachers do their best to live up to this expectation and offer answers to such questions in a very confident manner. What with all the competition, they are under pressure to adopt such a role; if they don't, there are other teachers who will. However, although it is comforting to think you are in the hands of someone who knows everything, from the spiritual point of view it simply isn't necessary to have such a teacher. Someone who is spiritually enlightened may very well be entirely ignorant about quite a number of things, although this is something some people find it difficult to believe.

The Buddha would have known less about geography than most children of today. If he had considered the matter at all, he would presumably have thought that the world he lived in was dominated by a great central mountain called Mount Sumeru, rising out of the ocean and surrounded by seven mountain ranges, this being the traditional Indian view.[277] In fact, it is hard for us to imagine how limited was the range of information available to the Buddha. We do not, therefore, have to subscribe to what the Buddha may have thought about geography, or any of the other physical sciences, in order to gain insight into the nature of reality. By the same token, the Buddha's limited grasp of matters that we take for granted does not affect his spiritual knowledge in the least.

In other words, spiritual realization is quite compatible with scientific ignorance, and when the one is expressed through the medium of the other, it is important to distinguish between the two, and not to feel that in order to benefit from the teaching we have to swallow the scientific ignorance with it. Some modern Buddhists try to find in the scriptures teachings that seem to anticipate the discoveries of modern science,[278] but this is entirely to misunderstand the nature of spiritual and transcendental knowledge. Even supposing that the Buddha had indeed anticipated the theory of relativity, say, or quantum physics, this would not prove he was Enlightened.

A Buddha, for example, would know that a car was conditioned, and he would not therefore be attached to it; but he wouldn't necessarily be able to tell you how it worked. In other words, he could have a deep spiritual understanding of the car without any mechanical understanding of it whatsoever. The two kinds of knowledge are entirely distinct. The Buddha would be seeing the car in its reality, but in another sense he would know nothing about it. He would know only that it was part of conditioned existence.

To appeal to science on behalf of Buddhism is basically to appeal to authority. In the modern world not everyone accepts authority of the religious kind, but a great deal of trust is placed in the authority of science. The scientist is the person who knows: science by very definition is knowledge; so if Buddhism agrees with science – or so the argument goes – Buddhism must be in the right. If a scientist speaks in favour of the spiritual life or Buddhism or meditation, that will enhance their standing in the eyes of many people. People from traditional Buddhist cultures seem to be particularly keen on presenting Buddhism in science-friendly terms. Conscious of the waning prestige of Buddhism in their country, they try to make a case for the congruence of their faith with science. In so doing, they may imagine they are thereby strengthening Buddhism, but what they are really doing is submitting the spiritual authority of the Dharma to what they see – or imagine other people may see – as the greater authority of science.

Similar claims have been made on behalf of the ancient Indian wisdom of the Vedas. Hindus will sometimes say that if you only look deeply enough into the *Rigveda*, you will find all the instructions you need in order to build a nuclear device.[279] They will tell you in all seriousness that the ancient Indians knew how to make atom bombs, but simply chose not to do so. Again, it is as though science was the real authority. But this is to tread on dangerous ground. Science, after all, is always changing: the science of today is not the science of yesterday, nor will it be the science of tomorrow. It is not as though there is an absolutely established body of scientific truth that everyone can accept. More importantly, any appeal on behalf of a spiritual tradition to scientific or any other authority comes from being unsure of one's ground, which in turn is likely to come from having little or no spiritual experience of one's own to fall back on. There is a more general misunderstanding at work here too: the assumption that spiritual knowledge is related in some way to mundane knowledge, that someone who studies philosophy or comparative religion is more likely to be able to understand the truths of Buddhism than someone who is a gardener or a window cleaner. But Buddhism can only be understood by virtue of spiritual insight, and spiritual insight has nothing to do with intellectual understanding.

It is even possible that the more highly educated and intellectual a person is, the less likely they will be able fully to appreciate – really to take in – the essence of Buddhism as a felt experience. They may be able to master the philosophical teachings and even write about them, though without sufficient spiritual experience they are likely to become confused and miss the point. To be a Buddhist is to understand certain spiritual principles and do your utmost to put these into practice.

Any idea we have of knowing something carries a certain assumption about the true nature of the thing known, its relation to the knower, and the kind of knowledge achieved. A flower, for example, can be known in a certain way by dissecting and classifying it. But an equally valid and for most people much more rewarding kind of knowledge of the flower depends not upon recognizing its botanical species, but seeing in its impermanent beauty a reminder of universal impermanence, including one's own impermanence.

In his essay 'East and West',[280] D. T. Suzuki makes an interesting comparison between two poems, one by a Japanese Zen poet and the other by the nineteenth-century English poet Alfred, Lord Tennyson. The two poems are about the same subject: a flower growing in a wall. Suzuki remarks that whereas the Zen poet just contemplates the flower in the usual Zen way, the English poet cannot help taking hold of it, both literally and metaphorically:

Flower in the crannied wall,
I pluck you out of the crannies,
I hold you here, root and all, in my hand,
Little flower – but if I could understand
What you are, root and all, and all in all,
I should know what God and man is.[281]

According to Suzuki, this poem illustrates an attitude towards nature, and perhaps towards life in general, that is peculiarly Christian. The English poet cannot just leave the flower growing where it is. He has to pluck it out, roots and all, and subject it to his musings on the nature of God and man. Suzuki suggests that if Tennyson had simply allowed the flower to grow where it was while he contemplated it rather than yanking it out of the wall, he might have gained some insight into its nature. As it is, he gets nowhere. Suzuki's point is well made, but it has also to be said that English poetry tends to be more complex than Zen poetry, and one should be careful not to make assumptions about the poet's intentions. There is almost certainly an element of impersonation in the poem – that is, one should not identify the poem's viewpoint as being too precisely that of the poet. In view of the richness of the poetic tradition in which Tennyson was writing, it seems probable that the irony and pathos of this collision of the philosopher and the scientist over the flower would not have been lost on him.

So from a spiritual point of view, how much intellectual knowledge of the Dharma do we need? The simple answer is: probably a lot less than we think. However, the role that study plays in our practice can owe as much to temperament as to necessity. Buddhism traditionally makes a distinction between what is termed the *dhammānusārin*, the 'doctrine-follower', and the *saddhānusārin*, the 'faith-follower', and it seems that people belong to one or the other of these types.[282] For the faith-follower, personal contact with the teacher is much more important than study. Faith-followers are not inclined to bother with studying the Dharma much beyond the personal precepts and instructions their teacher gives them; they are not concerned to learn more than a few basic principles that they can put into practice personally. The doctrine-follower, by comparison, wants to know all about Buddhism in all its aspects, perhaps not even just the doctrines of their own school, and they are therefore not so dependent on the teacher. They like to work things out for themselves, and to find out what other people have thought and said and done in other times and other cultures.

Both types of person are capable of practising Buddhism, inasmuch as both are 'followers': they both follow the Dharma in the sense of trying to be true to it, although in very different ways. The doctrine-follower is much more than a mere intellectual or scholar, just as the faith-follower is more than a sentimental devotee of the Buddha. If we seek examples of each type, the Buddha's companion Ānanda comes to mind as representative of the faith-follower, while another of the Buddha's most famous disciples, Śāriputra, is clearly a doctrine-follower. In the context of Tibetan Buddhism, if Je Tsongkhapa is very much the doctrine-follower, Milarepa is equally obviously the faith-follower.

The two approaches do not seem to combine naturally in the same person, and most people are clearly either one or the other. You might find yourself switching from one type to the other at different times in your life, but you are unlikely to be able to combine them fully at the same time, though you can do your best to balance out your main tendency. Doctrine-followers at their best have broad sympathies, while faith-followers at their best are deep and intense. The risk for doctrine-followers is that they may become too wide in their sympathies, spreading themselves too thinly and thus becoming shallow in their practice. Meanwhile, faith-followers run the risk of becoming too narrow, even a little fanatical, and unable to understand people with very different ways of practising the Dharma. To guard against such risks, all you can do is make time for study if you have strong faith and devotion, or balance your predilection for learning, if that is the case, with devotional practice.

But even for the faith-follower, a basic level of intellectual understanding is indispensable to spiritual progress, and this is something Nāgārjuna goes on to illustrate later in the *Precious Garland*. It is not enough to store up merit by making offerings to shrines and stupas, by chanting the sacred scriptures, or even by moral action. You have to engage with the deeper truth of things, and this must involve the intellect as well as the emotions, wisdom as well as faith. Ultimately we are looking for a quality of wisdom that supersedes conventional understanding. The term wisdom is therefore open to misunderstanding if it is distinguished from faith in too rigid a way. Wisdom is not a cognitive as distinct from an emotional faculty. One cannot speak of wisdom in terms either of 'knowing' or of 'feeling'. It is both, once it is experienced at a high enough level. It is an intuitive understanding and also an intuitive feeling. In other words, at a higher level there is no real distinction between faith and wisdom, or devotion and understanding. They are not experienced separately or even jointly. It is comparable to the experience of being deeply engaged in a conversation. You are thinking and feeling at the same time, and it is not possible to distinguish between the two: the thought is the feeling and the feeling is the thought. The attainment of wisdom is like this, albeit at a much higher level.

So Nāgārjuna's aim in the *Precious Garland* is not to generate an *understanding* of the Dharma in the king, but to generate the Dharma itself, just as the Buddha is described not as speaking *about* the Dharma, but as *speaking* Dharma. Nāgārjuna doesn't want to talk *about* the truth. He wants to *awaken* the truth. He is reminding the king of his inherent potential for Enlightenment, for establishing the practices and becoming thereby a vessel of the Dharma.

> Due to having faith one relies on the practices,
> Due to having wisdom one truly knows.
> Of these two, wisdom is the chief,
> Faith is its prerequisite. (5)

To summarize this verse: it is through faith that you are able to commit yourself to the practices, and it is through the practices that you achieve high status. It is then through wisdom that you attain definite goodness and break the hold on your mind of the desire for happiness and high status. Nāgārjuna's interpretation of faith here seems to be pitched at quite a low level; he seems to be suggesting that it is relatively unimportant compared with wisdom. It is true that the word 'wisdom' implies intellectual cognition, and by definition gives the emotional side of things less emphasis. But to think of it in this way is to miss the heart of the matter. To understand the true relationship between faith and wisdom we do well to consider the teaching of the five spiritual faculties.[283] Here, faith and wisdom are equal and coordinate, each balancing the other, without any suggestion that faith is somehow less important than wisdom. Following this teaching, one cannot say that wisdom is the 'chief' over faith any more than faith is the 'chief' over wisdom. One might just as well say that wisdom is the prerequisite of faith as that faith is the prerequisite of wisdom.

But many modern Buddhist writers, especially Theravādins, share Nāgārjuna's emphasis here. One sign of this is the translation of *śraddhā* as 'confidence'.[284] Confidence is certainly one level of its meaning, and faith at this level, as Nāgārjuna says, enables you to rely on the practices. But it is not the whole meaning of faith, because ultimately the wisdom through which you achieve definite goodness needs to be balanced with a higher faith. When it is linked with wisdom, faith is a total emotional response – even an aesthetic response – to the spiritual ideal, to the virtues with which the Buddha is adorned. It includes confidence and trust, but there is also a strong element of devotion. For Nāgārjuna, faith in this sense is generally every bit as important as wisdom, so perhaps here he should be paraphrased as follows: It is through confidence that one comes to rely on the practices, which will then bring about the arising of wisdom joined with faith, by which 'one truly knows'. Of these two, wisdom joined with faith is the chief, and confidence secondary, even though confidence is needed in order to bring the higher spiritual quality of wisdom/faith into being.

> One who does not neglect the practices
> Through desire, hatred, fear, or bewilderment
> Is known as one of faith,
> A superior vessel for definite goodness. (6)

You need faith if you are to lead the spiritual life.[285] It is through faith that undermining and distracting emotions such as craving, hatred, and fear are overcome. Faith is also needed to counteract spiritual ignorance, by which I mean an essentially emotional resistance to spiritual practice under the guise of a pseudo-objective depreciation of its value. It is possible to temporarily hold these negative states at bay in meditation, and thus to enjoy a deeper state of absorption and concentration, and no doubt faith at a very basic level is required if we are to practise meditation in this way. However, a much deeper faith is needed in order to commit oneself to a path of practice that promises to destroy the very roots of those negative states. Faith does not come on its own. It is connected with refined positive emotions such as friendliness, compassion, joy and equanimity (the four *brahma vihāras*)[286] and also with devotion. To these one can add the positive counterparts of the hindrances to meditation: contentment, patience, energy, and concentration. Without these qualities little spiritual progress can be made. You may want to be free of negative emotions, but you cannot just push them away; they must be replaced with something more positive.

The immediate benefit that we can expect from Buddhist practice is not that it will make us happier and more contented or even psychologically healthy, at least not in the way that we normally think of these qualities. What we can hope for is that it will help us to be more emotionally positive, though in a refined sense. Taking up Buddhism should help us become more interested in other people, more able to empathize with them, more willing to rejoice in other people's happiness, and less likely to fall into states of dejection or elation as the result of everyday circumstances. Above all, it should bring us a joy that is not dependent on ordinary human happiness or contentment.

In very simple terms faith is a deep enjoyment of the contemplation of the ideal. As Nāgārjuna says in an earlier verse of the *Precious Garland*, faith is the 'quintessence of the means' of happiness. When you contemplate the Buddha ideal, or the figure of the historical Śākyamuni, and experience a deep happiness, that is faith. Faith means rejoicing in your practice and being fascinated by the spiritual ideal, which in itself will make you want to get on with your practice. Rejoicing in the Buddha's qualities, you will feel happy, and getting on with your spiritual practice is a natural expression of that happiness. In this way you are carried along in your practice by your faith. So faith is not mere belief in this or that doctrine; it is a response of delight and fascination, much more like one's emotional response to a beautiful painting or piece of music or landscape.

Faith is not a sort of investment plan. You're not putting in a lot of laborious practice in the belief that you will reap dividends later on. It may be necessary at a very early stage to grit your teeth and carry on regardless, but you should not accept that this is just the way things are. You should always be looking to emerge into a feeling of happiness about what you are doing. If there's no joy in your spiritual life, there's no faith either. Without joy, there may be belief, but no faith.

In simple terms, Buddhist faith may be said to consist in rejoicing in the Buddha's full realization of his spiritual potential, and trusting that you yourself are capable of reaching the same goal. By contrast, John Middleton Murry, writing about Cardinal Newman, observed that the cardinal believed in God but did not trust him.[287] This must be terrible: to have a firm belief that your fate is in the hands of someone who cannot be trusted to look after you! You can never be quite sure whether your wretched accumulation of virtues is going to see you through or whether some long-forgotten unconfessed sin may not trip you up and cast you straight down into hell. Even if you have forgotten it, you can be sure that the vengeful Jehovah of the Old Testament has not. Believing in God is like having an angry father; you know he's there, and you don't trust him not to turn round and give you a theophanic clip round the ear from time to time. At the very least, our Christian conditioning may encourage us to think of the spiritual life as essentially sweat, grind and struggle, and this is no basis for the arising of faith in the true sense of the term.

These Old Testament attitudes are very often the aspects of Christianity that linger in the post-Christian consciousness, and they seep into the ways in which some Western people relate to Buddhism. Of course there is more to Christianity than this. One has only to look around medieval cathedrals, listen to the best of Christian devotional music, or read the words of the King James Bible, to get some sense that there is a healthier kind of Christian faith, based on an awareness of what the Bible calls 'the beauty of holiness'.[288] Nor can we say that Buddhism is all sweetness and light. Clearly the Dharma poses a threat to the ego, and to have to confront the reality of *śūnyatā* can be terrifying (even though the threat holds no danger because it threatens what in any case is unreal).

In one of the Mahāyāna *sūtras* Ānanda is asked what initially attracted him to Buddhism, and he says that it was the personal appearance of the Buddha. When he saw a beautiful light shining from the Buddha's body – the radiance of all his past meritorious deeds – he was so overwhelmed that he simply had to become a disciple.[289] For him it was an aesthetic as much as a spiritual experience. However, with all its disciplines and restrictions, religious faith and practice is often regarded in the West as being rather unattractive, even grim and forbidding. I remember that on my return to England in the 1960s I led a celebration of the festival of Wesak, the anniversary of the Buddha's attainment of Enlightenment, at the invitation of the London Buddhist Society. As I gave my little talk, I couldn't help noticing how glum everyone seemed at the idea that the Buddha had attained Enlightenment and shown them the path to Nirvāṇa. They seemed rather sorry that he had gone to all that trouble! By contrast, in early Buddhist scriptures like the *Mahāvastu*,[290] the whole text is suffused with an atmosphere of rejoicing in the Buddha. Everybody is happy that a Buddha has arisen in the world. It is almost as though life has become one great long celebration.

The Buddhists I encountered at that Wesak meeting in London were very different from the monks I had known in the East. A Buddhist monk is supposed to have given up everything. He has no home, no wife, no job. And yet even the oldest and most infirm of them is cheerful and even jolly much of the time. Contrary to popular belief, not all monks are highly spiritual people, devoting their time to silent meditation or study of the *sūtras*. They are by no means otherworldly. Yet they do not chafe at the life of renunciation. In freeing them from worldly attachments, it leaves them happy and carefree, like schoolboys on holiday. Even if they do not experience deep compassion, they generally feel sorry for lay people, with their worldly cares and responsibilities. Renunciation even seems to keep them young. A layman of 50 may be beginning to show his years, but a monk of the same age often looks quite boyish.

If there is one thing above all others that is lacking in Western Buddhism it is perhaps the atmosphere of joy that we find in the older Buddhist texts and in traditional Buddhist societies. We could start to remedy this by celebrating traditional Buddhist festivals in a more colourful and joyful manner. After all, the spiritual life is a happy life. If you cannot be happy following the spiritual path and living in accordance with the Dharma, how are you ever going to be happy? Buddhism may not be easy, but even at its most difficult, it should certainly not be miserable.

This is a constant theme in the *Songs of Milarepa*. The Tibetan yogi Milarepa lived a life of extreme physical hardship, but communicated his joy in the Dharma through his songs. One of the stories about Milarepa describes a young man who, even as he is reduced to suicidal despair by Milarepa's initial refusal to take him on as a disciple, declares, 'I have never been so happy as today.'[291] The spiritual life is sometimes like that: you may be experiencing real suffering, and at the same time you have never been so happy in your life. This is happiness in a deeper sense than mere pleasurable feeling – it is the happiness that comes from faith. The way of life to which this faith leads you may sometimes be difficult, but you know in your heart of hearts that you are on the right track.

2

THE ESSENCE OF THE MATTER

> 'I am not, I will not be.
> I have not, I will not have',
> That frightens all the childish
> And extinguishes fear in the wise. (26)

The doctrine of definite goodness is what we might call Buddhism proper, or the true Dharma. This is the essence of the matter: no 'I', and therefore no 'mine'. What we experience as the 'I', what we experience as 'myself', is not an ultimately real entity. There is, therefore, no question of 'me' as I experience myself being really and truly here, either in the present or in the future. Since there is in reality no 'me' in the ultimate sense, there is no question of my possessing anything, either now or later on: 'I have not, I will not have.' No self, no possessions.

The ordinary person will take this as meaning 'You simply don't exist', and that must surely be seen as a very terrible thing. This is meant to be the path of liberation, but when they first come across this teaching, very few people are going to experience it as being liberating. It is natural to feel that it negates one's whole being, and this is very difficult to accept. The doctrine of definite goodness spells the death of the ego, and when we realize that the ego is pretty well everything with which we identify, it feels like *our* death. However, what the doctrines are really pointing out is that what you take for reality, that is to say yourself, is not the be-all and end-all of existence that you take it for. It is not that you are completely non-existent or unreal. It is rather that you do not exist in the way you think you do. There is another dimension of your experience that is more real, and in contrast with this reality, what you take to be real is an illusion. Indeed, far from being a threat, to the wise this doctrine 'kills fear'. All fear, after all, arises out of one's desire to preserve and protect the ego. But if the ego is shown to be an illusion, one's fears on its behalf are extinguished. You see that there is no one to lose anything, so you have nothing to lose. If you have no 'I', you save yourself a world of trouble.

This may sound simple, and in fact it *is* simple, but getting a real sense of it is not. It is subtle and elusive. Sometimes you may get a fleeting glimpse of it at the moment of waking. Perhaps you catch the tail-end of a dream and realize that for what seems like hours you have been living some other life in some other world or dimension. Because it has so little connection with your daily life, it slips away from you almost immediately, but at such times you may get the feeling that there is another life behind your normal waking existence. It is easy to forget this other life, but we return to it again and again when we dream; and while we are in it, we identify with it just as we identify with our daily life. In the Indian tradition generally, though perhaps more within the Vedic tradition than in Buddhism, it is customary to reflect upon the fact that we have another existence in the world of dreams. This other dimension of consciousness is regarded as being as real in its own way as our 'normal' waking experience. Within Tibetan Buddhism, 'dream yoga', one of the six yogas of Nāropā, is an attempt to prolong awareness into the dream state, so that you dream consciously and learn to direct your dreams.[292] Eventually this practice awakens you to the fact that waking consciousness is only the tip of an iceberg. You spend hours every night dreaming – so where do you go, what do you do? Is your dream life not part of your life? Does it not have an effect upon your state of mind?

The Vedic tradition attaches particular importance to the state of dreamless sleep.[293] No object is experienced, and therefore the ego is not experienced either, so deep sleep is regarded as a kind of unconscious or negative state of union with Brahman. From a Buddhist point of view, however, it is not a state of real insight or Enlightenment, because there is no awareness in it, neither waking consciousness nor dream consciousness, and with the reawakening of consciousness from the state of deep sleep the ego returns. Nor do you remember anything of that state of deep dreamless sleep. However, it certainly provides daily evidence for the fact that the mind is not limited to ordinary waking consciousness. It has other dimensions, which we play down because they seriously undermine the claims of the waking self to be the whole of us. But why should the waking consciousness appropriate our total being? Why should it proclaim the 'I' as the totality of our existence? We are more than that, bigger, more multifaceted.

People who have experimented with consciousness-altering drugs tend to be more aware of these other realms of being than most people. Although they will not have entered them with either discipline or consistency, they have nevertheless had a direct experience of the fact that what we normally think of as the finite human personality is only a very small part of what is actually there. In meditation we have the opportunity to enter into further levels or dimensions of mind in a more integrated and sustained way. People who are not very imaginative are often bemused by the ability of those who have a cultivated or creative inner life to enjoy themselves without many material rewards or satisfactions. Anyone who meditates should be able, at least for a while, to live with even fewer of the material supports upon which the ego relies. Even if you lose everything – your money, your job, even your freedom – you know that you have inner resources upon which you can draw. You can still explore the infinite riches of your dream life, and the depths of your mind as revealed in meditation.

Not only is the 'I' only one small aspect of the self; it is one, moreover, that is constantly changing. As we realize the other dimensions that are accessible to us, we should be able to see that the ego, with all its petty anxieties and resentments, is not as important as it thinks it is. Otherwise, we confine ourselves to a narrow band of the total spectrum of our experience, as if the colour orange were to claim that it was the only colour, and that the other colours of the rainbow were somehow unreal or imagined. The ego is highly adaptable, of course, and will subtly appropriate experiences wherever it can do so. We have to be careful not to posit some kind of self-existent, absolutely real 'big self' to which we go forth from our 'small self'. However, reality can only be reached through an expansion of consciousness, through bringing all the bands of the whole spectrum of consciousness together, not by simply focusing on our present experience.

By him who speaks only to help beings,
It was said that all beings
Have arisen from the conception of 'I'
And are enveloped with the conception of 'mine'. (27)

Our conception of separate beings arises from the conception of 'I'. This is not to say that without the conception of 'I' you have non-being. Without the 'I' you have neither being nor non-being. The 'I' thought is the seed from which our sense of being arises. Enveloping this seed of being there is a wider conception of 'mine', representing the extent of its possessions. Here am I, sitting in the midst of my possessions: my house, my car, my land, my wife, my family, my football team, my religion. All my possessions act as a kind of tent protecting the conception of 'I', creating the little cocoon that is my world and that fills out the 'I', giving it a sense of solidity and permanence. 'I' and 'mine' are therefore very closely intertwined. The envelope protects, but it also limits. It is as though the 'I', the sense of self, sets an inner limit, while the sense of 'mine' sets an outer one.

Nāgārjuna's designation of the Buddha as one who speaks only to help beings gives us an insight into the nature of the Enlightened mind. Even when he is asking someone to do something, as when he asks Meghiya to stay with him and not go and meditate, his own need for a companion is not at the forefront of his mind.[294] Likewise, even when he speaks of the non-existence of the ego or self, his message is one of compassion, loving-kindness, and sympathetic joy. He is not out to deprive us of anything. Indeed, he is doing quite the opposite.

When considering these teachings, we have to be careful that we do not approach the Dharma with a negative self-view. If our gut-feeling is that we have or are a self, it can feel as if the Dharma is going to take something away from us that is central to who we are, when in fact the Dharma is there to help us see ourselves, whatever we may be, more clearly. Perhaps it is better simply to see ourselves as limited. Instead of challenging ourselves to explode our deluded conception of the self directly, it may be more helpful to think of breaking out of the closed circle of self-interest that is the emotional expression of our delusion. We can think of expanding that circle through the cultivation of *mettā* or loving-kindness until our self-interest is absorbed in a concern for the welfare of all living beings.[295] Overcoming ego is not just an idea; it is an experience, a way of life.

'The "I" exists, the "mine" exists.'
These are wrong as ultimates,
For the two are not (established)
By a thorough consciousness of reality just as it is. (28)

The key phrase here is 'wrong as ultimates'. 'I' and 'mine' are real experiences, but they have only a provisional validity. Experience the 'I', acknowledge your possessions as your own, as 'mine', but don't take these notions as the last word on the subject; don't take these inner horizons as giving you any idea of the true extent of your mind, your world, your reality. Why? Because this is how the Enlightened consciousness, which sees things as they really are, experiences 'I' and 'mine': it sees them as only relatively real, not absolutely real. It expands beyond the 'I', the 'mine'. Growth is not just up; it is not just a two-dimensional development. It takes place in all directions. It is therefore not always very obvious. Sometimes you may feel as though you are not growing spiritually, but it may be that you are developing in ways, in directions, that you have not been able to envisage.

The mental and physical aggregates arise
From the conception of 'I' which is false in fact.
How could what is grown
From a false seed be true? (29)

The five aggregates (*skandhas*) are: *rūpa* (form), *vedanā* (feeling), *saṃjñā* (Pāli *saññā*) (perception), *saṃskāra* (volition), and *vijñāna* (Pāli *viññāṇa*) (consciousness). They make up the various constituents of the psychophysical organism. When Nāgārjuna refers to what is grown from a false seed, he is referring to the traditional teaching that we are reborn out of ignorance. So again he employs an exclusively negative approach to the ego with a view to getting rid of it completely, at a stroke. It's as though he's not prepared to admit that there is any truth in the ego at all. But how are we to respond to this analysis creatively? Another way of looking at the mental and physical aggregates is to see them as representing a kind of concretization of the ego, a rather rigid structure, closed in on itself. Our task is to open this structure out. Rather than trying to put the ego out of reckoning altogether, it may be better to change the way we see it, to see it less as a thing and more as a way of functioning, or a way of being.

The language we use can be less than helpful when it comes to the ego. Expressions like 'transcending the ego' create a lot of confusion by apparently fixing something non-existent in the form of an apparent object of knowledge. The result is nonsensical: we talk of getting rid of something that never existed or even denying this object of intense interest and concern any reality at all. 'The ego', we say, 'is not real.' If we're not careful, we can spend a lot of time talking about something that does not exist in such a way that it becomes more real to us than it was before we started making so much of it.

The ego doesn't exist even on an empirical or relative level, let alone as a real object of perfect wisdom. At the same time, the term refers to a genuine experience. We have habits of selfishness, and our task is to transform these habits. If we introduce an imaginary object called the ego or the 'I' into the discussion, we complicate the process unnecessarily. You are functioning as an 'ego' when you are closed in on yourself, when you shut yourself off from other people. When you are more outward-going and expansive, on the other hand, when you are engaging with the concerns of others, you are functioning from 'non-ego'. These are two very different experiences: one reactive, the other creative. In a reactive state you feel cold and hard, as though there's a tight little ball inside you, or as if you are constantly circling back on yourself. But in a creative state you feel free and open, expansive and flowing; instead of the little ball there is warmth, radiation, a spiralling outwards and upwards. Note that I am using the *image* of expanding and contracting, which like all images has to be understood properly. It is not that the ego is expanding or contracting. The ego is the contraction of one's being around a delusion, and non-ego is the expansion of one's being. But this expansion is not just inflation. It is a mode of action that does not feed or reinforce that delusion.

This gives us a way of working in accordance with our nature. As we know, sometimes we function in one way, sometimes in the other. If we can be aware of which function is operative at any one time, we are in a position to do something about it, either to sustain it or to break out of it. It is not as if there is a thing called 'ego' that we have to worry about 'having' and 'getting rid of'. It is rather that there is a more satisfying way of living. It may be that you do experience 'something': something hard, knotted and tight, something lodged like a billiard ball in your gullet. You may well feel you need somehow to vomit it up. But there's nothing actually there – that's the point. It is a snarl in a skein of wool, a tangle or knot. It just has to be loosened, opened, unravelled, not cut out. At the same time, that knot is a real knot. We can experience ourselves as ego, and that is a real experience. The ego is a way of behaving, a kind of revolving upon your own axis. It is a particular kind of limitation placed upon experience, a non-expansion or blockage of energy. This fact makes it possible to become free of it, here and now, by behaving in a non-egoistic way, by going out from yourself, by orbiting around something bigger than yourself. In this way you refine the ego out of existence.

Instead of saying that the ego does not exist or that it is not real, you could say instead that to be constantly turning in upon yourself is not the most satisfying form of existence. There are better options available to you. Instead of saying to yourself, 'Just drop the ego', you can say, 'Let yourself open up a little' or even 'Let yourself go.' To the extent that you think of others with genuine concern, you are non-egoistic. Even if you are just thinking of your own wife and children, that is an important step towards being non-egoistic. Thinking about your family is certainly a more effective way of beginning to realize the truth of what Nāgārjuna is saying here than just reading about it and understanding it intellectually.

Paraphrasing Nāgārjuna's verse, we can say: 'Having seen that the egocentric way of behaving is not the best way in which one can behave, one abandons that way of behaving and embarks on a more expansive and other-regarding way of behaving.' As a result of that spiralling outwards of one's being, one's experience of oneself is no longer fixed, rigid, and closed. That is, you become so expansive, so engaged with and interested in the needs of others, that the possibility of going back to that old constrained and self-regarding behaviour no longer exists. The process of your expansion has gathered such momentum that it is now irreversible. It is not that you have somehow jettisoned this thing called 'ego', this extra baggage you do not now need; it is simply that the whole momentum of your being is so creative, so outward-looking, that to behave selfishly has become impossible. It would be against your very nature, and as such quite perverse. This point is what is traditionally known in Buddhism as the point of Stream Entry.[296]

3
IMAGES OF EMPTINESS

Next, Nāgārjuna uses a sequence of images to express, or give some sense of, the nature of emptiness or *śūnyatā*: an empty mirror, a wheel of fire, and a mirage.

THE EMPTY MIRROR

Just as it is said
That an image of one's face is seen
Depending on a mirror
But does not really exist (as a face),

So the conception of 'I' exists
Dependent on the aggregates,
But like the image of one's face
The 'I' does not at all really exist.

Just as without depending on a mirror
The image of one's face is not seen,
So too the conception of 'I' does not exist
Without depending on the aggregates. (31–3)

To see the reflection of your face, you need to look into a mirror. Without the mirror, there is no reflection. In this image Nāgārjuna is saying that it is the same with the *skandhas*. Due to their existence, you see in them an 'I', a self, and if they did not exist, the idea of a self could not arise. The fact of the matter is that you do have physical form, you do have consciousness, feeling, perceptions, and volition, and it is on this basis that you are able to be aware of something you think of as yourself. Of course it works the other way round as well: the *skandhas* arise from the conception of 'I'. It's a reciprocal relation, a mutual arising, but here just one side of it is emphasized.

In the case of the mirror, the reflection you see does not exist within the mirror. This idea of what you look like only arises in the way it does because you have looked into the mirror and interpreted what you see as you – which in a sense it is. But in another sense it is not you at all. The aggregates do not include the 'I', just as the mirror, as an object, does not include the reflection of the face. At the same time the aggregates are who you are in a truer sense than is the 'I'.

Your reflection in the mirror only arises upon the basis of the mirror being there to receive it. Likewise, the self you perceive when you become aware of physical form, feeling, perception, volition, and consciousness arises upon the basis of those five processes. Nāgārjuna is not suggesting that the aggregates are non-existent, any more than the mirror is non-existent. They represent a particular view of one's existence. The 'I' is an extreme version, a sort of concretization of that view.

The *skandhas*, like the elements, only exist, or possess an identity, due to their relationship with things other than themselves. The idea of 'form' only has meaning inasmuch as we are able to make a distinction between form and, say, feeling, or consciousness, and the same goes for the other aggregates. In each case, it is the activity of consciousness that enables us to make the distinction. Just as 'short' has no existence without 'tall', or cause without effect, the individual *skandhas* are no more substantial than is the illusory 'self' they appear to support.

Nāgārjuna's image of course has its limitations. The point to stress here is that the reflection of your face that you can see in the mirror is by no means the whole of you. It is a two-dimensional presentation of one aspect of you. All the other aspects of what you are – your dream life, your meditative experience, your memories of the past, your mindfulness, your ideals and aspirations, your relationships with others, and so on – are absent from that two-dimensional image. The mirror, like the *skandhas*, is itself dependent upon other factors for its existence.

The reflection arises upon the basis of an object deployed as a mirror by an embodied intelligence with organs of vision. Likewise, the *skandhas* do not exist as separate objects apart from the intelligence that is trying to understand its own processes by means of them. This having been said, it must be emphasized that analogies between consciousness and an object of consciousness, however elusive – such as a reflection – are potentially very misleading. The ego does not exist as a thing, so it is not an object of consciousness but a way of being conscious of things, a way of being, of behaving. Nor is it really even that. It is not an *it*, not *an* anything. The ego is like a reflection only in a very limited, specific sense.

Such images need to be understood in terms of what they might mean for us in quite practical, everyday ways. The question is not 'Do I have an ego or not?' but 'Am I looking out beyond what I already know, exploring new avenues, or am I simply going round the same old treadmill of my habits, my established views, my likes and dislikes? Am I stuck with a fixed idea of who and what I am?'

Nāgārjuna's starting point is the understanding that it is because we have an (imagined) ego to begin with that we are egoistic. But we can go a little further and say that because we can be egoistic we can also be altruistic or non-egoistic. If we develop Nāgārjuna's image on that basis we can say that the mirror can either reflect a face or reflect reality, which is empty. Both are possibilities for you, even if only one of them, the empty mirror, reflects you as you really are. Just as the same mirror can either reflect the face of the watcher or a world without fixed and permanent objects, so consciousness can either contract around a clearly defined 'self' in the limited sense or break out of that self-referential view of things. It can be reactive or creative, expansive or contracting, free or trapped. Imagine, say, looking in the mirror and seeing myriad facets of yourself, connecting you with everyone in the world, with everything in the universe. The empty mirror is an image for a consciousness that is not constrained by always referring to some static image of what you think you are.

When the Superior Ānanda[297]
Heard what this means,
He attained the eye of doctrine[298]
And repeatedly spoke of it to monastics. (34)

By 'superior' is meant something more like 'senior', and it probably translates the term *sthavira*.[299] The 'eye of doctrine' is the *dharmacakṣu*, the Dharma Eye: the eye that sees the truth. To 'attain the eye of the Dharma' is a common idiom in the Pāli and Sanskrit scriptures. It means to develop this 'gnostic' spiritual faculty for the direct vision of truth. It is of course a non-dual vision; it is as if you see with a single eye. The result of this depth of insight is that one feels impelled to teach other people how to gain insight themselves. It is not like a job that you take on. When Ānanda had attained insight into what Nāgārjuna calls the doctrines of definite goodness, he could not hold back from sharing it with others. The energy it released in him could not be contained because it came out of the depths of his being. It co-existed with his life, and could not be switched off. According to the available records, after the Buddha's *parinirvāṇa*, Ānanda gained full Enlightenment and had a large following, becoming revered almost as a second Buddha within his lifetime.

BOUND UPON A WHEEL OF FIRE

> As long the aggregates are conceived,
> So long thereby does the conception of 'I' exist
> Further, when the conception of 'I' exists,
> There is action, and from it there also is birth. (35)

You misconceive the aggregates of *rūpa*, *vedanā*, *saṃjñā*, *saṃskāra*, and *vijñāna* when you think of them as static and unchanging things instead of processes of continual flux and transformation. It is when you start to experience what is essentially a process as something static that the 'I' comes into existence. But the 'I' that is aware that you are doing this and starts to reverse the process is not quite the 'I' that is actually doing it, and this raises all sorts of mysterious and confusing questions. Who is it that gets rid of the ego? Who is it that gains Enlightenment? How can the ego get rid of itself? How do we get rid of something that doesn't exist? However, these are the sorts of question into which the Buddha did not think it useful to inquire. He simply said that when you reverse the process, when you stop trying to stem the flow, when you stop seeing the dynamic as static, then you will understand those things, and not before.

Birth considered as a result of action means in this context *re*-birth – that is, the repetition of an old pattern. When you try to arrest the flow, when you try to make what is dynamic into something static, you cannot prevent that dynamic process from going on, but you set up a patterning that gives an appearance of stasis. The continuing repetition of that pattern is what we call rebirth. Action that results in rebirth is habitual reaction rather than creative action. It expresses only the limitations inherent in that pattern. It is repeating the old patterning into another life, and that repetition reinforces the tendency to go on repeating the pattern. When this idea of an 'I' dominates consciousness, therefore, it leads to the arising through rebirth of a personality that is, in its significant aspects, very much like the old one. In simple terms rebirth means repeating old patterns and putting off being truly creative.

> With these three pathways mutually causing each other
> Without a beginning, a middle, or an end,
> This wheel of cyclic existence
> Turns like the 'wheel' of a firebrand. (36)

A firebrand whirled around in the hand produces the illusion of a circle or wheel of fire, a suggestive image for the wheel of cyclic existence, a world we see in terms of things that are in fact illusions formed out of repeated actions. The three pathways are presumably (though this is not completely clear) the misconception of the true nature of the *skandhas*, the misconception of an 'I' based on them, and the action of the 'I', which eventually results in rebirth. In other words, if you fail to see the aggregates in their true nature (i.e. as subject to the three *lakṣaṇas*) you will form the wrong conception of a 'self' or 'I', and the actions performed by this 'self' or 'I' will repeat the old pattern that has been set up. Because it has been repeated so often and, in a way, so successfully, it is virtually – though not quite – impossible to stop.

The 'three pathways' produce one another in a pattern of mutual causality. That is, none of them exists on its own, so none of them is capable of beginning the process. Nor can you conceive of their beginning or ending. You are in the midst of it all, you are part of it, you are these pathways, so how can you see the beginning or end of them?

> Because this wheel is not obtained from self, other,
> Or from both, in the past, the present, or the future,
> The conception of 'I' is overcome,
> And thereby action and rebirth. (37)

This is hardly possible to explain; you either see it or you don't. The 'wheel is not obtained from self' because the self is part of the wheel. Similarly, it is not obtained from what is other than the self, or both from the self and the non-self in the past, present, or future, because these too are part of the wheel. The wheel doesn't arise in dependence upon anything else, and therefore it doesn't cease in dependence upon anything else either. This is important because it means that there is nothing outside the process, this endless going round, to bring it to a halt. The conception of an 'I' ceases when you see the whole wheel as being no more than a self-contained process. It is the self that perpetuates the illusion, and the self alone that is instrumental in its ceasing. The conception of an 'I' ceases when you see that there is no possibility of stepping outside your experience – the wheel – and being a self or 'I' who possesses that experience. Then of course there can be no action based upon the conception of 'I', and no rebirth.

The difficulty in communicating this idea is that one must speak as though the 'I' were real, since otherwise you cannot refer to 'it' at all. One traditional way of explaining this point is for the teacher to close his hand into a fist. When he opens his hand, what has happened to the fist? Does it still exist, or has it ceased to exist? Are the hand and the fist the same, or are they different? Are they both, or are they neither? Similarly, when you become Enlightened, what happens to your ego? It goes the same way as the fist. It is inappropriate to say that it continues to exist, that it does not continue to exist, or both, or neither. There was in reality no fist apart from the open hand you see now. Likewise, there never was an ego apart from the egoless reality that seemed to replace it, and that ego therefore never ceased to exist either. We can think of the open hand with its display of fingers as the aggregates. When the hand and fingers are closed up into a fist, then we have the ego. When the hand and fingers are opened, what has happened to the ego? Can you really say that the ego once existed but that now it does not? Can you say that the ego never existed, either then or now? Perhaps we should drop the idea of the fist and say that at first we saw a closed hand, and now we see an open one.

The problem of the illusory ego is to some extent linguistic. Something non-existent has the same nominative status as something real. Once it is named, even as being non-existent, it starts to play a syntactically substantive role. This unconscious sleight of hand is regularly exploited by the Zen masters. In one well-known story, the master asks the disciple, 'What are you carrying in your hand?' When the student replies that he is not carrying anything, the master says, 'Well then, put it down.' The illusory burden is of course the ego, the 'I'.

One who sees how cause and effect
Are produced and destroyed
Does not regard the world
As really existent or really non-existent. (38)

This verse is Nāgārjuna's summary of the difficult question of the non-existent ego. If it exists, how can you get rid of it? If it does not exist, how is it able to create so much trouble? The best course is to see things in terms of cause and effect: not as things that are produced and destroyed but as interlinked processes, emerging in dependence on one another.[300]

FEAR OF FEARLESSNESS

One who has heard thus the doctrine extinguishing
All suffering, but does not examine it
And fears the fearless state
Trembles due to ignorance.

That all these will not exist in nirvāṇa
Does not frighten you,
Why does their non-existence
Explained here cause you fright? (39–40)

Once we have been introduced to this doctrine of definite goodness, we can do one of two things: we can reflect upon it, engage with it, and consider how to apply it, or we can forget it or ignore it. According to Nāgārjuna we adopt this second course out of fear. So another paradox rears its head: we fear being fearless. Fear being always on account of the ego, one result of seeing through the ego is that we become fearless.

However, the 'I' that must do the seeing is also the 'I' that must be seen through. We necessarily fear this 'demise' of our delusion. Who will guarantee our safety if we are fearless? The confusion here arises out of our inability to imagine being without the 'I' and therefore without fear. When we try to imagine the 'I' itself being fearless, this seems impossible. We imagine that not wanting to look around for security, for things to rely on, will make us feel insecure. We even fear being free of suffering. We are comfortable with our fear and misery, and we would feel very unsure of our ground without them.

We fear fearlessness in the same way that we fear non-violence. To act non-violently certainly appears to make one more vulnerable. You are dropping your defences, leaving yourself more open, more exposed. However, this very vulnerability can be disarming, and even when it doesn't succeed in disarming aggression, the lack of desire for retaliation and security renders you much less vulnerable at a mental and emotional level. You do not feed the escalating verbal aggression out of which most physical violence issues. At its most developed, non-violence is equivalent to non-ego; there is no fixed identification with the threatened self, and therefore no fear for it, and no violence in defence of it.[301]

For Nāgārjuna, fear of fearlessness provides the material for a polemical dig at the Buddhist opponents of the Madhyamaka doctrine. Beneath their rejection Nāgārjuna detects a deep unease with the Dharma, an unconscious terror of what they themselves teach. The traditional teaching is that on the attainment of Enlightenment, there is no further rebirth – that is, that when the Enlightened individual dies, the *skandhas* that were the basis of his existence will not come together again. The follower of the Hīnayāna is obviously going to be happy with the idea that in the state of Nirvāṇa there should be no *skandhas*. Nāgārjuna is suggesting, however, that the Hīnayāna position is inconsistent. If the Hīnayānist is inspired by the consideration that 'all these' aggregates will not exist in Nirvāṇa, why should he be so alarmed by their non-existence now? Neither the ego nor the five *skandhas* have ever existed as absolutely real entities, and the attainment of Enlightenment is the point at which one fully realizes that truth. If, therefore, a follower of the Hīnayāna is happy to think that the five *skandhas* have no existence in the state of Nirvāṇa, he should be equally happy to realize that they do not really exist here and now. If he is not prepared to countenance this corollary, he cannot really be taking his own teaching seriously.

This is not just ancient academic hair-splitting. Modern Buddhists who happily contemplate the future dissolution of the ego would probably change their tune were the dissolution of their ego to be about to happen right now. St Augustine's famous prayer, 'Oh Lord, make me chaste, but not yet,' is a rueful insight into the inner conflict of the spiritual life.[302] There is a parallel Buddhist story of an old lady who comes to her local temple every day to pray to the Buddha. 'Come and take me to Nirvāṇa, away from this sorrowful existence' is her fervent and regular plea to the temple's huge Buddha figure. One day the monk at this temple decides to teach her a lesson. He creeps behind the statue of the Buddha while she is on her knees before it, begging to be released from the sufferings of *saṃsāra*, and he booms out, 'Your prayers are answered. I am coming for you – now!' With this unearthly response still echoing round the walls of the shrine, she is on her feet and running for the door, crying out, 'Won't the Buddha let me have my little joke?'[303]

This is very often the attitude with which we approach our practice of the Dharma. We may think we are meditating in order to gain insight here and now, but is this really what we want? Do we not rather want to have a few more good rebirths? Enlightenment is after all a kind of death – the end of everything we rely on and identify with. And how ready are we even for death in the ordinary sense? Having read the *Tibetan Book of the Dead*, or studied the lives of the great Buddhist renunciants like Milarepa, we might claim, 'I'm quite ready to die at any time,' but once death starts actually looming over us it is a different story. 'Any time' in the next thirty or fifty years feels rather different from 'any time' in the next week, say.

But if we do not want to go now, then essentially we do not want to go at all. If we really wanted Enlightenment in the future, we would really want it now. And if we are not interested in Enlightenment at the moment, how can we hold to the wish for Enlightenment in the future? We cannot really be genuinely happy with the idea of gaining Enlightenment after, say, ten million rebirths, but not with the idea of gaining it right now, if such a thing were possible. It is not, after all, that the ego will become non-existent at some future date. Nāgārjuna's whole argument here is that the ego is non-existent at this very moment.

All this is not to suggest that Enlightenment might be sprung on us before we are ready for it. Indeed, it is the preparation, the getting yourself ready, that sets up the momentum that will carry you, eventually, to the goal. But we do need to be clear what 'goal' means. It is not in some other place that the nature of reality becomes apparent; if we could only realize the fact, it is already manifesting here and now.

THE NON-DEFINITION OF NIRVĀṆA

> 'In liberation there is no self and are no aggregates.'
> If liberation is asserted thus,
> Why is the removal here of the self
> And of the aggregates not liked by you?
>
> If nirvāṇa is not a non-thing,
> Just how could it have thingness?
> The extinction of the misconception
> Of things and non-things is called nirvāṇa. (41–2)

Nāgārjuna evidently feels the need, based upon the thinking current in his time, to address this issue in terms of things rather than processes, and thus characterize Nirvāṇa in essentially negative terms as the extinction of the misconception of things and non-things. A more positive way of putting this would be to say that liberation consists in seeing processes rather than things. Nāgārjuna's language of 'non-things' and 'thingness' is a little cryptic, to say the least. This is because the answer to the question he poses is not available to the conditioned mind. It is the conditioned mind that asks questions, but it is also the conditioned mind that finds certain answers unintelligible, and the same conditioned mind that finds this rather frustrating. In the Unconditioned mind, however, this frustration with the lack of an answer is simply not there. The answer is no longer necessary, as the question itself is no longer there. In the state of mind in which you ask the question, you cannot get a meaningful answer, while in the state of mind in which you can get the answer, you cannot meaningfully ask the question.

Throughout the Mahāyāna teachings we find an idea of Nirvāṇa that is not any sort of thing or space or state of being, or any kind of personal existence. It is not subject to any kind of limitation or definition whatsoever. It is not even defined as being opposed to *saṃsāra*. It is called the *apratiṣṭhita* Nirvāṇa, the 'non-established' or 'unlocalized'

Nirvāṇa. It is not established outside *saṃsāra*. It does not exist here as distinct from there. It is the Nirvāṇa of no fixed point. Nāgārjuna speaks here of Nirvāṇa as the extinction of misconceptions of Nirvāṇa as being either a thing or not a thing. But the fact that it is not nothing does not mean that it is any kind of thing. He is saying, in other words, that while we can talk about Nirvāṇa, we cannot do so in any way that really limits or defines it. At the same time it is also the extinction of the misconception of Nirvāṇa as being either limited or unlimited. That it is not unlimited does not mean that it is limited.

If we think of Nirvāṇa as a fixed point, however subtle or sublime, to which we may attain and of which we may take possession, we are really thinking of it as a glorified ego state. Nirvāṇa is not a sort of spiritual retirement home far from the madding crowd of suffering humanity, where we can settle down to enjoy our well-earned pension. Nirvāṇa is not a destination at which we arrive: it is the life of Enlightenment. It is a way of living, a process of perfectibility to which you can see no end. Nirvāṇa is the way you live, the way you have your being, when you have gone beyond the limitations of conditioned consciousness.

It is probably unwise to say that Nirvāṇa is not a terminus, but we can certainly say that while it may be an end, we cannot see that end. All we can imagine from our standpoint is the process of growth and development stretching before us, one vista giving way to another, unendingly. What we see perhaps is a kind of vanishing point created by our fixed and limited perspective or vision, whereas in reality the lines apparently converging at a point upon the horizon remain parallel. We may see in our mind's eye a vanishing point that we call Nirvāṇa, but this is only to say that we have reached the limits of the conditioned mind. That end point for the conditioned mind is where Nirvāṇa no doubt begins a yet further process of growth and development. The *White Lotus Sūtra* offers an image for this necessarily limited vision of the goal. In it, the Buddha speaks of a magic city which he has conjured up in order to encourage weary travellers to continue their journey. But when they get there, they find that it is no more than a halfway house.[304] Similarly, beyond our ordinary conception of Nirvāṇa there are higher, broader, deeper Nirvāṇas, to which we have no conceptual access at all.

Nāgārjuna's emphasis on the practices productive of high status, such as generosity and moral living, reflects the spiritual principle that any goal becomes a new starting point. Nāgārjuna's intention is that the king should commit himself to such practices so as to achieve high status, peace of mind, happiness and further success, as well as develop the higher practices that will carry him towards definite goodness. To put it another way, Nirvāṇa is a process just as *saṃsāra* is a process. The process of conditioned co-production (*pratītya-samutpāda*) that characterizes *saṃsāra* also characterizes Nirvāṇa, although it works in a different way. If *saṃsāra* is thought of as a cyclical process, then Nirvāṇa may be imagined as a kind of spiral. According to the teaching of the *nidānas* there are twelve links or *nidānas* making up the cycle of *saṃsāra*, which may be summarized as follows: our present rebirth arises in dependence on ignorance; craving arises in dependence on sense contact and the feeling associated with that contact, and grasping on the basis of craving, leading to death and another rebirth. But there are also twelve positive *nidānas* making up a spiral path leading from an awareness of the suffering (*duḥkha*) bound up with the cycle of *saṃsāra*. Faith arises in dependence on suffering; joy in dependence on faith, and after that rapture, and then bliss and concentration; knowledge and vision of things as they really are arises on the basis of concentration, and the series culminates with knowledge of the destruction of the *āśravas* or 'cankers' (craving for sense pleasures, craving for existence, and ignorance).[305]

This is the creative mind taken to its highest degree of development. But it does not mark an end to the spiral process. It is a jumping-off point for further development, the last visible stage of a process that continues indefinitely. Nirvāṇa is a term used to indicate the unlimited nature of the process of growth and development, a final term to designate the fact that there can be no end to that positive process, no final turn of the spiral. Enlightenment is a life, but not in the sense that it goes on and on in time; it is a living process that continues beyond time, indeed, beyond the very distinction between time and timelessness.

EMPTINESS AS A MIRAGE

A form seen from a distance
Is seen clearly by those nearby.
If a mirage were water, why
Is water not seen by those nearby?

The way this world is seen
As real by those afar,
Is not so seen by those nearby
For whom it is signless like a mirage.

Just as a mirage is seemingly water
But not water and does not in fact exist (as water),
So the aggregates are seemingly a self
But not a self and do not exist in fact. (52–4)

The simile of the mirage is a popular one in Indian thought, and especially in Mahāyāna Buddhism. If you see something from a distance, you do not see it very clearly. If someone is standing nearer than you are to whatever you are looking at, they will usually be able to see it much more clearly than you can. In the case of the mirage, however, which is an optical illusion – most commonly of water in the desert – the opposite is true. From a distance, you see what seems to be water, but as you approach it you find that there is no water there but only desert. This is the nature of a mirage: what you see from a distance you do not see when you come closer. If you think that the water you see will quench your thirst, you will inevitably be disappointed when you get nearer and find that there is only desert.

The spiritually immature, who do not examine their experience of the world closely enough to see it as it really is, see a world of substantial things, peopled by fixed selves. The spiritually mature, who reflect on their experience mindfully and dispassionately, realize that there is really nothing substantial, nothing fixed there at all. There is no water in the desert. If you really look closely at your experience, without losing sight of it in emotional reactions to it, you will see that it is not real in quite the way you took it to be; it is only provisionally, relatively real. This idea is one to which we have, unsurprisingly, a deep resistance. The arising of true insight, when we see things as they really are, has therefore to occur at a very deep level. However, when such insight does arise, the qualities that the things around us seemed to possess when our vision was distorted by craving, aversion, or indifference fade away like a mirage when we come closer and see them as they really are. The poet Thomas Campbell observed that ''tis distance lends enchantment to the view',[306] and this is certainly our situation in the world. We are enchanted by a mirage that promises to quench our 'thirst' for something permanent, substantial, and satisfying, but which never does so.

Just as the *skandhas* or aggregates seem to add up to something that is actually there, in the form of a substantial fixed self, so the mirage really appears to be water. We certainly do see something, but what we see is not really water. Similarly, the aggregates are there, but they do not amount to or include the ego-self that we read into them. What we see from a distance, so to speak, is the ego-self. But when we look more closely all we find are the *skandhas*, and when we go closer still and investigate each *skandha* individually, we find that they too do not exist as distinct, independent entities.

In the following verse, Nāgārjuna qualifies this to rule out any possibility of misinterpreting his teaching as simple nihilism.

> Having thought a mirage to be water
> And then having gone there,
> Someone would just be stupid to surmise
> 'That water does not exist.' (55)

The mere fact that one is able to mistake the mirage for water means that there is indeed something for which the mirage can be mistaken. Water does exist; it just doesn't exist where you think it does when you are taken in by the mirage. Similarly, although the self does not in fact possess the qualities of permanence and changelessness, which we wrongly attribute to it, those qualities do exist elsewhere. If you did not find the qualities of the Unconditioned in conditioned things, such as the self and its objects, you would be foolish to conclude from this that those qualities did not exist at all. Discovering that there is no water to be found in the mirage, you would be foolish to conclude that there is no such thing as water anywhere. Yet this is exactly what we do when we look in the wrong place for happiness, security, permanence, truth, or beauty. Having exhausted the possibilities for satisfaction in our quest to find these qualities where we expect to find them, we assume that they are not to be found anywhere. In fact, they are available to us here and now, but only if we change the whole direction of our life. This means abandoning habits of mind so deeply ingrained that we can barely envisage any other way of being. It means abandoning the search for happiness altogether, and instead following the path of ethical action from which happiness arises as an unintended, albeit very welcome, by-product.

> If through correct and true knowledge
> (Such wise persons) do not assert existence and non-existence
> And thereby (you think) that they follow non-existence,
> Why should they not be followers of existence?
>
> If from refuting existence
> Non-existence would accrue to them,
> Why from refuting non-existence
> Would existence not accrue to them?
>
> They implicitly have no nihilistic thesis
> And also have no nihilistic behavior
> And due to relying on (the path to) enlightenment have no nihilistic thought.
> Hence how can they be regarded as nihilists? (58–60)

As a follower of the Madhyamaka tradition, Nāgārjuna asserts neither existence nor non-existence, neither eternalism nor nihilism. However, with its talk of the void and the extinction of the ego, the Śūnyavāda, or 'way of emptiness' (another name for the Madhyamaka),[307] can quite pardonably be mistaken for a nihilistic philosophy. And in Nāgārjuna's time other Buddhists, presumably followers of the Hīnayāna, did regard it in this way. In response to this misunderstanding, Nāgārjuna points out that the Śūnyavāda refutes both eternalism and nihilism. If he comes to be accused of being a nihilist because he refutes the inherent existence of things, then he could also be accused of the opposite. After all, he also refutes the nihilistic view that things do not exist at all. Why not accuse him, then, of being an eternalist? In other words, he is trying to show that the Hīnayānist objections are self-contradictory.

The next point Nāgārjuna makes is that followers of the Śūnyavāda have as their declared aim *samyaksambodhi*, complete and perfect Enlightenment. How, with this goal in view, can their doctrine, ethics, or thinking be nihilistic? It is, after all, the same *bodhi* as that to which their critics aspire – not a state of non-existence. In order to arrive at this same goal, they both must follow essentially the same ethical code, essentially the same practices of meditation, and essentially the same teachings about Enlightenment.

4
NOTHING LEFT AT ALL?

> Ask the Sāṃkhyas, the followers of Kaṇaḍa, Nirgranthas,
> And the worldly proponents of a person and aggregates,
> Whether they propound
> What passes beyond 'is' and 'is not'. (61)

Here, Nāgārjuna throws down a challenge to various non-Buddhist schools. The 'worldly ones', Lokāyatikas, are of course the materialists.[308] The Sāṃkhyas make an absolute distinction between the material world (*prakṛti*) and the spiritual world (*puruṣa*) and they uphold a philosophy of causation called *satkāryavāda*, the view that cause and effect are identical. The followers of Kaṇaḍa are the Vaiśeṣikas, or pluralists, who attempt to analyse experience into its ultimate elements.[309] The Nirgranthas are the Jains, whose tradition was founded by a near-contemporary of the Buddha called Mahāvīra.[310] In one way or another, all these spiritual traditions uphold a belief in the absolute reality of the person and the aggregates. So Nāgārjuna issues his challenge. Ask them, he says, if they have a teaching that goes beyond all concepts whatsoever, a teaching that sees through the dualism of existence and non-existence.

The Śūnyavāda is nihilistic to those whose reality is wholly mundane. It seems nihilistic only if what it negates is seen as everything. To paraphrase a passage towards the end of *The World as Will and Idea*, Schopenhauer in effect observes that to one to whom the world 'with all its suns and galaxies' is everything, Nirvāṇa is nothing.[311] If you were to speak to the man in the street about the inherent meaninglessness of worldly life, and were to suggest to him that there could be a way of life in which there was no job, no marriage, no family, no football, he would say that this would leave him with nothing. For him, life without a job and so on is no life at all. Or if you see sex, or having fun, or making money, or even the arts, as everything, then the Dharma, when it suggests that these things are of no real importance in the larger scheme of things, can appear nihilistic. Thus Buddhism generally can be seen as nihilistic from the worldly point of view.

Critics of the Śūnyavāda doctrine may renounce mundane life in favour of the spiritual life, but ultimately they remain mired in the mundane world so long as they take their renunciation as having some kind of absolute validity, so long as they get caught up in the idea of the spiritual life and identify with it absolutely. If, for you, conceptualized reality is everything, when concepts are repudiated, nothing is left. And the Śūnyavāda does just this: it repudiates all concepts. For someone who has no real spiritual experience, whose whole life is bound up with knowledge as mediated by concepts, this is indeed a teaching of non-existence or nihilism.

Renunciation is not an absolute value. You give up what is relatively satisfying in order to attain something that is truly satisfying. The idea is not to throw away the good that you find in the things you enjoy, but to imagine that good refined and heightened to an infinite degree. If, for example, you obtain great satisfaction from your family, and for you family life is everything, you certainly won't want to give that up. The Buddhist invitation is simply to imagine a much wider family, what you might call the 'spiritual family', a circle of spiritual friendship that is as loyal and selfless as any parent should be towards their offspring. This is the ideal of the sangha. Of course, the reality is that the sangha is rarely quite as generous and kind and forgiving as it ideally should be, but that is what ideals are for – to give us something to aim towards.

There is no profit in shielding ourselves from the truth of things, which is that worldly pleasures and attachments are unsure and impermanent. Nor can we duck the challenges that this truth gives us. Sooner or later we have to confront the demands of the spiritual life, which may not be at all easy. But when we do so our purpose will be to grow and develop. We have to put aside certain activities and values that we have perhaps held dear in the past, in order to realize greater things.

The self is negated with similar provisos. If you fully identify with the ego-self, there is little to be gained from renouncing it unless at the same time you can see the possibility of transcending it. It should be questioned and broken down only in order to reveal a sense of identity that is infinitely more refined. It is put in its proper place as a lower self in order that you may realize what you are in a much higher sense.

Giving things up need not involve hardship, so long as you remain in good contact with your spiritual friends. If, for example, you are married, you need to seek out other married members of the sangha and find out how they manage to be fully committed to the spiritual life while fulfilling their responsibilities as husbands and wives, fathers and mothers. Likewise, if you are attracted to the life of a homeless and celibate wanderer, you can go to people who are already living in that way and talk to them about how they took up that lifestyle in the first place and how they live it on a daily basis.

It is not a question of some theoretical principle that you must follow in order to be a good Buddhist. It is about transforming your life in a way that does justice to what you are and what you wish to be. If you are not sure that some course of action is feasible, check it out with others who have followed it successfully. This is one of the very great benefits of the sangha. Here are other people, not very different from yourself, who are actually involved in the kind of life that you are thinking of leading. The teachings of Śūnyavāda, of the *Diamond Sūtra*, or of the Zen masters, mean very little without the community of committed followers who know from their own experience how to put those teachings into practice.

> Thereby know that the ambrosia
> Of the Buddha's teaching is called profound,
> An exclusive doctrine passing
> Far beyond 'is' and 'is not'. (62)

It is because the Buddha's teaching goes beyond ideas of existence and non-existence, beyond all concepts, that it is called profound. It is called ambrosia or nectar (*amṛta*) in order to suggest the complete suffusion of the experience of emptiness with the profound bliss that comes with the extinction of suffering.

How could the world exist in fact,
With a nature passed beyond the three times,
Not going when disintegrating, not coming,
And not staying even for an instant?

Because the coming, going, and staying,
Of the world and nirvāṇa do not exist
As (their own) reality, what difference
Is there in fact between the two?

If, due to the non-existence of staying,
Production and cessation do not exist as (their own) reality,
How could production, staying,
And ceasing exist in fact? (63–5)

In this rather obscure passage, Nāgārjuna asks how if, in the ultimate sense, there can be no past, present, or future, the world itself can exist as perceived in those terms. We perceive the world in terms of time, of its being a process of arising, continuing, and stopping. But in reality there is no coming or going or remaining, no production, cessation, or staying. Each process exists only in a relative sense, in relation to its opposite. Not that the world is ultimately unreal. What we read into the world is unreal, including the distinction between real and unreal. *Saṃsāra* and *nirvāṇa* are not eternally distinct realities. The distinction between them comes from our dualistic way of thinking, our delusion that we can categorize the world and what is beyond the world, separate *saṃsāra* and *nirvāṇa* in any way other than as a practical expedient.[312]

Nāgārjuna is not putting forward this proposition to win assent on a conceptual level. He is not asserting a philosophy, not teaching a monism. His intention is the practical one of clearing away the dualistic views that obscure the path to Enlightenment. The point is that we cannot help but think dualistically, even while we are engaged in uprooting dualistic concepts. As soon as you envisage a distinction between being dualistic and being non-dualistic, you are being dualistic. But you have to do this in order to have any chance of breaking down your dualistic vision.

It is the paradox of the goose in the bottle. Even though you cannot get the goose out of the bottle without either breaking the bottle or injuring the goose, that is what you have to do. You can overcome dualism only by initially adopting a dualistic standpoint. As the Tantrics were to say later on, you have to get rid of dirt with dirt. It is like the traditional Indian way of washing clothes. You take mud from the river and use it like soap, rubbing it into the clothes and then rinsing them out. In this way you use dirt to get rid of dirt.[313] Or it is like sailing against the wind by tacking this way and that. You use the wind that is blowing against you to make progress against the wind. Likewise, you get rid of concepts with concepts, dualism by means of dualism.

WHAT IS THIS MOMENT?

If always changing,
How are things non-momentary?
If not changing,
How can they be altered in fact?

Do they become momentary
Through partial or complete disintegration?
Because an inequality is not apprehended,
This momentariness cannot be admitted either way.

If momentary, then it becomes entirely non-existent;
Hence how could it be old?
Also if non-momentary, it is constant;
Hence how could it be old?

Just as a moment has an end, so a beginning
And a middle must be considered.
Thus due to this triple nature of a moment
There is no momentary abiding of the world.

Also the beginning, middle, and end
Are to be analyzed like a moment.
Therefore beginning, middle, and end
Are also not (produced) from self or other. (66–70)

A school of Buddhist thought in Nāgārjuna's time held that nothing lasted for more than a split second, and that what seemed to be things were just a sequence of *dharmas* popping up – each for a split second – and then disappearing. If these *dharmas* were very similar, they created an illusion of a single thing, like the way a motion picture creates the illusion of continuity out of a succession of separate images or frames. It is this philosophy of momentariness (*kṣaṇikavāda*) that Nāgārjuna has in his sights in these verses.[314] The main problem with it is that it attempts to explain flow, continuity, process, change, or coming and going, by discontinuity, by positing a succession of discrete entities, which is contradictory. Nāgārjuna points out that if one of these moments, however tiny, appears and disappears, then logically it must have a beginning, a middle, and an end. That is, it is divisible into these three elements at the very least. Therefore, no moment can be said to be absolutely irreducible. Anything you decide to call a moment must consist of further moments, themselves infinitely divisible in their turn. There is, in fact, nothing that exists momentarily at all. The world itself does not exist 'momentarily' even for a moment.

WHAT IS THIS OBJECT?

> Due to having many parts there is no unity,
> There is not anything without parts.
> Further, without 'one', there is not 'many'.
> Also, without existence there is no non-existence. (71)

The Abhidharma's analysis of the world of our experience into *dharmas*, conceived as the ultimate components of existence, gets the same treatment as the philosophy of momentariness.[315] What Nāgārjuna has done with respect to time, he now does with regard to space.

Anything conceived as a separable entity must logically be subject to further analysis. There is nothing that cannot be subdivided into parts, so nothing you can call 'one' can have any inherent existence. You can never get down to something that can be characterized simply as 'one'. As soon as you have 'one' you also have 'many'. Similarly, every part is itself a whole that can be analysed into further parts. Whether it is the one and the many, or the whole and its parts, the terms are co-relative. One cannot therefore regard the parts as real and the whole as unreal, which is what the Abhidharma does, any more than one can regard the whole as real and the parts as essentially unreal, which is more like the conventional way people see things.

Again Nāgārjuna is examining the way we lose sight of the reality of any concept, and the truth behind any kind of distinction. This truth is that whatever that concept may be, it is dependent upon its opposite, upon whatever it is distinct from. Whole philosophical schools are built upon this fundamental error. They invest a concept with ultimate reality, when in fact it owes its 'existence' to what it is not.

THE END OF THE WORLD

> If it is thought that through disintegration or an antidote
> An existent becomes non-existent,
> Then how without an existent
> Could there be disintegration or an antidote?
>
> Hence in fact there is no disappearance
> Of the world through nirvāṇa.
> Asked whether the world has an end
> The Conqueror remained silent. (72–3)

The idea of a poison and its antidote is another case of interdependent duality; the antidote exists only in relation to the poison. Thus *nirvāṇa*, as the antidote to the sufferings of conditioned existence, exists only in relation to those sufferings, to *saṃsāra*. For *nirvāṇa* to be there, suffering has to be there as well.[316] So long as you hold on to the idea of an end to suffering, there can be no end to suffering. You cannot have one without the other. The path that leads away from suffering exists only in relation to its point of departure, which is suffering itself. Hence you can never arrive at *nirvāṇa*, at least as conceived in terms of the antidote to the suffering of *saṃsāra*. *Nirvāṇa* as the cessation of suffering is like getting out of prison and leaving the prison still there behind you. Real freedom is where there is no prison at all, and even, we might say, where there is no freedom either: no prison and therefore no freedom from prison. In the same way, freedom from the world is not real freedom. The real freedom is where there is no world and no freedom from the world.

Abstruse as this idea may sound, it can be applied even at a quite ordinary level of spiritual practice. If when you meditate you are simply concerned to get away from a certain aspect of your experience, you will not get very far. Mindfulness is the practice of being present with the whole of your experience, bad as well as good, painful as well as pleasant. Even negative states of mind must at some point be *transformed*, not just pushed away.

THE GROUND BENEATH OUR FEET

> Because he did not teach this profound doctrine
> To worldly beings who were not receptacles,
> The All-Knowing is therefore known
> By the wise to be omniscient.
>
> Thus the doctrine of definite goodness
> Was taught by the perfect Buddhas
> The seers of reality, as profound,
> Unapprehendable and baseless. (74–5)

In his opening paean to the Buddha, Nāgārjuna acknowledges him as 'all-knowing'. He now tells us in what way the Buddha is omniscient, since this omniscience is not what we usually understand by the term. It consists, he tells us, simply in knowing whom to teach and what to teach them. It is not so much a question of the amount of the information, but of its relevance. It is a knowledge that is unapprehendable in that it is not to be understood in dualistic terms. It is baseless, firstly, in that it does not depend on anything else. It is not an amassing of facts that might be learned from someone; it comes from within. Secondly, it is baseless in that the Buddha's teaching does not provide a platform for false views.[317]

> Frightened by this baseless doctrine,
> Delighting in a base, not passing
> Beyond existence and non-existence,
> Unintelligent beings ruin themselves. (76)

The adjective 'baseless' used in conjunction with the noun 'doctrine' might seem to suggest, pejoratively, that the doctrine is unreliable and untrue. However, in this context it means that the content or meaning of the doctrine is baseless in the sense that it is not to be settled down in, or rested upon, or relied on for security, or taken as having absolute validity.[318]

If we truly get a sense of transcendental wisdom, we are frightened by it, because it teaches that there is nothing for us to settle down in, nothing in the world that is ultimately real. Yet our lives are dedicated to seeking fulfilment by stemming the flow of experience, by setting up false ideas of things, of self and other. We try to turn the impermanent into something permanent. We approach a situation that is in reality free and fluid and deal with it as if it was fixed, settled, 'a base'. We need it to be settled so that we can settle down in it. We delight in a base in the sense of feeling secure in our dependence upon impermanent 'things', our grasping after existence or non-existence. If we do nothing to get beyond this reliance upon concepts, we are without a firm footing in reality, and so we ruin and waste our life.

Much of the time, even, we do not properly *delight* in a base. We do not really *relish* where we are, yet it does not occur to us to look further. We may want to move from a small house to a bigger house, or exchange a small car for a bigger car, but we don't think of moving from houses and cars and so on as our base to a more spiritual base. In our fear of the unknown, we prefer to hang on discontentedly to the base we have rather than trying to move towards a better one.

If we are not in fact able to delight in a base, and do not feel frightened by this 'baseless doctrine', it may be that we are not ready for such a doctrine. We have to start from where we are, which may mean starting from an apparently secure but in reality unreliable base. We may be locked into a negative view of things and be unable to commit ourselves to anything. In order to transcend any kind of a base, we need a positive and provisionally secure base from which to begin. If we do not feel the ground beneath our feet, how can we experience it as it really is? How can we experience existence as baseless unless we can first rest our weight fully on that base?

The sangha is meant to provide an emotionally positive, open-ended base, allowing us room to grow and develop, and ideally encouraging us always to move beyond whatever base we make of it. It will even provide a base in which we may take a quite healthy delight. There can be nothing wrong with enjoying the things around us, so long as what we delight in leads us on to other interests, other 'bases' that are more refined, more subtle and more ethical. Following such a path, the 'base' in which you delight eventually drops away altogether. All we have to do is keep letting go of what we think we know; we have to avoid settling down in any sense of being sure of ourselves, of being secure in the absolute validity of our perspective.

Being able to settle down in a way that is committed but at the same time provisional is very much a matter of integration. It is a matter of bringing your emotions and desires into harmony with your ideals and highest aspirations, so that you are no longer thrown hither and thither by your whims and fancies. At the same time, you are aware that however rewarding or enjoyable a situation may be, it is neither permanent nor ultimately fulfilling. You will not, therefore, become so settled in it that you lose sight of your higher aspirations. You enjoy the meditation group, the Buddhist movement, the centre or community, the retreat facility, the right livelihood business, only to the extent that these situations enable you to grow and develop. But if need be, you are ready to move on. You do not 'delight in a base' in the sense of getting entrenched in your situation, expecting other members of the group or community to reinforce your little habits and settled ways. You will not resent new people with new ideas, nor will you assume that this is where you will continue indefinitely.

It is important not to apply Nāgārjuna's warning here too literally. A necessary condition of ascending a flight of steps is that you will for an instant rest on each step in turn. Even this image is not to be taken too literally, if it suggests an attitude of skipping lightly from one step to the next. Setting no great store by anything, and feeling no human attachment or responsibility at all, is nihilism, not spiritual maturity. The mind that is not driven by its attachments is one thing; the butterfly mind is quite another.

In his teaching of high status and definite goodness, Nāgārjuna seems to be saying that although we should avoid gathering useless things, we still need to gather things of relative value. Whatever they are, however, they should be appreciated as things that cannot be relied on in an absolute sense. We need to see that any situation is conditioned and impermanent, and that we may need to move on from it at some point if we are to grow.

O King, lest you be ruined
I will explain through the scriptures
The mode of the supramundane, just as it is,
The reality not partaking of dualism.

This profundity endowed with meanings drawn (from scriptures)
And beyond ill-deeds and meritorious deeds
Has not been tasted by those who fear the baseless –
The others – the Forders – and even by our own. (78–9)

The 'Forders' are the leaders of various non-Buddhist philosophical schools, and 'ourselves' may refer to those Buddhists, such as the followers of the Hīnayāna, who do not accept the Madhyamaka viewpoint. In a more profound sense, it can be taken to refer to the inherent ungraspableness of any doctrinal presentation of reality. There is in reality no one who tastes, nor any doctrine to be tasted. The doctrine of emptiness is not tasted by those who do not accept it; nor is it tasted even by those who accept it in all its profundity.

5
ELEMENTS AND ARGUMENTS

CONVINCING US TO DOUBT

A person is not earth, not water,
Not fire, not wind, not space,
Not consciousness, and not all of them.
What person is there other than these?

Just as the person is not real
Due to being a composite of six constituents,
So each of the constituents also
Is not real due to being a composite.

The aggregates are not the self, they are not in it,
It is not in them, without them it is not,
It is not mixed with the aggregates like fire and fuel,
Therefore how can the self exist?

The three elements are not earth, they are not in it,
It is not in them, without them it is not;
Since this also applies to each,
The elements, like the self, are false.

Earth, water, fire, and wind
Individually also do not inherently exist.
When any three are absent, an individual one does not exist.
When one is absent, the three also do not exist.

If when three are absent, an individual one does not exist
And if when one is absent, the three also do not exist,
Then each itself does not exist.
How could a composite be produced?

Otherwise, if each itself exists,
Why without fuel is there no fire?
Likewise why is there no water, wind, or earth
Without motility, obstructiveness, or cohesion?

If (it is answered that) fire is well known (not to exist without fuel
But the other three elements exist by way of their own entities),
How could your three exist in themselves
Without the others? It is impossible for the three
Not to accord with dependent-arising.

How could those – that themselves
Exist individually – be mutually dependent?
How could those – that do not themselves
Exist individually – be mutually dependent?

If it is the case that they do not themselves exist individually,
But where there is one, the other three exist,
Then if unmixed, they are not in one place,
And if mixed, they do not themselves exist individually.

The elements do not themselves exist individually,
So how could their own individual characters exist?
What do not themselves individually exist cannot predominate;
Their characters are regarded as conventionalities.

This mode (of refutation) is also to be applied
To colours, odours, tastes, and objects of touch;

Eye, consciousness, and form;
Ignorance, action, and birth;

Agent, object, and action,
Number, possession, cause and effect,
Time, short and long, and so forth,
Name and name-bearer as well. (80–92)

Whether people are really converted by such close reasoning, or really change the way they experience their life because of it, is perhaps questionable, especially today. Our experience shows us that the self does exist, at least in certain quite definite respects, and we seem to be able to accept the evident absence of the self within the elements as a puzzle, a living contradiction, perhaps in the same way that we accept the paradoxes of modern science. However, the ancient Indians had what seems to have been a misplaced trust in the power of logical reasoning – either that or they responded to hard logical argument in a way that people these days do not. We tend to be suspicious of any argument that is made too watertight. It can seem rather too clever to be convincing, signalling desperation and doubt more than confidence. Who is he really trying to convince, we ask ourselves, me or himself? If we are not motivated by simple, straightforward arguments, is complicating them the solution? Nāgārjuna would certainly seem to believe so, as his argument here becomes rather more sophisticated than seems strictly useful.

For whatever reason, the thoroughly worked, not to say overworked, logical argument seems to have been necessary to appeal to the ancient Indian mind. In Nāgārjuna's time, great public debates involving famous rival teachers were common in India. The defeated teacher would have to become the disciple of his vanquisher, taking all his disciples with him. This was how seriously public debate was taken in those days. Today, people might wonder what all the fuss was about. Just because you have lost an argument does not mean that your position is necessarily wrong. It may just mean that your opponent is more skilled at argument than you are, not that he has the truth on his side. Why make such a big change to your life simply because you have been defeated in a debate?

But this attitude persisted in India down the centuries. Śāntideva, a Madhyamaka teacher of a later period, certainly has it. In the

Bodhicaryāvatāra, for example, he puts forward all sorts of ingenious reasons why we should not give way to anger, but their overall effect can be curiously irritating, and therefore self-defeating.[319] When his arguments become too relentlessly unanswerable you begin to distrust them. Yes, it is illogical to be angry, and yes, the ego is an illusion – as many neuroscientists and psychiatrists confirm today – but the question is not whether that can be accepted on a purely conceptual level, but whether the truth of the argument is experienced and absorbed emotionally.

Even in present-day Tibet we find that the Gelugpas, who follow the Madhyamaka tradition, have a cast-iron faith in the power of logic to convey the essential truth of the Dharma. Whereas Milarepa, the founder of the Kagyupa tradition, goes almost entirely by inspiration and personal experience, Je Tsongkhapa, the great Gelugpa teacher, follows the guidance of the scriptures and strict reasoning. Of course, Tsongkhapa brings his own experience to bear upon his understanding, but personal experience is not usually at the forefront of his teaching.

In Europe, too, the scholastic philosophers and theologians of the Middle Ages displayed a tremendous faith in the power of reason and logic. The ancient Greek world also leaves the impression of people relishing the use of reason, not only taking it seriously but being fascinated by it. And yet, like those of Nāgārjuna, the arguments of Socrates seem sometimes less than compelling, even sophistical. Maybe we do not need all that much logical proof of the nature of reality. The real proof of any pudding is in the eating. When we try to understand and interpret the ancient teachings of the Madhyamaka for ourselves, it is important to bear in mind their real purpose and relate the arguments to our own experience of life.

All the same, there is method in the exhaustive way Nāgārjuna hunts the rational mind out of its holes. To be brought up sharp against the limitations of one's ordinary consciousness is utterly frustrating, but nonetheless entirely necessary if one is to apprehend the truth of things. To imagine that you have arrived at that point when you have not even stretched your ordinary consciousness is a big mistake. It is by exhausting the possibilities of rational thought that we enable the truth of things to reveal itself. There is no use in giving up on the possibilities of penetrating reality with the dualistic mind prematurely. In fact, there should be no conscious decision to renounce the cutting edge of reason in our search for truth. Such a decision can only be another ploy by the conceptualizing mind to grasp at the truth, one that short-circuits the quest altogether. Only when one has truly arrived at the limits of one's thinking, one might say, can one become aware that the truth cannot be thought, that it can only, in the final instance, be experienced directly for what it is.

First Nāgārjuna recaps some of the basics of his doctrine. A person is composite, and the constituents of that composite are themselves composite. A person is not to be identified with any one of the five aggregates or six elements, nor with a combination of all of them, nor with an existence apart from them. They are not in the self, nor is the self in them, and yet without them the self has no existence. Following this argument, you begin to get the idea of the self, of 'being' in the ultimate sense, as something self-contradictory, even absurd, to the extent that you begin to doubt your own existence.

The aggregates and the elements cannot be said either to exist or not to exist. Nāgārjuna shows, at length, that the elements depend upon one another for their existence, which means that they must exist, and at the same time he shows that they cannot exist in the sense of having an independent existence. If we think of things as embodying a varying mixture of the elements, and say simply that what we conventionally acknowledge as 'earth' is always a mixture of the elements in which earth predominates, then how can we identify 'earth' as an individual element at all? The same goes for the perceptual situation, in which eye, consciousness, and form all arise in dependence upon one another. Sense consciousness and external forms are two poles of a single process; they are not ultimately separate. Nor can we say even that ignorance is real in the sense of being ultimately separable from the karmic actions to which it gives rise and which eventually result in rebirth. We are a process in which we may identify elements like ignorance, skilful or unskilful actions, and so on for practical purposes, but these elements have no independent reality.

The relationship between the things we distinguish in the world, especially between the self and those elements of its experience with which it identifies most closely, is thus shown to be impossible to pin down. The way the self is usually taken for granted as existing is shown to be quite literally baseless. Indeed, the self oughtn't to be there at all. The idea of a self in the ordinary sense is quite illogical, even self-contradictory. In other words, Nāgārjuna is trying to transform our experience of ourselves, trying to get us out of the habit of taking ourselves as seriously as we usually do, trying to stop us from settling down in ourselves as though we were something fixed and final. He wants to return us to what Walt Whitman calls 'the terrible doubt of appearances', or what in the Zen tradition is often referred to as the 'Great Doubt'.[320] He wants to shake our confidence in the reality of what we now experience as our 'self'.

Are we immediately shaken by the logical inconsistencies in our view of ourselves? Probably not. But we can reflect more closely upon that view. We can look out for the little manifestations in our daily life of the essential incoherence of our assumptions about that life. We can start by reflecting on what has brought us to where we are now. We can look back, for example, and see how we have changed over time. In so doing, we can be aware that further change is possible. We might reflect in this way: I am not the finished article; what I am now is not fixed and final. I am still on the assembly line. I am still in transition. What I am now I shall not be tomorrow. There may be growth in some areas, deterioration in others. How real, therefore, is the self with which I identify today?

Impermanence cannot be fully understood simply as a concept. We know perfectly well that things are impermanent, but in our heart of hearts we understand what this means and we are deeply afraid. Impermanence has to be experienced in ourselves and the world around us, moment by moment. We must also respect the power of this truth, and recognize how deeply we resist it. In the city, we see houses and office blocks coming down, and new ones going up. Shops close and new ones open. In the countryside, we see that the corn that was standing yesterday has today been harvested; only the straw remains, gathered in bales. Nature itself is a constant round of birth and death, bloom and fade, erosion and sedimentation, crack and slide. What we see today will not be there tomorrow. How real, therefore, is the world we see today? We may imagine that all this is too obvious to need reflecting upon, but it is our facile dismissal of the obvious that holds reality at bay.

EXCHANGING ILLUSORY WATER FOR REAL NECTAR

> Earth, water, fire, and wind,
> Tall and short, subtle and coarse,
> As well as virtue and so forth are said by the Subduer
> To cease in the consciousness (of reality).

Earth, water, fire, and wind
Do not have a chance
In the face of that undemonstrable consciousness,
Complete lord over the limitless.

Here long and short, subtle and coarse,
Virtue and non-virtue,
And here names and forms
All are ceased. (93–5)

These verses describe how the 'lord over the limitless' sees into reality itself. The Enlightened consciousness sees through conditioned existence. That is, it sees through the attempt by the conditioned consciousness to catch reality in the net of concepts or 'names', catching in that net both ideas of the self and what is not the self. However, Nāgārjuna's concern as always is to address the unenlightened mind's assumption that if reality is not to be found among its objects, it is to be found nowhere. If the 'things' we catch in our net of names prove to be empty of reality, if reality slips through that net, however finely woven it may be, this does not mean that reality is nothing. It means that a net of concepts can in the end catch only concepts.

All those that earlier appeared to consciousness
Because of not knowing that (reality)
Will later cease for consciousness in that way
Because of knowing that (reality).

All these phenomena of beings
Are seen as fuel for the fire of consciousness.
They are pacified through being burned
By the light of true discrimination. (96–7)

The first of these two verses is especially cryptic, but it can be illustrated by going back to the analogy of the mirage in the desert. When you get near to the mirage, it is not that you see nothing at all, but that what you see is not the water you expected to find. Instead, you see what was really there all along. The appearance of the water ceases, and you see what was behind that illusion. The reality of things is missed because we see those things as 'things' rather than as unreal appearances. When the reality behind phenomena appears, those phenomena are seen through.

> The reality is later ascertained
> Of what was formerly imputed by ignorance.
> When a thing is not found,
> How can there be a non-thing?
>
> Because the phenomena of forms
> Are only names, space too is only a name.
> Without the elements how could forms exist?
> Therefore even 'name-only' does not exist.
>
> Feelings, discriminations, compositional factors,
> And consciousnesses are to be considered
> Like the elements and the self.
> Thereby the six constituents are selfless. (98–100)

'When a thing is not found, how can there be a non-thing?' This, too, can be understood in the light of the analogy of the mirage. What you falsely perceived to be water is later clearly seen to be desert. When that water is not found, nothing has been destroyed, nothing has been lost, since the water was never there in the first place. Similarly, in Nirvāṇa, nothing is lost. It is not as though *saṃsāra* no longer exists, or has been destroyed, but rather that you have realized the true nature of *saṃsāra*. If the 'thing' was never there in the first place, you are not left with a lack of a thing. Even the idea of 'name-only' is itself just a name, an idea. Emptiness itself is empty.[321] When Nirvāṇa is described as 'void' it is only natural for people to imagine it in terms of what it will not be – no wives or husbands, no children, no job, no pleasures and enjoyments, no world. But, in fact, Nirvāṇa is a state not of deprivation, but of fulfilment. It is not that you lose things, but that you have the reality of things.

Let us further consider this analogy of the mirage of water in a way that brings us a little closer to how Enlightenment positively changes our experience. When we look at the mirage, we think we can see water, and of course that is probably what we want – so we go towards it looking forward to slaking our thirst. If when we came close to it we found something even better than water to drink, we might not have found what we were expecting to find, but we certainly would not complain. If we were to find a fountain of wine instead, in the sense of the wine of life, the blissful essential nectar of Enlightenment (*amṛta*), we would be so delighted with what we had found that we would forget the very idea of the water we once imagined it to be. Having given up our belief in the water, we do not think of what we have found as 'non-water'.

It is a little like the view that people might take of monks or hermits or anyone who adopts some kind of 'restricted' lifestyle – even temporarily as on retreat. People look at you and ask, 'What have you got? You have no career, no money, no television, no decent clothes, no meat, no alcohol. Where's the fun in that?' There is no ready answer to this. Of course, monks usually seem happy enough, and people who go on retreat often say they have benefited hugely from the experience, but it is difficult to explain quite why or how that is the case in terms that people who have not experienced the situation for themselves will understand.

6
TRUTHS AND ILLUSIONS

LOOKING FOR THE PLANTAIN'S CORE

Just as when a banana tree
With all its parts is torn apart, there is nothing,
So when a person having the (six) constituents
Is divided, it is the same.

Therefore the Conquerors said,
'All phenomena are selfless.'
Since this is so, all six constituents
Have been delineated as selfless for you.

Thus neither self nor non-self
Are to be apprehended as real.
Therefore the Great Subduer rejected
Views of self and non-self. (101–3)

The banana tree is a well-known Buddhist simile. The plantain or banana tree does not have a solid core, being made up of layers like an onion, so that if you try to get at the essence of the banana tree by stripping off its successive layers, eventually you come to nothing at all. Likewise, when you practise the reflection on the six elements, stripping away earth, then water, fire, air, space, and finally consciousness, you end up with nothing.

It is the method of stripping away the various constituents that is the object of Nāgārjuna's attention here. It is essentially the Hīnayāna approach, and Nāgārjuna's criticism of it is that it does not take the process far enough. The truth of *anātman* (Pāli *anattā*) is not just the absence of self in the obvious sense; it is the absence of self in anything whatsoever. The way we reify things, craving and resenting what we take to be permanent entities that can be grasped or pushed away, is a direct reflection of our belief in the fixed self. Therefore to regard the self as illusory, and the six constituents as real, is a pointless exercise.

Even the view of non-self is wrong inasmuch as it is a view, and therefore something to which the self becomes attached. There is no point in congratulating yourself on dispatching self-view when the view of non-self has become simply a more subtle self-view. The only way we can see through the self is to be, to some extent at least, free from attachment and hatred at the most subtle level. In order to understand any Buddhist doctrine properly we have to identify it as relative truth, and not take it as absolute truth. We have to rely on relative truth for the purpose of clear thinking, and in order at least to understand where absolute truth is not to be found; but this relative truth includes the understanding that ultimate truth can be neither thought about nor spoken about.

THE LIMITS OF THE WORLD

> Sights, sounds, and so forth were said by the Subduer
> Not to be true and not to be false.
> If from one position its opposite arises,
> Both do not exist in fact.
>
> Thus ultimately this world
> Is beyond truth and falsity,
> Therefore the Subduer does not assert
> That it really exists or does not.
>
> (Knowing that) these in all ways do not exist,
> How could the All-Knower say
> They have limits or no limits,
> Or have both or neither? (104–6)

Those things which can be smelled, tasted, touched, and thought, i.e. the objects of the senses, are said by the Buddha to be neither absolutely real nor absolutely unreal, and Nāgārjuna goes on to offer a logical explanation for this. His argument is that to exist absolutely means to exist independently, which is impossible for anything that arises in dependence upon causes and conditions. If the existence of something necessarily involves the existence of its opposite, then that thing cannot be said to be absolutely real. Any conditioned thing comes into being in dependence upon that which it is not, upon its own non-existence. There is no life without death, no being without non-being, no light without darkness, no truth without falsehood, no craving without hatred, no absolute without the relative. And of course vice versa: if things are not absolutely real, they are not absolutely unreal either. Like a mirage, the world is there in a sense. Just as the mirage is there as an object of the sense of sight, so the world is experienced as being there; but it is not experienced as a really existing object.

Nāgārjuna goes on to refer to what are usually termed the fourteen 'inexpressibles'. These comprise four basic questions upon which the Buddha would not speak, which become fourteen on the basis of the formulaic ways in which they may be addressed. Two of them are to do with our relationship with the body. Thus the life principle (*jīva*) cannot be said to be identical with the physical body (*rūpa*), nor entirely separate from it. Four more questions deal with what happens to a Buddha after his death or *parinirvāṇa*: it cannot be said that he exists, or that he does not exist, or that he is both existent and non-existent, or that he is neither existent nor non-existent. All these four possibilities are inexpressible. The other eight 'inexpressibles' concern whether or not the universe is eternal, and whether or not it is infinite. 'Space' cannot be said to be finite or limited in extent, nor can it be said to be unlimited or infinite, nor both, nor neither. The same goes for the question of whether or not the universe is eternal.[322]

Of the fourteen questions, twelve illustrate the traditional four alternative positions that can logically be taken with regard to the metaphysical status of things. Thus, if it cannot be said that the world has a limit, we must go on to propose that it has no limit; and if neither of these positions can be upheld, then we must posit that it is both limited and unlimited; and if this position is also rejected, then we are left with the only possibility open to us, that it is neither limited nor unlimited; but this too is not the case.

The reality of conditioned existence, being dependent on causes and conditions, cannot be said to be finite or infinite, because if it has an existence that is only relative, like that of a mirage, the question of its real existence doesn't arise. The question of duration cannot apply to something that does not have any substantial existence of its own in the first place. The same may be said of the nature of space. It is generally held by idealist philosophers that space is not a thing in the sense of an empty box in which things are deposited. Space is a mode of our perception. It is not so much part of what we see as part of our perceptual apparatus, as is time. If we accept that space is an aspect of consciousness itself, there is no question of space, of the universe, being either finite or infinite.

From the Buddhist point of view, therefore, to try to ascertain whether the world is finite or infinite is quite mistaken; there is no question of its being either. One might say that while for certain practical purposes it is useful to assume that the universe is finite, for other practical purposes it is useful to assume that it is infinite. Scientists, for example, treat the universe as a discrete entity with boundaries of some kind, even though they may not be able to describe those boundaries in terms that can be understood except perhaps in terms of mathematics. On the other hand, philosophically speaking, however far the mind reaches out into the universe there must be further to go. But this is not to say that the universe as such is either finite or infinite, or indeed both, or even neither, because like any other conditioned thing it is not a self-existent reality.

THE ILLUSORY ELEPHANT

'Innumerable Buddhas have come,
And likewise will come and are here at present.
There are zillions of sentient beings,
And in addition the Buddhas intend to abide in the three times.

'The extinguishing of the world in the three
Times does not cause it to increase,
Then why was the All-Knower silent
About the limits of the world?'

That which is secret for a common being
Is the profound doctrine,
The world is like an illusion,
The ambrosia of the Buddha's teaching.

Just as the production and disintegration
Of an illusory elephant are seen,
But the production and disintegration
Do not really exist,

So the production and disintegration
Of the illusion-like world are seen,
But the production and disintegration
Do not ultimately exist.

Just as an illusory elephant,
Being only a bewildering of consciousness,
Does not come from anywhere,
Nor go anywhere, nor really stay,

So the illusion-like world,
Being only a bewildering of consciousness,
Does not come from anywhere,
Nor go anywhere, nor really stay.

Thus it has a nature beyond the three times.
Other than as the imputation of a convention
What world is there in fact
Which would exist or not?

For this reason the Buddha
Except for keeping silent, said nothing
About the fourfold format: having or
Not having a limit, both, or neither. (107–15)

The illusory elephant appears again and again in Buddhist philosophical literature. Just like the mirage, the elephant is not really there, it having been conjured up by a magician. But if the magician destroys the illusion he has produced, no elephant has been killed. The elephant did not exist in the first place, and it is impossible for anything that does not exist to be destroyed.

This, essentially, is Nāgārjuna's answer to an objection raised by certain philosophers of his time. The objection is based on the premise that there are no new sentient beings coming into existence, and that since innumerable Buddhas are dedicated to effecting their liberation from the world, which will decrease their numbers, eventually all beings must attain liberation. Now inasmuch as the conditioned world is the creation of conditioned consciousness, the world itself must eventually have an end: the world is made up of beings, thus no more beings, no more world. So why did the Buddha stay silent on the subject of the end of the world? There is a similar, more modern concern for anyone who contemplates the Buddhist doctrine of rebirth. In view of the population explosion in recent times, where do all the extra 'souls' come from? Do they come from another world, another planet, or another realm of being altogether?

According to Nāgārjuna, the world cannot really come to an end.[373] Like the illusory elephant, since it never really came into existence, it cannot really go out of existence either. Having no real existence, it cannot be said to be either finite or infinite. In reality the world does not come from anywhere, does not go anywhere, and does not even stay. When we say that the world neither exists nor does not exist, we are thinking of its existence in space. But the reality of the world is beyond space. Similarly, the true nature of the world is also beyond time. It neither comes into existence nor passes out of existence. To say, 'the world exists', or 'the world does not exist', or 'the world will have an end', is to speak in conventional terms. Such terms enable us to communicate with one another, but the concepts employed are not to be taken as having ultimate validity. For this reason the Buddha kept silent about the limits of the world. The nature of the world is beyond categorization. In the face of the intractable nature of objective truth with respect to such issues, silence is the appropriate attitude.

THE BODY OF THE DHARMA

> When the body, which is unclean,
> Coarse, an object of the senses,

Does not stay in the mind (as having a nature of uncleanliness
 and pain),
Although it is continually in view,

Then how could this doctrine
Which is most subtle, profound,
Baseless, and not manifest,
Easily appear to the mind?

Realizing that because of its profundity
This doctrine is difficult for beings to understand,
The Subduer, having become enlightened
(At first) turned away from teaching doctrine.

This doctrine wrongly understood
Causes the unwise to be ruined
Because they sink into the uncleanliness
Of nihilistic views.

Further, the stupid who fancy
Themselves wise, having a nature
Ruined by rejecting (emptiness), go headfirst
To a terrible hell due to their wrong understanding.

Just as one comes to ruin
Through wrong eating but obtains
Long life, freedom from disease,
Strength, and pleasures through right eating,

So one comes to ruin
Through wrong understanding
But obtains bliss and highest enlightenment
Through right understanding. (116–22)

We do not even see the true nature of our own physical body, with which we are in contact every moment of every day, so how can we be expected to see the true nature of the world, subtle and profound as this is? Elsewhere in the *Ratnāvalī*, Nāgārjuna gives the traditional skilful means of viewing the body as impure or unlovely (*aśubha*).[324] Suffice to say in this context that our inability to perceive the impurity of the body is cited here to illustrate the low level of awareness of the ordinary mind. It is as if to say that wisdom begins at home, where we live day by day, in the body.

Given the enormous gulf in understanding between the ordinary everyday consciousness and the Enlightened consciousness, it is understandable that after his attainment of Enlightenment the Buddha was at first reluctant to teach the Dharma. So far as he was concerned in his newly Enlightened state, the truth of the nature of reality was incommunicable to ordinary people, deeply entrenched as they were in worldly ways.

He was not thinking of matters of morality and discipline, or even of meditation, hard though these things were for people to master. It was the truth of conditionality that the Buddha felt would be too great a challenge for ordinary people. Teachings like this run completely against the grain of our whole way of thinking and, more importantly, our whole way of being. Thus it was only at the prompting of the great *deva* Brahmā Sahampati, who reminded him that there were yet some beings 'with little dust on their eyes', that the Buddha changed his mind. What he did not change, however, was his belief that his teaching was supremely difficult to master.[325]

Having thoroughly exposed the general unreadiness of the ordinary mind for transcendental wisdom, Nāgārjuna warns of two dangerous extremes into which the unwise and unwary are liable to fall when they attempt to grasp the teaching. When you think you have understood it you are liable either to reject it, or else to accept it as a nihilistic teaching. To fall into either of these extremes is disastrous. Nāgārjuna elsewhere famously remarks that if you misunderstand the Śūnyavāda, the teaching of emptiness,[326] you are like someone who is poisoned by the only medicine that can cure them of their sickness. He takes a similar line here, as he returns to a consideration of the body, comparing the process of taking in food with that of taking in the teaching. It is significant that we naturally speak of 'digesting' information in the sense of absorbing it, making it ours, making it part of us. The information or teaching has to descend from the head into the heart and stomach, even into our limbs, into the way we move and act. And, in the case of both food and teachings, what we take in may nourish us, but it may poison us too.

This is perhaps surprising. We tend to think of the truth as purely objective and invariably beneficial. The important thing, we imagine, is to 'get our heads around it', as the saying goes. But Nāgārjuna draws attention here to the fact that the truth needs the right 'vessel' before it can operate as Dharma. It is possible to take in the teaching in a way that causes delusion and suffering. An obvious example of misunderstanding the doctrine is literal-mindedness with respect to teachings like the *tathāgatagarbha*, the 'womb of Enlightenment' doctrine.[327] This teaching, which reminds us that Buddhahood is our true nature here and now, can be misunderstood as suggesting that we are already Enlightened and that to make any effort to attain Enlightenment is therefore deluded.

Sometimes we gobble down too much, or treat ourselves to teachings that are a little too rich for us. Sometimes we are simply not ready for theoretical teachings that require some preparatory understanding and practice. Another way to get indigestion is to take in different kinds of teaching which, though they may be nourishing when taken separately, are mutually incompatible. Different presentations of the doctrine, Zen and Shin for example, may be ultimately tending in the same direction, towards liberation, but they may take very different routes. Zen relies on 'self-power' (*jiriki*), whereas the devotional approach of Shin is a matter of dependence on 'other-power' (*tariki*), in which one surrenders any attempt to attain Enlightenment by one's own efforts and relies entirely on the compassion of Amitābha.[328] The two paths have a common goal, and both involve complete commitment, but they will not work together.

CLARITY

> Therefore having forsaken with respect to this (doctrine of
> emptiness)
> Nihilistic views and rejection,
> Be supremely intent on correct understanding,
> For the sake of achieving all aims.
>
> If this doctrine is not understood thoroughly,
> The conception of an 'I' prevails,
> Hence come virtuous and non-virtuous actions
> Which give rise to good and bad rebirths. (123–4)

Nāgārjuna's final instruction in his account of the doctrines of definite goodness, before he returns to the subject of high status, is that we should try to understand the doctrines correctly. It might seem odd that this needed saying at all, let alone that it should form his final message to the king on the subject. But it serves to remind us that in our approach to the teaching many of us have a deep resistance to clarity. How far do we really want to expose ourselves to the clear light of the Dharma? Some people imagine that if they mean well, and have a vague idea of the teachings, that will be enough. They seem to imagine that it is somehow not in keeping with the spirit of the Dharma to be clear and precise in one's thinking, and that the rational mind should be left well out of it. Nāgārjuna is quite clear, however, that if we do not understand the teaching correctly, we are not going to see through the conception of an 'I', of the self as a mere idea, to the true reality of things. If *śūnyatā* is not properly and clearly understood, the result is an ego-based life, whatever else we may do in the way of spiritual practice.

On the other hand, let us not take the word 'doctrine' too literally. It does not refer simply to conceptual formulations of the teaching as objects of intellectual understanding. To understand the doctrine means not just knowing the ideas but realizing the nature of voidness as an experience, a way of living. How much if anything you need to know about Buddhism to be a Buddhist and to realize something at least of the goal of Buddhism is an interesting question. It depends upon what one means by Buddhism, of course. Buddhism is whatever frees us from the grip of the ego, and you would be unlikely to get very far without the encouragement of others who have had at least some personal experience of the egoless state themselves. This means being involved in a tradition in which this teaching and this experience is familiar and accepted. But you do not need to know very much yourself, certainly not all the niceties of Madhyamaka philosophy.

7

AN ADVENTURE WITH NO END IN SIGHT

PLEASURE AND PAIN

Although Universal Monarchs rule
Over the four continents, their pleasures
Are regarded as only two –
The physical and the mental.

Physical feelings of pleasure
Are only a lessening of pain.
Mental pleasures are made by thought,
Created only by conceptuality.

All the wealth of worldly pleasures
Are just a lessening of suffering,
Or are only (creations of) thought,
Hence they are in fact not meaningful.

Just one by one there is enjoyment
Of continents, countries, towns, homes,
Conveyances, seats, clothing, beds,
Food, drink, elephants, horses, and women.

When the mind has any (one of these as its object)
Due to it there is said to be pleasure,
But since at that time no attention is paid to the others,
The others are not then in fact meaningful (causes of pleasure).

When (all) five senses, eye and so forth,
(Simultaneously) apprehend their objects,
A thought (of pleasure) does not refer (to all of them),
Therefore at that time they do not (all) give pleasure.

Whenever any of the (five) objects is known
(As pleasurable) by one of the (five) senses,
Then the remaining (objects) are not so known by the remaining (senses).
Since they then are not meaningful (causes of pleasure). (346–52)

By 'mental pleasures' Nāgārjuna means ambitions, plans, dreams, whether sleeping or waking, and entertainment (in our case, perhaps reading, listening to the radio, watching television, gambling, and so on). They are ways in which we distract ourselves from the tedium of ordinary life. Advertisements, for example, are often designed to create mental pleasure. I was surprised once – though perhaps I should not have been – to discover that advertisements for summer holidays start appearing early in January. In the midst of winter one is tempted by thoughts of golden sands and palm trees, and this kind of happy anticipation helps to keep one going through the winter months. Such pleasure is not purely mental because it is largely an anticipation of physical pleasure. Even in the most refined of mental pleasures, like meditation or art, the pleasure is felt in the body. In the higher stages of meditation sense consciousness is inhibited, so that you may not hear or feel anything. But the sense of floating that this withdrawal from the senses seems to induce in the mind suggests that the connection between mind and body remains. Likewise, it is virtually impossible to enjoy physical pleasure that is unaccompanied by mental activity. Sexual pleasure is often bound up with mental projections, and being massaged may be valued for its effect on the mind as much as on the body. Perhaps the nearest one could get to a pure physical pleasure would be to drink, on a very hot day, a cup of very cold water.

However, in this section Nāgārjuna is concerned to show that pleasure and pain are less real than we assume. Firstly, universal monarchs for all their power have no greater capacity for pleasure than anyone else. They have just physical pleasure and mental pleasure. They have the same six senses as anyone else. However exquisite the pleasures you can enjoy, the organism can take only so much before it is surfeited.

The king has enormous choice, he has anything and everything at his disposal; but this wealth does not multiply his pleasure. Perhaps there are three or four thousand women in his harem; but he can enjoy only one of them at a time. The same goes for everything else he possesses. Just because he owns a thousand horses, it doesn't mean to say he *enjoys* a thousand horses. He can ride only one at a time. He may have a hundred shirts, but he can wear no more shirts than a man who owns just one. He might enjoy the thought that he possesses all those things, and that each day he wakes up with a different woman and puts on a new shirt. No doubt a man with one shirt would be very pleased to have another one, but the pleasure would not last; he would soon feel the same as he did before. A third shirt would give him nothing like the same pleasure. The more we acquire, the less enjoyment our 'pleasures' bring. In fact, they may bring worries. If you are wearing your only shirt, you know where it is – on your back. But if you have a hundred shirts, they need a lot of looking after; and one can imagine the difficulties of having a multitude of women all competing with one another for your favour. So the idea that multiplying our possessions multiplies our enjoyment is an illusion. It is understandable that we are fooled by it, but if we are mindful, and examine our experience closely, we should be able to see through the illusion.

The same principle applies to the five senses. When you enjoy something, you will rarely be experiencing the pleasure through more than one sense organ. You may try, but one sense will tend to predominate. Indeed, in a mix of pleasures, the different pleasures can distract from each other. Nāgārjuna's point is that when you are awake all five senses are functioning, but only one sense at a time experiences pleasure. The experience of the others is at best neutral, or even disagreeable. Two senses experiencing pleasure at the same time is probably the best we can hope for. The nineteenth-century cleric and wit Sydney Smith famously imagined heaven as being like eating pâté de foie gras to the sound of trumpets, and perhaps he knew from experience that these particular pleasures complemented each other.[329] However, in general, you cannot really concentrate on one pleasure without the other being a distraction. Your enjoyment of a beautiful piece of music, for instance, may be spoiled by a sudden bad smell or a draught.

A late nineteenth-century French novel, *Against Nature*,[330] explores this theme. Its hero, Des Esseintes, isolates himself in his castle from the pleasures and pains of the world outside, and tries to make sure that everything within the castle is perfectly adapted to his enjoyment. Everything is uniquely beautiful; everything has just the right smell and the right taste and makes the right sound. He rids himself of anything that is not perfectly agreeable to him. Of course, all he is doing is increasing his sensitivity, thus making himself more susceptible to pain. In the end his scheme of pleasure breaks down, and he cannot enjoy anything.

Sometimes we have an experience of intense pleasure, but the intensity is necessarily fleeting. We get used to the pleasure, for the senses are quite quickly jaded. There were ancient kings who did their best to make the most of the immense variety of pleasures available to them, and who virtually destroyed themselves in the process. They couldn't sustain it. In such circumstances the whole psychophysical organism starts resisting. It seems to have been a source of human frustration in all ages, even to the present day, that we can only enjoy one thing at a time, and that we cannot even enjoy that one thing for very long. Yet few of us are prepared to accept the evidence for this fact.

One is quickly surfeited, even by the most refined aesthetic pleasure. For instance, if you go to a large art gallery, you may very much enjoy the first room, and perhaps the second, but after that, even though the paintings are extremely beautiful, and though you may have come a long way to see them, you cannot take in any more. You just want to go and have a cup of coffee. It can be quite a disappointment, like realizing at a feast that you have no room for the delicious dessert.

Culture-guzzling package holidays represent our unwillingness to acknowledge this reality. People say, 'I saw this famous old church. Now was it in Paris or was it Berlin? I guess it might have been Amsterdam.' For them, everything beautiful merges into one vaguely stimulating but rather exhausting experience. They can remember occasional details, but not necessarily what it was or where it was, or even why they saw it. All they really know is that it cost them a lot of money. This is why they take so many photographs. They hope to have the leisure when they get home to take in the sights that they didn't have time to look at when they were actually there.

There is a certain self-delusion that lurks in our consumption of pleasure. How often, for example, is one really carried away by a piece of music or a painting or poem? I suspect that such pleasures are more elusive than most of us care to admit. We have to be in a certain mood. Having had an intense aesthetic experience once, we expose ourselves again and again to the kind of work that produced it originally, and declare how much we like it. But more often than not, we are just not in the mood to appreciate it fully. It is clear that some people have a greater capacity for enjoying the arts than others, but even in their case the enjoyment is limited. Should you read poetry all day, even, you might get perhaps no more than two or three moments of aesthetic exhilaration from it.

Even meditation, while it can be genuinely and deeply pleasurable, does not guarantee pleasure every time you practise it. You may be feeling a strong – even a blissful – positive emotion, but you may also be aware that your knee is hurting or your back is aching. You may also experience an unaccountable urge to get up and end the meditation, as though a gravitational pull was exerting itself. What does this say about our relationship with pleasure? How comfortable are we with it? Most people rarely experience true ecstasy. To be able to feel intense pleasure and joy, you have to have a certain amount of energy bubbling up within you. It is not going to come from the pleasurable objects themselves. At our best, most of us feel moderately content most of the day with, if we are lucky, a few gentle highlights when we feel quite good – but our experience of pleasure usually doesn't go much beyond this. A retreat with others is usually our best chance of achieving a markedly higher level of happiness than we can manage in ordinary life, and this seems to be mainly a matter of collective energies bubbling over. It is always good to see such high spirits on a retreat, even if the mood is not exactly one of spiritual exaltation. Such ordinary, innocent happiness is rare enough.

Some religious texts talk about the need to give up worldly pleasure or happiness, but I would personally like to see people giving up their attachment to worldly misery. I would like to see them enjoying more of the simple pleasures of life. Many of those who are supposed to be wallowing in worldly pleasure, and who have everything at their command, tend to look miserable, gaunt, and even irritable.

So far, so uncontroversial. But can it be true that all bodily pleasures are no more than a lessening of pain? Is there no possibility of pure, unadulterated pleasure? It may seem unlikely, but this is the case. What we take for pleasure is only a slight amelioration of pain. Underlying any pleasure is a substratum of *duḥkha*, the basic unsatisfactoriness of conditioned existence. Whether or not we acknowledge it, we have an uninterrupted baseline of negative feeling that never altogether goes away. A weekend break might seem like an opportunity to forget your troubles, but at the back of your mind will be some unresolved crisis at the office, or some problem with the neighbours at home, and the thought of that may never really leave you all through the weekend.

Even without any obvious cause for concern to keep us from being absorbed in a pleasurable situation, our pleasure is necessarily limited. Unless you are mindful of the fact that it is impermanent, your pleasure will entail a painful limitation of your being anyway, inasmuch as you are unconsciously holding that awareness of impermanence at bay all the time. You can enjoy that object fully only by limiting your mindfulness. This is difficult for us to appreciate; we cannot be aware of that limitation if we have never experienced what it is to be without it. Nevertheless, it produces a quietly uncomfortable or uneasy feeling at the back of the mind that cannot be banished.

We might conclude that there can be no completely unalloyed physical pleasure because all pleasure is a distraction from the basic unsatisfactoriness or inadequacy of conditioned existence. You obtain something that you have looked forward to for a long time, and even while you are enjoying it, there is deep in your consciousness the feeling that after all it is not as enjoyable as you had thought it would be. You eat, for example, to alleviate the pain of hunger, and much of the pleasure involved is in achieving this end. Any particularly strong desire can be quite painful, because in so far as you are not getting what you want there is an element of frustration in it. You acquire the desired object not because you really want it but to assuage the desire for it. This is not really true enjoyment.

Goethe's *Faust* provides a dramatic illustration of what Nāgārjuna is saying. Mephistopheles strikes a bargain with Faust by which he promises to give Faust any object of enjoyment, any power or pleasure he wants. He is able, for example, to give him Helen of Troy, the most beautiful woman who ever lived. The bargain is that if Faust ever said, 'Stop, this is a totally satisfying experience!' his soul would then go to Mephistopheles. But of course Faust is never able to say that. He never does find anything so completely satisfying or enjoyable that he wants it to last for ever; so Mephistopheles fails to win his wager and consequently loses Faust's soul. This is a parable of human desire, showing that it cannot be satisfied by anything mundane. There is always some fly in the ointment, some imperfection, to any experience. Feelings of pleasure do exist, but they are only the scratching of an itch: it may be pleasant to scratch the itch but it is better not to have the itch at all.

We have all experienced this frustration in one connection or another. The trick is to notice what the experience of pleasure really consists in, moment by moment. As you are planning some kind of pleasure for yourself, as well as when you are actually experiencing the pleasure, notice the pleasant feeling when it arises together with any accompanying unpleasant feeling. Notice even the resistance to examining your experience so closely, and any resistance to the idea of losing the craving for pleasure.

All this is not to say that we should stop craving pleasure. According to Buddhism, we just have to wake up to the fact that our craving for pleasure is in vain, because we don't enjoy our pleasures as truly and fully as we imagine we do. We scratch the old itch a bit, that's all. Some people, of course, carefully cultivate their itches for the sake of the satisfaction they get from scratching them. This is called being devoted to a life of pleasure.

How unsatisfactory desire can feel can be gauged by considering our more obviously neurotic cravings: those emerging out of a dull feeling of frustration, boredom, and emptiness. We look for something pleasurable in order to fill that void and relieve the boredom, at least partially and temporarily. You eat a chocolate or drink a cup of tea or put on a piece of music not so much for the positive enjoyment of such things but more because you don't know what else to do. It is these kinds of craving that should concern us most, more than those that arise out of a strong, healthy appetite. And the way to deal with them is to regard the boredom itself as a positive opportunity. It is like having to deal with fear, anger, or indeed craving, or any other negative mental state. It is an opportunity to experience the energy that is usually drained away by distractions. When you are really bored, the best thing you can do is sit down and let yourself experience the boredom more fully. It may not be a deep or satisfying state, but at least you are not indulging in the things with which you usually cover up this kind of experience. Your real state of mind is more nakedly exposed, because for the time being there are no distractions. If you can stay with the experience of boredom, you can try to feel your way through into something deeper, truer and more spontaneous within yourself.

This is likely to be more helpful than trying to force a more positive state into being or rushing to alleviate the boredom with a distraction. After a while you should find that the boredom passes. You will start to feel more positive simply by virtue of experiencing yourself more truly. And feeling more positive, you will probably want to get on with actually doing something positive. But if the minute you start feeling bored you turn on the radio or pick up the newspaper or ring somebody up, then you've lost the opportunity with which the boredom has presented you.

Boredom is an intermediate state between being in touch with deeper and truer levels within oneself and just being distracted. For the time being you're neither the one nor the other – hence the feeling of emptiness. You are neither really in touch with yourself nor being distracted from the fact that you are not really in touch with yourself. You have neither a truer, deeper enjoyment, nor a superficial enjoyment. At such a time, you can either rush into a superficial, transitory enjoyment, or else you can wait for true enjoyment to arise from within. Usually the state of boredom will not last more than a few hours.

There are, though, two different kinds of situation in which boredom arises. First, there is the boredom of not having anything to do, in which case you may end up asleep. It can take a lot of energy to hold yourself back from going in search of distractions, but just by falling asleep you will be refreshing yourself from deeper resources within you. Second, there is the boredom of doing something you find uninteresting. You may be working hard, but there are significant strata of your mind that are not engaged in what you are doing. The work itself is not a distraction and at the same time it prevents you from distracting yourself with something else. Whether in such a case you should carry on working or stop in order to gather together some more positive energies depends on circumstances, on how objectively important the work is.

Nothing is intrinsically boring. Anything can be boring if you have to do it all the time, but the same thing can be interesting when done occasionally, and quite restful when done more regularly. When you are not actively stimulated by what you are doing, you can occupy yourself with your own thoughts or just experience your own general positivity. But not for eight hours a day. Everyone needs a balance of relatively undemanding activity and more challenging, interesting work. When the balance is wrong, stress or boredom is the result. Where this balance lies depends on the individual. In general, the more creative you are, the more easily bored you get and the less easily distracted you are from that boredom. A dull, unimaginative person is less easily bored and by the same token more tolerant of distraction. Give some people piped music, cups of tea, and a bit of a chat at intervals, and they can do repetitive work year after year.

Boredom is connected with not being able to express your energies. When someone starts talking to you, for example, you might be quite interested in what they are saying, but if they ramble on and on, and give you no opportunity to respond, you will probably start to feel bored. Your energy is being frustrated. Boredom is also connected with not being able to be yourself. You start feeling bored when too little of yourself is involved in what you are doing. When work is too repetitive to stimulate your energies, you are being prevented, effectively, from being fully involved. You are drying up inside; there is an empty space where there should have been an active, spontaneous individual. If you were a young civil servant and you got an important and complicated directive from higher up, you might have a lot of fun working out how to implement it. But if after a few years the inventive, creative part of you stopped being involved, you might well start to find the work boring.

Once you start analysing things in this way, you may begin wondering whether you have ever experienced real pleasure. If you arrive home from a day's outing and someone asks, 'Did you have a good time?' unless the day was a disaster you will probably reply, 'Yes, I really enjoyed it.' But did you? No doubt doing something different is refreshing, but when you think about the day in detail, you will probably find it to have been, like most things, a mixed experience. We give the label 'pleasure' to certain experiences perhaps because they involve giving way to certain appetites, or even merely spending money, and we don't like to question the label because then we would have to change our ideas about life.

THE BIAS OF MEMORY

> The mind apprehends the image of a past object
> Which has been apprehended by the senses
> And imagines and fancies
> It to be pleasurable. (353)

As adults, most of us look back to our childhood as a time of innocent happiness. Children are told that schooldays are the happiest time of their lives. Children themselves, of course, may take a different view. They think, reasonably enough, that they will be happy when they are grown up and able to do what they want to do, when they can eat all the chocolate they like and play all day and never be told to go to bed and not have to wash their necks.

Nostalgia, or a sentimental dwelling on the past, is the way we create pleasure out of past unhappiness. The past is all the more pleasurable the further we are away from it. We settle down in the past, consolidating our identity more and more round it as we feed our attachment to what we are remembering. We choose the past over the present or the future, trying to console or compensate ourselves for the present by turning over in our mind the supposed joys of the past.

Different people have different attachments. Some people are nostalgic, some people live for the present in a very narrow, mindless way, while others live for the pleasures of the future. One of the benefits of going on a spiritual retreat is that the past and future both fade into the background. What you have been worrying about seems much less important; what you are going back to and what you will be doing there seem like another world. You are in the present not in the sense of being lost in the concerns of the present, but in the sense of being simply aware.

Our natural tendency is to soften or even forget the harsher features of the past. If we took a more clear-eyed view of it, though, we would have to contemplate a less rosy, more painful reality. As this would become our present experience for as long as we continued to think of the past, it would make our present experience itself more painful. Because we want to experience pleasure rather than pain, we naturally and automatically edit the past when we think about it. Not all our painful experiences can be edited out so easily, but this editing process works on many of the disagreeable details of our lives.

You may even come to see a painful situation in the past as so positively pleasurable that you start thinking of revisiting it. Forgetting the lesson that this situation has taught you, you turn the pain into a sort of wistful melancholy. A certain fascination about that difficult situation lures you back into it and you can end up going through much the same thing all over again, if under slightly different circumstances.

In this connection it could be helpful to keep a diary, which would give you a counterweight of evidence against the sweetening bias of memory. The positive and pleasant experiences would take their natural place among the more difficult ones, and in this context pleasant memories could achieve a more truly Proustian poignancy and intensity. In his great novel *The Remembrance of Things Past* Proust's narrator recounts various intensely joyful moments in his childhood, which he re-experiences through little events or accidents in his mature life. But he doesn't bathe these memories in a warm glow. There are equally intense painful experiences, from which an adult is no less excluded than he is from the pleasures of childhood. Proust writes, 'The true paradises are the paradises that one has lost.' And he says of the life of the Duchess of Guermantes, that it 'appeared to me to be a paradise I would never enter'.[331]

However, the re-experiencing of a moment in childhood (rather than merely remembering it) produces a sort of transcendence of time and space in one's mind. It is that transcendence that is the real joy, not the rosy misapprehension of a particular time in one's life. It is worth considering that this transcendence of time and space does in fact take us closer to how things really are. For example, from reading the *Udāna* or some of the other books of the Pāli canon one can get a vivid sense of the Buddha as he may actually have appeared to people, and of what life in the early days of Buddhism may have been like. I have occasionally had an odd feeling of being in very much the same sort of situation as some of the early disciples of the Buddha. Once, when I was in New Zealand, I found myself wandering in a remote part of the country, in the company of a few friends, and talking with them about the Dharma as if it were something just revealed to mankind. I had a slightly uncanny but powerful sense of the millennia between me and those original followers of the Buddha just falling away. In such cases one can feel that one is not just imagining something taking place, but that one is actually present. You can be meditating, and it might as well be the fourth or fifth century BCE; and when you open your eyes there is a moment perhaps before your personal historical location swims back into perception.

If you do recapture some vivid experience from your earlier life, a question arises. Given that your experience repeats, at least momentarily, your experience then, where are you? Are you there or are you here? In that moment you cannot tell. You are both here *and* there. In that sense, or to that extent, you transcend time. When you experience what you experienced as a child, given that it is a child's experience, are you now a child or are you an adult? You are of course both, and neither. In a sense you have transcended time. Your experience momentarily bridges the past and the present, giving you a strange impression that time is illusory. It is as though your experience contains the past and the present.

Allowing our imagination to link us directly with past and even future ages can be a useful exercise, helping us to break out of the cocoon of the present, and out of our tendency to identify completely with our present situation. Wherever we may now find ourselves, we can reflect on what we would see and hear around us if we were to go back a hundred years, or a thousand years, or even ten million years. Where we are walking may even have once been under the sea. Reflections like this can take away the ground from under our feet and remind us that the world we see is not the fixed reality we take it for.

THE PERMANENT POSSIBILITY OF SENSATION

Also the one sense which here (in the world
Is said to) know one object,
Is meaningless without an object,
And the object also is meaningless without it.

Just as a child is said to be born
In dependence on a father and a mother,
So a (visual) consciousness is said to arise
In dependence on an eye sense and on a form. (354–5)

It is a basic Buddhist tenet that, as the second of these two verses reminds us, consciousness is conditioned. It arises from the interaction of the senses with their respective objects, which themselves arise in dependence upon consciousness as well as on each other. From this the Abhidharma concludes that there is a consciousness for every sense organ. Thus 'eye consciousness' arises in dependence on the contact of the organ of sight with the visual object. The Abhidharma lists first the six senses (including the mind in the ordinary sense of the term), then the twelve *āyatanas* or 'bases', which are the six senses and their respective objects. Finally, it enumerates the eighteen *dhātus* or 'spheres', which comprise both senses and objects together with their corresponding consciousnesses.[332]

In the case of the visual sense, the eye perceives an object of a certain shape and colour. Without an object for it to perceive that sense organ ceases to be a sense organ. Conversely, there can be no object of perception without a perceiving sense organ. This is why John Stuart Mill defined matter as the permanent possibility of sensation.[333] Matter is not an entity that is there all the time, waiting to be perceived. It is the permanent possibility of that sort of experience occurring when a sense organ comes into contact with its appropriate object.

There is no object without a subject. There is no subject without an object. Neither exists independently. So if a thing cannot exist except in dependence on some other thing, can it be said truly to exist at all? If the object of sight can exist only in relation to the sense organ of sight, and vice versa, can either of them be said to be real? Here we come back to *śūnyatā* or emptiness: each is 'empty' of independent existence, and hence is only relatively real. And if the production of pleasure is dependent on these unreal sense organs and their unreal objects, how can the pleasure itself be real?

NO TIME LIKE THE PRESENT

Past and future objects
And the senses are meaningless,

So too are present objects
Since they are not distinct from these two. (356)

Nāgārjuna goes on to undermine our belief in pleasure by questioning its temporal context. Past, present, and future objects all depend upon one another, so that they are only relatively real. They are not real in themselves. The notion that things are in the past is dependent upon the notion that they were once in the present and before that they were in the future. The future, by virtue of its being the future, will become the past. Present objects are of the same conditioned nature as past and future objects, since the present moment can always be subdivided. The present is only a moving boundary or edge between the past and the future. It is where the two edges meet: it does not have an independent existence. The present is the term we apply to our experience of the future continually becoming past. To talk of being 'in the now' really means being out of time altogether. There is no 'now' where one can be. We say 'all the time' but that makes no sense either. One can accumulate as much of nothing as one likes; it will still add up to nothing.

If the present does not exist, the past does not exist either, because what is past is made up of what was once present. The same goes for the future, because the future is made up of what will be present. Every past was once a present; every future will be a present. Nāgārjuna is trying to bring us to an experience of time as unreal: he says that the present is unreal because, as he has already shown, past and future are unreal. One can also say that past and future are unreal because the present is unreal, since this amounts to the same thing.

How, asks Nāgārjuna, can a real pleasure arise from unreal senses and their unreal sense objects? Whether in the past, present, or future, the pleasure cannot be grasped or secured in any way. There is nothing there. You cannot be anywhere other than here and now, but nor can you really even be here and now. There is no 'being' at any point in time at all. The now that is the only point at which you can be is outside time, and therefore outside any sense of a subject as opposed to an object. There is no 'you' there, and therefore no 'being'.

The thought that pleasure is unreal, though at the same time basically frustrating or painful, helps to free us from our attachment to it, and it is at this point that we realize that pain too is unreal. This is unlikely to happen the other way round. Trying to take pain as unreal while taking pleasure as real can only be a self-serving fantasy, as a result of which we dig ourselves deeper into self-delusion. If pleasure is grasped at as a self-existent reality, pain will feel if anything even more real.

Living in the present is good, but with the arising of insight one realizes that strictly speaking there is no present moment in which to live, and that one cannot live in time at all. And one can only live beyond time when one is not affected by either pleasure or pain. Without repressing your feelings, without being alienated, you learn to treat pleasure and pain as being the same, and therefore do not react to them.

Thus, being in the present is not a matter of grasping at the present. It is about not anticipating the future or hanging onto the past. Its concern is with how we see ourselves. If we say, 'This is me, this is how I am, take me as I am,' we are limiting ourselves by identifying with what we are now. We are not prepared to respond *creatively* to the present.

CHASING SHADOWS

Just as due to error the eye perceives
A (whirling) firebrand as a wheel,
So the senses apprehend
Present objects (as if real).

The senses and their objects are regarded
As being composed of the elements,
Since the elements are meaningless individually,
These also are meaningless in fact.

If the elements are each different,
It follows that there could be fire without fuel.
If mixed, they would be characterless.
Such is also to be ascertained about the other elements.

Because the elements are thus meaningless in both these ways,
So too is a composite,
Because a composite is meaningless
So too are forms meaningless in fact.

Also because consciousness, feelings,
Discriminations, and compositional factors
Altogether and individually are without essential factuality,
(Pleasures) are not ultimately meaningful.

Just as a lessening of pain
Is fancied to be a pleasure in fact,
So destruction of pleasure
Is also fancied to be pain.

Thus attachment to meeting with pleasure
And attachment to separating from pain
Are to be abandoned because they do not inherently exist.
Thereby those who see thus are liberated. (357–63)

Illustrations like that of the whirling firebrand, which we have already met in this text, do not prove anything; they just make clearer something that is independently known. The image itself is clear enough. One whirls a firebrand around to give an impression of a wheel of fire. But is what one sees really a wheel of fire? No, one has created an illusion of one. The eye is deceived by the speed of the firebrand's circular motion. The real issue, though, is what this image is meant to illustrate. Except in the case of simple illusions like this one, how else do we experience present objects in a way that we know them not to be? After all, the image is striking because it is taken as anomalous. How do we get from this particular anomaly to a general rule that 'the senses apprehend present objects (as if real)' when they are illusory?

We have to look into things a bit more deeply, see what is really going on, see through our assumptions. Is there anything that is not in the process of changing, decaying, from one moment to the next? As with the wheel of fire, we know intellectually what is happening, but because we do not actually perceive what is going on, we happily ignore what we know to be true. And when we finally have to face the truth, we become downcast. It is as if we went about with our eyes half closed, allowing ourselves to be mesmerized.

Still trying to convince the king of the unreality of his pleasures, Nāgārjuna then breaks the senses and their objects down into their constituent elements: earth, water, fire, air, space, and consciousness.

Those pleasures cannot be any more real than the elements out of which they are composed. Nāgārjuna is saying that you cannot distinguish the elements from one another completely; the element fire cannot have an independent existence from the element earth. Fire needs the earth element (and the air element, for that matter) as its fuel. On the other hand, if they were mixed together they would lose their specific characteristics. Hence they are neither different from one another, nor the same.[334] Our pleasures are made up of nothing beyond these elements, which disappear when they are looked at closely. Out of these unreal elements we make our unreal sense organs and sense objects. And these unreal sense organs and sense objects produce an unreal consciousness – and an unreal pleasure.[335]

What do we mean when we say that one thing is composed out of other things? Here Nāgārjuna asserts that the idea of composition itself is untenable. Can we really say that the wheel of fire is 'composed' of a moving firebrand? No, because time is unreal, fire is unreal, and – as Nāgārjuna has proved elsewhere (at least to his own satisfaction) – movement is impossible as well.[336] 'Composition' suggests a number of things put together to form a whole. But a lot of nothing still adds up to nothing. Yet we insist on reifying even the most obviously insubstantial aspects of our experience. Is ignorance or attachment something that we can get rid of, or something we just have to drop? Ignorance is simply a word. If there really was such a thing as ignorance it could not be removed. One can only get rid of ignorance because it is not there. One can drop one's attachment because one is not holding onto it. The same goes for pleasure (and pain).

For the experience of pleasure to be possible in any real sense, there must be a real framework within which that experience can take place. And Nāgārjuna has been concerned to show the unreality of the framework within which pleasure is considered to be experienced in order to cast doubt on the reality of that pleasure. Demolish the framework, and the pleasure also collapses. The spiritual life, by contrast, is a real framework. Or, to put it another way, one could say that real satisfaction is possible only outside time. Of course, such satisfaction is not what we imagine it to be. Real satisfaction is what we would call 'lasting satisfaction', which is impossible because 'lasting' means continuing within time, and time involves change. Lasting satisfaction is possible only outside time, where the question of its lasting does not arise.

Abstruse and over-ingenious as these arguments may seem, such mental gymnastics were highly appreciated in ancient India. It seems that the Buddha's down-to-earth, common-sense approach was superseded quite early on by such dialectics. I have certainly had the experience myself in India of having to field quite intellectual questions from orthodox Brahmins. No doubt Nāgārjuna grew up with this mindset, as he was formerly an orthodox Brahmin himself. But generally speaking, unlike Nāgārjuna, the super-subtle Brahmin tends to remain a Brahmin, with all his prejudices intact.

Those of us who are fortunate enough to be more simple-minded still manage to offer considerable resistance to the reality that Nāgārjuna is uncovering here. Just as we take a temporary and partial relief from pain to be pleasure, we also take a surrender of pleasure to be pain. We imagine that giving up the imaginary pleasures with which we alleviate our fundamentally painful existence must itself be painful. In fact, though, our predominant feeling may well be one of relief, freedom, and release from the sense of being in thrall to our desires – certainly in the long run.

Nāgārjuna's argument is meant to be a challenge to the importance of the place that pleasure and pain hold in our ordinary lives. Most of the time, if not all the time, we are instinctively searching for what is pleasurable and trying to separate ourselves from what is painful. We are probably not aware of the extent to which we do this. But unconsciously, we build our lives around these two things, making all sorts of adjustments and arrangements, taking all sorts of steps and measures, to ensure that we continue to experience as much pleasure and contentment and as little suffering and difficulty as possible, almost regardless of other considerations.

Because pleasure and pain do not inherently exist Nāgārjuna is suggesting that a life that is oriented towards finding pleasure and avoiding pain is one that is not oriented towards reality; it is therefore an unreal life – the conditioned in pursuit of the conditioned.[337] It is a chasing after moving shadows. Such a life, he says, should be abandoned. At least, we need to reduce the extent to which these two drives dominate our lives. Making the pursuit of pleasure and the avoidance of pain one's overriding priority means that one is considering pleasure and pain to be more real than they actually are. A life of this kind is therefore based on unreality.

What sees (reality)?
Conventionally it is said to be the mind,
For without mental factors there is no mind
(And hence minds and mental factors) are meaningless, due to which it is not asserted that they are simultaneous.

Knowing thus correctly, just as it is,
That transmigrating beings do not exist in fact,
One passes (from suffering) not subject (to rebirth and hence) without appropriating (rebirth),
Like a fire without its cause.

Bodhisattvas also who have seen it thus,
Seek perfect enlightenment with certainty,
They maintain a connection between lives
Until enlightenment only through their compassion. (364–6)

When we assume that it is the mind that cognizes the nature of reality, we are thinking of the mind defined as 'awareness of an object', not as defined in any other way. But how do you know that it is the mind that sees the object, let alone that it sees reality? What you need is a 'second mind' to see the first mind, and see that it does in fact see reality. However, this requires a third mind to see the second, and a fourth to see the third, and so on. The search for such certainty is a fruitless regression to infinity. Consequently, it is only in a manner of speaking that one says that the mind sees reality. Mind itself cannot be considered to be an existent entity: it is a complex of a number of mental factors.[338] If the mind is unreal, there is no question of its perceiving an object, least of all of its perceiving reality, nor even of a second mind seeing it doing so. Conventionally we see and speak dualistically, in terms of subject and object. It is the only way in which it is possible for us to speak. Reality, therefore, unless it is thought of as dualistic, cannot be described as a subject or, as here, as an object of perception.

A point that Nāgārjuna does not make is that you no more need a second mind in order to perceive the fact that the first mind perceives than you need a second light to show you that the light you have in the first place is giving light. It is by the light given by the original light that you see *that* it is giving light. By the light by which the mind perceives its object, you can see *that* the mind is perceiving its object. A second mind is surplus to requirements. Hence the mind is said to be 'self-luminous'.[339]

One of the implications of the refutation of a self-existent mind is that the so-called living being (*jīva*) lacks a basis in reality. If you can absorb this truth without falling into nihilism – that is, without losing the thread of compassion that binds you to beings – you are a bodhisattva. It is not that you regard living beings as absolutely non-existent, but you regard yourself and others as having a relative and contingent existence. In other words, by its very nature any kind of existence, as we are able to understand it, is relative. When one sees things in this way one is free from grasping, and therefore no longer subject to rebirth. There is no one there to do the grasping.

What the bodhisattvas are certain of is their goal. They are certain that there is such a thing as Enlightenment, because they have already had some preliminary glimpses of it in the form of some insight into the truth of non-ego. They have seen that a higher transcendental dimension is attainable. They then hold back from arriving at the goal out of compassion for other beings. This is the popularized if dualistic Mahāyāna view that the bodhisattva, in Dr Matics' phrase, 'hovers between being and non-being'.[340] That is, he or she holds back from becoming completely immersed in *nirvāṇa* without, of course, becoming completely immersed in *saṃsāra*. He or she keeps in contact with *nirvāṇa*, with the ultimate spiritual dimension, through wisdom, and keeps in contact with *saṃsāra*, continuing the series of births and rebirths, through compassion. In a deeper sense the bodhisattva has passed beyond the duality between *saṃsāra* and *nirvāṇa*. There is no question of their deciding, through compassion, to continue existing. They see no difference between remaining in the *saṃsāra* and not remaining in it. For them, wisdom and compassion, *nirvāṇa* and *saṃsāra*, are one.

In Tibet many lamas were believed to be bodhisattvas who remained in the world and did not enter into Nirvāṇa so that they could help other living beings. It was also believed that they could be identified when young and brought back to their original monasteries. But one must distinguish here between two kinds of rebirth. According to orthodox Buddhist belief, everybody is reborn, including great lamas. In theory one could go out and identify any child as having been a specific person in his or her previous life. But only a few of these rebirths can be of bodhisattvas. When you identify a child as having been an abbot who died a few years before, it does not follow that he is necessarily an 'incarnate bodhisattva'. If that abbot himself was a bodhisattva then yes, the little boy will be a bodhisattva, but if the abbot was not a bodhisattva, the little boy will not be one either.

I was talking once to Christmas Humphreys about these 'reincarnate' lamas or *tulkus* and something he said seemed to sum up the plain facts of the situation in many cases. He remarked, 'I don't know what all the fuss is about incarnate lamas. What are they, after all? They're just the Buddhist equivalent of the local vicar reborn.' In the West we are very impressed if someone is presented as being the thirteenth incarnation of such and such an abbot of such and such a monastery; and the fact that the line has been maintained over many centuries, the lama being rediscovered over and over again, is no doubt impressive. But it does not necessarily mean that he is an incarnate bodhisattva. Remembering details of a previous life is certainly no guarantee of spiritual attainment. Dhardo Rimpoche once told me that it was his personal opinion, and the belief of quite a number of other lamas, that in Tibet there were among the two thousand officially recognized *tulkus* no more than six or seven, or at the most eight, who really were incarnate bodhisattvas.

A bodhisattva is one in whom the *bodhicitta* has arisen. An incarnate bodhisattva would be someone who had reached the eighth *bhūmi*, where the renunciation of Nirvāṇa for oneself becomes a real possibility, and that is a very advanced stage indeed.[341] Nāgārjuna himself, according to one tradition, was a bodhisattva of the second *bhūmi*. So one sees how difficult it is to be an incarnate bodhisattva.

It is a question of how deep our understanding of the nature of reality goes, of how 'intuitive' it becomes. And the way to deepen our understanding is to remind ourselves constantly that any understanding we do have has its limitations. After all, once our understanding has matured a little, we look back on our former confidence and think, 'How could I ever have kidded myself that I understood *that*? I didn't understand it at all.' We need the imagination to be able to project that mature reflection into a possible future in which our present knowledge will appear just as jejune. The spiritual life is an adventure with no end in sight. When we say, 'Now, finally, I understand,' we are really only just beginning.

8
TO END AS WE BEGAN

A SEVENFOLD PUJA

Therefore in the presence of an image
Or monument or something else
Say these twenty stanzas
Three times every day.

Going for refuge with all forms of respect
To the Buddhas, excellent Doctrine,
Supreme Community, and Bodhisattvas,
I bow down to all that are worthy of honour.

I will turn away from all ill deeds
And thoroughly take up all meritorious actions.
I will admire all the merits
Of all embodied beings.

With bowed head and joined palms
I petition the perfect Buddhas
To turn the wheel of doctrine and remain
As long as transmigrating beings remain.

Through the merit of having done thus
And through the merit that I did earlier and will do
May all sentient beings aspire
To the highest enlightenment.

May all sentient beings have all the stainless faculties,
Release from all conditions of non-leisure,
Freedom of action
And endowment with good livelihood.

Also may all embodied beings
Have jewels in their hands,
And may all the limitless necessities of life remain
Unconsumed as long as there is cyclic existence.

May all women at all times
Become supreme persons.
May all embodied beings have
The intelligence (of wisdom) and the legs (of ethics).

May embodied beings have a pleasant complexion,
Good physique, great splendor,
A pleasing appearance, freedom from disease,
Strength, and long life.

May all be skilled in the means (to extinguish suffering),
And have liberation from all suffering,
Inclination to the Three Jewels,
And the great wealth of Buddha's doctrine.

May they be adorned with love, compassion, joy,
Even-mindedness (devoid of) the afflictive emotions,
Giving, ethics, patience, effort,
Concentration, and wisdom.

Completing the two collections (of merit and wisdom),
May they have the brilliant marks and beautiful features (even
  while on the path),
And may they cross without interruption
The ten inconceivable grounds.

May I also be adorned completely
With those and all other good qualities,
Be freed from defects,
And have superior love for all sentient beings.

May I perfect all the virtues
For which all embodied beings hope,
And may I always relieve
The sufferings of all embodied beings.

May those beings in all worlds
Who are distressed through fear
Become entirely fearless
Even though merely hearing my name.

Through seeing or thinking of me or only hearing my name
May beings attain great joy,
Naturalness free from error,
Definiteness toward complete enlightenment,

And the five clairvoyances
Throughout their continuum of lives.
May I always in all ways bring
Help and happiness to all sentient beings.

May I always without harm
Simultaneously stop
All beings in all worlds
Who wish to commit ill deeds.

May I always be an object of enjoyment
For all sentient beings according to their wish
And without interference, as are the earth,
Water, fire, wind, herbs, and wild forests.

May I be as dear to sentient beings as their own life,
And may they be even more dear to me.
May their ill deeds fructify for me,
And all my virtues fructify for them.

As long as any sentient being
Anywhere has not been liberated,
May I remain (in the world) for the sake of that being
Though I have attained highest enlightenment.

If the merit of saying this
Had form, it would never fit
Into realms of worlds as numerous
As sand grains of the Ganges. (465–86)

Nāgārjuna recommends the recitation of these twenty-two verses, as a devotional practice, three times a day, that is, morning, noon, and night. This pattern of practice comes from the Brahminic tradition, a tradition going back to the Vedic period, of reciting the mantra of salutation to the sun at sunrise, at midday, and at sunset. It should be said that all the verses of the text of the *Ratnāvalī* would originally have been chanted, and in this way one learned them by heart. It seems that the people of ancient India did not read silently, and when they read verses aloud, they chanted. In India today children still learn their lessons by repeating them aloud in a sort of sing-song.

These verses evidently provided Śāntideva with the model for the confession in the second chapter of his *Bodhicaryāvatāra*, from which the verses of our Sevenfold Puja have been taken. The sequence varies slightly, as it does in other sources. Śāntideva's ordering runs thus: worship, salutation, Going for Refuge, confession of faults, rejoicing in merits, entreaty and supplication, and finally transference of merits. Nāgārjuna's, on the other hand, starts with Going for Refuge, then worship and salutation. Nor do Nāgārjuna's verses cover the different sections of the Sevenfold Puja equally. Some of them are referred to merely in passing, most of his verses being taken up with the transference of merits. But in passages like these it becomes clear that Śāntideva and Nāgārjuna belong to the same tradition. Both combine penetrating philosophical insight with intense devotion.

I am not sure that I would recommend reciting the Sevenfold Puja three times daily on a regular basis. The danger would be that it would become a chore. What I would say is that if you really felt like performing a puja, it would not matter so much if you did not get round to doing it, but if you did not feel in the mood, you probably ought to find time for it. As in the case of meditation, resistance is best confronted.

One should not forget that in the *Ratnāvalī* Nāgārjuna is offering the king teachings that will be suitable for him in the event of his deciding to become a monk. If he was reciting the Sevenfold Puja on his own he would presumably have to set up the shrine himself. And when you have to set things up yourself, you will naturally tend to enter into the appropriate devotional mood.

Nāgārjuna's emphasis is heavily on the conclusion of the sequence. For him the transference or dedication of merit is very much the point of the whole practice, and it becomes what the Tibetans call a prayer of good wishes, expressing a supremely positive attitude towards all living beings. For Nāgārjuna, becoming Enlightened is the way in which one can help beings most effectively. On his becoming a Buddha he wants his very name to bring joy to beings. Such is the power of a word, a name; and hence the power of a mantra. A mantra is in a sense the name of the Buddha or Bodhisattva, and when you recite or repeat it, it puts you in touch with all the qualities of that Buddha or Bodhisattva. This is one of the reasons why the repetition of a mantra is considered to be so important. It is the essence of who they are. If you repeat the mantra, the Buddha or Bodhisattva will be there. The mantra is in a way a short and simple prayer, in which you identify yourself with the Buddha or Bodhisattva that you aspire to become.

TSONGKHAPA'S *THE THREE CHIEF PATHS*

EDITORIAL NOTE

Sangharakshita's foregoing two commentaries on Nāgārjuna's *Precious Garland* describe a path of regular steps leading from the attainment of worldly 'high status' to the highest level of 'definite goodness', or transcendental insight. The following translation of Tsongkhapa's *Three Chief Paths* outlines a similar progression, involving in this case the renunciation of worldly entanglements, the development of *bodhicitta* on that basis, and the cultivation of wisdom. Like Nāgārjuna's *Precious Garland*, *The Three Chief Paths* is presented in concise, densely-packed verses that are not always easy to understand. For this reason, readers may require more in the way of explanation than that provided by Sangharakshita's brief introduction, informative as it is. In the absence of further commentary by Sangharakshita on his translation, readers are therefore directed to Geshe Wangyal's *Door of Liberation*, which offers an alternative rendering of Tsongkhapa's root text accompanied by a commentary by the Fourth Panchen Lama, Tenpe Nyima.[342] The Lama's commentary gives detailed instructions for meditation based on Tsongkhapa's verses including advice on how to carry the practice forward into everyday life. Taken together, they make up an all-inclusive scheme of practice for anyone wishing to commit themselves wholeheartedly to Tsongkhapa's teaching of *The Three Chief Paths*.

A NOTE ON THE TRANSLATION

Je Tsongkhapa's verses on *The Three Chief Paths* was translated from a traditional Tibetan text by Sangharakshita with the assistance of Mr Trethong on the instruction of His Holiness the Dalai Lama. His Holiness commissioned the work following Sangharakshita's move to Kalimpong in 1957. It was published in London in the November 1960 edition of the *Middle Way* (vol. 35, no. 3).

INTRODUCTION

by Sangharakshita

Jetsün Tsongkhapa (1357–1419 CE),[343] founder of the school known as the Gelug or 'virtuous ones', is one of the greatest figures in the history of Tibetan Buddhism. As reformer, organizer, teacher, and writer he is perhaps unrivalled. In Tibet and Mongolia, as well as in other Tibetan-speaking parts of the Buddhist world, his writings have enjoyed down to the present day a prestige and popularity similar to that attaching to those of Ācārya Buddhaghosa in the Theravāda countries of South-East Asia and those of Dōgen in Japan.

The works of Tsongkhapa comprise eighteen volumes, together with another nineteen for those of his two principal disciples, which are considered inseparable from his own writings. Some are commentaries on scriptural texts, others original works. As an example of the first, mention may be made of his monumental *sNags-rim chen-mo,* an exposition of the *Guhyasamāja Tantra* (comprising volume 3) and the commentary on the *Abhisamayālaṃkāra* with Haribhadra's *Vṛtti* (vol. 17 and two-thirds of vol. 18). Undoubtedly the most celebrated of the original works is the *Lam-rim chen-mo,* 'The Great Stages of the Path' (vol. 13), which forms the basis for the religious education of all monks belonging to the Gelug school. There are also an abridgement (*Lam-rim chung-ba*)[344] and analysis of contents (*sa-bcad*), of 201 and 14 leaves respectively, of the *Lam-rim chen-mo,* which is itself based on the *Bodhipathapradīpa* or 'Lamp of the Path to Enlightenment' of the great Indian teacher Atīśa. Says Lobsang Phuntsok Lhalungpa,

'Whatever Tsongkhapa wrote on any subject is precise and accurate, clear in expression, and profound in meaning. His beautiful literary style is unique in Tibetan literature. His practical teaching is extremely systematic, with graded courses embodying the teachings of the three stages of development.'[345]

These characteristics are exemplified in our present text, 'The Three Chief Paths [to Enlightenment]', one of Tsongkhapa's short but important minor works. The three paths, or stages, are those of 'withdrawal' *(niḥsaraṇa)*; 'generation of the Enlightenment-mind' (*bodhicitta-utpāda*); and 'insight into conditioned co-production' (*pratītya-samutpāda*). After making his obeisance to the holy lamas, or gurus, the author declares his intention of expounding the essence of the Buddha's teaching. The first stage, that of withdrawal, he says, is reached when, having reflected in various ways on the rarity of a well-endowed human existence, on the inescapability of the fruits of one's actions, and the miseries of continued rebirth, one experiences an intense aversion even for pleasant states of phenomenal existence and longs day and night for deliverance. Attainment of Nirvāṇa for the sake of oneself alone is not, however, the ultimate goal. By reflecting on the sufferings endured by sentient beings, all of whom have been our own mothers in previous lives, one develops compassion, and out of this compassion resolves to strive for the attainment of Supreme Enlightenment for the sake of all – thus generating the *bodhicitta* and reaching the second stage. But attachment to phenomenal existence can be totally destroyed only by means of insight into the underlyng reality of things. One therefore strives to reach the third stage, that of 'insight'. According to Tsongkhapa this consists in apprehending the conditioned co-production, which comprises, in his teaching, not only the casual sequence of *dharmas,* both conditioned and unconditioned, but also the ineffable Emptiness (*śūnyatā*), which is their real nature. Yet until the essential non-duality of these has been realized the Buddha's meaning has not been fathomed to its depth: Nirvāṇa and *saṃsāra* are the same reality seen from opposite points of view. Understanding how each one appears as the other, and cancelling out 'positive' views with the 'apparent truth' of casual connection and 'negative' views with the 'absolute truth' of Emptiness, one will avoid all extreme views and attain the final goal. In conclusion, Jetsun Tsongkhapa exhorts his disciples, to whom the work is addressed, to

Je Tsongkhapa

realize the essence of the Three Paths for themselves by protracted solitary meditation.

The present version of this text, the first of Tsongkhapa's works to be published in English, has been checked against the rather lengthy and academic commentary of Phabongkhapa, a celebrated Gelug scholar whom the modern monks of Sera regard as their Lama.[316]

Acknowledgement should be made of the great help received from Mr John Driver, of Kalimpong, and Mr Trethong, the officer deputed by His Holiness the Dalai Lama to assist me in producing the following work, undertaken at short notice in response to His Holiness's special request.

Bhikshu Sangharakshita
Triyana Vardhana Vihara
Kalimpong
26 October 2503/1959

JE TSONGKHAPA'S VERSES ON *THE THREE CHIEF PATHS*

(Rje btsun tsong kha pa'i gsung lam gyi gtso bo rnam gsum gyi rtsa ba)[347]

THE TEXT[348]

The Obeisance

Obeisance to the Holy Lamas!

The essential meaning of all Buddha-Teachings,[349]
The Path commended by the Buddha-Sons,[350]
That food of those, blessed, who desire deliverance,
I shall relate, according to my ability.

Those who, not adhering to the pleasures of existence
But striving to make fruitful their opportunities and advantages,[351]
Place their trust in the Path that Buddhas[352] delight in:
Let those blessed ones listen with open mind!

Part 1: Withdrawal[353]

Without a pure withdrawal there is no means
To still the longing for a happy outcome of the sea of existence;
And by craving for existence, too, those who have bodies
Are fettered all about: therefore first seek withdrawal.

The fancies of this life are banished by keeping in mind
That we have no time to spare of opportunities and advantages hard to find;[354]
The fancies of the hereafter are banished by repeatedly thinking
Of acts and their fruits infallible, the miseries of the Round.

When, by so practising, there is born not even
For a moment desire for the Round's well-being
And a sense of longing for Deliverance, all day and night,
Arises, then it is that withdrawal is born.

Part 2: Generation of the bodhi-mind

But since that withdrawal too, unless controlled
By a pure 'mind-generation' does not become the cause
Of Unsurpassed Enlightenment's consummate felicity
Intelligent ones should generate the excellent Bodhi-mind.

Swept along by the flow of the four violent rivers,[355]
Tied with the tight bonds of acts hard to reverse,
Trapped inside[356] the iron net of ego-attitudes,[357]
Encompassed by the great gloom of ignorance's dark:

Born in unlimited existences, and in their births
Three miseries[358] torment them without cease:
In circumstances like this are – our mothers![359]
Think of their state and then generate the excellent Bodhi-mind.

Part 3: Insight into conditioned co-production[360]

Since, if they don't possess the insight[361] that apprehends the underlying Reality,
Even those practised in Withdrawal and the Bodhi-mind
Cannot cut off the root of existence,
Work at techniques to apprehend Conditioned Co-production.[362]

He who sees the never-failing
Cause-and-fruit of all *dharmas* temporal and eternal[363]

And has destroyed whatever is the basis of imagination,
Has entered the Path beloved of the Buddhas.

The apparent – the infallible Conditioned Co-production –
And the Void – free of predication[364] – the two understandings,
As long as they appear separate, for so long
Is the Sage's[365] thought still unrealized.

When without alternation, simultaneously
At the moment of seeing the unfailing Conditioned Co-production
One destroys all fixed ideas and conceptual forms,[366]
Then is the investigation of views complete.

If one knows how there appears as cause-and-fruit
Emptiness – clearing the negative extreme with the empty
And the positive extreme with the apparent – moreover,
He will not fall a prey to views which hold to an extreme.

Concluding exhortation

When one has realized as they are, for oneself, the quick
Of the Three Principal Paths in that manner,
Wait upon solitude, beget the strength of assiduity,
And speedily effect a lasting counsel, O Sons!

KNOW YOUR MIND

The Psychological Dimension of Ethics in Buddhism

EDITORIAL NOTE

Know Your Mind is drawn from the transcript of a seminar on Herbert Guenther's *Mind In Buddhist Psychology* conducted at Padmaloka in the summer of 1976. The seminar was high on the list of those considered by Sangharakshita to be especially worthy of publication by the Spoken Word Project. Consequently, Vidyadevi and the late Jinananda prepared the text during the mid-1990s. Over that period, Sangharakshita gave much of his time to checking and considering the text at various stages. As Vidyadevi and Jinananda note in their preface to their first edition, the resulting style was quite different from Sangharakshita's own preferred mode of writing and they acknowledge that he had been, as they put it, 'most patient in restoring the occasional stretched point to its true proportions'. *Know Your Mind* was published by Windhorse Publications in 1998. The book is by no means casual reading. Two minor changes have therefore been introduced to the earlier published version as aids to understanding. Firstly, with the aim of making the text more accessible to the non-academic reader, additional subheadings have been included as thematic markers along the way. Secondly, and for similar reasons, some of Sangharakshita's forays into other topics have been relocated to endnotes, so as to leave his main ideas more clearly in view.

In preparing the original text for publication the editors acknowledge the invaluable role of Silabhadra, who provided the original transcripts; and of Kamalashila, Sagaramati, and Asanga, who gave the benefit of their substantial knowledge of the field, supplying many useful corrections and suggestions. Asanga checked all the Sanskrit and Pāli terms, and spared much time to help with elusive endnote information at a time when he was hard at work on the final details of his own book. Thanks also go to Shantavira and the late Dhivati, Windhorse Publications' remarkable copy-editors, who, to quote the book's original editors, have left 'no cross-reference cryptic and no metaphor mixed'.

We also acknowledge with gratitude the publishers' permission to quote extracts from Herbert V. Guenther and Leslie S. Kawamura (trans.), *Mind in Buddhist Psychology*, Dharma Publishing, Berkeley 1975, and the page references supplied below refer to that edition.

INTRODUCTION

Is there such a thing as Buddhist psychology?

It should be admitted right at the outset that there is really no such thing as Buddhist psychology. In the West we may speak of Buddhist ethics, Buddhist philosophy, Buddhist logic, Buddhist epistemology, and so on, but the teaching of Buddhism as a whole is a fully integrated tradition. It's all of one piece, as it were; take up any one aspect of it, and all the others automatically follow. The danger of specializing in one area of study or another is that one tends to lose sight of its connections with other subjects, or even the subject from which it originally sprang – and this has indeed happened at times in the history of what I am calling Buddhist psychology.

At the same time, of course, the term is not entirely inappropriate, if one simply understands it to refer to Buddhism's teachings about the nature and functioning of the mind, especially as this has a bearing on the spiritual life in general, and on meditation in particular. Buddhist psychology is not just a descriptive science; it has no purpose other than to be put into practice. And its practical use lies in enabling us to recognize what is going on in our own minds, to discriminate between positive and valuable mental events and negative or unhelpful ones, between real vision and subjective views. It starts from the basis that we play a part in creating the world we find ourselves in, and that the only effective way to improve our situation is to take responsibility for it – which means taking responsibility for our mental states.

According to Buddhism our predicament arises out of our ignorance.

Ignorance (Sanskrit *avidyā*) is traditionally likened to drunkenness, while the volitions (*saṃskāras*) that arise from ignorance are compared to actions committed whilst in a state of drunkenness. This perception of the human condition may seem extreme, but it is no more than sober fact. Sometimes we don't realize the extent of the damage we do simply because we don't know what we are doing. We initiate things, we say things, we get involved with people, and in doing so we inevitably set up problems. Although we sometimes become aware that our lives are more or less made up of the problems we create in this way, very often we don't even see them as problems – and this is a problem in itself.

Of course, there is no question of trying to stay on the safe side by putting off doing anything at all until we are Enlightened; to live, we must act, and we are therefore bound to make mistakes. But if we can understand what we are doing, we can break the reactive patterns that cause us to create the same problems over and over again. And the way to break those reactive patterns that bring us so much suffering is to set up different patterns of thought, feeling, and behaviour.

Once one sees one's predicament clearly, once one knows where one is starting from, one is in a position to perceive the choices before one, which gives one a certain degree of freedom. It isn't absolute freedom – one can't choose one's starting point – but one is free to choose what one makes of one's situation. Where one *is* is less important than whether or not one *knows* where one is. There is a freedom which arises out of knowing oneself and knowing the possibility of evolving beyond one's present condition.

That freedom is, however, double-edged. The mind is not a thing; it is not, as Guenther puts it in the introduction to his translation of *Mind in Buddhist Psychology*, 'a static entity or a mere state or function of consciousness'.[367] It consists solely in its activities. 'It' is therefore always changing, always moving. But it can move either creatively or reactively. At every moment the mind is confronted with the choice of repeating old patterns and going round in circles or rearranging the pattern and setting up more positive conditions for spiritual growth. At every moment there is the possibility of moving forward and also the possibility of just moving round and thus not really moving at all. We are free to develop our awareness of the spiritual path, to look for solutions; and we are also free to sink back into unconsciousness and stop asking questions. Furthermore, mental states cannot be compartmentalized.

Painful and harmful states of mind cannot be shut away somewhere while we develop mindfulness, joy, and kindness. At any one time we are either encouraging positive mental states or reinforcing negative ones.

If one makes the effort to develop in a positive direction, one's life assumes a more serious meaning as one takes responsibility for it. One realizes for oneself the necessity, almost, of a certain way of living. This is what it means to follow the Buddhist path.

Buddhism is presented as a path or way, but this is only a manner of speaking. The path is a symbol, representing the fact that we can change, we can develop. If we know what we are now and what we can become, we can take steps to effect that transition. We have the capacity, and the freedom, to perceive and to realize our best interests.

According to the Pāli idiom, we *develop* the path.[368] It is not 'something out there', an objective thing. We *are* the path. If we think of it as something out there, like a road or track, we may get stuck with an unhelpful notion of the spiritual discipline required in order to follow it. One is not following the Buddhist path if one feels that one is being driven along it like a sheep, rather wishing one could stray off and have a nibble on some succulent wayside shrub or flower.

There is certainly an objective criterion of development which one has to understand and act upon, but the path itself is not out there; it is in here. There is no question of forcing oneself to follow a particular track or go in a particular direction. The path simply represents the individual solution to one's own particular predicament. If you know and understand yourself as you are now, that puts you in a position to develop in your own way. The path is you in the process of organizing your mental states in such a way that growth and development will take place in a positive direction.

AN EXHAUSTIVE SCIENCE OF MIND

This recognition and organization of mental states became the overwhelming preoccupation of generations of Buddhist scholars. What became known as the Abhidharma absorbed the best efforts of some of the finest minds in Buddhist history over a period of a thousand years. Although in some respects there was a degeneration into scholasticism, the zeal of these scholars for their tremendous task was very much connected with their commitment to the spiritual path. Their desire to understand mind and mental states stemmed from their commitment to following the Buddha's teaching. 'Cease to do evil. Learn to do good. Purify your mind.'[369] This was their starting point.

But what was the mind? How could it be understood? This, over centuries, they sought to fathom. They didn't just think in terms of what in the West we would call psychological health; they were inspired by the Buddha's vision of the infinite, transcendental potential of the human mind. The Abhidharma could be described as an exhaustive science of mind – although it is not really possible to speak of the mind as a subject of study like any other, because in a sense the mind doing the studying cannot be at the same time the object of that study. As we explore the Abhidharma we have constantly to take this into account if we are to derive practical benefit from it. It is true that Buddhism appeals to observation to verify its account of the nature of things, but this method of observation is not like a laboratory experiment; it always remains personal. In the case of Buddhist psychology it consists in introspection, in watching oneself – seeing how one reacts to things, for example.

So although in a sense the Abhidharmikas were 'Buddhist psychologists', in speaking of Buddhist psychology we have to beware of limiting our conception of Buddhism. This is a real danger for the simple reason that the English language, reflecting the limitations of the general Western idea of mind, does not have words to recognize or describe higher states of consciousness (the Sanskrit term is *dhyāna*). A conscious state of mind in which there is no perception of external things, in which the senses do not function, in which there is no mental activity in the usual sense, is simply not recognized. Such states are not, therefore, included in the denotation of the term 'psyche' or 'mind'; and this means that to speak of Buddhism as a method of psychological development automatically suggests that the development one has in mind falls short of *dhyāna*.

The range of experience over and above what the term 'psychological' generally covers may be referred to by the term 'spiritual'. In this way, the 'spiritual life' comes to mean a life organized for the production of skilful mental states, especially as represented by the *dhyānas*, so as to form a foundation for the experience of Enlightenment.

We also need to find a way of referring to the distinction between states of mind which are attained temporarily, and those whose attainment constitutes a permanent change. Spiritual states of mind are not necessarily permanent; as is all too clear, one can be feeling 'spiritual' at one moment, and far from spiritual the next. It is possible, however, to achieve continuously positive and refined states of mind. At a certain point, one sustains such deep insight into the nature of reality that one's uninterrupted progress towards Enlightenment is guaranteed. This is known traditionally in Buddhism as 'entering the stream' an experience that may be described as transcendental. We thus have three terms – psychological, spiritual, and transcendental – to describe different phases in the development of consciousness. Although the term 'psychological' refers to the mind or psyche, and although it is the human mind, in a manner of speaking, that experiences *dhyāna* and transcendental insight, it may be limiting, even misleading, to refer to Buddhism as a method of psychological growth.

As well as being cautious about the use of the term 'psychological', we also need to be careful in using the word 'mind', which, in the context of the Western theistic and even post-theistic tradition, is limited in the sense that a distinction is drawn between the human mind and the 'mind of God'. According to the Buddha's teaching, however, there is no limit to the human mind, and nothing – at least potentially – beyond its reach; it has a vast, literally inconceivable, significance. For a Buddhist, the expression 'merely human' does not make sense; nor does the idea that one could have faith in a revelation on the basis that it had come from a realm beyond the compass of the human mind.

MIND AS ACTUAL EXPERIENCE

To begin an exploration of the nature of mind in Buddhist psychology, we need to remind ourselves that 'mind' and 'mental events' are concepts – concepts that may form a basis for an understanding of the reality to which they refer. Essentially, concepts arise in two ways. Firstly, one can hypothesize the existence of the thing one names on the basis of an idea or theory (this is a 'concept by postulation'). This is the starting point of many Western philosophers, although some – Hume, for example – can be said to arrive at concepts more by the second method, which is simply to name a direct perceptual experience (this is a 'concept by intuition').[370] The concept of mind in Buddhist psychology belongs to this second category. It is arrived at not by a deduction from abstract ideas or general principles, but by way of induction from actual experience. That is, it is not a metaphysical principle (Mind with a capital M – as in 'Mind over Matter'); nor does it stand for the individual ego, postulated as something distinct from the mental events it 'experiences'. In Buddhism 'mind' is conceived of in the same way that we conceive of a tree, say. Just as we experience an assemblage of sensory data – trunk, branches, leaves – and call it a tree, so we experience a range of mental events and call it 'mind'. And just as there is no meaning to the word 'tree' beyond what we can experience personally, so there is no meaning – there are no connotations – to the term 'mind' beyond what we can apprehend for ourselves.

Because mind in Buddhism refers to something that is experienced by direct perception, every point made in this book is verifiable from personal experience, provided we are prepared to examine our experience honestly. The inner tranquillity, clarity, and insight that can be developed through meditation practice is not merely helpful to this process of examination, but absolutely necessary to it. From a Buddhist point of view, to try to philosophize, or even think clearly, without getting one's negative mental states out of the way is going to be a flawed enterprise. Whatever efforts one makes to come to a true understanding of reality, if one has not given attention to the mental state with which one approaches the matter, one will inevitably see things in terms of one's own craving, hatred, fear, and delusion. In Buddhism, therefore, there is no philosophy without meditation. One has to rise above one's limited, personal, or individual standpoint, at least to some extent, and be relatively free from negative mental states, in order to see the truth.

This book has two aims: to present the picture of mind and mental events that centuries of Abhidharma scholarship brought into focus, and to act as a practical guide to mental states for meditators, showing how the various mental events may be recognized, and which are to be eradicated and which cultivated so that psychological health, spiritual insights, and ultimately transcendental knowledge may be attained.

The first part of the book is of necessity fairly theoretical; in it we trace the background of the Abhidharma, and introduce the work *The Necklace of Clear Understanding*, on which the rest of the book is a kind of commentary, before going on to look at the Abhidharma's understanding of mind and mental events. In the second part we take a fairly detailed look at the mental events themselves, and in doing so build up a picture of the kind of spiritual life needed to support the cultivation of positive states of mind.

I
THE FIRST BUDDHIST ANALYSTS

The spiritual and scholastic undertaking represented by the term 'Abhidharma' is very ambitious. Its origins may be traced back to the general intellectual background in the context of which early Buddhists strove to express their own distinctive vision. Of all the systems of thought prevailing at the time, that of the Sāṃkhya school of Indian philosophy is said to be the closest in spirit to that developed by the Buddha himself. Indeed, it may be significant that the Buddha was born and brought up in Kapilavastu, the city connected with the pre-Buddhist sage Kapila, who is traditionally regarded as the founder of the Sāṃkhya school.

Sāṃkhya literally means counting, numbering, or enumerating. The Sāṃkhya school tried to enumerate the elements of existence, in a way that seems to foreshadow the greatly more sophisticated and refined analysis of the Abhidharma. It was the Sāṃkhya philosophers who first, as far as we know, thought in terms of the five elements – earth, water, fire, air, and space – and conceived of consciousness as a sixth sense, as well as differentiating a sort of supermind.[371]

The adherents of the Sāṃkhya school were not the only early Indian philosophers to attempt such an analysis of the universe. It seems that it was a very strong trend in Indian thought generally to try to understand existence by breaking it up into its constituent parts. One finds the same thing in ancient Greece, in the writings of Democritus, for example. In Indian thought generally one could say that there are two major trends:

a pluralistic trend which tends to be associated with the non-brahminical tradition, and a more monistic trend which tends to be associated with the brahminical tradition. Included in the pluralistic schools of thought are the Sāṃkhya, the Abhidharma in its various forms, the Jains, and also the Nyāya-Vaiśeṣika school.

In his *Buddhacarita* (an account of the life of the Buddha), Aśvaghoṣa gives a fairly detailed, although not very clear, account of the Sāṃkhya philosophy, and represents the Buddha as refuting it systematically, which would suggest that there was some danger of Buddhism's being confused with Sāṃkhya thought at the time he was writing. Some scholars have certainly seen a continuity between the Sāṃkhya school and the Abhidharma, although there are all sorts of philosophical difficulties in tracing it. The difference between the two could be said to be that the Sāṃkhya analysis is more cosmological than psychological, while the Buddhist analysis is predominantly psychological.

A VAST SORTING-OUT

The classifications of the Abhidharma itself began to be compiled during the period of several hundred years after the Buddha's lifetime when his teachings were still being passed on by word of mouth. Basically, the Abhidharma began as a vast sorting-out operation. During the Buddha's life he must have given thousands, even tens of thousands, of discourses, and answered thousands of questions; and around him was always a circle of disciples who, as best they could, learned by heart whatever he said. They treasured these teachings, reflected on them, repeated them to one another, and in this way committed to memory what the Buddha had taught them. When they were old they transmitted what they had learned to their own disciples, and they to their disciples in turn. This process of oral transmission went on for at least four hundred years, and in this way the teaching was preserved for posterity.

So there was an enormous floating mass of material in existence, but to begin with it was not systematically arranged. Long discourses were mixed up with short ones, poetry with prose, teachings about the mind with teachings about the elements, teachings about cosmology mixed up with history and legend and biography. Over the years, however, some of the more brilliant scholars, those whose minds were more retentive, started to organize the teachings systematically. The result of this sorting-out process – which took hundreds of years – is what we call the Abhidharma.

One of the chief virtues of the Abhidharma was that it clarified Buddhist terminology, comparing the usage of a term in one context with its usage in another, so that a term like, say, 'Nirvāṇa' could be used with full confidence as to its precise meaning. This clarity of definition is one reason we still use terms that derive from the ancient Indian languages Pāli and Sanskrit.

The Abhidharmikas also arranged all the teachings into different groupings so that they might be related to each other more easily and grasped in their entirety. It was only natural that the Buddha's followers should want to settle all the disparate points he made on various occasions into some kind of system. Thus, for example, in the *Visuddhimagga*, the 'Path of Purity', Buddhaghosa, the great Theravādin scholar of the fifth century CE, collated all the Buddha's teachings on meditation into a single clear system.[372]

This was the great achievement of the Abhidharma, which came to dominate Indian Buddhism for about a thousand years, so that an understanding of it is crucial to an understanding of Indian Buddhist thought. At the same time, it must be admitted that the Abhidharma had its negative side. One could say that it banished the human element from Buddhism, removing from the teachings all biographical and historical material, and banishing myth, legend, and above all poetry. In the Abhidharma the impersonal, the scientific, and the rational reigned supreme.[373]

TWO TRADITIONS

As the Abhidharma developed there emerged two great traditions, the Theravāda and the Sarvāstivāda, each of which eventually committed to writing its own distinctive version of the Abhidharma teachings.[374] The Theravāda version was written down in the Pāli language – so that strictly speaking we should refer to the Theravāda Abhidhamma, that being the Pāli equivalent of the Sanskrit Abhidharma – and forms part of the Theravāda Pāli canon. The Sarvāstivāda Abhidharma, which was originally written down in Sanskrit, is, in translation, part of the Chinese canon, the original Sanskrit texts having been lost.

Both sets of teachings consist of seven substantial books, but although there is some overlap between the two sets of books, essentially they cover different ground.[375] The Theravādins regarded the material contained in *their* Abhidhamma texts as having been preached by the Buddha to his deceased mother in the Tuṣita *devaloka*, a higher heavenly realm. Then, the tradition says, the Buddha repeated these teachings to Śāriputra, the wisest of his disciples, and in that way the Abhidharma tradition was handed down.[376] The Sarvāstivādins, on the other hand, frankly admitted that the contents of their Abhidharma texts were the work of disciples.

Not everything about the project of the Abhidharma was plain sailing. Differing interpretations of the teachings among the early schools were gathered together in the *Kathāvatthu*, the 'Matters of Discussion', which is one of the seven books of the Theravāda Abhidhamma. In the *Kathāvatthu* some views are definitely rejected, but others are left unsettled; we are just given the views of the different schools and left to make up our own minds. Both sets of teachings form one of the three *piṭakas* or 'baskets' into which Buddhist canonical literature is divided: the Vinaya Piṭaka (the 'books of the discipline'); the Sūtra Piṭaka (Pāli Sutta Piṭaka, the collection of discourses); and the Abhidharma Piṭaka (Pāli Abhidhamma Piṭaka). There is some overlap between the ground covered in the Sūtra Piṭaka and that in the Abhidharma Piṭaka. However, very early on, the Abhidharma took a direction of which the other *piṭakas* give little hint.

BASIC BUILDING BLOCKS

It wasn't long before the Abhidharma started to go far beyond its original objectives. From analysing and classifying the Buddha's teachings, it went many steps further, to start analysing and classifying the whole universe, indeed the whole of existence. For a start, the Abhidharmikas were uncompromising in their use of language. Out went expressions like *sattva* (being), *pudgala* (person), and *puruṣa* (self), which might be taken as suggesting that the notion of a self might have some substance in reality. Through clear thinking in meditation, experience was analysed down until the irreducible elements of existence were identified. The Abhidharmikas chose to refer to these elements, beyond which analysis could not go, as *dharmas* – a technical usage quite distinct from the usual use of the word 'Dharma' in Buddhism to mean the Buddha's doctrine or teaching.

Thus the Abhidharmikas developed a sort of psychophysical atomism. They conceived of *dharmas* as being a limited number of ultimately real, discrete elements which together comprehended the whole of existence – mental, physical, and spiritual, conscious, and non-conscious. These elements – the Theravādins counted 170, the Sarvāstivādins 75 – included physical constituents – the elements of earth, water, fire, and air, qualities such as agility and elasticity, as well as food and other things – and mental constituents, some skilful, like faith and mindfulness, some unskilful, like anger and wrong views, and some neutral, being coloured by the *dharmas* with which they were associated.

NOT DRY AS DUST

Both the Theravādins and the Sarvāstivādins divided *dharmas* into two groups, *saṃskṛta dharmas* and *asaṃskṛta dharmas*. These terms literally mean 'compounded' and 'uncompounded', but they are sometimes translated as 'conditioned' and 'unconditioned'. According to the Theravāda there was only one unconditioned *dharma*, Nirvāṇa, while the Sarvāstivāda identified three: two kinds of Nirvāṇa and space. But for both schools of the Abhidharma tradition, this distinction between conditioned and unconditioned *dharmas* was not a distinction between real and unreal. This is rather important. All these ultimate elements were thought of as being equally real, as being ultimate in the sense that no one of them could be reduced to any other of them. And this, in fact, was a kind of heresy, as we shall see.

Even this brief description should be enough to show that the Abhidharmikas' conception of *dharmas* was very different from the fundamental particles of Western science. There is an analogy, though, in that, just as for a certain phase of scientific history atoms were held to be the irreducible 'building blocks' of which the material universe was constructed, so the Abhidharmikas held that *dharmas* could not be broken down into further components of experience. (And, just as particle physics has come up with a completely different way of seeing things, so the Buddhist tradition later exposed the limitations of the Abhidharma's conception of *dharmas*, as we shall see.) The Abhidharmikas went on to say that this irreducibility made *dharmas* real in a sense that what we conventionally take to be real – ourselves, tables, and so on – is not. In this way the Abhidharma came to occupy a particular philosophical position which has been called by Dr Radhakrishnan 'pluralistic realism'; and the term 'Abhidharma', which originally simply meant 'pertaining to the Dharma', came to be taken as meaning 'the higher doctrine'.

It was the Buddha who began the tradition of the classification of phenomena, although, as we shall see, the Abhidharmikas eventually departed from his system of classification. He inherited from Upanishadic tradition a distinction between *nāma* (name) and *rūpa* (form); and he broadened this out to analyse the whole of compounded existence into five *skandhas* (heaps): *rūpa* or form; *vedanā* or feeling; *saṃjñā* or perception; *saṃskāra* or volition; and *vijñāna* or consciousness.[377] But why did he do this?

It appears that he wanted to counteract a static view of existence and our experience of it. He wanted to break down apparently solid and stable things, not into smaller things, but into *processes*. Take, for instance, *vedanā*, 'feeling'. It is not that there is a thing called feeling that is one of five separate things that make up the human personality; *vedanā* is simply a process which, interacting with other processes, makes up our experience of ourselves.

It is important that we understand the Buddha's analysis – and the Abhidharma's analysis that followed – in this way. Otherwise, perhaps under the influence of scientific materialism, we can easily get the impression that the Abhidharma is positing a pseudo-scientific reductionism of all that is distinctively human to a collection of impersonal elements. From here we can start to imagine that reality is the dust to which we reduce everything – and this might reinforce the common, but mistaken, impression that Buddhism is nihilistic. But, on the contrary, this way of seeing things offers a vision of the possibility of human growth and development. The analysis of the *skandhas* – according to which one sees that what we think of as the self is made up of these five 'heaps', all of which are continually changing – is tremendously inspiring. If the self was really permanent and unchanging, human growth would be impossible. Only the reality of impermanence offers the possibility of change.

DEPARTURE FROM THE *SŪTRAS*

Having made the distinction between conditioned and unconditioned *dharmas*, the Abhidharma went on to divide conditioned *dharmas* into groups; and it was here that it departed from the *sūtra* tradition – that is, from the tradition of unsystematized Buddhism. The *sūtras* preserved the teaching of the five *skandhas*, these five 'heaps'; that was their only classification of phenomenal existence. But the Abhidharma adopted a quite different classification, positing three or four main categories of conditioned existence as an alternative to the five *skandhas*. The first category, though, was just the same as the first of the *skandhas*: *rūpa* or material form. It is the epistemological object; Guenther says '*Rūpa* ... is a name for an objective constituent in a perceptual situation.'[378] In other words, *rūpa* is 'what' we perceive in our experience. It is not matter conceived as separate from a perceiver. We are concerned simply with the fact that there is something in our experience that is intractable, that resists us in various ways.

Rūpa is traditionally described in terms of the four great elements or *mahābhūtas*: solidity, fluidity, temperature or radiation, and expansiveness or atmospheric movement. The term *mahābhūta* can also be translated as 'great magical transformation' or 'great spirit' – which, in connection with *rūpa*, reminds us that we really have no way of knowing what we are in contact with when our senses give us information about the 'objective' world. Our senses give us a sense of perception through sight, hearing, taste, touch, and smell; but we have no evidence of what may be objectively there apart from that mediated by our senses.

So in a way *rūpa* is a great mystery. One could go so far as to say that the idea that we are in contact with a thing is no more than a linguistic fiction – although the Abhidharmikas themselves would not go that far.

WALKING INTO A MYSTERY

As the Abhidharma texts sometimes say, *dharmas* have not merely 'conceptually constructed existence' (*prajñaptisat*); they have 'more than conceptually constructed existence' (*dravyasat*).[379] So there is no need to disbelieve our senses when they tell us we are in contact with something; certainly if we walk into a door, that door is more than a 'linguistic fiction' as far as we are concerned. The point is that, while we may be in contact with something, we have no way of knowing *what* exactly we are in contact with except through our senses. Interestingly, the implication of the term *mahābhūta* is that we are in contact with something living rather than inert physical matter. Apparently one should understand the Abhidharma's idea of the four elements not as a primitive attempt at science but as referring to living symbols representing different manifestations of energy.

Of course, for the Abhidharma the elements of earth, water, fire, and air were just four of the kinds of the *dharmas* they identified as *rūpa*. According to the Theravāda, there were twenty-eight such *dharmas*, while in this first category the Sarvāstivāda placed just eleven *dharmas*. The second and third categories posited by the Abhidharmikas as an alternative to the five *skandhas* are what we are concerned with in this book; here is where the Abhidharma's analytical philosophy became an analytical psychology. The second category is mind or consciousness (*citta*), and the third consists of mental concomitants or mental events, functions associated with mind (*caitta* in Sanskrit, the equivalent of the Pāli *cetasika*).

MIND AND MENTAL OBJECTS

So far the Theravādin and Sarvāstivādin traditions were in agreement. However, they differed when it came to the way they classified mind and mental events. As far as the second category is concerned, the Theravādins thought in terms of 89 different *cittas*, including *kuśala* (skilful), *akuśala* (unskilful), and *avyākṛta* (neutral) mental states. As for the third category, mental events, they listed 52 *cetasikas*, considering each type of *citta* to be characterized by a particular combination of mental events. The Sarvāstivādins, on the other hand, while identifying 46 mental events (*caittas*), recognized only one single *citta*, arguing that mind is essentially one, because although there are many mental states, they are all phenomena of consciousness itself; they are not independent.

For the Theravādins, these three categories covered the whole of conditioned existence comprehensively, but the Sarvāstivādins came up with a fourth category, *cittaviprayuktasaṃskāra*, 'factors dissociated from mind', which basically consists of all those factors that do not fall under the other three headings; it includes, for example, a list of the various possible kinds of conditionality, or causal relationship.

Altogether the Sarvāstivādins identified 72 compounded *dharmas* and three uncompounded ones – that is, two types of Nirvāṇa (before and after *parinirvāṇa*) and space – while the Theravādins enumerated

169 compounded *dharmas* and one uncompounded one. Most of these *dharmas* are mental, because the whole project of the Abhidharma was geared to the spiritual purpose of meditation. However, all of them, whether compounded or uncompounded, were supposed to be equally real, inasmuch as together they made up the irreducible building blocks of existence. On this basis the Abhidharma embarked on a massive cross-referencing operation.

SEEKING GOOD ADVICE

Abhidharma literature was by no means confined to the two sets of seven books; those constituted only a beginning. Subsequently hundreds of other works were produced, but among all the writers of Abhidharma texts two in particular stand out, both of them belonging to the fifth century CE. On the Theravādin side was the great scholastic commentator Buddhaghosa, author of the *Visuddhimagga*, the 'Path of Purity'; he was a native of India but lived and worked in Sri Lanka. And among the Sarvāstivādins was Vasubandhu, the author of the *Abhidharmakośa*, who lived and worked in north-west India, and – as we shall see – in his old age became a follower of the Mahāyāna.

Some of the discussions and classifications of the Abhidharma are very helpful, but others are less so. We must therefore study it in the analytical and critical spirit of the Abhidharma itself – not swallowing it whole, as it were. If we were to swallow everything indiscriminately, perhaps with the attitude that everything that comes out of India or Tibet or Japan must be wonderful, we would probably get intellectual, spiritual, or aesthetic indigestion. We need to learn to discriminate – which will mean seeking good advice.

In the Pāli canon the Buddha tells a story to illustrate the danger of imitating Enlightened behaviour without Enlightened experience. He says there were once some elephants who pulled up lotus stalks from a pond and washed them carefully before eating them – and those elephants thrived. But some younger elephants, uninstructed by their elders, went to the pond and ate the roots just as they were, covered in mud. 'That was not good for either their looks or their health, and they incurred death and deadly suffering because of that.'[380] The moral of the story is, of course, that we mustn't follow even a good example unthinkingly.

It was this critical spirit that led to the arising of a new phase of the history of the Abhidharma which swept away many of the earlier ideas.

A FRESH EMPHASIS

This new initiative was part of the Mahāyāna tradition of Indian Buddhism, which arose in order to counter the increasingly narrow focus of some of the schools subsequently characterized (though not by themselves) by the term Hīnayāna, 'the Lesser Way'. The Mahāyāna gave a fresh emphasis to Buddhist practice – to devotion, metaphysics, and meditation – and to making the Dharma available to everyone, whether monk or lay person. And when it came to philosophy, the Mahāyāna flatly denied the reality of *dharmas* as ultimately existent entities. Just as the self was empty, so, the Mahāyānists insisted, were *dharmas*. Anything we think we can identify as real is in reality empty of self-nature (*svabhāva*).

That the earlier schools should have gone so far as to assert the existence of a certain fixed number of material and non-material elements, themselves irreducible, to which all the phenomena of existence were capable of being reduced, was a very serious thing. Central to Buddhism from the very beginning had been the doctrine of *anātman* – 'no-self' – which denied that in the absolute sense there existed in any object, whether transcendental or mundane, an eternal, unchanging principle of individuality or selfhood. As we have seen, it was in order to counter the wrong belief in absolute selfhood that the Buddha himself analysed the so-called person into the five *skandhas* (Pāli *khandhas*), showing that apart from these psychophysical phenomena, which were in a state of perpetual flux, there existed no unchanging psychic substratum corresponding to the *ātman* as conceived by certain non-Buddhist schools.

Ironically, although it was the Buddha's analysis of existence into the *skandhas* that the Abhidharmikas made it their special business to develop, the analysis they ended up with in fact contradicted the *anātman* doctrine. While they still maintained that the *pudgala* (person) or *ātman* (self) was nothing but an assemblage of evanescent parts, as we have seen, they saw the parts themselves as being real – as being, in fact, absolute realities. This was a deviation from orthodoxy of the most disastrous type. As the Mahāyānists saw, it was in effect a repudiation of the doctrine of *anātman*, for the conception of permanent individuality had not been superseded, but simply transferred from the whole to its parts.

In order to counteract this tendency to deviate into the heretical extreme of eternalism (*śāśvatavāda*), the Mahāyānists brought forward their doctrine – in reality a reversion to the Buddha's own position – of *sarvadharmāḥ-śūnyatā*, 'emptiness of all *dharmas*'. *Dharmas*, they said, not being self-existent, but arising in dependence on conditions, could not rightly be regarded as absolute realities, any more than the self.

The link between the earlier 'Hīnayāna' Abhidhamma and the Mahāyāna's development of Abhidharma doctrine is Asaṅga, who lived in north-west India in the fourth or fifth century CE. His *Abhidharmasamuccaya*, 'Collection of the Abhidharma',[381] is an abridgement of the first two chapters of his *Yogācārabhūmi*, which harnesses the Sarvāstivāda – i.e. Hīnayāna – Abhidharma teaching to the 'Greater Way' of the Mahāyāna. As we will see, the *Abhidharmasamuccaya*'s analysis of mind and mental events differs slightly from the Sarvāstivādin classification, producing a different and slightly longer list of mental events (51 instead of 46).

While Asaṅga was always a Mahāyānist, his older brother Vasubandhu came to the Mahāyāna point of view rather later in his Buddhist life. He had become the greatest teacher of the Sarvāstivāda school, and had compiled the major work of Abhidharma in Sanskrit, the *Abhidharmakośa* or 'Treasury of Abhidharma',[382] when Asaṅga persuaded him to take up the practices of the Mahāyāna. Vasubandhu's major work is the product of this transition; he wrote a commentary on his own *Abhidharmakośa*, the *Abhidharmakośabhāṣya*, criticizing the Sarvāstivādin view from a Sautrāntika position. Vasubandhu subsequently became a great teacher of the Yogācāra school of the Mahāyāna, second only to Asaṅga himself.

YOGĀCĀRA AND MADHYAMAKA

The Yogācāra is one of the two major schools of the Indian Mahāyāna tradition, the other being the Madhyamaka; but the two schools are closely interconnected, the difference really amounting to predominant emphasis. Very broadly, one might say that the Yogācāra took a more psychological approach, while the Madhyamaka was more logical, metaphysical, or even dialectical. The Yogācāra was more closely concerned with meditative experience, one could say, whereas the Madhyamaka's preoccupation was with abstract truth.

The Madhyamaka school probably began around the first or second century CE with Nāgārjuna, who tried to show the non-reality of what we take to be real by exposing its contradictory nature. He gave logical reasons why it cannot possibly exist, proving that every formulation we construct to describe or identify the nature of reality is riddled with contradictions – including even the categories of Buddhist thought. He demolished everything except for *śūnyatā* – *śūnyatā* stripped, that is, of any conceptual content. It has to be admitted that some of Nāgārjuna's 'sound logical reasons' have been shown to be fallacious, but his was an audacious project. Perhaps one could say that the only Western philosophical method that compares with what he tried to do is the Eleatic method of Parmenides. But whereas Parmenides embarked upon this spiritual exercise in the interests of absolute being, Nāgārjuna did so in the interests of *śūnyatā* or 'emptiness'.[383]

Nāgārjuna, therefore, and the adherents of the Madhyamaka school with him, while they certainly meditated, relied, on the whole, upon sustained philosophical thinking. The Yogācāra, on the other hand, although it had a strong philosophical basis, relied upon meditation. The very name Yogācāra means the practice of yoga in the sense of meditation. The philosophy that emerged out of the meditation of the Yogācārins was established upon the idea of *citta-mātra* or Mind Only, which in some respects comes close to the immaterialism of Bishop Berkeley, the British eighteenth-century empirical philosopher.

Citta-mātra denies the reality of matter as a separate category from mind. What we perceive are not external objects as such, not objects as opposed to ourselves, the subject. We perceive 'mental impressions', that is all. The significance of this insight is that if you remove the notion of an object, you also effectively remove the notion of a subject. There can be no sense of a subject without the sense of an object, and vice versa. In this way you break down the notion of a self that is separate from the world, to be left with Mind Only. This Mind Only is, by definition, not 'mind' as opposed to 'matter', and thus not mind in the limited way we usually understand the term.

So, over centuries, the scholars of Mahāyāna Buddhism developed and refined the Abhidharma vision of the universe which the Theravādins and Sarvāstivādins derived from their own understanding of the Buddha's teaching. If one looks at, say, the *Abhidharmakośabhāṣya*, in which Vasubandhu comments on the discussion by other scholars of his own verses, his quotations from different teachers and schools give an impression of a vigorous discussion that carried on for centuries. The Abhidharma is known as 'the delight of the learned' because if one is an academically-minded individual one can happily spend a lifetime immersed in one branch or another of this kind of study. One hardly notices the years passing, the decades rolling by, as one burrows deeper and deeper into one's favourite Abhidharma topic. Some at least of the scholars of the Abhidharma certainly meditated on what they studied, and their contributions to the debate embodied real spiritual insight. But the danger is that the Abhidharma becomes a delightful hobby, an end in itself, and one loses sight of the Abhidharma's original spiritual purpose.

GELUG AND NYINGMA

In Tibet, the Yogācāra and the Madhyamaka were brought together, and lamas of all schools have always studied works from both traditions. It is generally difficult to compartmentalize Tibetan Buddhists – and this is true, too, of the later phases of Indian Buddhism. Very often monks would devote many years to studying the Abhidharma and logic, say, and then just take off to become wandering yogis and practise Tantric disciplines. However, within a general free flow of ideas, certain patterns may be discerned.

Of the two main schools of Tibetan Buddhism, the Gelug and Nyingma schools, it could perhaps be said that the Nyingmapas, founded by Padmasambhava, are the heirs of the Yogācāra tradition, inasmuch as they emphasize meditation and direct experience. The Gelugpas are more influenced by the Madhyamaka tradition, and tend to regard the Yogācāra as, in a sense, a slightly lower truth, a sort of preamble to the full truth of the Madhyamaka system.

There is, therefore, no separate school of Yogācāra Abhidharma in Tibetan Buddhism. However, although it is evident that the Nyingmapas take their inspiration from the Yogācāra, of the two schools the Gelug tradition is the more closely connected with the original Indian Buddhist literature, including the Yogācāra literature.

The Gelugpas go in for the study of the *sūtras*, the Abhidharma, the Vinaya, logic, and epistemology, while the Nyingmapas concentrate on the tantras, the *terma* literature, and the writings of the teachers of their own school.

THE NECKLACE OF CLEAR UNDERSTANDING

It is no surprise, therefore, to find that Yeshe Gyaltsen (1713–1793), the author of the text on which this commentary will be based, *The Necklace of Clear Understanding*,[384] is a Tibetan Buddhist of the Gelug school. But he does not offer any particular line of Gelugpa interpretation. Though he includes quotations from Tsongkhapa (the founder of the Gelugpa tradition) and from Tsongkhapa's disciples, he is clearly at pains to interpret faithfully the original Yogācāra Abhidharma tradition as expounded by Asaṅga in the *Abhidharmasamuccaya*. Basically, he follows the Yogācāra tradition with regard to mind and mental events only so far as it is more or less in tune with the Madhyamaka.

In its form, *The Necklace of Clear Understanding* follows a pattern quite commonly found in Buddhist literature. The author writes a series of verses that express what he has to say as concisely as possible (for purposes of memorization, perhaps) and then explains each verse with a prose commentary. As it is a commentary on his own work, it is called an autocommentary. No doubt it would be possible to offer a further commentary on his autocommentary, but for the purposes of introducing the basic outlines of the Abhidharma this would probably be counter-productive. I shall therefore simply base my comments on the overall layout and scope of Yeshe Gyaltsen's work, drawing on his quotations and comments as appropriate, together with an occasional reference to other works. *The Necklace of Clear Understanding* is quite elementary and therefore a good introduction to what is probably the most important and useful part of the whole subject.

Of course, Yeshe Gyaltsen himself was in the position of being able to draw on what by his lifetime amounted to two thousand years of Abhidharma tradition. He himself writes very much in the spirit of the earliest Abhidharmikas, always focusing on the practical spiritual import of the teaching, and avoiding getting into detailed discussion of abstract matters.

There is one other work from which I will draw a number of definitions and explanations: the *Cheng Weishi Lun*, or *Doctrine of Mere-Consciousness*, which is the basic text of the Chinese branch of the Yogācāra. It was written by the Chinese pilgrim, translator, and scholar Xuanzang, and consists of a set of thirty of Vasubandhu's verses on the Vijñāvāda/Yogācāra teaching, explained and commented on by Xuanzang. In Sanskrit, Vasubandhu's text is known as the *Vijñaptimātratāsiddhi-triṃśikā*, the 'Treatise on the Establishment (or Proof) of Vijñāpti-only'. Xuanzang's commentary on Vasubandhu's work is based on ten Indian commentaries, but relies mainly on that of Dharmapāla, who was abbot of the great Indian Buddhist university Nālandā in the sixth century CE, and upon whose interpretation of the Yogācāra Xuanzang established the Faxiang (*dharma* characteristics) school when he returned to China.[385]

Just to complete the picture of the lineage of this teaching, I should add a word or two about the context in which *The Necklace of Clear Understanding* has been translated by Dr Guenther and Dr Kawamura. Until fairly recently, Dr Guenther was labouring in the field of Buddhist psychology virtually single-handed. Today, however, important new texts are becoming available in translation almost every year, and this process will no doubt go on for quite a few more decades. The impact of Buddhism on the intellectual and spiritual life of the West in the twentieth century has already been quite dramatic, and the publication of more difficult texts, like those which deal with the Abhidharma, should begin to deepen that impact.

A NEW TRADITION OF STUDY

Although a lot of useful academic work has been done in Tibetan studies over the last few decades, pioneered especially by Japanese scholars, what is required now is a sifting process to isolate the really useful texts from those which are less so. Practically speaking, we don't really need so very many Buddhist texts. We don't need to master the entire field of Buddhist literature in order to practise Buddhism. Take Buddhist logic, for example: however interesting a development it might be from an academic point of view, it is questionable whether it really has any relevance for practising Buddhists in the West.

A creative response to this influx of Buddhist literature into Western culture is therefore required. The only period in Buddhist history to which we can look for a parallel to the present one is the time when Indian texts first started to be translated into Chinese, and the Chinese literati were having to try to get to grips with this mysterious new literature, adjusting to it and assimilating it as best they could. The Tibetans, by contrast, had no highly developed pre-Buddhistic civilization to enable them to make the kind of evaluation or response to Buddhism that was made in medieval China, and which is being made in Europe today.

However, the unsophisticated acceptance of Buddhism by the Tibetans had some obvious spiritual advantages. The danger of the sophisticated response to Buddhist teachings in the West is that it trivializes them: Zen, for example, becomes – as a friend of mine observed, writing about London Buddhist circles in the early 1960s – 'the witty word among the teacups'.

Another danger, already hinted at, is that the whole teaching becomes psychologized – that is, its reference point becomes psychological in the restrictive sense rather than spiritual and transcendental. There is no foolproof safeguard against this; the unenlightened mind will always find a way. The best we can do is develop a tradition of study and interpretation to ensure that texts are not just left at large, so to speak, for anybody to misunderstand. What we need to keep in view is the essentially practical nature of the Abhidharma, both in aiding meditation practice through enabling us to discriminate between skilful and unskilful mental states, and in helping us to realize that what we usually think of as our self is just an ever-changing combination of mental states – a realization which is, for any Buddhist, of supreme importance.

2

ANALYSING THE PATH TO ENLIGHTENMENT

In the introduction to his translation of *The Necklace of Clear Understanding*, Dr Guenther chooses to introduce the Buddhist path, or the 'way', as he calls it, not in terms of the most universally known formulations, but according to a more obscure one: the path of five stages. This is a Sarvāstivādin formulation which was taken up by the Mahāyāna. (Vasubandhu outlines it in his *Abhidharmakośa*.) Instead of the eight limbs of the Noble Eightfold Path, or the basic threefold analysis of Buddhist practice into ethics, meditation, and wisdom, we have the five stages of the path – or, more literally, the five paths. According to some later commentators all Buddhist practices and teachings can be accommodated within this framework. Although such an enterprise would probably be a little over-ambitious, the five *mārgas* certainly provide an illuminating breakdown of what Buddhists are trying to do with their lives. The five stages are: the path of accumulation or preparation; the path of practice or application; the path of insight; the path of transformation; and the path of no more learning.[386]

ACCUMULATION

In the first stage, the path of accumulation (*saṃbhāra-mārga*), one establishes a foundation of relative integration by accumulating certain moral, intellectual, and spiritual qualities. This accumulation stage basically consists of three degrees of intensity. The first is represented by the practice of the four foundations of mindfulness. This involves being constantly aware of one's body – its position and movement; of one's feelings, pleasant, painful, and neutral, and one's emotions; of one's thoughts as they arise; and of ultimate reality. This last aspect of mindfulness involves developing a general awareness of ultimate reality by, for example (to take the method proposed by the Abhidharma), analysing things into their constituent *dharmas*.

According to the Hīnayāna tradition this practice is a self-sufficient path to Enlightenment, but the Mahāyāna saw the notion of trying to go the whole way by force of mindfulness as a bit dry.[387] For the Mahāyāna, mindfulness is therefore the key practice only at the most elementary level of one's spiritual career. This is not at all to suggest that mindfulness can be dispensed with once one has progressed beyond the nursery slopes of the spiritual life; it is more that a deep and full experience of mindfulness requires the support of other practices.

It is sometimes suggested, particularly in Theravādin literature, that if one just observes an unskilful mental state, it will eventually disappear; but anyone who has tried this will know that it doesn't always work. However, one can take a more active approach, represented by another aspect of the path of accumulation, the four right efforts. These are: to remove the unskilful states that have arisen in one's mind; to prevent further unskilful mental states from arising; to maintain and develop skilful states of mind; and to bring into being further skilful mental states.[388]

With the practice of mindfulness one is just observing what is going on, but when one takes up the four right efforts as a practice one works much more dynamically with one's mental states. No longer the passive observer of one's own mental processes, one actively works to change them. It is said that by means of this practice one will establish a connection with the purely spiritual stage of the path in one's next life. Whether or not it is necessary to have this kind of sense of a continuity of lives in order to follow the path, we will consider later.

A prime example of the practice of the four foundations of mindfulness is the meditation called the mindfulness of breathing, while another basic Buddhist meditation practice, the development of loving-kindness (*maitrī bhāvanā*, Pāli *mettā bhāvanā*), is clearly representative of the four right efforts.[389]

The practice of mindfulness is powerful, and the development of positive emotion is even more radical and effective. But one can go even further, to tap the energy which becomes available when one has gone beyond the conflict involved in weeding out the unskilful and cultivating the skilful, to gain access to energy that was previously caught up in negative emotions. Having got rid of unskilful mental states, or at least held them at bay, the victory is virtually won when one moves on to the four *ṛddhipādas*, the 'bases of psychic power'. These are: *chanda, vīrya, citta*, and *mīmāṃsā*.[390]

Chanda means 'thrust, urge, desire'; it is the whole force of one's will bent in a certain direction. With the development of *chanda*, one's interest in the path is fully aroused. With the second *ṛddhipāda*, *vīrya* or energy, one brings all one's vigour into play; one's energies are fully aroused. When one establishes the third *ṛddhipāda*, *citta*, which means 'mind' or 'heart', one really puts one's heart into what one is doing. And with the fourth, *mīmāṃsā* or 'investigation', one goes into the matter thoroughly; one is fully alert.

With this level of integration one begins to develop an effective measure of transcendental insight. The different traditions are not clear about whether or not one's contact with the transcendental becomes irrevocable at this point, but one certainly makes some sort of connection with it, by way of what is called the linkage or *gotrabhū*. This is a rather obscure aspect of the path of the five stages. It represents the point at which one becomes involved with a particular spiritual lineage; that is, when one determines which particular aspect of the transcendental path one will be following – whether that of the *arhant*, the *pratyekabuddha*, or the bodhisattva.

PRACTICE

Having traversed the path of accumulation, one is ready to undertake the path of practice – *prayoga-mārga*. By now it is no longer a struggle – one is in a position to meditate effectively, and to bring one's energy to bear on something – so one applies oneself to penetrating the four noble truths, or any of the basic doctrinal formulations. Then one enters into a sub-stage of the path of practice, that of 'meditative heat'. Heat is generated by energy, and the intensity of one's practice generates, in the course of one's meditation, a sort of inner or psychic heat called *tapas*.

The term comes from a root meaning 'glow' or 'burn', and it is the oldest Indo-Aryan, Vedic word for what we now call spiritual practice or discipline. This psychic heat has a sort of melting effect, melting the hardness and rigidity of one's whole mental structure, softening it, making it more pliable.

At this point the five spiritual faculties come into play. One develops faith, energy, mindfulness, meditative absorption, and a modicum of wisdom, or *prajñā*.[391] Finally one experiences what is called the supreme worldly state, the highest mundane realization. One has gone as far as one can possibly go in terms of mundane development, in terms of human health in the ordinary sense.

ACTIVATION

As a result of the path of practice, one has a flash of pure insight, which can gradually be increased. Having mobilized all one's energies and become more open and pliable, one enters upon the path of seeing (*darśana-mārga*), in which one has some direct vision of the truth. One has a detailed insight into the four noble truths, and into the nature of mind and mental events.

In the light of that breakthrough into the transcendental, a gradual transformation of one's whole being takes place. This is the path of cultivation (*bhāvanā-mārga*), and according to Mahāyāna tradition it takes a very long time indeed to follow this path to the end. Paul Williams says,

> All the remaining nine bodhisattva stages, as well as the other perfections, occur during this path [the path of cultivation] which (short of adopting Tantric practice, which can lead to Buddhahood in one lifetime) is said to take aeons of compassionate activity and striving to follow to its end.[392]

But eventually, however long it takes, one experiences a permanent transformation of oneself, at every level and in every aspect, in accordance with that vision. And as one works to reorganize one's existence, that experience of Perfect Vision continues to develop until one gains full Enlightenment, when one has no more to learn.

It might be objected that this last stage, the path of fulfilment or 'no more learning' (*niṣṭhā-mārga*), cannot be counted as a stage in any meaningful sense, since it is the goal itself. However, this is to take the idea of Enlightenment too literally. In reality it is not a full stop. Enlightenment abounds in compassionate activities that are completely spontaneous. You don't just settle down and twiddle your thumbs. In fact, the stage of no more learning is called by the Tibetan teacher Gampopa, in the *Jewel Ornament of Liberation*, the stage of Buddha activity.[393]

In this way the path as a whole is laid out in regular steps, as five distinct stages. In practice, as with other formulations of the path, most people approach it in a more irregular way. Perhaps one starts – never having given the spiritual life any serious thought – with a flash of insight – that is, with stage three. One may even try to move on to stage four and embark on the path of transformation; but one will find that the vision and the transformation are not sufficient to sustain one at this level, so that one will need to go back and start at the beginning. One may not necessarily start with the path of accumulation, but one will have to go back to it at some point in order to consolidate the attainments that technically belong to the more advanced stages of the path.

In the end one needs to follow what, following Zhiyi, I have sometimes called a path of regular steps. This is where discipline comes in. Unfortunately, the word 'discipline' has negative connotations for many people. Most of us don't like the idea of submitting our unique individuality to someone else's notion of what is good for us. However, without in any way condemning a healthy resistance to pressures imposed by others, it is true to say that those who can remain positive, inspired, and spontaneous through following their own natural inclinations without the need for any discipline, whether imposed by others or by themselves, are very rare indeed. Most people, if they allow themselves to do what they please, do nothing very constructive, and end up feeling dull, listless, and uninspired.

In a sense, it comes down to energy. If our energies are unintegrated, they work against one another. Galvanizing them, getting them working in harmony together, requires some element of discipline, of imposed order. Paradoxically, inspiration and spontaneity are the product of discipline and regular practice. There is a gradual build-up of energy which gains momentum until finally we break free of all habits whatsoever, whether negative and unconscious, or positive and disciplined. It is only at this point that the need for conscious regular effort in our practice drops away. When our energies are integrated without depending on discipline to bring them together, when integration is our normal state, when our energies are always immediately available – that is when we can be simply spontaneous.

WHY YOU NEED THIS BOOK

The nature of the path of five stages gives some idea of the need for the study of mind and mental events which was the preoccupation of the Abhidharmikas, and which the present work will consider. If, for example, one is to remove unskilful mental states and develop skilful ones, one needs to be able to distinguish skilful from unskilful, to recognize exactly what is going on in one's own mind.

But first, of course, one needs to feel inspired to do so. The very fact that our energies are not integrated means that we are certain to be in conflict about how much effort we want to put into spiritual practice. Our inspirations are all too likely to be sabotaged by something in us that says 'Why bother?' To keep ourselves inspired to follow the path of regular steps, we need constantly to remind ourselves of why we are following the path, of who we can become if we work on our minds in this way.

Such a need for inspiration is acknowledged by Yeshe Gyaltsen at the very beginning of *The Necklace of Clear Understanding*. He begins the text with some 'verses of veneration and intention', which put him, and the reader with some understanding of the Buddhist tradition, directly in contact with his sources of inspiration, historical and archetypal exemplars of how to follow the path.

Crucial to all study of the Dharma is the way we approach it, our attitude and our intention. There is only one real reason for studying the Dharma, and this needs to be acknowledged right at the start, particularly in the case of the Abhidharma, where one can all too easily lose sight of the wood for the trees. So one needs to be clear about one's motivation; and one may purify one's motivation by establishing a devotional attitude. Here are the verses with which Yeshe Gyaltsen does so.

VERSES OF VENERATION

I bow with folded hands to him who is inseparable from
Lord Mañjughoṣa, the reverend and excellent teacher.
And I pray that he may accept me in his love for all times.

I bow to the supreme protector, Śākyamuni,
Who illumines the world where he looks
By his Omniscience from which all obscuring darkness
Has gone and who has fulfilled the two requisites
By the power of his spirituality.

From the bottom of my heart, I fold my hands devotedly
To the invincible Lord, Buddha's representative,
Known as Maitreyanātha in all the three times
Because he showers his love on all beings.

I bow to the most supreme leaders from among the
Six ornaments of India, renowned as the Great Charioteers
Who, having been predicted by the Sugata himself,
Illumined the auspicious Buddha Teachings, profound and vast.

I bow to 'Jam-mgon Lama worthy of praise
Like the Buddha-sun to unfold again and let bloom forth
The forest of Sūtras, Tantras, and commentaries,
Like the thousand-petalled lotus, in this country
Surrounded by snow-capped mountains.

May the light of the sun-like reverend Guru
Reside forever in the petal of the lotus-like heart
Brightening the mental eye
That views the auspicious path
By merely seeing a ray of his charismatic activity.

Even if others do not benefit from talk by people like me,
I am dealing here with the mind and mental events
Because I have been urged by others and because
I want to increase the training of my own mind. (pp. 3–4)

So here, in a manner very typical of the Tibetan tradition, our author shows his respect and love for his teachers and inspirations, both historical and archetypal. Mañjughoṣa, the first named, is a manifestation of Mañjuśrī, the Bodhisattva of Wisdom. *Mañju* means 'gentle', 'soft', or 'auspicious', and *ghoṣa* is 'speech' or 'voice', so Mañjughoṣa is 'he of gentle voice'. There is a softness about him – a spiritual softness, a gentle glow – no hardness, no rigidity. 'He of gentle voice' is, however, an embodiment of transcendental wisdom, and in his right hand he holds aloft a flaming sword – an apparently violent appearance which doesn't seem to go with his gentle name. But this contrast itself directs us to think again about the true nature of wisdom.

When I was seven or eight I went to see a film about the Crusades. It was rather a corny film, I seem to remember, but there was an episode in it which made a strong impression on me. This was the scene in which Richard the Lion-Heart meets Saladin and wishes to demonstrate to the Saracen prince his great prowess with the sword. He calls for a great log of wood to be brought in; it is placed across two trestles, and with a single blow of his sword he cuts it in two. But Saladin just smiles and calls for his own sword. Then, unsheathing it, he orders that a piece of silk should be tossed up into the air and allowed to fall across the blade. And of course the sword is so sharp that the piece of silk falls on either side of the blade, severed in two.

So we don't have to think of Mañjuśrī cutting through all delusions by ferociously swinging his sword and bringing it down with a crash, like Richard the Lion-Heart cutting through his log. The kind of wisdom he represents is much more subtle and gentle – and devastating – than that.

Mañjuśrī is also called Kumārabhūta: 'he who has become a youth' or 'he who is youthful'. There is a definition of beauty in Sanskrit poetics: 'Beauty is like that which, from instant to instant, is always new.'[394] Mañjuśrī is represented as being beautiful and never growing old because the experience of wisdom is like that: it is always fresh, always new, always young. The experience of Enlightenment never grows old or stale. One never grows tired of it; it renews itself from moment to moment. The beauty, the magic of it, never fades away.

In this first verse the author bows to 'him who is inseparable from Mañjughoṣa' – that is, the author's own teacher, though we are not given his name. He is saluted as the living embodiment of Mañjughoṣa because he is a Gelug teacher. Mañjughoṣa is a particularly important figure for the Gelugpas, and they all regard the founder of their school, Tsongkhapa, as a manifestation of Mañjughoṣa. Indeed, Mañjughoṣa is the inspirational source of the whole Madhyamaka lineage, in the same way that the bodhisattva Maitreya is particularly associated with the Yogācāra lineage.

MERIT AND WISDOM

Next, Yeshe Gyaltsen pays his respects to the Buddha Śākyamuni, the historical Buddha of our own era. He refers to Śākyamuni as being omniscient, but the word should not be taken literally; the historical Buddha claimed omniscience only with regard to what constituted the path to Enlightenment and the obstacles to that path.[395] The 'two requisites' are *puṇya* (merit) and *jñāna* (wisdom). To understand this, one has to appreciate another of the paths delineated by the Buddhist tradition – this time by the Mahāyāna. This is the path of the bodhisattva. The bodhisattva is said to practise six *pāramitās* or perfections: giving, ethics, energy, patience, meditation, and wisdom. The first five perfections represent the accumulation of merit, while the sixth, *prajñā*, is said to represent the accumulation of wisdom.

Mundane perfection, in other words, is represented by the first five *pāramitās*; one could even say that they represent the fullest possible psychological and spiritual development. The sixth, on the other hand, represents comprehensive transcendental insight, beyond mundane, psychological, and even spiritual perfection. So *puṇya* and *jñāna*, the two 'requisites' or 'accumulations', represent a twofold perfection made up of the consummation of the mundane and the consummation of the transcendental, united in the person of the Buddha, Śākyamuni. Iconographically, *puṇya* is symbolized by the halo around the Buddha's body and *jñāna* by the halo around his head.

THE TUṢITA HEAVEN

Now Yeshe Gyaltsen turns his devotional attention to Maitreyanātha, 'the invincible Lord, Buddha's representative'. Who exactly he is referring to is a moot point. Some would say that the reference is to

Asaṅga, generally regarded as the founder of the Yogācāra school. According to tradition, Asaṅga received his inspiration from Maitreya, the bodhisattva who is said to be waiting for the right moment – when all record of the Dharma has been lost – to take his last rebirth on earth, in which he will gain full Enlightenment and reintroduce the Dharma into the world. He is waiting in the highest of the heavens of the world of form, the Tuṣita ('contented') heaven, which is where bodhisattvas are born before their final human rebirth. It is said that the five books of teachings written by Asaṅga were not just inspired by Maitreya, but actually revealed to him by the bodhisattva. The books, therefore, naturally became known as the 'Five Books of Maitreya'. Some Western scholars are unable to give credence to this account of the originator of the tradition, and suggest that this Maitreya must have been a human teacher who later became confused with the bodhisattva of that name. Dr Guenther sorts the problem out with a neat theory of his own, which is that this accredited author is in fact Asaṅga himself, because some texts refer to the author not as Maitreya but as Maitreyanātha: 'he whose master (*nātha*) is Maitreya'. In this way Guenther comes to the conclusion that the 'Five Books of Maitreya' were authored by Asaṅga under the inspiration of Maitreya.

However, this is a controversial view which would find little favour in some quarters, particularly those of the Tibetan tradition. According to tradition, we are looking at a bodhisattva here – whether Maitreya or Maitreyanātha – rather than Asaṅga or any other human teacher. We cannot discount the possibility that Maitreya or Maitreyanātha was in actuality a human teacher. But the fact that Asaṅga is referred to in the next verse rather counts against the likelihood that his is the true identity of Maitreyanātha – at least as far as the author of this text is concerned.

SIX PRECIOUS ORNAMENTS

The 'six ornaments of India', often depicted in Indian paintings as three sets of pairs, are Nāgārjuna and Āryadeva, Asaṅga and Vasubandhu, and Dignāga and Dharmakīrti. They are all great teachers: Nāgārjuna and Āryadeva of the Madhyamaka tradition; Asaṅga and Vasubandhu of the Yogācāra; and Dignāga and Dharmakīrti of the tradition of Buddhist logic that grew out of the Yogācāra.[396]

They all embody an aspect of the bodhisattva ideal that is sometimes overlooked: the idea that the bodhisattva should be able to teach and convert all beings – that is, rid them of their wrong views. To this end it was necessary – in the highly sophisticated intellectual climate of the Indian Middle Ages at least – to be well-versed in logic and rhetoric. In fact, for more than a thousand years, Indians of all schools, both Buddhist and non-Buddhist, engaged in great public debates with each other, a ding-dong battle that ended only with the disappearance of Buddhism itself from the soil of India.

The only comparable intellectual era, so far as Europe is concerned, is the scholastic period of medieval philosophy, which was much more short-lived. And it would be fair to say that the Indian thinkers conducted their debates at a much more rigorous, exacting, and sophisticated level than that achieved by the medieval schoolmen of Christendom in their controversies, tightly disputed as these were. In this milieu the possession of a finely-honed command of logic became so important that it eventually became an end in itself – thus setting up an inevitable reaction, which to some extent arose in the form of the whole Vajrayāna movement. The Vajrayāna reasserted the primacy of direct spiritual experience and stressed the importance of meditation as the most direct means to that end, while tending to dismiss logic almost entirely. Even so, the old debates continued to be rehearsed. Right down into the nineteenth century Tibetan Buddhist teachers were still busily refuting the views of medieval thinkers, both Hindu and Buddhist, who had been dead for up to a thousand years, such was their determination not to let a wrong view pass uncorrected.

Just how many people are capable of deriving real spiritual benefit and inspiration from the cerebral path carved out by the formidable intellects of the six ornaments of India is hard to say. What one can count on throughout the writings of Nāgārjuna, Asaṅga, and Vasubandhu is a definite and powerful overall spiritual orientation, however much the traditions they seeded may have degenerated later on. From that point of view, rather than reading modern interpreters and commentators on, say, the Madhyamaka, one might be better off reading the original works, just plunging straight into Nāgārjuna's *Mūlamadhyamakakārikā*, the key work of the whole Madhyamaka tradition, perhaps balancing it with Śāntideva's *Bodhicaryāvatāra* for something a bit more practical, and looking to Nāgārjuna's *Ratnāvalī* for a general survey of the Mahāyāna.

However, it has to be said that some Madhyamaka works, including the *Mūlamadhyamakakārikā* itself, are extremely obscure; to make sense of them, one may need the help of modern commentaries, some of which are very good.[397]

The six ornaments of India are 'renowned as the Great Charioteers', that is, the charioteers 'of men who are ready to be tamed'. This is the sense in which the word appears as one of the Buddha's titles in the *Tiratana Vandanā*, the 'Salutation to the Three Jewels'. They are 'predicted' by the Sugata[398] in the sense that the Buddha has, according to followers of the Mahāyāna, especially in Tibet, predicted their coming in certain *sūtras*. Nāgārjuna, for example, is said to be referred to in the *Laṅkāvatāra Sūtra*, though the word that bears the weight of this interpretation (it appears in the *Sagāthakam* section) is actually Nāgāhvaya.[399]

The writer of the verses bows to 'Jam-mgon, which means 'Mañjunātha' – 'he whose master is Mañjuśrī' – by which the author designates Tsongkhapa, whose voluminous writings explain and clarify the *sūtras*, tantras, and Indian commentaries. Tsongkhapa never left Tibet to visit India, as many other teachers did, so he did indeed produce all this work 'surrounded by snow-capped mountains'. Tsongkhapa is singled out here because he is the founder of the Gelug school, which is the dominant tradition of Tibetan Buddhism.

Through these verses of veneration, our author generates in himself – and us, he hopes – a sense of intention, a wish to emulate those whose spiritual greatness he celebrates. We ourselves will be able to find our own ways of doing this, whether by contemplating those qualities of Buddhas or Bodhisattvas to which we are drawn, or by deriving inspiration from our friends and spiritual teachers. But dwelling on such sources of inspiration is not the only way to move us to follow the spiritual path. There is another; and it is to this that Yeshe Gyaltsen now turns, in his introduction to *The Necklace of Clear Understanding*: 'Introduction to Mind and Mental Events'.

3

WHAT'S THE POINT?

Having called upon the sources of inspiration as an incentive to embark on the Buddhist path, Yeshe Gyaltsen now turns to another strong motivation for spiritual practice. To begin with, he distinguishes between two kinds of people: those who think only of this world and this life, who are content with acquiring material things and pursuing mundane goals, and those who take into account the implications of the law of karma with regard to a future life, and on the basis of this consideration start thinking in ethical and spiritual terms. This is the traditional assumption with regard to what motivates people in their practice of Buddhism: that what one is seeking is a good rebirth, and that spiritual practice will be a means to that end.

This, of course, would have been the prevailing view in India at the time of the Buddha, but in the modern West we are not necessarily going to find it easy to go along with it. In fact, the Buddha himself does not seem to have put the kind of emphasis on karma and rebirth that so many Buddhists did later on. This is understandable. He had already gained Enlightenment, and his disciples were eager to do the same. If one's aim is to gain Enlightenment, a state beyond the conditions of life and death, there is little need to consider future lives.

The great Tibetan yogi Milarepa attained Enlightenment in one lifetime, though in his case it was not that he did not consider the long view, but that he could not afford to take it. Having lived a wicked and murderous life before he converted to Buddhism, he perceived that no accumulation of merit he might gather in the life he had left could outweigh his evil actions sufficiently to divert his course away from a rebirth in the hell realms, where he would probably have remained for aeons upon aeons. His only hope was to gain Enlightenment in one lifetime, starting from scratch.

It was assumed by many that he must have practised all sorts of virtues and perfections over many, many lifetimes, but he himself always insisted that he began his spiritual practice with no merit to his credit at all. So although Milarepa himself had a powerful appreciation of the implications of karma and rebirth, he does at the same time provide a model for anyone who has difficulty with these ideas.[400]

In fact, there is no need to assent to the idea of karma and rebirth in order to be a practising Buddhist. Any account of Buddhism as traditionally handed down tends to bring it in at some point, but there are plenty of texts and teachings which present the path simply as the path, making no reference to karma and rebirth at all. If the Buddhist tradition holds good, then as one's understanding deepens the truth of karma and rebirth will presumably become clearer. After all, Buddhists have disagreed over many things, but no teacher of any school or sect has ever suggested that belief in karma and rebirth might be a wrong view – except in the sense that time itself, mundane existence itself, is not ultimately real.[401] The idea of rebirth, one could say, follows logically upon the fundamental tenet of Buddhism that actions have consequences. However, one doesn't have to be completely logical in order to follow the Buddhist path, and it is possible to draw motivation for one's practice by considering the operation of karma in this life without necessarily taking rebirth into account.

Of course, however logical belief in it may be, rebirth is not the only possible answer to the universal question 'What happens when we die?' For many people the Buddhist conception of rebirth seems more or less self-evident. But there are, obviously, other views on the matter. In fact there are three, or possibly four, views to choose from. The first view is that one will exist after death – in heaven or elsewhere, though not again on earth – but that one did not exist before this life. This is the Christian view, or, at least, that is the view which has been held almost universally throughout Christian history. One or two of the early Greek Christian scholars, like Origen, did believe in some sort of pre-existence before physical birth.[402] Their idea was that the soul, which one inherited from one's parents, ultimately came from Adam.

This belief – which amounted to a belief in a sort of group soul of which one's individual soul is a part – was known as Traductionism (because one's soul is 'traduced' or conveyed from Adam).

Christian opinion is more divided on what happens after death. Some believe that the soul created by God is immortal, and that it eventually goes to heaven or hell – or, in the case of unchristened babies, to Limbo – for all eternity. Others take the view that the soul is created mortal and dies with the death of the body until it is revived, either shortly after death or – according to, for example, Seventh Day Adventists and Jehovah's Witnesses – at the time of the Last Judgement. Then one goes either to heaven or to hell – though the Seventh Day Adventists replace eternal torment with a much kinder final solution for the condemned, which is that God simply annihilates them.

The second possible view is the strictly materialist one: the belief that there is just this life with no kind of existence whatsoever before or after. There is, theoretically speaking, also a third possibility which would be the view that there is just this life and a succession of previous lives, but no next life – but no one, to the best of my knowledge, actually holds this view. Finally, the fourth possible view is that there is a past life or lives, a present life, and a future life or lives.[403]

TRAILING CLOUDS OF GLORY

Most people find that one of these views seems more satisfactory than the others. No one view is altogether free from difficulties; but I have come to the conclusion that the idea of rebirth fits best. And the most telling confirmation of this lies not in some objective intellectual demonstration but in a feeling – a quite definite and powerful feeling – that develops through one's life.

This is something one can't appreciate when one is young, unless one is rather exceptional. But as one gets older, one starts seeing that one's whole life has had a certain clear direction or tendency which cannot fully be accounted for by any accumulation of circumstances within this present life, but which definitely seems to originate from what one can only assume is a previous life. Furthermore, one gets a strong feeling that this trend isn't just going to stop, but will continue after one's death. If one is relatively observant and reflective I think one cannot but entertain quite seriously the idea that one has come into this life with a propensity, even an agenda, already in place and that one will project it – project oneself – beyond the conclusion of one's life.

One can get a sense of this from telling one's life story to a friend or friends. This is a useful and powerful practice which often brings to the surface half-forgotten aspects of one's life and allows one to discover patterns in one's experience. And one theme that frequently emerges as one tells one's life story is a sense that in the business of growing up something important has been lost along the way. Quite a number of people have this feeling, that when they were young, before they got caught up in worldly responsibilities, they really did have a sense of what life was all about, before it all got overlaid by the dense complex of adult experience. It's as though we lose contact with our true feelings, our true self, even – not just in a psychological way that requires some psychotherapeutic solution, but in a definitely spiritual way.

In our early years many of us have experiences or feelings that seem to belong not to this world but elsewhere – or that even seem to indicate that we *belong* elsewhere. A few years later, when one starts to think and feel as an individual without yet being weighed down with responsibilities, one wants to find one's way back to one's origins, back to a truer, more innocent experience, and take that as one's starting point.

All this is not to suggest that there is some kind of primeval innocence about a child, or that children are in some way in touch with the Absolute. Unfortunately, one can get a sentimental and mistaken impression of this sort from some of the English poets: Vaughan, for example: 'Happy those early days when I / Shined in my Angel-infancy';[404] or Wordsworth: 'trailing clouds of glory do we come / From God who is our home'.[405] Wordsworth himself is a very clear, though unusual, example of someone who achieved a true vision in early adolescence which he managed to sustain well into his thirties. William Blake is another – indeed, he never really lost contact with his childhood. Though he was a very mature person he never grew up at all in the sense of becoming corrupted with (in Traherne's phrase) 'the dirty devices of the world'.[406]

There will always be people who say that it is a necessary part of one's development to taste something of the dirty devices of this world, but this is a wrong view. Ideally, one should try to remain an adolescent in this positive sense for as long as possible. One should seek to deepen one's vision, to mature it – but not to lose it. To return to the idea of rebirth, it's as though when we are young we are in touch with something from a previous life. One may not be aware of it as a small child, but as one comes up to adolescence one becomes old enough to have a sense of it – though not, perhaps, old enough to appreciate how precious it is, or how easily it is lost.

Such experiences lead many people to see the idea of rebirth as quite reasonable, even obvious. However, if we find it difficult to take it to heart as our Tibetan author would like us to, we do not thereby lose our motivation for the spiritual life – at least, not necessarily. In fact, in some Buddhist countries the doctrine of karma and rebirth sometimes provides an excuse for postponing any real spiritual effort. It is even said that it isn't possible to gain Enlightenment any longer – the Buddha lived so long ago and there aren't any Enlightened teachers around any more – so our best bet is to accumulate merit, hope for good rebirths, and wait a few thousand years for the next Buddha to reappear, in the hope that we will get a chance to become his disciples. That will be the time to make an effort to gain Enlightenment. So some people believe – but it is a disastrously wrong view. It is better to disbelieve in karma and rebirth and follow the path anyway than to believe in karma and rebirth and make that one's excuse for not following the path here and now.

THE MODERN PERSPECTIVE

Yeshe Gyaltsen's assumption that it is concern for one's future rebirth that motivates one to take up Buddhism is simply not the way most people think in the West today. People tend to become interested in Buddhism, or start practising meditation, because it seems to offer a solution to psychological problems, or an intellectually respectable alternative to a purely materialist philosophy. Many practising Buddhists may be said to take a frankly agnostic or even sceptical attitude to the idea of rebirth. The very survival of human life on this planet is an issue that seems to many of us more pressing than any consideration of future rebirths.

Nowadays we can see things happening much more quickly than people could in more traditional and stable societies. It seems as though the whole process of life has speeded up, so that we can see the results of karma in this life itself. We are continually made aware through the media that we are teetering on the edge of global catastrophe, and this deepens our sense of responsibility. Never mind future lives; if we don't act now something terrible will happen in *this* life. (Of course, one can also think in terms of the consequences of our actions for future generations.) On a more personal level, too, one may conclude that only through some kind of spiritual development will one be able to transcend one's immediate painful conditions in this life. In these ways it is possible to accept the principle of karma within the much narrower context and more limited timescale of a single lifespan. Some people derive sufficient inspiration from thinking in terms of transforming their lives and the world around them, without needing to consider a long view of futurity at all.

Alternatively, one can take a completely opposite, more positive, perspective to that recommended by our author. Within the framework of karma and rebirth, one is usually thinking in terms of escaping from something. Some Tibetan lamas teaching in the West make a point of describing in vivid detail all the different hells and heavens that await us – what will happen to you if you do this, what will happen to you if you do that – and this uncompromising, even dogmatic laying down of traditional doctrine evidently has a strong effect. But many western Buddhists see this approach as unnecessarily fundamentalist. For them the spiritual life has its own intrinsic appeal which overrides the fear of any unpleasant contingencies attendant upon the worldly life, whether here and now or in the future. This innate love for the spiritual life should be encouraged. There are people who do not need to be told that they will suffer if they follow the worldly life, because they see spiritual development as good in itself.

Of course, the doctrine of karma and rebirth need not be intimidating. Some people are positively invigorated by the prospect of practising the spiritual life for life after life after life, gathering momentum over aeons of time and visiting all sorts of Buddha-worlds as described in the Mahāyāna *sūtras*. That others will find the mind-boggling duration of three *asaṃkhyeyas*[407] of lifetimes simply depressing testifies to the necessity of developing an appropriate motivation of one's own.

KARMA

But whatever we think about rebirth, we can still take karma seriously. Karma, it should be noted, is only one of the five levels on which conditionality operates. This is an aspect of the teaching that is not always made explicit in the Mahāyāna, although it is standard Theravādin teaching.[408] (Indeed, not all Mahāyāna Buddhists would even agree that conditionality is multifaceted in this way; in some Mahāyāna traditions karma has become very dominant indeed.) But taking the Theravādin line on this, we can say that everything that happens does so as the result of a network of conditions, involving causal links which can be of a physical, biological, psychological, karmic, or transcendental nature. While karma – the level on which our skilful actions bring happiness for us and our unskilful actions bring suffering – is a causal factor in our lives, it does not follow that everything that happens to us is a result of our karma. Nonetheless, an understanding of the karmic level of conditionality is crucial to us because it is something on which we can rely. If we act skilfully, joy is sure to follow; if we act unskilfully, we are letting ourselves in for suffering we could have avoided.

This insight can be traced back to the very earliest Buddhist teachings, to the first two verses of the *Dhammapada*, which state:

> (Unskilful) mental states are preceded by mind, led by mind, and made up of mind. If one speaks or acts with an impure mind suffering follows him even as the cart-wheel follows the hoof of the ox.
>
> (Skilful) mental states are preceded by mind, led by mind, and made up of mind. If one speaks or acts with a pure mind happiness follows him like his shadow.[409]

So, as these verses make clear, there is a connection between our mind and the nature of our future life or lives. According to the doctrine of karma and rebirth, our actions have a direct effect on our own being by modifying the patterns of habit, the conscious and unconscious volitional drives, which constitute the most essential part of us. This 'essential nature' is not unchangeable; on the contrary, it can change in any direction at any time. It carries on through death and into another rebirth, in accordance with the karma that has accumulated during the previous life.

To delve briefly into the implications of this as outlined in Buddhist tradition, we can say that these volitional drives, modified by karma, take an appropriate physical embodiment. For a predominantly human consciousness, this will be a human form; for an angelic consciousness it will be the form of a god; for an animal consciousness, an animal form; and so on. Of course, the new form one assumes is not 'off the peg', as it were. There are said to be innumerable classes of beings – Buddhists in Eastern countries have had no difficulty with the notion of the existence of all kinds of what the scriptures call non-human beings – but the variety of beings even within each class that we know of is enormous. More than that, each individual living being is in some way unique, and has a unique history and future. And to the extent that they are unique, to that extent individual living beings have the potential to modify the habit-volitions that make them up in order to promote their growth towards higher levels of consciousness. As human beings we are able to do this through various practices known collectively as the Dharma, or the way to Enlightenment, or Buddhism. Some forms of living beings, like animals, are in no position to take advantage of these practices; beings that are in a good position to do so may be said to have a precious opportunity which should not be thoughtlessly squandered.[410]

DEEPER WATERS

> As long as there is the belief in the *skandhas*,
> There will come from them a belief in a self.
> When there is a belief in an ego, then there is *karma*.
> From this, there will come (re)birth. (p. 5)
> Nāgārjuna

Here Yeshe Gyaltsen brings in the first of his many quotations from the Mahāyāna tradition. And with this little verse from the sage Nāgārjuna he plunges us into deep water – or, at least, into a more Abhidharmic perspective on rebirth.

The *skandhas* are, as we have seen, the five constituents making up the psychophysical organism that we call the self. They are: form, feeling, perception, volition, and consciousness. The Buddha exposed the insubstantial nature of the self by analysing one's experience of oneself into these five heaps or aggregates. But here Nāgārjuna points out that one should take care not to make the mistake of regarding the *skandhas* themselves as being substantial. To do this is to take something that exists merely empirically to be ultimately and permanently existent, effectively rebuilding a false belief in the self. So long as there is that fixed point of reference in the form of an ego, there will be an indefinite repetition of the pattern in the form of rebirth.

The whole process can also be seen at work within this life itself – indeed, within each minute of our lives. We are constantly reaffirming our belief in the discrete and substantial existence of the *skandhas*, thus giving rise to a self which acts in a particular way, as a result of which our present ego-ridden existence undergoes a manner of rebirth from instant to instant. This mistaken assumption – that the self, comprising the physical body, feelings, perceptions, impulses, and consciousness, is a real entity – gives rise to behaviour which in turn supports that mistaken assumption, until the adoption of positive conditioning eventually unravels all conditionings whatsoever, and we are able to see things as they really are.

KARMA FORMATIONS

> The root of *saṃsāra* is motivation.
> Therefore, the wise do not make plans.
> The unwise, therefore, become agents
> Because they see only unwiseness. (p. 6)

This verse from Nāgārjuna's *Madhyamakakārikā* is not as contentious as the translation makes it appear. What Nāgārjuna says in fact is that the root of *saṃsāra* – compounded existence – is the fourth of the five *skandhas*, the *saṃskāras*, more straightforwardly rendered as volitions, impulses, or karma formations. They are only 'motivations' inasmuch as they are based on a belief in a fixed self. So it is not that 'the wise' do not make plans (which is simply untrue) but that they do not set up *saṃskāras*. The wise do not make plans only in so far as plans are the production of a rigid mental attitude, where the framing of that plan and the projection of its realization fulfils some neurotic need, so that one is unable to adapt or adjust it in the light of changed circumstances. The wise are fully equal to each and every situation as it arises, so the plans they make are always provisional.[411]

> The seeds for the possible worlds are concepts.
> The objects are their field of activity.
> Āryadeva, *Catuḥśataka*

The Buddha himself said, 'Thus, all terror
And also the countless frustrations
Come from the mind.' (p. 6)
Śāntideva, *Bodhicaryāvatāra*

In these terse statements is contained an immense idea: that whatever world we find ourselves in owes its origin to ideas in the mind. Hence the overwhelming importance of the study of mind and mental events for the spiritual welfare of all beings – because mind and mental events are what constitute karma. This is the traditional and appropriate motivation for the study of the Abhidharma: the fact that mind and mental events together with the law of karma determine one's whole future, both in this life and throughout future lives.

TO DO IS TO BE, TO BE IS TO DO

One could say that everything that happens in the universe – from a personal point of view – can be divided into two great classes: things that happen to us and things we do. Many of our experiences come into the first category. It rains, for instance, and we just experience the rain. We have nothing to do with making it rain; it just happens to us. Then, secondly, there are things we do: things we initiate, things in respect of which we are active rather than passive.

The Buddhist viewpoint ties these two categories together by saying that what happens to us, our present *vipāka* (*vipāka* means 'fruit'), is the product of things we have done in the past – that is, the product of past karma. This term *vipāka* (or *karma-vipāka*) is of crucial importance to any discussion of mind and mental events.

The symbol known as the Tibetan wheel of life, but more accurately called the 'wheel of becoming' (*bhavacakra*), gives a graphic illustration of the workings of karma and *karma-vipāka*. The outer rim of the wheel illustrates what are known as the 'twelve links' (*nidānas*) of compounded existence. Although these links are popularly associated with the symbolism of Tibetan Buddhism, in fact they derive from the Buddha's own description of the insight he gained into the nature of human existence.[412]

We have already come across the first two links of the chain – ignorance (*avidyā*) and 'karma formations' (*saṃskāras*). These refer

The Tibetan wheel of life

to the past life, reflecting the process by which, acting on the basis of ignorance, we formed the karmic propensities that have shaped our present life. The next eight links show the process of this life. The karma of our past life bears fruit (*vipāka*) in the form of consciousness (*vijñāna*), in dependence upon which arise the five *skandhas*. From the *skandhas* come the six senses (*ṣaḍāyatanas* – mind being considered as a sixth sense), in dependence upon which arises contact (*spārśa*); and this in turns leads to feeling (*vedanā*). These five links are all *karma-vipāka*; they are all 'things that happen to us' in the sense that we have no choice about their arising: they arise in dependence upon our past karma.

But the next link is different. At this point we do have a choice. On our response depends the future course of events; we are back in the realm of 'things we do'. At this point we can create fresh karma by craving (*tṛṣṇā*) which leads to grasping (*upādāna*) and becoming (*bhāva*). The momentum of this karmic process leads to a future rebirth – hence the last two links of the chain, birth (*jāti*) and decay-and-death (*jarāmaraṇa*), a compressed and therefore grim snapshot of one's future life.

Alternatively, if we can learn to respond to pleasant feeling without craving and to unpleasant feeling without aversion, we set up fresh karma which will ultimately lead us beyond the wheel of life and death altogether, towards Enlightenment. Through the 'things we do', in other words, we can direct the 'things that will happen to us' in the future. From a Buddhist, especially an Abhidharmic, perspective, it is the things we do with our minds – in other words, our mental events – that make all the difference. All this it will be the concern of this commentary to explore in some detail.

SUNNY INTERVALS

However, as we have seen, not everything we experience is the *direct* result of things we have done. According to the doctrine of the five *niyamas*, whatever happens to us may be the result of a combination of five types of conditionality, only one of which consists of our ethical choices. The others represent the conditions that obtain within the general context of human existence.

Many of the things that happen to us simply arise out of the environment in which we find ourselves. Suppose, for example, that bad weather is preventing one from doing something one really wants to do. The rain is not necessarily the karmic consequence – the *vipāka* – of one's having once stopped somebody else from doing what they wanted to do, perhaps in some previous existence; that would be to take the law of karma too literally.

However, although what happens to us may do so as a result of physical, biological, psychological, or even transcendental factors, as well as arising from our karma, one could argue that these other factors have, indirectly, a karmic origin. For example, if bad weather sometimes stops one from doing what one wants to do, one could say that this is a result of one's having been born as a particular psychophysical organism inhabiting a particular kind of world in which it rains from time to time. And how has one come to be in possession of this particular psychophysical organism? Because of previous karmas one has performed. According to this line of reasoning, one could conclude that everything we experience *is* in fact a *vipāka* of previous karmas, though not in a literal 'eye for an eye, tooth for a tooth' sense.

This indirect karma could also be called collective karma; though this term has no traditional provenance, the Sarvāstivādin texts make it clear that such karmic concatenations occur.[413] One could even go as far as to say that a world comes into existence, so to speak, because a number of beings have performed the same kind of actions, thereby setting up the same kind of results. This congeries of common *vipāka* constitutes their world, which they also – broadly speaking – perceive in common. The same principle applies in the case of a Pure Land: by virtue of his infinitely powerful volition a Buddha is able to set up a whole ideal environment single-handedly, but others who have managed to 'tune in' to this Pure Land can also be reborn into it.[414]

The fundamental implication is that volition is a creative force that is capable of producing what we would call objective consequences. Expressions such as 'It's just a thought' are simply not Buddhistic. A thought is, in a sense, everything. Thought is a force; thought is a power; thought is an energy. But what exactly is it that this energy produces? What do we mean by the objective consequences produced by volitions?

We cannot say that thought creates matter. What we can say is that thought produces *rūpa*, 'the objective content of a perceptual situation', as Guenther puts it.[415] So while we may say that our experience has an objective pole, just as there is a subjective pole, we should not go as far as to think in terms of an object which is actually out there waiting for us to perceive it.

One may also create karma with regard to specific individuals. The *Jātaka* tales suggest as much, anyway. When the Buddha relates one of these stories of something that is supposed to have happened millions of years ago, he says that such-and-such a figure was himself, that another was Ānanda (the Buddha's companion), and yet another was Devadatta (the Buddha's opponent on many occasions). So the same dramatis personae are presented in each story. They travel down the ages together, appearing in different guises but standing in much the same relation to one another as they do in their historical incarnation. Devadatta, for example, is for lifetime after lifetime trying to kill the Buddha. It is as though he couldn't leave the Buddha alone. The Buddha was always there in his thoughts, so Devadatta always got reborn along with the Buddha. They somehow got tangled up together, for one rebirth after another.[416] The idea behind the *Jātaka* tales perhaps provides an explanation for the feeling one gets with certain people that one is picking up threads that were dropped a long time ago (though one wouldn't want to press this point towards unduly romantic conclusions).

The main point to be drawn from all this is that as one's mind is, so is one's karma. As one's karma is, so is one's rebirth. As one's rebirth is, so is one's happiness or one's suffering. And ultimately, with the attainment of Enlightenment, one is freed even from the alternation between happiness and suffering. The Buddhist tradition sums the whole matter up in one key phrase: actions have consequences; and, if we are uncomfortable with the notion of rebirth, we can readily see the truth of this even within our present life. All this depends on mind and mental events. But what is mind, and what are mental events? To these questions Yeshe Gyaltsen now turns his attention.

4
THE NATURE OF MIND

THE YOGĀCĀRA BACKGROUND

Our ordinary experience is firmly and securely based on subject–object dualism. All our knowledge, all our thinking, takes place within this framework – subject and object, me and you, 'me in here' and 'the world out there'. But the Enlightened mind, we are told, is completely free of such dualism. This, at least, is one of the key doctrines of the Yogācāra, or *citta-mātra*, the Mind Only school.[417]

Between the experience of non-duality and our ordinary, everyday dualistic consciousness, there is obviously a great gulf; and to move from the one experience to the other will entail a complete and absolute reversal of all our usual attitudes. This reversal, this great change – this great death and rebirth, even – is what the Yogācāra terms the *parāvṛtti*. Sometimes *parāvṛtti* is translated as 'revulsion', but this is not really satisfactory because it implies a psychological process rather than a spiritual and metaphysical one. It is much better to use the literal translation of *parāvṛtti* – 'turning about'.

As we have seen, *The Necklace of Clear Understanding* is more or less based on the Yogācāra tradition's understanding of mind. Before plunging with Yeshe Gyaltsen into the distinction between mind and mental events, therefore, we will look a little more closely at the Yogācāra's conception of mind, on which Gyaltsen's commentary largely rests.

Basically, the *citta-mātra* doctrine denies the reality of matter as a separate category from mind. The objects of our perception, it says, are not external objects as such, not objects as opposed to ourselves, the subject. We perceive mental impressions, that's all. The significance of this insight is that if one removes the notion of an object, one also effectively removes the notion of a subject. In this way one breaks down the notion of a self that is separate from the world, to be left with Mind Only. This Mind Only is not mind as opposed to matter, but a completely different conception of mind.

We have already come across the teaching of the five *skandhas*, which states that our experience can be analysed into five heaps or aggregates: form (*rūpa*), feeling (*vedanā*), perception (*saṃjñā*), volitions (*saṃskāras*), and consciousness (*vijñāna*). Contradicting the standard Abhidharma teaching, the Yogācāra made the bold statement that there is really only one *skandha*, *vijñāna* or consciousness, the other four being manifestations of *vijñāna*.[418] Having established this metaphysical position, the Yogācārins drew attention to its practical consequence: if you think in terms of an object, you will grasp at that object, they said; but if you see that what appears to be an object is in fact a transformation of mind, your experience is like someone who dreams that they are about to eat a delicious fruit. When they wake up, they realize that the fruit is just a product of their own mind, and they forget about it – the grasping is gone.

So, rather than being able to make a sharp distinction between subject and object, all one can really say is that there is a 'perceptual situation' (to use Guenther's expression) comprising two opposite poles. One pole is the experience of what I call myself, together with everything I have under my immediate control; that is the 'subjective content' of the perceptual situation. And then, at the opposite pole, there is everything and everyone that is independent of my direct control – the 'objective content' of the perceptual situation. When one becomes Enlightened, that perceptual situation still occurs, but one no longer identifies oneself with its subjective content, which means that the whole perceptual situation is expanded, clarified, illuminated, enlightened.

The Yogācāra interpretation is not so much that there is a thing called 'mind' and a thing called 'matter', and that the thing called matter is discovered actually to be mind. It's not like discovering that what one thought was a jug is in reality clay. It's more that *citta* or mind is the term applied to that undifferentiated substratum which has been polarized into subject and object, mind and matter. Mind and matter are just symbols for the two poles of the one perceptual situation, and it's sometimes very difficult to tell where one ends and the other begins. If one can attenuate that subject–object polarity a little, for example in meditation (the Yogācāra, remember, came out of meditative experience, not philosophical reasoning), then one's experience is transformed.

There is of course the question of how we all come to share more or less the same 'objective content'. The general, though perhaps rather implausible, Yogācāra view is that we have a common perception to the extent that we have a common karma – to the extent, that is, that we share a common mental outlook. The 'objects' more or less coincide because the 'subjects' more or less coincide. This consensus reality, however, is real for practical purposes only.

THE EXPERIENCE OF NON-DUAL AWARENESS

When you attain Enlightenment, the element of resistance to the objective content of the perceptual situation is no longer there. You no longer have a will that is separate from that of others. It's as though you utterly identify with others, and with what they are doing. You no longer want one thing while they want another, or want something from them that they are unwilling to give. What they want, you want; what you want, they want. You don't experience another person as a sort of brick wall that you are coming up against, and you no longer experience yourself as a separate and conflicting solid force. You experience others in a completely different way: they become diaphanous or transparent, because your will is not coming into collision with theirs. This completely different, more relaxed, lighter, and freer attitude, taken to the nth degree, is something of the nature of Enlightenment. The world is the same but you see it differently. Perhaps one could say that it's like what happens when you fall in love, only much more so. Even though everything is there as before, the world looks almost physically different.

The Yogācāra describes the process of becoming Enlightened in terms of the transformation of what it calls the eight *vijñānas* into the five *jñānas*. *Vijñāna* is usually translated as 'consciousness', but that is not exactly accurate. The prefix *vi-* means 'to divide' or 'to discriminate', and *jñāna* means 'knowledge' or 'awareness', so we can translate *vijñāna* as 'discriminating awareness'. *Vijñāna* therefore refers to awareness of an object not just in a pure mirror-like way but in a way which discriminates the object as being of a particular type and belonging to a particular class, species, or whatever. The first five *vijñānas* are the five 'sense *vijñānas*', the modes of discriminating awareness that operate through the five senses – through the eye with respect to form, the ear with respect to sound, and so on. Guenther uses the term 'perception' where other translators use 'consciousness', so that, for example, instead of 'eye-consciousness' we have – more correctly, in my view – 'visual perception'. In his commentary, Yeshe Gyaltsen classifies perceptions according to the sense organ through which they function or take place.

MANO-VIJÑĀNA

The sixth of the six categories of 'discriminating awareness' – perhaps surprisingly to anyone schooled in Western ways of thinking – is mind itself. In Buddhism, mind in the everyday sense is classified as a sort of sixth sense; it doesn't have a special elevated position above the five sense consciousnesses. The word being translated as mind here is *mano-vijñāna*, which Guenther translates as 'categorical perception'. This is mind as the simply mechanical or reactive process of perceiving mental objects (as opposed to *manas*, mind as – so to speak – the seat of ego identity). The idea of the mind as a sense 'organ' is a necessary corollary to the Buddhist conception of what Guenther terms the perceptual situation. The conventional Western view is that thoughts remain part of oneself as a subject set against a separate world of objects. But this is a limited viewpoint. It is akin to what William Blake calls the *ratio* of the senses, the split-off intellect, representing a process of induction from a narrow field of experience: you observe, you classify, you generalize, from the limited field of sense experience. When you look out, you construe a world of actually existing objects, and when you look within, you construe an actually existent self. Blake contrasts this ratio with Imagination, which is based upon, or is the expression of, the experience of the whole person.[419]

Unlike the conventional Western view, the Buddhist viewpoint recognizes thoughts as objects of perception along with any other objects. Just as objects flow through one's visual field, so do objects flow through one's cognitive field. One could even say that, in a sense, one's thoughts are even less a part of oneself than the objects of the other five senses, because it would seem that one has rather less control, generally speaking, over what one thinks than over what one sees, hears, tastes, smells, and feels. It seems unreasonable to identify oneself with a realm of experience over which one seems to have so little control.

According to Yogācāra philosophy there are two aspects of *mano-vijñāna*. The first of these is awareness of what we might describe as ideas of sense – in other words, the awareness of impressions presented by the five senses. The second aspect is awareness of ideas that arise independently of sense-perception, out of mind itself. This latter aspect of *mano-vijñāna* is of three kinds. First of all, there are the ideas and impressions that arise in the course of meditation, as when one experiences light that doesn't have its origin in any sense impression but comes from mind itself. Then, secondly, there are functions such as imagination, comparison, and reflection. If, for example, one's immediate impression of someone was that they were untrustworthy, this might be a subtle sense impression, but on the other hand it might be that one has in the past met someone who resembled this person in some way and who turned out to be untrustworthy. In this latter case one's impression would come under the heading of categorical perception (*mano-vijñāna*). Thirdly, there are images perceived in dreams, which again come not from sense impressions but directly from mind itself. Categorical perception, in short, covers any perception that does not come in through the physical senses. It is the perception of all kinds of mental operations, including recollections of experiences that originally came through the senses and also things that were never experienced through the senses at all.

The seventh consciousness or *vijñāna* is the *kliṣṭa-mano-vijñāna*. *Kliṣṭa* means 'afflicted' or 'suffering', and also 'defiled', defilement being a source of suffering; it has also been translated as 'tainted'. This mode of awareness, therefore, is afflicted, defiled, or tainted by a dualistic outlook. Whatever it experiences, it interprets in terms of a subject and an object – subject as self, and object as world or universe. Everything is seen in terms of pairs of opposites: good and bad, true and false, right and wrong, existence and non-existence, and so on. Of course, this dualistic mode of discriminative awareness or consciousness characterizes the way in which we usually live our lives.

The eighth consciousness is called the *ālaya-vijñāna*. *Ālaya* literally means a repository or store, or even treasury – as in 'Himalaya', which means 'repository of snow'. This store consciousness, one could say, has two aspects, the 'relative' or 'tainted' *ālaya* and the 'absolute' or 'pure' *ālaya*.[420]

The relative *ālaya* consists of, or contains, the impressions left deep in the mind by all our previous experiences. Whatever we have done or said or thought or experienced, a trace or residue of it remains there; nothing is absolutely lost. The Yogācāra school conceives of the impressions that are deposited in the *ālaya-vijñāna*, the consequences of our various thoughts and deeds, as being like seeds (*bījas*). In other words, these impressions are not passive; they are not like the impression left by a seal in a piece of wax. They are *active* impressions, left like seeds in the soil, and when conditions are favourable they sprout and produce fruits.

This subconscious collectivity of seeds sown by previous actions fructifies and evolves eventually into the six sense perceptions, plus the *kliṣṭa-mano-vijñāna* or ego-consciousness; and all these seven *vijñānas* together comprise the evolving consciousness which produces the illusion of the world as we know it. It is this *kliṣṭa-mano-vijñāna*, often referred to simply as *manas*, 'mind' or 'ego-consciousness', that interprets the impressions it receives from the other six *vijñānas* as representing an objectively existing external world, and at the same time interprets the *ālaya-vijñāna* itself as an objectively existing self.

The *ālaya* in its absolute aspect is reality itself, conceived of in terms of pure awareness free from all trace of subjectivity and objectivity. It is a pure, continuous, and non-dimensional – or even multidimensional – awareness in which there is nothing of which anyone is aware, nor anyone who is aware. It is awareness without subject and without object – something which it is scarcely possible for us to imagine.

TURNING ABOUT: A MIND CAPSIZED

The *āśraya-parāvṛtti*, the 'turning about in the deepest seat of consciousness', is brought about, according to the Yogācāra, by the accumulation of impressions – seeds – in the relative *ālaya*. Through spiritual practice, more and more pure seeds are gathered in the relative *ālaya*, and as these pure seeds accumulate, they put pressure on the impure seeds until in the end the impure seeds are pushed right out of the *ālaya*; it is this that constitutes the *parāvṛtti*. When the *parāvṛtti* occurs, the eight *vijñānas*, the eight modes of discriminating awareness, are transformed into five *jñānas* – five modes of pure, that is, non-discriminating, awareness or wisdom.

These five modes of pure awareness are represented in Mahāyāna iconography by five archetypal Buddhas, the five Buddhas of the mandala. The first five *vijñānas*, the sense consciousnesses, are transformed into the all-performing wisdom of the green Buddha, Amoghasiddhi. The *mano-vijñāna*, or mind consciousness, is transformed into the distinguishing

The mandala of the Five Buddhas

wisdom of the red Buddha, Amitābha. The *kliṣṭa-mano-vijñāna*, or defiled mind consciousness, becomes the wisdom of equality of the yellow Buddha, Ratnasambhava. The relative *ālaya* is transformed into the mirror-like wisdom of the dark blue Buddha, Akṣobhya. And the absolute *ālaya*, of course, does not need to be transformed at all; it is equivalent to the wisdom of the *dharmadhātu*, the wisdom of the universe perceived as fully pervaded by reality, the wisdom of the white Buddha, Vairocana.[421]

BUT IS IT TRUE?

The doctrine of the *ālaya-vijñāna* provides an explanation for how it is that we take illusory things like the self and the world to be real.[422]

Whether or not one accepts the idea of the *ālaya-vijñāna* depends, traditionally, on whether one takes it to be an explicit teaching or an implicit teaching.[423] Some teachers say that the word of the Buddha is at all times quite explicit and never requires any interpretation to bring out its real meaning. They say that reading something other than the explicit meaning into it falsifies it. The Yogācārins do not go this far; they accept the presence of implicit statements in the teachings. For example, according to the *Saṃdhinirmocana Sūtra*, an important scripture for the Yogācāra, the Perfection of Wisdom *sūtras* and the *Madhyamaka* itself should not be taken literally; the teaching of emptiness as presented in these texts is a skilful means.[424] But as far as the *ālaya-vijñāna* is concerned, the Yogācārins posit it on the basis of what they take as explicit statements in the teachings. It is on this basis that they declare the whole of reality to be Mind only.

The Madhyamaka school, by contrast, explains away references to the *ālaya-vijñāna* by saying that it is not to be understood explicitly; it is not to be taken in a literal, philosophical sense. Indeed, the Madhyamaka even goes so far as to say that even mental events – or what we think of as mental events – are illusory, just logical fictions.[425] On the other hand, texts which teach the universal emptiness of inherent existence are, for the follower of the Madhyamaka, to be taken literally, while the Yogācārin would have seen this – perhaps with good reason – as tantamount to nihilism.

In *The Necklace of Clear Understanding* Yeshe Gyaltsen chooses not to go into the seventh and eighth *vijñānas*; for practical spiritual purposes his main concern is with the first six, as we shall see. In his brief chapter on mind, however, he notes simply that one can gain Enlightenment by following either the Madhyamaka or the Yogācāra.[426] Though they are different teachings – different ways of looking at things – they lead ultimately to the same goal.

This serves as a reminder that all this analysis is intended for a practical purpose. Given the way things are – given that we see things dualistically, through the lens, as it were, of the defiled mind consciousness – we can learn to discriminate between positive, skilful mental states, which are to be cultivated, and negative, unskilful mental states, which are to be dropped. This is very basic Buddhism. In the Buddha's teaching of the seven factors of Enlightenment,[427] for example, the second factor (after mindfulness or awareness) is *dharma-vicaya*, investigation of mental events. The Abhidharma project developed this idea further by identifying and classifying a definitive range of positive and negative mental events. It is these that are the subject matter for the main body of Yeshe Gyaltsen's commentary.

First, though, he chooses to explore a crucial distinction: the difference between mind and mental events.

MIND AND MENTAL EVENTS DISTINGUISHED

1. Mind

Yeshe Gyaltsen begins his discussion by singling out a quotation from the *Madhyānta-Vibhānga*, one of the five books of Maitreya that Asaṅga taught to his brother Vasubandhu, who wrote notes and commentaries on all five books. This is the quotation:

> Seeing a thing belongs to mind.
> Seeing its specific characteristic belongs to a mental event. (p. 9)
>
> *Madhyānta-Vibhānga*

In his translation of the *Madhyānta-Vibhānga*, Stcherbatsky renders Vasubandhu's explanation of this statement as follows:

> This means – the Mind (itself, i.e. pure sensation) apprehends the Thing alone, (i.e., the Thing-in-Itself, the pure object). The mental

phenomena, such as e.g. feelings (pleasant and unpleasant) etc., apprehend its qualities, (i.e. the qualities of the Thing, pleasant or unpleasant)... (Vasubandhu says) 'among them the Mind apprehends the Thing alone.' Here the word 'alone' serves to exclude (every kind) of definiteness.[428]

In other words, mind is awareness of what Guenther calls 'facticity': awareness of the unique specificity of an object or, more simply, awareness that it is there. This does not include an awareness of any qualities as such, even qualities that differentiate that thing from other things. All this comes under the heading of mental events. As defined here, mind is a general, even vague, awareness. But it is vague only in cognitive terms. Though it does not assign the object to any particular class, it has a clear, direct apprehension of the object as being there;[429] it is a clear perception without conceptualization. It is almost as though one has an instant, a bare instant, of pure awareness before the mind starts to function with respect to what one perceives.

Just occasionally one becomes aware of a slight extension of that bare instant. For example, sometimes first thing in the morning when one wakes up, mental events can be quite slow to arise, and in the meantime one perceives without interpreting for a minute or two before mental events start coming into operation. In the usual course of things we swiftly move away from this experience, but it can be developed. In meditation one may move *towards* this quality of almost pure perception, which would seem to show that the potentiality of an experience of pure mind is already there, already functioning, if only in a very minor way.

2. Mental Events

An object having been apprehended, the mind tends to become involved with it in certain specific ways. It is interested in it or otherwise; it likes it or dislikes it, accepts it or rejects it; it is pleased or angered by it; it compares it with other things – and so on. These specific ways in which the mind becomes involved with an object are called in Pāli *cetasikas*, which means 'connected with mind', and in Sanskrit *caitta-dharmas*, 'that which pertains to mind': i.e. 'mental events' or 'mental concomitants'.

If I look at and become aware of a person, this is mind. But if I then start thinking, say, 'He's a bit taller than that other fellow' or 'I don't like the look of him,' these are mental events. It's possible, of course, for more than one mental event to be present at the same time; there can be whole complexes of them. Indeed, as we shall see, there are five mental events that are 'omnipresent'. Mental events arise as one engages oneself with the object more specifically and begins to apprehend or cognize its distinguishing qualities.

Mind and Mental Events Together and Apart[430]

One may wonder, though, how this interpretation of one's experience, this idea of a kind of hiatus between mind and mental events, squares with Yeshe Gyaltsen's next quotation, which appears authoritatively to contradict it:

> The mind and mental events are certainly together. (p. 10)
> *Abhidharmakośa*

I have suggested that it is possible for there to be awareness of an object without mental events coming into play. This does not, however, appear to be the conclusion we are being offered here. These two statements can be reconciled by the introduction of a third term: 'mind-as-such'. But why do we need this? Why can't we just say that mind is sometimes associated with mental events and sometimes not? The simple answer is that while one can have mind without mental events, one cannot have mental events without mind; and the mind one gets with mental events is different from the mind without them.

It's as though when mental events cease, mind in the sense of the consciousness that accompanies mental events also ceases. What one is left with then is 'mind as such'. If mind and mental events were twins, when one twin disappeared, the remaining twin would no longer be a twin. If mental events cease to exist – or have not yet arisen – mind is no longer the same; it 'becomes' or 'is replaced by' 'mind-as-such'.[431]

Yeshe Gyaltsen goes a little further than the *Abhidharmakośa*, saying that 'mind and mental events arise together, as far as time is concerned, and are of one and the same stuff'.[432] To say that mind and mental events are of the same stuff is to say rather more than that they are certainly together. Vasubandhu probably didn't feel that it was necessary to go as far as that. It is enough to assert that – because they are concerned with the same object at the same time – mind and mental events are certainly together.

For a further perspective on this, we can look to Dr Guenther's introductory notes to the text. Here Guenther suggests that the relationship between mind and mental events is like that between a father and his sons. The sons have a 'symmetrical' relationship to each other, whereas their relationship with their father is 'asymmetrical'. That is, if David is John's brother, then John is David's brother – the relationship is symmetrical. But if Peter is James's father, it does not follow that James is Peter's father; in that case the relationship is asymmetrical. So the mental events or concomitants stand in a symmetrical relationship to one another, because they all pertain to one and the same mind, but they all stand in an asymmetrical relationship to mind itself.[433]

It would be a mistake to gather from this, however, a notion of mind as a sort of stable centre or ego around which mental events come and go. It's not that first of all you get mind in its pristine glory and then mental events come along. Mind – in the sense in which the term is being used here – and mental events arise together. Generally speaking, in the instant one perceives an object the mental concomitants are there. In this sense the mind itself is a mental event – an elder brother, if you like, rather than a father. The 'father' is not mind but what Guenther calls the 'x-factor', in relation to which mind and mental events stand in a symmetrical relationship between themselves.The x-factor is 'mind-as-such', or mind as pure fact; this is the point of reference for both mind and mental events. If 'mind as such' can be represented by the image of a lake without any ripples, the ripples that arise can be said to have two sides to them (mind and mental events) which necessarily arise and cease at the same time.

So although we naturally tend to think of mental events as arriving subsequent to a kind of constantly present mind, in fact there is no real difference between mind and mental events: they simply perform different functions within the process of subject–object interaction. Mind can just as well be spoken of as itself a mental event. Following the Yogācāra's relational approach, we may even question whether mind exists at all. We may indeed ask this about all the terms we are using. 'Mind' and 'mental events' are useful ways of describing the process we experience, but they are not to be taken as a fixed and final description.

DESCRIBING THE INDESCRIBABLE

Mind, in short, cannot really be described at all, and to try to do so is to falsify it. Nonetheless, in trying to describe it we at least have a means of coming to an understanding of its true nature. The term 'mind-as-such' is metaphysical or epistemological rather than psychological, referring to mind as undescribed and thus unfalsified. We could therefore regard 'mind-as-such' or 'mind as pure fact' as an 'operational concept' that guards against our mistaking mind for some permanent and unchanging ego. It is the existence, so to speak, of 'mind as pure fact' which prevents us from absolutizing 'mind as described fact', i.e. taking it too literally. As nothing may be said about 'mind as pure fact', what we talk about when we speak of mind is termed by Guenther 'described fact', and 'described fact' is no more than our falsifying attempt to describe 'mind as pure fact'.[434]

To go with 'pure fact' and 'described fact', we have *vidyā*, or wisdom, and *avidyā*, or ignorance. *Vidyā*, which Guenther translates as 'pure awareness' or 'appreciative discrimination', is what perceives 'pure fact'; it is as though wisdom is 'mind as pure fact' in action. *Avidyā*, or 'absence of pure awareness' (usually translated as 'ignorance'), is what perceives 'described fact'. As ignorance is classified among the mental events, or concomitants, then mind itself, in a state of ignorance or lack of awareness, is also a mental concomitant.

Indeed, to take this very complex matter to its conclusion, the fact that we distinguish between mind and mental events at all is an instance of that ignorance which is itself a mental event. So the distinction between mind and mental events is not an absolute distinction, but an operational concept. One can't chop reality into mutually exclusive little bits and then put them together again to get at the truth. The only way to get at the truth is to stop cutting reality into little bits altogether.

DON'T TAKE IT LITERALLY

But wasn't the whole method of the Abhidharmikas to chop reality into bits in just this way? We have to be careful – and one could perhaps say that the Abhidharmikas themselves weren't ultimately quite careful enough about this – not to take this whole question of analysis too literally. Is it really possible to divide one part of a thing from the others, or is the division only notional? You can divide your nose from the rest of your face, but where does your nose end and the rest of your face begin? Is there an actual point? And if not, is not the division of the nose from the face arbitrary, at least to some extent? Or take time: we divide time into minutes, but is time really divided at all, let alone into minutes?

If you divide things, there is always a problem of how to put them together again. One can't help making these divisions for practical purposes, but it is dangerous to take those divisions as actually corresponding to realities. It is the mind that chops things up into bits; but reality does not consist of bits strung together. At the same time, we can't say that things are completely continuous, because we do see, if not differences, at least corrugations, so to speak, in reality. All we can do is use these concepts of continuity and being made up of parts appropriately.

From this perspective we may view the Abhidharma simply as playing with operational concepts for a certain practical purpose. It's an example of what the Tantrics call 'using dirt to get rid of dirt'.[435] It is the mental concomitant of 'lack of pure awareness'[436] that makes the distinction between mind and mental events; but by making this distinction, we can classify and sort out skilful mental events from unskilful ones. Living our spiritual life on that basis, we eventually go beyond unskilful mental events. Then we go beyond skilful mental events as well, and finally we go beyond the distinction between mind and mental events altogether.

PRACTICE IN PLACE OF THEORY

It is highly questionable whether the Abhidharmikas themselves would have looked at what they were doing in quite this way. Guenther, who looks at things very much from the Nyingma point of view, is at pains to point out that we have the Nyingma philosophers to thank for this perspective, for making a living experience of the Abhidharma tradition.[437] One might say that this perspective takes us a bit beyond the Abhidharma proper, but if it does, it does so quite justifiably.

Through spiritual practice, particularly with the development of *dhyāna* – *dhyāna* being a state of higher consciousness reached through the practice of meditation – the mental events become purer and fewer, until eventually, when one enters the realms of the *arūpa* or 'formless' *dhyānas*, one is left with the singleness of mind without any defilements whatsoever. This mind is not pure in the sense that the mental concomitants have dropped away. It is more that they have been absorbed and fully integrated. All the energy that had been bound up in those mental concomitants passes into mind itself, which remains as the pure perceiver. Nothing has been lost: it is a singleness of richness rather than poverty.

This singleness is reflected in the experience of the four *arūpa dhyānas*. When one enters the first of them, the sphere of infinite space, it is not as if one perceives an object 'out there' called space. It's more that mind proceeds without resistance or impediment. The usual interpretation of the second *arūpa dhyāna*, the sphere of infinite consciousness, is that in order to traverse infinite space, mind must itself be infinite. But it is perhaps more accurate to say that in this state of consciousness one becomes aware of the infinite range of the mind's activity. With the third *arūpa dhyāna* one begins to doubt whether there is an object at all, and also, therefore, whether there is, in a sense, a subject either. In this way one enters the sphere of 'no-thing-ness'. Finally, the sphere of neither perception nor non-perception carries this process a stage further. This is the 'highest worldly attainment' of the path of practice. One can enter the path of vision from any of the *dhyānas*, but the higher the *dhyāna*, the more concentrated energy there is behind the penetration that leads to vision.

HOW MIND AND MENTAL EVENTS GO TOGETHER

As we have seen, it is in the nature of mind to have attendant mental events. The Abhidharma, as one might expect, goes into the specifics of this relationship, and it does so by enumerating five 'functional co-relations', as Guenther rather awkwardly translates them (Hopkins gives 'five similarities' or 'five samenesses').[438] Correspondingly, it is in the nature of mental events to arise in conjunction with mind – and again, this happens through the five functional co-relations. According to the *Abhidharmakośa* they are: 'alike basis, alike objective reference, alike observable quality, alike time, [and] alike stuff'.[439]

So firstly, 'alike basis'. To understand this, we have to recollect the idea that in Buddhism mind is regarded as one of the six senses – the others being, of course, taste, touch, smell, sight, and hearing. The six sense faculties (which include mind) are the means by which mind perceives; there is no sense perception without a perceiving mind. The sense faculties therefore depend upon the mind in the same way as do mental events. Hence there is a common basis – an alike basis – for the senses (including the mind considered as a sense) and the mental events.

'Alike objective reference' means that mind and mental events refer to the same objects. 'Alike observable quality' refers to the fact that when mind is aware of the existence of a blue object, say, the mental events are concerned with the specific qualities of that same blue object. 'Alike time' means that mind and mental events refer to objects simultaneously.

As for 'alike stuff', this functional co-relation emphasizes that the mind which is associated with mental events is never pure mind. It bears a residue from previous situations (whether remembered or forgotten), a residue that has not exhausted itself within those situations, and which therefore goes on looking for a new situation into which it can project itself. Guenther helps to make this clearer by translating mind in this context as 'mental attitude'. It is this aspect of mind that the Theravāda school addresses in its enumeration of the eighty-nine *cittas*, the states or moods of the one original, pure *citta*.[440]

This perspective of the Theravādins helps to make sense of 'alike stuff'. If one perceives something with anger, for instance, then all the mental events that arise in that situation will also be imbued with anger (as it were). That is, if one looks at someone with anger, various mental events will arise – 'How ugly, how stupid, how unpleasant he is' – which will be of the same nature or 'stuff' (not a happy expression, this). Just as the object is coloured by mind, it is coloured more specifically by the mental events or functions. This goes for complexes of emotions as well: if the mind is one of mixed feelings, then the mental events will be of mixed feelings too. However, whereas the Theravāda focuses on the different forms in which mind appears – whether it be as mind-with-anger, mind-with-craving, or mind-of-the-plane-of-form, or even mind-of-the-formless-plane – the Sarvāstivāda and Yogācāra schools are more concerned with the oneness of mind.

The author of the *Abhidharmasamuccaya*, Asaṅga, comes up with a slightly different list of functional co-relations, replacing 'alike basis' with 'alike spheres and levels'.[441] 'Alike spheres and levels' refers to the possibility in meditation of moving into higher realms that are qualitatively different from everyday experience. If one's mind is dwelling in one realm, mental events proper to a different realm cannot also be present. When one is in a state of meditative absorption, say – and thus dwelling in the *rūpadhātu* (world of form) or the *arūpadhātu* (world of no-form) – then certain kinds of mental events like anger or craving will simply not arise. They can only arise in connection with an angry or craving mind, and the moment an angry or craving mind develops one falls back into the *kāmadhātu* (world of desire).

This is not to say that an unpleasant experience may not arise from time to time even in higher states of consciousness. Such an experience may constitute *karma-vipāka* – that is, it may be the result of the karma of, say, anger in the past. But if one does not react to that experience, not experiencing further anger in consequence of that unpleasant experience, and therefore not setting up fresh karma, then one's sphere or level of consciousness is unaffected by it.

REALMS OF EXPERIENCE

This discussion of spheres and realms plunges us into an area of Buddhist thought that so far we have encountered only briefly. The notion of different realms of experience or existence is one that can be taken literally, metaphorically, or even psychologically. For a literal depiction we can look again at the Tibetan wheel of life, which illustrates six different realms: the human realm, the animal realm, the realm of the gods, the realm of the warlike titans or *asuras*, the hell realm, and the realm of what are called hungry ghosts (*pretas*).

Buddhist cosmology envisages these realms as actually existing, and encompasses the possibility that one might be reborn in any one of them. One can equally think of the realms as symbolizing different mental states, our inner states being reflected in our experience of the external world – so that, for example, if we are very angry or miserable, the world seems a hellish place, while if our experience is refined and blissful, that will be reflected in an experience of the world that is similarly pleasurable and beautiful. As Milton's Satan says in *Paradise Lost*, 'The mind is its own place, and in itself / Can make a heaven of hell, a hell of heaven.'[442]

As the depiction of the realms in the wheel of life suggests, held as it is in the grip of the devouring monster called Time, these realms are not permanent. There are no such things as eternal damnation or everlasting paradise in the Buddhist scheme of things. Our birth into a realm is the result of our past karma, and our life in that particular realm will last only until that *karma-vipāka* is exhausted.

Another traditional classification of realms is threefold: the *kāmaloka* or *kāmadhātu*, the realm of sensuous experience or desire; the *rūpaloka* or *rūpadhātu*, the realm of (archetypal) form; and the *arūpaloka* or *arūpadhātu*, the 'formless' realm or sphere. The *kāmaloka* is the world of our ordinary experience; the *rūpaloka* and *arūpaloka*, which in Buddhist tradition are called 'god realms', relate to the experience of higher states of consciousness. So there is a correlation between this idea of realms and meditative experience; again, the connection is through mental states. We will go into this more in the next chapter when we consider the mental event termed 'feeling-tone'.

Returning to the two differing lists of functional co-relations between mind and mental events, it may seem as if Asaṅga's 'alike spheres and levels' amounts to something very different from the functional co-relation it displaces, 'alike basis'. However, I would suggest that they are, in fact, the same thing. What we have with the different spheres and levels are different levels of sense perception. On the level of the *kāmaloka* the physical senses come into play; in the *rūpaloka* it is the subtle senses; while in the *arūpaloka* there are, in a way, no senses at all. So 'alike basis' and 'alike spheres and levels' represent, perhaps, just different ways of looking at the same thing.

MIND AS ACTIVITY

So far, the main thing we have gathered is that 'mind' in Buddhism is not a term for a thing, an entity, but a relational term. Mind is a relationship with an object, an awareness that an object is there and that this object is a particular object. So mind or *citta* is not a passive registering or mirroring of things; it is a reaching out, as it were. This is one of the key insights of the Abhidharma.

Now, having set out the distinction between mind and mental events, Yeshe Gyaltsen goes on to reflect further on the nature of mind. He begins with three definitions of perception from the Mahāyāna tradition:

What is perception? It is a distinct awareness of what is before the mind.

Pañcaskandhaprakaraṇa

Perception is a process of singling out.

Abhidharmakośa

The individualizing perception by means of being aware of the mere factual presence of an object is the defining characteristic of the mind. (p. 14)

rGyal-tshab

rGyal-tshab's 'individualizing perception' is a perception that singles out a particular object – *this* man, say, rather than man in general.[443] So the term mind here is not used with regard to just a general awareness of things – to what psychologists call 'breadth of field awareness'. It refers to the process of singling out, when one's attention focuses on to just one thing.

It's as though when we perceive things in general we are in some sense passive, and what we register in this way is *vipāka*. We are born with senses as a result of karma, and the sense organs themselves are therefore *vipākas*, as are the experiences conveyed by those sense organs in the form of general perceptions. The general field of potential sense-objects that surrounds us at any given moment – our world – represents the fruit of previous karma. But once one starts singling out (and this is a conclusion of my own, not one to be found in the Abhidharma as far as I know) then some kind of motivation necessarily comes into play. This is the first stirring, as it were, of fresh karma.

So here again we see that mind is an activity. The mind that is associated with mental events is not a passive, mirror-like reflection of what is there. It is not, as the English philosopher John Locke has it, a *tabula rasa*, a blank wax tablet upon which objects of perception impress themselves. It is never like this; there is always a bit of movement here and there until our attention is seized by a particular object.

It is the adverting of the mind to a particular object that leads directly to what the Theravāda terms the *javana*,[444] the stage of volition; and it is at the *javana* stage of the perceptual process that karma is produced. Every process of perception includes these two elements: a stage of turning towards a particular object and, in dependence upon this, the *javana* at which volition or karma enters in. Where that singling out process ends and karma proper (in the sense of *javana*) begins it would be hard to say.

MENTAL EVENTS: TOOLS FOR PRACTICE

> They are whatever correspond to the mind. (p. 18)
> *Pañcaskandhaprakaraṇa*[445]

So mental events are whatever are in accordance with the general nature of the mind. In a way, they share that general nature. As the mind is, so are the mental events.

No list of mental events can be exhaustive; nor are the boundary lines between them always fixed. Any classification of them is solely to provide a tool for spiritual practice, allowing one to give provisional labels to one's experience, and thereby enabling oneself to transform one's life. This needs constantly to be borne in mind. As we have seen, the Sarvāstivādins number 46 mental events, while the Theravādins distinguish 52; but the Yogācārins, whose classification we will be following here, identify 51 different mental events, divided into six categories: five omnipresent mental events, five object-determining mental events, eleven positive mental events, six basic emotions (primary negative mental events), twenty proximate emotions (secondary negative mental events), and four variable mental events.[446] It is with the nature of these mental events that the second part of our commentary will be concerned. I will be referring to them according to Guenther's translations from the Tibetan, as well as adding alternative translations where appropriate. I will use the Sanskrit terms, not the Tibetan as in Guenther's text, simply because the main authority the Tibetan author cites for his definition of each mental event is Asaṅga's *Abhidharmasamuccaya*, which is written in Sanskrit.

5
THE PERCEPTUAL SITUATION

Loosely speaking, in every situation in which mind not only perceives an object but, as it were, moves towards it, five mental events are present. To be more accurate, one could say that the presence of the five omnipresent (*sarvatraga*) mental events is implicit in the very definition of what it means to experience an object. It's not that when one experiences an object these mental events are present. It's the other way round; when these mental events are present, one is experiencing an object.

We must go further: it cannot be asserted that there is an object there at all, nor a subject (oneself) to perceive it. All we can say is that a sort of network of these five mental events constitutes a perceptual situation within which there is a subjective content and an objective content. This is the case at all mundane levels of experience, including the higher states of *dhyāna*.

The five omnipresent mental events are: feeling (*vedanā*), recognition or identification (*saṃjñā*), directionality of mind (*cetanā*), contact (*spārśa*), and what Guenther calls 'egocentric demanding' (*manaskāra*), also translated as 'mental engagement' or 'attention'. So there is some overlap between the Abhidharma's analysis and earlier Buddhist classifications. Well, given that the entire Buddhist tradition is in agreement that the whole of mundane, compounded existence can be analysed into the five *skandhas*, there would have to be some correspondences.

From the Abhidharma's perspective, *rūpa* (form) is the objective content of the perceptual situation, which would leave the other four *skandhas* as constituting its subjective content. *Vijñāna* (consciousness), as we have seen, corresponds to mind; the illustration for the five *skandhas* on the Tibetan wheel of life is a boat with four passengers, one of whom – representing *vijñāna* – is steering.[447]

Among the omnipresent mental events we encounter two more of the five *skandhas*: *vedanā* (feeling) and *saṃjñā* (recognition), as well as *cetanā* (directionality of mind), which is roughly synonymous with *saṃskāra* (volition), the fifth *skandha*. To add to these three omnipresent mental events we have *spārśa* (contact), which also features as one of the twelve links of the wheel of life, and *manaskāra* ('egocentric demanding').

We shall now address each of the five omnipresent mental events in turn.

1. FEELING-TONE (*VEDANĀ*)

The Results of Action

Yeshe Gyaltsen begins his discussion of 'feeling-tone' with a quotation from the *Abhidharmasamuccaya*:

> What is the absolutely specific characteristic of feeling? It is to experience. That is to say, in any experience, what we experience is the individual maturation of any positive or negative action as its final result. (p. 19)

The second part of this description indicates that *vedanā* is the feeling-tone of our experience of *vipāka*, which is what we experience as the result of karma. That is, whatever one experiences, pleasant, painful, or neutral, represents – directly or indirectly – the maturation or result of skilful or unskilful action, whether of body, speech, or mind. In short, *vedanā* constitutes the final result of action.

The first part of the *Abhidharmasamuccaya*'s definition of *vedanā* is less helpful; 'It is to experience' is something of a tautology. But is it really possible to define feeling? We all know what feeling (as distinct from thought) is, but it would be impossible to communicate what feeling is like to someone who had never experienced it. Feeling cannot be described in terms of something else.

Conceptual terms can be used to communicate feelings in the sense that one can use concepts to indicate to someone something in their experience which is analogous to something one has experienced oneself. But it is impossible to communicate the feeling itself. My feeling is mine and your feeling is yours. All one can say is that one experiences the same *kind* of feeling that someone else experiences. If you stick a pin in yourself you feel something and perhaps you say 'ouch'; if you stick a pin into someone else and they make the sort of sound you made, you can infer that they have had a feeling of the kind that you had. You don't directly perceive their feeling, nor do they directly perceive yours.

Feelings and Emotions

It is important to distinguish feeling from emotion, though of course they are connected. One could say that feeling is the raw material out of which emotion is produced. The seventeenth-century Dutch philosopher Spinoza discusses this. If one has a feeling of pleasure, he says, and that feeling is accompanied by the idea of the external cause of the pleasure, then one feels an emotion of love towards the cause of that pleasure. If one has a feeling of pain and that feeling is accompanied by the idea of the cause of that pain, then one feels hatred towards the cause of the pain.[448]

The point to be emphasized with regard to emotions is that they are not produced automatically. We actively manufacture them out of the raw material of our feelings; they are actions of mind. If one has a painful experience, one can choose whether or not to manufacture hatred out of it. And if one chooses to do so, one has performed another unskilful karma which will make one liable to further painful sensations in the future.

As well as being one of the five *skandhas*, *vedanā* is one of the links of the chain of conditionality that binds us to the wheel of life from one life to the next. The crucial link or *nidāna*, the one that keeps the whole cycle of birth and death going, is the one following *vedanā*: *tṛṣṇā* or 'craving'. While *vedanā* is something that happens to us, *tṛṣṇā* is something we do. We are presented with feelings, but what we do with those feelings – whether we manufacture positive emotions or negative ones out of them – is our own choice. Feeling is passive, but emotion (as the word itself suggests) is active.

It is the possibility of responding creatively to our experience that gives us the opportunity of coming off the wheel of life. For example, in the meditation practice called the *mettā bhāvanā*, one develops a response of loving-kindness towards oneself and towards a good friend, and one then brings that naturally positive response to bear upon someone one ordinarily has little regard for, either positive or negative. In this way one starts to shift one's habitual reaction to other people in a more positive direction. One begins to develop genuine *mettā*, a response of warmth and care which is not simply the product of attachment.

When the mind is sufficiently imbued with *mettā*, even when one introduces the thought of someone one dislikes, this thought will not be unpleasant, even though it would normally give rise to an unpleasant feeling and therefore to hatred. So one can then proceed at least comparatively easily to develop *mettā* even towards this person. Eventually, when one attains real insight into the true nature of things, it becomes impossible for an unskilful mental state to arise in dependence upon a painful feeling.

Feeling is a conditioned phenomenon. It arises in dependence upon conditions and disappears when those conditions are removed. This has the important corollary that we can create or abrogate our own feelings by manipulating our impressions. If, for example, one feels depressed, one may know from experience that a day in the country will put one in a much more positive mood, that pleasurable feelings will arise in dependence upon some space and fresh air. So our feelings are to some extent under our control.

However, the feelings that arise as a direct result of karma are not altogether under our control. Unless circumstances are such that we are able to produce a counteractive karma we may simply have to bear that particular *vipāka*. If one takes adequate measures to change the circumstances that appear to be giving rise to one's discomfort and those measures fail to work, it may make sense to conclude that a particular unpleasant feeling is a direct result of karma.

Feeling is classified in several different ways: according to whether it is pleasant, unpleasant, or indifferent; according to whether it is a physical or a mental feeling; according to whether it is subjectivistic or transpersonal; according to which sense organ is involved; and, finally, according to whether it sustains attachment to or disentanglement from mundane existence.

Likes and Dislikes

First, Yeshe Gyaltsen tackles the question of pleasant, unpleasant, and indifferent feelings:

> 'Pleasant' is that which one would like to feel again (when the original feeling is over). 'Unpleasant' is what one would like to get rid of when it is present. 'Indifferent' is where neither of these two desires occur. (p. 20)
>
> *Pañcaskandhaprakaraṇa*

Striking as this statement is, things are not, of course, as simple as this. The myriad degrees of pleasure (*sukha*) and pain (*duḥkha*) we are subject to elicit more than just commensurate degrees of one and the same response. Different degrees of pleasant feelings elicit responses that range from 'Wouldn't it be nice if that happened again' to 'Let me make sure that happens again as soon as possible' and even to 'I must have another of these right now even though I haven't finished the first one yet.'

However, it is true that by and large the desire to repeat a pleasant experience takes place after the event whereas with unpleasant feelings there is generally no question of waiting until the unpleasant feeling is over and then thinking, 'Well, I wouldn't want that to happen again': one wants to be rid of it as soon as it starts. But again, our response to unpleasant experiences is not quite as straightforward as this. There are experiences that may be more troublesome to get rid of than to endure, so that one doesn't really think of getting rid of them (in which case, although they might feel unpleasant, they count as 'indifferent feelings' according to the criteria employed here); and at the other end of the scale there are feelings that are so unpleasant that, in order to be rid of them, one is prepared to put up with a lot of other disagreeable feelings – which again would have to be classed here as indifferent feelings.

Of course, in the end we want to be rid even of pleasant feelings. The physical organism has its limitations. If one has had a good meal, for example, one doesn't want to repeat the experience immediately. At more refined levels of sense experience, including some states of meditative concentration, one can sustain pleasant feelings for longer: one can perhaps enjoy listening to music, for example, for hours at a time. But a pleasant experience, at whatever level of refinement, if prolonged to the point where the psychophysical organism can no longer sustain it (if only because it needs to sleep), will gradually diminish in intensity and may even turn into an unpleasant experience.

This can also happen the other way round: one can get used to some unpleasant experiences to the point that one feels quite indifferent to them. Not just indifferent: with acquired tastes – tea, wine, modern art, and unfamiliar music, for example – very unpleasant experiences can subsequently change into very pleasant ones. Even extreme pain does not stay the same, and may, in some circumstances, change into pleasure. And in some very stressful situations, one can experience such a rapid alternation of pain and pleasure that it is hard to know which is which. People who have experienced the break-up of a sexual relationship sometimes say that there is an intense sense of loss, but at the same time there is an equally intense sense of relief at being free of all the insecurity and conflicts that the relationship entailed. In some circumstances at least, it is as if one is a switch flicking madly back and forth, from joy to sorrow and back again in a moment. At such times it is possible to see that pleasure and pain are, in a sense, the same thing. A change in attitude, and the one becomes the other. The switch is oneself and the flick is the change of attitude.

The Pursuit of Pleasure

So pleasure and pain are both in the end rather elusive. Pleasure is here defined as that which one wants to feel again, and it is that very wanting to feel it again which changes the pleasure into pain. As far as we are concerned, the problem usually seems to be how to get hold of whatever it is that provides the pleasant feeling, but it isn't really. But – as we realize if we examine our experience closely – it is wanting to get hold of the pleasure in the first place that starts to vitiate the very pleasure we crave. The more we grasp hold of pleasure, the more we find that what we are holding on to is pain. The solution to the paradox is to let go of pleasure as it comes to you:

> He who binds to himself a joy
> Does the wingèd life destroy
> But he who kisses the joy as it flies
> Lives in Eternity's sunrise.[449]

The ancient Greek philosopher Epicurus maintained that the pursuit of pleasure was the only rational purpose in life – in his conception, the highest pleasures being those of the mind: art, friendship, conversation, and so on.[450] It seems quite an attractive idea, but it doesn't work, because one becomes subject to the law of diminishing returns. If one devotes oneself to pleasure one ends up with nothing to enjoy, because in the end pleasure is really a by-product of something else. Certain things give us pleasure, but it is self-defeating to get involved in situations simply on account of the pleasure – even the refined pleasure – that they give us, regardless of any other value or interest they may have. The world may provide all sorts of conditions and supports for the attainment of satisfaction of one kind and another, but the real source of satisfaction is within oneself. Our own happiness depends on our overall attitude towards things, and what we ourselves do.

With awareness it is possible to enjoy pleasant feelings without allowing craving to arise. If one is sufficiently mindful while, say, eating good food, so that the pleasant feeling does not give rise to a desire to repeat that experience, then one will not be creating fresh karma. So being mindful does not involve starving out pleasure. It *is* possible, if one is mindful enough, to enjoy an experience without wanting it to continue or be repeated. Clearly one is on a knife-edge here and one has to find one's balance as one may – but becoming non-attached certainly does not mean losing one's feelings.

Feeling is, after all, an omnipresent mental event. If one is going to experience anything at all, there has to be feeling of some kind in that experience. And a certain amount of pleasure acts as a tonic for the system. One can enjoy the pleasure of the sunshine, the atmosphere of the early morning, or a walk in the forest, and feel a sense of openness, expansion, and liberation that goes beyond pleasure, in the ordinary sense at least. But one shouldn't just be trying to squeeze pleasure out of the situation; that would be counter-productive. Experience teaches us to keep mindfully aloof from situations in which pleasure is sooner or later connected with painful or unskilful mental states.

With pain, the same thing applies in reverse: the desire to be rid of pain actually contributes to it. If one is mindful of this fact, developing sufficient equanimity so that one no longer contributes to the pain in this way, one is also no longer creating karma (which doesn't necessarily mean that the pain goes away).

Indifference

As for indifferent or neutral feelings, there is the possibility of some confusion here. The word being translated as 'indifferent' or 'neutral' is *upekṣā*, but *upekṣā* has a variety of meanings. The same word is used to describe the culminating phase of the seven factors of Enlightenment, in which context it can be translated as 'non-attachment', 'equanimity', or even 'the higher indifference'; and we will also be discussing *upekṣā* as a positive mental event (see p. 582 below), in which context it is considered as a factor of meditation.

There is a great difference between *upekṣā* as an aspect of the feeling-tone that accompanies sense experience[451] and *upekṣā* as a factor of Enlightenment or a positive mental event. Indifference is a sense experience that is neither particularly pleasant nor particularly unpleasant, that one is bothered neither to prolong nor to get rid of. With *upekṣā* in the more positive sense, one is likewise concerned neither to prolong nor to get rid of the feelings one experiences, but this is not because the feelings themselves are neither pleasant nor unpleasant. That kind of *upekṣā* is not determined by sense experience at all. Pleasure and pain, however intense, do not impinge upon it.

Furthermore, it is not arrived at by getting rid of all pleasant and painful feelings. In fact, it arises out of the development of pleasant feeling – or rather, it arises as the culmination of the conscious development of positive emotion that has pleasant feeling as its fruit. *Upekṣā* in this sense is mind poised in a collected and deeply happy state that is unaffected by pleasure and pain. As a positive mental event it represents the full development of positive emotion, a deep emotional stability that is connected with the development of the fourth *dhyāna*. As the culminating factor of the seven factors of Enlightenment, one could even say that it is synonymous with Enlightenment itself.

What Indifference is Not

This is not, obviously, what is meant by *upekṣā* as a kind of feeling-tone. It is important to be clear on this point; indeed, perhaps the most useful thing to be said about this third category of *vedanā* is that it represents the sort of feelings which can easily be misidentified in various ways. Whether one can in fact classify indifferent or neutral feelings as a properly separate category on a par with pleasant feelings and painful feelings is of course questionable. All experience, all thought, is feeling-toned, even emotionally-toned. If pleasant feelings are those one wants to have repeated and unpleasant feelings are those one wants to be rid of, then a third category has to be introduced to represent feelings that fail to elicit either of these responses. But this suggests that indifferent feelings are either simply not intense enough to qualify as pleasant or unpleasant, or else consist in a rather complicated mix of pleasure and pain so that the two feelings cancel each other out and leave one at an emotional standstill. This kind of state is certainly not to be thought of as non-attachment – although it often is.

Another class of indifferent feeling that can be confused with non-attachment could be termed 'alienation'. This is a superficial, even superimposed, indifference where one doesn't allow oneself fully to experience a strong feeling or emotion because it doesn't fit in with the idea one has of oneself. If one were to acknowledge that one experienced such a feeling, one might have to acknowledge also that one was, for example, not as spiritually developed as one would like to think. So the kind of feeling that does not go with one's ideal picture of oneself gets locked away, and because this happens unconsciously, the energy caught up in that feeling gets locked away as well. Alienation from feeling and emotion is thus also alienation from energy. Though it is not an obviously strong feeling it is, in a way, much more dreadful than straightforwardly unpleasant feelings. The unpleasant or unacceptable feeling has not gone away; it is still there and still wielding its influence, but – being unconscious of its real nature – one is unable to do anything about it.

Physical and Mental Feeling

These three categories of feeling (pleasant, unpleasant, and indifferent) are further divided in terms of whether they are physical or mental. As far as physical feelings are concerned, Yeshe Gyaltsen chooses to illustrate the operation of the visual faculty, and by extension all the other physical sense faculties, with a quotation from Āryadeva's *Catuḥśataka* which offers an analogy with the faculty of touch:

> Darkness is everywhere just as the skin covers the whole body.
> (p. 21)

We inhabit a realm of sense perception called the skin, within which we experience particular physical feelings pertaining to the sense of touch when we come into contact with objects impinging on that particular realm of sense perception. Similarly, the realm of eye perception is the whole visual field; and a physical feeling pertaining to the sense of sight is whatever is experienced visually with regard to any object within that visual field. Āryadeva's usage of 'darkness' is somewhat obscure, but we can perhaps take it to mean the potential for light and visibility. 'Darkness is everywhere' in the sense that we are surrounded by a seamless visual field like a skin, which extends wherever the eye perceives. A visual feeling can presumably relate to the whole of this visual field or to any part of it.

Visual consciousness arises in dependence on the interaction of subject with object, of eye with visual form. This meeting of subject and object provides the field of operations, so to speak, where physical feeling takes place, whether that feeling be touch, sight, sound, smell, or taste. It is a particularly positive way of regarding our physical and sensory interaction with the world because it proposes not so much that objects are 'out there' as that we ourselves are 'out there'. The suggestion is that we need not think of our experience as wholly taking place within our fleshly envelope, that we have other, different kinds of sensory 'skin', so to speak. This enables us to realize a closer involvement with the objective world, carrying our experience of our subjective world beyond the crude confines of the flesh. It helps us to see that what we think of as object is, in fact, subject, or at least an extension of what we think of as subject. In short, it helps to break down the hard and fast distinction we maintain between subject and object.

Another Kind of Feeling

Feelings may further be categorized as being either subjectivistic or transpersonal. This classification distinguishes between what we are all able to recognize as feeling, and a kind of feeling which is outside commonly accepted notions of what feelings are. 'Transpersonal' feelings do not include a sense of possession; they are not felt as one's own because they are felt where there is no idea of a fixed, unchanging self. They are in some way equivalent to 'mind-as-such', the suggestion being that 'mind-as-such' has a sort of feeling-tone or feeling value. In other words, there can apparently be feelings without there being anyone around whose feelings they are.

But can we relate this to anything in our own experience? It's rather like picking up the atmosphere of a place, where one feels something that is not one's own, making contact with feelings that one has not produced oneself. But the idea of transpersonal feelings goes further than this. Perhaps one could say that one gets a sense of it in the *mettā bhāvanā* meditation practice, the development of loving-kindness. In the final stage of this practice one develops – or rather, one makes contact with – an 'impersonal *mettā*', a positive emotion that one has not actually produced, that is not a personal feeling.[452] It's like a stream or current of something 'out there' which one is able to channel through oneself. This isn't quite the same as the profundity of feeling that accompanies 'mind as such', but perhaps it gives us a clue as to what is meant by 'transpersonal feeling'.

One might still wonder, though, what on earth a 'transpersonal' unpleasant feeling might be. This would be an unpleasant feeling experienced by an *arhant* or even a Buddha as a result of unskilful actions committed prior to attaining Enlightenment. It is possible to have quite different feelings occurring at different levels at the same time. One can, at the same time as one stubs one's toe or traps one's finger in the car door, be overjoyed by some other event. Physical pain does not necessarily preclude joy in the mind. But in the case of the *arhant* who experiences the inner bliss that arises out of being free from the delusion of an ego, any headache he experiences is also unconnected with an ego. It is just there: it could be anybody's headache. It certainly does not diminish that inner bliss.

Conversely – to take the Mahāyānist viewpoint – just as the *arhant*'s suffering is not experienced as his own personal suffering, so the bodhisattva experiences the suffering of the world as if it were his or her own suffering. Where there is no distinction between subject and object there is no distinction between one's own suffering and that of other people. At the same time, there is no diminution of the bodhisattva's own inner bliss. The result is, in Tennyson's words, 'painless sympathy with pain'.[453]

The important point to take from this particular classification of feeling is that from the spiritual point of view we are trying to realize the experience of non-self rather than the experience of pleasant feelings.

In a sense, the experience of non-self is pleasant – but only in a sense. One can have that experience of non-self around any combination of pleasant, unpleasant, and neutral feelings; it doesn't matter. Whether those feelings are one's own or other people's doesn't matter either. One will try to get rid of the unpleasant ones and cultivate the pleasant ones, but whether one succeeds or fails doesn't make any difference to one's fundamental experience of non-selfhood – which in another sense, or on another level, has a very refined positive feeling value of its own.

Attached or Disentangled?

Feeling is further classified according to which particular sense organ is involved in giving rise to the feeling by making contact with its object. In this context mind itself counts as a sense faculty (associated, of course, with mental feelings). Finally, feeling is classified according to whether it sustains attachment to, or disentanglement from, mundane experience.

Yeshe Gyaltsen terms these 'a sustaining feeling of addiction' and 'a sustaining feeling of realization'. He goes on to say:

> The sustaining feeling of addiction occurs on the level of desiring sensuous things of this world. The sustaining feeling of realization is to turn away from being addicted to these things and occurs on the level of ... the first meditative stage.
>
> This division into two kinds of feelings is made here for the purpose of knowing how the strength of feeling itself may ... bring to light an existing desire or bring about detachment from this addiction through ... meditative concentration. But if one wants to know this more deeply, one should look up the *Abhidharmakośa*, the *Abhidharmasamuccaya*, and also the *byang-chub lam-rim* in order to prevent the three feelings of pleasure, pain, and indifference from becoming the cause of the three poisons. (p. 22)

The three poisons are ignorance, craving, and hatred. In the iconography of the Tibetan wheel of life they are represented by the pig, the cock, and the snake which circle endlessly at the very hub of the wheel (see p. 477). These three poisons arise from feelings of indifference, pleasure, and pain when these feelings lead to an addictive response – that is, attachment – 'on the level of desiring sensuous things of this world'.

This 'level' is more literally a 'realm': it is the *kāmaloka*, the realm of sensuous desire, which is where we are when consciousness is functioning in the ordinary way. The *kāmaloka* is what we might call the objective correlative of the experience of sensuous desire, just as the *rūpaloka*, the realm of form (or of archetypal form, as it is sometimes translated), is the objective correlative of the meditative experience. The 'experience' and the 'realm' are the same thing seen from different perspectives – subjective or objective. Like the term Pure Land, the idea of a realm need not be taken in a purely literal sense, but neither can it be simply reduced to a subjective experience.

A feeling of addiction is what sustains our existence on the *kāmaloka*. And this addiction is not just to pleasant feelings; it is the *strength* of our feelings – whether of pleasure or pain or dull indifference – that sustains our attachment. We cannot enjoy something intensely, flinging ourselves ravenously at it and really wallowing in it, without feeling intense craving. We cannot wallow in our own pain without indulging a corresponding degree of hatred. And we cannot sink into dull indifference without sinking into ignorance.

However, strength of feeling does not necessarily reinforce attachment. Once the feeling exists, it can go in either of two directions. It can deepen our involvement in the *kāmaloka*, in which case it is 'a sustaining feeling of addiction'. On the other hand it can be led into the *rūpaloka*, in which case it is 'a sustaining feeling of realization'.

This category is introduced, as Yeshe Gyaltsen says, because a distinction needs to be drawn between a feeling that is associated with an experience of the *kāmaloka* and a feeling – which may not otherwise be any different – experienced by someone who is developing feelings appropriate to the *rūpaloka*. One can't really turn away from the grosser pleasures of the senses unless one has had some taste of the pleasures of meditative concentration. One can hold oneself off from sense pleasures by force of will as a disciplinary measure, but in the end one has to find something better; and until one has had some experience of meditative pleasure one doesn't have anything better (unless one finds it in the realm of aesthetic experience).

If one applies oneself to meditation, one will relish ordinary pleasant feelings less, at least as long as one can sustain some degree of meditative absorption. For example, one would experience a good meal as pleasant, but only at a certain level. In comparison with the pleasure of the *rūpaloka* it would, in a sense, not be a pleasure at all. Experienced in this way such a feeling would be a 'sustaining feeling of realization' rather than a 'sustaining feeling of addiction'.

2. RECOGNITION OR CONCEPTUALIZATION (*SAṂJÑĀ*)[454]

> It is to know by association. (p. 23)
>
> *Abhidharmasamuccaya*

Saṃjñā is the second omnipresent mental event. The term is often translated as 'perception', but in fact it refers to a certain phase within the process of perception, which involves an act of cognition, a sort of mental labelling, that arises in dependence upon sense perception of an object. So *saṃjñā* is perception, but perception of a particular kind. It is not perception *of* something, but perception that something *is* this or that, which is quite a different matter. One perceives the characteristics of an object, and then makes a judgement based on pre-existing conceptions, labels, or names as to what those characteristics represent. So *saṃjñā* may be defined as 'judgemental perception' or simply 'apperception'. Its two aspects can be described thus: (a) *Naming:* Directly perceiving and simply naming the characteristics of an object without fitting those perceptions to a pre-existing proposition. (b) *Defining:* Identifying those characteristics that define or specify the object, and enable one to make a proposition as to what it is.

According to Yeshe Gyaltsen,

> The former deals with the specific characteristic of an apparent object in a conceptless perception and the latter deals with the specific characteristic of an apparent object in a judgemental perception. (p. 23)

On the one hand one perceives and recognizes characteristics possessed by an object; on the other, one perceives characteristics that the object shares – or does not share – with certain other objects. This second aspect is to do with definition in the sense of binding a thing to its correct genus and species (logically rather than biologically speaking). When one sees a chair or a leopard and recognizes what it is because one has seen one before, or identifies it from one's knowledge of domestic furniture or natural history, one is recognizing or identifying the 'specific characteristics of an apparent object in a judgemental perception'. One has seen the characteristics of the object and they correspond with an abstract, already labelled, idea in one's mind.

However, when in the Middle Ages Europeans saw an animal that looked like a cross between a lion and a panther and they called it a leo*(lion)*pard*(panther)*, they were simply naming characteristics without having a pre-existing idea of the object perceived. Although the animal had some recognizable qualities, it did not conform to any pre-existing proposition in the mind by which they could recognize or identify it. Similarly, when one identifies a colour, there is no proposition to be applied to the perception.

It wouldn't be quite correct, though, to describe this sort of conceptualization as a conceptless perception as opposed to a judgemental perception. Perceived characteristics of whatever kind are of course concepts, and identifying them requires judgement. The difference is that in the one case one is just labelling characteristics, while in the other one is labelling characteristics by which one is able to identify or recognize what something is. In both categories of *saṃjñā* one is dealing with concepts and making judgments; the difference is in the kind of mental activity involved.

If we attempt to describe how *saṃjñā* takes place, we need to bear in mind Dr Guenther's careful terminology in order to avoid conveying an assumption that there is necessarily an ontological, ultimately real object that corresponds in some way with the epistemological object, the object we know about.[455] Hence the term 'apparent object'. The way Guenther puts it, where there is a perceptual situation, a subjective constituent that we call the mind perceives an objective constituent that we call the object. So, you understand the proposition 'This is a leopard'; you know what it means. Then within the perceptual situation there is an objective constituent with certain qualities, and you, the subjective constituent, proceed to apply your proposition to this object. But those qualities belong to the objective constituent of the perceptual situation, not necessarily to an objectively existent object. And the same thing goes for you, the perceiver: you cannot infer from the fact that the perceptual situation has a subjective constituent that this refers to an objectively existent subject. What we conceive to be the case is not necessarily the same as what is really the case.

Making things clear: the four bases for *saṃjñā*

We have already been introduced to these in effect, but Yeshe Gyaltsen makes things clear with a list, which can be summarized thus: (a) What is perceived in immediate sense perception. (b) Trustworthy information as to what an object is. (c) Recognizing the characteristics of an object. (d) Understanding a proposition in such a way as to be able to apply it appropriately to a particular object.[456]

The six forms of sense base for saṃjñā

As *saṃjñā* arises on the basis of sense perception, it may be classified according to which of the six senses is involved in making contact with the object. You name or recognize or identify something from seeing, hearing, smelling, tasting, touching, or thinking it. In the case of the last of these – which Guenther terms ideational perception – the object of perception is of course thought itself of some kind: you define or identify or recognize a thought; 'Ah, that's the same thought I had last week', or 'I had that same thought in my dream.'

Levels of *saṃjñā*

Yeshe Gyaltsen goes on to list six 'levels' of identification, depending on the state of consciousness in which the object is perceived. First there's the level of conceptual understanding involved in *saṃjñā*. This has three strata: identification that accurately applies names to objects, identification that includes a reflection on the impermanence of the object, and identification that clarifies one's insight into the impermanence of the object. These three correspond to the 'three levels of wisdom': listening, reflecting, meditating.

Then there's a corresponding level of conceptual *mis*understanding involved in *saṃjñā*: that is, three bands of false identification corresponding to those of conceptual understanding.

Thirdly, there is limited *saṃjñā*: identification taking place on the level of the *kāmaloka*, the realm of sense desire, which is our normal, everyday experience. Here, one's identification has a range limited to that of the five senses and the ordinary mind.

Fourthly, we have *saṃjñā* involving an aesthetic perspective; and fifthly, identification involving an infinite or unlimited viewpoint. Sixthly, there is identification 'which is nothing whatsoever ... the idea of an experience which one would objectify as nothing'.[457]

Higher steps

So the field of one's identification or conceptualization progressively broadens out as one steps back from the narrow viewpoint of the *kāmaloka*. Once one has taken this step, one is able first to look at things from the aesthetic perspective, which involves a refinement and intensification of sensory perception and a condition of appreciative awareness, developing into a state of meditative concentration or *dhyāna*. The word 'aesthetic' has quite a broad range of connotations in English, but in this context the level of aesthetic perception could be said to comprise the *rūpa dhyānas*, the levels of meditative absorption corresponding to the plane of archetypal form.

On the basis of the fourth *rūpa dhyāna*, the four *arūpa* or formless *dhyānas* may be developed. The infinite viewpoint mentioned here would appear to refer to the first two of these *arūpa dhyānas*, the sphere of infinite space and the sphere of infinite consciousness. It would then be an obvious step to take 'identification of an experience which one would identify as nothing' as referring to the third *arūpa dhyāna*, the sphere of no-thing-ness, in which one does not discriminate one thing from another.

Whether this level refers not only to the third *arūpa dhyāna*, but also to the fourth *arūpa dhyāna*, the sphere of neither perception nor non-perception, it is hard to say. It may be that there is no exact correspondence here. Indeed, it may well be that the 'infinite viewpoint' of the previous level in this series refers to the *arūpa dhyānas* generally, and that this sixth level of identification now refers to an experience beyond them. Guenther habitually translates *śūnyatā* as 'nothing' or 'nothingness', so it is perhaps justifiable to assume that 'the idea of an experience which we would objectify as nothing' refers to the transcendental experience of *śūnyatā*.

Is nothing a thing?

At this point we have to address something of a conundrum. *Saṃjñā* is presented here as an omnipresent mental event, which implies that it is present in all states of consciousness. But this seems to contradict the teaching of the five meditation factors outlined by Buddhist tradition. In his *Visuddhimagga*, Buddhaghosa lists these as applied thought, sustained thought, rapture, bliss, and concentration.[458] All these factors need to be present if one is to enter into meditation in the full sense of the development of states of higher consciousness (the *dhyānas*). But according to tradition, as one progresses through the *dhyānas* these factors cease to be part of one's experience. So, when one moves from the first to the second *dhyāna*, the first two factors – applied thought (*vitarka*) and sustained thought (*vicāra*), sometimes translated as 'apprehension of an object' and 'investigation of an object', are no longer present. Furthermore, 'apprehension and investigation of an object' sounds more or less synonymous with *saṃjñā*. Does this mean that if *vitarka* and *vicāra* are no longer present, *saṃjñā* is not after all an omnipresent mental event?

To address this question, it would seem reasonable to assume that there *is* a form of identification in the higher *dhyānas*, but that it is too subtle and refined to come within the definition of *vitarka* and *vicāra*, which represent a comparatively coarse kind of mental functioning.

It's as well not to take the notion of identification in too crude a sense. Perhaps *saṃjñā* is capable of degrees of refinement that are difficult for us to conceive of. One may not, upon entering the third *dhyāna*, actually say to oneself 'bliss, bliss', as do monks recorded in the Pāli *suttas*, but one is certainly able to identify one's experience as being blissful.[459] Otherwise, how would one know afterwards what one had experienced? There must be some subtle thread of identification connecting one's *dhyāna* experience with one's everyday conceptualizing mind.

One must assume that the same goes for deep sleep. It seems that when one emerges from a state of higher consciousness or from sleep, one is able to haul back an impression of what was going on in that state which enables one to know that one was in *dhyāna* or asleep. If one has an experience of *dhyāna* which one never had before, one may, if one has a book on meditation, be able to say 'Ah, the experience I've had corresponds to the level of *dhyāna* described on page 495,' say.

Farewell to *saṃjñā*

For a further perspective on *saṃjñā* we can consider the sequence of twelve positive links that describe the spiritual path as it spirals away from the wheel of life towards Enlightenment. This positive spiral is mentioned in the Pāli canon but on the whole it is an aspect of the teaching that has been much neglected.[460] It starts from the point at which, rather than allowing feeling to turn into craving or aversion, one takes what could be called the spiritual initiative, recognizing that one's desires cannot be fulfilled in the mundane sphere. Out of this experience of unsatisfactoriness arises faith, in dependence upon which joy, rapture, calm, bliss, and concentration successively arise. On the basis of concentration arises knowledge and vision of things as they really are – which we can call insight, for short.

The arising of insight – the eighth link – is the beginning of the transcendental part of the spiral; once one has attained it, one has built up an unstoppable momentum towards Enlightenment. Then follow the stages called withdrawal, disentanglement, and freedom. (I am, of course, merely sketching the outline of a process about which much can be said.) From the point of view of understanding *saṃjñā*, the interesting link is the last one, which is synonymous with Enlightenment itself. It is called the knowledge of the destruction of the *āsravas* – that is, one recognizes that craving for sensuous pleasure, craving for existence, and ignorance, have been destroyed.

But this attainment certainly does not involve identification in the sense of *saṃjñā*. The Sanskrit term for it is *āsravakṣayajñāna*. *Jñana* is usually translated as 'knowledge' but in this context it's more like an instantaneous and direct awareness: you just see. It's not that a quick mental reckoning takes place and you realize 'Ah! the *āsravas* aren't there any longer. Excellent!' You simply see the empty space, so to speak, where the *āsravas* were. This recognition is not *saṃjñā*. The point is that *saṃjñā* is an aspect of all *mundane* experience, not transcendental experience.

Incidentally, what happens cognitively when one perceives the non-existence of something is exhaustively discussed in Indian logic. In the period after the demise of Buddhism in India the adherents of the ancient Nyāya school of Indian – mainly Bengali – logic were considerably exercised over questions about absences and their ontological status.

For example, what exactly is the object of one's cognition when that object is the absence of, say, a pot? It can't be the pot, because it isn't there. But how can one recognize a 'not-pot'?[461]

In the Buddhist tradition the Enlightenment experience is often described in negative terms: as an absence of the *āsravas*, say, or an experience of *śūnyatā* (emptiness), which is often described as the absence of inherent existence/self-nature (*svabhāva*) of entities. Such expressions help to minimize the possibility of mistaking Enlightenment for some kind of conceptual perception. It is in the very nature of the experience that it is inconceivable: you don't know what you have experienced in the way you do when you have experienced *dhyāna*, say.

However, we can still refer to the Enlightenment experience in conceptual terms. If you were to ask the Buddha, 'What is your experience?' and he said, 'It is *śūnyatā*,' he would have communicated at least something of the nature of the experience of Enlightenment by means of conceptualization or identification. Thus while the 'experience which one would objectify as nothing' remains ineffable, the *idea* of that experience comes within the bounds of *saṃjñā*.

3. DIRECTIONALITY OF MIND (*CETANĀ*)

> It is a mental activity that propels the mind forward.
> *Abhidharmasamuccaya*

> Just as iron cannot but be attracted by a magnet, so also the mind cannot but be set on an object by this mental event. (p. 26)
> Yeshe Gyaltsen

Cetanā, will, and life-force

The Sanskrit term for this omnipresent mental event, *cetanā*, is roughly equivalent in meaning to two other terms: karma and *saṃskāra*. The *saṃskāras* are one of the five *skandhas* or heaps making up the totality of the human personality. The *saṃskāras* heap is the one which, under the law of karma, leads to a particular rebirth; it is defined by the commentators as *karma-cetanā*, volitional action. At the same time, the Pāli texts say that *cetanā* equals karma.[462] Karma is that which produces consequences in the form of pleasant or painful experiences. *Cetanā*, one could say, is the same thing viewed from a less existential, more psychological viewpoint.

Cetanā is sometimes translated as 'volition' or 'will', but Guenther clearly wants to avoid giving to the term the Western philosophical connotations that hang about the term 'will'. In a footnote to the main text he says that it 'refers to the total psychic energy'.[463] So whereas volition or will refers to the sum of psychic energy available to the conscious subject, *cetanā* is the whole mind, both conscious and unconscious, seen as a stream of psychic energy moving in a certain direction.

The idea that *cetanā* is a 'mental activity that propels the mind forward' should not be taken too literally. It's not that there is a 'thing' called mind which is moving in a certain direction by means of a faculty of volition which it operates. *Cetanā* is the pressure forward of the whole subject towards its object, or the whole subject experienced as psychic impetus, one could say. All the time we are moving or turning towards an object – now this, now that. We are never just reflecting things or being aware of things. We always have an object in view. This is why *cetanā* is translated as 'directionality of mind'. It is the dynamic aspect of mind. There is a flow of energy towards something all the time.

Of course, some of the 'objects' of our attention are people – and as far as *they* are concerned they are not objects, but subjects. Only when one becomes aware that other people are subjects as well as objects, and that from their point of view one is oneself an object rather than a subject, can true communication take place. It is all too easy to experience *cetanā* just flowing out to people as objects, but if one is going to recognize other people as subjects, one has to realize that one is oneself the object of someone else's *cetanā*. To refuse to be an 'object' in this way (and one should be careful not to misunderstand the usage of this term) is to refuse to be in communication.

Of course, the ideal here is to transcend all questions of subject and object altogether, entering into a mysterious process of empathy in which the duality between subject and object is abrogated. Upon the attainment of Enlightenment there is no question of directionality of mind towards anything, because – in the absence of the distinction between subject and object – there is nothing there for one's mind to go towards. This is the state called the *apraṇihita*, the 'unbiased', one of the three liberations or three doors to Enlightenment.[464] The point is that one has no *egoistic* motive for doing anything, so that one is utterly free to respond, out of compassion, to whatever arises. One is left with just energy – both fully conscious and spontaneous. We may say, therefore, that the natural tendency of *cetanā* is to go in quite the opposite direction from Enlightenment.

Being an omnipresent mental event, *cetanā* does not come into operation solely on the initiative of the conscious mind, like volition or will. It is much broader and in a way more fundamental than volition in the ordinary sense – because even when one is not consciously moving towards an object, the mind always has an unconscious tendency to settle on this or that. *Cetanā* is a little like the idea of a life-force, except that the latter refers to a biological as well as a psychological drive.

A stream of life

It's possible to work out a kind of hierarchy here. If one thinks of matter in terms of energy, one can think of living beings in terms of consciousness as well as energy, and of self-conscious beings in terms of volition as well as consciousness and energy. In this sense, the whole universe can be considered as consisting of life or energy that coagulates into more or less separate forms of conscious life. It is as if the whole of life is a stream within which more concentrated currents flow.

So in building up a mental picture of the nature of the universe we should think neither in terms of mutually exclusive interlocking parts, nor of a sort of undifferentiated mass; the reality is somewhere in between. We are separate from each other and from the world, but there isn't a hard and fast division between us. What I think of as me and what you think of as you is in each case the centre of a particular coagulation of the common stream of life. It is difficult to tell where 'I' come to an end and 'you' begin. We shade into each other. It is because of this that we can have a sense – a real sense as opposed to an idea – of other forms of life.

However, in speaking of ourselves in this way, we also have to accept that our own personal coagulation can liquefy again, or disperse into a number of lumps. What one thinks of as oneself is just a tiny fraction of the limitlessly multidimensional nature of consciousness. It is apparently possible for one's personality to be so fragmented that when one dies the different streams of one's volitions drift off to form more than one rebirth. At the other end of the scale, it is also said to be possible for someone to be so integrated as to be able consciously to find rebirth in a number of different forms. For example, one of my own teachers, Jamyang Khyentse, was said to be one of five products of such a multiple reincarnation.

For most people, the stream connecting the different bits and pieces is sufficiently strong to keep them all together. But we need to be aware that the form we find ourselves in is a function of our volitional energies, and it is absurd to identify rigidly with that form. We are much more fluid than we appear to ourselves to be. It is therefore important to make the effort to identify imaginatively with others – for example, if one is young and one finds oneself getting impatient with an older person who can't keep up (whether physically or mentally); or if one thinks of oneself too rigidly as being British or Irish or Black or whatever.

Another idea that may help to distinguish the essential features of *cetanā* is the purely Theravādin concept of *bhavaṅga-sota* or 'life-stream'. This is the basic stream of existence, or becoming, underlying consciousness. It is an unconscious stream of past impressions which emerges on to a subconscious level or into full consciousness only when an external stimulus impinges upon it. According to a traditional analogy, *bhavaṅga* is represented by a man sound asleep under a mango tree, who wakes up only when a mango drops on his head. The external stimulus is by way of being a disturbance; *bhavaṅga-sota* essentially flows on independently of the conscious mind and of external stimuli.[465]

Cetanā, by contrast, is a flowing out towards external objects, and it can be both unconscious (or subconscious) and conscious. Like *bhavaṅga-sota*, *cetanā* goes on regardless, whether we like it or not; but whereas *bhavaṅga* is *karma-vipāka*, *cetanā* is karma. So we are back again to the crucial distinction between 'things that happen to us' and 'things we do'. And whereas we cannot be aware of *bhavaṅga*, we can be aware of the directionality of the mind, introduce some conscious guidance, and channel awareness towards skilful rather than unskilful objects.

Karma

It is popularly said that we create or produce karma by our actions, but karma actually consists in our volitional actions themselves; what we produce or create is the *result* of karma i.e. *karma-vipāka*. So it is a mistake to think that everything we are is the result of karma. The importance of *cetanā* lies in the fact that it represents that aspect of mind which is not the *result* of karma, but karma itself. We experience *karma-vipāka* in terms of feeling, but the directionality of mind, though it may be reinforced by past karma, is not itself *vipāka*, but fresh karma.

Karma is going on all the time. One might be forgiven for imagining that karma and *vipāka* alternate in some way, so that we are either creating *vipāka* or experiencing it, but in fact karma is going on even while we are experiencing its fruits. It's easy to get the idea that when we do certain things – give to a beggar, say, or steal something – that is karma, but that when we are not doing those things, karma is not going on. In fact, our whole life is karma. *We* are karma.

Of course, like *cetanā*, karma is not always conscious. Sometimes it is said that karma is what we do deliberately, but this mustn't be taken in too narrow a sense. Karmas develop their own momentum over lifetimes so that we don't always notice the general flow. Actions that start off as deliberate choices actually develop more karmic weight if they become our natural, even unconsidered, way of going on. What we usually think of as karmas are only the more noticeable ripples on the surface of the general flow of karma.

In that what makes something volitional is some degree of awareness, one could say that in a sense unmindfulness does not have karmic consequences. However, being unmindful confines one to a lower level of consciousness, making unmindfulness part of the general drift of unconscious tendencies which is part of volition and which *does* have karmic consequences.

Discussion of karma and its consequences of course leads to the consideration of rebirth. As we have already seen, it is quite possible to take the notion of karmic consequences seriously while retaining an agnostic stance on the subject of rebirth. But if one thinks in terms of future lives, in general terms one could say that an overall directionality of mind towards characteristically human acts ensures future life as an ordinary human being, while our more consciously determined actions represent more specific, more concentrated karmas which will result in certain specific situations and experiences within the general human context. We cannot stand back from karma as if we were separate from it. We are not things – we are drives. We *are* karma. And if this drive keeps up without serious modifications, we will be reborn more or less as we are now.

This is why in Buddhism so much importance is attached to the constant repetition of positive actions. If one constantly recites mantras and *sūtras*, if one constantly practises meditation, if one regularly performs pujas and practises generosity and kindness, if one's speech is consistently truthful, helpful, and harmonious, and if one's livelihood supports these practices, then all the time one is modifying the overall karmic flow that is one's directionality of mind or *cetanā*.

If one's directionality of mind is shifted profoundly enough, then one's future life will not necessarily be a human one. One may conceivably be reborn as a god in a 'heaven realm' – one corresponding to the level of *dhyāna* that one has habitually sustained in this life. On the other hand, if one's *cetanā* has habitually gone towards eating, drinking, and sex, and nothing but these activities, there is a chance that one will be reborn as an animal – though it would be difficult to shift one's directionality of mind as profoundly as that without dedicated effort. No doubt a few people succeed occasionally. The same must go for rebirth in any other realm apart from the human. An attitude of neurotic craving or hatred would have to be sustained constantly and intensely for years on end to ensure rebirth in the corresponding hell realm.

A legacy of *cetanā*

This question of the relative intensity of *cetanā* means that actions that are ostensibly more or less the same may have different consequences for different people. Two people may seem to be leading more or less the same kind of life, doing the same sort of things, but although the actions are the same, the *cetanā* and thus the karma may be much stronger for one of them than for the other. If what they are doing is ethically unskilful, one of them may have inherited from past positive karma a degree of pleasant *vipāka* which might reduce the intensity of the craving or hatred he or she brings to that action. On the other hand, if the same two people were performing ethically skilful actions, the one with good *vipāka* would perhaps be more prone to lose mindfulness and become over-elated, careless, or foolish, while the one with bad *vipāka* might find that adversity helped to concentrate the mind.

In short, one cannot tell from people's experience and actions precisely what is going on karmically. For example, in certain kinds of illness, especially fevers, it can happen that the mind seems to separate itself from the body, so that one becomes able to enter into quite profound reflections, and even into a state of awareness that virtually amounts to a higher state of consciousness, quite undisturbed by what is happening to the body. At the very least, a setback in life or a bout of physical suffering, if it is taken as a positive purgation or catharsis, cannot be looked upon simply as a bad thing.[466]

So *vipāka* does not determine karma. But if one performs certain karmas this will tend to enhance one's tendency to perform them. It is as if karma can gather momentum. Hence the insistence within Tibetan Buddhism on performing various practices as many times as possible – the traditional number is 100,000 prostrations, 100,000 mantras, and so on. And hence also the importance of going on retreat: through performing only positive actions over a continuous period, and at the same time greatly reducing the opportunities for unskilful mental action, one gets into the habit of it.

Ideally, of course, one wants to sustain the weighty positive karma of *dhyāna* or meditative absorption. (This expression 'weighty' karma refers to karma, whether positive or negative, that will have a decisive effect when it comes to one's rebirth.) Mantra recitation doesn't usually constitute weighty karma inasmuch as one tends not to want to keep the mantra going as one becomes more deeply concentrated. This is not to suggest that mantra recitation is merely a concentration technique – it is a devotional practice – but as one dwells ever more deeply on the meditation deity symbolized by the mantra, the repetition of the mantra drops away. But even at the level of recitation, if one can maintain it as a regular practice it becomes habitual; and it is generally this habitual karma, the overall karmic trend of one's being, which determines one's future life. In reciting mantras, to stay with that example, one is at the very least passing one's time in a highly skilful manner.

If by the time of death one has – as is quite usual – performed no weighty karma, whether positive, like meditation, or negative, like murder, one's rebirth will be consequent upon the overall directionality of mind, upon one's habitual karma in this life. From the Abhidharma point of view, therefore, what one does habitually is regarded as of extreme importance. If one calculated how much time one spent doing one's various activities, and the intensity of one's involvement in them, one could probably work out the sort of future life one could look forward to. (Just how objective one could be about such a calculation is, of course, open to question!)

The results of past action

In meditation, it is volition that produces *dhyāna*, but what one actually experiences in *dhyāna* is the fruit of that volition. The weighty positive karma of *dhyāna* is not the experience, but the volition. So while *dhyāna* may correspond – as *vipāka* – to the experience of the god realms, it differs inasmuch as the gods are unable to generate fresh karma. They are in a passive state of enjoyment, reaping the rewards of what they have done in the past but accumulating no fresh karma, whether good or bad. When the karma that caused them to be reborn as gods is exhausted, they slip down to a lower level or realm, depending on what residual karma they have to their credit. It is as though they are in such a state of bliss that they are stupefied by it, unable to exert themselves even so as to prolong that state of bliss. The gods are therefore not so much in a dhyānic state as in a world to which those in the *kāmaloka* have access through *dhyāna*. As a result of their experience of higher states of consciousness in past lives they have a very fine material body, which means that all their experience is correspondingly subtle and delicate, and in this sense enjoyable, but it is not truly dhyānic.

It is a little like what happens when one takes a psychedelic drug: certain areas of the mind are temporarily paralysed or inhibited, with the result that one experiences – depending on whether one's past karma has been skilful or unskilful – a 'good trip' or a 'bad trip'. In other words, one's capacity for volition, or karma, is swamped by one's experience of *vipāka*. It is as if – without stretching this illustration beyond the level of analogy – one's capacity for creating fresh karma is suspended, thus making way for the experience of whatever *vipāka* is there to be experienced at that time. The intensity of such experience, whether good or bad, naturally provides a fertile basis for the subsequent arising of fresh karma in the form of craving or aversion once the effect of the drug wears off.

One may say that the meditational experience has in technical terms a *saṃskāra* (volitional) aspect and a *vedanā* aspect. As one enters the *dhyānas* one experiences first the one and then the other. Once one is in *dhyāna*, though, one experiences only the *vedanā* aspect. Well, one can continue to put in volitional action even while one experiences *vedanā*, and thus deepen the experience, but a point may come when one ceases to generate further positive karma. The intensity of bliss tends to submerge the other positive mental events, though they must all be there in some form or other. This is why the Buddha says of his own experience of *dhyāna* that 'pleasure did not lay hold of my mind'; he did not allow himself to be side-tracked or swamped by the pleasure of meditation.

The ten creativities

Awareness moves towards an object through sense perception (which in the case of a mental object would, of course, be thought). Like *saṃjñā*, therefore, *cetanā* may be classified according to which of the six senses is involved.

> From a broad viewpoint,
> The paths of action are said to be ten
> According to their being wholesome and unwholesome. (p. 26)
> *Abhidharmakośa*

What this means is that *cetanā* is also classified in terms of the ten ethical precepts.[467] Strictly speaking, there is no limit to the different operations of *cetanā*, but the ten precepts may be said to adumbrate the most significant ways in which it functions. *Cetanā* being a purely mental operation, this makes it clear that the precepts are all actions of the mind, although the first three pertain to actions of body as well as mind, and the next four pertain to actions of speech as well as mind, so that just the last three of them pertain to mind alone.

As far as the classification of *cetanā* is concerned there are, as the above quotation from the *Abhidharmakośa* makes clear, two different sets of ways of action: wholesome and unwholesome. The quotation is also a reminder that what we more usually call vows or precepts are in fact pathways of skilful action, the ten avenues by which skilful karmas come out. Actions in the sense of karmas are movements in a certain direction, intentionalities, so the precepts could be called the ten skilful intentionalities, or even the ten creativities. They are not so much rules to observe as specific channels by which skilful karmas flow out. This is actually the sort of model put forward by the *Dhammapada*:

> Those who make channels for waters control the waters;
> Makers of arrows make the arrows straight;
> Carpenters control their timber;
> And the wise control their own minds.[468]

The idea is that water can either be used to irrigate and therefore nourish the crops, or it can be allowed to flood over the land and destroy everything. Similarly, the *daśa-kuśala-karma-pathas*, the ten paths of wholesome action, represent so many channels which one opens up for the waters of one's *cetanā* to flow into. *Cetanā*, after all, is always there; one can't block it without opening another channel for it to flow through. Having said this, the analogy is not to be pressed as far as to suggest that *cetanā* works according to the laws of mechanics; it is just an analogy. But the suggestion that ethics consist in giving a certain direction to energy is a revealing one.

4. CONTACT (*SPĀRŚA*)

> It is a determination, a transformation in the controlling power, which is in accordance with the three factors coming together. Its function is to provide a basis for feeling. (p. 27)
>
> *Abhidharmasamuccaya*

This is *spārśa*, the fourth omnipresent mental event.[469] The 'controlling power' translates the term *indriya*, which literally means the ruler but is more usually rendered as sense faculty, and here refers to the six sense faculties. (*Indriya* is also often rendered as 'sense-power', which preserves the connection with 'ruler'.)

So contact is a specific mode, a particular transformation, *in* the sense faculty. This takes place in the coming together of three factors: the object, the sense faculty, and the consciousness that arises when the two come together. It is of course possible for object and sense faculty to come together without being joined by consciousness, if consciousness happens to be completely withdrawn from the sense organ in question.

For example, if one is totally caught up in one's thoughts, one's eyes can be wide open without one's actually seeing anything. In this case, although the sense organ and the object have come together, contact in the sense of *spārśa* has not taken place.

So the sense faculty connects with an object, and then at least some degree of consciousness needs to be present for sense contact to take place. And when it does take place, then feeling (*vedanā*) arises. So contact provides a basis for feeling. Or – in terms of the *nidāna* chain – in dependence upon contact arises feeling. Put in the simplest terms, contact is a change that takes place in the sense faculty when that sense faculty connects with the appropriate sense object and gives rise to a certain kind of consciousness. This then makes possible the arising of feeling. There are of course six types of rapport or contact, depending on which sense faculty is involved in its operation.

To put it another way, when the sense faculty connects with an object, contact 'captures' the object; this is the modification of the sense faculty. Saying this, we must bear in mind that when we speak of all these various elements that go together to make contact happen, we are speaking not of things or entities but of relations – and not even relations between things, but simply the different terms in a relation.

With the modification of the sense faculty arises feeling, which is pleasant, unpleasant, or neutral. Then, if in place of just feeling pleasure we *take* pleasure, if we delight in the pleasant feeling, craving arises. Whether or not we allow feeling to develop into craving depends on the way we channel our *cetanā*. In terms of the *nidāna* chain, in dependence upon contact arises feeling, and in dependence upon feeling arises craving. Where feeling ends and craving begins is a question of where one ceases to be able to detach oneself quite easily from the object of the pleasant feeling. If it proves next to impossible to give up that object, craving is well established and karma has been set in vigorous motion.

Here we see a fundamental difference between the four omnipresent mental events we have discussed so far. Both contact and feeling are mental events that simply happen. The senses can come into contact with their appropriate objects without any particular movement on the part of mind. On the *nidāna* chain they are part of the effect process of the present life. Directionality and perception, on the other hand, belong to the cause process which takes us on to the next life; and so does the fifth omnipresent mental event, egocentric demanding.

5. EGOCENTRIC DEMANDING (*MANASKĀRA*)

> It is a continuity having the function of holding the mind to what has become its reference.
>
> *Abhidharmasamuccaya*

> The difference between directionality and egocentric demanding is that directionality brings the mind towards the object in a general move, while egocentric demanding makes the mind jump on this particular objective reference. (p. 28)
>
> Yeshe Gyaltsen

'Egocentric demanding' is Guenther's translation of *manaskāra*, which literally means 'mind-making'. It is a continuity in the sense that its nature is to go on, almost as if it becomes habitual – within a relatively short timescale, anyway. By 'its reference' is meant whatever object the mind has made contact with.[470]

In his *Buddhist Dictionary*, Nyanatiloka, quoting from Buddhaghosa's *Visuddhimagga*, gives us a clearer definition of *manaskāra* (Pāli *manasikāra*): it is the mind's first 'confrontation with an object' and 'binds the associated mental factors to the object'.[471]

It is difficult to establish an absolutely clear distinction between the different mental events. But perhaps we can say that if directionality or intentionality is like creeping up on the object, *manaskāra* is like the final spring. Of course, being an omnipresent mental event, it is not just the occasional pounce; it is something one does again and again (hence 'demanding'). So 'egocentric demanding' is quite good as an interpretative translation.

6
A STEADY FOCUS

In this chapter we are going to start getting a much more specific idea of how the Abhidharma's classifications of mental events are of practical use, especially in the practice of meditation. Here we are concerned with another group of five, the 'object-determining' mental events. The Sanskrit term is *viniyata*, which means 'restrained, checked, regulated, limited', but in this context it is taken to mean 'specific' or 'determining'. The object-determining mental events are those in which one applies oneself more particularly to the object of one's attention. They are object-determining in the sense that one determines that it shall be this object and not that object. One comes, as it were, much closer up to the object; these mental events are concerned with it in a much more vital and even dynamic manner than are the omnipresent mental events. The object-determining mental events are therefore brought into operation above all in the context of meditation, which is a process of applying oneself to a particular object with an increasing intensity of involvement.

1. INTEREST (*CHANDA*)

Again, Yeshe Gyaltsen starts his exposition with a quotation, this time from the *Abhidharmasamuccaya*:

> What is interest? It is the desire to endow a desired thing with this or that particular attribute, and has the function of laying the foundation for making a start on assiduous striving. (p. 29)

So this is *chanda*. Guenther translates it as 'interest'; one could also render it as 'eagerness'. Before you fix the mind on an object, you are, as it were, saying 'Let that be the object of my attention,' which implies making a definite effort with regard to that particular object. Obviously this is especially important within the context of meditation. And on the basis of interest the other object-determining mental events gradually come into play.

It is important to note about this, the first of the object-determining mental events,[472] that it is *not* an omnipresent mental event. Of course, this is not going to be news as far as most of us are concerned; we know very well that eagerness or *chanda* is not part of our experience all the time. Indeed, it is unfortunately possible to go through life without evincing much eagerness for anything whatsoever. This seems to be what being 'cool' or 'laid back' is about. Eagerness is something that has to be established and maintained; and it is established in conjunction with other qualities. In meditation, for example, one first has to appreciate the value of the meditative state itself. This is what stimulates interest or eagerness, which is the basis for endeavour or striving, which in turn leads to *praśrabdhi*, or 'integrated exhilaration'.

Eagerness, one could say, is the opposite of laziness, so that the overcoming of laziness and the development of eagerness are closely related. On the subject of laziness, Yeshe Gyaltsen quotes the Tibetan master Tsongkhapa:

> If one is unable to suppress laziness which delights in the non-inclination towards the practice of meditation and which delights in the factors not conducive to the practice, then one quickly loses all interest.... When one has attained a state of alertness which is satiated with happiness and pleasure both on the physical and mental level, and when one is not weary to apply himself day or night to what is positive, then laziness is overcome. In order to generate this alertness, it is important that one has the concentration which is the sustaining cause of the aforesaid state of alertness and that one makes this a continuous process. In order to have the power of concentration, one must have a strong and continuous involvement in concentration. In order that concentration be a sustaining cause factor, one must repeatedly invoke a firm conviction which enraptures one's whole mind

> because one has seen the virtues and value of concentration. To understand these qualities and processes in this order must be taken as the most essential point because they become clear and certain in seeing them in one's own experience. (pp. 29–30)
>
> *Lam-rim chen-mo*[473]

To summarize what Tsongkhapa is saying here: (a) Laziness must be overcome, because it prevents not only concentration, but continuity of concentration, in meditation. (b) Laziness can only be said to have been overcome when one experiences no resistance in meditation to applying oneself, day and night, to the positive, and continually feels both mental and physical bliss. (c) To generate this, one needs continuous concentration – that is, one needs to be involved constantly in the practice. (d) In order actually to achieve this level of involvement, one has repeatedly to invoke, in the course of practice, a firm conviction of its value – especially, presumably, when concentration is flagging.

So laziness is to devote oneself to and delight in something in a way that prevents one from devoting oneself to and delighting in something of greater value. We tend to think of laziness as being about lack of exertion, but the Buddhist idea of laziness is quite different – and quite revealing. For Gampopa, for example, the most extreme form of laziness is devoting oneself day and night to defeating enemies and making money.[474]

Being lazy really means being busy doing something that is not conducive to skilful mental states: one's busyness actually prevents one from being aware of what one might otherwise be engaging in. In fact, Tsongkhapa goes further than that: laziness, he is saying, is taking delight in the fact that one is not occupying oneself with something of higher value. It involves a sort of complacency and satisfaction in the fact that one is occupying oneself with lower things. To overcome laziness we need to be able to distinguish that which is worthwhile from that which is less so. This means that we need to think deeply about the implications of attaining concentrated mental states (*dhyāna*): what it will mean to attain *dhyāna* and what it will mean *not* to attain it. Eagerness (*chanda*) is based on this, and it is established to counteract laziness.

Tsongkhapa's remarks on laziness are especially important, according to Yeshe Gyaltsen, for those who are tempted to immerse themselves so deeply in various discussions and arguments about the teachings of Buddhism that they miss the whole point of them. However conscientiously one occupies oneself with the teachings, if one doesn't put them into practice, such occupation is no more than a form of laziness. This is not at all to say that Dharma study and Dharma practice are necessarily two different things. Study can be a method of practice just as meditation is. Study is, after all, an aspect of the first of the three wisdoms (listening, reflecting, and meditating).[475] Laziness sets in when one does not go on to reflect and meditate on the teachings one has studied.

2. INTENSIFIED INTEREST WHICH STAYS WITH ITS OBJECT (*ADHIMOKṢA*)

> It is to stick to the determined thing just as it has been determined, and the function of intensified interest is that it cannot be taken away. (p. 31)
>
> *Abhidharmasamuccaya*

Here Guenther chooses to translate *adhimokṣa*, sometimes translated as 'resolve' or 'determination', as 'intensified interest which stays with its object'. In this context it refers to an object of meditation, but in fact this resolve may be applied to anything. If the object is the Three Jewels of Buddhism: the Buddha, representing the ideal of Enlightenment, the Dharma, representing the Buddha's teaching, and the Sangha, the spiritual community of those who have realized the higher stages of the transcendental path – then the determination amounts to faith (*śraddhā*). Whereas *chanda*, as a firm conviction regarding the quality and value of higher mental states, will appear in some form at an elementary level of spiritual development, *adhimokṣa* is experienced only by a person who is really committed to the spiritual life.

3. INSPECTION (OR MINDFULNESS OR RECOLLECTION) (*SMṚTI*)

> It is not to let what one knows slip away from one's mind. Its function is not to be distracted. (p. 32)
>
> *Abhidharmasamuccaya*

Guenther gives us 'inspection', and *smṛti* is usually translated as 'mindfulness' or 'awareness', but in fact, as this quotation from the *Abhidharmasamuccaya* suggests, the primary meaning of the word is 'recollection' or even 'memory'. Sometimes *smṛti* quite clearly means recollection or memory, while in other contexts it refers to being aware of something here and now, and sometimes its meaning is a synthesis of the two, which one could term 'mindfulness'. The common characteristic is 'not to let what one knows slip out of the mind'. Whether the object is there in the present or whether it is remembered from the past, the practice of *smṛti* is about holding the object in mind. This is mindfulness.

We have already briefly encountered the 'four foundations of mindfulness' – mindfulness of body, of feelings, of thoughts, and of reality – as an aspect of the path of accumulation. One can go further, to cultivate what I would call four dimensions of mindfulness or awareness: awareness of things, awareness of self, awareness of others, and awareness of reality.

Aware of things

By awareness of things I mean awareness of the world around us, awareness of our material environment – awareness of nature, if you like. Of course, if we want to be aware of the world, we have to look at it and listen to it, but this is what very few of us ever manage to do. Most people, if challenged, would say that they have no time to stop and look at things. But if we really want to be aware of the world, we need to learn to look at it. We need to learn to look at the sky, at mountains (when we get the opportunity), at flowers, at rocks, at water, at fire – at the familiar things that are all around us, that are there all the time, but that we never really see. We need to look not just at 'poetic' things, but at everything we encounter in our everyday life, even brick walls and unemptied dustbins, if they happen to be what is around.

It is not only a question of looking. We need to learn to hear, to taste, to smell, to touch. No doubt the highest degree of perceptual awareness is possible through the sense of sight, but that does not mean that the other senses should be neglected. We should learn really to look not only at natural objects and familiar household things but, for example, at paintings, sculptures, and so on – things that we often take for granted as part of our cultural heritage. We can also learn to listen – to music, for example. (Many people have music on as a sort of background noise; whether it's Bach or the latest pop song they wouldn't be able to say – it's just a river of sound flowing through the background.) In so many ways we can increase our awareness of the world, both natural and cultural.

Aware of self

Secondly, we need to develop awareness of self. By this I don't mean anything very metaphysical; I mean simply awareness of the changing empirical self, which is in any case all that we usually experience. In Buddhism awareness of self is traditionally said to be of three kinds, of increasing degrees of subtlety. First, there is awareness of the body and its movements, including the breathing process, on which, of course, a whole concentration technique is based. According to tradition, as one moves about one should be aware of just how one is moving. If you are standing, be aware that you are standing. If you are sitting, be aware that you are sitting; experience yourself sitting. If you move your hand, be aware that you are moving your hand. If you close the door, be aware that you are closing the door. If you are holding a book, be aware that you are holding it.

If we practise in this way, even for a little while, we very speedily become aware that we have lapses of mindfulness. There are whole periods of time when we literally don't know what we're doing. Although being aware of the physical body is the simplest form of self-awareness, it is still very difficult. But it is nonetheless very important, because it is the foundation of all the other aspects of awareness of self.

From there we can go on to practising awareness of feeling, noticing whether our feeling-tone is pleasurable, painful, or a sort of neutral grey. Then we can become aware of our emotions, of whether we are experiencing love or hatred or fear or anxiety or desire or hope or jealousy or delight or expectation or disgust – or whatever. The important thing, whatever the emotional state we are in, is to know that we are experiencing it. If we can become aware of our whole emotional life in this way, we will find that this has a twofold effect: our negative emotions will tend to be dissolved – or at least brought very much under control – and our positive emotions will tend to be refined still further.

Aware of thoughts

Then there is awareness of thoughts. It has to be said that very few people really think at all. Usually thoughts just drift through our minds; they take possession of us, as it were. We don't know why they have come and very often we don't know where they have come from; they just come, and there seems to be very little we can do about it. We just have to tolerate them. Even in meditation we just have to watch the thoughts playing – rioting, even – in the playground of our mind, powerless to chase them away. They are not our own thoughts, really; we are not masters of them. All that is happening is that we are subject to a very loose association of ideas which is easily interrupted or redirected. But if we become aware of what is happening, if we cultivate awareness of our thoughts, our thinking becomes more purposeful. In a sense it becomes our own; it becomes an active rather than a passive process. Wandering thoughts are gradually eliminated, and we experience an altogether more peaceful and harmonious state of mind.

This is the traditional classification of awareness of self: awareness of the body and its movements, of feelings and emotional states, and of thoughts. But other classifications are also possible. We can speak, for example, in terms of various kinds of psychological conditioning – by which I mean the tendency for our actions to be determined, without our realizing it, by previous patterns of existence, often patterns laid down very early in life. This conditioning is of various kinds. We are conditioned by the fact that we are human beings and not animals, or rather that we are humanoid mammals as distinct from non-humanoid mammals. We are conditioned by the fact of being either male or female. We are conditioned by the place where we were born, by our race, by our nationality. We are conditioned by the social group to which we belong – by caste, by class, by profession, by party, even by religion. Such conditioning is also resolved by means of awareness of self, in that to the extent that we become aware that we are psychologically conditioned in these various ways, we can become free from that conditioning.

Aware of people and reality

The third dimension of awareness is awareness of people. Strange to say, this is a comparatively rare thing. Usually, as already discussed, we are aware of people not as people but as things, as objects, as bodies 'out there'. The extreme case, of course, is that of the infant, to whom 'mother' is just an object that gives warmth and nourishment. We like to think that we grow out of this sort of attitude to people, and to an extent we do, but not altogether. All too often in our personal lives we treat other people not as persons but as things. The way to start to change this is simply to learn to look at people. Only if we look at people can we be aware of them. And only if we are aware of them can we love them.

Fourthly, there's awareness of reality, which is of course the highest kind of awareness. Not that this dimension of awareness and the other dimensions are mutually exclusive. One can have glimpses of reality through awareness of nature, of the self, or of other people. But in this fourth dimension, one's awareness of reality is, as it were, direct. In what it actually consists it is very difficult to say, because it is beyond words, but we can perhaps say that it is synonymous with meditation in the highest sense – that is, with meditation as contemplation.

These dimensions of awareness or mindfulness are clearly fundamental to Buddhist practice. Mindfulness was a fundamental aspect of the Buddha's teaching – a whole *sutta* of the Pāli canon, the *Satipaṭṭhāna Sutta*, is devoted to an exposition of the four foundations of mindfulness – and clearly it is of great importance to the practice of the Abhidharma. It is a moot point, of course, how far this kind of awareness will take us; as we have seen, some would argue that simply being aware of a mental state is not enough to change it, while one could equally argue that the very act of becoming aware has a transformative power.

Recollection

In the context of the object-determining mental events, attention is being drawn to *smṛti* as recollection, which reminds us that here we are discussing a mental event. The term 'recollection' in English is ambiguous: it can mean the act of recollecting, in the sense of calling up a mental image pertaining to the past – that is, remembering something – but it can also mean the state of being recollected – being mindful and aware in the present.

As a spiritual practice, recollection may be said to be about remembering what is really important, what life is really about and what one is really supposed to be doing. 'Why am I here? What am I doing this for?' Recollection is often about waking up to the fact that one has strayed away from where one really wants to be. The Sanskrit term reserved for this particular type of recollection is *saṃprajanya*, sometimes translated as 'mindfulness of purpose' or 'mindfulness with clear comprehension'; we will encounter its opposite, *asaṃprajanya*, among the list of negative mental events.

When one recollects something one is, as it were, collecting together again what has been lost, even gathering up scattered energies. In recollecting one's purpose, one is recollecting one*self*. In a sense, though, one's ultimate purpose never falls into abeyance. There is no need to be remembering constantly that one is on the spiritual path in a strained and artificial way, but it's always there in the background. It's a bit like an electrified wire. If one does anything that begins to take one away from one's main purpose, one gets a little jolt from that undercurrent of recollection.

Memory

Perhaps it is worth adding that even *smṛti* in the straightforward sense of memory has its uses. Memory is quite an odd phenomenon. One has to remember that one has forgotten before one can remember again – that is, one can only recollect one's recollection by means of recollection. Things one wants to remember get submerged by other things, and they have to wait for an opportunity to surface into consciousness; it seems very often just a matter of chance whether one's memory gets jogged or not. The best one can do, perhaps, is set up appropriate conditions in advance for retrieving one's memory. The time-honoured method is to tie a knot in one's handkerchief, but one can set up more elaborate systems of association to stimulate the memory, or write things down, or even employ someone to remember things on one's behalf. Remembering things is so important that quite often we're seized with a feeling that we've forgotten something before we know what it is that we've forgotten – or we get a feeling we've forgotten something when we haven't at all.

There is very often a point to memory loss. When we're under stress, for example, it's sheer self-protection, a way of cutting down on the number of things we have to think about. If there are too many demands being made on us and we don't do anything about it consciously, we reduce the input unconsciously by simply forgetting things.

We also tend to forget things as we get older. When we're young we remember all sorts of details, very often quite trivial ones, because it is not yet clear to us what is going to be important and what is not. What will turn out to be peripheral may at the time look like a matter of great concern. As we get older and the general pattern of our life comes into focus, we want to intensify and deepen that focus, and our memory becomes more selective. As we strive to strengthen the basic pattern, which is presumably what we will carry over into our next life, the things that are irrelevant to the broad brush-strokes of our life cease to make an impression. By the time one gets to the end of one's life one may not be taking in anything that's going on, and one's memory may go altogether. One becomes like a child again, ready for one's next rebirth.

Practice

Smṛti is fundamental to spiritual practice; one cannot begin without it. Many devotional practices in particular help to recollect the mind in this general sense, and there is a series of practices that are specifically named the ten *anussatis* or recollections (*sati* being the Pāli version of the Sanskrit *smṛti*).[476] One of these practices is the *ānāpānasati*, the mindfulness of breathing; and another is the *buddhānussati* (Sanskrit *buddhānusmṛti*), which involves calling to mind what one has heard about the Buddha and his qualities.

Mindfulness of one's purpose can be lost just as one loses one's memory, but it involves losing something rather more fundamental than people's names or the day of the week. If you realize the importance of this kind of mindfulness, if you realize that if you lose it you lose, in a sense, everything, then you are going to want to do something a little more radical than tying a knot in your handkerchief to make sure you preserve it. And one very effective way is to develop spiritual friendship. Our friends may literally remind us in conceptual terms of our purpose in life, but we are also frequently reminded of what we are trying to do simply through observing their example.

4. INTENSE CONCENTRATION (*SAMĀDHI*)

The fourth object-determining mental event is *samādhi*, which in this context means one-pointedness of mind that stays with a mental object – that is, an object that is not perceived through the senses.[477] Yeshe Gyaltsen quotes the *Abhidharmasamuccaya*: 'Its function is to become the basis for awareness'.[478] But, remembering that most basic formulation of the Buddhist path, the threefold path, we can also say that *samādhi* is developed on the basis of ethics, and 'its function is to become the basis for awareness' in the sense of transcendental wisdom or insight. These are the three stages of the path: ethics, *samādhi*, wisdom.

For an important qualification to this definition of *samādhi* we can turn not to Yeshe Gyaltsen's commentary this time, but to the *Cheng Weishi Lun* of Xuanzang:

> The expression 'concentration of the mind' indicates that the mind is fixed where it wishes to be fixed, not that it is fixed on only one object. Otherwise, there would be no Samādhi on the 'Path of Insight into transcendental Truth' where the ascetic discerns and contemplates successively the eternal verities and where, in consequence, the object changes from moment to moment.[479]

This can be applied directly to one's meditation practice. Take, for example, the practice of visualizing a particular Buddha or bodhisattva. One may bring to mind the details of a visualized bodhisattva, concentrating now on this, now on that element of the visualization, but the idea is that one's concentration (*samādhi*) remains constant even while its object changes in this way. With the *mettā bhāvanā* practice likewise, the aim is to develop a quality of response, *mettā*, that remains constant whoever is the object of one's concentration. *Samādhi* is basically the ability to fix the mind where we wish during meditation.

Yeshe Gyaltsen lists four classes of mental object one may concentrate on.[480] The four are, to paraphrase his list: (a) That which is concerned with the development of *śīla*, morality. (b) That which is concerned with purifying emotions – i.e. by counteracting craving. (c) That which is concerned with developing the four 'abodes of the gods' (*brahma vihāras*): loving-kindness, compassion, sympathetic joy, and equanimity. (d) That which is concerned with the development of wisdom.

These four categories again cover the threefold path. The first refers to the ten precepts, while the second and third have as their aim the development of *samādhi* itself. The second category, reflecting as it does the need to counteract the powerful emotions of craving and lust, involves strong measures: meditation on the ten impurities and the various disgusting aspects of bodily existence, in particular the meditation on the stages of decomposition of a corpse. The third, designed to counter the opposite tendency, towards hatred and aversion, consists in the cultivation of positive emotion. And the fourth has as its aim the development of insight into the nature of reality, which involves reflection on the Dharma, including the teachings of the Abhidharma itself.

In his commentary Yeshe Gyaltsen makes it clear that it is only with reference to the *mental* product of perception – an inwardly perceived object – that concentration in the sense of *samādhi* develops. While it is quite common to focus on some external object (traditionally a coloured disc) in order to develop a preliminary degree of concentration, it would be a mistake to imagine that through doing this one could develop concentration in all its stages. The extreme form of this sort of wrong view is held by people who claim that they meditate 'all the time'. Awareness – being aware of what one perceives through one's external senses – is one thing, but *samādhi* is another. Perception through the five senses, indeed, plays no part in *samādhi*. It is possible to meditate with one's eyes open, but even then, once one is deeply concentrated, one is not concentrating on what is before one's eyes; in fact, one doesn't register any visual perception at all.

Having said that, we should remember that the conceptualizing mind also counts as one of the sense faculties, and that the same controlling faculty of mind (*indriya*) operates whether the eye perceives visual form or the mind perceives mental objects. However, whether one starts off by concentrating on some external object perceived through the five senses, or on an object perceived through the mental sense faculty[481], the mind one starts off with is not the same mind with which one ends up. The whole process is formulated by the Buddha as follows:

> The senses find refuge in the mind as a sixth sense, but the sixth sense finds refuge in mindfulness; and mindfulness finds refuge in 'release'.[482]

Visualization

> Whether it is real or not,
> Whatever becomes truly familiar
> When you have become fully conversant with it
> Results in a clear feeling of presence without subject–object dichotomy. (p. 36)
> *Pramāṇavarttika*

With this quotation from Dharmakīrti, Yeshe Gyaltsen takes us further into the heart of meditation practice, and more specifically visualization practice. You may take as your object of concentration something that can be said actually to exist outside your imagination (like a visualized bodhisattva) or an invented object (like a unicorn). Either way it is, as the object of your meditation, your own creation: you have produced it yourself. Although you perceive it as an object, your connection with it is actually subjective. When you become fully absorbed you become, as it were, one with the object, and it becomes one with you. If you focus on the object without thinking about it, you get a direct experience of it, not mediated by concepts. And as you 'change' the object, you change yourself, and so gradually the two become one.

Samādhi is not *prajñā*

Even if the object of one's meditation is a visualized bodhisattva, even if one merges with that object in *samādhi*, it is still the product of one's mundane mind. It is not the bodhisattva himself or herself. In terms of Tantric meditation practice, a clear distinction is made between the *samayasattva* and the *jñānasattva*. The *samayasattva*, sometimes translated as the 'convention being', is the bodhisattva visualized according to tradition but produced by one's own mind. The *jñānasattva* literally means the 'knowledge being' and – in a manner of speaking – it actually exists; that is, it is *not* a product of one's own mind.

By developing the *samayasattva*, one is preparing a counterpart of the *jñānasattva*, a sort of mundane simulacrum into which the transcendental original, so to speak, can descend, or through which it can manifest. One is tuning in to the *jñānasattva*, the actual Enlightened mind of the bodhisattva, through the mundane meditative experience of the *samayasattva*. When the one descends into the other then one is in contact with the bodhisattva, and that becomes a transcendental experience.

Of course, you don't necessarily have to know anything about the foregoing technicalities for a bodhisattva to appear to you. It may just happen by the sheer impetus of your spiritual practice; you may have a vision. But until it does happen, however it happens, though you may be so absorbed that you can no longer distinguish between yourself and the visualized image, the visualization still remains no more than an image, your own mental creation.

5. APPRECIATIVE DISCRIMINATION (*PRAJÑĀ*)

> Its function is to avoid any confusion or doubt. (p. 37)
> *Abhidharmasamuccaya*

Prajñā,[483] which is often translated simply as 'wisdom' or 'knowledge', is the culmination and purpose of meditation. With *prajñā*, one is able to sort out the qualities of the compounded from those of the Uncompounded, distinguishing clearly between that which is impermanent, insubstantial, painful, and unlovely, and that which is permanent, real, blissful, and beautiful. (This distinction is one which, without *prajñā*, one is simply unable to make. Subject to what the Buddhist tradition calls the four *viparyāsas*, the four 'topsy-turvy views', we are prey to the delusion that what is impermanent is permanent, what is insubstantial is substantial, and so on.)[484]

With *prajñā* one sees the positive as positive (*kuśala* or skilful), the negative as negative (*akuśala* or unskilful), and the neutral – that which is neither positive or negative – as neutral (*avyākṛta*). *Prajñā* is also characterized as 'appreciative' because it is not just intellectual but value-toned, as Guenther would say.[485]

According to Yeshe Gyaltsen's commentary, there are four kinds of knowledge to be cultivated for the attainment of appreciative discrimination: (*a*) *Awareness of what must be done:* Knowledge of activity that is spiritually fitting. (b) *Awareness of relationship:* Knowledge of the kind of relationships that follow from the principle of dependent origination; that is, the relationship between actions and their consequences, karma and *vipāka* – and, indeed, the whole network of relationships elucidated in the Abhidharma. (c) *Awareness of attaining proper validity:* Knowledge of that which is ultimately valid and irrefutable, and of how it is to be obtained. (d) *Awareness of the absolute real:* Knowledge of the Uncompounded itself.[486]

We will discuss further characteristics of this supreme mental event under 'Non-deludedness' – which is the same thing viewed as a positive mental event rather than an object-determining mental event – and under 'Lack of intrinsic awareness'.

Three *yānas*, three views

With the concept of *prajñā* we come to the main locus of contention between the Hīnayāna and the Mahāyāna. According to the Hīnayāna, *prajñā* consists essentially in seeing what we usually think of as the self in terms of its constituent *dharmas*. The Abhidharma is the systematic study of these *dharmas* so as to preclude the possibility that one might think of the psychophysical organism as a self.

The Mahāyāna, on the other hand, sees *prajñā* in terms of the intuition of *śūnyatā*. It regards the Abhidharma's classification of *dharmas* as purely provisional and pertaining to relative or conventional truth, holding that the *dharmas* into which the Abhidharma breaks down the psychophysical organism can themselves be broken down indefinitely. *Dharmas* are not entities, as far as the Mahāyāna is concerned; they are only concepts, and all concepts must be transcended if *prajñā* is to be attained – *prajñā* consisting, as the Mahāyāna maintains, in the intuition or realization of *śūnyatā*, or the emptiness of all concepts. So this – according to some opinions at least – is the Mahāyāna criticism of the Hīnayāna.

The Vajrayāna in its turn would say that the realization of *śūnyatā* in the Mahāyāna is itself limited in that it is purely mental – not that it is merely rational, but that it takes place on just the mental plane. The Vajrayāna is concerned with the direct experience of *śūnyatā*, and maintains that this must involve not only mind but also speech and even the body. The Tantra therefore speaks not just in terms of Enlightenment, but in terms of attaining the *trikāya* – that is, the completely transformed body, speech, and mind – of the Buddha. The idea is that the involvement of all the energies of the psychophysical organism in the process of actually experiencing *śūnyatā* leads to a much more thoroughgoing and complete realization.

In the end, of course, each *yāna* sees the previous one from its own special point of view; whether a real point of view is being criticized when the Hīnayāna or Mahāyāna position is being assailed is open to question. What we can probably say is that a certain solidifying of concepts or settling down with ideas is being criticized in each case. If one reads some of the earliest Pāli texts, for example, one finds little trace of what the Mahāyāna calls the Hīnayāna. Sometimes in the *Sutta-Nipāta* or the *Udāna* one feels as though one is not only in Mahāyāna territory, but even in touch with the Vajrayāna. The three *yānas* constitute a useful framework of reference, but this framework should not be applied too rigidly to the historical material involved.

A progression

The object-determining mental events clearly represent a progressive series, leading from interest, which may or may not be applied to meditation, all the way to intense concentration, which leaves the external, sense-based world behind altogether. However, the culmination of the series, *prajñā*, brings us back, in a sense, to where we started, because wisdom operates whether or not one is in a meditative state of consciousness. Once one has it one doesn't ever lose it, even when one is out and about in the world. One may not be absorbed in *dhyāna*, but one's *prajñā* is alive and functioning.

When one is experiencing *prajñā*, whatever one does there is no absolutely real subject doing it, and no absolutely real object to apply oneself to either. So with the arising of *prajñā* one gets as close to an object as one can possibly get: the object is known as it really is. It is known, in other words, not as an object, ultimately speaking, at all, but as a temporary condensation of conditions which our own propensity for identification (*saṃjñā*) has labelled as a specific object.

The experience of *prajñā* or transcendental insight is a paradoxical thing. It seems, at least in the early stages, to come from outside oneself, though this impression may be corrected by subsequent experience. At the same time it clearly arises in the midst of oneself. It negates one completely and finally, but at the same time it represents one's true individuality.

Prajñā is of course different from Nirvāṇa, which is described as a *dhātu*, a sphere or realm, not simply a state of mind. At least, this is the Hīnayāna Abhidharma point of view. Nirvāṇa, your Hīnayāna Abhidharmika would say, is an objective reality, existing above and beyond the mundane, independently of whether anybody experiences it or not. This is what makes it ultimately real. It's not dependent upon our experience in order to be what it is. However, it is the nature of reality that it is not to be spoken of in terms either of subject or of object. This is why it can be described either as if it were an experience or as if it existed altogether independently of one's experience. So there is no right answer; all one can do is be aware of the limitations of either approach.

7

THE CREATIVE MIND AT WORK

Having outlined the object-determining mental events, Yeshe Gyaltsen moves on to consider the Abhidharma's next classification: the eleven positive (*kuśala*) mental events. The positive mental events come before the negative ones perhaps because it is considered healthier to examine the negative on the basis of an exploration of the positive. (The Indian tradition generally, however, would seem to favour putting it the opposite way round, at least in such teachings as the famous verse from the *Dhammapada*: 'Cease to do evil, learn to do good, purify the heart.')[487]

These eleven are not intended to enumerate a fixed and limited number of mental states. Still, it is notable that just eleven positive mental events are deemed sufficient to set against twenty-six negative ones. The reason for this is no doubt that, as the saying goes, 'There are many ways of being bad, but only one way of being good.' To put it another way, there's a greater variety of sinners than of saints, which is probably why the wicked are regarded as so much more interesting than the good.

Of course, careful consideration of human nature reveals on the one hand what has been termed the banality of evil, and on the other the strong sense of individuality that is an inescapable characteristic of the highly integrated person. But there is no doubt that one follows the 'primrose way to the everlasting bonfire' (as the porter in Shakespeare's *Macbeth*, Act II, scene ii, colourfully describes the downward path) in one's own little way, whereas through becoming more developed one comes to have more and more in common with other more evolved individuals. By their very nature positive mental events tend to cohere, to integrate more and more with each other. A positive action or mental state will partake in some sense of all of the positive mental events, inasmuch as if one of them is definitely absent then one is not in a totally positive mental state. Negative mental events, on the other hand, have the opposite tendency: they represent forces of disintegration, they are more differentiated, and there are therefore more of them.

The eleven positive mental events are simply different aspects of the creative mind. They do not represent a cumulative, graded series like, for example, the seven *bodhyaṅgas.*[488] But there are various connections between the eleven positive mental events and the *bodhyaṅgas*; in particular, the second *bodhyaṅga*, *dharma-vicaya*, is specifically concerned with reviewing one's own mental events, analysing and understanding them. It is, one could say, a practical application of Abhidharmic thinking in the context of meditation.

If one were to take up this practice at the most basic level one would begin by analysing one's mental state simply in terms of the three skilful and unskilful roots: 'Is craving present in my mind? Or hatred? Or delusion?' – and so on. One just follows the rise and fall of mental events in this way. If one keeps it up for long enough and gets competent enough at it, one's attention remains constant even as its object changes. In principle, this is what is meant by *vipaśyanā* meditation.[489]

1. CONFIDENCE-TRUST (OR FAITH) (*ŚRADDHĀ*)

Faith (or confidence-trust, as Guenther translates *śraddhā*) has to come first. It is enumerated first in all the different traditions of the Abhidharma, which is perhaps indicative of its importance. It provides the basis for sustained interest, interest in turn supports the application of effort, and effort is what makes the development of other positive mental events possible.

> It is a deep conviction, lucidity, and longing for those things which are real, have value, and are possible. It functions as the basis of sustained interest. (p. 38)

This quotation, which Yeshe Gyaltsen selects from the *Abhidharma-samuccaya*, specifies three aspects of faith. One could read it as saying that faith consists in deep conviction of what is real, lucidity as to what has value, and longing for what is possible. These three aspects may be found enumerated in various places in the Pāli canon, almost like stock phrases, as if together they made up a formulaic description of faith.

Real

According to Xuanzang the first of these, which he describes as 'the deep understanding of, and the ardent desire for, realities, qualities, and capacities' signifies 'profound faith in, and understanding of, dharmas, that is, in very broad terms, really existing 'things', or principles (verities)'[490]. Yeshe Gyaltsen further identifies the object of this aspect of faith as the law of karma, the fact that if one performs certain actions then certain consequences will inevitably follow.

The second quality of faith is lucidity, a limpidity of mind, a state of serenity, clarity, and a very refined sort of contentment. Yeshe Gyaltsen observes that this comes from an acknowledgement of 'such valuables as' the Three Jewels (the Buddha, Dharma, and Sangha), but we should be clear about what this means. This lucid mind does not arise from a cool, objective recognition of the value of the Three Jewels. It is a response to them, a response which at once introduces a certain order and clarity into one's life and mind. Things are sorted out: there are certain things one is going to do, and certain things one is not going to do. Conflict and indecision give way to a great relief and clarity.

The third aspect of faith is a 'longing for those things which ... are possible'. This explanation is enlarged upon in the *Vijñaptimātratāsiddhi-śāstra*: 'This signifies the profound faith in one's own power to attain and realize all good mundane and supramundane dharmas, and produce the desire and aspiration for them.'[491] Again, Yeshe Gyaltsen draws out the principle in terms of a specific and fundamental doctrine – in this case, the four noble truths: 'When we know that through our efforts these truths can be realized, we certainly will do so.'[492] Faith is therefore the confidence that one may oneself attain the path and the goal represented by the Dharma.

Faith and pleasure

Faith is further characterized by distinguishing it from the mental event with which it is most easily confused: pleasure. Enjoying something – 'getting something out of it' – is different from putting faith in it. Yet, if we're not careful, we don't just enjoy and appreciate ordinary mundane things, we believe in them, we get into them, we emotionally invest in them. The essential difference between faith and pleasure is that the one is unequivocally positive, whereas the other may be positive or negative.

It is not so much that one should not – to use the example offered by Yeshe Gyaltsen[493] – trust one's wife and children, as that one should not trust *in* them. One cannot repose absolute confidence in them. We know this, of course. The admonition 'Put not your trust in princes' is familiar enough to most of us.[494] But it does not stop us from doing it. We repose our trust where we cannot really expect to find ultimate security or happiness. It starts when we are very young, when we are absolutely dependent on our parents for our security, and full satisfaction seems an achievable goal. Though we may be forced to withdraw this naive trust in life, we retain a need to commit ourselves emotionally, and we therefore give our commitment to the things we enjoy and the people we love. We think, 'Well, what else is there?' We know how uncertain life is, we know how dangerous it is to rely on that which is uncertain, but we don't see any other way. The test comes when what we like is taken away from us: our distress and disappointment is the measure of the trust we reposed in whatever, or whoever, it was we liked or loved.

Our apparently infinite capacity for disappointment comes from this tendency to lump pleasure and faith together. When we start to distinguish them, however, Yeshe Gyaltsen maintains that we have four alternative ways to experience them. His list of the alternatives is certainly to the point: (1) liking something but not trusting, (2) trusting but not liking, (3) both, (4) neither.

To elaborate on these a little, firstly, one may like something which is of the mundane world – whether appropriately (wife and children) or inappropriately (getting intoxicated or gormandizing) – but without trusting in it. One reserves faith or trust for the source of one's highest values. This is where some people have trouble with God. It has been said of Cardinal Newman, for example, that he *believed* in God but he didn't trust him.[495]

Secondly, one may trust without liking. One may understand and have faith in, for example, the law of karma – one understands that one's every action will have results – but one doesn't like it much. One doesn't like to have to think about the results of one's unskilful actions. Or there may be a particular spiritual practice which one trusts, believing in its efficacy, but which one doesn't relish much. When faith arose in Milarepa, for example, he didn't like its implications in terms of his future rebirths, should he fail to realize Enlightenment there and then in that lifetime; nor did he enjoy what his teacher put him through in order to prepare him for spiritual practice.

Thirdly, it is possible to have both liking and trust. There is the possibility of joy in one's faith: one is *happy* to trust in the law of karma. If one has practised the Dharma, one is able to rejoice in the merit arising from skilful actions, both one's own and those of other people. When one sees the positive results of spiritual practice one starts to like it, even if it is difficult, demanding practice. However painful it may be to bring about positive change, when one starts liking that positive change, one's attitude to the practice itself will change from faith without joy to joyful faith. We can perhaps observe this development most clearly in our attitude to others who are following the spiritual life. Faith involves a genuine appreciation of and trust in one's spiritual friends as spiritual friends, while at the same time we may like them just as plain friends.

But in the fourth case, where there is neither liking nor trust, all avenues towards happiness of any kind seem closed, and the result is a state of anger and frustration.

Devotion

> Confidence [or faith] ... removes arrogance and becomes the root of devotion. (p. 41)
>
> *Ratnolkānāma-dhāraṇī*

Devotion is an expression of faith, in thoughts, words, and deeds. And faith expresses itself in a sense of humility, gratitude, and devotion towards one's ideal. It is one thing to respect the Buddha as a great teacher, a great thinker, a great reformer, but it is quite another thing – quite a distinct mental event in fact – to respect him as the Enlightened One. Acknowledging the Buddha as the Buddha inevitably prompts one to act – not with a view to *using* the object of one's faith for one's own ends, but simply in order to devote oneself to it.

Unfortunately, devotion is not always an expression of faith. In fact, it is very rarely this. Devotion in the sense of *bhakti* can be delightful and emotionally fulfilling – decorating shrines can give one a great deal of aesthetic pleasure – but smiles and garlands do not add up to true devotion as an expression of faith. In other words, there are two levels of devotion, one antecedent to faith, the other the outcome of faith. The first level has its own value, because it may lead to a genuine receptivity to the Dharma. But devotion as an expression of faith is quite distinct; it is more calm, more serious.

Faith can be identified in a certain sense of care, responsibility, and respect. The precise word is lacking in English, but the quality of mind we should look out for goes back in a way to the old meaning – perhaps the original meaning – of the word 'religion'. It means observing certain things very carefully and mindfully; one is circumspect and scrupulous, even (in this very positive context) fearful, in the way one goes about devotional practice.

It is a very positive thing to decorate a shrine with a genuine feeling of aesthetic pleasure and a certain sense of devotion. But it's possible to do the same thing without that sense of pleasure, and for that to be even more positive – if, that is, one is doing it simply out of faith. When Tibetan Buddhists undertake to perform 100,000 prostrations, say, they do not expect to be getting something out of it all the time. Part of the point of such a massively extended practice is to be able to keep going with it even when one's inspiration dries up and one feels one is just going through the motions.

Faith is not belief in the sense of the acceptance of a set of doctrines; nor is it feeling, whether pleasant, unpleasant, or neutral. It is a separate kind of mental event, a particular kind of emotion felt for the highest spiritual values, especially as represented by the Three Jewels. The test of faith is whether one is able to act on it in the absence of any kind of gratification whatsoever, any kind of pleasurable feeling or emotion associated with the object of one's faith.

Of course, this is by no means always, or even often, going to be the case. But when there is no pleasure, not even spiritual pleasure, to fall back on – when in the midst of a desert of suffering one stays faithful to one's practice – then one can be sure that it really is faith that sustains one's practice. Again taking the example of Milarepa, when his teacher was making him build towers and knock them down again, he had faith even in the complete absence, at least for a while, of any pleasurable feeling at all.

There is a typical story of St Francis on this topic. He and his Little Brothers were having a discussion as to what was the greatest enjoyment they had ever experienced. One said, 'When I was caught up in contemplative rapture – that was the greatest pleasure.' Another said, 'When I was preaching the Word of God and I was carried away by devotion – that was the greatest pleasure.' Each of them had something to relate in this way – and then it was St Francis's turn. He said, 'It's a cold, dark, windy, rainy night. You've had nothing to eat, you've been walking all day, and you've lost your way. You'd give anything for a good hot dinner beside a roaring fire. But you're lost in a wood and the wolves are howling. Then you see a light through the trees, and there's a cottage, with smoke drifting from the chimney. So you knock at the door and it opens ... and a woman shouts at you, "Off with you, you miserable, good-for-nothing friar. There's nothing for you here," and slams the door. *That* is the greatest enjoyment.'[496]

St Francis's inner joy is so great that it can transcend all those experiences. It just burns all the brighter. Standing on nothing, not even an enjoyable religious experience, it comes purely from within. This is the kind of faith which is a positive mental event, a positive emotion. If one has it, even though one may be having immense difficulties in some way, one is quite happy: one has faith and that's all one needs. There is – there has to be – a certain kind of pleasure in faith, but it is quite different from the kind of pleasure that is unrelated to faith.

Faith and culture

Faith is the indispensable emotional or volitional element of any experience of insight into the nature of reality. It is not like plunging optimistically into the dark. It is not blind. There are degrees of faith, obviously – sometimes one may have enough faith to commit oneself without enough to feel total conviction – but faith contains at least a degree of certainty, a degree of knowledge. In Buddhism there is no association of faith with uncertainty. Once one has experienced real faith of this kind, one may forget it from time to time but one never actually loses it. And if one hasn't experienced it then it seems that one cannot help confusing it with simply feeling very good about the spiritual life.

It may therefore seem contradictory to go on to observe that faith seems definitely to inhere in a whole culture – were it not for the fact that in some cultures faith is just as evidently almost entirely missing. When I was living in Kalimpong, almost all the Tibetans I met had some touch of real faith, and many had it to a quite marked degree. I hope I am not lending enchantment to the view of the Tibetan people in the early days of their diaspora, but I think that in general my conclusion does hold good: that Tibetan culture is, or at least was, a culture of faith.

It would surprise many Western people to learn that, for their part, the Tibetans regard the Indian people as deeply irreligious. The fact that we in the West conventionally hold a diametrically opposite view simply highlights the stark materialism and cynicism of our own culture, and the degree to which we have lost touch with any understanding of what faith really is. It is because we have no sense of the real meaning of faith that we regard devotion as somehow naive and superstitious – which of course it is when it is not an expression of faith. Faith is nurtured by a climate of faith, and great spiritual teachers arise in a culture that is able to recognize them. Conversely, it is very difficult to develop faith within a materialist culture, because there is no awareness that anything is missing.

Quite a high proportion of Western Buddhists seem to be ex-Roman Catholics; perhaps this is because as children they had drummed into them the idea that the worldly life isn't everything. If one is brought up Catholic, even if one loses one's faith in the Church, it seems that one still needs to go on looking for something to replace it. Roman Catholics take their faith very seriously indeed, which is why they tend to avoid any serious attempt at dialogue with other faiths. They understand the nature of faith sufficiently clearly to appreciate that such a dialogue is more well-intentioned than meaningful.

I knew a Japanese monk who experienced a clever, not to say Jesuitical, example of non-dialogue from the Vatican. On his way to England he had stopped over in Rome, and being the head of a Buddhist sect in Japan he had secured an audience with the Pope. He was really delighted with what the Pope said during their interview; the pontiff apparently spoke very appreciatively about Buddhism and sent him off with a letter as a record of their amicable exchange. The monk was so overjoyed at this that I asked to have a look at this letter. Although it was on Vatican notepaper it had not been signed by anyone, nor was it addressed to anyone, and all it said was that Buddhism was a very good human teaching. The monk did not see the implication of this statement, but of course the point being made was that Christianity was, by contrast, divine revelation, the teaching of the son of God. So while Buddhism is no longer, at least on the diplomatic level, regarded by the Catholic church as totally false or evil, it is dismissed as a 'human teaching' on a par, say, with the philosophy of Socrates. It is not recognized as a faith.

Faith is action; it is karma, one could say, very weighty karma, although it is not technically classified as such. One might even say (and it is with technicalities like this that the Abhidharma gets a little tricky, so one must tread carefully) that it isn't just weighty karma. When it is categorized as 'lucidity' and 'longing' (though not 'deep conviction') faith is tinged with the transcendental. When as a Buddhist one has faith, one goes for Refuge to the Three Jewels; and the determination to go for Refuge carries that transcendental trace.

But faith is inherent in any positive mental state; it doesn't have to be faith in the Three Jewels as such. It can manifest as simply a vague but powerful inkling of something higher, a conviction that there is something more. Wordsworth describes this sort of feeling:

> ... a sense sublime
> Of something far more deeply interfused,
> Whose dwelling is the light of setting suns,
> And the round ocean and the living air,
> And the blue sky, and in the mind of man.[497]

2. SELF-RESPECT (OR SHAME) (*HRĪ*)[498]

> ... if self respect and decorum are not there, one is incapable of restraining any evil action. (p. 43)
>
> Yeshe Gyaltsen

Yeshe Gyaltsen links this second positive mental event with the third one (translated as 'decorum') because they are regarded as a pair throughout the Buddhist tradition. In the Pāli canon they are jointly referred to as the two *lokapālas*, the two guardians of the world: *hiri* and *ottappa* in Pāli or *hrī* and *apatrāpya* in Sanskrit.[499] They are the guardians of the world because there would be no social order, no civilized existence, without them. The idea that they are the only restraint on our evil actions is perhaps hyperbole, but they are mentioned in all schools of Buddhism and considered very important indeed.

In his very brief remarks on *hrī* (which is translated as 'self-respect'), Yeshe Gyaltsen says, paraphrasing the *Abhidharmasamuccaya*:

> Self-respect ... is to refrain from what is objectionable by having made oneself the norm. (p. 42)

Having made oneself 'the norm' one is setting oneself the highest standards of behaviour. This is self-respect. There are certain courses of action that one's self-respect will not allow one to follow. They just would not be proper, not becoming, not worthy. One would be demeaning oneself to do such things. In its highest development – in the Tantric context – this is what is called '*vajra* pride' or 'Buddha pride': one wants to act according to the dictates of one's essential Buddha-nature.

An interesting association is suggested by Lama Govinda in his discussion of the archetypal Buddha Amitābha in *Foundations of Tibetan Mysticism*. Amitābha's colour is red, and his *bīja* mantra or sacred seed syllable is in fact this word, *hrīḥ*, which literally means 'to blush', 'to feel shame'. Govinda suggests that the colour represents the blush of shame, that is, one's own self-respect responding to one's wrongdoing: 'What makes us blush is the shame we feel in the presence of our better knowledge, our conscience.'[500]

3. DECORUM (OR RESPECT FOR WISE OPINION) (*APATRĀPYA*)

Yeshe Gyaltsen goes on to define *apatrāpya* as:

> to refrain from evil action ... 'because others will despise me'. The primary realm of restraint is the fear that one's guru and teacher and other people deserving respect would be annoyed. (p. 42)

This definition should not be misunderstood.[501] *Apatrāpya* is not about slavishly bowing to external pressure, public opinion, and conventional proprieties, which Guenther's translation of it as decorum would suggest. The more usual definition, in both Pāli and Sanskrit texts, is 'not doing something for which one would be blamed by the wise' and this makes things much clearer.[502]

The essence of the term's meaning is a wish to avoid doing anything that will disappoint people whom one respects as one's spiritual friends, especially those one considers wiser than one is oneself. 'Respect for wise opinion' seems the best translation.

There is no question of being motivated by a feeling of guilt. Guilt is associated with a fear of the withdrawal of affection – but our spiritual friends are not going to withdraw their affection and care, however badly we behave. So there is nothing to fear in that respect. We need be afraid only of letting them down.

In the interests of peace and quiet one may well want to conform to models of behaviour deemed acceptable by society in general, in so far as these do not hinder one's spiritual development. But one has to know what one is doing, and take care that one is not conforming simply out of fear of arousing the disapproval, execration, scorn, or ridicule of society at large. I have sometimes referred to the distinction between 'society', or the aspects of society with which one is personally in contact, and the sangha, which in the broadest sense means the community of men and women who follow the Buddha's teaching, as the distinction between the 'group' and the 'spiritual community'.[503] One must be able to distinguish between the group and the spiritual community, and between conforming to the expectations of the group and living up to the expectations of other members of the spiritual community. Sometimes, indeed, it may be necessary to incur the disapproval of the group in order not to incur the disapprobation of the spiritual community.

It is a question of what one believes in, where one places one's faith. The first three positive mental events are closely related: 'self-respect' implies faith in oneself, while 'fear of blame' implies faith in others. Obviously these other people one has faith in will be spiritual friends: one will have faith both that they have one's best interests at heart, and that they have the insight to know what one's best interests are, to know what is helpful to do and what isn't. The whole point of *apatrāpya* is not to submit to other people's ideas of what one should be doing – ideas that other people want to impose on one – but to follow the ideal that one has chosen for oneself, with the help of certain people, whom one has also chosen.

Having a true regard for your spiritual friends, and knowing that they really want you to make progress, you don't want to make them unhappy by doing something that is going to get in the way of your spiritual development. Trusting them to help reinforce your better self against your weaker self, you are able to use their expectations of you as a support in moments of weakness, and perhaps as an inspiration in times of strength. You have chosen them as spiritual friends because you share their view – or at least your better self shares their view. Of course, it may be that sometimes *they* will need the support of your better self too: sometimes *apatrāpya* is mutually interchangeable between spiritual friends, so that each fears the blame of the other. It needn't be a one-way thing.

Spiritual friendship

It follows that in order to develop *apatrāpya* one needs to be in good, almost familiar contact with the spiritual community, with one's spiritual friends. It's vital never to isolate oneself from the people one looks up to when one is at one's best. A distant and apparently slightly threatening body of people becomes, in one's mind, a kind of authority; it is this sort of perception which probably gives rise to the inappropriate idea that *apatrāpya* is about 'fearing' that others will be annoyed or despise one. Real *apatrāpya* is more like a concern that one's spiritual friends will be troubled, perhaps grieved or even hurt – there isn't the precise word for the emotion in English – by one's unskilful action. And for this kind of mental event to become operative one needs regular contact with 'the wise'. It is not enough just to fear that they might get to hear about what one is doing.

Nor is it enough to regard the Buddhas and Bodhisattvas as one's spiritual friends in this regard. Ideally, one needs actual contact with an actual person. After all, Christians believe that 'the eyes of the Lord are in every place, beholding the evil and the good' and that God sees literally everything that they do. But how many good Catholics are as afraid of God as they are of the local priest?

This is the kind of frailty that draws the withering scorn of Alexander Pope, in whose *Horatian Satires*, Paxton, the Solicitor to the Treasury, declares that men utterly unafraid to disobey God tremble at the very idea of public disgrace.

> Yes, I am proud; I must be proud to see
> Men not afraid of God, afraid of me.[504]

It is therefore safer not to rely entirely on one's ability to fear the discommendation of the Buddhas and Bodhisattvas. At the same time though, this kind of relationship with the Āryasaṅgha, with those who have gained Enlightenment through following the Dharma, can be very beneficial. Of course, there is much that could be said about the nature of this relationship; we have had a hint of it in Yeshe Gyaltsen's verses of praise – but here perhaps we can simply make the connection with the idea of protection. The Buddhas and Bodhisattvas are said to be protectors. They represent the qualities – wisdom, compassion, purity, energy – we ourselves have the potential to develop in their fullness, and in that sense they protect our aspirations to fulfil our potential.

Likewise, *hrī* and *apatrāpya* are called the protectors of the world; but they can also be considered to be protectors of oneself and one's spiritual practice.[505] For example, if one takes a vow in front of a shrine, one is consciously drawing to oneself the protection of *apatrāpya* or fear of blame. One is calling upon the Buddha, the Bodhisattvas, and one's personal friends to witness one's vow, so that they will know the precise standard of behaviour to expect of one with regard to one's practice.

4. NON-ATTACHMENT (*ALOBHA*)[506]

In its most exalted sense, non-attachment is to be not attached to compounded existence or *saṃsāra* – that is, not attached to the three *dhātus* or worlds: of sense desire, of archetypal form, and of no-form. Non-attachment is ultimately, therefore, to be free of attachment to the highest heaven realms, even the most refined levels of meditative experience. According to the *Vijñaptimātratāsiddhi-śāstra*,

> It is the nature of this Caitta to remain detached from, and uninfluenced by, the three states of mortal existence in the three Dhātus and the causes of this triple existence. Its special activity consists in counteracting covetousness and accomplishing good deeds.[507]

Non-attachment or *alobha* (literally, non-greed) is not one of the most popular virtues. It can sound like a purely negative state, consisting merely in the absence of attachment. But as a positive mental event in its own right there must be more to it than this. Non-attachment is not a sort of bloodless lack of interest, although the term might seem to suggest it. It provides the basis for positive action – 'accomplishing good deeds'. In fact, one can only become non-attached by being selectively and consciously attached to what is skilful and positive.

Non-attachment is not quite the same as detachment. 'Detachment' suggests that one's attachment is taken away from something: there are previous or potential objects of attachment from which one has detached oneself. But non-attachment has no reference to any particular object. The traditional image for the condition of non-attachment is that of thistledown blown on the wind.

One is serene, confident, balanced in oneself. One doesn't settle on or stick to things, because one is self-contained. One doesn't feel the need to reach out for something to make one feel better, to make one whole or complete. One doesn't need to be appropriating things or people so as to feel fulfilled. One doesn't insist on keeping certain elements of experience to oneself, or maintaining certain patterns of experience that support a particular idea of oneself. One has the confidence and the wider vision to be free from being neurotically involved with things. As should be clear, generosity is intrinsic to this positive mental event.

The true individual

Being non-attached does not mean being self-contained in a hard-edged way. It is not quite the same as being self-sufficient, which might imply a certain self-protectiveness, even a certain insecurity. If non-attachment means being self-contained, it is also about being an individual, being self-aware, objective, responsible, and sensitive. It is not about self-assertion. Of course, if circumstances require it one has to know how to stand up for oneself, but it is not intrinsic to being an individual to be asserting oneself all the time.

Self-assertiveness is not an intrinsic part of the definition of the true individual,[508] because there are all sorts of circumstances that don't call for it. Self-assertion may simply be evidence of a dependence on the group, a sense of one's own weakness in relation to a projected authority. It's true that an individual is strong, but one should take care not to throw one's weight around with the mistaken view that one is thereby expressing one's individuality. People who demand to be treated 'as an individual' are often simply demanding attention, or claiming special treatment and indulgence.

Non-attachment is a state of individuality, independence, freedom, and creativity, but these are qualities of mind. You don't require them to be recognized by others, and you don't feel that they are under threat when someone resists letting you have your own way, because these qualities are developed in conjunction with responsibility and concern for others. So non-attachment is a state of equilibrium. You don't have to please everybody all the time; but you don't feel you have to displease them either. And if someone tries to pressure you, you may feel sorry or amused, but you don't feel pressured or threatened in any way.

5. NON-HATRED (*ADVEṢA*)

Yeshe Gyaltsen, again treating the subject very briefly, chooses to illustrate this fifth positive mental event with a quotation from the *Abhidharmasamuccaya*:

> It is the absence of the intention to torment sentient beings, to quarrel with frustrating situations, and to inflict suffering on those who are the cause of frustration. (p. 43)

To this we may add, from the *Vijñaptimātratāsiddhi-śāstra*:

> It is the nature of this Caitta to remain non-irritated by the three kinds of suffering and their causes. The three kinds of suffering are: suffering produced by direct causes, suffering by loss or deprivation, and suffering by the passing away or impermanence of all things.[509]

Adveṣa or non-hatred means, firstly, not wanting to hurt people who have given us no cause to hate them. Hatred is the way we react to suffering; and we don't necessarily feel the need to discriminate clearly between worthy and not so worthy objects of our hatred. We simply feel a need to hate someone. Secondly, *adveṣa* means not getting angry with unsatisfactory situations – which means, ultimately, not even raging against the inevitable decay and passing away of things. Thirdly, it means not feeling any ill will towards people who have hurt us, even if they have done so deliberately. *Adveṣa* is not to react to suffering in any of these ways. Although hatred certainly produces suffering – inasmuch as hatred is, at the very least, an immediately painful experience – suffering does not have to produce hatred. We can cultivate *adveṣa* instead.

Attachment

Non-hatred as the absence of the intention to inflict harm also means that one is not providing any occasion for hatred in others. Hatred spawns more hatred; it is contagious. Hatred causes both oneself and others to suffer, and that suffering carries both oneself and others on to further hatred and further suffering. This seems quite obvious: one doesn't inflict suffering directly, and one doesn't deprive someone of what they value, because, apart from anything else, to do so would cause hatred to arise in them.

However, there is the implication in the quotation from the *Vijñapti-mātratāsiddhi-śāstra* that one can become an object of hatred simply by being impermanent. You can be totally faithful to someone all your life, but when you die the person left behind can feel real resentment, as though it were your fault. 'Why did this have to happen to me?' they think, 'Why did you have to die just now, when I needed you so much?' It's irrational, but it happens. Resentment *is* irrational. Even if someone has an accident or contracts a disease through no fault of their own, and they need looking after, it seems that as the carer one naturally feels resentful from time to time. This is not to say that we are responsible for other people's hatred of us; even the Buddha was hated by some people.

There is a close relationship between hatred and attachment; perhaps this is most evident in the context of sexual relationships. One could say perhaps that where attachment is present in a sexual relationship, hatred is bound to arise sooner or later. Are they so very surprising, those terrible fights and quarrels that flare up between sexual partners? They are the inevitable fruit of attachment. If there are no flare-ups, if you can go on for a number of years without violent hatred breaking out, and without just getting into a rut, the likelihood is that attachment is not strongly present and that the relationship is relatively healthy.

But in a sense a healthy relationship ceases to be a relationship. The very term suggests that you are officially together, that you've got to be together, and woe betide anybody who sees you as separate people or treats you as two distinct individuals.

Double negatives

> When a good mind is born, whatever may be its object of perception, it always manifests itself as non-attachment in regard to existence and non-irritation in regard to suffering. This means that non-covetousness and non-anger are established in relation to 'existence' and 'suffering', but it is not necessary for the mind actually to consider existence and suffering in order to manifest these two Caittas. Similarly, the sense of shame and that of integrity are established in relation to good and evil, but it is not necessary for the mind actually to experience good and evil in order to manifest these two Caittas. It follows from this that non-covetousness and non-anger accompany all good minds.[510]
>
> *Vijñaptimātratāsiddhi-śāstra*

All these terms – shame, fear of blame by the wise, non-attachment, and non-hatred – represent positive mental events, not just negative mental events that have somehow failed to materialize. In order to experience or manifest them, one doesn't have to be tempted to do something shameful or blameworthy, or feel on the brink of attachment or aversion. It may seem misleading that grammatically negative expressions are used for positive qualities, but this is a general characteristic of Pāli and Sanskrit; the addition of *a-* as a prefix produces the negative counterpart of a word, rather as adding the prefix 'non-' does in English (so that here we have *dveṣa* meaning 'hatred' and *adveṣa* meaning non-hatred).

It is not usual in English, though, to refer to positive qualities in this 'double negative' sort of way. But there is one obvious example of an English word which is constructed in this way: the word 'immortal'. It literally means 'absence of mortality', but of course it has a very positive connotation of its own. Terms like non-hatred need to be recognized as carrying a similarly positive connotation.

But if 'non-hatred' is not merely the absence of hatred, if it is a positive quality in itself, why is that quality not just termed, say, love or *maitrī* (Pāli *mettā*)? Actually, there is a real point to expressing certain qualities in terms of their opposites, because they acquire thereby an elusiveness that is essential to their meaning. Yes, these qualities are hard to get at through this negative terminology, but that may not be such a bad thing. Faced with these 'negative' terms,[511] we have to ask ourselves, 'What is actually meant here?' The word itself does not allow us to imagine that we know all about it just because we know what the word means. We begin to realize that we have to get a sense of the thing itself – *alobha* or *adveṣa* – as an experience in order to understand what it is about; it isn't enough just to be able to make clear sense of the label. And in fact there is a distinction between these 'negative' expressions and their positive counterparts. For example, loving-kindness goes beyond non-hatred. If you are in a situation where someone is making things very difficult or unpleasant for you, you can experience non-hatred without necessarily experiencing loving-kindness, which suggests that the two are distinct mental events.[512]

In the *Bodhicaryāvatāra*, Śāntideva – apparently following Mahāyāna tradition – regards *kṣānti* (patience) as the positive counterpart of hatred or anger. *Kṣānti* is a form of awareness, an awareness of suffering in which one does not react with anger. It is even a form of transcendental insight in that it arises together with the next positive mental event, non-deludedness. The way Śāntideva puts it, here are all these people effectively helping you to practise *kṣānti* by giving you a hard time – and what do you do? You get angry with them, you poor deluded fool![513]

A positive mental event

While non-hatred and non-attachment support each other – inasmuch as there can be no hatred without attachment, and no attachment without hatred – both are brought into being only through 'non-deludedness', the mental event which follows. Together, these three fundamental positive mental events form the three wholesome roots of all positive action.

6. NON-DELUDEDNESS (*AMOHA*)

> It is a thorough comprehension of (practical) knowledge that comes from maturation, instructions, thinking and understanding,... (p. 44)

This is part of the quotation from the *Abhidharmasamuccaya* with which Yeshe Gyaltsen begins his commentary on the positive mental event non-deludedness. He goes on to remark:

> It is a distinct discriminatory awareness to counteract the deludedness that has its cause in either what one has been born into or what one has acquired. (p. 44)

So non-deludedness or *amoha* is a thorough knowledge that comes in four different ways. It arises firstly from maturation, by which is meant the natural intelligence one is born with, as a result (*vipāka*) of having developed one's moral and intellectual understanding in the past. The other three ways consist in the active cultivation of non-deludedness through the three knowledges: *śruta-mayī-prajñā*, *cintā-mayī-prajñā*, *bhāvanā-mayī-prajñā*: literally 'the wisdom arising from hearing, the wisdom arising from thinking/reflecting, and the wisdom arising from meditation'.

The first of these is the understanding one gets from instruction – that is, Dharma study, ideally with one's teacher. The second is the result of consideration: thinking, reflecting, turning the teachings over in one's own mind, and relating them to one's own experience. And the third knowledge comes from understanding or intuition, which refers to meditation: focusing on the teaching while in a state of meditative concentration, and thereby gaining insight into it, making a real experience of it, actually being changed by it. So learning provides the raw material for thinking which in turn provides the raw material for meditation.

Prajñā and *amoha*

We get another angle on this from the *Vijñaptimātratāsiddhi-śāstra*[514]

> According to one opinion, non-delusion is of the same nature as discernment [i.e. *prajñā*], because the Abhidharma says that 'non-delusion has as its essential nature the certitude which arises from retribution, instruction, demonstration, and intuition'.... Although non-delusion is discernment by nature and is essentially a special Caitta, still, in order to indicate that the good aspect of discernment possesses a superior power for the accomplishment of good acts, it is separately regarded as a 'good Caitta' ...

According to another opinion (Dharmapāla), non-delusion is not discernment; it has a separate self-nature. For it is directly opposed to ignorance and, like non-covetousness and non-anger, it is comprised among the roots of good ...

It is true that the *Abhidharmasamuccaya* says that non-delusion is discernment by nature; but this text explains the nature of non-delusion in terms of its cause and fruit.... The cause of non-delusion is discernment.[515]

The point of controversy here is whether or not non-deludedness is the same as 'discernment' (by which is meant *prajñā* or wisdom). If they are the same, why is *prajñā* a 'special *caitta*' (what Guenther calls an object-determining mental event) while non-deludedness is a 'good *caitta*' (i.e. a positive mental event)? But if they are different, why is non-delusion defined by the Abhidharma in such terms as to suggest that it is *prajñā*?[516] We may say that the controversy is more apparent than real. We have to remember that we are concerned not with things, but with relations.[517] Object-determining mental events have the function of getting to ever closer grips with the object, and wisdom does this by dispelling doubt. Non-deludedness, on the other hand, is a positive mental event in its own right. It is not that it confronts or gets to grips with the object but that it provides the basis 'for the accomplishment of good acts', 'for not becoming involved in evil behaviour'.

It is tempting to try to simplify things by seeing non-delusion as *prajñā* manifesting on a different level, so to speak. However, the Abhidharma is very careful to avoid using this kind of language. Yeshe Gyaltsen describes non-deludedness as a '*distinct* discriminatory awareness' – in other words, a special form of wisdom that counteracts delusion or ignorance as to what is skilful and what is unskilful. This is why Guenther adds the word 'practical': 'It is a thorough comprehension of (practical) knowledge'. In brief, therefore, *amoha* is a positive mental event that is *prajñā* (primarily an object-determining mental event) in its aspect of distinguishing in practical terms between what is skilful and what is unskilful.[518]

Being and doing

Appreciative discrimination (*prajñā*) is, if you like, concerned with knowing what *is*, while non-deludedness is concerned with knowing what to do. It seems that most people tend, perhaps by temperament, to be more interested in one than the other, but it is generally metaphysics that holds the greater appeal; questions of ethics tend to be dismissed as being dry or boring. Certainly when I was young – in my late teens and even my early twenties – I was much more interested in knowing 'what is' than in knowing 'what to do'. It was as though what one did more or less took care of itself, leaving the mind free to think about 'what is'.

For example, I remember that when as a young soldier in the last war I was stationed in Singapore, some friends asked me why I was not a vegetarian. As it happened I had simply never thought about it before. I'd never thought, 'Is it skilful or unskilful to eat meat? Would it not be more skilful to become a vegetarian?' In several years of reading books about Buddhism it had never crossed my mind to question my own behaviour in this way. But when it was questioned *for* me I realized at once that a Buddhist had to try to be a vegetarian, which is what I did. But it was not the sort of thing I was interested in. I was interested in knowing about *śūnyatā*, the One Mind, and so on, not in knowing which actions were skilful and which were not. That came very much later on.

Very generally, one could say that the sort of people who want to know 'what is' attend lectures and read books on Buddhism, while those who want to know 'what to do' go along to meditation classes and join in other Buddhist activities. Perhaps it is a question of age, responsibility, and experience. If one has had some involvement with the world, one will have had to live with the choices one has made, perhaps for a long time, which will make one realize the importance of knowing how to behave skilfully. When one is young, on the other hand, one is less likely to have this sort of perspective; one's focus is more likely to be on wanting to know things as they are in reality.

Theory and practice

This distinction is not, of course, between knowing and doing, theory and practice, but between two kinds of theory. Having developed an understanding of what is skilful and what isn't, one still has to put that theory into practice. As well as maintaining a balance between these two aspects of knowledge one needs also to maintain a balance between knowing why one practises and actually practising. This is *amoha*, non-deludedness, the vital link between the ultimate metaphysical questions and our own existential situation. The Abhidharma tradition considers it so important that it enumerates non-deludedness as a skilful mental event in its own right.

We can think of *amoha* as the practical aspect of *prajñā*, and this emphasis reflects what it's actually like to become involved with Buddhism. In a sense one has already determined 'what is' by the very fact of having taken up the practice of Buddhism. One has accepted that Enlightenment is the ultimate goal, that the transcendental is there beyond one's mundane experience of the world, and that one is trying to work towards that. One acknowledges that it is a long way off, and that in the meantime one just has to get on with whatever lies to hand. One presses on with one's meditation, gets on with one's work, cultivates one's spiritual friendships, goes on retreat, and all the rest of it. Whether in the end one is going to experience the Void, or the One Mind, one can probably quite safely wait and see.

This is the attitude of many practising Buddhists, including monks in the East, particularly if they have no great aptitude for metaphysics. They don't think too often or too deeply about the whys and wherefores of their practice. It has to be said that some Theravādins take this attitude too far and completely ignore ultimate questions of metaphysics, even claiming that the Buddha told his followers not to think about such matters. This is, of course, a mistake. What could be more practical and down-to-earth than exploring the true nature of reality?

However, there is a great deal of sense in making up one's mind once and for all about the general spiritual pattern within which one needs to work and then fully involving oneself in it. This doesn't mean becoming mechanical and superficial and getting in a rut. After all, one's regular practice includes meditation, mindfulness, reflection, and study. As Candrakīrti robustly puts it, 'Those who go through the day without wondering about the existence or non-existence of things are not fit to be called human.' But wondering about the existence or non-existence of things does not mean questioning the very basis of one's practice. It does not mean constantly wondering whether perhaps the Sufis or the

Vedāntins have a more profound conception of 'what is' than is to be found in Buddhism.

The aspect of one's practice which does need consideration from time to time is the question of what is truly and deeply skilful and what isn't. From time to time one may need to review one's practice and see if any modification is required – but not all the time. One can't stop every minute of the day to work everything out all over again. Once, as a result of some thought and investigation, one has made the decision to accept a particular pattern of spiritual practice – because it seems to be a positive, helpful one – one has to commit oneself to it, otherwise one will never be able to test its validity for oneself. If one is always questioning it one cannot very well commit oneself to it, and then one will never know anything much about it anyway. One is likely to arrive at some kind of Perfect Vision – actually seeing 'what is' and indeed also 'what to do' – not by working out 'what is', or even 'what to do', but by getting on with regular practice.

An eternal legacy

Non-deludedness is cultivated through studying the Buddha's teachings in one form or another. Yeshe Gyaltsen lists twelve different classes of teaching (collectively known as *dharmapravacana*, 'Exposition of the Doctrine') identified by the Sarvāstivādins (though the Theravādins recognize only the first nine). The first five are: *sūtras* (discourses in prose), *geyas* (mixed prose and verse), *vyākaraṇas* (predictions to Enlightenment), *gāthās* (verses), and *udānas* (inspired utterances). The sixth class of scripture is the *nidāna*. *Nidāna* means 'connection', and the connection is usually between the past and the present via, say, a *jātaka* story. Whereas a *jātaka* is simply the story of one of the Buddha's past lives, a *nidāna* makes the connection with the present, with one character in the story being identified as the Buddha's companion Ānanda, another as the Buddha, and so on. *Nidāna* also means a continuous narrative – for instance, a connected account of certain events in the life of the Buddha.

The other classes of scripture are *avadānas* (heroic deeds of disciples of the Buddha in their previous lives), *itivṛttakas* ('Thus it was said' – sayings of the Buddha), *jātakas* (birth stories), *vaipulyas* (extended discourses), *adbhuta-dharmas* (miraculous happenings), and *upadeśas* (instructions).[519]

Yeshe Gyaltsen goes on to point out that the teachings may also be classified according to the three *piṭakas* or baskets: the Sūtra Piṭaka, the Vinaya Piṭaka, and the Abhidharma Piṭaka. We can get an idea of the balance of the content of these three collections by considering to what extent they cover the stages of the path: *śīla*, *samādhi*, and *prajñā*. One could estimate that the *sūtras* – or rather the *suttas* – of the Pāli canon deal more or less equally with all three; by and large, the *vinaya* is concerned with *śīla* and *samādhi*; while the Abhidharma is devoted entirely to the development of *prajñā* through a review of the *dharmas*. (According to the Hīnayāna, especially as developed in the Abhidharma, *prajñā* consists in an understanding of the content of the Abhidharma itself.)

The product of wisdom

The Vinaya Piṭaka is conventionally regarded as consisting in a specifically monastic code of rules, but this is not really so. The original separation of *sūtra* from *vinaya* occurred as part of the oral tradition, before these teachings were written down – and before the first compilation of the Abhidharma – and it was meant simply to distinguish the teachings as a whole from an account of their practical application in terms of 'discipline', particularly as exemplified in the everyday activity of the Buddha himself.

The Vinaya is, therefore, the product of non-deludedness or *amoha*; it is the product of practical wisdom. It is not simply a matter of observing rules. In fact, thinking exclusively in terms of observing rules can have a deleterious effect, spiritually speaking, in that you get depressed when you break a rule and elated when you keep one. One also inevitably seems to attach too much importance to certain rules, and this unbalanced view of one's practice leads one to veer from one emotional extreme to another. It is fair enough to standardize skilful mental attitudes in the form of rules, though this term is perhaps not ideal; but the point of them is to help one do what is skilful in a regular and consistent manner.

This is perhaps clearer if we think in terms of precepts rather than rules. Of course, the rules of the Vinaya were originally laid down as specific applications of the ethical precepts; many of them had reference to the specific cultural situation of the time, and make little sense today.

But in general, rules – appropriate rules – give stability to one's whole life, and thus in fact remove elation and despondency. So it is less a matter of observing rules than of having a firm basis to fall back on, a disciplined way of life that protects one against ups and downs.

Fuel for meditation

The cultivation of non-delusion is not, therefore, a matter of learning rules any more than it is a matter of amassing facts. This said, study of some kind is probably essential:

> Knowing little, the blind men do not know how to bring
> contemplation to life.
> Because they lack that, they cannot think of anything. (p. 47)
> Aśvaghoṣa

Of course, one has to be careful in criticizing the way other people go about their practice. One has to make due allowance for differences of temperament: there are doctrine-followers (*dharmānusārins*), who are particularly stimulated and inspired by study; and there are faith-followers (*śraddhānusārins*), who are much more concerned with actual practice: meditation, maintaining close contact with their teacher, and so on.[520]

However, taken to extremes, either of these approaches can leave us high and dry. If we don't develop *śruta-mayī-prajñā* (the wisdom arising from studying the Dharma) and *cintā-mayī-prajñā* (the wisdom arising from reflecting on what we have studied), we will not be able to develop *bhāvanā-mayī-prajñā*, the transcendental insight that arises from meditating upon what we have studied and reflected on. In short, we will have nothing to meditate on.

On the other hand, some of the more learned *geshes*, particularly of the Gelugpa tradition, get so deeply into study that they make no time, even towards the end of their lives, for meditation. I have met one or two Tibetan *geshes* who say that meditation isn't necessary, although this is not the orthodox Gelugpa view. Some even openly scoff at the tantras: 'What is the point of all this ringing of bells and banging of drums?' they say. 'Buddhism is really all about metaphysics and logic!' What we all need, of course, is a balance; the lives of Buddhism's most eminent practitioners exemplify a balanced approach. Padmasambhava, for example, was a great scholar as well as a great yogi, and even Milarepa had a comprehensive knowledge of the tantras.

Roots and levels

Taking the three wholesome roots of non-attachment, non-hatred, and non-deludedness together, we find they can be experienced at three different levels. On the first level, the three poisons (that is, their negative counterparts, attachment, hatred, and delusion) are overcome as regards this life, but they have been displaced on to a future life, perhaps in heaven. At this level, while one has no attachment to this life – one knows it is impermanent – one is attached to the idea of a permanent heaven, and woe betide anyone who gainsays that. The second level represents the *arhant* ideal of the Hīnayāna – at least according to the Mahāyāna. According to this, while there may be no attachment to any form of satisfaction whatsoever, whether now or in future lives, there is still a very refined attachment to the attainment of Nirvāṇa itself. This allows for a third level to be posited by the followers of the Mahāyāna, who look forward not to a Nirvāṇa that can be localized or particularized in straightforward contradistinction to *saṃsāra*, but to the *apratiṣṭhita nirvāṇa*, that is, a non-localized or, more literally, non-established or non-abiding Nirvāṇa.[521] Even in the attainment of Nirvāṇa, it seems, there is to be no settling down.

7. DILIGENCE (OR ENERGY IN PURSUIT OF THE GOOD) (*VĪRYA*)

Vīrya is another of those terms for which there is no adequate English translation. In fact, even the Sanskrit word did not originally carry the full meaning that it bears as a specifically Buddhist term. It means 'strength' or 'energy', but in the Buddhist context it means more than this. For a start it has a purely positive connotation. The important corollary is that energy as such is not necessarily *vīrya*, or even necessarily positive. It is commonly assumed that 'freeing up one's energy' is somehow positive in a spiritual sense, but in fact it is positive only when the energy freed up is directed towards the positive.

We get a truer feeling for the idea of *vīrya* if we take the emphasis away from the notion of energy altogether and translate it as intentness on, or a powerful inclination towards – in the literal sense of bending towards – the skilful. This also helps to emphasize the fact that we are talking about a mental event here – not simply busying oneself doing good. That is, *vīrya* is a mental event that expresses itself in action; it is not the activity itself.

Yeshe Gyaltsen has quite a lot to say about *vīrya* (which Guenther translates as 'diligence'). Here we will focus on one of the quotations given from the *Abhidharmasamuccaya*, a list of five kinds or stages of *vīrya*:

a. Diligence which is ever ready

Gyaltsen elaborates on this with the help of a quotation from the *Pāramitāsamāsanāma*:

> When the mind, having been released from the
> frustrations of
> One's round of *saṃsāra*, becomes ever active,
> Immovable and infinite, that (mind) becomes possessed of
> The capacity towards the wholesome which is a brave mode of
> action,
> And is said to be the first of the pure things to be grasped. (p. 50)

This is the pure capacity for *vīrya*, before it has been manifested in action. It is the readiness to apply oneself. Yeshe Gyaltsen characterizes this stage as 'to put on the heavy armour', which is quite a common idiom in Buddhist texts – as it is in the Christian tradition: St Paul talks of putting on the full armour of Christ, for example. The spirit of the image is clearly voiced in the words of William Blake:

> Bring me my bow of burning gold:
> Bring me my arrows of desire:
> Bring me my spear: O clouds, unfold,
> Bring me my chariot of fire.
>
> I will not cease from mental fight,
> Nor shall my sword sleep in my hand,
> Till we have built Jerusalem
> In England's green and pleasant land.[522]

Putting on armour simply means getting ready for battle. We should be careful not to take from the phrase the impression of a hard, rigid, resistant attitude being adopted. *Vīrya* is not about sealing oneself off.[523] We should also be careful not to take the idea that *vīrya* is 'the first of the pure things to be grasped' too simplistically. We have already been told that *śraddhā*, for example, is the spiritual quality upon which all others depend; from which we can only conclude that these positive qualities are not to be found as separate entities. They tend to arise together; in a sense they are aspects of each other. Where there is energy in pursuit of the good, there one will find some measure of faith, and vice versa.

b. Diligence which is applied work

When one actually gets down to applying oneself, one exhibits *vīrya* in two quite different ways. One can steadily plod along the path one knows one needs to follow even though it may currently be a rather joyless exercise; or one can follow the same path enthusiastically. These two modes of *vīrya* may seem different, but the first will eventually lead to the second. Directing one's energies towards what one knows to be wholesome in a steady, systematic, persistent way – albeit without a lot of joy – will have positive effects, and enthusiasm will naturally tend to arise more and more as one keeps going.

The second can unfortunately give way to the first from time to time as well – one's enthusiasm can sometimes melt away – and then *vīrya* consists in carrying on without it. The crucial point is that enthusiasm is not necessary in order to keep up a steady practice. To say 'I don't really feel inspired about doing this (whatever it is), so it would be better if I didn't get involved,' is a rationalization, a specious excuse for laziness. Motivation, enthusiasm, and inspiration will arise as long as we just get on with the job.

c. Diligence which does not lose heart

This is *vīrya* as stout-heartedness, applying oneself with courage and confidence, not losing heart in moments of personal frailty. It calls for a measure of *śraddhā* in the sense of confidence in one's own potential.

d. Diligence which does not turn back

One may take it upon oneself to achieve a certain goal and, having foreseen quite clearly all the obstacles that are likely to arise, one may estimate that one has the resources to fulfil the task one has set oneself. But what happens when one runs up against an obstacle that one had not anticipated? One may quite reasonably feel like saying, 'This was not in the bargain. What has arisen is outside the range of conditions under which I was prepared to make an effort. Sorry.' But one needs to realize that in fact this almost always happens. Some unforeseen difficulty or other almost always crops up, whatever one is trying to do. If what one is trying to do is skilful, this is where *vīrya* – in the sense of applying oneself with complete thoroughness, not turning back – comes in. One doesn't abandon one's original intention just because the going has become more difficult than one had expected.

e. Diligence which is never satisfied

Whatever one has achieved, however exalted it may be, one never rests on one's laurels. The very nature of *vīrya* is that it goes on and on, as long as there is something higher to be achieved – and of course there always is. When, in the *White Lotus Sūtra*, the Buddha announces this fact to an enormous gathering of bodhisattvas, *arhants*, Stream Entrants, laymen, laywomen, *rākṣasas*, *gandharvas*, and many other beings, it is altogether too much for some of them. Five thousand 'persons of overbearing arrogance' simply walk out. The revelation that they cannot rest satisfied with their attainment is just too much.[524] One could say that *vīrya* in this sense involves a perception and understanding of the full extent of development, represented by the path.

8. ALERTNESS (OR TRANQUILLITY) (*PRAŚRABDHI*)

Physical and mental

Guenther's translation of *praśrabdhi*, 'alertness', will not do at all. Many of his translations are exceptionally precise and helpful, but sometimes it seems that he translates the word but not the meaning. He is at pains to call upon contemporary, philosophical, linguistic, and analytical terminology in constructing his translations but he doesn't always relate the result back to actual spiritual experience, even though he always made much of the Tantric emphasis on 'actual experience'. Like Caroline Rhys Davids' notorious translation of *jhāna* (the Pāli equivalent of *dhyāna*) as 'musing', Guenther's translation of the Tibetan word for *praśrabdhi*, however correct from a philological point of view, does not help us to understand what is actually being talked about.

Literally, *praśrabdhi* is tranquillity, relaxation, calming down. What, though, is being calmed down? We can get an idea of this from considering *praśrabdhi* as the fifth of the twelve positive *nidānas* or links comprising the spiral path that leads us from the endless wheel of compounded existence to Enlightenment.[525] It comes between *prīti* (ecstasy or rapture) and *sukha* (bliss), and it signifies the whole process of calming down and releasing unresolved energy in *dhyāna* (higher meditative states).

As we have already seen (p. 518 above), all five factors of meditation are present in the first level of *dhyāna*: *vitarka* and *vicāra* (initial thought and sustained thought), *ekāgratā* (concentration), *prīti* (rapture), and *sukha* (bliss). As absorption deepens, thought dies away and one experiences a clear, conceptless concentration together with ecstasy and bliss. Then, as absorption deepens still further, the element of physical ecstasy – *prīti* – is increasingly contained by or assimilated into a growing experience of purely mental bliss – *sukha*. This process of containment or assimilation is *praśrabdhi*; it is by means of *praśrabdhi* that absorption deepens.

Yeshe Gyaltsen asserts that *praśrabdhi* is twofold:

> Physical alertness means that when through the power of concentration the sluggishness of the body, which does not allow one to do anything, has been overcome, one feels light like cotton floating in the air and the body can be made to work towards any positive value one wishes. Mental alertness means that when through the power of concentration, mental sluggishness has been removed, the mind moves on towards its object without friction and can operate smoothly. (p. 53)

Thus there are two aspects of *praśrabdhi*. It is physical, though not in the sense of the physical body but in the sense of the mental factors of feeling (*vedanā*), perception (*saṃjñā*), and motivation (*saṃskāras*), which subside as the attention is withdrawn from the body and its concerns. And it is also mental, in that the unconscious energy which arises in the form of physical ecstasy is absorbed into the experience of purely mental bliss.

It would seem as though in the state of *prīti* deeper sources of energy are tapped, blocked energy is released, and the upward rush of that energy is experienced as intensely pleasurable in a bubbly sort of way. But it isn't completely integrated and it may even bubble over – as one is sitting in meditation, one may start laughing or twitching or shaking. All this is unintegrated energy breaking out in various ways. It is possible to find oneself completely taken by surprise and thrown off balance.

As *praśrabdhi* begins to develop, the effervescence subsides, but one doesn't return to a comparatively emotionless state: one is left with a feeling of exhilaration which is no longer out of control. The rapture does not disappear, or even lessen. It simply contributes to the intensification of the blissful feeling, giving it a light, floating quality, while at the same time it becomes quieter, so to speak, more pure and stable.

This is in no way a passive state – in fact it makes it very easy to do anything, either mentally or physically. Everything becomes very pleasant, flowing, smooth, spontaneous. *Praśrabdhi*, sometimes translated as 'pliancy', makes the mind pliable, adaptable, easily worked with. Obviously, a very useful quality.

9. CONCERN (OR NON-HEEDLESSNESS) (*APRAMĀDA*)

> From taking its stand on non-attachment, non-hatred, and non-deludedness coupled with diligence, it considers whatever is positive and protects the mind against things which cannot satisfy. (p. 54)
>
> *Abhidharmasamuccaya*

This is *apramāda*. The very last words the Buddha spoke before he died were apparently (in Pāli) *appamādena sampādetha*, usually translated 'With mindfulness, strive on.'[526] But *apramāda*, which is sometimes translated 'conscientiousness', means mindfulness in a special active sense: it is to keep up mindful attention in order to guard against unskilful action. A very full account of this quality appears in a beautiful little memoir of Surendranath Dasgupta by his wife Surama. Dasgupta was possibly the greatest Indian scholar of modern times and also a distinguished Bengali poet. His wife's account of his life includes a large number of letters he wrote to her, from one of which are extracted the following reflections on *apramāda*:

> The word *pramāda* means inadvertence. In simple Bengali it means lack of attention. Therefore the term '*a-pramāda*' will mean absence of inattention.... But ... why should the scriptures use the word in a negative form, i.e. instead of emphasizing attention ... why should they speak of 'lack of inattention'?
>
> The word '*pramatta*' ([he] who is under *pramāda*) means a drunkard or a lunatic.... So we see the word '*pramāda*' means error, ignorance, drunkenness, inadvertence or carelessness and laxity.... The negative particle [prefix] *a-* stands here in the sense of the 'least amount' of *pramāda*. Therefore *apramāda* does not mean that we have been able to eliminate *pramāda* completely, but that we have been able to reduce it.... All the time, inattention and errors are trying to get hold of us, but our mind, keeping alert all the time, is trying to drive them away.
>
> [*Apramāda*] is not one of those functions of the mind which we call accomplished or stabilised. In *apramāda* we get the idea of a movement or a process. The brightness of intellect, tenacity and firmness are steady characters of the mind. But *apramāda* is of the nature of movement. Our mind is always drawn towards small achievements in the outside world. We have, therefore, to withdraw our mind from those small interests, keep it alert so that we are not dragged into a current to other goals, and we have to be very careful that we are moving towards the achievement which we value and which we desire.
>
> [*Apramāda*] is not the same as the presence of attention, because the attention that we require for study is punctuated with gaps; we try to collect knowledge and move on from one object to another. Therefore our attention also shifts from object to object. It is not like the continuous flow of the River Ganges.... Therefore, we should distinguish between *apramāda* ... and the presence of attention, by accepting the former as an attribute of the spirit.[527]

So according to Dasgupta *apramāda* is expressed in this negative form because it is not a quality that is achieved, but a process, an activity, that one engages in. Because things are always happening we have to be continually on our guard, continually taking precautions against the ever-present possibility of being taken unawares. If *vīrya* is like arming oneself, then *apramāda* is the battle itself – in other words, one needs *vīrya* to apply *apramāda*. But though energy in pursuit of the good provides one with the spiritual fuel to advance along the whole front of one's spiritual practice – developing the positive as well as warding off the negative – the main thrust of one's practice at the outset of one's spiritual life is generally to engage this quality of non-heedlessness.

Clearly, non-heedlessness is supported by mindfulness, especially by mindfulness of purpose (*saṃprajanya*). But it should not be confused with mindfulness as such – as it is in the common translation of the Buddha's famous last words. As we have seen, *smṛti* is firstly 'recollection' in the sense of calling up something of the past, and secondly 'mindfulness' in the sense of being aware in the present, whether that awareness is of one's body, one's thoughts, one's feelings, or the Dharma itself. When, as a result of directing one's awareness towards the Dharma, one gains insight into the truth, that awareness becomes knowledge in the sense of *prajñā*.

Non-heedlessness, however, is mindfulness in an essentially defensive posture – the quality of being on the alert for interruptions, temptations, and unskilful states. It is of crucial importance; indeed, as the *Dhammapada* suggests, it is the difference between life and death:

> Non-heedlessness is the basis of immortality. Negligence is the state of death.[528]

10. EQUANIMITY (*UPEKṢĀ*)

> It is a mind which abides in the state of non-attachment, non-hatred, and non-deludedness coupled with assiduousness [*vīrya*].... It is a state where mind remains what it is – a state of being calm and a spontaneous presence of mind. Its function is not to provide occasions for emotional instability. (p. 55)
>
> *Abhidharmasamuccaya*

As we have already seen, there are three levels or types of equanimity or *upekṣā*. The first is 'hedonic indifference',[529] a state of indifference with regard to feelings coming in through the senses. We are all familiar with this basic level of *upekṣā* – which is in no way a positive mental event – and we need to be careful not to confuse it with the others.

The third form of *upekṣā* is synonymous with Nirvāṇa, and it is in this sense that it occurs as the seventh and last of the *bodhyaṅgas* or factors of Enlightenment. As we have seen, it is a state of equilibrium with regard to all mundane things whatsoever. From the Mahāyāna point of view it is a state of equilibrium between *saṃsāra* and *nirvāṇa*. One might also describe it as a state of metaphysical axiality: that is, one becomes – in a manner of speaking – the axis upon which the universe turns. Again, this third level of *upekṣā* should not be confused with the second level, which is the positive mental event under discussion here.

This second level – *upekṣā* as a positive mental event – is equanimity as a factor of the fourth *dhyāna*. We have seen that the higher one's consciousness progresses through the four *dhyānas*, the fewer the mental factors: not that mental factors are eliminated, but they become more and more fully integrated with one another. This gradual process of consolidation, integration, and refinement leads towards a state of greater and greater stability.

In the third *dhyāna* the factor of physical ecstasy is absorbed into the factor of bliss through the process of *praśrabdhi*, so that one is left with just the factors of bliss and one-pointedness or concentration[530]. And in the fourth *dhyāna* the process continues. The bliss becomes transformed into *upekṣā* or equanimity, while one-pointedness becomes unshakeable. So equanimity in this sense is the strength that comes from complete emotional integration and stability.

11. NON-VIOLENCE (*AVIHIṂSĀ*)

To quote from Yeshe Gyaltsen's own commentary:

> Non-violence is patient acceptance [*kṣānti*] which expresses itself in the sentiment of how wonderful it would be if suffering sentient beings could be released from all their frustrations …

To fulfill the *vinaya*, it is necessary to carry about a water strainer in order to avoid harming life in water. Since a person who does not carry a water strainer is one who goes against loving kindness taught by the Buddha, he must be uprooted from his foundation of harming another and be earnestly advised of the need to actualize the four attitudes by which one becomes an ascetic, namely,

1. Even if one is reviled, he should not revile in return.
2. Even if one is angered, he should not retaliate with anger.
3. Even if one is struck, he should not strike back.
4. Even if someone pries into one's affair, he should not pry into someone else's affair.

... the renunciation of violence is the quintessence of the teaching. (pp. 57–8)

Avihiṃsā or abstention from harming is the first and most fundamental of the precepts; in a sense, any breach of the precepts is an act of violence. At the same time, inasmuch as it is about not having even the slightest idea of harming any living being – that is, in that it is a positive mental event – it is very closely akin to loving-kindness (*mettā*) and even compassion (*karuṇā*).

Of course, the principle of non-violence is virtually synonymous with Buddhism in many people's minds, but it still seems that Buddhists themselves rather take it for granted. There's much more to it than one might think; it means an entirely different mode of operating. Sometimes I have characterized it as operating according to the 'love mode' rather than the 'power mode'. But if one thinks about it, a great deal of life in society is based on force, on the power mode. Exercising power isn't just about literal violence; it includes emotional blackmail, and all sorts of subtle methods of coercion.

But if one wants to follow a spiritual life one has more or less to abandon the power mode and operate in accordance with the love mode. Sometimes one may be in a situation in which the use of power is necessary; for example, if you run a business and someone owes you money, it may be necessary eventually to take him to court, which is in a sense invoking force. If you know that he has money, that may be the best thing to do; but if, on the other hand, you are aware that he is in real financial difficulties, you may decide not to pursue the matter.

Within the spiritual community power should never be used, because that would be to negate everything the spiritual community stands for. If you use violence towards someone, whether overtly or covertly, you are not treating him as an individual. To the extent that one does act violently, even to the extent of speaking harshly, one places oneself outside the spiritual community.

A diet of non-violence

The principle of non-violence is to be practised not just with regard to other people, but also with regard to animals, and to our environment. The water strainer Yeshe Gyaltsen refers to is one of the 'eight requisites', the eight things with which monks are provided when they are ordained, together with the three robes, the needle and thread, the bowl, the razor blade, and the girdle.[531] Presumably without a water strainer it would have been all too easy, when drinking from pools and rivers, inadvertently to swallow all sorts of minute living things.

This is just one indication of how seriously the first Buddhists took their practice of non-violence. But how far do we need to carry this principle of *avihiṃsā*? The Buddha made a clear distinction between what is intentional and what is unintentional – so that if you accidentally swallow a fly, say, this does not constitute bad karma. (This is implicit in the doctrine that karma equals *cetanā*.) However, for Mahāvīra, the founder of Jainism, even the unintentional taking of life was bad karma. Therefore, whereas the followers of the Buddha were enjoined simply to take reasonable precautions, the Jains went to extreme lengths – wearing masks over their faces and sweeping the ground before them – so as to avoid the remotest possibility of swallowing or stepping on any insects. Of course, with the discovery of microscopic living organisms, the Jain position is very difficult to sustain.

How far one takes one's practice of *avihiṃsā* in this respect will depend upon one's sensitivity; perhaps the best thing is to take it just a little bit further than one's sensitivity to the issue demands. One very basic aspect of practising *avihiṃsā* is being vegetarian. Perhaps you still eat cheese, drink cow's milk, or wear leather shoes, but you draw a firm line at actually eating meat. If one is not a vegetarian, there must be a question mark over whether one is really a Buddhist at all.

For me one of the saddest experiences of living in the East was that so many people calling themselves Buddhists – particularly Buddhist monks – were so unwilling to consider becoming vegetarian. Chinese, Vietnamese, Korean, and Indian monks were almost invariably vegetarian, as were some Sinhalese *bhikkhus*, but the Japanese and Thais were not, and among the Burmese there was a real prejudice against vegetarians, amounting in some cases almost to hatred. Their attitude was that vegetarians were trying to go one better than the Buddha himself. They used to say that the Buddha ate meat, that he didn't insist on vegetarianism. And this is quite true; he made no hard and fast rule about it.

At least, this is true for the Pāli canon. The rule that the Buddha did make, according to the Pāli texts, was that 'meat is not to be accepted (as almsfood) in three cases: if one has seen, heard, or suspects that the animal was specially killed for the monk'.[532] In a later Mahāyāna scripture, the *Laṅkāvatāra Sūtra*, on the other hand, the Buddha is quoted as saying, in the chapter 'On Meat-eating': 'It is not true, Mahāmati, that meat is proper food and permissible for the *śrāvaka* when [the victim] was not killed by himself, when he did not order others to kill it, when it was not specifically meant for him.'[533] So here is a hard and fast rule supposedly made by the Buddha *insisting* on vegetarianism.

Special cases

But in the Buddha's day, if you were a wandering monk, as the Buddha himself was, your practice was to take what you were given; and living in a carnivorous society, you would be given meat. Under those conditions the Buddhist attitude would be that inasmuch as you were leading an ascetic life, living on alms, and practising indifference towards food, these factors would counterbalance the unskilfulness inherent in actually eating meat. Illustrative of this attitude is the story of a famous ascetic who ate somebody's thumb which, as a result of a nasty accident in the preparation of some food, had ended up in his bowl. Because he made a point of not picking and choosing, he ate the thumb along with everything else.[534] If you are practising extreme asceticism of this kind, vegetarianism doesn't come into it. But if you have a choice about what you eat, you also have a responsibility, particularly if you can influence the society you live in by choosing to be vegetarian.

I used to make this point to some of my Thai *bhikkhu* friends and they would say, 'But what can we do? The lay people always give us meat, and we don't want to hurt their feelings by refusing what we are offered.' And it is true that whereas in some cultures the meat is served separately from the vegetables, every Thai dish has meat in it – sometimes pork, chicken, and fish all in the same meal. But the fact is that the lay people were their disciples. The monks were scrupulously insistent on the correct etiquette being observed in the matter of *how* food was offered to them – what to say, how to bow, and so forth – so it should have been possible over a period of several hundred years to persuade the lay people to offer vegetarian food. The Vietnamese had managed it among a laity with the same appetite for meat. It is not as if there was any shortage of vegetables.

In this respect Tibet is a special case. The land yields practically nothing in the way of fruit and vegetables so Tibetan Buddhists have been traditionally obliged to eat meat – which is fair enough: if the alternative to eating meat is starvation, one must eat what is available. The Tibetans never tried to pretend that what they did was skilful – but when vegetables did become available to them, they generally continued to eat meat. I used to be told that, coming as they did from a meat-eating country, their constitution required meat.

The Thais used this argument too. If one pointed out that Westerners like myself also came from meat-eating countries and still managed to make the transition to a vegetarian diet, they would laugh and say, 'Well, your mind is very strong.' No doubt there are a few vegetarians among the Thais and the Burmese as well, but they have to keep quiet about it unless they are very eminent indeed, as otherwise they are looked upon as 'holy Joes' who want to show everyone else up. The whole subject is fraught with embarrassment and guilt for them and therefore arouses quite irrational reactions at times.

Non-violence is not, of course, just about being vegetarian. It might even be said that in many parts of India an exaggerated importance is attached to this particular expression of the principle. One can extort money from the poor, one can be a usurer, one can let one's cow die of starvation, but as long as one is a vegetarian one has nothing to worry about, spiritually speaking, while if one is not strictly vegetarian, any attempt one makes to lead any kind of spiritual life is dismissed out of hand. Of course, this is just an illustration of the way we exaggerate the importance of whatever we ourselves are able to achieve and minimize the significance of whatever we are disinclined to attempt.

The letter of the law

The *vinaya* itself, it has to be said, provides any number of convenient issues upon which one may appear to take a moral stand. I remember a friend telling me that a German monk in the Thai tradition once told him off for offering him a cup of tea while he was standing up. 'Don't you know the Vinaya?' he said. In fact, there is no Vinaya rule about what is really just a matter of Indian etiquette, but a lot of monks like to stand on ceremony in this way.

However, just as a clever lawyer can probably find that everyone is breaking the law in some way, likewise one can fault even the strictest monk over some point of Vinaya. For example, one is not supposed to shave one's face without shaving one's head, but virtually all monks ignore this rule, as they shave every day but get their heads shaved only once a fortnight.[535]

If Theravādin monks are open to the charge of losing sight of fundamental spiritual principles in favour of the minutiae of the Vinaya, it should be said in mitigation that – in Sri Lanka anyway – they do tend to be in thrall to the laity, who of course can hardly be expected to make such distinctions. The laity in Sri Lanka are vicarious Buddhists: they have no spiritual ambitions themselves; the monks are expected to earn merit on behalf of the whole community in return for their support. If they contribute a son to the Order a couple can certainly look forward to going to heaven when they die, so a lot of monks have been pushed into ordination.

Not that it isn't a pleasant enough existence being a monk: there's plenty to do – teaching, building temples, engaging in various cultural activities. The *bhikkhus* constitute a set of kind, generous, and good-natured bachelors, but generally not much more than that. And they tend to be nagged and bullied, even terrorized by the laity. For example, if it's getting on for twelve o'clock, the lay people, especially the women, will say 'Come along, come along – it's time you were eating your lunch.' They keep a close eye on what 'their' monks are up to so that they can say, 'Oh, our monks are pure, very pure, not like all those Japanese monks, you know!'

The positive mental events as subjects for reflection[536]

Yeshe Gyaltsen ends his chapter on the eleven positive mental events with remarks on the general characteristics of positive mental events and the categories of circumstances under which they arise. His enumerations of these are clearly not exhaustive, but they do provide a starting point for one's own personal reflections.

To begin with, he lists five characteristics of positive mental events that are wholesome by their very nature.[537] To elaborate a little on what he has to say:

a. *Wholesome by their very nature:* They are positive in themselves, without reference to other factors; that is, they need no qualification. So they may be termed the eleven *primary* positive mental events.

b. *Wholesome by being related:* They involve an association of mind and mental events by means of the five functional co-relations (see p. 495 above). That is, where there is a positive mental event, mind and mental events are, as it were, permeated by the same feeling, they refer to the same object, and so on.

c. *Wholesome by being related to that which follows:* Although they are positive in themselves, they are the basis for further production of the positive.

d. *Wholesome by inspiring:* They are positive on account of the fact that they have been inspired by faith; or by virtue of the inspiring quality of faith.

e. *Wholesome in the ultimate sense:* They are positive in the ultimate sense; that is, they are not positive as opposed to negative – they have no negative mirror image. They are Positive with a capital P, as it were – like Plato's concept of the Good.

In considering these characteristics, we need to bear in mind that positive mental events are not actual entities. This should in any case be clear from the fact that there is a certain amount of overlap between them, and that each one obviously arises in some kind of relation with other positive mental events.

Bringing the positive mental events into being[538]

Yeshe Gyaltsen goes on to enumerate eight occasions for the arising of the positive mental events.[539]

Innate

Firstly, they may be innate; that is, we may carry over a predilection for or inclination towards the positive from a previous existence. The implication is that our mental states, and indeed our qualities in general, are determined, at least to some extent, by a general attitude that would seem to have been there from birth. Handel, for instance, had a quite unmusical background and ancestry, and yet displayed an outstanding interest in and aptitude for music from a very early age.

Setting up conditions

Secondly, they may be developed through being involved in the setting up of the essential conditions for the attainment of Enlightenment in one's own life: spiritual friendship, Dharma study, attention, mindfulness, watchfulness, and realization of what leads to the attainment of Enlightenment – i.e. Going for Refuge to the Three Jewels.

Skilful action

Thirdly, positive mental events may arise in association with some kind of skilful action. They produce skilful actions and they also arise as a result of skilful actions. There are, of course, very few actions, apart from involuntary ones, that are wholly unaccompanied by intentional – and therefore positive or negative – mental activity, so it's really a question of the degree of volition or intentionality brought to an action. An act of giving, for example, might be accompanied by warm, generous feelings, or by a sort of half-conscious contempt. It might even be stimulated by quite mixed motives, and might also give rise to quite mixed emotions. On the other hand, we cannot say that a good action is entirely a question of the quality of intention behind it. Good and evil cannot be thought of in terms of just actions or just intentions; they involve a combination of both.

The *saṃgraha-vastus*

Fourthly, they may arise through the four means of conversion (*saṃgraha-vastus*) exercised by a bodhisattva: *dāna* or generosity, *priya-vāditā* or kindly speech, *arthacaryā* or exhortation and encouragement, and *samānārthatā* or exemplification.[540]

An integrated attitude

Fifthly, positive mental events may arise by way of a thoroughly integrated attitude behind one's action, ensuring, from a mundane point of view, the best possible return in terms of *puṇya* or merit. Yeshe Gyaltsen cites as an example 'special bright pure actions that make one attain heaven or the good things in life'.[541] By this is meant actions producing mundane merit, as opposed to merit leading to Enlightenment.[542] The only necessary distinction between an action to which accrues mundane merit and one that produces real merit is in the intention behind the action. Apart from that the action may be equally 'special, bright, and pure'.

Overcoming negative mental states, the cessation of craving, and Enlightenment

Sixthly, they may arise with the overcoming of negative mental states. Seventhly, they may arise with the cessation of craving and thus the end of suffering. And eighthly, once Enlightenment has been attained, positive mental events arise simply in dependence upon positive mental events.

8
FORCES OF DISINTEGRATION

Yeshe Gyaltsen has taken us to the pinnacle of life's potential, the most positive experience possible: Enlightenment. Now, scarcely pausing for breath, he plunges us into the subject with which the rest of his – and our – commentary is concerned: negative mental events. It's a shock, but a salutary one; it is simply a fact of spiritual life that as well as understanding how to recognize and cultivate positive mental states, we need to know how to spot and deal with negative ones.

According to the Abhidharma there are six basic negative emotions and twenty proximate negative emotions. Yeshe Gyaltsen's enumeration of the characteristics of negative mental events – which he offers as a counterpart to his general remarks about positive mental events – makes a good starting point. First he lists five characteristics of 'negative mental events that are unwholesome by their very nature'. Here they are, together with a few explanatory comments of my own:

a. *Unwholesome by its very nature:* The six basic negative emotions and the twenty proximate negative emotions are negative in themselves, under all circumstances. They can't become wholesome, or be interpreted as wholesome, under any circumstances, even by being related to something else that is wholesome.

b. *Unwholesome by being related:* A negative mental event is associated with a simultaneously and similarly negative mind.

c. *Unwholesome by being related to that which follows:* Negative mental events provide the basis for the development of further negative mental events.

d. *Unwholesome by inspiring:* Negative mental events inspire all sorts of unskilful activities of body and speech.

e. *Unwholesome in the ultimate sense:* We must be clear about this final characteristic. In fact, of course, everything within *saṃsāra* is ultimately negative, inasmuch as it is not Nirvāṇa. It may be true that from the perspective of Nirvāṇa one no longer stands upon the distinction between the positive and the negative, but this perspective takes us beyond the Abhidharma altogether, and one should be very cautious indeed about deciding that one has gone beyond the perspective of the Abhidharma. If one does go beyond it, all well and good, but one cannot invoke, as it were, the Perfection of Wisdom hypothetically.

But although in a sense everything within *saṃsāra* is ultimately unsatisfactory, we should not derive from this the notion that *saṃsāra* is completely negative. Quite the contrary. We have, after all, already seen that positive mental events may arise that have a purely mundane result, but they remain positive for all that. The experience of *dhyāna*, for example, may bring about no more than happiness in this world and the next, but this cannot be said to be an unsatisfactory result in anything but an ultimate sense.

From an absolute, metaphysical perspective, even pleasant, positive experiences constitute *duḥkha*, in so far as they do not constitute Enlightenment, but as experiences they remain positive and pleasant. There should be no mistake about this: a jaundiced, cynical, pessimistic, negative attitude towards the world is no basis for any kind of spiritual realization. To dismiss the relatively skilful, the relatively wholesome, and the relatively positive as being unskilful, unwholesome, and negative is itself simply unskilful, unwholesome, and negative. As long as one is in *saṃsāra*, one can't afford to take up negative attitudes towards it. It is possible to have a positive experience of disillusionment, but this is quite different from disgruntlement; in fact, one can be disillusioned with things in the sense of seeing their limitations even while one is thoroughly enjoying them.

Doctrine and method

We in the West are particularly prone to miss the point that there is that which is relatively positive as distinct from the absolutely positive. We tend not to see this on account of the ethical absolutism we have inherited from the Judaeo-Christian tradition, which gives us the idea that there are things which are absolutely right and things which are absolutely wrong. To take just one example, from the Judaeo-Christian viewpoint it cannot under any circumstances be right to bow down to a graven image: that is absolutely wrong. The Muslims have much the same feeling with regard to what they call 'joining others with God' – any deviation from strict monotheism is absolutely wrong. One could not, as a Muslim or a Christian, say that polytheistic worship, mistaken though it may be, is better than no worship at all.

The Buddhist position may be summarized as comprising a distinction between doctrine and method. In doctrinal terms, all compounded existence – according to the first of the four 'noble truths' – is ultimately *duḥkha*; it is unwholesome in that it is not Nirvāṇa. But methodologically speaking, one cannot make any progress towards Nirvāṇa – via the fourth noble truth – unless one distinguishes, within *saṃsāra*, between the relatively unwholesome and the relatively wholesome, so that one may move from the one to the other. Thus one needs to be able to perceive that a good retreat is more wholesome and positive – and even more enjoyable – than a good party, say, even while recognizing that both are ultimately unsatisfactory inasmuch as one remains unenlightened.

How negativity arises

Yeshe Gyaltsen goes on to list seven occasions for the arising of negative mental events.[543] Again, to elaborate a little on his list:

a. One may be innately predisposed to unskilful mental states as a result of volitions carried over from a previous life.

b. One may develop unskilful mental states by involving oneself with unskilful influences.

c. One may develop unskilful mental states through performing unskilful actions.

d. One may develop unskilful mental states by harming sentient beings. (Logically speaking this category is supererogatory; it is enumerated separately presumably to emphasize the fact that non-violence or non-harm is the central point of the Buddha's teaching.)

e. One may pursue the unskilful with such thoroughness as to ensure rebirth in the hell realms.

f. One may harbour views that obstruct the path towards Enlightenment.

g. One may harbour views that actually destroy all possibility of spiritual development.

It is evident from this list of Yeshe Gyaltsen's that clear thinking is going to be of crucial importance when it comes to avoiding the arising of negative mental events. The various categories of wrong views will be discussed more fully and systematically later in this chapter, under the heading of the sixth of the *mūlakleśas*. But here one might observe that there are two 'pernicious views' of a general nature that are traditionally mentioned: the view that actions do not have consequences; and the view that no beings exist in the world who have realized higher stages of spiritual development.[544]

There are also some pseudo-Zen views that are dangerous in this way – like the idea that we are all in some sense Enlightened already, or that it is useless to make any effort to attain Enlightenment, or that we have Buddhahood within us if we could only wake up to the fact. To these one may add the idea that any attempt at spiritual development is spiritual materialism, and the misunderstanding that occasionally finds currency in the West to the effect that there is no place for emotion in the spiritual life, that all emotion is to be overcome. This last one fits in nicely with the idea that everything in *saṃsāra* is negative, and appeals particularly to people who are most comfortable cultivating aversion or hatred. It is quite easy for plain hatred of the mundane to disguise itself as disillusionment with the mundane.

The mystic Orient

We cannot simply accept the truth of everything that comes out of the East. Sometimes the problem is one of translation from one language or culture to another, but occasionally, unfortunately, there is a real degeneration of the teaching. We have already taken account of the dangers of an attachment to study for its own sake. At the other end of the spectrum, one can meet with supposed Tantric practitioners who can only be described as charlatans.

The Tantra can seem to be an easier path as well as a higher path – and what could be more attractive than that? It seems to condone certain things that other paths do not condone; and it also seems that with the Tantra one doesn't have to give anything up. In a certain sense that is true, but it is true in a profound sense which is simply not accessible to the person who enters upon it without proper preparation. The Tantra looks like a very relaxed way of going about things, but actually it is a knife-edge path.

It is a similar note of caution that Yeshe Gyaltsen sounds in a few verses which, he says, 'are meant to summarize what has been said so far' – and which also serve as a good introduction to the commentary on the six basic emotions that follows:

> The eye of intelligence which distinguishes the path from that which is not
> Is blinded by the foul waters of the fools and idiots.
> To claim that one can walk the path and scale the spiritual levels by using an artificial staff
> That resembles the *dharma* is too ridiculous for words.
>
> Oh friends with intelligence and sustained interest,
> If you want to search for the jewel that elevates your mind to the two positive qualities,
> Then follow Tsong-kha-pa, the supreme Bodhisattva, and
> Dive deep into the ocean of the Buddha's words which is like a Wish-fulfilling Gem. (pp. 63–4)

The six basic emotions (*mūlakleśas*)

The Sanskrit term being translated as basic (or negative) emotion here is *kleśa*, which means both 'that which torments' and 'that which defiles'. Thus one could translate it as 'defiling passion' – except that modern usage fails to connect the term passion with its original meaning of 'suffering'. We tend to think of passion as meaning uncontrolled emotion of any kind, but with the *kleśas* we are dealing with unequivocally negative emotions. These first six are the *mūlakleśas*, the negative roots from which all other negative mental events grow.

While the positive emotions are characterized essentially by an underlying quality of calm and serenity, the defiling passions have a quality of ego-centred restlessness. It is true that positive emotion may sometimes contain a certain amount of effervescence or rapture (*prīti*), but this is a transitional phase in the process of developing the calm and stable condition of bliss (*sukha*). *Prīti* – the experience of submerged energy, as it were, rushing to the surface – is certainly not ego-centred restlessness.

The six basic emotions are, as translated by Guenther, cupidity-attachment, anger, arrogance, lack of intrinsic awareness, indecision, and opinionatedness. So here we have variants of the three poisons – usually referred to as greed, hatred, and delusion – together with arrogance, indecision, and 'opinionatedness', often referred to as 'wrong views'.

1. CUPIDITY-ATTACHMENT (*RĀGA*)

> Cupidity-attachment is a hankering after any pleasurable external or internal object by taking it as pleasing to oneself. (p. 65)
>
> Tsongkhapa

This is *rāga*. The term is often used interchangeably with *lobha*, but there is a difference of connotation, *lobha* generally being translated as 'craving' while *rāga* is more powerful, more like 'passionate attachment'. In the Tantric context *rāga* sometimes carries a positive connotation, but in the context of the Abhidharma it refers to a purely negative emotion. Neither *lobha* nor *rāga* may therefore be translated simply by the word 'desire' – because, of course, desire is not necessarily negative. For example, the bodhisattva's desire that all beings may attain Enlightenment is utterly positive.

What makes cupidity or craving or passionate attachment negative is that it involves desiring pleasure from the object one is attached to. This can get quite complicated. For example, there's the do-gooder. Do-gooders don't actually want to make others happy; they want to make themselves happy, using others as the means. This is not to say, of course, that doing others good for the sake of what one gets out of it personally, whether in terms of personal development or in any other way, is at all a bad thing, as long as one is aware of what one is doing. The trouble is that one is not always aware of one's motivations. The harm sometimes caused by do-gooders arises from the difficulty of detecting in oneself the subtler manifestations of craving or attachment.

Craving may be experienced in relation to an object in the present, the past, or the future; and it may be experienced in relation to the *kāmaloka*, the realm of sense desire, or, at a more subtle level, in relation to the *rūpaloka* or the *arūpaloka*, the realms corresponding to the experience of *dhyāna*. Craving does not arise when one is actually experiencing *dhyāna*, because *dhyāna* by its very nature does not include negative mental states. But in the absence of *prajñā* craving can arise in anticipation or recollection of the experience of *dhyāna*.

Indeed, craving of a very subtle kind is still present even in a non-returner, that is, in one whose transcendental insight has broken through the first five fetters of mundane existence.[545] With all this accomplished there is still desire for existence in the world of form and desire for existence in the formless world (the sixth and seventh fetters) to be overcome.

In *dhyāna*, *lobha*, *dveṣa*, and *moha* are just suspended, not destroyed. Only *prajñā* can remove them permanently. In *dhyāna* they are simply held in abeyance. But they cannot be held in abeyance indefinitely. Sooner or later they will reassert themselves and one will then come out of *dhyāna*. One may even say (though the Abhidharma does not go this far in its discussion) that throughout the *dhyāna* experience there is a potentiality of negative mental states present, a substratum of unmanifested *kleśas* waiting to come to fruition.

Imagination

Craving is obviously very difficult to eradicate, but a useful approach to changing this, and indeed any other negative state of mind, is to use the imagination. Dr Johnson once defined imagination as the capacity to emancipate oneself from one's present experience and project oneself into the past or the future. He was thinking of the term in a rather negative sense, but in this context his simple definition highlights a capacity we all have and use when it suits us. It doesn't always suit us to use it, of course. When we indulge ourselves without considering the fact that our actions will have consequences, when we do not consider how others will be affected by what we do, all this can, in a way, be put down to a basic failure of imagination.

Through the imagination we can emancipate ourselves from our own experience and project ourselves into the experience of someone else, or foresee the possible consequences of our present actions. Imagination is really a matter of clarity. When we are in the grip of craving we are blinded by our present experience. When we're carried away by, say, sexual passion, present experience sweeps away our ability to imagine someone else's needs and feelings, or what might happen as a result of our passion. All thoughts of past, present, and future, this world and the next, disappear. It is only after one has had what one wanted that one's imagination slips into gear again and one thinks, 'Oh my God, how will her husband feel?' It is as if one has been in a dream.

This is why the poet Shelley speaks of morals in terms of imagination.[546] Ethics are about going out of oneself, not being limited by one's present mode of being. Giving, for example, is simply a matter of feeling the needs of another person as vividly as one feels one's own needs. It is a matter of imagination. Seen in this way, ethics are not about keeping a tight rein on oneself, but about freeing one's imagination, being less bound by one's present situation.

2. ANGER (*PRATIGHA*)

> It is a vindictive attitude towards sentient beings, towards frustration, and towards that which gives rise to one's frustrations. Its function is to serve as a basis for fault-finding and for never finding even a moment of happiness. (p. 66)
>
> *Abhidharmasamuccaya*

Pratigha is generally a kind of blind rage or fury, but its description here as a 'vindictive attitude' implies that it also has an element of hatred.

Hatred, though, translates another Sanskrit word, *dveṣa*. And, of course, hatred and anger are different things. Hatred involves a definite intention to do someone harm, but anger is more like an explosive release of energy with a view to breaking through an obstacle. One can get angry with someone without wishing to do them any harm; someone obstructs one's energy and this frustrated energy just accumulates until one cannot contain it any longer.

Anger

Of course, anger cannot be said to be a skilful mental state, because it does burst out in a violent manner; yet it can be deployed quite skilfully in that it is quite possible to get really angry and be careful at the same time not to do any real harm or actual damage. Anger, one could say, is not entirely incompatible with *maitrī*, at least in the long run. The average person experiences anger much more often than hatred; and this anger, paradoxically, is directed mostly towards one's nearest and dearest – that is, those who are going to be treading on one's corns on a regular basis.

For some people, experiencing anger can be a step forward. If a strong feeling like desire or anger gets repressed, perhaps because one is afraid to face one's own disapproval by fully experiencing it, one can be angry or full of craving, say, without knowing it. Indeed, failing to acknowledge what one is feeling enables it to develop into an ever more powerful negative emotion. In this way, by not allowing oneself to feel anger or desire, one becomes repressed or alienated.

Being alienated from one's most powerful emotions also means being alienated from one's energy. It is then very important to re-contact one's emotions in almost any way one can. All of which is not to say that someone who is placid and easily contented must be in some way alienated or repressed; they might just be gentle and innocent by nature. Nor would one want to suggest that becoming angry is a necessary element in one's relations with others. It can often be the case that one begins to seethe with anger as a result of not having been firm and direct about something in the first place. This said, one should not necessarily be afraid of getting angry – as long as one is very careful that one's anger does not develop into hatred.

Hatred

There can never be any justification for hatred. As a 'vindictive attitude' – he's done you down and you want to get even by doing him down – hatred has a lot to do with egotism; it involves a subtle sense of one's having been diminished in the eyes of others. Suppose someone abuses you. You can think, 'Well, he just lost his temper. He said some foolish things, but in the end it's his problem, not mine.' If you take that attitude, you won't feel put down, and you won't need to get even – because you feel 'even' anyway. Your evenness has not been disturbed. Alternatively, you may think, 'Oh, he has called me a fool – who is he to call me a fool? He has made me look a fool in the eyes of others.' If you think like this – that other people's opinion of you matters so much – you are going to get very angry indeed, because you have been hurt in this crucially sensitive place.

Sympathy

If *maitrī* is the opposite of hatred, tea and sympathy generally is not. There is very often something false about sympathy. People who are not genuinely pleased when one is in a very positive mood are going to be delighted when one is feeling low because they can then start to be sympathetic, relishing their own superior position in the guise of being warm and kind. This satisfaction in someone else's weakness, as well as being corrupting for the perpetrator, reinforces the weakness of the recipient. It is all the more damaging for both parties because its true nature as a very subtle form of hatred or malice goes unrecognized.

Ironically enough, instead of detaching oneself from the source of one's suffering one seems to want to get closer to it – perhaps in order to get even. *Pratigha* cannot, therefore, be translated as 'aversion', which simply means 'turning away'. One becomes as attached to one's enemies as one does to one's friends – and this negative attachment is of a particularly unhealthy and neurotic kind. It may even appear in the context of a sexual relationship, where a couple have no truly positive feelings for each other. It is possible, as I have suggested, to express anger towards one's nearest and dearest, but it is also possible for a couple to stay together in order to satisfy their hatred of each other, rather than quietly going their separate ways.

Ridiculous hatred

There is no limit to the range of possible objects of hatred. One can feel hatred towards oneself, towards friends, towards animals, towards inanimate objects, towards people one has known in the past, even towards future or prospective situations. It arises from paranoia – the feeling that others have it in for us – and from an insistence on finding a source for our suffering. It is the rage of the victim for redress; it is the way we avoid taking ultimate responsibility for the state we find ourselves in.

The Mahāyāna regards hatred as the worst of negative mental states – certainly as worse than craving, because craving at least shows some affinity for life, for people, and holds out at least the possibility of experiencing some pleasure, however transient. But hatred does not allow us to enjoy those ordinary pleasures that are available. This is why it is sometimes said that hatred is ridiculous. In a hateful mental state we don't want something pleasant; we actually want something painful.

In a hateful mood, if we can find something unpleasant, some fault or weakness, we are pleased. If someone tries to cheer us up, or placate us, or show us that we don't need to feel hatred, we're displeased because our hatred is precious to us – we don't want it taken away from us, and we will hate anyone who tries to take it away. We even find ourselves saying, 'I've every right to be angry!' as if claiming the privilege of enjoying some rare pleasure.

What we are trying to claim, of course, is that our anger is righteous indignation. However, whether indignation or anger can really ever be counted as righteous is open to question. There may be moments of crisis when some kind of high-energy vociferation or action is called for. If, for instance, one saw someone beating a child, one might experience a sudden hot anger which would lead one to say or do something drastic to stop that person engaging in that unskilful action. Or if someone appeared to be about to do something stupidly dangerous to themselves or to others, then again some sort of high-energy response would be in order. But righteous indignation in any sense other than this is generally going to be unskilful. An outburst may make one feel better oneself, but it is not going to do anything to enhance one's relations with the people against whom it is directed. In any situation where one might be inclined to get impatient or angry, one will find that the exercise of patience and persistence is the more skilful and effective option.

Even when it comes to discussing the ideals that one holds most dear, there is no justification for getting angry. One may be able to browbeat someone into submission by getting hot under the collar, but one will not convince them thereby. Wrong views with regard to the spiritual life generally have deep roots and they need to be dug out with patient persistence. It is no use just hacking away wildly at them. Outbursts of righteous indignation are only going to reinforce those wrong views.

Hatred is unskilful not only with regard to its effect on others; it has grievously deleterious effects on the person doing the hating. It alienates our friends. It makes us act recklessly. It takes away our capacity to judge what is skilful and what is unskilful. We are unable to take pleasure in anything. It is traditionally said to make one ugly – it certainly makes one unattractive. It even takes away one's sleep (conversely, one of the benefits of *maitrī* is said to be that it gives one sound sleep). Ultimately, one falls into subhuman, demonic states: that is, one becomes something worse than just a bad human being – one becomes a demon, a being dedicated purely to negative and destructive ends.

Psychological types

Hatred is linked with greed (cupidity-attachment) and ignorance (lack of intrinsic awareness) in a familiar trio – the three poisons or poisonous roots. They are all present in the unenlightened mind, in varying degrees. In the *Visuddhimagga*, Buddhaghosa identifies three different psychological types or temperaments (*caritas*) based upon them: the greed type, the hate type, and the delusion type.[547]

The greed type basically finds life more pleasant than painful. That is the starting point for the formation of that particular kind of temperament. Presumably as a result of having performed skilful actions in the past, the greed type experiences pleasant *vipākas* rather more than unpleasant ones, and therefore tends to experience craving more than hatred. Buddhaghosa describes the behaviour of each type in terms of the monastic life – because that was the usual context within which his work would be studied – and he says that the greed type would favour brightly-coloured robes: everybody's robes would of course be yellow, but those of the greed type would be *bright* yellow. The greed type would also eat nicely, making his rice and curry into neat balls and popping them gracefully into his mouth. When he sweeps the floor he does so smoothly and thoroughly, including the corners; when he walks he goes elegantly, wearing his robe neatly and correctly (with the upper robe exactly four inches shorter than the lower robe) and when he speaks his voice is mellifluous and gentle.

The hate type is just the opposite. He is a person for whom existence is definitely more painful than pleasant, putting him in a general mood of irritation and resentment. Everything he does will be performed impatiently, carelessly, or harshly, reflecting his darker and more disagreeable view of the world.

Finally, the deluded type is one whose experience of pleasure and pain is fairly equally mixed. Sometimes he finds life pleasant, but then circumstances change and life seems altogether unpleasant. So he would not be able to make up his mind on the matter once and for all. He couldn't really say whether life was pleasant or not, and it probably wouldn't occur to him to try.

There are three refined versions of these three types. The greed type tends to become the devotee, the faith type. The hate type on the other hand becomes the wisdom type; that is, in the same way that the hate type sees the faults of the hated object, wisdom sees the faults of compounded existence. As for the deluded type, he or she becomes what is usually called the intelligence type. Whereas wisdom is the faculty that sees through things, that penetrates through the compounded to the Uncompounded, intelligence is a more versatile, creative, faculty. A standard definition of intelligence is 'an ability to use concepts creatively'; while wisdom brushes aside concepts in order to penetrate to the reality behind them, intelligence is the ability to express what wisdom sees, to communicate what that reality is and how it is realized. So to begin with one needs faith, which is replaced by *karuṇā* (compassion) when wisdom is attained – and finally one needs intelligence to communicate the content of that realization.[548]

3. ARROGANCE (*MĀNA*)

> It is an inflated mind as to what is perishable and its function is to serve as the basis for disrespect and frustrations. (p. 68)
>
> *Abhidharmasamuccaya*

Māna is arrogance as distinct from pride. There is a healthy pride that guards one from doing things of which one should be ashamed; and one can have a healthy confidence that one is capable of achieving worthy ends. But arrogance is different; it is an inflated idea of oneself in comparison with others. Of course, one cannot help making comparisons, and although making any sort of comparison is very subtly unskilful, there is probably little harm in objectively recognizing that one is in various respects superior, equal, or inferior to others. Practically speaking, one may certainly need to be able to make a judgement as to who is best qualified to do a particular task. But if one wants to make something of this state of affairs – whether or not it really is the case – if one insists on some kind of recognition, or relishes the fact that one is better at something than other people are, this is arrogance.

Seven kinds of arrogance

Yeshe Gyaltsen distinguishes seven different varieties of arrogance:

a. You overvalue yourself in comparison with others who are less gifted, less wealthy, less successful, and so on, than you are. You look down on them in an overbearing way, like Lord Curzon in the anonymous verse:

> My name is George Nathaniel Curzon,
> I am a most superior person.[549]

Though Lord Curzon was indeed very able, his arrogance was such that he was said to have died of disappointment at not becoming Prime Minister.

b. You imagine that you are superior to your peers, to those who are, in fact, your equals.

c. You fancy yourself superior to those who are, in fact, your superiors.

d. You are unable to identify with anything other than your own five *skandhas* – that is, other than your body, feelings, perception, volitional impulses, and consciousness. You firmly identify yourself with the five *skandhas*, which in effect is to see oneself as the centre of the universe. This is obviously quite a subtle form of arrogance.

e. You boast of your achievements or your position, whether or not they represent any real attainment. This includes arrogance with regard to social class, physique, age, and education, and it is well expressed in the celebrated couplet about Benjamin Jowett, the Master of Balliol College in Oxford:

> I am Master of this College:
> What I don't know isn't knowledge.[550]

f. You take an inordinate pride in your humility; that is, your arrogance comes in disguise. This can be illustrated by a little story concerning a meeting between representatives of the different orders of the Catholic church. The Dominican says 'Of course we Dominicans are the most learned order,' and the Jesuit says 'Yes, but we are certainly foremost in the educational sphere.' Then the Franciscan pipes up, a little diffidently, and says: 'Well, that's all perfectly true, but I rather think that when it comes to humility, we're the tops.'

In fact, one cannot actually cultivate humility. There is a well-known story about Mahatma Gandhi, who was quite keen on inculcating humility in his followers. He drew up a list of rules for those who were involved with his ashram, and right at the top he put 'Practise humility.' But someone pointed out to him that real humility can never be self-consciously cultivated, so he crossed it out and wrote at the bottom of the list 'All these to be practised in the spirit of humility.'

Humility is necessarily unselfconscious. Other people may see it in you, but the moment you see it yourself it's no longer there. Indeed, when it is a deliberate attitude, humility seems to be entirely negative, a sort of grovelling posture. (One thinks of the odious Uriah Heep in Dickens' *David Copperfield*.) However, if arrogance serves as the basis for disrespect then non-arrogance should serve as the basis for respect. If one cultivates respect, or even reverence, which of course can readily be cultivated in a very positive manner, one can more or less forget about the need for humility, because humility naturally comes with reverence.

g. The seventh variety of arrogance is 'inverted arrogance'. You are proud of, say, having got drunk and made a fool of yourself; or having come bottom of the class at school. Instead of feeling sorry or ashamed you feel, perhaps, that such failings or weaknesses make you more interesting as a person; or you may simply want to get attention, and think that the way to get it is by playing the fool. You belittle yourself, you pretend to be more stupid than you really are. People are sometimes even proud of having made a mess of their life. It is possible to be proud of being ignorant, of having no education, of being blunt or rude or brutal, of being hard and cynical.

The consequences of arrogance

These are the traditional seven forms of arrogance; but we don't have to stop there. For example, there is a kind of vicarious arrogance whereby you attach yourself to someone you admire and, while having no personal ambition to emulate their achievements, bask in their reflected glory: 'My teacher is better than your teacher.' There is also the arrogance of egalitarianism: you refuse to recognize that anyone can be truly superior to anyone else. Some people take this to the extreme of saying – to use the current expression – that a Buddha, for example, is not 'more developed' than other people so much as 'differently developed'.

The karmic consequence of arrogance, from the traditional point of view, is that one is reborn in particularly humble circumstances. More immediately, one makes it very difficult for oneself to learn anything, because one fails to recognize one's own limitations and thus one's need to learn. One also fails to recognize those from whom one might learn, because one is unable to acknowledge their superiority to oneself.

This could perhaps be said to be a particular problem in the West, where we have recently developed a social climate in which teachers are not greatly respected. The respect is not there basically because the values that the teachers are supposed to stand for and pass on, including the cultural heritage of the community, are not valued by the society they serve. A further problem derives from the way some of us have been brought up to regard religion as something that cannot be taught. In the traditional religion of the West, Christianity, the emphasis is not generally on methods. One can learn its history, one can study the Bible, but on the whole most people are not taught how to practise religion in the way that one can be taught how to practise carpentry or law or architecture. Certainly there is nothing in the West really equivalent to the passing on of knowledge from teacher to disciple which is so much part of Eastern religious tradition.

Integral to arrogance is the negative mental event which follows it here, lack of intrinsic awareness. We are arrogant on the basis of failing to see the true nature of things, and thus failing to see that we really have nothing to be arrogant about. The way to overcome a tendency to arrogance is therefore to reflect on the Dharma – on impermanence, the four noble truths, and so on.

4. LACK OF INTRINSIC AWARENESS (*AVIDYĀ*)

> It is a lack of being aware to one's fullest capacity and it covers the three realms of life. Its function is to serve as a basis for mistaken stubbornness, doubt and emotionality about the entities of reality. (p. 72)
>
> *Abhidharmasamuccaya*

The existence of *avidyā* as a negative mental event suggests that one can't be unaware of reality in a purely privative sense. Ignorance of reality has consequences: it automatically plunges one into confusion and bewilderment, which lead to a course of misguided thought and action. It's not just that one doesn't know something; one doesn't know that one doesn't know. Lack of intrinsic awareness (*avidyā*) represents a stubborn refusal to accept anything that might threaten one's ego-identity. The more one lacks intrinsic awareness, the more one digs one's heels in against developing that awareness. *Avidyā* is a resistance, a rigidity, a lack of receptivity. This underlines the fact that theory and practice are not separate. Ideas cannot be kept separate from action; if one is confused in thought, one will blunder in what one does.

Lack of intrinsic awareness is of two kinds. Firstly, there is lack of practical wisdom; that is, not being able to distinguish clearly between what is skilful and what is unskilful, and thus not perceiving the consequences of one's actions, not appreciating the law of karma. The result is suffering and rebirths in painful realms.

Secondly, lack of intrinsic awareness consists in lack of *prajñā*, in the sense of not knowing 'mind-as-such'. Even though one may have realized practical wisdom to the extent of ensuring good future rebirths, one is still short of attaining to ultimate wisdom and thus one's happiness is still subject to impermanence. Even in the formless *dhyanas*, if one has not broken the first fetter – *satkāyadṛṣṭi* or self-view – one will still have a subtle but very strong experience of the self or ego.

There is a Pāli term, *mahaggata*, meaning 'grown great', which refers to what is generally called 'expanded consciousness'. It is possible to dwell in very refined states of expanded consciousness while still lacking intrinsic awareness. Simply to expand one's consciousness is not enough – unless one expands it beyond all limits whatsoever, in which case one is no longer the starting point of the expansion and there is no longer a centre from which one expands. The *dhyānas* are called *mahaggatacitta* in that unlimited sense.

A certain kind of awareness

Avidyā is usually rendered simply as 'ignorance', but Guenther's interpretive translation – 'lack of intrinsic awareness' – is very helpful. The word 'awareness' carries quite a broad range of meanings in English; what precisely should we understand by it here? For Guenther, wisdom has an appreciative, even an aesthetic, character.[551] It can be described in aesthetic terms because it represents an essentially non-utilitarian vision of things. Inasmuch as one is not looking for what one can get out of the world for oneself, one's vision is appreciative – one appreciates things for their own sake. One is satisfied purely to contemplate things, to appreciate them, even to become absorbed in them. Schopenhauer draws the same sort of parallel between aesthetic and mystical experience.[552] According to him, in both there is a suspension of what he terms '*der Wille*' which, as he interprets it, is the selfish and blind urge of life that is the source of our suffering.

There is then the question of how one functions in the world with this aesthetic appreciative awareness. But in practice, no such question arises. One has to make use of things; the only difference is that one's overall orientation is not a selfish, egoistic one. Making use of things in this way – to meet one's own objective needs and to help other people – does not conflict or interfere with one's intrinsic awareness at all. The nature of intrinsic awareness is that it produces spontaneous activity without any such conflict or problem.

Taking the aesthetic analogy again, there is on the one hand the aesthetic vision of the finished work of art, and on the other the concrete work of art in the making. The artist makes use of certain materials and tools within the overall context of his or her vision of the finished work of art, with the intention of making something – a painting, a poem, a piece of music – that conforms to his or her imaginative vision of what it should be. It is said of Mozart, for instance, that before writing a symphony, he heard the whole composition simultaneously, in a single moment, in his mind. This sort of vivid pre-apprehension of the work to be produced seems to be characteristic of the very greatest artists. The work of creation is done before they even start. It is all there already, like a great spool waiting to be unrolled; they have just to translate the work from eternity into time.

Likewise, if one has an experience of intrinsic awareness, one could say that while this experience takes place on the plane of the absolute, one is at the same time working to make life on the relative plane of existence conform to that vision or to manifest it. All one's energies, all one's activities on the relative plane, are directed towards that end, and therefore take place within the overall context of one's aesthetic perception. Everything one does is geared towards the transformation of the everyday world, through the manifestation of that experience of intrinsic awareness.

The realm of goal-oriented activity, inasmuch as it is not ego-related, takes place within what I have elsewhere called the greater mandala of essentially useless, appreciative awareness.[553] One may have realized the greater mandala for oneself, but as far as the world in the midst of which one is working is concerned – and as far as one is concerned oneself as well, inasmuch as one is identifying oneself with that world – it is still an ideal to be realized. This is the dual nature of the bodhisattva: he or she is in *nirvāṇa* and at the same time in *saṃsāra*, working along with other beings towards *nirvāṇa*.

Avidyā

When one loses that aesthetic appreciation, when one loses that awareness, one falls into bewilderment and confusion, and then one wants to make use of things, to manipulate them for one's own satisfaction. That is *avidyā*, the first of the twelve *nidānas* or links on the wheel of life, in dependence upon which arise the *saṃskāras*, the second *nidāna*. As we have seen, the relation between the first two *nidānas* is traditionally likened to the relation between the state of drunkenness and the actions of body, speech, and mind inspired by that drunkenness. Hence *avidyā* is not just ignorance, but an emotional darkness, on the basis of which all other *kleśas* arise. *Avidyā* is therefore the root of *saṃsāra*. Once intrinsic awareness has been lost, there can only follow an uninterrupted sequence of confused actions. This said, *avidyā* is not all bad, in so far as these essentially confused actions will include skilful as well as unskilful ones. They will all spring from a lack of intrinsic awareness, but some at least may help to 'restore' it.

Three terms, many meanings

The three terms *vidyā*, *prajñā*, and *jñāna* are very closely related, and between them they cover the characteristics of what we may call awareness of reality. They are not used altogether consistently throughout the Buddhist canon, but it is certainly possible to work out a standard usage based on the way they are generally applied.

Guenther's translation of *avidyā* in this context as 'lack of intrinsic awareness' suggests – whether or not Guenther consciously intends this – that *vidyā* is the basic, original awareness which 'subsequently' becomes overlaid or obscured. As for *jñāna*, this term is usually translated by Guenther as just 'awareness' – presumably the same awareness of which *avidyā* is the lack. Perhaps one could say that the difference between *vidyā* and *jñāna* is that whereas *vidyā* is the awareness that has been lost, *jñāna* is the awareness that has been regained.

And where does *prajñā* come in? In terms of the six perfections or *pāramitās* practised by the bodhisattva, *prajñā* is the sixth or final *pāramitā*. There exists, however, another series of ten *pāramitās* and in this formulation *prajñā* is explicitly distinguished from *jñāna*, which appears as the culmination of the series.[554] Taking this perspective, one might say that *prajñā* could mean awareness in the process of its emergence or, expressed slightly differently, it could mean *jñāna* in action. When one is applying *jñāna*, or awareness, to something so as to know it as it actually is, that application of awareness could be called *prajñā*.

As the dynamic function of awareness – as *jñāna* in action – *prajñā* is thus the main counter-agent to *avidyā*. Recalling the formulation of the three kinds of wisdom considered earlier, in which *prajñā* appears at each stage, one could go as far as to say that to develop *prajñā* is to follow the path. First one studies the teachings – that is, one practises *śruta-mayī-prajñā*; then one reflects on those teachings – *cintā-mayī-prajñā*; finally one meditates on them – *bhāvanā-mayī-prajñā*. The first two kinds of *prajñā* support the third, which is transcendental *prajñā* proper. One could also say that the first two are the foundations of the meditation – *samādhi* – that is required to transform those first two kinds of *prajñā*, study and reflection, into wisdom in its fullness.

Prajñā and *samādhi*

At the same time, *prajñā* is the support of *samādhi*; meditators commonly alternate between *śamatha* (calming) meditation practices and *vipaśyanā* (insight) practices. If you develop a certain level of *samādhi* you may use that concentrated energy to penetrate into reality – that is, to develop *prajñā*. But the depth of that penetration will be limited by the level of concentrated energy behind it; so to deepen your experience of *prajñā* you have to channel your effort into deepening your experience of *samādhi*. Or, to take another approach, you can make the *samādhi* you have previously experienced the basis for the development of *prajñā* – by, for instance, reflecting on the impermanence, and hence the unsatisfactoriness, of the *samādhi* experience. As one gets further and further along the path, the two reinforce each other until they become indistinguishable: *samādhi-prajñā*. *Samādhi* becomes the internal dimension of *prajñā*, *prajñā* the external dimension of *samādhi*.

To put the matter simply, we can refer to *prajñā* as awareness in the making, *vidyā* as intrinsic awareness that has been lost, and *jñāna* as recovered awareness. But this is to speak in terms of time. It would be more accurate to speak of a falling away from eternity and a gradual return to the realization of being in eternity, beyond the vicissitudes of temporal existence. However, this is still misleading, because it suggests a certain point when we bite the apple and fall from grace, fall away from eternity, and another point when we are restored to eternity. In reality, it is not that we fell from grace at some point in the past; each of us is falling from eternity now, at every instant. But we do not have to look at it quite so negatively; intrinsic awareness, after all, really is intrinsic: it is there within us, within our reach, all the time.

5. INDECISION (*VICIKITSĀ*)

> It is to be in two minds about the truth. (p. 74)
> *Abhidharmasamuccaya*

Vicikitsā is doubt, but not doubt of a purely intellectual, abstract kind. It is not just being unsure about what is the case, or questioning things, or thinking things through for oneself. Quite the contrary, *vicikitsā* is an emotional inability to make up one's mind one way or the other. It is, in short, the kind of doubt that manifests as indecisiveness, a cognitive event that carries a reaction in its wake in the same way that, say, *avidyā* comes with the *saṃskāras* in its wake. Doubt and indecision are in a way two sides – the cognitive and the reactive – of the same negative mental event. Just as a fundamental unclarity leads to unskilful action, so the function of doubt is to lead to indecisiveness. If one is in two minds about what is good or right, that will inhibit one from acting. Unless one knows for sure what one should be doing one cannot act decisively, thoroughly, vigorously. As the Zen saying goes, 'Whatever you do, don't wobble.'[555]

Vicikitsā is doubt and indecision with regard to the Dharma, with regard to what we know at some level to be the truth. It concerns the conflict between what I have sometimes called the gravitational pull of the conditioned or compounded and the gravitational pull of the Unconditioned or Uncompounded.[556] By 'conditioned' I mean everything that is within the wheel of life, everything that is within *saṃsāra*, everything that is marked by impermanence, unsatisfactoriness, and insubstantiality, while the Uncompounded – Nirvāṇa – is free of these constraints. We know that if we do make up our mind, then *ipso facto* we commit ourselves to a certain line of action which, even if we recognize it as being positive, may also be uncomfortable, even painful. We are going to have to let go of our attachments, we are going to have to give. There is also the consideration that resolving this conflict in favour of Nirvāṇa is going to be ultimately and essentially irreversible. By contrast, a decision in favour of the compounded cannot stand for ever and is therefore not really a decision at all. Such a 'decision' is characterized by doubt and indecision.

That is to look at the nature of this mental event on a grand scale. But this inability, this unwillingness to make a decision, needs first of all to be addressed at quite an ordinary, basic level. Sometimes we are faced with an important, perhaps complex, issue about which it is genuinely difficult to come to a decision, perhaps because of insufficient information. But very often we are indecisive about trivial things, about which we are simply unwilling to commit ourselves through timidity or laziness or obstinacy.

Being indecisive can give weak people a sense of power, if in doing so they can keep others waiting. Children try to get attention in this way: you offer them a box of chocolates, and the longer they can draw out the business of choosing which one they're going to take, the longer they have your attention. It may be appropriate sometimes to indulge children in this way, but not adults. On the other hand, dithering can mean surrendering power in that a ditherer is often waiting for circumstances – which usually means other people's decisions – to make the decision for them. In the meantime, their indecision tends to have the effect of making others anxious.

Doubt as a negative mental event is essentially a response to the truth, so doubt in this sense is not present where one has not yet perceived what the truth actually is. One can be so confused as to be unaware that there are any alternatives to choose from. One may think, for example, that 'it's all one', that all religions have the same truth as their goal, or that there is literally no difference between *saṃsāra* and *nirvāṇa*, and that one need not therefore distinguish between skilful and unskilful actions. In this way one may avoid doubt and indecision, by remaining in a dark cloud of unawareness. If, on the other hand, one experiences some kind of doubt while in the process of trying to perceive or understand more clearly, this is obviously not doubt as a negative mental event.

Clarity

The counter-agent to doubt in the negative sense is clarity of thought. But how do we clarify our thinking? To begin with, we need to appreciate that clear thinking is not developed on its own. The whole of our spiritual life – at least indirectly – contributes to clarity of mind in some way. One starts off, therefore, by adopting skilful modes of action even though they do not necessarily spring naturally and spontaneously from one's mental state. This is going to be easier for some people than others.

If one is a faith-follower one may tend to get caught up in other people's skilful modes of action and work out the reason for it afterwards – which is fair enough. This sort of enthusiastic mentality certainly helps to get one's spiritual life off the ground in the early stages – as long as one's enthusiasm has lighted upon the right object, i.e. the Dharma. However, the answer to doubt and indecision is not indiscriminate enthusiasm, but clarity. If one is a faith-follower one may not appear to experience much doubt and indecision, but one will still need to develop clarity.

If one is a doctrine-follower, on the other hand, one will want to make sure exactly what one is letting oneself in for. One will see perhaps quite early on the implications of becoming a Buddhist in terms of one's whole way of life. One doesn't want to make big, perhaps painful decisions for the sake of something that is not going to stand up to rational scrutiny, or that is not going to produce happiness and joy, in the long term if not in the short term. This sort of careful examination of the Dharma is not doubt and indecision but clear thinking.

One's doubt and indecision is one's own, and one has to make one's own decisions. However, others can help one clarify the issues involved. Some people go to a divination system of one kind or another for help. If one consults, say, the *I Ching*, one is saying, in effect, 'Let's leave it to the wise old man: see what he says.' But what he generally says is 'Well, if you do this, perhaps something like that will follow.' One still has to make up one's own mind; the exercise has simply concentrated one's mind more clearly and coolly on the situation.

A more straightforward way of objectifying one's situation is to talk with an actual person – a spiritual friend – who will help one to clarify the issues. For instance, one may want to follow a certain line of action, but feel afraid or guilty about doing so. There may be a conflict between a desire to do what one wants to do and a desire to meet other people's expectations: if one's desire to please other people is very strong one may well want to sacrifice one's own wishes in order to retain their approval. Alternatively, there may be a conflict between the needs of an objective situation and what seem to be one's own personal needs; again, it is a matter of delicate judgement to decide how to balance the one against the other. Unless one can become aware of these conflicts, which are often quite unconscious, one will remain more or less in their power. What one needs is for someone to encourage one to admit that 'Yes, I'd like to do that – but ...' and help one sort out what the 'but' amounts to and whether or not it is valid. They may even venture an opinion – but without pressurizing one into accepting it.

A good listener

If one is the person being approached for clarification one needs to bear in mind that some people are going to be inclined to take one's opinion as an implicit directive; they will not just hear what one says, but do as one says. In that case one has to be careful to refrain from giving one's opinion at all. It can also happen that one's clarity can make someone who is naturally confused even more confused because it brings them up against all sorts of unconscious impulses and assumptions which they are unable to rationalize. They may say 'Yes, I understand' but that understanding is perhaps just on a superficial rational level, while deep down they're saying 'No, no!'

Real clarity is not about offering someone some sort of straightforward, common-sense solution and then telling them to pull their socks up and get on with it. It involves understanding their underlying confusion, taking into account their deeply-rooted difficulties and objections, while at the same time being uncompromisingly clear with oneself. If someone comes to you for help, are you going to be sufficiently concerned for them that you are prepared to ask them some hard questions or point out that there are some difficult choices to be made?

Sometimes when one is being soft with others one is really being soft with oneself. One doesn't want to appear to be making life more difficult for someone, one doesn't want to be involved in someone else's suffering – not because of their pain but because their pain hurts oneself. Perhaps one feels guilty; or one may be emotionally dependent on being a popular, easy-going person. So it is not as simple as it seems. One needs to be clear about one's own problems as well as those of the other person; otherwise one won't be of much use in helping them solve anything.

Clear thinking

Doubt and indecision lie at the root of our difficulties with the spiritual life, and that is where we have to bring clear thinking to bear. If one doesn't really believe that it is possible to develop as an individual, one won't be able to put into that development the energy that will enable one to develop. If one is unsure about the value or effectiveness of meditation, so that one does it with an attitude of just seeing how it will turn out, hoping something will come of practising it, one probably won't get very far. One can't start off with no doubts whatsoever, but there must be at least some sort of willing suspension of disbelief; one must have a degree of conviction sufficient to fuel one's practice with the requisite energy and decisiveness and thus produce a result tangible enough to confirm the rightness of the original decision. In this way there is a possibility of something tentative and provisional being proven on the anvil of experience.

For example, perhaps one believes that psychological development is possible but one is not sure about the whole idea of spiritual development – or vice versa. Either way, one has to be clear about what these notions actually amount to before one decides to commit oneself to them. The reason we so often fail to put in the commitment required to realize our ideals is that we have not addressed our underlying doubt and indecision about them.

Does one, for instance, really believe in the non-reality of the self? What *is* the self? In what sense is it unreal? And has one thought out one's position as regards oriental Buddhism and Buddhism in the West? As regards the three *yānas* – the Hīnayāna, the Mahāyāna, the Vajrayāna? As regards the *arhant* ideal and the bodhisattva ideal? Is one trying to be an *arhant*, or a bodhisattva? Or has one vaguely kept the two ideas (which are supposed to be ideals) in different compartments of one's mind, unsure how they might hang together – except that one day one somehow feels that it's time to get down to being an *arhant*, while the next it's the bodhisattva spirit that seems the thing.

One probably feels it's hardly worth thinking about, but inasmuch as one cares about these ideals at all, one hopes that in the long run they'll turn out to be more or less the same thing. Perhaps one likes to be pragmatic: perhaps one thinks that abstract theorizing and metaphysics are all right if you like that sort of thing, but they butter no parsnips. One has perhaps picked up the idea that the truth of things is not to be approached through the rational mind at all, but that it will suddenly vouchsafe itself while one is muddling along, and then everything will become clear.

But it is not going to be like this. One penetrates beyond the rational by way of exhausting the resources of the rational mind. The thing is not going to be achieved except through the tension of the rational mind stretching itself to its limit. Even more immediately practical matters require more clear thinking than we generally like to afford them. Why exactly should one be a vegetarian, for instance – what are the principles involved? Or why does one meditate – what actually is the point? You can't just say, 'If you're a Buddhist, these are the things you do.' Well, you can, but you won't thereby make much of an impression on a sceptical non-Buddhist.

It may be true that not everything one does as a Buddhist is fully susceptible to rational analysis. The Dharma does point towards something beyond the grasp of the rational mind. But there are rational considerations that certainly do arise, and which may be communicated in response to enquiries about why you do what you do. There can be a false humility in admitting that you have no clear idea about what you are doing.

Fortunately, if one has the idea at the back of one's mind that it is rather unspiritual to be too clear about things, the Abhidharma is there to put one right. As should be quite clear by now, the Abhidharma hammers home at every point the crucial importance of distinguishing very precisely and accurately between what is skilful and what is unskilful.

6. OPINIONATEDNESS (*DṚṢṬI*)

Opinionatedness is Guenther's translation of *dṛṣṭi*, which literally means a sight, a view, a vision, a perspective. It means seeing things in a particular way, from a particular point of view – the implication being that this view or perspective, whatever it may be, is a limited, narrow one. It is, in fact, *mithyā-dṛṣṭi* (Pāli *micchā-diṭṭhi*) or 'wrong view', that view which is under the influence of *kleśa* – as opposed to *samyag-dṛṣṭi*, right or perfect view.

In some of the earliest Pāli texts the Buddha is reported to have said that 'the Tathāgata is free from all views'[557] – including even right view. The term 'right view' is a contradiction in terms, from that absolute – so to speak – point of view. But from our own point of view, we need right view in order to displace wrong view. Only then will we be able to go beyond views altogether.

So *samyag-dṛṣṭi* is not a closed system of ideas to which one permanently adheres, but a skilful attitude provisionally adopted in order to get rid of unskilful states of mind. It is a wrong view, therefore, to believe that one must give up all views in order to attain to right or perfect view. One cannot realize absolute truth without taking one's stand upon relative truth. To be paradoxical, one could say that all views are wrong views, and one of them is that one should give up all views.

One does encounter people with this kind of wrong view from time to time, people who profess a sort of intellectual and even spiritual hospitality or open-mindedness. They don't want to confine themselves to any particular philosophy or religion. They aspire to a universal vision – which is, practically speaking, beyond them. Without right views, there is no basis for right action, no basis for ethics. And without right action there is no possibility of attaining to universal vision. Only a Tathāgata has no views; while this should certainly be one's aim, one can realize it only by taking one's stand upon right views and practising on that basis.

According to Yeshe Gyaltsen's commentary there are five kinds of *dṛṣṭi*: they are – and here I am giving my own translations rather than Guenther's – fixed self-view, extreme views, attachment to ideologies, attachment to moral codes and religious observances, and wrong views regarding actions and their consequences.

a. Self-view

> It is any acceptance, claim, opinion as dogma, fiction and opinion about the five psychophysical constituents as a (eternal) self or as belonging to a self, and its function is to serve as a basis for all other views. (pp. 74–5)

This is the text Yeshe Gyaltsen quotes from the *Abhidharmasamuccaya*. He goes on to give his own interpretation of what it means:

> *Acceptance* insofar as one is not afraid of what is contrary to every evidence;
> *Claim* insofar as one is involved with objects which are contrary to all evidence;
> *Opinion as dogma* insofar as one has rationalized it;

> *Fiction* insofar as one is enamored with it;
> *Opinion* insofar as one makes it the content of one's thinking.
> (p. 75)

Self-view is the fundamental wrong view underlying all the others. It is the view that the five *skandhas* add up to, or contain, or form an aspect of, or can be identified with, the idea of a self or ego. The wrong view arises because one posits an absolutely substantial self on the basis of one's psychophysical experience.

We fondly embrace the assumption that we are absolutely real: that the self we experience has some ultimate validity. This misunderstanding constitutes the frame of reference within which all our other views are held. It is not just the content of our thinking. It is, as it were, the 'continent', of our thinking, the 'continuous land' upon which we live and act. It is as if as human beings we are entranced or mesmerized by this misunderstanding, even sometimes proceeding to rationalize it into the basis of a philosophy or religion.

All this is despite the evidence of the Buddha's experience and teaching, and in fact the evidence of our own reason and observation. It doesn't appear to us to be evidence, of course, because we have adopted an interpretation of our experience which is not in accord with the experience of Enlightenment, and which does not allow us to appreciate the evidence available to the Enlightened mind.

We present our views in rational terms even though they are based on an essentially irrational premise – that is, on our emotional need to believe in our own secure and unchanging ego-identity. On an ordinary day-to-day level we rationalize in this way all the time. To justify our viewpoints or actions we provide reasoned explanations which serve to disguise the true reasons for them. We like to dress up our gut reactions as rational responses to make them respectable. Then we amass more and more evidence and argument on top of the original purely personal feeling. It is possible eventually to elaborate a whole philosophy out of certain basic personal human weaknesses. One begins with a certain experience of oneself and refuses to consider any evidence that challenges this experience. On the basis of this false idea of oneself one becomes involved with objects, and this whole position is presented as a philosophy or religion. One then proceeds to become attached to this view, even enamoured of it, and eventually it becomes consolidated into certain assumptions which one never subsequently questions.

Any philosophy that is not the product of an Enlightened mind is inevitably constructed in basically this way. The rationalizations are all too easily observable, even though they may be shot through with profound insights. It is sobering to reflect that all the systematic philosophies we have, and perhaps even all the religions as well, are pseudo-rational presentations, at least on a certain level, of experiences that are essentially limited. One could even go as far as to say that any systematically worked-out view must be suspected of being a rationalization in some sense.

This is why Nietzsche wrote in the form of strings of aphorisms, especially toward the end of his life. Each aphorism represents an intuition, an insight, but he doesn't attempt to string all the insights together and work them into a comprehensive system of thought. It is significant that his *Thus Spake Zarathustra* is presented as poetry rather than philosophy. If one really wants to get to the truth of things, to the heart of the matter, the imagination is arguably a more reliable faculty than the intellect alone, and the poet a more reliable guide than the philosopher.

A path of practice

There are said to be twenty possible forms of self-view.[558] This figure is arrived at by distinguishing four different ways of projecting the idea of a self on to each of the five *skandhas* (form, feeling, perception, volition, consciousness), making twenty in all. If one takes form or body (*rūpa*), for example, one could say:

i. I am my body and nothing beyond that. My body is my self; my self is my body. Body and self are identical.

ii. The body is possessed by the self as something apart from and beyond the body. This is a common idea of the nature of the soul, that there is a psychic element, identified as the self, to which the body belongs.

iii. The self is located within the body.

iv. The body is located within the self – that is, the self is a wider non-material entity within which the body is contained.

One may apply this series of possibilities to each of the *skandhas* individually, or indeed to all five *skandhas* collectively. None of these views is consonant with the reality that whatever we think of as a self is no self. This is an aspect of the insight one gains when one becomes Enlightened. A statement about the Buddha's own experience of himself is to be found among what are called the 'fourteen inexpressibles' (Sanskrit *avyākṛtavastūni*) although the 'statement' is really a non-statement. There is nothing to be said about the Buddha's experience; it is literally ineffable.

Unanswered questions

The fourteen inexpressibles emerge from a conversation between the Buddha and the wanderer Vacchagotta.[559] Vacchagotta asked the Buddha a series of questions, each presented as two (four in the case of the last question) alternative views, according to the conventions of Indian logic. The first two sets of questions concerned whether or not the universe is eternal and whether or not it is infinite.

The third question was whether or not the Buddha – and by extension any other fully Enlightened being – can be said to exist after death; or whether he simultaneously exists in one sense and does not exist in another sense; or whether he neither exists nor does not exist. The Buddha rejected all these alternative views as to his status after death. None of them fits the case, he said, and to hold any one of them would be to hold a wrong view. Even during his lifetime, so the Buddha said, he is inconceivable. How can one even consider the nature of his existence after his death?

Vacchagotta's fourth question is the one we are concerned with here. Can it be said that the *jīvitindriya*, the life principle or life faculty, is identical with this physical body? This is a question of a kind that still exercises thinkers today: whether life, or mind, or whatever you like to call it, is identical with the physical body or not. The Buddha rejects both views. In doing so, it's as though he is refusing to accept the assumption that the relation between body and life can be discussed in terms of their being either one thing or two.

In fact, it is impossible to think in terms of absolute dualities of any kind. Once one has a duality one is faced with the problem of reconciling it, which in the case of an absolute duality is impossible. So it's not a question of reducing what we think of as body to what we think of as life, or vice versa. The Buddha is suggesting that we shouldn't think in these terms at all. Perhaps we should follow Blake and say 'The body is that portion of the soul which is perceptible by the senses in this age.'[560]

The Buddhist position would appear to be that one always has a body of some kind; it isn't always a *physical* body. If you encounter a dead body, you don't get the impression that the person himself or herself is actually there in the body. Even though it looks just like them, you don't feel that you are in the presence of that person. But put it the other way round: supposing you have the experience of encountering someone who is dead – by which I mean a purely mental experience of them, not seeing a ghost – do you experience them as a sort of disembodied intelligence or spirit? Well, no – if you've ever had that sort of experience you will know that you experience them as having a body. It isn't a physical body, but they have a body, just as they had during their lifetime.

Or take the case of so-called out-of-the-body experiences: even though one has the experience of withdrawing from the body, one still feels complete – one still has subtle sense-experience. That is, one is in possession of what in the Pāli texts is termed the *manomayakāya* or 'body made of mind'[561] – through which one has supersensory experience: telepathy, clairaudience, and so on. So the body does not necessarily have to have a material medium. 'Body' is more like a principle of configuration, a unitive principle.

In short, whether or not the body one experiences at any one time can be said to be identical with one's 'life principle' is impossible to say. The whole question of the nature of the body is philosophically quite abstruse. It is not essentially the physical body, even though that may be the way one experiences it at the moment, because clearly one can leave the physical body, whether through death or an out-of-the-body experience; but equally clearly, one doesn't get away from having a body completely. In the *bardo* of death one could say that one has a body, albeit of a different kind from that that one had while alive. Furthermore, one is always connected to a physical body, if only potentially, in terms of one's karma generating a future material existence.

The *nirmāṇakāya*

But a Buddha is said to have gone beyond birth and death – and yet he still has a body. How is this? Well, one's own physical body, the experience one has in dependence upon the body and its organs, is a *vipāka*; it comes to each of us as a result of our past karma. Our bodies are, in a sense, our past catching up with us. This is true also of the Buddha. One could say – although any statement about this matter is necessarily cryptic – that in realizing the non-duality of *saṃsāra* and *nirvāṇa*, one no more ceases to have a body than one continues to have a body. In short, once one is Enlightened, no statement as to the relationship between one's Enlightened being and one's physical body is appropriate.

And, as the entire Abhidharma tradition goes to considerable lengths to show, our own physical existence is more mysterious than we usually think. 'Who am I?' is a question most of us leave behind with our adolescence, but it continues to be relevant. There is no 'me' apart from the flow of physical and mental events, apart from the five *skandhas*, which continually change. Deep down we don't really believe this; and yet, as I say, the evidence is there for us to experience.

The meditation practice called the contemplation of the six elements has as its specific purpose the overcoming of the wrong view that one has a fixed, permanent self. In the course of the practice one reflects that each of the elements of which one's body is composed – earth, water, fire, air, space, and consciousness – is not really one's own. When one dies, one will have to give back these elements to the universe; they have only been 'borrowed' for the duration of one's life. Even one's consciousness, once it is no longer bound up with the body, cannot really be said to be one's own.

b. Extreme view

> It is any acceptance, claim, opinion as dogma, fiction and opinion which is completely biased taking the five original elements as eternal existence or as non-existence, and its function is to prevent

gaining certainty through the understanding of reality as it comes through the middle way. (p. 77)

Abhidharmasamuccaya

To some extent we have already dealt with extreme views. There are the two extreme views we may hold with regard to views themselves. On the one hand we may adopt a dogmatic, possessive attitude towards views, clinging to them as though they did fully express ultimate truth. The opposite extreme view is to consider it unnecessary to have any views at all, even skilful views, right views.

The 'inexpressibles' also represent extreme views, to which the only appropriate reply was for the Buddha to stay silent. His silence was not the silence of ignorance, or of suspension of judgement; nor was it even simply the *āryan* silence, the noble silence of the second *dhyāna*, when the thought processes of *vitarka* and *vicāra* are suspended. All the alternative views he was offered were inapplicable, and he knew no explanation could be articulated in words, so he remained in the silence of the Enlightened mind.

Traditionally, the extreme views which are held to be representative are eternalism and nihilism: the view that the self is eternally existent, and the view that the self is totally non-existent.[562] In ancient India these two views concerned whether or not the self survived death in some form. The eternalist view was that the self persisted unchanged from life to life; this is akin to the Christian view of the soul, that it survives death intact and goes on to heaven, hell, or limbo. The nihilistic view was that the whole psychophysical organism was totally annihilated at the moment of death – which is of course the common, modern, secular view.

Such is, we may say, the psychological aspect of these two extreme views. They may also be put in a more metaphysical context. This version offers the view that mundane existence, in terms of the five *skandhas*, is ultimately real in some way, and at the other extreme the view that it is completely unreal and illusory at every level.

Anātman

Thirdly, in ethical terms, eternalism and nihilism may be interpreted as the two extremes of self-indulgence and self-torture. It is possible to see self-indulgence – in the philosophy of 'eat, drink, and be merry, for tomorrow we die' – as a form of nihilism. And it is possible to see self-torture – for the purpose of releasing the eternal soul from its prison – as a form of eternalism. However, this is just from the viewpoint of the traditional idea of the two extremes as representing attitudes to the possibility of life after death. It is probably more true to the psychological reality to say that self-indulgence expresses a belief in the absolute reality of mundane existence, while self-torture expresses self-hatred, and thus a desire for self-destruction and, by extension, for the destruction of mundane existence.

The Buddhist doctrine of *anātman*, no-self, is unfortunately sometimes interpreted in such terms as to appeal to this tendency towards self-destruction. If this teaching is interpreted as a total negation of the self, it will be very attractive to people who want to express their own self-hatred. Quite a few people seem to have this sort of attitude, a fascination with the *anātman* doctrine as an essentially life-denying principle. But the idea that the doctrine of no-self declares life to be worthless, meaningless, and in fact non-existent, is simply not Buddhist.

The *anātman* doctrine can also be used as a way of avoiding personal responsibility, or of sitting on one's natural energies. Anything one decides to do, particularly in an energetic or wholehearted way, becomes an expression of ego and thus doctrinally suspect. Again, this is a wrong view. The goal of Buddhahood is to go beyond the individual self, not to regress from the achievement of individual selfhood.

The ego is no more than the tendency to absolutize one's present state of being. It is not a thing, but a faulty interpretation. One is seeing something that just isn't there. The individual is there in a process of continuous change and therefore of ever-present potential development; delusion may also be there, in the form of a belief in a fixed, unchanging self or essence or soul. But that fixed, unchanging self or essence or soul or ego is not there; it never was, and it never will be. And because it isn't there, one can't do anything with it – get rid of it, go beyond it, or whatever. The best thing to do as far as the ego is concerned is just to forget about it.

We are not just an absence of self; we are an absence of *fixed* self, a flow of ever-changing components, physical and mental. The Buddha himself was evidently a powerfully distinct individual, with a very clear idea of who or what he was. To have self-view means to identify oneself with a sort of cross-section of the flow of *skandhas* and imagine that one can arrest the flow at that point. It is just a state of arrested development, like being a child who says, 'When I grow up I'm going to fill my house with toys and eat sweets all day,' unable to imagine the transformation involved in growing up.

The Middle Way

The five *skandhas* – the world which we experience as both subject and object – is neither the ultimate reality (because according to the Buddha's Enlightened experience things are not as we perceive them) nor completely illusory (because our experience, unenlightened though it may be, has its own validity on its own level). It is in response to our tendency to embrace one or another of such extreme views – which are of course reflected in various philosophies and dogmas, both Western and Eastern – that the Middle Way was formulated.

The Middle Way is to see the five *skandhas* as having a conventional or relative existence – that is, to see them as having arisen in dependence upon causes and conditions. If the extreme views are to see conditioned existence as either unconditioned or totally illusory, the Middle Way is to see the conditioned as what it is, simply conditioned. We tend to treat concepts like existence and non-existence, reality and non-reality, as absolutes, whereas so far as conditioned or relative existence is concerned (and conditioned existence is where we are when we make these distinctions) there are no absolutes.

Everything conditioned, everything phenomenal, everything mundane, arises in dependence on conditions and ceases in the absence of those conditions. The world is not completely real, but neither is it absolutely unreal. It is there to be experienced, we are involved in it, but it is not to be mistaken for absolute reality, for something that exists in an ultimate sense. It's as simple as that. It's the Middle Way, the way in which Buddhism sees the world. Really, it is just common sense.

But, of course, we want absolutes. The Buddhist approach is to get us to think for ourselves, to see into the complexity of the situation we find ourselves in, all the different factors involved, trying to understand it truly and honestly, not sliding off that Middle Way into easy answers. To think about something objectively in this way can be very frustrating. It also takes courage, because it means taking responsibility for one's conclusions.

A false sense of security

Most people put their faith and trust in someone who makes a strong impression, someone who is very emphatic and certain and self-confident. If you try to be careful about what you are saying, introducing qualifications where appropriate and suggesting that yours is only a certain way of looking at things, that there are other ways, and that one will have to make up one's own mind, you will make a comparatively feeble impression. On the whole, people want to know what to think, which means something black and white. They want certainty. What they are certain about is less important to them than the certainty itself. They will believe any farrago of nonsense as long as they have permission to believe in it absolutely. It is not clarity but certainty they are looking for. Certainty is security; and being exposed to the difficulties and confusions of having to think seriously is to be thrown into insecurity.

Many people seem to want to rush to take up views where, one may say, angels fear to tread. I have noticed this in, for example, Hindus with a smattering of religious knowledge. I remember on one occasion when I took the public jeep from Kalimpong to Siliguri, I was sitting in the front next to the driver when there was a hold-up of some sort, and the Bihari policeman who was controlling things, seeing there was a sadhu in yellow robes – i.e. myself – waiting there, and having nothing better to do for the moment, strolled up and started asking the usual questions: 'Are you a holy man?' and so on. Then he began to tell me all about how the universe had evolved from Brahman, and how it was all unreal, and how the soul was the same as God. He held forth in this way for about fifteen minutes and then strolled off again. There was a Tibetan Buddhist sitting behind me who had observed all this with mounting horror: 'That man was talking about the Dharma,' he said at last, as if he couldn't believe his ears. That someone with a few undigested religious notions rattling around in his head should shoot his mouth off about them, in public, to a total stranger, had left him almost speechless.

As a Buddhist one finds that one has to resist a tendency in people to look for absolutist views. They might ask about a certain gifted but wayward Buddhist teacher, 'Is so-and-so a bodhisattva or is he a total fake?' Of course, the fact is that such a person is a complex human being and worthy of more than a snap judgement either way – or even somewhere precisely in between. Or someone might say, 'What's the Buddhist view on such and such: hanging, abortion, astrology, extra-marital sex?' What they want is a definite, simple answer to take away with them.

But there is no 'Buddhist view' as such; there is no hierarchy of authority from which to draw one's views. One can have one's own view as a Buddhist, but it will not have the stamp of authority that Christians have from God or the Bible or the Pope. And people generally want the kind of security one gets from a source of authoritative judgements. As a Buddhist, the best one can do sometimes is to say, 'Here are the four noble truths. Do what you can with these.'

By looking for ready-made 'Buddhist' answers – the party line – people also want to be able to categorize one as a Buddhist. Just as people say 'He's an Aries,' or 'She's a greed type,' or 'He's an accountant,' and think they've got that person dealt with, classified, docketed; likewise, if they can categorize Buddhism, then they can put one in the Buddhist category. Again, one needs to resist this tendency. It's a way of dismissing you, disposing of you, not being concerned with you as an individual. What to think of you has been settled by the fact that you are a Buddhist. This is not to say that one should be afraid of saying that one is a Buddhist – or an accountant, for that matter – but that one should not imagine (or hope) that being a Buddhist puts one as an individual in a category.

c. Attachment to ideologies

> It is any acceptance, claim, opinion as dogma, fiction and opinion to hold the five psychophysical constituents – as far as they are occasions of an opinion about them – as the supreme, the principle, the particularly sublime, and the absolutely real. Its function is to serve as the basis for becoming even more enmeshed in wrong views. (p. 77)
>
> *Abhidharmasamuccaya*

We have seen how an ideology is established. First of all one has a *dṛṣṭi*, a view, representing a certain limited and emotionally negative perspective. One rationalizes this into a philosophical position or ideology, and then one proceeds to become attached to that position, to cling to that ideology. To take a simple example, someone who felt very unsure of himself, inadequate, insecure, might perhaps be drawn to some form of, say, fascist ideology. Embracing that ideology would make him feel more sure of himself, so he would then become more and more attached to it, and more and more certain in his adherence to it. Not all ideologies are as unskilful as this, of course, but an element of wrong view is always going to be there somewhere.

A mixture of motives

Clinging to ideologies means fixing our attitudes so that we won't have to think or feel or see for ourselves. Faced with the fundamental issues of life and finding there are no obvious easy answers to them, we find security in a certain limited perspective, which we formulate into a set of views. Almost all of us do this to some degree: our personal desires, whims, and perhaps neuroses bring all kinds of views or rationalizations in their wake. Some of these we are aware of, others not. But usually our wrong views underpin the emotional basis for the way we look at the world. In a sense we *exude* our wrong views – they aren't just there as a little intellectual tangle we've got into in a little corner of the brain.

We will probably find that even our involvement with the Dharma is at least partly based upon these views, these ideologies. It is almost inevitable that we start off with impure motives. We probably have some cherished notions that we associate with Buddhism, that we feel Buddhism ought to endorse, but into which we do not enquire too deeply, for fear of being disappointed. This is where the trouble starts. If we have embraced Buddhism for the wrong reasons – which is quite common – we need to make sure that we don't cling to it in such a way as to reinforce the original weakness on account of which we embraced it in the first place. Otherwise we will be embracing not Buddhism but our own preconceived views, which we can hold even more tightly because we imagine that they are sanctioned by the Dharma.

Take the example of the person who comes to the Dharma with a mistaken view of the doctrine of *anātman*, interpreting it as a total negation of the self, unconsciously finding it attractive because it seems to reflect their own self-hatred. They might then study this subject that they find so fascinating, research it, even write books on it. Finally they might become a well-known expert on the *anātmavāda*. In this way their whole life would have revolved around their basic neurosis and the rationalization built upon it.

The idea of self

Right view with regard to the self is that in truth or in reality it is a non-self. However, one can hold this view in one of two ways. One can adopt it as a skilful attitude by which one will be able to progress towards eventually transcending all views whatsoever, or else one can adhere to it as a dogma. It is possible to adopt the *anātmavāda* (the doctrine of no-self) in an unskilful, egoistic way.

This is certainly a criticism that might be levelled at some Theravādins, that they have had a tendency to advocate the *anātmavāda* in an aggressive, even belligerent manner, violently criticizing anyone who professed the opposite view. Not that these Theravādins always understood quite what they were talking about, but they were still very attached to their doctrine as a key element in their cultural and intellectual heritage, something which clearly marked them off from Hindus. One of my own teachers, Jagdish Kashyap, once remarked in the course of a lecture he was giving in Sri Lanka that one could not understand what *anātman* meant without first understanding what *ātman* or self meant. He was shouted down by the monks in the audience, who said that they didn't want him 'bringing his Hindu philosophy here'.

Such is clinging to ideology in a Buddhist context. This kind of unskilful attitude towards that which is specifically meant to help one to be skilful is a serious matter. As Candrakīrti says, if the medicine itself becomes poisonous, where will you turn for the treatment you need?[563]

A lighter touch

It is clear that sometimes what is technically a wrong view may temporarily serve a skilful purpose. For example, on the basis of a belief in an essential self or soul one may perform certain skilful actions; and on the basis of the skilful mental states arising from those actions one may realize that the idea of a self or soul could not be in accordance with reality. Up to this point that wrong view has served a useful purpose. The fact of the matter is that, until such time as we are Enlightened, we need a self; in fact, most of us actually need to strengthen and define our individuality. In the Pāli scriptures the Buddha himself speaks of 'making the self strong'[564] – because a weak self is simply not capable of sustaining the shattering experience of transcendental insight.

The crucial issue is not so much whether the view held is right or wrong, but the manner in which it is held. If one holds it sufficiently lightly, so that one is able eventually to see its limitations and discard it, then at the very least one will be able to move forward. Right view that is treated as dogma is being taken as an end in itself. It is then no longer useful and therefore no longer right view. Right view must always be held as what Guenther calls an operational concept. It is all right to believe that as a Buddhist one's operational concepts are reliable, effective, and long-lasting, but only if one keeps bearing in mind that they are still only operational concepts.

A dogmatic attitude towards right views turns them, practically speaking, into wrong views. If you try to hit someone over the head with Buddhist truth, it effectively ceases to be Buddhist truth. In any case, we have no idea at all at present what the Enlightened state – the state of realized non-ego – is like. Even to describe it as a state of non-selfhood gives us so little idea of it as to be conceivably quite misleading.

The Pudgalavāda

The followers of an ancient Hīnayāna school called the Pudgalavāda provide an interesting slant on this issue. They posited the existence of a *pudgala* or person which is distinct from the concept of *ātman* or self, supporting this view by referring to texts such as the *Tiratana Vandanā* which speak of the eight noble *pudgalas* (Pāli *aṭṭha-ariya-puggalas*), and pointing out that the Buddha refers to himself as a *pudgala*: 'There is a *pudgala* who has arisen for the benefit of the world.'[565] So they advanced the idea of a *pudgalavāda* which is not an *ātmavāda* – a position which can be defended rationally. Their opponents, of course, interpreted the key texts which the Pudgalavādins cited in support of their views differently, holding that the *pudgalavāda* was in fact a form of *ātmavāda*. However, the other Hīnayāna schools admitted that Pudgalavādins could gain Enlightenment.

So the view advanced by Edward Conze in his important account of Buddhist philosophy, *Buddhist Thought in India*, that the Pudgalavādins were not really Buddhists, does not ring true.[566] This view – that early converts to Buddhism, unable to give up their Brahminical belief in the ultimate reality of the *ātman*, tried to smuggle in their heresy in the guise of *pudgala* or *ālaya* or *bhavaṅga* – rather misses the point. In India at this time the discussion was not conducted in terms of whether or not the Pudgalavādins were really Buddhists. The term 'Buddhist' itself hardly existed. The important point, which all parties recognized, was that they were all trying to gain Enlightenment.

The more fruitful line of inquiry is to ask: why did they introduce this doctrine? If we reflect that the Buddha himself continued, even after his Enlightenment, to experience himself as himself, the answer seems clear enough. If the Theravādins reject the *pudgala* doctrine out of hand, this is perhaps because it is a purely metaphysical position, and they are sometimes quite unsophisticated, even naive, when it comes to metaphysics.

The fact is that although the Pudgalavāda school and its own recension of the scriptures have not survived it was one of the most important schools of early Buddhism. As it happens, one of the most respected Pāli scholars of modern times, A. P. Buddhadatta, came to the conclusion that they were right. Nobody bothered him about it; it was just considered a mild eccentricity on his part to be a Pudgalavādin.[567]

In the end we should have the attitude of the true Mādhyamika – the follower of the Middle Way – which is to find the truth and be receptive to it, whatever it might turn out to be, even if it threatens everything that up till now we have based our life upon. To some extent, it is bound to do this – if it is really the truth – and we should be prepared for that.

d. Attachment to moral codes and religious observances

> Its function is to serve as the basis for uselessness. (p. 78)
> *Abhidharmasamuccaya*

It is said that there are ten 'fetters' (Sanskrit *saṃyojana*, Pāli *samyojana*)[568] which hold us back from the ultimate freedom which is Enlightenment, and the breaking of the first three, according to tradition, is synonymous with the dawning of transcendental insight. The first two fetters are 'fixed self view' and 'doubt with regard to the Three Jewels'. *Śīlavrataparāmarśa* is the third. *Śīla* means 'ethics', and in this context it refers to a formulation of rules or precepts, while *vrata*, which literally means 'vow', is a pre-Buddhist, Vedic term for a certain kind of brahminical observance. And *parāmarśa* means 'being attached to, hanging on, being under the influence of'. A good interpretive translation of this term would therefore be 'clinging to ethical formalism and conventional religion as ends in themselves'. To be bound by this fetter is to think that observing the outward forms of religious observance purely mechanically or compulsively will suffice to bring about deliverance from compounded existence. It is a superstitious belief in the inherent spiritual or salvific efficacy of, say, bathing in the River Ganges, going on pilgrimage to Mecca, receiving absolution from a priest, and so on.

It is crucial to one's spiritual progress that one should break these three fetters, so it is a good idea to approach them from every angle. I have sometimes described them in psychological terms with 'fixed self view' rendered as habit, 'doubt with regard to the Three Jewels' as vagueness, and 'attachment to moral codes and religious observances' as superficiality,[569] while in social terms they could be described as attachment to psychology, philosophy, and religion. So here we are concerned with an essentially superficial approach to spiritual practice – that is, religion.

Saṃsāra

Saṃsāra is essentially an expression of compulsiveness. The fixed sense of self, the ego, is essentially compulsive, inasmuch as it has continually to reinforce its fixation by going over the same ground again and again. Such practices as bathing in the Ganges and so on are inherently egoistic acts, inasmuch as their rationale is based on the idea of a separate, unchanging self to be liberated or admitted to heaven or paradise. Such attachment to conventional religious or ethical observances simply binds us more securely to *saṃsāra*.

Buddhism itself, of course, has its own tendency towards this form of attachment. In Theravāda Buddhism, for example, many people are strongly convinced that things like shaving one's head, wearing yellow robes, and not eating after twelve o'clock make one a monk – and that these things are the most fundamental prerequisites to being a monk. But this is simply ethical formalism in the guise of Buddhism. In fact it is worse than that, because although the Theravāda itself recognizes that these observances are matters of conventional rather than natural morality, if you try flouting these conventions in a Theravādin country, you will find you have committed a major offence.

There was an Indian *bhikkhu* I knew who spent a number of years in Sri Lanka, and it happened once that he picked up a severe cold in the head. He was staying up in the hills where it can get quite cold and – being an Indian – he put on a small woollen cap. This provoked a tremendous hullaballoo: there were pictures of him in the paper under such headlines as 'the shameless monk who wears a woollen cap' and people hooted after him in the street. For years afterwards he was nicknamed 'the cap-wearing *bhikkhu*'. Of course, this happened over forty years ago; no doubt the Theravāda is more relaxed about adherence to its conventional observances than it used to be.

Western equivalents

When I returned to England after spending many years living as a *bhikkhu* in India, I myself provoked an astonishing reaction when I started letting my hair grow – this was while I was still wearing robes. This caused disquiet not just in Theravādin circles; Mahāyānists and even Zen Buddhists all seemed to find it quite upsetting. It seemed that ethical formalism was creeping into British Buddhism although it had only been going for a few decades. So I let my hair grow longer and longer. After a lecture one evening several people came up to speak to me about the length of my hair, which by now amounted to a couple of inches, and one of them said, 'I don't know why you are growing your hair so long – it is really upsetting everybody. We don't know what it means.'

I found it very interesting that the length of my hair should be a subject of such deep concern to so many people. Even Christmas Humphreys, who was supposed to be very broad-minded, was not, I came to understand, altogether happy about this deviation from the religious proprieties by one whom he had personally admonished to regard himself as the Buddhist equivalent of the Vicar of Hampstead. When I eventually gave up wearing robes, there were some people who were rather pleased – and as with the issue of the hair, their approbation was not always for the right reasons – but there were others who were deeply upset, feeling that this was tantamount to giving up Buddhism.

This whole episode was something of an eye-opener for me, and when I set up the Friends of the Western Buddhist Order I tried to discourage any creeping paralysis of the forms and institutions through which we practise and spread the Dharma. It still happens, of course – people are heard to say, 'Well, this is the way we do things in the FWBO.' But in fact, things in the Buddhist movement I started are generally the way they are because I once thought, 'That's how we'll do things for now.' Within the FWBO, nothing apart from the centrality of Going for Refuge to the Three Jewels is set in stone. There isn't one right way of doing things – there never has been.

Of course in communicating the Dharma one should be responsible about this; one should draw on past experience, and not encourage mere self-expression. And we have already discussed the value of discipline, of rules, in the spiritual life. However, a certain margin of creative variation is not only permissible, but desirable. Every once in a while one needs to re-examine everything with a completely open mind. Maybe one could even go right back to the Buddha's way of doing things – just going from place to place, and talking to people.

The idea that one has to break away from religion and morality as ordinarily understood before one can really start to make any progress on the path is a radical one, even for Buddhists. But it is quite literally what one has to do. One is wasting one's time otherwise. The third fetter is really about fear of breaking the rules. But why is one afraid of breaking the rules? Basically, it is because one doesn't trust oneself. One thinks, 'Well, if I don't observe the rules, who knows what will happen? All hell may break loose.' And yes, perhaps it will.

e. Wrong views

> It is the denial of cause and effect and of action and its result....
> Its function is to eradicate the good ... (p. 79)
>
> *Abhidharmasamuccaya*

This category concerns wrong views regarding actions and their consequences. They are given a category of their own because wrong views of this kind will undermine the spiritual life completely, making any kind of development on the path impossible. In this respect they are, so to speak, the cardinal wrong views. Traditionally there are four:

denial of cause, denial of effect, denial of oneself as an ethical agent, and denial of the attainments of the Buddhas and Bodhisattvas.

Denial of cause

The first of these, denial of cause, is the wilful refusal to acknowledge any meaningful distinction between good and bad actions – that is, the wilful refusal to recognize the ethical content of actions. This is a wrong view that used to have some currency in some 'beat' Zen circles.[570] One would assume what one imagined to be the viewpoint of the Enlightened mind which has gone beyond mundane distinctions, including that between good and evil, or skilful and unskilful.[571]

In fact, the Enlightened mind unquestionably perceives the difference between good and evil. If you are Enlightened you will look at compounded existence and perceive what is appropriate to or pertains to it, and this will include the necessary distinction between what is skilful and what is unskilful. Or rather, you will at least seem to others to be recommending skilful courses of action and deprecating unskilful ones. Whether you yourself see things in that way is another matter. What we may be sure of is that an Enlightened one will perceive the ethical implications of our actions far more clearly than we do.

Denial of effect

The second of these wrong views, denial of effect, is the wilful refusal to acknowledge any meaningful distinction between good and bad actions in terms of their consequences – specifically karmic ones. This may be a straightforward conclusion arising from the first wrong view, or it may be that no effectual ethical connection between action and experience, karma and *vipāka*, is recognized at all.

Of course, causation is not a straightforward matter, which is why it is better to think in terms of conditionality. In the Indian philosophical tradition, there are two opposing viewpoints with regard to the relationship between cause and effect. The followers of the Satkāryavāda school of thought, which brought together the Sāṃkhyas and the Advaita-Vedāntins, believe that there is essentially no difference between cause and effect, that effect is a transformation of cause, cause in another form. Various illustrations are given in support of this thesis. For instance, one can say that when water freezes, water is the cause, and ice is the effect; that when clay is formed and baked, the clay is the cause, and the pot is the effect; and that when gold ornaments are made, again, the effect is a transformation of the cause. That is the view of the Satkāryavādins. The opposite viewpoint, the view of the Asatkāryavādins, is that cause and effect are totally distinct. When there is an acorn and then much later there is an oak tree, it seems clear that the tree is not simply a transformation of the acorn, even though the acorn is the cause of the tree. Cause and effect are, according to this view, quite different.[572]

The Buddhist view is that the whole question is artificial, because from a practical point of view it is not necessary to assert either of these positions. Ice arises in dependence upon water; the oak arises in dependence upon the acorn. There is no need to say more than this. Besides, as Nāgārjuna points out, if cause and effect are identical there can be no causation. Similarly, if cause and effect are different, no causation is possible.

The idea of conditionality is effectively the idea of causation employed in modern science. When we use the term cause it should be understood to mean the condition in dependence on which an event is observed to occur. But although there is an event, in the sense of a happening, there is no 'thing' to which something has happened. There is only a process.

From an ethical perspective, the point is that actions have consequences. Unskilful actions of body, speech, and mind do not come from nowhere and do not disappear without leaving a trace. We cannot say that suffering is caused by the *kleśas*, but we can certainly observe that we suffer when we are subject to the *kleśas*.

Denial of agency

The third wrong view with respect to actions and their consequences is denial of oneself as an ethical agent: the wilful refusal to recognize that one's relationship with others, as well as with oneself, has an ethical dimension. Our actions affect others, and they affect us too, not only in the immediate future, but with respect to future lives as well. Our past and our future are the product to some degree of our ethical decisions.

The crucial relationship from an ethical point of view is traditionally the relationship with one's mother and father. If one doesn't recognize a special duty or moral responsibility towards them, one may well have lost one's moral bearings altogether (assuming that one's early ethical training did come from one's mother and father). The family in which one grows up, in other words, is said to be the training ground for the maintenance and cultivation of ethical relationships in later life.

The socialization of a child takes time and skill. When it is done well, it produces an ethically aware individual, someone who has a positive attitude towards other human beings, who actually wants to be kind and generous, and who has a positive attitude towards society generally, and can find their place in it. When it is done badly it produces someone who would sell their own grandmother for sixpence, and who has a negative and destructive attitude towards society as a whole – an attitude sometimes quite consciously and irresponsibly instilled in children, with very dangerous long-term results.

Another way of denying that one is an ethical agent is to take the view – perhaps a particularly modern one – that life, even spiritual life, is simply about doing what we feel like doing. Sooner or later, this viewpoint is more or less bound to lead to an over-valuation of the sexual relationship. This is not to say that sexual activity is necessarily unskilful on its own basic level. At the most unrefined mundane level, it is good not to be sexually blocked. There are those whose emotional development is held back by their being sexually repressed, who are unable to free up their emotions at any more subtle level than that of their sexuality. Unless some exceptional spontaneous spiritual experience arises to break through this emotional blockage, straightforward sexual experience may be the answer.[573]

The idea that there is nothing to feel guilty about in one's sexuality is for many of us quite new. Because of the atmosphere of guilt that, even subconsciously, still surrounds the issue of sex, Western people sometimes find it difficult to accept sex simply for what it is – just sex. It has to be dignified, it has to be awarded some kind of spiritual validation. If one feels that there is something wrong with sex, one wants it sprinkled with religious rose-water, so to speak, to make it all right. This is perhaps one reason why even quite secular people like to have a church wedding, for example. And it is why some people who would like to be Buddhists refer to their sexual relationship in terms of the Tantra – girlfriends becoming *ḍākinīs*, coupling becoming the union of wisdom and compassion, and so on. They don't want to face the fact that a purely mundane preoccupation occupies a large, perhaps central place in their life, and that a truly spiritual commitment would require a shift in their priorities.

No doubt a sexual experience can reach such a pitch of intensity that one is tempted to make some spiritual claims for it. But there is a simple test to apply here: does faith in the Three Jewels come into it anywhere? Is that intense experience compatible with a simultaneous experience of faith? Is the overall orientation of the emotion involved in that experience in the direction of what the Three Jewels represents – that is, faith in the transcendental? I would suggest that the actual experience of faith is incompatible with any quite defined sexual experience, that it will inhibit and even dissolve the sexual experience. The two cannot occur simultaneously.[574]

In not recognizing the experience for what it is, one lays oneself open to a twofold error. That is, as well as not distinguishing the skilful from the unskilful, it also involves not distinguishing clearly between lower and higher orders of skilfulness. The danger is that one tries to invest something occupying a lower order of skilfulness with the prestige and mystique of something that belongs to a higher order, so as to justify one's attachment to that less skilful experience.

Denial of the ideal

The fourth of these wrong views, denial of the attainments of the Buddhas and Bodhisattvas,[575] is the wilful refusal to recognize the possibility of liberation from compounded existence – and not just in the abstract. It is the wilful refusal to recognize the concrete reality of the Buddhist ideal as embodied in historical and even contemporary figures. It is to disbelieve that anyone has in the past or the present achieved a level of development that is qualitatively different from ordinary human existence, such as to represent an irreversible shift in their being towards an ever clearer and more compassionate realization of the true nature of existence. With this wrong view one immediately limits the range of one's own vision.

This attitude is probably more prevalent among ex-Protestants than among ex-Catholics because Catholics have at least been brought up with the concrete possibility of the attainment of sainthood embodied in the lives of historical individuals right up to the present day. Protestants, however, through their objection to the worship of saints, lost the notion of sanctity as representing a different and higher level of human development. The whole idea of attaining a particular level of sanctity that is recognized as marking one off from ordinary human goodness is regarded as rather suspect in a Protestant society.

Ex-Protestants tend to think in terms of 'Believe and you will be saved.' If they do accept the possibility of some kind of transformation they tend to think of it as a dramatic, even sensational group experience (mediated, perhaps, by an evangelical preacher). They don't tend to think in terms of spiritual evolution. If they take up meditation, they think of it as a way of being at peace with oneself, of being happy and comfortable with oneself on one's own level, not as a way of moving towards the permanent attainment of a state far beyond that level. Those who resist the possibility of radical change are really looking to reinforce their existing attitude, their existing way of life. If they take up meditation it is for the same reason that most people go to church – to partake of whatever consolation and emotional positivity they can find there, to enable them to carry on with mundane life.

The whole idea that one may develop into a substantially better kind of human being can be undermined by the assumption, widely current today, that no one is better than anyone else. The fact that you are more aware, more positive, more kind, more thoughtful, more energetic than other people, is not supposed actually to make you a better person than others. After all, it may be argued, other people have not had your advantages. You are not more developed; you are differently developed. One of the reasons that festivals celebrating the attainment of Buddhas and Bodhisattvas like Śākyamuni or Padmasambhava are so important is that they overturn this wrong view by drawing our attention not only to the path to Enlightenment but also to actual exemplars of the attainment of its goal.

Forces of disintegration

This analysis of the various categories of wrong view does not by any means exhaust the subject. The *Brahmajāla Sutta* of the Pāli canon, for example, deals with sixty-two wrong views. This is the first *sutta* of the first *piṭaka* of the Pāli canon.[576] That may be coincidental – after all, the Pāli canon had to start with something – but one would like to suppose that the compilers of the oral tradition knew what they were about in this as in other matters. The suggestion is that one has to get these wrong views out of the way before one can have access to the rest of the Dharma – before, that is, one can commence the spiritual life at all. The *Brahmajāla Sutta* is the 'great net' in which all wrong views are caught – that is, all the wrong views that were current in India at that time among both Buddhist and non-Buddhist spiritual practitioners. No doubt we could fish up a lot more that we have to contend with today.

One of these sixty-two wrong views is the notion that the universe is the creation of Īśvara, or God. To us, this rejection of the idea of a creator god is one of the defining ideas of Buddhism as a world religion, but in fact the Buddha at no point goes into it in any great detail, simply because it does not seem to have been a very popular view in his time. In a sense, the question is dealt with in the first two of the fourteen inexpressibles: the view that the world is eternal and the view that the world is not eternal. The belief that the universe was created by God – or indeed the belief that it started by chance or necessity – represents one extreme view; the other is the view that the universe is eternal. One might think that one of these views has to be right, but Buddhism rejects all of them.

The reason for this is that – according, at least, to the Yogācāra perspective – wherever there is the perceiving mind, there must be an object. Every attempt to account for the beginning of the universe, for example, is based on the assumption that one can rewind the spool of the universe in one's mind and eventually come to a point where the mind is not confronted by an object. But this is not possible; it is a wrong view to think so. The Yogācārin might say that the question of whether the universe is eternal or not eternal is unanswerable precisely because the question assumes (incorrectly) that there is a *mind-independent* universe to which the attributes 'eternal' or 'not eternal' might be attached.

To use a traditional Buddhist analogy, one could take the following question: 'Is the horn of a rabbit big or small?'[577] The horn of a rabbit cannot be big or small because there is no horn of a rabbit to have such attributes. A non-existent entity cannot have attributes! Likewise with the question 'Is the (mind-independent) universe eternal or not eternal?' The (mind-independent) universe cannot be eternal or not-eternal because there is no (mind-independent) universe to have the attributes 'eternal' or 'not-eternal'. Thus, the question is 'unanswerable', because it involves an unwarranted assumption. In modern logical terms, this is an example of the informal fallacy called the 'complex question'.

9
FACTORS OF INSTABILITY

The following twenty negative emotions are the *upakleśas*. Guenther calls them the proximate factors of instability – that is, they hang around the six *kleśas* as subordinate forms of them. If the *kleśas* are the root defilements, the *upakleśas* could be called the branch defilements. Another way of looking at them would be to call them more complex forms, or developments, of the *mūlakleśas*.

We are given a good many more negative mental events than positive ones, and no doubt one could extend the list considerably – more so, at least, than in the case of the positive mental events. It may even be that we have developed fresh and virulent strains of negative mental events in the time since the Abhidharma was first compiled. However, we may take some comfort from the fact that a small number of positive mental events will suffice to counteract a larger number of negative ones. Much of the importance of this list lies simply in its identification of the demons we create for ourselves. There will probably be some we didn't even realize existed. But once identified, they cease to be demons and become just problems to be worked with.

1. INDIGNATION OR RAGE (*KRODHA*)

> It is a vindictive intention which is associated with anger when the chance to hurt is near at hand. Its function is to become the basis

of taking hold of a knife, killing, and preparing to strike. (p. 82)
Abhidharmasamuccaya

Krodha is a further development of *pratigha*. Essentially it means 'readiness to strike', being the immediate intention to do harm on the arising of an opportunity to do so – for example, if a stick, knife, or other weapon lies to hand. If *krodha* is present in one's mind, as well as bearing the intention to harm, one has now fixed on the means to carry it out. Whether or not one actually does so is another matter, though it seems that *krodha* can be interpreted as including the actual deed. Perhaps it is most useful to identify three critical stages in this deteriorating mental state: first comes the general intention to do harm, or hatred, next is rage, or the immediate intention to inflict specific damage, and finally comes the actual infliction of harm, or 'fury'.

As already discussed, experiencing one's anger can be a necessary stage in becoming integrated; anger should not be unconsciously blocked off as this can lead to alienation from the sources of one's energy. This is basic therapeutic wisdom, and it is all well and good. But we must now emphasize another, more important consideration to bear in mind with regard to this sort of negative mental event.

If we were to continue with the psychotherapeutic angle, we might describe rage and fury in terms of psychological tension. When one conceives of the means by which one may express one's rage, it is as if something snaps and one experiences a sudden release of tension. One has let off steam. One has probably even freed up energy. But here we are concerned not with psychology but with ethics. What is under discussion is the immediate intention to inflict suffering on someone else – a much more critical issue than whether or not one is becoming more integrated. If we can seriously think of violence towards another person – or even kicking the cat – in terms of our own psychological states, this in itself suggests that we have lost sight of the ethical perspective.

This self-referential approach is sometimes even built into the way people practise the *mettā bhāvanā* (Sanskrit *maitrī*), which is, of course, the most effective counter-agent to hatred, rage, and fury. It seems that some people do this practice not so much as an exercise in wishing that other people should be well and happy, but rather as a means to make themselves feel more 'positive'. The aim of the practice, however, is not just to feel good in oneself, but to develop a positive attitude towards others in order to be able, when occasion offers, to express that positive attitude in action. Obviously one needs to have a psychologically skilful approach, but the psychological is not an end in itself. One cannot hope to develop skilful mental states without considering what one actually ends up doing as the fruit of those mental states. It is useless wishing people well in a purely theoretical way.

This is very much the Mahāyāna approach: to keep one's spiritual practice free from too great a concern with the preciousness of one's own mental states. If one can make sure that one actually does something genuinely altruistic from time to time, or at least takes on some work that is truly beneficial to others, this is the most effective way of keeping the ethical dimension from being crowded out by the psychological.

In my very early days as a Buddhist I wrote a skit which apparently became something of a talking point among the *bhikkhus* of the day. It was about an irascible and ill-natured gentleman (a more or less imaginary character) who was a great advocate of the *mettā bhāvanā* practice. He edited a Buddhist newspaper, writing all sorts of furious articles which savagely slated pretty well everything and everybody. His telegraphic address was 'Metta, Colombo'. In this little skit I described him sitting on his bed every morning and radiating *mettā* – this being the way the practice used to be described. One morning while he was radiating *mettā* to the four quarters of the globe, the servant boy happened to come in with his morning cup of tea – which the gentleman took after completing his *mettā* radiation – and tripped, dropping the cup and its contents all over the carpet and rather breaking up the meditative atmosphere. In a moment, the gentleman had seized the boy by the scruff of the neck and soundly thrashed him, saying 'You idiot! Can't you look where you're going when I'm radiating *mettā*?'

2. RESENTMENT (*UPANĀHA*)

> It is not letting go of an obsession which develops through association with the anger which underlies it. (p. 83)
>
> *Abhidharmasamuccaya*

In Robert Burns' poem 'Tam o'Shanter', while the eponymous hero is at the pub, his wife waits at home, 'nursing her wrath to keep it warm'. This is *upanāha*, resentment, brooding over an injury, bearing a grudge.

We want to go on being angry; we rather enjoy it, we cultivate it. We even cherish our anger. We won't let go – we refuse just to put up with the fact that we have suffered an injury.

Resentment is a pervasive form of negativity, and its very nature is to hang around situations which people feel helpless to change – a job or a marriage, perhaps – in which one feels put upon or put down or injured in some way. Our resentment gives our ego the sense that when the opportunity arises, it will be able to even the score. Even if there is no likelihood that we will be able to effect any kind of revenge, our resentment still gives us an obscure sense that we are getting our own back, albeit in a very ill-directed and pointless way.

Even though we are the only person really suffering from it, we feel we have a right to our resentment. We look back at a situation that has made us angry, feeling again the anger it has evoked, savouring that feeling, and turning the situation over and over in our mind. Most of us carry around a certain quantum of negativity that can show itself at a moment's notice if someone gets in our way. But if we build upon and work up our irritation or annoyance, that quantum of negativity becomes a steady, well-banked fire of resentment.

A hot-house atmosphere

So resentment needs to be checked in the early stages, like depression or sexual infatuation, because its very nature is to perpetuate itself as a settled mental state. If we don't nip it in the bud, there is very little we can do about it later on. Once we have allowed ourselves to get deeply into it, there isn't any straightforward way of extricating ourselves. Resentment is cumulative; it gathers a quiet momentum of its own. If we don't bring it out in the open when we first become aware of what is going on, it can become so strong that we may be afraid of taking the lid off at all. We may feel that we have lost control of it altogether and that if we start to express our feelings we may end up doing actual injury to the object of our resentment. It may be that the other person is not even aware of our resentment, so again we can be afraid of the effect of revealing our true feelings.

It has to be said that resentment is a notable feature of many marriages. A certain pattern of behaviour is established early on, and niggling dissatisfactions grow up in that hot-house atmosphere over many years until one is eaten up with resentment. And yet one's spouse may be totally unaware of the problem, fondly imagining that one loves them. I have known some older women particularly who have found it almost impossible to practise meditation on account of their feelings of resentment, accumulated over decades.

So resentment can become a crippling affliction. We need to be prepared to let go of it, even if it may be uncomfortable from an egoistic point of view to do so, and to let go of the idea that there is any point to it whatsoever. If we really can't let go, we are going to need to tackle it directly with the other person or persons involved, even though this may also be an uncomfortable experience. If the situation is really difficult to handle, we may need to ask for the help of a third party.

3. SLYNESS-CONCEALMENT (*MRAKṢA*)

> It is to perpetuate a state of unresolvedness because of its association with dullness and stubbornness when one is urged towards something positive. Slyness-concealment has the function of preventing one from making a clean break with it and feeling relieved. (p. 84)
>
> *Abhidharmasamuccaya*

Mrakṣa is sometimes translated as 'hypocrisy'. However, hypocrisy usually suggests the deliberate and systematic adoption of a mode of behaviour in order to conceal one's real intentions, whereas *mrakṣa* implies a context in which one has at least professed to set out on the spiritual path and in which one has quite a deep involvement with the spiritual community. *Mrakṣa* will arise only when one has committed oneself – more especially when one has publicly committed oneself – to certain ethical and spiritual standards that one shares with other members of the spiritual community.

At that point one may discover that there is something in one's life which is incompatible with one's spiritual commitment, but which one is unwilling to give up. It becomes a sore and sensitive area that one is not prepared to discuss with anybody, especially not with one's spiritual friends. Yes, you feel guilty; you know that what you are doing is unskilful. But you are determined to hang on to this pet weakness. You don't come clean and confess it because you would then be openly confronting the fact that you were doing something unskilful – and you would also be urged by your friends to give it up, so as to clear the path to more positive states.

Taboo

'It is to perpetuate a state of unresolvedness' because in concealing one's fault from others one is also in a sense concealing it from oneself, in that one is not really facing up to its implications, which are that it is obstructing the realization of the positive. One is sort of hoping to muddle through somehow. Thus it is not unconnected with *vicikitsā*, doubt and indecision. One may even start to rationalize one's unskilful behaviour, find all sorts of arguments to justify it. Because one is avoiding clarity, one's state of mind becomes duller and duller. One's friends may be aware that there is something wrong, that one is not making progress for some reason, and they may try to get one to bring one's difficulty out into the open. But one stubbornly pretends that there's nothing the matter.

As long as there is this sacred area of one's life that is off-limits as far as one's friends are concerned, one is effectively closing oneself off from them. One becomes increasingly out of touch – not because of one's unskilful activity (otherwise we should all be out of touch with each other most of the time) but because one insists on holding back from communicating, to those who are supposed to be one's friends, something that is evidently a very pressing problem. The longer one puts off coming clean with one's friends, the more difficult it becomes to do it, and the stronger becomes one's commitment to one's pet weakness. So this *upakleśa* of slyness-concealment, once it becomes entrenched, is one of the most problematic to deal with.

The danger is that one will eventually break off contact with one's spiritual friends altogether, in favour of people who are less demanding. At this point, the most important thing is to feel that your spiritual friends are on your side, that they are not against you. If they really are your friends, they will do their best to maintain contact even though you may be getting quite defensive and isolated as a result of your secrecy and feelings of guilt.

The principal antidote to slyness-concealment is confession of faults. Ideally we should be open with our friends all the time, and anything obstructing communication should be cleared up at once, so confession should be an everyday practice. But what is confession?

Confession

It is not just admission or acknowledgement of what we have done. It is true that in a legal context admission and confession are more or less interchangeable expressions; they are interchangeable, however, only if they are both taken to have only a psychological significance. But confession in a spiritual context is primarily not a psychological but an ethical act. If we confess to a spiritually unskilful action there is obviously a psychological element there, inasmuch as we are referring to a mental attitude, something pertaining to our own psyche. But there is more to it than this. Indeed, the psychology of the Abhidharma as a whole is not just about psychology. Although it does involve becoming a healthy human being, it is also about developing beyond that level.

When we confess to an unskilful action we are confessing to a failure to live up to our own ideals. We are invoking a norm, a set of ethical and spiritual ideals that we have accepted for ourselves, and that we share with other members of the spiritual community. These ideals are not imposed upon us. There is no veiled threat behind them that if we don't try to live by them we'll be in big trouble. It is this, in fact, that makes them truly ethical and spiritual ideals. And it is this also that makes a refusal to confess one's ethical failures so damaging towards one's integrity as an individual.

A general confession – 'I'm afraid I sometimes behave rather badly' – is not enough. To be effective, confession should be very specific, and it should be addressed to someone who understands the seriousness of what we are confessing. If we have any doubt about whether or not to confess something, we need to make a particular point of confessing it, because that doubt is quite likely to be the first stirrings of slyness-concealment. As its name suggests, it is a slippery customer that has to be watched out for carefully.

We should ideally confess to the person we have offended, but if they don't share our ideals, all we can really do is make an *admission* to them. To make our confession in the spiritual sense, we will need to talk to someone else who understands the Buddhist distinction between skilful and unskilful. In this case it is more important to make the confession than to make the admission.

Teacher and disciple

Confession has been an aspect of the relationship between teacher and disciple in the Buddhist tradition from the earliest times. It is customary in any well-ordered monastic situation for the pupil to go to the teacher every morning and evening and confess any unskilful actions they are aware of having committed during those twelve hours, and ask for forgiveness for any they are not aware of. One says, 'Whatever faults I have committed of body, speech, and mind, please forgive me.' And the teacher says '*Khamāmi, khamāmi*,' 'I forgive, I forgive.'

This practice differs from Catholic confession and absolution in that the teacher doesn't forgive on behalf of God; in fact, he doesn't forgive offences committed against anyone apart from himself. It is a purely personal exchange. One is asking forgiveness for any offences committed against him personally. If, for example, one had committed an offence against the rules of the order, then that would be dealt with by the order as a whole. However, in respect of offences that don't concern him personally, the teacher can, if not forgive, certainly listen to one's confession and advise one what to do, or what practice to take up, to help one avoid repeating that particular fault.

If – as is usual among modern Western Buddhists – one is not in a traditional teacher–disciple situation but part of a spiritual community, confession can still be very much part of one's spiritual life. Spiritual friends (*kalyāṇa mitras*) can help one another a great deal through mutual confession and exploration of how to act more skilfully in future.

The Āryasaṅgha

There is a Tibetan practice, originally deriving from the Sarvāstivāda school, of confessing to the thirty-five Buddhas of confession, who each preside over a different set of the monastic rules. That is, one confesses to whichever Buddha presides over the set of rules that includes the rule that one has transgressed. It is important, though, not to misunderstand this idea of confessing to the Buddhas. When Buddhist texts speak of asking forgiveness of the Buddhas and Bodhisattvas, this is not to say that the Buddhas might not forgive one if one didn't placate them.

After all, what is forgiveness? It is to let someone off the consequences of their action in terms of one's own personal reaction to it. It is to say that in effect the matter is now closed, the slate is wiped clean. No vicious circle of action and reaction, offence and retaliation, has been initiated. But as far as the Buddhas are concerned, one's breaking a precept is no offence to them. It is essentially an offence against oneself – because one will be reaping the *vipāka* of one's karma in the future. In that sense one is going to have to forgive oneself. Of course, as already discussed, one should be careful not to be too self-referential; as well as harming oneself through one's action one will in most cases have caused harm to someone else. One cannot forgive oneself on their behalf, so to speak. Nor can one effectively confess to oneself, though it may be a start. If one is truly to overcome slyness-concealment, one needs to confess to those one respects most, as well as to the person one has offended.

4. SPITE (OR DEFENSIVENESS) (*PRADĀŚA*)

> It is a vindictive attitude preceded by indignation and resentment, forming part of anger, and its function is to become the basis for harsh and strong words…
> *Abhidharmasamuccaya*

> It is the urge to use harsh words of disagreement due to anger and resentment when others raise one's shortcomings… (pp. 84–5)
> Yeshe Gyaltsen

Pradāśa is a vindictive mental event that gives rise not to injurious action but to unskilful speech. Yeshe Gyaltsen goes a little further than the *Abhidharmasamuccaya* does, linking it with the specific situation of receiving criticism, and thus suggesting that this *upakleśa* is directly connected with the previous one. If we are in the grip of slyness-concealment and we are taxed with our shortcomings, we are likely to react defensively. Instead of accepting criticism from our friends in a positive manner, on the basis of trust in their goodwill, we react with anger and resentment – basically because we know that we are in a weak position. We bluster: 'I'm not getting angry,' 'It's not me who's in a sulk!' 'What's your problem?' 'I don't know why you always misunderstand me,' 'You're just projecting your own anger on to me,' 'Back off, will you – I just need some space to sort myself out,' 'You're always saying that – why can't you say something positive for a change?'

We should watch for this word 'always' in these situations – 'always' comes up a lot when one is reacting in this way. But the fact is that one doesn't *always* say or do whatever one is said to be doing or saying: the statement 'You're always doing that' doesn't make sense. What is meant is really something like 'I'm aware that there's a problem here that I need to address, but I can't bring myself to be rational about it.' But instead of being able to say this, one absolutizes the other person's action, completely identifying them with it. What the expression 'You're always ...' signals is that one's reaction is out of all proportion to what has been said or done, and one cannot be treated on the assumption that one is in a rational state of mind.

This is defensiveness. We distract attention from the objective situation by attacking the *bona fides* of the person who points it out, or playing the injured innocent, or whatever. An element of paranoia can develop such that we begin to imagine that other people disapprove of us when they have said nothing at all; we start to react to criticism that no one has yet thought of except ourselves. Before we create that kind of rift between ourselves and our friends we have to be prepared to be open with them, having sufficient confidence in them to be able to confess our shortcomings.

Positive feedback

If you are the person doing the criticizing, it should be done in a skilful manner, with kindness and encouragement. Nor should there be any pretence that you yourself are well clear of that particular shortcoming. In fact, it is a good idea to be explicit about this, and say, perhaps, 'I know this failing only too well from my own experience of it – why don't we tackle it together?' If you are not Enlightened, you won't go far wrong if you make this your approach every time, because whatever the fault, it will be yours too, at least to some extent.

If you just say 'Don't be dishonest with yourself,' you are tacitly suggesting that dishonesty is the other person's problem, not something you have to work to overcome yourself. You're on much safer ground if you say 'Let's face it, we aren't always as honest with ourselves as we might be.' This should be said in full consciousness that it really is something you yourself need to work on as well. 'We are simply concerned with the elimination of unskilful mental states; whether they are yours or mine is virtually irrelevant. Let's work together to eliminate unskilful mental states from the world.' This is the bodhisattva attitude.

It is always easy to see the faults of others, but pointing them out can be an unskilful activity in itself. For example, one may criticize someone as a pre-emptive strike. This can be a stratagem of slyness-concealment: one conceals one's own faults by getting one's criticism in first. In this sort of case there needs to be a responsible person around to disentangle all the mutual recriminations.

It also happens that someone can be made a scapegoat if for one reason or another they aren't very popular. Some people even seem to invite being targeted in this way. If you go around as though you have a notice pinned to your back saying 'Please kick me,' there will always be people who are happy to oblige. Of course, to victimize someone in this way – even in the name of humour – is terribly unskilful.

In the Zen tradition, the teacher himself sometimes picks on an individual quite deliberately – not, of course, a vulnerable person, but someone who is perhaps rather arrogant and pleased with himself – and makes him see himself as no more than a mass of faults. This is a dangerous approach and should be resorted to only by experienced teachers who definitely have that person's welfare at heart, and who can clearly distinguish between, on the one hand, helping someone to break through, and on the other pushing them to break down. Only very robust people with strong natural self-confidence can stand up to that sort of treatment and benefit from it.

5. JEALOUSY (OR ENVY) (*ĪRṢYĀ*)

> It is a highly perturbed state of mind associated with aversion-hatred which is unable to bear other's excellencies by being overly attached to gain and honour. (pp. 84–5)
>
> *Abhidharmasamuccaya*

This is *īrṣyā*. It is either envy, which one feels with regard to something one doesn't have but would like to have, or jealousy, which one feels with regard to something of which one is already in possession and is afraid to lose.[578]

With envy one feels a sense of poverty in oneself, one feels unfulfilled, one craves whatever one believes will enrich one's life – and one sees someone else who has, or seems to have, what one craves oneself. The result is a mixture of craving and hatred. Envy seems to be a particularly shameful *upakleśa* to have to admit to, because effectively one hates someone either for their happiness or their good qualities, which can only seem perverse. It is also associated with a feeling of poverty and impotence: instead of being galvanized to emulate someone else's achievements, you resent them because they show you up. As Iago says of Cassio in Shakespeare's *Othello*:

> He hath a daily beauty in his life
> That makes me ugly;[579]

Antidotes

The antidote to envy is simple: it is to practise what the Buddhist tradition calls rejoicing in merits, being happy in the happiness of others, appreciating the good qualities of others. Another antidote is to associate with people who will appreciate one's own qualities. As so very often with negative mental events, the damage is done in childhood. If you find, when people thank you profusely, or make it clear how much they appreciate you, that you feel uncomfortable, or even get upset, what you are finding difficult to handle is probably a sense of lack of appreciation in the past when you were very young, which is triggered by the appreciation you are experiencing in the present. You feel regret and unhappiness at not having been appreciated in the crucial early years. You have basically never learned to take appreciation: in a perverse way, it doesn't seem right. You therefore respond with self-deprecation, which usually signals that you neither deserve nor need appreciation.

It is often said that power corrupts; but lack of power also corrupts. The corruption that comes from lack of power is envy and jealousy, resentment, discontent, disgruntlement, sourness, inadequacy, emotional sterility, and general negativity. This inner corruption can be addressed by questioning who one thinks one really is. We should perhaps look particularly at what we think of as our better self. This is the self that we like to identify with, the self that tries to keep all our other selves in order. It might feel quite comfortable to have that acceptable, respectable self in charge. But what if it's the wrong self in the chair? Is there some powerful self that is undermining the whole show? Is there some other submerged self that is more truly oneself?

According to Nietzsche, real progress begins when one has the courage to baptize the worst in oneself as the best.[580] He is putting it very strongly, but one can see what he means. You baptize, even sanctify or consecrate, that unacknowledged, apparently less desirable side of you, your 'worst' side. It's a useful exercise sometimes to ask oneself 'What do I really consider to be the worst thing about myself, what am I really ashamed of?' – and then look at it positively.

Jealousy

Jealousy is of course most often associated with our relationships, particularly sexual ones. Again, it can begin in childhood, perhaps especially for one who, having been an only child, is suddenly ousted from centre stage – as it appears – by the arrival of a second child. The jealousy that arises can be very intense indeed – it can even become murderous – though it may be covered up by an excessive demonstration of affection towards the younger sibling, so that the jealousy turns into over-protectiveness.

This is a very common source of jealousy, but it is by no means the only one. Jealousy seems to stem from a basic insecurity which can arise in any number of ways. If one has no worth in one's own eyes, if one does not feel that one is a lovable person, one will become dependent on someone else's love towards one for all one's emotional security. Instead of one's basic worth as a person being one's own property, so to speak, it is experienced only in the form of someone else's regard.

If, therefore, there is any threat of that person's regard being transferred to someone else, then what is under threat is one's whole value as a person. One risks losing not just someone one loves and values, but one's own value to oneself. If they go they will take away with them one's very identity. Jealousy is the fear of being destroyed, almost. It is in this way that jealousy can give rise to murder. To need love of a romantic or possessive kind is neurotic and should be shaken off in any way one can. It should certainly not be idealized.

To need good will, companionship, and warmth is by contrast quite healthy and positive. On the basis of this need for companionship one can then go further and develop something more, which is spiritual fellowship: sangha. Of course, there are always going to be people who simply get their healthy human needs met within the healthy human environment of the spiritual community. This is fine; the spiritual community has a great deal to offer people on the ordinary, positive level of just being human, even if they are not ready to go for Refuge to the Three Jewels.

6. AVARICE (OR ACQUISITIVENESS) (*MĀTSARYA*)

> It is an over-concern with the material things in life, stemming from over-attachment to wealth and honour... (pp. 85–6)
> *Abhidharmasamuccaya*

It is not just that one is attached to the things of this world; one holds them to be all that matters. *Mātsarya* is an almost obsessive concern with material things – with power, prestige, wealth, and possessions. The implication of this attitude is that these things have an absolute value, that once one has them one will be able to hold on to them for good. The assumption is that one can make real, solid acquisitions. One's life becomes devoted to the pursuit of these things such that one loses sight of their real value, even in material terms. They become ends in themselves rather than the means of satisfying straightforward human desires.

This attitude of possessiveness and acquisitiveness is often quite transparent, but equally often it flourishes behind a sincere spiritual or at least anti-materialist intent. These are sometimes parodied as 'Hampstead hippies' and 'champagne socialists', people who take a very critical attitude towards the society within which they continue to live rather well. There are also those who profess to be very concerned to avoid 'spiritual materialism' while being far less exercised – if at all – about freeing themselves from ordinary materialism. That is, they are very careful not to make their spiritual practice an occasion for attachment, while continuing to live rather comfortable lives.

In all these ways it is possible to do things with the appearance of not doing them. If it were slightly more consciously done one would put these examples under the heading of slyness-concealment, or perhaps the heading of defensiveness: criticizing a weakness that one wants to conceal in oneself. In fact, materialism or possessiveness and acquisitiveness is such a pervasive feature of our society that it can all too easily absorb anti-materialist impulses and make good business enterprises out of them.

The antidote to possessiveness is simple enough: it is generosity. It is also to contemplate the impermanence of material things, our own impermanence, and the fragility and evanescence of our hold upon worldly things.

7. DECEIT (OR PRETENCE) (*MĀYĀ*)

> It is a display of what is not a real quality and is associated with both [craving] and [ignorance] by being overly attached to wealth and honour. Its function is to provide a basis for a perverse life-style. (p. 86)
>
> *Abhidharmasamuccaya*

Māyā literally means a magic show – one sees something that isn't there. This is what pretence amounts to: a sort of trick. One pretends to be what one is not in order to gain wealth or honour – to which one is over-attached. One certainly would have to be over-attached to them in order to perform day in, day out, year in, year out, which is what pretending to be what one is not inevitably involves. One has to be systematic, one can't let the mask slip for a moment. One's whole lifestyle has to be harnessed to the task of keeping the lie going.

However, one has to tread a fine line between being honest about one's weaknesses and simply indulging them. One should never affect to experience positive mental events that are not in fact present in one's experience; at the same time it is truly said that one becomes a bodhisattva by behaving like a bodhisattva. The middle way here clearly involves openness and confession.

Being recognized as a Buddhist, particularly as an ordained Buddhist, you have to step carefully between these extremes. On the one hand, you are, once ordained, in some sense accountable. You stand there as an ethical individual. You can't say 'Well, everyone fiddles their tax returns, don't they?' Other people know that you are a committed Buddhist. And you know that they know. You therefore can't afford to slip up: you are expected to behave in at least a reasonable, human, considerate, and mindful manner. Even if the rest of the Order may let you off lightly, the general public won't. You have, in short, to maintain certain standards.

On the other hand, you have to avoid playing up to other people's projections.[581] You have to make sure that when you are teaching meditation other people don't see you as some kind of meditation master. When you give a talk you have to make sure that you don't get carried away with your own rhetoric, with your ability to manipulate an audience's emotions. The larger the audience, the easier it is for a practised speaker to make this mass of people do or feel or think precisely what he or she wants; and this is a very dangerous power. You can make them laugh or cry or riot; all that is required is a certain theatrical talent.

Strictly speaking, the theatricality of the actor cannot be categorized under the heading of this *upakleśa*, because an actor would never pretend to be, say, Hamlet, as a matter of actual fact. However, the danger for an actor is that he or she may fall almost inadvertently into a whole series of pretences, not distinguishing clearly between theatre and real life, between the personalities they assume and their own personality. They find themselves putting on a bit of a performance all the time, and gradually their own personality loses any kind of definition. What one can safely say, probably, is that the more completely an actor enters the character he or she is playing, the more pure a medium he or she is for the role, and thus the less there is of exhibitionism in the performance. The less one obtrudes the idea of oneself performing into one's work, the better one's chance as an actor of keeping performance and exhibitionism out of one's personality. The same goes for public speaking. One can pour out one's heart and soul, or one can put on a bit of an act; and one may find it difficult to tell the difference oneself – though one's friends should be able to.

Five different forms of pretence are distinguished by Yeshe Gyaltsen:[582]

a. *Hypocrisy:* the deliberate and continuous adoption of a way of life that is designed to make you appear to be other than you are.

b. *Flattery:* feigned admiration of someone to butter them up, followed by extravagant admiration of their property in the hope that they will want to give you some of it.

c. *Overpraise:* servile accord with someone's views, soft soaping, toadying, boot-licking, in order to get something out of someone.

d. *Evaluating by possessions:* making others ashamed to enjoy something so that you can enjoy it yourself.

e. *Seeking wealth by wealth:* You let people know how you are used to being treated and rewarded, the covert message being that they should not disappoint your expectations. The size of the limousine you are driven in signals not how much leg room you like to have in the back, but how much money you expect to be paid.

8. DISHONESTY (*ŚĀṬHYA*)

> These two, deceit and dishonesty, are counted among the four bleak things referred to in the *Kāśyapaparivarta*.
>
> Yeshe Gyaltsen

> I am constantly living
> Under the watchful eyes of
> The Buddhas and Bodhisattvas
> Who have unlimited vision. (p. 88)
>
> *Bodhicaryāvatāra*

Śāṭhya is a more straightforward form of covering up the truth than *mrakṣa* (slyness-concealment). It is dishonesty resorted to simply for the sake of worldly advantage, whether material or social, whether for wealth or for honour.

The answer to it is equally straightforward: one won't get away with it. Never mind for a moment 'the watchful eyes of the Buddhas and Bodhisattvas'. One's friends and associates, especially if they have some experience of the world, are not taken in to the extent one likes to think. Sometimes the truth comes out in most surprising ways. Certainly a politician can never count on keeping his or her dishonesty from coming to light at some point in the future.

The four bleak things are:

a. *To lie to one's teacher, or to any other member of the spiritual community.* To deceive someone by telling a lie essentially breaks the link between you. There can be no healthy human relationship without the trust and confidence that arises from a mutual respect for the truth. When one tries to deceive those who are more highly developed than one is oneself, one is closing oneself off to their influence, and to their teaching inasmuch as they embody or represent it. More than that, one is effectively shutting oneself off from the spiritual life, in that one is shutting oneself off from those sources of spiritual inspiration and instruction. It is not as if one has anything to fear from them. If one can't be open and honest with one's teacher and one's spiritual friends, who can one be open with? And the most serious way one can deceive one's teacher or spiritual friends is by trying to mislead them as to one's mental state, or one's spiritual practice.

b. *To undermine the skilful intentions of others.* This is not just discouragement. For example, we may want to dampen down someone's enthusiasm. This can be an expression of ill will or disgruntlement – we just want to get at them; or it may be that we feel threatened by their energy – we're afraid we won't be able to keep up, so our natural reaction is to want to discourage them. We perhaps invoke the middle way – as if the middle way were between enthusiasm and apathy – saying, 'Don't let your enthusiasm carry you away. If you were realistic, you'd see that your scheme would never work.' So there can be an element of dishonesty here.

But the second bleak thing is more than this. It is to raise doubts in the mind of someone who is happily doing something positive and creative, perhaps by questioning their motivation. Perhaps we are jealous: we want to bring this person down a peg or two, show them and others who calls the shots. Sometimes people do this because they think it shows their own superior insight and psychological penetration, their understanding of human nature. But it's a very cheap form of wisdom, to interpret a good action in terms of some unconsciously unskilful motivation, and to present this interpretation as fact. It is easy to undermine someone's confidence. Even when it is genuine, confidence may not necessarily be very firmly established.

The cheap or pseudo psycho-analytical approach is essentially irresponsible. It is, ethically speaking, unaware. One is so fascinated by the depth and subtlety of one's psychological analysis that one fails to consider the possible effect of one's words on the other person.

A responsible attitude

We think of awareness as being one of the most important characteristics of the true individual. But when we take the awareness of others – the second of the four dimensions of awareness outlined earlier (see p. 536 above) – we can, if we are not careful, think of it exclusively in psychological terms. It is possible to think of being aware of someone as simply seeing what they're like or how they are as an individual quite separate from oneself, overlooking the fact that in being aware of someone one is putting oneself in relationship with that person.[583]

This is where the ethical dimension comes in. The psychological dimension is useful and necessary, but it is not enough. Even if the other person is at the centre of one's attention, that in itself is not necessarily to be truly aware of them. If one is in love with someone, for example, one may be aware of them all the time – aware, at least, of one's projection onto them – but oblivious to the real effect on them of one's words and actions, oblivious as to whether one is helping or harming them.

If one is aware of oneself as an individual and of the relationship between oneself and the other person, one is aware of the effect one has on them and the effect they have on oneself. It follows that one has a certain responsibility for the effect one has on them. Awareness of someone implies the adoption of an ethically responsible attitude towards them. This is the attitude of the bodhisattva – that one does not separate the needs of others from one's own needs.

c. *To say nothing in praise of those who sincerely practise the spiritual life.* This is to be dishonest by omission; it is akin to slyness-concealment. By choosing not to draw attention to something skilful and wholesome, one is pretending it isn't there. In referring to particular people who are dedicating their lives to the Dharma, for example, if one doesn't ever mention their most conspicuous feature – that they are noticeably developing as individuals – this is a passive lie. If one sees someone who is evidently making an inspired effort to be clearer and kinder, and if an occasion arises when it would be appropriate to remark on that person's merits and qualities, but one just keeps quiet, making no acknowledgement of them whatsoever, even if it is just to nod in agreement with someone else, then this is a bleak thing. Or, to take a more complex and serious situation, it might happen that someone was being generally slandered and one knew the truth, but said nothing – perhaps because one was afraid of being on one's own with one's opinion. This, again, would be a bleak thing indeed.

d. *To praise others insincerely.* You may think someone doesn't deserve praise, but you praise them anyway, perhaps because you want something from them, or because everyone else praises them and you're afraid to suffer the consequences of standing up for your own convictions. Alternatively, you may praise someone who you know is worthy of praise, but your heart isn't in it because you bear a secret grudge against them. Or else you 'damn with faint praise': your praise of someone is a backhanded way of slighting them.

These are the four bleak things that drain the life out of one's spiritual practice. But if dishonesty is not in itself quite evidently bleak enough to warn us away from it, the traditional antidote is to remind ourselves that we are 'constantly living under the watchful eyes of the Buddhas and Bodhisattvas'.

A watchful eye

If one feels a little uncomfortable about this it may be to do with one's general Christian background: the idea that God, the judge, jury, and executioner, is everywhere, totting up one's sins. But one can drop this idea completely; there is no need to feel that one is stuck with it for ever. If any sense of dread or mistrust arises with respect to the 'Buddhas and Bodhisattvas watching over us', one has to keep reminding oneself that the Buddhas and Bodhisattvas have nothing to do with meting out justice. They do not administer the law of karma. They may see all sorts of unskilful things about you but at the same time they are completely 'with' you. It's not that they are going to approve or indulge your wrongdoing – not at all – but they aren't going to withdraw their compassion. There is no personal disapproval, although this can be very difficult to accept or even imagine.

In a sense, they don't care. In a sense, from their point of view, all these things that seem so important to us are utterly trivial. The Buddhas and Bodhisattvas aren't going to bother themselves with approving of one bit of us and disapproving of another bit. They are concerned to get us out of the whole mess. And part of the mess is – from their very much higher point of view – that we bother ourselves so much about our little skilful habits and our little unskilful ones (though we personally can deal with this part of our mess only after we have bothered ourselves about these things a very great deal). So we have to imagine the Buddhas' and Bodhisattvas' view of us as being quite different from our own or from that of any kind of authority figure – or any kind of 'indulgent uncle' figure, for that matter.

9. MENTAL INFLATION (OR SELF-INTOXICATION) (*MADA*)

> It is joy and rapture associated with passion-lust ...
> *Abhidharmasamuccaya*

> An inflated mind is the root of unconcern.
> Never treat a poor bhikṣu with contempt
> Or you may not find salvation in an aeon.
> *Adhyāśayasaṃcodanasūtra*

> Look at the vainglory of your social status and appearance,
> Your learning, your youth, and your power as your enemies.
> (p. 89)
> *Suhṛllekha*

Mada arises when one is so pleased, even infatuated and inflated, with being young and healthy, good looking, and successful, intelligent, well-bred, and so on, that one becomes unmindful. It is not simply the possession of these advantages that is the problem; after all, if one is young and energetic one can direct one's youthful energy in a skilful direction. But if one is intoxicated with one's youth and energy, one is unlikely to be thinking about one's direction at all.

Mada is a happy and joyful feeling that puts you off your guard. When things are going your way and you feel good about yourself – that is often the time when you start to make mistakes. You lose awareness of the fragility of your vaunted advantages over others and imagine that you can walk on water. Sometimes when someone is at the peak of their career everything suddenly starts to go wrong, because success has gone to their head and they have become careless. One also has to watch for this sort of mental inflation when one is doing something at which one is something of an expert. If you are so sure of your expertise, you may start to skimp on the preparations, stop applying the attention to detail that made you an expert in the first place, and this will soon begin to show. It can certainly happen with one's meditation practice.

If you're in this inflated state you don't bother about other people very much, except to the extent of comparing them unfavourably with yourself. Self-intoxication can manifest as a contempt for others who are old or infirm or ugly or unsuccessful or not as clever as you are, and a disregard for their difficulties. It's a kind of egotism: you feel a satisfaction that you're young and beautiful, and that others are not.

The *Adhyāśayasaṃcodana Sūtra*'s warning not to treat the poor *bhikṣu* with contempt might be directed at the laity, enjoining them not to be so intoxicated with worldly pleasures that they look down on the humble *bhikṣu*. However, if we consider that this is a Mahāyāna text it becomes clear that it is not only the laity who are in danger of despising the *bhikṣus*. It is the bodhisattva – the aspiring bodhisattva – who is being addressed here as well as the ordinary laity. Don't think, it says, that with all your fine notions of saving all sentient beings you can afford to look down upon the ordinary *bhikṣu* just practising the precepts. You may well be in for a fall.

10. MALICE (*VIHIṂSĀ*)

> It belongs to the emotion anger, lacks loving kindness, pity, and affection, and has the function of treating others abusively.
>
> *Abhidharmasamuccaya*

> … 'lack of loving kindness' is one's own inclination to treat others abusively. 'Lack of pity' is the inclination to induce others to treat others abusively. 'Lack of affection' is to be pleased when one hears or sees others acting in such a way. (pp. 89–90)
>
> Yeshe Gyaltsen

This is *vihiṃsā*. *Hiṃsā* means 'harm' and *vi-* is an emphatic prefix, so *vihiṃsā* is to inflict extreme harm. It is cruelty, the deliberate infliction of pain and suffering for the sake of the gratification it gives you. It is not just hatred, wanting to harm someone in particular; it is getting a taste for the infliction of harm itself, taking pleasure in the suffering of others. There is an admixture of craving with hatred.

Although this seems to be a very perverse and distorted mental state, it is evidently one that forms a significant component in the make-up of many people's minds. The malice of little boys is almost proverbial – pulling the wings off flies, tormenting cats, and so forth – and it would seem that with most people this element becomes socialized, but not necessarily eliminated. Western culture has a long tradition of staging spectacles of bloodthirsty violence, whether in the Roman arena, in Renaissance art, on the Elizabethan and Jacobean stage. It is there too in modern film and television – not to speak of bear-baiting, bullfights, and public hangings. Malice clearly finds expression, even just on an imaginative level, in some of the highest and most refined manifestations of Western culture as well as in the most obviously depraved. Perhaps it is the gratification by proxy of this dangerous *upakleśa* that effectively keeps it under control from a social point of view.

A quantum of negativity

From an individual perspective, it would seem that people have a stable quantum of negativity that remains more or less the same whatever their circumstances, give or take the occasional mood swing, and that some people have a bigger quantum of negativity than others.[584] If one is a Buddhist practising the *mettā bhāvanā*, what does one do with that quantum of negativity once one becomes aware of one's habitual projections of it on to various people or groups of people? One can withdraw those projections, only to find that one's negativity manifests in connection with the people one is living with. Obviously one is going to want to overcome this negativity completely, but as a stepping-stone it may help to find some impersonal object for one's negativity to fix on to. For example, one can direct one's aggression towards ideas or attitudes, say, or spelling mistakes, rather than the people who disseminate them. Or, more simply, one may channel one's aggression into some harmless sporting activity.

Malice is considered in Buddhism to be the worst of all possible mental events to entertain. Hence, if one deliberately decides to see a film, say, that one knows will include the closely observed depiction of people being tortured or killed, one has to reflect on one's motives. Such graphic depictions are simply unnecessary; the issue of violence can be addressed with terrifying immediacy without the necessity for the direct gratification of malice.

11. SHAMELESSNESS (*ĀHRĪKYA*)

> [*Āhrīkya*] is not restraining oneself by taking one's perversions as one's norm....
> [*Anapatrāpya*] is not restraining oneself by taking others as the norm. (p. 90)
>
> *Abhidharmasamuccaya*

Āhrīkya and *anapatrāpya* (the next factor) form a pair as the direct opposites of the pair of positive mental events *hrī* and *apatrāpya*.

Āhrīkya, shamelessness or lack of self-respect, is not just being unskilful. It is to perform a habitual unskilful action as if it were good, as if it were a principle by which you stand. You say, perhaps, 'Well yes, I am rather hot-tempered. That's just the way I am, and you'd better get used to it.' The suggestion is that you know that what you are doing is unskilful, you know what the Buddhist ideal truly consists in, but you obstinately refuse to accept the implications of that ideal for your own practice. Your weakness is not to be questioned. Against your better judgement you have drawn a line across the path of your development that has hardened into a basic principle by which you approach everything else. Anything that is incompatible with the bad habit that you have accepted as your norm must be rejected.

It is not even that you're rationalizing your position. It's not as if you're saying that going to the pub every night is your skilful means or that you don't tell people you're vegetarian when they offer to cook for you because you don't want to put them to any trouble. Lack of self-respect is not that you persuade yourself that the unskilful things you want to do are really skilful. Nor is shamelessness to do with just being a bit weak, yielding to external pressures, say. It is when you don't – or rather won't – care that what you do is unskilful. You're going to do it anyway, and that's all there is to it.

12. LACK OF SENSE OF PROPRIETY (*ANAPATRĀPYA*)

Lack of respect for wise opinion is obviously similar to shamelessness; but whereas shamelessness is resistance to one's own better judgement, lack of respect for wise opinion is resistance to the better judgement of others, a lack of sensitivity to others. In our earlier exploration of *apatrāpya*, the positive equivalent of this *upakleśa* (see pp. 558–61 above), we emphasized the importance of not submitting to the assumed verities of conventional opinion, stressing that one should distinguish between 'wise opinion' and simply conventional opinion. However, lack of respect for wise opinion implies not just that we respect the wisdom of certain people and then choose to ignore their opinions. It means that we are not open to the wisdom of others at all. We are not receptive. We don't care what anybody thinks. In discarding respect for conventional opinion, therefore, we should be careful that we are not simply rationalizing a general contempt for others, an arrogant posture of self-sufficiency. The fact is that we have to depend on others for guidance up to a certain point. We cannot make progress at any level unless we cultivate an openness to wiser counsel, a receptivity to the possibility that others may be wiser than ourselves, particularly with regard to our own spiritual needs.

The root of these *upakleśas* is lack of love for oneself. This is why one does not heed one's own ethical perceptions or the opinions of the wise – of other people, that is, who have one's welfare at heart and truly understand one's situation. If one doesn't love oneself, or care for oneself very deeply, one cannot believe that others might care about one's welfare.

Self love

It is difficult to recognize that one has a deficiency in self-love – firstly, because it generally begins in early childhood in one's experience of one's parents, and secondly, because a healthy self-love can easily be confused with various forms of unhealthy self-regard – like selfishness, narcissism, egotism, or solipsism – which actually derive from lack of real self-love.

Again, we find here the importance of asserting the ethical dimension as distinct from the psychological. It is not enough to know oneself in a psychoanalytical way. True self-knowledge must include self-love; you can't be an ethical individual unless you love yourself. This healthy self-love is comparatively rare. People who find it difficult to love themselves are going to find it difficult to receive love from others as well. But usually the way people come round to a positive self-regard is through becoming convinced, eventually, that someone else really does wish them well. It is, I think, very unusual for this to happen in a romantic context; in a sexual relationship the friendship and the element of *mettā* tends to get swamped by attachment and possessiveness.

By healthy self-love is meant self-*mettā* – non-exclusive love, love that cannot be grasped in an egoistic way. Romantic love is grasped at as compensation for lack of self-love. If you are aware that someone also has genuine goodwill for you, you can come to feel genuine goodwill for yourself; but this is quite different from using someone's love to fill the sense of inner emptiness with a temporary substitute for self-love. In the one case you learn to love yourself by being with someone who loves you, who feels *mettā* for you; you come to realize that another person feels that you are genuinely worthwhile, and begin to appreciate your own worth for yourself. In the other case you let the other person love you because you can't do it yourself. They do it for you, and you never learn to love yourself.

Unfortunately, if you feel that only romantic love will fill the aching void inside, you may not be sensitive to *mettā*, which may seem rather cold and impersonal and rarefied. Even if someone is showing real goodwill and kindness by their actions, you may experience their *mettā* as a lack of interest or concern. If what you are looking for is a strong emotional attachment, then disinterested concern and warmth and kindness, however powerfully felt, will quite possibly not touch you. However, *mettā* is almost certainly what someone who has no shame or no respect for wise opinion really needs, because what they are missing is real interest in their own welfare and development.

13. GLOOMINESS (OR STAGNATION) (*STYĀNA*)

> It is the way in which the mind cannot function properly and is associated with listlessness. (p. 91)
>
> *Abhidharmasamuccaya*

Styāna literally means stiffness or stagnation. It is a state of emotional blockage that has hardened into a sort of paralysis in which you are bound, costive, and nothing is moving at all. Nothing can go out, nothing can come in. It is a chronic physical and mental heaviness to the point of petrifaction in which everything has more or less closed down. It is quite a complex state, emotionally speaking, and likely to be the result of a build-up of a number of negative mental factors over time.

Like many of the other *upakleśas*, stagnation is difficult to get out of by oneself because one almost doesn't want to be helped. When one is resentful, anxious, or depressed for one reason or another, one can get into a state where one says 'There's nothing you can do. I'm finished.' One can no longer even see a way to retrace one's steps or undo the harm one has done oneself without determined and skilful intervention from one's friends. In these extreme and entrenched states there is generally resistance to being helped, but when one is extremely lethargic, one hasn't even got sufficient energy moving around to summon up resistance.

Probably the easiest way to get energy moving again is through the body, through physical exercise. However, this state is a negative *mental* event, even if it expresses itself to some extent in physical terms, so at some point it has to be addressed on a mental or emotional level. One has to look for its real origins, which are probably in the area of unresolved conflict, or blocked or repressed emotion – anger or fear, say. It's a kind of depressive state, a tendency which is easily recognizable in that when one has succumbed to it, one becomes dull, gloomy, and listless, at least for a time. In its fully developed form, however, it is quite unusual.

14. EBULLIENCE (*AUDDHATYA*)

> It is restlessness of mind which is associated with [craving] that gets involved with things considered to be enjoyable. Its function is to obstruct quietness. (p. 92)
>
> *Abhidharmasamuccaya*

Auddhatya is a sort of recklessness; an excited, emotional turmoil; hilarity; scattered, unmindful liveliness – with reference specifically to pleasurable objects. You are like a greedy child let loose in a sweetshop, intoxicated by the pleasurable objects you encounter, always in search of a good time. You get so excited, darting from one enjoyable object to another, that you're unable to settle upon any one of them. Young girls in fashionable clothes shops seem to be in this sort of state sometimes. (The atmosphere in bookshops – with which I am personally rather more familiar – by contrast seems altogether heavier – a heavy atmosphere of greed.) The chief characteristic of this *upakleśa* is an unintegrated, irresponsible, and thus essentially selfish bubbly energy.

Clearly, ebullience is the opposite extreme to the previous *upakleśa*, stagnation, and moderate forms of the pair of them can be seen to alternate in the same person, as in manic depression. Some creative people in particular seem to swing between moods of dull depression and vigorous elation – except that the concentration involved in their creative energy makes this a completely different state from the negative one under discussion here.

This is one reason why one needs to be precise in examining mental events; otherwise it is quite possible to confuse a positive mental event with a negative one.

In fact, one might say that creative inspiration in the sense of *prīti* and creative energy in the sense of *vīrya* are the positive counterparts of this *upakleśa*, ebullience. There is a distinguishing psychological element – freed-up energy – which the negative mental event shares with the positive ones. The difference is that *vīrya* is specifically 'energy in pursuit of the good'; it has an essentially ethical reference.

We tend to think of energy, and even *vīrya*, in psychological terms. If one feels full of positive, fairly benign energy, for most of us that'll do. If we can free up our energies, that is enough. We'll settle for that. However, if we accept the whole psychological model of human development as self-sufficient, as an end in itself, we are left with a self-centred, self-indulgent, and thus very limited idea of what we are about.

15. LACK OF TRUST (OR NON-FAITH) (*ĀŚRADDHYA*)

> It is the mind associated with [ignorance] which does not have deep conviction, has lack of [faith], and has no desire for things positive. It provides the basis for laziness.
>
> *Abhidharmasamuccaya*

> It is a preponderance of dullness which is not conducive to [faith]. (p. 93)
>
> Yeshe Gyaltsen

There is more to non-faith than simply the absence of faith. In this state we are lazy with respect to positive things, with respect to the development of positive mental states. We have no appreciation of the value of those positive things, nor even any very deep conviction about their existence, and therefore no definite drive in their direction or clear volition to realize them.

We don't appreciate the fact that our actions have consequences and we therefore don't make any particular effort to act skilfully and avoid unskilful activity. We don't really understand the value of the Three Jewels and we therefore don't commit ourselves to them, we don't go for Refuge to them. And of course without faith in the transcendental, without faith in the possibility of Enlightenment, we are not going to be interested in them. In this way lack of faith is the link between dullness in the sense of not appreciating what the Dharma really means, and laziness in the sense of not practising the Dharma.

Faith is a very precise mental event. It represents a quite distinctive – one might even say unique – kind of emotion, and it is actually very rare. One may be affected, moved, and inspired by one's experience of Buddhism, but this does not necessarily amount to faith. If, for example, one attends a Buddhist centre regularly, one may find it a very congenial place: warm, friendly, peaceful, colourful; one may appreciate its positive effect on one's mental state; one may be moved and inspired by the possibilities of spiritual development that it opens up. But faith is more than this.

Commitment

When one wishes to be ordained as a Buddhist, for example – and here I am thinking in particular of my own order, the Western Buddhist Order – one can 'do all the right things', and still be asked to wait. Of course it is natural to wonder what one has to do to be considered ready for ordination. One may well feel that one has done enough to earn promotion. One may even go off the idea of this particular Buddhist order and go to another Buddhist group that will accept one more readily. Or one may reconcile oneself to the situation by persuading oneself that the waiting time is a sort of test, or that people in the order are prejudiced against one for one reason or another.

But the fact of the matter is more straightforward than this. If one seeks ordination as a sort of natural process of promotion within the group, which one can earn by good works, so to speak, one has no real idea of what ordination, or Going for Refuge to the Three Jewels, or commitment, or faith, is really about. This might sound strange, but people can be devoted Buddhists for years without having any idea whatsoever of what faith means. They'll talk in terms of faith and commitment, but they'll use these terms without understanding them at all. It isn't that they have a partial understanding which they can gradually build upon; they haven't any inkling of what these things really mean.

It can be difficult to detect this absence of understanding beneath all the right attitudes they express and their genuinely positive feelings about the Dharma and the spiritual life. But it's as if a certain faculty is missing, a faculty that one needs if one is to perceive the Three Jewels in such a way that one may be said to have faith in them. And it can take quite a long time to develop this faculty.

Pleasure

It is possible, of course, to confuse faith with pleasure. One can read a book like *The Life of Milarepa* and be inspired by the vicarious experience of all that meditation, all that spiritual practice, all that attainment of higher mental states – but being stirred up in this way does not constitute faith. A book may even inspire one to meditate, but unless this is more than a wish for enhanced or pleasurable experiences in meditation, it is not faith. The pleasures of religious literature can be a sort of indulgence, particularly if one gets through a lot of it at once. The danger is that one ends up consuming books like boxes of chocolates.

The same thing goes for one's Buddhist friends. They may be good company, they may be helpful, they may provide positive support and advice, one may trust them – but to have *faith* in spiritual friends involves an attitude towards them which is qualitatively different from the appreciative pleasure one takes in them as friends. If the positive group revolves around pleasure at some more or less refined level, the spiritual community by contrast revolves around faith.

One could say that faith is the single significant element missing from the purely psychological or therapeutic model of human development. There is a great deal of happiness, energy, pleasure in the positive sense, even joy, to be found in various psychological and therapeutic circles – but no faith. There may sometimes be a spiritual dimension of some kind, but not a transcendental dimension.

As we have already seen in our discussion of *śraddhā* as a positive mental event (see pp. 550–7 above), faith is not to be associated with pleasure at all. Some of the Christian mystics make this point very firmly. They warn that one should carry on with one's contemplations regardless of what they call 'sensible consolations', and that one should not regard the withdrawal of such pleasures of meditation as a sign that one is not making progress. This condition is best known under the term coined by St John of the Cross as the 'dark night of the senses'. (There is, of course, no Buddhist analogy for what he terms the 'dark night of the soul', when the presence of God seems to be withdrawn). Conversely, the fact that one feels good with regard to some allegedly religious or spiritual object does not mean that one necessarily has faith in it.

Faith

To awaken the faculty of faith, one needs to bridge the gap between the emotions and the intellect, and to do this it is not enough just to try to balance these two areas of one's experience. The problem lies with our limited conception of what 'intellect' means. Originally, the word meant a higher, intuitive power to see directly into the truth of things. Now that its meaning has been debased into simply the power of reasoning, we are left short of a vital concept.

It is possible to be drawn to the Dharma for intellectual reasons (though such a motivation could never, obviously, be *purely* rational). One can also be attracted through an emotional response, or a combination of the two. But none of this is enough. Faith involves the stimulation of something else, the stirring into life of an imaginal, visionary faculty, which is the total reaction of the whole being when confronted by the ideal, whether embodied in human form or in the teaching.

Without the operation of this spiritual faculty of the imagination, the emotions and the intellect remain dissociated from each other. In a sense, the imagination, in the sense in which I am using the term, is a separate faculty from reason and emotion, but it operates with them in the form of a psycho-spiritual network – that is, its nature is to unite reason and emotion.

We may begin by becoming involved with Buddhism academically, organizationally, or socially. We have to catch hold wherever we can. But whatever bit we get hold of is not actually Buddhism. It's not that one can get a clear idea of the Dharma, and then all one has to do is introduce a little emotion, a little warmth. No. If one looks at the Dharma rationally and coldly, one will already have a distorted idea of it. In integrating the emotions with the intellect, faith changes the way we see things.

Unfortunately, many people are in the situation of thinking, or even knowing or believing, 'This is what I ought to do,' but not wanting to do it. One should be able to work with this, but if the conflict becomes too extreme, one will need to go right back and address the question: 'How did I come to be the kind of person who knows what is good for me but doesn't feel like doing anything about it?' In order to re-contact one's feelings one has to go back to doing what one really wants to do and work towards one's ideals from that basis.

16. LAZINESS (*KAUSĪDYA*)

> It is an unwilling mind, associated with [ignorance], relying on the pleasures of drowsiness, lying down and not getting up. Its function is to obstruct and hinder one in applying himself to positive things. (p. 94)
>
> *Abhidharmasamuccaya*

While *kausīdya* is generally interpreted in terms of 'drowsiness, lying down and not getting up', we shouldn't come away with the idea that we counteract it simply by being more energetic. It is essentially an unwillingness to apply oneself to positive things, so it may equally well express itself in energetic activity, if that activity is directed towards an unwholesome end. Satan finds work for idle hands. We have already touched on this topic in our discussion of the object-determining mental event *chanda* or eagerness (see pp. 533–5 above).

It would seem that laziness can involve the expenditure of plenty of energy, but it is expended inappropriately – that is, it is not a question of blocked energy so much as active resistance to appropriate activity. We all need to relax from time to time, but for a healthy person to prolong the period of relaxation beyond its natural limits means either that their energy has stagnated – which is *styāna* – or that they are lazy, which is different. Laziness is not an inability to mobilize energy, but an unwillingness to mobilize available energy towards a positive end.

Dr Johnson was very conscious of being a lazy person, and he regretted it bitterly. He made regular resolutions to remedy this defect in his character, but to no avail. He used to write in bed, because he didn't get up till late, and he said that if a sheet he was using blew onto the floor he would write what he had written over again on a fresh sheet to avoid the trouble of getting out of bed to pick it up. However, among many other things he single-handedly compiled his great English dictionary, so he can't have been short on energy; he did manage to do the things he needed to do, despite his laziness.

Laziness is perhaps a weakness that Buddhists particularly need to guard against. I remember seeing a book called *The Lazy Man's Guide to Enlightenment*; this sort of nonsense seems to appeal to people who become interested in Buddhism. Laziness is often what attracts people to the advanced teachings of Zen Buddhism, which emphasize the teaching that the Dharma is a raft, to be left behind once one has crossed the river of *saṃsāra*.[585] The way these teachings are sometimes presented in the West gives the impression that one can discard the raft before one has bothered to make use of it at all.

Even without such manifestly wrong views, there is a constant danger of settling down wherever one finds oneself comfortable. The spiritual life is so rewarding on all kinds of levels that one can always be tempted basically to stay put. Quite early on one discovers how to operate effectively and happily on a straightforward human level, how to live a happy, healthy life, how to communicate well and so on, and one can think, 'Well, I'll settle for this.' Even if one gets over this stage, even if one is apparently meditating eight hours a day, it can still be that one is just treading water, just enjoying the fruits of one's practice. It's like wallowing in bed just because it's warm and comfortable – you cling on to that half-dreaming state and resist the challenge of the new day.

This is laziness. It is associated with ignorance because what is lacking is vision. What is lacking is a 'divine discontent' – not disgruntlement, but a sense of continual striving towards an ideal, an awareness of the limitations of the mundane (the compounded, the psychological, the hedonic) sufficient to keep taking one beyond oneself.

17. UNCONCERN (OR HEEDLESSNESS) (*PRAMĀDA*)

> It is to persevere in passion-lust, aversion-hatred, and [ignorance] aggravated by laziness. It is not to attend to what is positive and so also is not to protect the mind from those things which cannot provide lasting satisfaction. (p. 94)
>
> *Abhidharmasamuccaya*

We have seen that one can give way to laziness at any point before Stream Entry. When one stops making an effort in response to the pull of the Unconditioned, one is effectively giving way to the pull of the conditioned. We may have the sense that we want to stay just where we are for a while, but this is impossible. If we aren't moving forward, we're slipping back.

If we persist in this course, there comes a point where we let go completely; we cease to offer any resistance at all to the *kleśas* and *upakleśas*. We just don't care any more about what is happening. This is heedlessness or *pramāda*. It's a sort of lack of responsibility towards oneself. We no longer bother to protect the mind from negative mental events. We let everything slide.

It's like someone who 'lets themselves go', who stops taking care of their appearance. One becomes a spiritual slattern, ethically down at heel. Or it's like someone who just stops bothering to keep their house in repair. There are broken panes of glass in the windows, the roof leaks in several places, doors are coming off their hinges, floorboards are loose, and they don't even try any more to keep dust from gathering and dead leaves from blowing in, and cats and dogs from fouling the place wherever they like. If one could see one's spiritual condition when one no longer bothers about it, this is more or less how it would appear.

If we become heedless out of craving it is like someone who lets their house go to rack and ruin because they sit about all day drinking. Our mind gets so taken up with the objects of our craving that we hardly notice, let alone care, what sort of state of mind we're in.

If we become heedless out of hatred it's as if we're much more concerned to make our neighbour suffer – breaking his windows and trampling on his flower beds – than we are to look after our own property: we are so intent on inflicting harm that we are unconcerned about our own interests.

And if we become heedless out of ignorance we are like someone who is so dull-witted that they don't know any better than to let their house become a shambles. In this case we are simply unaware of the serious consequences of allowing negative mental events to take over our minds. We allow the *kleśas* and *upakleśas* to run riot either because we don't think it matters or perhaps because we think that being mindful or watchful is not good for us, or else because it has never occurred to us to consider the question at all.

Just as a house will not keep itself in good repair, so with the mind. One has to watch for the leak in the roof, stains on the carpet need to be cleared up and so on. Likewise one has to guard against ethical and spiritual deterioration. Indeed, the case of the mind is more perilous than this comparison suggests, because it is not just a thing that is subject to disintegration – rather, it is in ever-present danger of being actively invaded. One has to maintain – with the help of one's friends – a constant posture of non-heedlessness.

18. FORGETFULNESS (OR UNRECOLLECTEDNESS OR UNMINDFULNESS) (*MUṢITASMṚTITĀ*)

> It is a flash of awareness in which the mind is not made clear and forgets immediately the positive thing because it is an attention to an emotionally tainted object.
>
> Yeshe Gyaltsen

> It functions as the basis of distraction. (p. 95)
>
> *Abhidharmasamuccaya*

If one is experiencing *muṣitasmṛtitā*, one adverts to a positive object, but very fleetingly, because the mind is immediately pulled away from it by other, purely negative, factors. It is not simply forgetfulness – one can be forgetful of anything, positive or negative. Here, the object is a positive one. The mind happens to alight on a positive object but we don't properly appreciate the nature of that positive object. It makes a very weak impression, so that our attention is at once snatched away.

This is what happens – according to the *Tibetan Book of the Dead* – when we have a glimpse of the clear light of Reality in the *bardo* and our consciousness is unable to sustain this vision. On a more basic level it also happens in meditation. Meditation is essentially easy: all one has to do is sit down and concentrate on one's breathing. That's it. If one were a balanced, happy, and integrated person one would be able to become more and more absorbed in the breath without any trouble. So it's not that it's difficult to concentrate on the breathing. The difficulty is to keep one's attention from being drawn away by distractions – i.e. negative mental events. So in a sense, *muṣitasmṛtitā* is forgetfulness of oneself.

Forgetfulness is the inability to retain the impression of the positive. If you read a book while you're in a negative state of mind, for example, it won't make any impression at all. You may pass the words across your mind but they just don't register, they don't mean anything to you – whereas at another time they might sink in very deeply. Negative emotions have such a hold over us that we can't fix the attention on anything positive long enough to begin to come under its influence. So we forget all about it. Clearly the counter-agent to this *upakleśa* is mindfulness.

19. INATTENTIVENESS (OR PURPOSELESSNESS) (*ASAṂPRAJANYA*)

> It is an emotionally tainted discriminating awareness which lacks watchfulness with regard to the activities of body, speech, and mind and is not associated with carefulness.... This inattentiveness becomes the foundation for falling from one's level of being ... (p. 96)
>
> Yeshe Gyaltsen

This is the negative mental event which consists in the lack of *saṃprajanya*, usually translated as 'mindfulness of purpose'. If one does not stay continually aware of one's purpose and aim in life – which for a Buddhist is ultimately the attainment of Enlightenment – one will succumb to *asaṃprajanya*, which could be described as a sort of neurotic introspection with no clear purpose or point. One can be aware in some degree of what is going on in one's own mind, one can even have a measure of faith in the possibility of attaining to higher states of being, but if one isn't fully mindful – that is, if one isn't watchful with regard to one's mental states, one's speech, and one's actions – one will 'fall from one's level of being' to a lower level of existence through the process of karma and rebirth.

If one does not bring one's activities of body, speech, and mind into line with one's discriminating awareness and one's faith – that is, if one's approach is purely psychological – one will come to grief. If one is careless or cavalier with regard to ethics, no amount of discriminating awareness will save one. The point is that it is possible to examine and analyse one's mental states without actually being mindful or watchful with regard to them any more than to one's speech and physical actions. If one is preoccupied with one's mental states in this unhealthy, even neurotic way to such an extent that one doesn't heed the ethical implications of those mental states in terms of one's actions of body, speech, and mind, there is bound to be an overall deterioration in one's level of being.

This is because one's level of being is determined by one's volitional actions, by whether they are skilful or unskilful, not by whether or not one feels good while performing those actions. Unfortunately, there is a tendency in the West to be far more concerned about the complexities of one's inner psychological states than about the much simpler questions of how to live an ethical life. One may perhaps fear, for example, that giving up some unskilful activity may disrupt the free flow of one's energies: it may well do this, but one should then be able to redirect that energy into a more skilful activity.

It is true that Buddhist ethics are ethics of intention, but this does not mean that they are simply about how we feel; rather, they are about our intentions with regard to objective situations. If we are to act skilfully, we need to focus our attention on the objective situation rather than on ourselves and how we feel about what we are doing.

It may be reasonable to expect to get something out of what we do, at least occasionally, but the paradox is that we are only going to get something out of it to the extent that our focus is not on getting anything out of it at all.

20. DESULTORINESS (OR DISTRACTION) (*VIKṢEPA*)

> It is to be a scatter-brain and belongs to the categories of [greed, hatred, and ignorance]. Its function is to obstruct one from becoming free of [greed]. (p. 96)
>
> *Abhidharmasamuccaya*

Vikṣepa literally means a sort of tossing about of awareness. Your distractedness consists in a kind of tossing and turning, as you stagger or flounder from one thing to another. There are traditionally six varieties of this *upakleśa*,[586] though one could no doubt think of others.[587] Each of the six will now be examined in turn.

a. *Desultoriness* qua *desultoriness:* In this state, one is distracted from one's meditation through sense perception of one kind or another: a fly lands on one's arm, one smells something, one hears something. When one is not particularly concentrated, whatever it is cannot but impinge upon one's consciousness and distract one, if only momentarily, and this is *vikṣepa*. When one *is* concentrated, on the other hand, there can be a sound going on, say, but one's reception of it is inhibited by one's state of concentration. One may be aware of a very subtle, muffled noise, but it is not definite enough to cause one's mind to go towards it. One becomes aware of what one has heard, one names or identifies it, only when one comes out of the state of concentration.

b. *Desultoriness regarding the without:* This kind of distraction occurs in the context of insight practice and refers specifically to consciousness being drawn to the opposite of what one is trying to realize. One drifts away from one's concentration on the real nature of compounded things and become distracted by their illusory qualities. For example, one may be reflecting or meditating on the impermanence of something but become unable to fix one's mind on that object in such a way as to penetrate into its impermanence, because one starts relishing it as if it were permanent. Or – to take a rather shocking example – one may be practising the *aśubha bhāvanā*, fixing one's mind on the inherent unloveliness of compounded things by contemplating a corpse; but then one's mind may drift off to think of other bodies that are very much alive and really rather lovely. In ways such as this one can lose sight of the real characteristics of the object of concentration and start grasping its unreal characteristics.

c. *Desultoriness regarding the within:* In this instance of *vikṣepa*, one becomes distracted in meditation through getting caught up in various negative mental states. One becomes more and more involved and fascinated with one's inner experience, with one's subjective states of mind, instead of becoming more and more deeply absorbed in the object of one's meditation. It is a mental restlessness.

d. *Desultoriness regarding defining characteristics: Vikṣepa* in this sense is the state of being distracted by the opinions of others as to what meditation practice one should be doing. Not being firm enough in one's purpose, one has to rush off and try every new method one hears about. In this way one drifts from one method of practice to another. This kind of distraction comes from lack of confidence, from being unduly influenced by the recommendations of others. It also comes from placing too much faith in the particular method; that is, one clings to the idea that if one could only find the right method of practice all one's difficulties would be over.

e. *Desultoriness of inappropriate action:* One's distraction consists in being drawn to practices based on perverse or topsy-turvy views, and one takes up these activities, one after another, with a conceited sense that one is getting into something positive. The perverse or topsy-turvy views meant here are those expressed in a list called the four *viparyāsas*, the four perversities; these are to take the perishable as imperishable, the painful as pleasant, the impure as pure, and the devoid of self as possessing self.[588] So one drifts from one pseudo-positive thing to another, from one personal growth therapy to another, from one 'deep and meaningful' experience to another. All the time one thinks that one is getting somewhere; one thinks that one's life is becoming more and more rich and significant. As one guzzles one 'profound life-changing experience' after another one gathers an inflated idea of one's own psychological and spiritual development.

f. *Desultoriness by rationalization:* This is essentially about the positive taking one away from the even more positive. One is distracted from the highest ideals by intermediate attainments. Thus the popular Mahāyāna view is that the ideal of the *arhant* can become a distraction from the bodhisattva ideal, that one can settle for a limited form of Enlightenment for oneself alone. In fact, it's more that one can become distracted by the limited progress to be made in one's practice of the Dharma when one makes a point of going it alone – i.e. leaving the Sangha refuge out of one's practice. To take another example, the first *dhyāna* is a thoroughly positive state of mind, but it becomes a distraction if one doesn't move on from it to the even more integrated states represented by the higher *dhyānas*. All the *dhyānas* are equally positive inasmuch as they are all positive and not negative, just as all shades of blue are blue inasmuch as they are all blue and not red or yellow. But of course some blues are bluer than others, and likewise some *dhyānas* represent a greater degree of integration than others.

10
UNCLASSIFIABLE MIND

These last four mental events, the *aniyatas* – torpor, worry, initial application of mind, and sustained application of mind – are essentially unclassifiable; that is, they cannot be classed as necessarily positive, or negative, or neutral, or object-determining or whatever.

1. DROWSINESS (OR TORPOR) (*MIDDHA*)

> ... during the night sleep is appropriate for increasing the ability of the body to attend to positive tasks;... The negative aspect of sleep which is emotionally tainted makes one dread positive tasks which must be done. (p. 100)
>
> Yeshe Gyaltsen

Middha is like the kind of state one is in after a heavy meal. It's primarily a physical state, but it does of course have mental repercussions, and these may be either positive or negative depending on circumstances. If the mind is in a drowsy state it may drift either way. As for an Enlightened mind, according to the Theravādin tradition, the *arhant* is liable to torpor, *middha*, but not to its mental equivalent, *thīna*.[589]

The state of torpor or drowsiness does obviously involve a loss of energy; because one is in a hazy, even passive state, one drifts in the direction of one's natural inclination, whether that is positive or negative. In meditation it may involve withdrawing inward, away from the object of meditation. One might think that meditation is all about withdrawing inward anyway, but in fact it involves all one's energies going out towards a single object 'out there'. The state of torpor is the opposite of this, because it takes one back into oneself.

Sleep

The sleep state, though, cannot be said to involve the loss of energy. It is a recuperative state. One may feel drowsy, go to sleep, and as a result bounce out of bed ready and happy to get on with something positive. Alternatively, and most unfortunately, one may wake up with a freshly renewed negative state of mind, or a negative state consisting in a disinclination to wake up at all.

Of course, the differences between people are particularly evident when it comes to sleep patterns. Some people need more sleep than others. Some like to get up early, while others seem to be naturally late risers and are more active late at night. Some people take longer to emerge from sleep than others; they may be a little slower in their reactions, a little less sharp or wakeful. One particular sleep pattern is not in itself more virtuous than another. And even within one's own pattern one may sometimes need to make allowances. If one has been overactive and one's system needs a rest, there may be a natural and healthy reluctance to get out of bed. There is certainly no particular virtue in needing less sleep than other people. In deciding how much sleep one needs, one just has to take into consideration one's constitution, temperament, and age. Having taken all that into account, one should be able to rise from sleep with a healthy and optimistic inclination to get on with positive activity.

Of course, to sleep is to dream – and dreaming is one way of staying in touch with the imaginative part of one's mind. If one is preoccupied with abstract ideas to the exclusion of more imaginative mental activity, it's as though a whole side of oneself dies away. Take Charles Darwin, for example. Of course he was by no means an uncreative or sterile collector of scientific data, and as a young man he had a vivid appreciation of poetry; but when after twenty-five or thirty years of intense scientific work he turned one day to his Shakespeare, he discovered to his dismay that he was completely unable to enjoy poetry. He had simply lost that faculty, and apparently he never regained it.

The Spectre

This one-sidedness is represented in the writings of William Blake by what he calls the Spectre, which is reason split off from feeling.[590] According to Blake, the prime examples of the Spectre were to be found in the scientific and philosophical community of his day; he cited Bacon, Locke, and Newton. In other words, science and philosophy do not express the whole person. The natural expression of the integrated human being is the Imagination, which for Blake is only realized when Spectre and Emanation come together.

When one takes up the spiritual life, one needs to engage one's emotions with one's spiritual practice, and integrate one's intellectual life with one's emotional life. It is characteristic of someone who is governed by Blake's Spectre (and this seems a most appropriate term) that they can think their way quite effectively around anything, even feelings – which means that they find it easy to go through the motions. If one is of this type, rather than trying to work away at developing one's emotional side, one might do best to lie around for a while doing nothing – dozing, sleeping, dreaming even – until real feelings start floating up. Then one can move on to working at developing those feelings, perhaps through making a connection with the arts or with devotional practice.

It can be useful to study Blake, especially the so-called Prophetic Books, because they cannot be reduced to a cut-and-dried system; they contain contradictions that cannot be reconciled. This is, indeed, part of their message: that the Spectre cannot have everything under its control. In trying to sort out the tangle of Blake's symbolism, the Spectre defeats itself: if you want every symbol and every statement to have one definable meaning and one definable relationship to every other symbol and statement, you are going to get very frustrated. But if you just plunge into the poetry and absorb its direct emotional impact, the general drift of Blake's meaning is quite clear.

Tantra

I had a similar experience when I first started exploring the Tantric disciplines. I very much wanted to fit them all into a neat, overall synthesis, but I found that this just couldn't be done. However you arrange the material, there are always loose ends trailing all over the place. In the end I concluded that this was in some sense intentional. You can never get an overall view of the Tantra. But if you accept that you can only ever have a partial view of it, and that you get this view by engaging with the material rather than by standing back from it, you can at least get a precise *feel* for it. One might go so far as to say that nothing that is thoroughly amenable to rational analysis will satisfy us for long. A language, for example, needs to be rich in ambiguities in order to serve our needs fully.

So although torpor, drowsiness, dreams, and sleep may well represent negative mental states in the form of dullness and laziness, they are also our most direct connection with a whole realm of experience that we ignore at our peril. They represent a perspective that we need to maintain especially within the context of the Abhidharma, in which we find an attempt to rationalize the Buddha's teaching, to make it all hang together in an orderly fashion, to reduce it to its 'essentials' by removing all the 'extraneous' elements of biography, history, myth, and poetry. Useful as this exercise may be, particularly in certain details – such as in this analysis of mind and mental events – we must constantly bear in mind the limitations inherent in the whole approach of the Abhidharma.

In the autobiography of Geshe Rabten, who studied and wrote extensively on Abhidharma topics, it is striking that, in trying to describe to Westerners what a Tibetan monastery was like, he chose the image of a factory, evoking a picture of the machinery of the monastery whirring away and turning out monks, and everybody very busy on the production line. That Geshe Rabten should choose this little image, as so often with small details, is very telling.

Dream worlds

It is a useful practice to meditate or recite devotional verses or repeat mantras just before going to sleep; in this way one can prolong awareness into the sleep state, and one's dreams are then more likely to have spiritual significance. One can have valuable experiences in dreams that are simply not accessible in the waking state. It seems that a lot goes on in dreams that doesn't proceed parallel with one's waking life but takes a direction of its own. Our dream experience may touch, even burst through, our waking life at times, but it has, in a sense, a life of its own. It's as though the life dominated by one's waking consciousness is only a narrow segment of one's total life. A lot is happening on other levels, or other dimensions, of one's being, beyond even what one normally thinks of as one's individuality. Perhaps one is even living a quite different life on some other level – even in another world, in a sense – of which, with one's conscious mind, one is not aware. 'It' is no more aware of 'you' than 'you' are aware of 'it', but they are somehow both aspects or dimensions of 'you' in the broader sense, and they may very occasionally cross paths. What one has to guard against is taking one's stand on rational consciousness and from there appropriating that other realm of experience by trying to analyse it, explain it, understand it, translate it into completely rational terms. By controlling it in this way one avoids having to experience it. In a way asking what dreams, symbols, and myths 'mean' is beside the point.

Having said that, I can remember receiving a very clear message from my own dreams at one time. Many years ago I used to have a recurring dream of a woman scolding me. She wasn't anybody I knew, and I couldn't make out what she was complaining about, but she was very angry. Sometimes I would meet her; sometimes she would just be on the telephone. At first I was rather puzzled by these dreams, because I wasn't on bad terms with any particular woman. But finally I realized what it was about. She was my imagination, my creativity, if you like, and she was protesting that she wasn't getting enough attention. So I learned from this – I eased up on the Abhidharma and picked up a volume of poetry from time to time – and I haven't heard from her now for very many years.

Branch closure

The more one looks at the stable ego the more it is seen to disintegrate. It's just a very weak thread of waking consciousness artificially holding together a large bundle of disparate materials. In the case of the ordinary person the unifying factor is the physical body – the only relatively stable component of our experience – so for all practical purposes one's body is who one is. This is why the Buddha said on one occasion that to identify with the body is a less serious error than to identify with the mind.[591] The implication is that to think of the mental and emotional turmoil that is the mind as the locus of one's sense of an unchanging self is clearly absurd, but one might be forgiven for thinking of one's body as oneself.

However, if one can develop some awareness of the multidimensional nature of consciousness one can begin to get one's everyday sense-consciousness into perspective. Then when one dies – to risk using an image which is just as utilitarian as Geshe Rabten's factory but which may help to make things clear – it's like a man who is involved in a number of different businesses, one of which has folded. On the level of that little business there is total failure, but within the totality of all his interests and operations, it's not so important. He'll probably be able to open another business and transfer the staff there.

2. WORRY (*KAUKṚTYA*)

> Its function is to obstruct the mind from becoming settled. (p. 101)
> *Abhidharmasamuccaya*

Worry can be positive if one can do something to allay it, and if it leads one to do something useful and appropriate about it; if, that is, it is a spur to appropriate action. It can act as a useful message from one's subconscious mind that one has overlooked something. In the case of Milarepa, for example, worry and regret about the very serious karmic consequences of his previous evil actions drove him to seek Enlightenment in that very lifetime, as the only alternative to being reborn in the hell realms.

If, on the other hand, there is nothing you can do about what you're worried about, or the time has passed for doing anything about it, or if your worry effectively undermines what you are doing to allay it, it is negative, it's anxiety. If Milarepa had continued to worry after realizing what he had to do, or had worried that he wasn't going to be able to attain Enlightenment, such worrying would have been pointless and harmful. If in the middle of the night you think, 'Oh, I don't think I locked the front door,' that is perhaps appropriate worry. But if you go downstairs, check the door, go back to bed, then continue to worry about whether you checked it properly, that is inappropriate worry, or anxiety.

Freud explains anxiety as arising when one is trying to keep the lid on powerful feelings that one regards as negative. You don't allow yourself to experience those feelings so far as to acknowledge them properly, but at the same time you can't exclude them altogether, so you feel a sort of diffuse, floating anxiety all the time which attaches itself to particular situations. This happens because you are not acknowledging some factor in your life that is very important to you, and that bubbles up despite all your efforts to keep the lid on. Again, we are dealing here with the split between the rational and the emotional. The problem comes when we worry about external, 'objective' things without addressing the emotional source of our anxieties, whatever that might be.

Having done all one can reasonably do in a given situation, one should be able to sit back and forget all about it. If one finds oneself continuing to worry that something may go wrong, this might be because one hasn't fully accepted the truth of the situation: the fact that something may indeed go wrong. Sometimes we want more certainty than life by its very nature is able to give. In the end we feel uncertain because life itelf is uncertain, although we don't want to accept this fact. We can never have complete certainty; we can't be certain beyond all doubt that we will live until lunchtime. All we can do is go on with our life in the absence of any complete certainty.

3 & 4. SELECTIVENESS AND DISCURSIVENESS (OR INITIAL APPLICATION OF MIND AND SUSTAINED APPLICATION OF MIND)

> [Initial application of mind] is a rough estimate of the thing under consideration and [sustained application of mind] is an exact investigation of it. (p. 102)
>
> Yeshe Gyaltsen

These two mental events – *vitarka* and *vicāra* – occasionally get mentioned separately, but they are usually referred to as a pair, especially in connection with the first and second *dhyānas*. As we have already seen (see p. 624 above), they represent the kind of mental activity that is present in the first *dhyāna* and absent in the higher *dhyānas*. In simple terms, they are 'thinking of' and 'thinking about'. Traditionally they are likened to seizing a pot with one hand – *vitarka* – and scouring it round with the other – *vicāra*. On the one hand one has got a mental hold of the object without knowing anything about it while on the other, one investigates it in detail.[592]

These two mental events may be positive – as when you bring a friend to mind and consider their good qualities; or they may be negative –

as when you bring to mind some attractive object and think how nice it would be to possess it. Thus *vitarka* and *vicāra* are variable mental events; they may be positive, negative, or neutral.

However, in the context of the Abhidharma's analysis of mind and mental events, one might ask whether there is any real distinction to be drawn between *vitarka* and mind. Can we not say that *vitarka* is mind and *vicāra* is mental events in general? As we know by now, mind is defined as that which perceives an object – no object, no mind – while *vitarka* is defined as an actual apprehension of the object. But where perception of the object ends and apprehension of the object begins would be difficult to say – though there must be some difference, otherwise *vitarka* would be classified as mind, not as a mental event. It is not as if this apprehension is 'recognition' because recognition is a separate mental event – *saṃjñā*. Really one would think that *vitarka* as a mental event should be superfluous, because what seems to be the function of *vitarka* is performed well enough by mind.

The difference would seem to be that *vitarka* is just one of the functions of mind, inasmuch as the object of *vitarka* is a mental object, whereas the mind perceives perceptual objects in general – that is, objects of ordinary sense perception as well as objects of mental or 'categorical' perception. Furthermore, the objects of perception of the mind in the higher *dhyānas* are not possible objects of *vitarka*; so it would seem that *vitarka* represents just the coarser-grained element of mind.

Thus even in the Abhidharma we find loose ends. There isn't really a definite fixed number of separate entities; there are all sorts of overlaps between mental events. In this case we seem to have a complete overlap of one by another, *vitarka* by mind viewed as a mental event. So, after all, we shouldn't take the idea of mind and mental events too literally. Mind isn't distinct from mental events. They are all – and the Mahāyāna teachers of the Abhidharma stress this, as we have seen – operational concepts.

CONCLUSION: MAKING THE MOST OF ANALYSIS

> Those who do wrong actions become the helpers of Anaṅga (Cupid)
> And become degenerate by the clouds of stupidity
> Which are the waves of this degenerate age, and thus
> They become inflated by seeing this degeneration as the best possible world. (p. 113)

This is one of the sequence of verses with which Yeshe Gyaltsen ends his exploration of mind in Buddhist psychology. A legend recounted in one of the Hindu Purāṇas explains how this figure of Anaṅga – which means 'limbless' or 'bodyless' – got his name.[593] Once upon a time – indeed, for thousands of years – the god Shiva was engaged in his austerities, completely oblivious to what was happening in the world. And during this period the world was being troubled by a terrible demon. The gods held a council to decide what to do about it, and eventually a great *rishi* told them that the demon could be destroyed only by a son of Shiva. At first this seemed to be more of a theoretical than a practical resolution of the difficulty, because, of course, Shiva was immersed in his solitary meditations in the Himalayas and thus in no mood to beget a son. Anyway, the gods decided to do what they could, and they deputed Kāmadeva, the Hindu god of love (like the Roman Cupid) to seek out Shiva and shoot one of his flowery arrows at him. So Kāmadeva set off and found Shiva. He was just drawing his bow when Shiva suddenly, for an instant, emerged from his contemplation, opened his third eye, and threw out a great flame that consumed the little love-god to nothing.

Clouds of stupidity

Ever since then, Kāmadeva has been invisible. But although we can't see him, he's still in business just as before. When he is up to his tricks we are not even aware of it, so we have to be on our guard. Because it is very easy to be fascinated by the mundane, and rather more difficult to be fascinated by the transcendental.[594]

In doing wrong actions we are playing into the hands of Anaṅga – that is, we are often not really aware of our unskilfulness. We 'become degenerate by the clouds of stupidity' upon which we attempt to establish our lives. One might suppose that during the twentieth century we have jettisoned what seemed to many people to be the facile optimism of the Victorian age with its enthusiastic faith in human progress. Not a bit of it. It is nowadays generally held in libertarian, egalitarian, socially progressive, technologically advanced, liberal democracies that these represent an ideal to which the rest of the world should aspire. However, one could certainly take the view that these 'ideal' societies actually represent a plunging degeneration, without any clarity of values or sense of community. So yes, unfortunately, we do see this degeneration as the best possible world. And at the heart of this degeneration is muddle over what is skilful and what is unskilful, what is positive and what is negative.

Self and other

Even when we conclude that the way forward, for ourselves and for the world, is to follow a spiritual path, we may still be muddled when it comes to determining the nature of spiritual development. The Abhidharma's analysis takes place within an overall context of spiritual practice, which is, of course, about self-development. But the very notion of self-development can undermine itself if it is interpreted too narrowly. It is true that Buddhism emphasizes the importance of being concerned for oneself as well as for others, but it also emphasizes the importance of being concerned for others as well as for oneself. One may have to overcome a tendency to see the spiritual life as being to do with the negation of the self; but at some point one needs to see it as basically about devoting oneself to the welfare of others – and looking after oneself as well, incidentally.

Yes, one needs to discover the importance to one's self-development of one's relationships with other people. One needs to realize the importance within one's programme of self-development of being kind and generous towards other people. It is at least a start to realize that time and energy spent looking after other people's development does not mean time lost with regard to one's own. That is at least something. Some people don't even get that far: they think that any time spent on behalf of others is lost as far as their own spiritual development is concerned. But having brought the existence of other people into consideration, one has to move on from regarding other people and what one does for them as simply a means towards one's own spiritual ends. Other people, one has to realize, have a value of their own.

Perhaps one starts practising the *mettā bhāvanā* with a view to getting into higher states of consciousness, becoming a better person, even gaining Enlightenment. One takes other people as objects for the development of one's *mettā*: one wishes other people well so that one will become a better, happier person. But the practice only works if one really does become concerned about the welfare of others; and when that happens one loses interest in one's original reason for doing the practice. One's own personal development can no longer be a separate issue from the spiritual welfare of other people.

It is within the framework of the dichotomy between self and other that all our thought and experience takes place. As far as ordinary experience goes, this dichotomy is irreducible. We cannot talk our way round it. So on the level of empirical, relative reality, we need a double approach. As reality has bifurcated into subject and object, we have to approach it not only via the self, but also via the other.

In fact, it could be said that the best way to approach reality is via the other, because we naturally approach it from the point of view of the self anyway. It comes naturally to us to feel that we count, and perhaps that our nearest and dearest count, but that others hardly count at all. By helping others one begins to register that others are just as real and just as important as one is oneself, and one engages in something which one can be certain will be helping to break down the subject–object dichotomy.

However you try to approach ultimate reality it is always *you* doing it; and as long as you are trying to attain it for yourself, you will fail in this endeavour. There is no possibility of you yourself attaining to ultimate reality. Only you plus others can do it. *Prajñā* (wisdom) is the culmination of the self-oriented approach, *karuṇā* (compassion) is the culmination of the others-oriented approach, and in non-dual reality these two necessarily coalesce.

If, therefore, one's approach to the realization of ultimate reality is with a view to realizing it for oneself, if it is – with all the benevolent feeling for others in the world – essentially for one's own benefit, then there is no breaking down of the dichotomy of subject and object, and therefore no realization. To put it very simply, it is not enough to feel unselfish – one has to *be* unselfish, which means acting unselfishly. This is the only way to break down the barrier between subject and object. Self and other have to become interchangeable as the source of motive for one's actions. One realizes as a matter of *fact* that there is no difference between self and other. This is the vision of the bodhisattva: that there is no Nirvāṇa for oneself (however benevolent one may feel towards others) at all. Hence the importance of the traditional practice of dedicating one's merits, which involves wishing that any merit one has gained from one's actions may benefit not just oneself but all beings. Whenever one does something positive, one needs to make sure one isn't trying to appropriate the benefits for oneself; otherwise those benefits will in a sense be frittered away.

One may think, 'Surely it's best to look after myself first. Then, when I have a bit more experience and understand other people's needs better, I can move on to looking after them as well.' But one can just as easily turn the argument round: why not look after others first? Then, when one has a bit more experience and understands one's own real needs better, one can move on to looking after oneself as well. One can't go wrong with this approach. As long as one is doing things for others, or doing useful things with no thought of self-gratification, one can be sure that one is taking steps towards the real aim of any kind of spiritual practice.

Aesthetic appreciation and refinement

If we value the psychological too much and the ethical not enough, the spiritual life becomes a sort of refined, pseudo-spiritual, hedonic aestheticism. Of course, refining and concentrating one's experience is inherent in spiritual practice; but is one refining one's experience of the self–other dichotomy, or is one simply refining one's experience of selfhood? If one is bent on refining one's subjectivity in the context of an awareness of the dichotomy, all well and good. But if one is concerned with increasingly more refined experiences of oneself while becoming resentful about other people somehow getting in the way of one's enjoyment of or devotion to those refined experiences, clearly something has gone awry.

One cannot refine oneself out of the mundane world altogether; there always has to be something that is being refined. For example, in one of the monasteries of Tibet in the old days there was, so I have heard, an enormous vat in which they brewed tea every day for all the hundreds of monks. In fact, tea had been brewed in the same vat for about six hundred years, since the days of Tsongkhapa. And every day they left a little bit at the bottom, so that every monk in every generation had an infinitesimal drop of the very tea Tsongkhapa himself had partaken of. By this process, however diluted Tsongkhapa's tea became, it was still there. Adapting the image for present purposes, we can see that our attitude to compounded existence is much the same. We might try our utmost to refine the duality of subject-and-object out of existence, but like Tsongkhapa's tea, this is impossible so long as the slightest trace of it remains. The only solution is to make a bold existential leap and throw out the very last drop.

There is of course the ideal of aesthetic appreciation in a higher, contemplative, objective sense: through delighting in something for its own sake, one loses oneself in the object. But this needs to be distinguished from a subjective aesthetic appreciation in the sense of enjoying an object, at however subtle a level, for one's own individualistic gratification – which cannot, by itself, lead to liberation. One may say that *samādhi* represents the most refined levels of this purely subjective pleasure. But on its own, without transcendental insight, *samādhi* cannot produce Enlightenment: the culmination of the spiritual life is not just some great wonderful experience for oneself.

One does not attain an ideal of objective aesthetic appreciation in which one achieves a dissolution of the self in the object without practical reference to the ethical dimension. In a way one could say that one can't dissolve oneself in contemplation of the object without dissolving others in that object too, and one can do that only by devoting oneself to others. Really, what we are trying to dissolve is the subject–object dichotomy itself. The one value of ultimate reality must be approached from two directions: from wisdom and from compassion.

So one should be concerned neither just with oneself, nor just with others, but with self *and* others. It's impossible to have one without the other; they are interconnected. Any unselfish act is the expression of some kind of apprehension or experience or realization of this reality, at the very least an aspiration towards that understanding.

Being unselfish basically involves taking on responsibilities. Of course, most people take on major responsibilities by becoming parents, and develop a measure of unselfishness. But if some people choose not to take on domestic responsibilities in order to follow the spiritual path, it would be a big mistake to take from this the notion that the spiritual life involves avoiding responsibility. Quite the opposite. In the same way that one makes time for one's meditation practice, one should make time for disinterested activity on behalf of others – that is, responsibilities. It is a good idea not to be too particular about exactly what jobs one takes on to do; a choosy attitude will obviously undermine the whole project of breaking down the subject–object dichotomy. And to float around with no responsibilities at all, with no sense that what one does should be in some way for others' benefit, is for most people quite dangerous.

Taking on responsibilities means not just agreeing to do things for people, but also carrying out what one has agreed to do at the time one agreed to do it. It means keeping one's word. If one doesn't keep one's word, and if others are inconvenienced thereby, it means one is not really aware of other people, it means a lack of responsibility – which means a lack of ethical identity. Very often people give their word very lightly and easily because they know they aren't going to be very particular about keeping it – so their word is not really their word. Then come the blustering excuses: 'Look, I didn't say I'd definitely do it; I said I'd do it if I could – I just haven't got round to it yet. I've had a lot on.'

It also happens that the person who has to do something is not the person who agreed to do it. We can be so unintegrated that when we volunteer to do something, it is just a part of us that volunteers – the part of us that happens to be uppermost at the time, the part that wants a bit of attention and approval, the part that wants to be slapped on the back for being such a good sport. This part of us probably does want to do what we have volunteered to do. But once we have had the attention and sense of self-worth we wanted, this part subsides and disappears. When the time comes for doing whatever it is we said we would do, some other part of us is uppermost, a part that isn't interested in what we volunteered for but has other interests entirely.

To show willing is fine so long as everyone knows that that's all one is doing, but it isn't really good enough if others are led to believe that what one is volunteering to do is actually going to get done. Unfortunately, some people seem to think that being willing is, morally speaking, tantamount to actually doing, or that one should get some credit for offering, even if one doesn't quite manage to get round to fulfilling that offer. This is not the attitude of the ethical individual. The ethical individual is aware and responsible and integrated, which means that they are concerned about others, and act in a way that reflects that concern. Only an integrated person can be trusted, only an integrated person has an ethical identity.

The list of mental events we have been exploring here is not exhaustive. Indeed, it may be that the ancient people of India had different emotional emphases from our own, and that we need to seek to identify further mental events, appropriate to the particular emotional colouring we have developed in more recent times. But what should be clear from an examination of the traditional analysis of mind and mental events is that by becoming more aware of precisely how the mind works and how the activity of the mind is expressed in actions of speech and body, we can move with more direction and focus in our spiritual practice. We can become more aware of our mental states and the actions of speech and body that arise out of them and in turn give rise to further mental states. We can identify mental events as being helpful or hindering, and can move to build on them or counteract them more swiftly and accurately.

Whatever we have come to understand in the course of studying the Abhidharma must be practically applied, both in meditation and in other situations, but the real purpose of the Abhidharma analysis of mind and mental events is to bring us to an understanding, an experience, of ourselves. This understanding is to perceive that those ever-changing and developing mental events actually constitute in themselves what we usually think of as the self. It is to watch one's whole idea of one's self dissolve in the continuous flow of mental events.

But, to balance this, we need to move beyond a narrow concern with our personal mental states towards a realization of our true nature through a wholehearted and authentic engagement with the interests and concerns of others. Only in this way will we begin to approach the perspective of the Enlightened mind.

APPENDIX

THE FIFTY-ONE MENTAL EVENTS (*CAITTA*)

These translations are those used by Sangharakshita in the text. Alternative translations from J. Hopkins, *Meditation on Emptiness*, are shown in square brackets. The Sanskrit equivalent is shown in italics.

The five omnipresent mental events (*sarvatraga*)

1. Feeling-tone (*vedanā*)
2. Recognition or conceptualization [discrimination] (*saṃjñā*)
3. Directionality of Mind [intention] (*cetanā*)
4. Contact (*spārśa*)
5. Egocentric demanding [mental engagement] (*manaskāra*)

The five object-determining mental events (*viniyata*)

1. Interest [aspiration] (*chanda*)
2. Intensified interest which stays with its object [belief] (*adhimokṣa*)
3. Inspection (or mindfulness or recollection) (*smṛti*)
4. Intense concentration [stabilization] (*samādhi*)
5. Appreciative discrimination [knowledge] (*prajñā*)

The eleven positive mental events (*kuśala*)

1. Confidence-trust (or faith) (*śraddhā*)
2. Self-respect (or shame) (*hrī*)
3. Decorum (or respect for wise opinion) [embarrassment] (*apatrāpya*)
4. Non-attachment (*alobha*)
5. Non-hatred (*adveṣa*)
6. Non-deludedness [non-ignorance] (*amoha*)
7. Diligence (or energy in pursuit of the good) [effort] (*vīrya*)
8. Alertness (or tranquillity) [pliancy] (*praśrabdhi*)
9. Concern (or non-heedlessness) [conscientiousness] (*apramāda*)
10. Equanimity (*upekṣā*)
11. Non-violence [non-harmfulness] (*avihiṃsā*)

The six basic emotions (*mūlakleśa*)

1. Cupidity-attachment [desire] (*rāga*)
2. Anger (*pratigha*)
3. Arrogance [pride] (*māna*)
4. Lack of intrinsic awareness [ignorance] (*avidyā*)
5. Indecision [doubt] (*vicikitsā*)
6. Opinionatedness [afflicted view] (*dṛṣṭi*)

The twenty proximate factors of instability (*upakleśa*)

1. Indignation (or rage) [belligerence] (*krodha*)
2. Resentment (*upanāha*)
3. Slyness-concealment [concealment] (*mrakṣa*)
4. Spite (or defensiveness) (*pradāśa*)
5. Jealousy (or envy) (*īrṣyā*)
6. Avarice (or acquisitiveness) [miserliness] (*mātsarya*)
7. Deceit (or pretence) (*māyā*)
8. Dishonesty [dissimulation] (*śāṭhya*)
9. Mental inflation (or self-intoxication) [haughtiness] (*mada*)
10. Malice [harmfulness] (*vihiṃsā*)
11. Shamelessness [non-shame] (*āhrīkya*)
12. Lack of sense of propriety [non-embarrassment] (*anapatrāpya*)

13. Gloominess (or stagnation) [lethargy] (*styāna*)
14. Ebullience [excitement] (*auddhatya*)
15. Lack of trust (or non-faith) (*āśraddhya*)
16. Laziness (*kausīdya*)
17. Unconcern (or heedlessness) [non-conscientiousness] (*pramāda*)
18. Forgetfulness (or unrecollectedness or unmindfulness) (*muṣitasmṛtitā*)
19. Inattentiveness (or purposelessness) [non-introspection] (*asaṃprajanya*)
20. Desultoriness (or distraction) (*vikṣepa*)

The four variables (*aniyata*)

1. Drowsiness (or torpor) [sleep] (*middha*)
2. Worry [contrition] (*kaukṛtya*)
3. Initial application of mind [investigation] (*vitarka*)
4. Sustained application of mind [analysis] (*vicāra*)

FURTHER READING

Asaṅga's *Abhidharmasamuccaya* is available in an English translation by Sara Boin-Webb (Asian Humanities Press, 2001). This is a translation of a French version translated and annotated by Walpola Rahula (École française d'extrême-orient, Paris 1971).

Asaṅga, *The Summary of the Great Vehicle*, translated from the Chinese of Paramātha by John P. Keenan, Numata Center for Buddhist Translation and Research, Berkeley Calif. 1992.

Paul J. Griffiths et al. (trans.), *The Realm of Awakening*, a translation and study of the tenth chapter of Asaṅga's *Mahāyānasaṅgraha*, Oxford University Press, Oxford 1989.

Vasubandhu's *Abhidharmakośa(bhāṣya)* is available as *Abhidharmakośabhāṣyam*, English translation by Leo M. Pruden from the French translation by Louis de la Vallée Poussin (4 vols.), Asian Humanities Press, Berkeley Calif. 1988–90.

Ganganatha Jha. (trans.), *The Tattvasaṅgraha of Shāntarakṣita: With the Commentary of Kamalashīla*, 2 vols., Motilal Banarsidass, Delhi 1986.

NĀGĀRJUNA'S *MŪLAMADHYAMAKAKĀRIKĀ*

Various translations are available, for example:

D. J. Kalupahana, *Nāgārjuna: The Philosophy of the Middle Way*, State University of New York Press, Albany 1986.

B. Bocking, *Nāgārjuna in China: A Translation of the Middle Treatise*, Edwin Mellen, Albany 1995.
J. L. Garfield, *The Fundamental Wisdom of the Middle Way*, OUP, Oxford 1995.
K. K. Inada, *Nāgārjuna*, Hokuseido, Tokyo 1970.

RATNĀVALĪ

For an English translation see J. Hopkins et al (trans.), *The Precious Garland and the Song of the Four Mindfulnesses*. George Allen and Unwin, London 1975.

ABHIDHARMA

Nyanaponika Thera, *Abhidhamma Studies: Researches in Buddhist Psychology*, Buddhist Publication Society, Kandy 1976.
W. F. Jayasuriya, *The Psychology and Philosophy of Buddhism: An Introduction to the Abhidhamma*, Buddhist Missionary Society, Kuala Lumpur 1976.
Lama Anagarika Govinda, *The Psychological Attitude of Early Buddhist Philosophy and its Systematic Representation According to Abhidhamma Tradition*, Motilal Banarsidass, Delhi 1991.
H. V. Guenther, *Philosophy and Psychology in the Abhidharma*, Motilal Banarsidass, Delhi 1991.
Nyanatiloka Mahāthera, *Guide Through the Abhidharma-Piṭaka*, Buddhist Publication Society, Kandy 1971.

SOME OF TSONGKHAPA'S PRINCIPAL WRITINGS

'Great Exposition of the Stages of the Path' (*Lam rim chen mo*). Partial translation by A. Wayman in *Calming the Mind and Discerning the Real*, Columbia, New York 1978; partial translation by E. Napper, *Dependent-Arising and Emptiness*, Wisdom, London 1989.
'Essence of the Good Explanations, Treatise Discriminating What is to be Interpreted and the Definitive' (*drang ba dang nges pa'i don rnam par ba'i bstan bcos legs bshad snying po*). Translation by Robert Thurman in *Tsong Khapa's Speech of Gold in the Essence of True Eloquence*, Princeton University Press, Princeton 1984.

'Great Exposition of Special Insight' (*lhag mthongchen mo*). Translation by Alex Wayman in *Calming the Mind and Discerning the Real*, Columbia University Press, New York 1978.
'Great Exposition of Secret Mantra (*sngags rim chen mo*). Chapter 1: translation by Jeffrey Hopkins in *Tantra in Tibet*, George Allen and Unwin, London 1977. Chapters 2 and 3: translation by Jeffrey Hopkins in *Yoga of Tibet*, George Allen and Unwin, London 1981.
'The Three Principal Aspects of the Path' (*lam gtso rnam gsum*). Translation by Geshe Wangyal in *The Door of Liberation*, Lotsawa, New York 1978, pp. 126–60. Translation by Jeffrey Hopkins and Geshe Sopa in *Practice and Theory of Tibetan Buddhism*, Grove Press, New York 1976, pp. 1–47. See also the translation by Jeffrey Hopkins (including commentary by the Dalai Lama), in Tenzin Gyatso, *Kindness, Clarity, and Insight*, Snow Lion, Ithaca NY 1984, pp. 118–56.
'Praise of Dependent-Arising' (*rten 'brel bstod pa*). Translation by Geshe Wangyal in *The Door of Liberation*, Lotsawa, New York 1978, pp. 117–25.
'Ocean of Reasoning, Explanation of (Nāgārjuna's) Fundamental Treatise on the Middle Way Called "Wisdom"'. Translation of chapter 2 in Jeffrey Hopkins, *Chapter Two of Ocean of Reasoning by Tsong-ka-pa*, Library of Tibetan Works and Archives, Dharamsala 1974.

YOGĀCĀRA

P. Williams, *Mahāyāna Buddhism: The Doctrinal Foundations*, Routledge, London 1989, pp. 77–95.
S. Anaker, *Seven Works of Vasubandhu, the Buddhist Psychological Doctor*, Motilal Banarsidass, Delhi 1984.
P. Griffiths, *On Being Mindless: Buddhist Meditation and the Mind-Body Problem*, Open Court, La Salle 1986, pp. 76–106.
G. M. Nagao, *Mādhyamika and Yogācāra: A Study of Mahāyāna Philosophies*, L. S. Kawamura (trans.), State University of New York Press, Albany 1991.
J. D. Willis, *On Knowing Reality*, Columbia University Press, New York 1979.

Chhote Lal Tripathi, *The Problem of Knowledge in Yogacara Buddhism*, Bharat-Bhararti, Varanasi 1972.

Traditional life stories of Nāgārjuna, Āryadeva, Asaṅga, Vasubandhu, Candrakīrti, Dignāga, etc:

Lama Chimpa and Alaka Chattopadhyaya (trans.), *Tāranātha's History of Buddhism in India*, Motilal Banarsidass, Delhi 1990.

NOTES AND REFERENCES

Notes appended with (S) are by Sangharakshita. Those appended with (EC) are by Edward Conze.

FOREWORD

1 Vajragupta, *The Triratna Story*, Windhorse Publications, Cambridge 2010, p. 17.
2 *Terma* is a Buddhist Tantric term that literally means 'treasure'. Traditionally, *terma* teachings have been left hidden away by a great teacher, ready to be found by future generations.
3 See for example, Stephen W. Porges, *Pocket Guide to Polyvagal Theory*, Norton, New York 2017.
4 p. 483 below.
5 p. 540 below.
6 p. 332 below.
7 p. 377 below.
8 p. 366 below.
9 p. 265 below.
10 p. 233 below.
11 p. 341 below.
12 p. 399 below.
13 p. 621 below.
14 See for example Kathy L. Kain, Peter Levine, Stephen J. Terrell, *Nurturing Resilience*, North Atlantic Books, Berkeley 2018, and Bessel van der Kolk, *The Body Keeps the Score*, Memories of Ages Press, La Vergne 2021.
15 p. 376 below.
16 This echoes what Sangharakshita refers to as 'the sequence of twelve positive links that describe the spiritual path as it spirals away from the wheel of life towards Enlightenment.' See p. 519 below.
17 *What is the Dharma*, *Complete Works*, vol. 3, p. 227.

OFFERING OF THE MANDALA

18 Dhardo Rimpoche (1917–1990), an eminent Tibetan lama of the Gelugpa tradition, was educated at Drepung Monastery. He founded the Indo-Tibetan Buddhist Cultural Institute in Kalimpong in 1952, and Sangharakshita met him there the following year, later receiving the bodhisattva ordination from him. Dhardo Rimpoche is described by Sangharakshita as a man 'perhaps embodying the bodhisattva ideal to a greater extent than anybody I had met'. (*The History of My Going for Refuge*, *Complete Works*, vol. 2, p. 471.) For a complete biography, see Suvajra, *The Wheel and the Diamond: The Life of Dhardo Tulku*, Windhorse Publications, Glasgow 1991. Jnanasiddhi has edited a collection of tributes to Dhardo Rimpoche as Sara Hagel (ed.), *Dhardo Rimpoche: A Celebration*, Windhorse Publications, Birmingham 2000; and Sangharakshita offers his own accolade in *Precious Teachers*, *Complete Works*, vol. 22, pp. 420ff.

THE WAY TO WISDOM

19 Edward Conze, *The Way of Wisdom: the Five Spiritual Faculties* (Wheel publication no. 65/66), Buddhist Publication Society, Kandy, first published in 1964 (available at accesstoinsight.org).

20 *Indriya* (Sanskrit and Pāli); variously translated as 'faculties', 'controlling faculties', 'spiritual faculties'. The same five qualities are called powers (*bala*) if emphasis is on the fact that they are 'unshakable by their opposites'. (S) The word *indriya* is derived from the Vedic god Indra, the ruler of the gods in the ancient pantheon. Hence the word suggests the idea of dominance or control. (EC) Among many canonical references to the five *indriyas*, *Saṃyutta Nikāya* v.193ff. describes them in various ways in a section on the faculties. See Bhikkhu Bodhi (trans.), *The Connected Discourses of the Buddha*, Wisdom Publications, Somerville 2000, pp. 1668ff; or F. L. Woodward (trans.), *The Book of the Kindred Sayings*, part 5, Pali Text Society, London 1979, pp. 169ff. See also Sangharakshita in *A Survey of Buddhism*, *Complete Works*, vol. 1, pp. 279–94.

21 Beyond a certain point on the spiritual path, one's practice has sufficient momentum to guarantee that one will continue to progress towards Enlightenment; there is no further danger of falling back. This point was called by the Buddha 'Stream Entry', and someone who has reached

it is thus a 'Stream Entrant'. For more on Stream Entry, see, for example, *What is the Dharma?*,*Complete Works*, vol. 3, pp. 241–57. Among the many references to Stream Entry in the Pāli canon, the *Saṃyutta Nikāya* has a whole section devoted to the subject. See Bhikkhu Bodhi (trans.), *The Connected Discourses of the Buddha*, Wisdom Publications, Boston 2000, pp. 1788–837; or F. L. Woodward (trans.), *Kindred Sayings*, part 5, Pali Text Society, London 1979, pp. 296–351.

22 E. Conze (ed.), *Buddhist Texts Through the Ages*, Harper & Row, New York 1964.

23 The Tibetan name for the work usually known as the *Tibetan Book of the Dead* is *Bardo Thödol*, which literally means 'the liberation through hearing in the in-between state' (i.e. the *bardo*). The text, said to have been composed by the eighth-century guru of Tibet, Padmasambhava, is traditionally spoken to a corpse, guiding the consciousness of the deceased through the post-death experience in the *bardo*. See Francesca Fremantle and Chogyam Trungpa (trans.), *The Tibetan Book of the Dead*, Shambhala Publications, Boston and London 1987. For more about the *bardo*, see 'Aspects of Buddhist Psychology 5', *Complete Works*, vol. 12, pp. 194–208. See also Shenpen Hookham, *There's More to Dying Than Death*, Windhorse Publications, Cambridge 2006, which offers a Tibetan Buddhist approach to death based on meditation practised here and now.

24 'Faith is the seed' in *Kasibhāradvāja Sutta, Sutta-Nipāta* 1.4, verse 2.

25 Bad faith or *male fides* (Latin) is a legal term meaning to knowingly deceive someone. In existentialist philosophy, bad faith (*mauvaise foi*) also refers to an individual's adoption of a range of inauthentic values under pressure to conform to those of wider society. The English existentialist Colin Wilson considers this alienated individual to be typical of modern social life. See Colin Wilson, *The Outsider*, Gollancz, London 1956.

26 For instance, God signalled his approval of a number of Old Testament figures by bestowing material wealth upon them. These include Abraham (Genesis 13:1–7), Isaac (Genesis 26:12–14), Jacob (Genesis 30:43), Joseph (Genesis 39:2–6), Solomon (1 Kings 3:13), and Job (Job 42:10–17).

27 The Padmaloka seminar took place following the 'Oil Crisis' of 1973, when Arab members of the Organization of Petroleum Exporting Countries (OPEC) unexpectedly

raised the price of crude oil. By 1974, when world oil prices had climbed to four times their previous level, some Arabs found themselves among the richest people in the world.

28 There are two varieties of artichoke. Globe artichokes (*Cynara scolymus*) are tall-standing plants often cultivated in the flower garden. Their large globular flower buds can also be cooked and eaten. The Jerusalem artichoke (*Helianthus tuberosus*) is a garden vegetable that produces underground tubers, similar to potatoes.

29 For now we see through a glass, darkly, but then face to face. Now I know in part; but then shall I know, even as also I am known.

Corinthians 13:12.

30 For more on the life of St Bruno, including the anecdote related here, see John Stoughton D. D., *Golden Legends of the Olden Time*, Hodder & Stoughton, London 1885, pp. 211ff.

31 See for example Sir Edwin Arnold's epic poem recounting the life of the Buddha, *The Light of Asia* (Windhorse Publications, Birmingham 1999). Sir Edwin Arnold (1832–1904) was an English poet and journalist. The *Lalitavistara Sūtra*, upon which Arnold's poem is based, also makes for inspired reading. The *sūtra* is published as Gwendolyn Bays (trans.), *The Voice of the Buddha*, Dharma Publishing, Berkeley 1983.

32 For example, Dr Jim B. Tucker's account of his research into past-life memory at the University of Virginia Medical School's Division of Perceptual Studies. Jim B. Tucker, *Return to Life*, St Martin's Griffin, New York 2015.

33 Joseph Head and S. L. Cranston (eds.), *Reincarnation: The Phoenix Fire Mystery*, Crown Publishers Inc, New York 1977. (S)

34 The theosophical movement, 'the synthesis of science, religion, and philosophy' was the inspiration of Russian-born Helena Petrovna Blavatsky (1831–1891). Her *Isis Unveiled* was published in 1877.

35 Christmas Humphreys, *Both Sides of the Circle*, George Allen and Unwin, London 1978, p. 33. (S)

36 Christmas Humphreys (1901–1983), was an English barrister, and later a judge, whose theosophical interests led him to Buddhism. The Buddhist Lodge of the Theosophical Society was one of the first Buddhist organizations in Europe. After breaking away from the Theosophical Society in 1926, it was renamed the Buddhist Society. Humphreys was its president until the end of his life.

37 'Friends' here are people involved with the Friends of

the Western Buddhist Order (FWBO), the original name of the Triratna Buddhist Community. The name was changed at Sangharakshita's request in 2010.

38 It was Edward Conze who termed *pratītya-samutpāda* 'conditioned co-production'; see, for example, the introduction to his translation of *The Large Sūtra on Perfect Wisdom*, University of California Press, Berkeley 1984, p. 14. This fundamental Buddhist doctrine is expressed in the Pāli canon (*Majjhima Nikāya* i.32) thus: 'This being, that becomes, from the arising of this, that arises; this not becoming, that does not become; from the ceasing of this, that ceases.' See Bhikkhu Ñāṇamoli and Bhikkhu Bodhi (trans.), *The Middle Length Discourses of the Buddha*, Wisdom Publications, Boston 1995, p. 655; or I. B. Horner (trans.), *The Collection of the Middle Length Sayings*, vol. ii, Pali Text Society, Oxford 1994, p. 229. In other words, all things arise and cease in dependence on conditions. For a detailed introduction to the *pratītya-samutpāda* doctrine, see Sangharakshita, *A Survey of Buddhism*, *Complete Works*, vol. 1, pp. 88ff. For a general introduction to *śūnyatā*, see Sangharakshita, *What is the Dharma?*,*Complete Works*, vol. 3, pp. 230–8.

39 The *saddhānusārin* (faith-follower) and the *dhammānusārin* (doctrine-follower) are two of the group of seven *ariya-puggalas* (noble disciples) enumerated in the Pāli canon. See, for example, the *Cūḷagopālaka Sutta, Majjhima Nikāya* 34 (i.227):

> Just as that tender calf just born, being urged on by its mother's lowing, also breasted the stream of the Ganges and got safely across to the further shore, so too, those *bhikkhus* who are Dharma-followers and faith-followers – by breasting Māra's stream they too will get safely to the further shore.

See Bhikkhu Ñāṇamoli and Bhikkhu Bodhi (trans.), *The Middle Length Discourses of the Buddha*, Wisdom Publications, Boston 1995, p. 321; or I. B. Horner (trans.), *The Collection of the Middle Length Sayings*, vol. i, Pali Text Society, London 1976, p. 279. Sangharakshita introduces the two terms at the beginning of his talk 'A Vision of Human Existence', published in *Buddhism for Today and Tomorrow*, Windhorse Publications, Birmingham 1996, pp. 24–5 (*Complete Works*, vol. 11).

40 S. Radhakrishnan (trans.), *Bhagavad Gītā*, Blackie & Son, Bombay 1971, p. 343. (S)

41 In the interest of brevity, the following passage has been omitted from Conze's original text:

> The break with the normal social environment is, of course, complete only in the case of the monk who, as the formula goes, 'in faith forsakes his home'. To a lesser extent it must be carried out by every practitioner of the Dharma, who must 'live apart' from his society, in spirit if not in fact. The company of others and the help we expect from them are usually a mainstay of our sense of security. By going for refuge to the Buddha and the Sangha one turns from the visible and tangible to the invisible and elusive.

42 The Āryasaṅgha or Noble Order comprises all those who have attained at least the level of Stream Entry. For more detail, see *A Survey of Buddhism*, *Complete Works*, vol. 1, pp. 177–8.

43 The Children of God was an apocalyptic Christian evangelist cult that began in 1960s California and incorporated elements of hippie culture. The Hare Krishna movement consists of devotees of the Maharishi Mahesh Yogi (1915–2008), an Indian guru who rose to fame when members of the English pop group the Beatles became his disciples in the 1960s. The Divine Light Mission gained prominence in the West under the leadership of Prem Rawat, also known as Guru Maharaj Ji. In the early 1980s, Rawat rebranded the movement as Elan Vital, which was listed as a cult in a 1996 French parliamentary commission report. Scientology is an organization based on beliefs and practices invented by American science fiction author L. Ron Hubbard (1911–1986). Sun Myung Moon (1920–2012) was the founder of the Unification Church, which promoted a mixture of Christianity and Confucianism and later built a massive business empire in South Korea and the United States. All these groups targeted young people as converts in the late 1970s.

44 Sangharakshita draws a distinction between a social 'group' and a 'spiritual community'. Examples of groups include the family, one's nationality, occupation, and so on. The 'positive group' is one of a number of terms Sangharakshita uses to describe the journey from being a group member to membership of the spiritual community as a true individual. A 'true individual' is someone who is 'sufficiently integrated as an individual as to be able to make a valid commitment to the path to Enlightenment' and is thus

able to associate with others of like mind in the spiritual community. See, for example, *What is the Sangha?*,*Complete Works*, vol. 3, pp. 457–8.

45 'Enlightenment as Experience and as Non-Experience' appears in print in Sangharakshita, *The Taste of Freedom*, Windhorse Publications, Birmingham 1997, pp. 58–60 (*Complete Works*, vol. 11).

46 See note 37 above.

47 The Order *mettā bhāvanā* is a meditation in which Order members sit to practise the *mettā bhāvanā* at a given time each month with a special focus on fellow members of the Order.

48 Buddhaghosa, *Visuddhimagga* 102 (3.75) in Bhikkhu Ñāṇamoli (trans.), *The Path of Purification*, Buddhist Publication Society, Kandy 1991, pp. 101–2, or Pe Maung Tin (trans.), *The Path of Purity*, Pali Text Society, London 1975, pp. 118–19.

49 In the Abhidharma, faith (*śraddhā*) is the first of the eleven positive mental events. For more about the role of faith as a positive mental event, see pp. 550–7 below.

50 Buddhaghosa was a Theravādin Buddhist commentator, translator, and philosopher of fifth-century Sri Lanka. He is the author of the *Visuddhimagga*, which is Conze's basic source in *The Way of Wisdom*. The *Visuddhimagga* is a wide-ranging compilation of older Sinhala commentaries on Theravāda doctrine and practice and for that reason a major source of reference for meditators. See Bhikkhu Ñāṇamoli (trans.), *The Path of Purification*, Buddhist Publication Society, Kandy 1991; or Pe Maung Tin (trans.), *The Path of Purity*, Pali Text Society, London 1975.

51 In the interest of brevity, the following has been omitted from Conze's original text:

> It multiplies the distractions from the sensory world to such an extent that the calm of the invisible world is harder to reach than ever. It exposes the citizen to so great a variety of conflicting viewpoints, that he finds it hard to make a choice.

52 In the Buddha's time, there were already six schools of classical Indian philosophy. These are the schools of Yoga, Nyāya, Vaiśeṣika, Mīmāṃsā, Vedānta, and Sāṃkhya. See S. Radhakrishnan, *Indian Philosophy*, Oxford University Press, Delhi 1998, vol. ii, p. 28.

53 Joseph Head and S. L. Cranston (eds.), *Reincarnation: The Phoenix Fire Mystery*, Crown Publishers Inc., New York 1977. (S)

54 In the interest of brevity, the following has been omitted from Conze's original text:

The fourth 'superknowledge' is the recollection of one's own previous rebirths, and the fifth, the knowledge of the rebirths of other people, by which one 'sees that whatever happens to them happens in accordance with their deeds'. There are many well-authenticated cases of persons spontaneously remembering certain details of one or the other of their own previous lives, and these people obviously have an additional reason for belief in rebirth which is lacking in those who cannot recall ever having lived before. Full certitude on the issue is, however, given to those only who can, on the basis of the fourth *jhāna* and by taking definite prescribed and disciplined steps on emerging from that *jhāna*, 'recall their manifold former lives,' according to the well-known formula, 'there I was, that was my name, that was my family, that was my caste, such was my food, this was the happiness, this the suffering which I experienced, this was the duration of my life-span. Deceased there I was born elsewhere and there had this name, etc.' When a monk has practised properly and successfully, 'these things become as clear to him as if lit up by a lamp'. (*Visuddhimagga* 13.23)

55 *Bardo* literally means 'in-between state', in this case between death and future rebirth. For more about the *bardo*, see 'The Psycho-Spiritual Symbolism of *the Tibetan Book of the Dead*', *Complete Works*, vol. 12, pp. 194–208. Acheron, one of the five rivers of the underworld in ancient Greek mythology, is mentioned in the *Inferno* of Dante Alighieri, canto 3, where the newly dead are ferried across to enter the circles of hell. Cerberus, the terrifying three-headed dog, appears in Dante's *Inferno*, canto 6, standing guard to ensure that those who enter never return.

56 Presuming that Sangharakshita is implying that Christianity is the most intolerant religion, then his *From Genesis to the Diamond Sūtra* provides additional background to his thinking, especially chapter 3. See *Complete Works*, vol. 13, pp. 548–62.

57 The Mind Body Spirit Festival first took place at the Olympia Exhibition Centre in London in 1977. Here 'universalism' refers to the view that all religious teachings are equally true and lead equally to the same ultimate experience. It should be noted that this use of the term differs from its use in Christian theology.

58 'Relative' here means conventional as opposed to ultimate truth. Sangharakshita

explains Nāgārjuna's teaching of absolute and relative truth in *A Survey of Buddhism*, *Complete Works*, vol. 1, pp. 264–71. See also Nāgārjuna, *Mūla-madhyamakakārikā*, xxiv.8–10.

59 The Buddha identified five orders of conditionality, five *niyamas*, as Buddhaghosa subsequently called them: physical inorganic; physical organic (i.e. biological); psychological; karmic; and transcendental. Unless one has the insight of a Buddha, one cannot be sure which *niyamas* have brought about what particular effect.

The example usually given is that of a fever. If one gets a fever, it may be a chill caused by a sudden change in temperature; or one may have caught a viral infection; or perhaps one has succumbed to illness as a result of some kind of mental strain; or it may have been caused by an unskilful action committed in the past; or it may even be the effect on one's system of transcendental insight. Thus the same end result may have been brought about by something physical, something biological, something psychological, something karmic, or something transcendental – or a combination of two or more of these. *What is the Dharma?*, *Complete Works*, vol. 3, p. 316. See also *The Three Jewels*, *Complete Works*, vol. 2, pp. 69–70. The five orders of conditionality or *niyamas* are enumerated by Buddhaghosa in his commentary on the *Dhammasaṅgaṇī*, the first book of the Abhidhamma Piṭaka; see Pe Maung Tin (trans.), *The Expositor*, vol. ii, ch. 10, Pali Text Society, London 1921. p. 360; also in Buddhaghosa's commentary on the *Dīgha Nikāya*, published as W. Stede (eds.), *Sumaṅgala-vilāsinī*, part 2, Pali Text Society, London 1931, p. 360 (not available in English translation). Another of Sangharakshita's sources is C. A. F. Rhys Davids, *Buddhism: A Study of the Buddhist Norm*, Williams and Norgate, London 1912, pp. 118–9.

60 For example:

> Within an erber, and a garden fair
> With floures growe, and herbes vertuous.
> Of which the savour swete was and the eyr.

Geoffrey Chaucer, 'The Court of Love' in Rev. W. Skeat (ed.), *Chaucerian and Other Pieces*, Clarendon Press, Oxford 1897, p. 429.

61 In the Abhidharma, vigour (*vīrya*) is the seventh of the eleven positive mental events. For more about vigour as a

mental event, see pp. 574–5 below.

62 *Visuddhimagga* 129–30 (4.45–9). See Bhikkhu Ñāṇamoli (trans.), *The Path of Purification*, Buddhist Publication Society, Kandy 1991, pp. 128–9.

63 i.e. the Friends of the Western Buddhist Order, latterly known as the Triratna Buddhist Community.

64 'Just sitting' is a practice integral to Sangharakshita's 'system of meditation'. In a meditation posture, one aims to allow bodily and mental events to change and pass on without obstruction, maintaining continuous attention in the present moment. It is also an important practice in the Tibetan Kagyupa tradition and in the Vajrayāna generally. 'Just sitting' was outlined in a talk given by Sangharakshita on the Order convention in 1978. Since then, other Order members have elaborated on the practice. See, for example, Kamalashila, *Buddhist Meditation*, Windhorse Publications, Cambridge 2012, pp. 32–44.

65 Don Quixote de la Mancha is the protagonist of the picaresque novel *Don Quixote* (1605–1615) by Miguel de Cervantes y Saavedra (1547–1616). In a series of adventures, its elderly hero sets out to right the world's wrongs, inspired by tales of gallant knight-errant romances.

In the interest of brevity, the following passage has been omitted from Conze's original text:

> 'Cervantes' novel gives a fine and detailed description of all the chief attributes of faith. Don Quixote vigorously, fearlessly, without complaining, and even serenely endures all tribulations because he wants to help others, all of them equally, according to their needs. When he dashes into the middle of the boiling lake, he reaches the very height of self-abandonment of which faith as such is capable. 'And just when he does not know what will happen to him, he finds himself among flowery fields beautiful beyond those of Elysium'.

66 Don Quixote fights 'commending himself to God and his mistress' and he feels himself as an instrument of Dulcinea who infuses valour into his arms. 'She fights in me, she is victorious in me, and I live and breathe in her, receive life and being itself from her.' He thus belongs to a large band of those who sustain their faith by the love of a feminine being, and his Dulcinea corresponds to the Virgin Mary of the Catholics and to the Tārā and Prajñāpāramitā of Mahāyāna Buddhism. (EC)

67 R. H. Blyth, *Zen in English Literature*, Hokuseido Press, Tokyo 1948, pp. 199, 201. (EC) Conze is citing mainly the Japanese names of Chinese patriarchs. Hakuin Ekaku (c.1686–c.1769) was a key figure of the Rinzai Zen school of Japan, and is one of the four Japanese 'teachers of the past' on the Triratna Refuge Tree. Rinzai refers to Linji Yixuan (Pinyin *Línjì Yìxuán*; Japanese *Rinzai Gigen*), the founder of the Linji school of Chan Buddhism during Tang dynasty China. He died in 866 CE. Eno refers to the Sixth Chinese patriarch, Huineng (Pinyin *Dàjiàn Huìnéng*; Japanese *Daikan Enō*) (638–713 CE). Daruma is the Japanese name of Bodhidharma, a semi-legendary Buddhist monk who lived during the fifth or sixth century. He is known as *Dámó* in China and is traditionally credited as the first Chinese patriarch, having first brought Buddhism into that country. For a description of the Triratna Refuge Tree see Kulananda, *Teachers of Enlightenment*, Windhorse Publications, Birmingham 2000.

68 Jianzhi Sengcan (Pinyin *Jiànzhì Sēngcàn*) (?496–?606) is known as the Third Chinese Patriarch of Chan after Bodhidharma and Thirtieth Patriarch after Siddhārtha Gautama Buddha. Sengcan is best known as the reputed author of the poem, Xinxin Ming (Pinyin Xìnxīn Míng), or 'Inscription on Faith in Mind'. The year and place of Sengcan's birth is unknown.

In the interest of brevity, the following has been omitted from Conze's original text:

> I admit that I have always liked Don Quixote for saying that the 'perfection' of madness does not consist in going 'mad for some actual reason or other', but 'in running mad without the least constraint or necessity'. But still I cannot help feeling that there is some difference, intangible perhaps, but nevertheless real, between the perfection of madness and the perfection of wisdom.

69 Reginald Horace Blyth (1898–1964) was an English author and follower of Japanese culture. The influence of his writings on Zen and haiku poetry, particularly among the San Francisco and Beat Generation writers of the 1950s and 1960s, may have contributed to the popular belief that haiku poetry and Buddhism are in some way connected.

70 Christmas Humphreys also claims that 'Alice (Through the Looking-Glass) describes the Path more accurately than any of the glorious Scriptures of the world' and that 'Alice, of course, whether in Wonderland or through the Looking-Glass,

is full of Zen.' Christmas Humphreys, *Zen Buddhism*, Heinemann, London 1949, pp. 112–13, 189.

71 'Zen is the most irrational, inconceivable thing in the world'. D. T. Suzuki, *Essays in Zen Buddhism*, first series, Rider, London 1958, p. 23.

72 Lewis Carroll was the pen name of Charles Lutwidge Dodgson (1832–1898), a deacon of the Church of England and an Oxford mathematics lecturer. *Alice's Adventures in Wonderland* (1865) and *Through the Looking-glass and What Alice Found There* (1871) brought him immediate fame and he began friendships with many notable figures in Victorian society. Under his real name, Dodgson published a number of significant works on mathematics and logic, and was also an accomplished photographer.

73 Colin Wilson (1931–2013) was an English novelist and existentialist philosopher. In *The Outsider*, Wilson sets out a theory of social alienation based on the existentialist idea of bad faith (*mauvaise foi*). In this view, under pressure to conform to the norms of society at large, individuals are misled into rejecting their innate destiny as free-thinking human beings and adopt instead a range of inauthentic values. Wilson calls this alienated individual 'the Outsider' and considers such a personality characteristic of modern society. See Colin Wilson, *The Outsider*, Gollancz, London 1956.

74 *Visuddhimagga* 129 (4.45–9). See Bhikkhu Ñāṇamoli (trans.), *The Path of Purification*, Buddhist Publication Society, Kandy 1991, pp. 128–9.

75 *Akṣayamati Sūtra* (quoted in *Śikṣā-samuccaya*) in Edward Conze (trans.), *Buddhist Texts Through the Ages*, Shambhala Publications, Boston 1990, p. 185.

76 *Milindapañha* (*The Questions of King Milinda*) 36 (2.1.11) in Edward Conze (trans.), *Buddhist Scriptures*, Penguin Books, Harmondsworth 1987, p. 156. Both this and the previous quotation are from the Appendix to *The Way of Wisdom*, a short anthology of translations that was not studied on the seminar. (S)

77 James 'Jim' Sharples was born in 1946 in South Africa and emigrated to New Zealand in the early 1970s. His Mitra ceremony was conducted by Sangharakshita in 1975 on a visit to New Zealand and he was ordained as Vipula in 1979. In 1981, together with Dharmamati and Dipankara, Vipula formed a men's community in Sydney, helping start Triratna activities in Australia.

78 Purna was ordained in 1975 during Sangharakshita's first visit to New Zealand. Purna

was attracted to Buddhism as a teenager and had travelled to India in his early twenties to find a teacher. Returning to New Zealand, he had connected with Sangharakshita through reading *A Survey of Buddhism* and listening to recordings of lectures. In Bethnal Green in London, in the late 1970s, he lived and worked in the old fire station that became the London Buddhist Centre. In the early 1980s, Purna lived in India for three years as an *anagārika* and worked closely with Lokamitra in the early days of the Triratna Buddhist Order and Community there. Purna has been a private preceptor since 2005 and is active in the Preceptors' College and men's Order convening in New Zealand and Australia. Purna is mentioned frequently in Sangharakshita's *Travel Letters* (*Complete Works*, vol. 24).

79 Sukhavati, meaning 'full of bliss', was the name given to the community at the London Buddhist Centre, which had been created from a derelict fire station over the preceding three years. The work had demanded great energy and commitment, especially when, to begin with, there was neither electricity for heating, nor windows to keep out the cold. The renovation team lived, worked, and practised Dharma together on the construction project, which provided valuable experience in building and fundraising for those involved, as well as in 'team-based right livelihood' and community living. The project inspired similar initiatives across the Triratna Buddhist Community, in places as far apart as Helsinki and New Zealand and the hills of Wales. The success of Sukhavati was in some sense, however, only half the story, being a single-sex project limited to men. It would take the creation of Taraloka Retreat Centre five years later to provide a similarly pivotal situation for the women's wing of the Triratna Buddhist Community.

For more on Sukhavati, see Vajragupta, *The Triratna Story*, Windhorse Publications, Cambridge 2010, chapter 2.

80 This is one of the Zen stories compiled by Paul Reps in the late 1950s. The story concerns Baizhang Huaihai (Pinyin *Bǎizhàng Huáihái*; Japanese *Hyakujō Ekai*) (720–814) a Zen master during the Tang dynasty. It was Baizhang's practice, even at the age of 80, to work alongside his pupils doing manual work around the monastery grounds. His disciples were unable to persuade him to do otherwise and in desperation they finally hid the old master's gardening tools. Paul Reps continues:

> That day the master did not eat. The next day he did not

eat, nor the next. 'He may be angry because we have hidden his tools,' the pupils surmised. 'We had better put them back.' The day they did, the teacher worked and ate the same as before. In the evening he instructed them: 'No work, no food.'

Paul Reps, *Zen Flesh, Zen Bones*, Tuttle, Rutland 1970, pp. 89–90.

81 Aryatara is the name of a Buddhist men's community in Croydon, Surrey. At the time of the seminar, Aryatara also housed a public Buddhist centre.

82 Amaravati was a large, dilapidated old house in Wanstead, East London that was renovated by a team of women to accommodate a residential community in 1977.

83 Pundarika (Pāli *puṇḍarīka*, 'white lotus') was the very first Triratna Buddhist centre. Founded by Buddhadasa in 1972, it occupied a small, disused factory building in Archway, North London.

84 Faith lends itself to emotional excitement; vigour to the excitement of doing things and wanting to do more; wisdom to the excitement of discovery. (EC)

85 In the Abhidharma, mindfulness (*smṛti*, which Conze renders here as *smriti*) is the third of the five object-determining mental events. For more about mindfulness as a mental event, see pp. 535–41 below.

86 Sangharakshita first came across communication exercises in India. The procedure is for participants to form pairs and take part in a formalized verbal exchange emptied of objective meaning. The focus therefore falls upon the direct experience of the communicative situation as it unfolds stage by stage between the partners. The exercises, which are generally found to be a lively source of energy, were originally developed by educationalist Muriel Payne, author of *Creative Education* (1958), whom Sangharakshita met in the 1950s. See 'Some Bombay Friends' in *Adhisthana Writings*, *Complete Works*, vol. 26, pp. 561–2.

87 *Kirtan* originates in the Vedic *anukīrtana* tradition. It refers to a meeting in which one or more singers recite legends, spiritual teachings, or words of devotion to a deity. The meeting is characterized by high states of emotion as the audience engages with the performance, repeating the words or replying in call-and-response, and offering up their own expressions of emotion from time to time. (S) See for example *The Rainbow Road from Tooting Broadway to Kalimpong*, *Complete Works*, vol. 20, pp. 185–90.

88 The term *samādhi* takes on a number of meanings depending

on its context. Considered as the fourth of the five object-determining mental events, *samādhi* can be understood as an awareness that is firmly fixed or established on its object. See pp. 542–5 below.

89 See *The Taste of Freedom*, Windhorse Publications, Birmingham 1997, pp. 27–48 (*Complete Works*, vol. 11).

90 The Chogyal ('Dharma kings' or *dharmarājas*) were the Buddhist monarchs of the former kingdom of Sikkim from 1642 until 1975 when the monarchy was abolished and Sikkim became an Indian state.

91 *Visuddhimagga* 129–30 (4.45–9); see Bhikkhu Ñāṇamoli (trans.), *The Path of Purification*, Buddhist Publication Society, Kandy 1991, pp. 128–9. See also *Saṃyutta Nikāya* v.115 (46.53); Bhikkhu Bodhi (trans.), *The Connected Discourses of the Buddha*, Wisdom Publications, Somerville 2000, p. 1607; or F. L. Woodward (trans.), *The Book of the Kindred Sayings*, part 5, Pali Text Society, London 1979, p. 98.

92 *Majjhima Nikāya* 10 (i.57). The commentary to this passage should be consulted. It has been translated in Bhikkhu Soma, *The Way of Mindfulness*, 1949, pp. 18–31. (EC)

93 For more on the division of the whole of existence into *dharmas*, see p. 442 and p. 546 below. One of the meanings of *dharma* is 'mental object, representation'. What Conze calls the '*dharma*-theory' thus forms the basis for the analysis of consciousness into 'mind' and 'mental events'. This is the central focus of Sangharakshita's *Know Your Mind*, pp. 429ff in this volume.

94 Recollection, as understood by Christian monastics, involves the withdrawal of the mind from earthly affairs in order to attend to God and divine things. Consideration, on the other hand, means thinking carefully about the consequences of one's intended actions. Bernard of Clairvaux (1090–1153) was the main instigator of the Second Crusade against the Turks (1146–1149). The Crusade's military failure caused Bernard to send an apology to the Pope inserted in the second part of his *De Consideratione*, where he attributes the crusaders' defeats to the pressing weight of their sins.

95 For the Eightfold Path see *The Buddha's Noble Eightfold Path* in *Complete Works*, vol. 1, pp. 469ff. The 'five cardinal virtues' are what Conze calls the *indriyas*, or spiritual faculties, which are the subject of the present work. For an account of the seven *bodhyaṅgas*, see Sangharakshita, *Buddha Mind*, Windhorse Publications,

Birmingham 2001, pp. 55–61 (*Complete Works*, vol. 11).

96 For more on the four applications of mindfulness, see *Living with Awareness*, Windhorse Publications, Birmingham 2003, p. 134 (*Complete Works*, vol. 15).

97 *Skandha* literally means 'heap' or 'aggregate'. The Buddha taught that what we think of as the self or personality is made up of five 'heaps': *rūpa* (form), *vedanā* (feeling), *samjñā* (perception), *saṃskāras* (volitions), and *vijñāna* (consciousness). *Saṃyutta Nikāya* iii.1–188 has a whole section on the *skandhas* (Pāli *khandhas*), the *Khandhasaṃyutta*; see Bhikkhu Bodhi (trans.), *The Connected Discourses of the Buddha*, Wisdom Publications, Somerville 2000, pp. 853–983; or F. L. Woodward (trans.), *The Book of the Kindred Sayings*, part 3, Pali Text Society, London 1975, pp. 1–154.

98 For more on the four dimensions of awareness, see *The Buddha's Noble Eightfold Path*, *Complete Works*, vol. 1, pp. 567–78. Sangharakshita sometimes refers to these as four 'levels' of awareness. These four levels, or dimensions, of awareness are not to be confused with the 'four foundations of mindfulness': awareness of the body, feelings, consciousness, and mental objects – outlined in, for example, the *Mahāsatipaṭṭhāna Sutta*, *Dīgha Nikāya* 22; see M. Walshe (trans.), *The Long Discourses of the Buddha*, Wisdom Publications, Boston 1995, pp. 335–50; or T. W. and C. A. F. Rhys Davids (trans.), *Dialogues of the Buddha*, part 2, Pali Text Society, London 1971, pp. 327–37.

99 Sangharakshita may have been referring, for example, to Nyanaponika Thera, *The Heart of Buddhist Meditation*, Samuel Weiser, New York 1970.

100 The Canadian monk was Ananda Bodhi, and the incident is related in greater detail in *Moving Against the Stream*, *Complete Works*, vol. 23, pp. 71–3.

101 In the Abhidharma, this mental factor is termed by *vikṣepa*, or distraction, and is the last of the twenty 'proximate factors of instability' (*upakleśa*). For more on *vikṣepa* see pp. 680–2 below.

102 Recollection of the Buddha or, in Sanskrit, *buddhānusmṛti* (Pāli *buddhānussati*), is the contemplation of the qualities of the Buddha. It is familiar to many Buddhists from the *Tiratana Vandanā* or 'Praises to the Three Jewels'. Buddhaghosa wrote extensively on the practice at *Visuddhimagga* 198–213: 'Recollection of the Enlightened One'. See Bhikkhu Ñāṇamoli (trans.), *The Path of Purification*, Buddhist

Publication Society, Kandy 1991, pp. 192–209.

103 TM or Transcendental Meditation is a technique taught by the Maharishi Mahesh Yogi (1915–2008), an Indian guru who rose to fame when members of the English pop group the Beatles became his disciples in the 1960s. The TM method is based on the recitation of a mantra.

104 In addition, Sangharakshita's commentary on the *White Lotus Sūtra* notes a correspondence between what he calls 'the metaphysics of potentiality' and the language of the Upanishads with regard to Brahman. See *The Drama of Cosmic Enlightenment*, *Complete Works*, vol. 16, p. 62. See also *Bṛhadāraṇyaka Upaniṣad* 1.4.

105 A likely reference to the *tathāgatagarbha* doctrine. In *Early Writings* Sangharakshita quotes S. N. Dasgupta on the position of Aśvaghoṣa with regard to the *tathāgatagarbha* doctrine:

> He held that in the soul two aspects may be distinguished – the aspect as thatness (*bhūtatathatā*) and the aspect as the cycle of birth and death (*saṃsāra*).... It embraces two principles, (1) enlightenment, (2) non-enlightenment.

S. N. Dasgupta quoted in Sangharakshita, *Early Writings 1944–1954*, *Complete Works*, vol. 7, p. 202. See also note 327 below.

106 This belief in a static creation, known as 'preformationism', can be contrasted with Aristotle's more developmental theory of 'epigenesis'. For more on medieval debates around the nature of generation, see Lois N. Magner, *A History of the Life Sciences*, Marcel Dekker, New York 1994, pp. 172ff.

107 *Aṅguttara Nikāya* i.10: 'This consciousness (*citta*) is luminous, but it is defiled by adventitious defilements.' See F. L. Woodward (trans.), *The Book of the Gradual Sayings*, vol. i, Pali Text Society, Oxford 2000, p. 8; or Bhikkhu Bodhi (trans.), *The Numerical Discourses of the Buddha*, Wisdom Publications, Somerville 2012, p. 97.

108 *Ātmavāda* refers to the Hindu conception of the spiritual path (the 'way of the soul'). In his 1948 article 'Progress and Religion' Sangharakshita discusses it (as Ātmanism), saying:

> The materialist and Ātmanist views ... are, in spite of the fact that in one sense they represent opposite poles of thought, identical inasmuch as they equally invalidate the ideal of progress and in fact preclude it altogether.

Early Writings 1944–1954, *Complete Works*, vol. 7, p. 166.

109 Kenneth K. Inada translates Nāgārjuna's statement on emptiness and co-arising as:

> All is possible when
> emptiness is possible.
> Nothing is possible when
> emptiness is impossible.

Nāgārjuna, *Mūlamadhyamaka-kārikā*, trans. Kenneth K. Inada, Hokuseido Press, Tokyo 1970, p. 147.

110 In the interest of brevity, the following has been omitted from Conze's original text:

> The expectation is that conscious attention will disintegrate the power of the enemies, diminish their number, and dissociate them from the ego. However diverse in nature the numerous exercises which come under the heading of mindfulness may seem to be, they all have in common this one purpose, that of guarding the incipient and growing calm in one's heart.

111 For more on Guenther's notion of an 'operational concept', see, for example, Herbert W. Guenther, *Philosophy and Psychology in the Abhidharma*, Buddha Vihara, Lucknow 1957, p. 349, where he states:

> The term self-concept is a purely operational term and not a theory about a Self. It is nothing concrete and existent.

112 In the interest of brevity, the following passage from Conze's original text has been omitted:

> The practice of mindfulness is not confined to taking note of what enters the mind by way of the sense-organs. One also tries to determine what is allowed to enter, and to generally reduce the number of sensory impacts by restraining the use of the physical organ, e.g. when one walks with eyes directed only a few feet or yards ahead. In addition, by an effort of the will one refuses to cooperate with one's habitual impulses in building up a mere casual observation into a thing of moment [sic] to which one returns again and again. Finally the intruder is weakened and worn down by appropriate reflections. He is kept out of the heart and devalued as trivial, as already passed, as nothing in particular, and by thinking that 'this does not concern me at all, this means nothing to me, it is only a waste when salvation and Nirvāṇa are considered'.

113 This is *cetanā*, or 'mental activity that propels the mind forward'. In the Abhidharma, directionality of mind (*cetanā*) is the third of the five omnipresent mental events. For more about *cetanā* as a mental event, see pp. 520–9 below.

114 Pāli *ānāpānasati*. For extracts from Sangharakshita's writings on the mindfulness of breathing practice see *The Purpose and Practice of Buddhist Meditation*, *Complete Works*, vol. 5, pp. 57–70.

115 Herbert V. Guenther and Leslie S. Kawamura (trans.), *Mind in Buddhist Psychology*, Dharma Publishing, Berkeley 1975. Sangharakshita's *Know Your Mind*, included in this volume, is a commentary on this work.

116 'The Dark Night of the Soul' (*La noche oscura del alma*) is a poem by the Spanish mystic, St John of the Cross (1542–1591). St John joined the Carmelite order as a young man, but his later attempts to bring about its reform led to imprisonment. It was during his incarceration that he composed much of his 'Spiritual Canticle' (1577). 'The Dark Night of the Soul' was written in 1585 and the following year he added a detailed commentary describing the two kinds of Night which the soul that seeks God must endure, the first being a night of sense, and the second, experienced only rarely, and only by those further along the path to God, the Dark Night of the Soul.

117 For a discussion of the salient events in the Buddha's life see *Who is the Buddha?*, *Complete Works*, vol. 3, pp. 18–33.

118 In the interest of brevity, the following passage has been omitted from Conze's original text:

> But if the monastic life is a necessary condition for these virtues, why talk about them at all? Partly because it is salutary, though painful, that we should see their absence in us, and partly because they constitute the subjective counterpart of the scriptures which we read. The Suttas describe the world as it appears on a spiritual level on which concentration and wisdom have come to maturity. The understanding of the scriptures is furthered by an understanding of the subjective attitude which corresponds to them. And so, although we are forced to go beyond the range of our immediate experience, and although the description tends to become more intangible as it rises to loftier heights, we will now, leaving aside the higher ranges of mindfulness, try to explain the traditional definitions of concentration and wisdom, as they are handed down to us.

119 The *Middle Way* is the journal of the Buddhist Society in London. Wheel publications are produced by the Buddhist Publication Society, whose library of literature on Theravāda

Buddhism is based in Sri Lanka. For the *Visuddhimagga* of Buddhaghosa, see Bhikkhu Ñāṇamoli (trans.), *The Path of Purification*, Buddhist Publication Society, Kandy 1991; or Pe Maung Tin (trans.), *The Path of Purity*, Pali Text Society, London 1975.

120 According to the Abhidharma, *samādhi*, or concentration, is one of the five 'object determining mental events' which must necessarily be present as a factor in the continued awareness of any object. See pp. 542–5 below.

121 The *dhyānas* are the levels of higher consciousness identified by the Buddha. They are most often experienced in meditation, though the lower *dhyānas* may occur in other circumstances. There are four '*dhyānas* of the world of form' (*rūpa dhyānas*) and four 'formless *dhyānas*' (*arūpa dhyānas*); the sphere of infinite space and the sphere of infinite consciousness are the first and second *arūpa dhyānas*. For more about the *dhyānas*, see *The Bodhisattva Ideal, Complete Works*, vol. 4, pp. 144–67; and *The Purpose and Practice of Buddhist Meditation*, *Complete Works*, vol. 5, pp. 231–79.

122 For more on the five hindrances, ibid., pp. 311–55.

123 Sense desire (*kāmachanda*).

124 Ill will (*vyāpāda*).

125 Sloth and torpor (*styāna-middha*).

126 The five *dhyāna* factors are (1) initial application (*vitarka*), (2) sustained application (*vicāra*), (3) joy (*prīti*), (4) happiness (*sukha*), and (5) one-pointedness (*ekāgratā*). They are enumerated by the Buddha in the *Anupada Sutta, Majjhima Nikāya* 111 (i.25–9); see Bhikkhu Ñāṇamoli and Bhikkhu Bodhi (trans.), *The Middle Length Discourses of the Buddha*, Wisdom Publications, Boston 1995, p. 899, or I. B. Horner (trans.), *The Collection of the Middle Length Sayings*, vol. iii, Pali Text Society, Oxford 1993, p. 78. For Sangharakshita's commentary, see *The Purpose and Practice of Buddhist Meditation*, *Complete Works*, vol. 5, pp. 242–3.

127 *Saṃyutta Nikāya* iii.13 (22.5); *Visuddhimagga* 438 (14.7) (EC).

128 For example *Abhidharmakośa* vi, pp. 142–4. See Vasubandhu, *Abhidharmakośabhāṣya*, vol. vi, trans. L. de la Valleé Poussin, translated into English by L. M. Pruden, Asian Humanities Press, Berkeley 1991.

129 *Triṃśikā* by Vasubandhu. See S. Levi (ed.), *Vijñaptimātratāsiddhi*, Champion, Paris 1925. (EC)

130 Sangharakshita refers again to the three 'knowledges' or 'wisdoms' on p. 567 below. See also *What is the Dharma?*, *Complete Works*, vol. 3, pp. 301–3. The three

wisdoms are enumerated in, for example, the *Saṅgīti Sutta, Dīgha Nikāya* 33 (iii.219); see M. Walshe (trans.), *The Long Discourses of the Buddha*, Wisdom Publications, Boston 1995, p. 486; or T. W. and C. A. F. Rhys Davids (trans.), *Dialogues of the Buddha*, part 3, Pali Text Society, London 1971, p. 212.

131 See commentary in *Aṭṭhasālinī*, PTS 1897, 147–9. (EC) This text is presumably Conze's own translation. See also Pe Maung Tin (trans.), *The Expositor (Aṭṭhasālinī)*, vol. i, Pali Text Society, London 1921, p. 196.

132 *Indriya. Aṭṭhasālinī* 122:

> Through overwhelming ignorance it is a 'dominant' in the sense of 'dominant influence'; or it is a 'dominant' because by exercising discernment (*dassana*) it dominates (associated *dharmas*). (EC)

Ibid. p. 162.

133 *Aṭṭhasālinī*, 123:

> As a clever surgeon knows which foods are suitable and which are not, so wisdom, when it arises, understands *dharmas* as wholesome or unwholesome, serviceable or unserviceable, low or exalted, dark or bright, similar or dissimilar.

See Maung Tin, ibid. Similarly *Abhidharmakośa* i.3, ii.154. (EC)

134 *Dharma*; the four holy truths (*Aṭṭhasālinī*). (EC)

135 *Vebhabyā; aniccādīnaṃ vibhāvanā-bhāva-vasena*. Or 'a critical attitude'? (EC)

136 Or 'examination'. (EC)

137 Or 'breadth'. Wisdom is rich and abundant, or massive. (EC)

138 *Medhā*; also 'mental power'. 'As lightning destroys even stone-pillars, so wisdom smashes the defilements; alternatively, it is able to grasp and bear in mind'. (EC)

139 *Milindapañha* 39 (2.1.14):

> It is like a lamp, O king, which a man might introduce into a house in darkness. When the lamp had been brought in it would dispel the darkness, cause radiance to arise, and light to shine forth, and make the objects there plainly visible.

T. W. Rhys Davids (trans.), *The Questions of King Milinda*, part 1, Motilal Banarsidass, Delhi 1992, pp. 61–2.

140 Because it gives delight, is worthy of respect (or 'variegated') hard to get and hard to manifest, incomparable and a source of enjoyment to illustrious beings. (EC)

141 *Milindapañha* 32 (2.1.8), as translated in Edward Conze, *Buddhist Scriptures*, Penguin Books, Harmondsworth, 1987, pp. 151–2. (EC)

142 *Kleśa*, meaning 'that which defiles', refers to the three

'unwholesome roots' (*akuśala-mūla*) of greed, hatred, and delusion or ignorance. For more about the *kleśas*, see Sangharakshita, *Know Your Mind*, pp. 596ff below.

143 *Aṭṭhasālinī* 123: 'This penetration is unfaltering (*akkhalita*), like the penetration of an arrow shot by a skilled archer'. (EC) See Pe Maung Tin (trans.) *The Expositor (Aṭṭhasālinī)*, vol. i, Pali Text Society, London 1921, p. 162.

144 *Visuddhimagga* 438 (14.7). *Dhammasabhāva-paṭivedhalakkhaṇā paññā; dhammānaṃ sabhāvapaṭicchādaka-mohandhakāra-viddhaṃsanarasā*. (EC) See Bhikkhu Ñāṇamoli (trans.), *The Path of Purification*, Buddhist Publication Society, Kandy 1991, p. 437.

145 For more about *ḍākas* and *ḍākinīs*, see *Creative Symbols of Tantric Buddhism*, *Complete Works*, vol. 13, pp. 221–47.

146 In the Hindu spiritual tradition there are said to be four paths to God. These four kinds of yoga – as well as others – are explained to Prince Arjuna by his charioteer, Krishna, in the *Bhagavad Gītā*. The four paths are the path of *jñāna yoga*, or knowledge and contemplation (chapter 5); *karma yoga*, or active service (chapter 3); *bhakti yoga*, or love and devotion to the ideal (chapter 12); and *rāja yoga*, or meditation (chapter 9).

147 An *arhant* is a Buddhist 'saint' who has attained individual Nirvāṇa, having broken the five 'higher fetters'. These are: *rūpa-rāga* and *arūpa-rāga*, or craving for existence in the world of pure form and in the formless world; *māna* or conceit; *auddhatya*, restlessness; and *avidyā* or lack of a clear understanding of reality. See also under 'arahant' in T. W. Rhys Davids and W. Stede, *Pāli–English Dictionary*, Motilal Banarsidass, Delhi 1993, p. 77. *Rāga, māna, auddhatya*, and *avidya* are all classed as negative mental events, and more is said about each of them in *Know Your Mind* in this volume. For *rāga*, see pp. 596–8, for *māna*, see p. 603–7, for *auddhatya*, see p. 670–1, and for *avidyā* see pp. 607–11 below.

148 Rudolf Otto, (1869–1937) was a German theologian whose exploration of the 'awe-inspiring' element in religious experience is outlined in his most important work, *Das Heilige* (1917) published in English as *The Idea of the Holy* (1923). Otto was the originator of the term 'numinous', from the Latin *numen*, meaning 'divine will', and refers to the above-mentioned awe-inspiring quality.

149 Sangharakshita writes of John Driver in his volume of memoirs, *In the Sign of the Golden Wheel*. Having been given some *sādhanas* (visualizations) by his teacher, Jamyang Khyentse Rimpoche, he continues,

> They arrived a few weeks later. Naturally they were in Tibetan, which I did not understand, least of all the classical Tibetan in which the texts were composed. Luckily I had a friend who did understand it and who, moreover, was willing to translate my texts for me. The friend was John Driver, an English scholar of about my own age who was doing research into the Nyingma tantras for a doctoral thesis. Dreamy and absent-minded (or at least appearing so), he lived with his wife Anne and their two – later three – daughters within the Scottish Mission compound called the White House, but which, for the purposes of our correspondence, we renamed the White Tara House.

Complete Works, vol. 22, p. 403.

150 The fullest surviving account of Candragomin's life comes from the Tibetan lama Tāranātha (1575–1634), who praises him alongside Śāntideva, 'famed among the learned as the two wonderful master-teachers (*ācārya*)' of Mahāyāna Buddhism. In Tāranātha's account, the socially engaged generosity of the layman Candragomin is contrasted with the strict bookishness of his contemporary, the ordained monk Candrakīrti. For more on Candragomin, see M. Tatz, 'The Life of Candragomin in Tibetan Historical Tradition', (1982) *Tibet Journal*, 7 (3), 3–22, from which the above quotation comes. Candragomin's writings also include the *Śiṣyalekha* or 'Letter to a Disciple' published by Dharma Publishing as 'Mātṛceṭa, Candragomin' in Michael Hahn (trans.), *Invitation to Enlightenment*, Dharma Publishing, Berkeley 1999.

151 C. M. Chen (Yogi Chen) was a Zen practitioner and teacher with whom Sangharakshita studied during his time in the Himalayan town of Kalimpong. See *Precious Teachers*, *Complete Works*, vol. 22, pp. 532–41.

152 *Puṇya*: merit; *jñāna*: knowledge or understanding. Sangharakshita clarifies the relationship between *puṇya* and *jñāna* in *Know Your Mind*. See p. 463 below.

153 *Siddhis*: attainments.

154 Five *jñānas*: the five Buddha-knowledges or wisdoms represent the five aspects of Enlightenment, usually personified in Tibetan Buddhist iconography as five Buddhas

of various colours. They are the sublimated forms of the 'eight *vijñānas*', the modes of discriminating awareness which operate through the five physical senses and three aspects of mind. For more on the *vijñānas* and their transformation into the five *jñānas*, see pp. 483ff. below.

155 *Bhūmis*: the ten 'grounds' or stages to be attained in the course of the bodhisattva's career. See also note 341 below.

156 i.e. Avalokiteśvara, the bodhisattva of compassion.

157 *Bhūtas* are malignant and formless elemental spirits said to inhabit the north-east quarter of the universe, while *vetālas* are zombie-like beings returned from the dead. Both have much in common with *pretas*, or hungry ghosts.

158 The Jambu is one of the heavenly rivers, containing gold of exquisite purity.

159 *Ṛddhi*: psychic powers, such as the ability to pass through solid objects, walk on water, fly through the air, and touch the sun and moon.

160 *Śrīvatsa* also refers to the knot of eternity, one of the eight auspicious symbols (*aṣṭamaṅgala*) of Tibetan Buddhism.

161 *Dhyāna*: states of absorption characteristic of *śamatha* meditation. *Samādhi*: states of meditative concentration. *Vimokṣa*: liberation from mundane existence.

162 Brahmā, Viṣṇu, and Mahādeva are three aspects of the supreme divinity in the mythology of the Vedas. Brahmā is referred to as 'the Creator', i.e. of the universe; Vishnu is known as 'the Preserver' who protects and transforms existence; and Mahādeva, otherwise known as Shiva, is 'the Destroyer', controller of time and bringer of destruction at the end of creation.

163 *Bhaṭṭārakī*: a female Vedic deity, also 'head-ornament of Shiva'.

164 The five *kāyas* of the Buddha are the *dharmakāya*, or 'body of reality'; the *sambhogakāya*, or 'body of enjoyment'; the *nirmāṇakāya*, or 'transformation body'; the *vajrakāya*, or 'body of the unchanging natural state'; and the *abhisambodhikāya*, or 'perfect *kāya* of complete awakening'.

165 *Kleśas*: mental defilements. See note 142 above.

166 Māmakī represents a wisdom that makes no distinction between beings. Yellow in colour, she is the consort of the Buddha Ratnasambhava. *Locanā* is associated with pure awareness. Pale blue in colour, she is the consort of the Buddha Akṣobhya. Pāṇḍaravāsinī is a female manifestation of Avalokiteśvara. She is white in colour and has much in common with Guanyin, the

bodhisattva of compassion in the Chinese tradition.

167 *Prapañca*: the mental tendency to proliferate concepts with the result that an illusory 'self' arises.

LIVING ETHICALLY

168 Translated with a commentary in Jay L. Garfield, *The Fundamental Wisdom of the Middle Way*, Oxford University Press, Oxford 1995.

169 To quote Sangharakshita,

> According to an ancient and widespread belief, the great sage [Nāgārjuna] recovered the *Prajñāpāramitā* from the depths of the ocean, where since the days of the Buddha the *nāgas* had preserved it. Buddhist art depicts him seated on a raft, while a *nāga* maiden, emerging from the waves, presents him with a volume generally identified with the *Large Prajñāpāramitā* 'in One Hundred Thousand Lines'.

The Eternal Legacy, *Complete Works*, vol. 14, p. 135.

170 Published in English as Jeffrey Hopkins, *Buddhist Advice for Living and Liberation*, Snow Lion, New York 1998.

171 Emptiness, or *śūnyatā*, is the central teaching of the Madhyamaka school of the Mahāyāna. It refers to the absence of intrinsic nature (*svabhāva*) in anything that might conventionally be regarded as really existent. For more on emptiness, see *Living Wisely* in this volume, especially chapter 3, 'Images of Emptiness', pp. 346ff.

172 The Sātavāhana dynasty prevailed some time between the mid-first century BCE and the early third century CE, occupying an area that included the Deccan, Andhra, and the west coast of India. Although Sātavahana rulers were Hindus claiming Brahmanical status, they nonetheless offered generous support to Buddhist monasteries, and were sponsors of Buddhist art and architecture, including the stupa at Amaravati in Andhra Pradesh.

173 The ten ethical precepts are addressed in verses 8–9 (see pp. 175ff below), and the fifty-seven faults to be abandoned in verses 402ff. (p. 268 below).

174 For the historical background, see for example Andrew Skilton, *A Concise History of Buddhism*, Windhorse Publications, Birmingham 1997, especially chapter 17, 'The Tantra and Vajrayāna Buddhism'.

175 Ibid.

176 Milarepa (c.1052–c.1135) was a renowned yogi associated with the Kagyu school of Tibetan Buddhism and famed for his songs through which he communicated his inner realizations to his disciples. Tsongkhapa (1357–1419) is credited with the formation

of the Tibetan Gelug school and the founding of Ganden monastery. His works include a detailed commentary on the *Mūlamadhyamakakārikā* of Nāgārjuna. See rJe Tsong Khapa, *Ocean of Reasoning*, trans. Geshe Ngawang Samten and Jay L. Garfield, Oxford University Press, Oxford 2006.

177 See Andrew Skilton, *A Concise History of Buddhism*, Windhorse Publications, Birmingham 1997, chapter 11, 'Origins of the Mahāyāna'.

178 See ibid., p. 82.

179 For Sangharakshita's commentary on some of the Perfection of Wisdom *sūtras* see *Wisdom Beyond Words* in *Complete Works*, vol. 14. One of the earliest Mahāyāna Perfection of Wisdom *sūtras* is the *Vajracchedikā Prajñāpāramitā* or *Diamond Sūtra*. See also E. Conze (trans.), *The Perfection of Wisdom in Eight Thousand Lines and its Verse Summary*, Four Seasons Foundation, San Francisco 1995. The *Daśabhūmika Sūtra* appears as the chapter 26 of Thomas Cleary (trans.), *The Flower Ornament Scripture (Avataṃsaka Sūtra)*, Shambhala Publications, Boston 1993, pp. 695–811.

180 The Abhidharma is the third of the three baskets (*tripiṭaka*) or collections of the Buddha's words. It consists of a number of highly scholastic treatises which define technical terms, arrange doctrines in numerical order, and present a systematic exposition of the Buddha's teaching. For a short introduction to the Abhidharma, see chapter 1 of Sangharakshita, *Know Your Mind*, pp. 439ff, in this volume.

181 The Tibetan wheel of life depicts six realms of existence: those of human beings, gods, *asuras* or anti-gods, animals, hell-beings, and *pretas* or hungry ghosts. (See p. 477.) According to tradition, one can be born into any of these realms, but once the karma that resulted in one's birth into a particular realm is exhausted, one may be reborn in another. This teaching is taken literally by some Buddhists, metaphorically or psychologically by others. For more information see, for example, Kulananda, *The Wheel of Life*, Windhorse Publications, Birmingham 2000.

182 *Ariyapariyesanā Sutta*, *Majjhima Nikāya* i.168.

183 The eight 'conditions of non-leisure' (*akṣaṇa*), also translated 'inopportune births', are listed in the *Dharma-saṃgraha*, an extensive glossary of Sanskrit Buddhist technical terms attributed to Nāgārjuna. They are: *narakopapatti* (rebirth in hell); *tiryag-upapatti* (rebirth in the animal kingdom); *yama-lokopapatti* (rebirth in the realm of Yama – a

kind of limbo region similar to purgatory and ruled by the god Yama); *pratyanta-janapadopapatti* (rebirth in the border regions where the Dharma is unknown); *dīrghāyuṣa-devopapatti* (rebirth among the gods of long life); *indriya-vikalatā* (rebirth with impaired faculties); *mithyā-dṛṣṭi* (rebirth with wrong view); and *cittotpādarāgitatā* (rebirth with a mind intent on passion). See Nāgārjuna, *Dharmasaṃgrahaḥ*, Central University of Tibetan Studies, Sarnath, Varanasi 2013, section 134. See also Master Dōgen's 'Instructions for the Cook':

> One should also reflect on what our lives might have been had we been born in one of the realms of hell, as an insatiable spirit, as some lowly animal, or as a demon. How difficult our lives would be if we suffered the misfortunes of these four circumstances or any other of the eight misfortunate conditions.

Zen Master Dōgen and Kōshō Uchiyama Rōshi, *How to Cook Your Life*, trans. Thomas Wright, Shambhala Publications, Boston 2013, p. 19.

184 See note 171 above. For more on emptiness, see pp. 346ff. below.

185

> The first test of love is that it knows no bargain. So long as you see a man love another to get something, you may know that it is not love; it is shopkeeper's love. Wherever there is any question of buying or selling, it is no more love. So when any man is praying to God: 'Give me this and give me that,' it is not love. How can it be? I give you my little prayer, and you give me something in return; that is what it is, mere shop-keeping.

Vivekananda, *Speeches And Writings*, Natesan & Co., Madras 1927, p. 410.

186 For more on deceit (*māyā*) as a negative mental event, see pp. 657–9 below.

187 Romans 12:20.

188 *Bodhicaryāvatāra* 6.43. See, for example, Śāntideva, *Bodhicaryāvatāra*, trans. K. Crosby and A. Skilton, Windhorse Publications, Birmingham 2002, p. 72.

189 For more on the *bodhicitta* or 'awakening of the bodhi heart' see *The Bodhisattva Ideal, Complete Works*, vol. 4, pp. 27–54.

190 The ten precepts are listed in, for example, the *Kūṭadanta Sutta, Dīgha Nikāya* 5 (i.140). See T. W. Rhys Davids (trans.), *Dialogues of the Buddha*, part 1, Pali Text Society, London 1973, p. 173; or M. Walshe (trans.) *The Long Discourses of the Buddha*, Wisdom Publications, Boston

1995, p. 137. See also the *Sevitabbāsevitabba Sutta*, 'To Be Cultivated and Not To be Cultivated', *Majjhima Nikāya* 114 (iii.47–50) in I. B. Horner (trans.), *The Collection of the Middle Length Sayings*, vol. iii, Pali Text Society, Oxford 1993, pp. 94ff; or Bhikkhu Ñāṇamoli and Bhikkhu Bodhi (trans.), *The Middle Length Discourses of the Buddha*, Wisdom Publications, Boston 1995, pp. 914–17. See also Sangharakshita, *The Ten Pillars of Buddhism*, *Complete Works*, vol. 2, pp. 469ff.

191 For more on cruelty (*vihiṃsā*) as a negative mental event, see pp. 664–6 below.

192 The mindfulness of breathing or *ānāpānasati* is one of the most widely-practised meditations in Buddhism. For more details of this meditation and the *mettā bhāvanā*, see, for example, Kamalashila, *Buddhist Meditation*, Windhorse Publications, Cambridge 2012, or Bodhipaksa, *Wildmind: A Step-by-Step Guide to Meditation*, Windhorse Publications, Cambridge 2010.

193 William Shakespeare, *Richard II*, Act I, Scene iii.

194 The difference between them is that the Pāli verses compare Buddhist practices with Vedic ones, whereas Nāgārjuna is comparing one important Buddhist practice with another (S). *Dhammapada* 100 in Sangharakshita (trans.), *Dhammapada*, Windhorse Publications, Birmingham 2001. (*Complete Works*, vol. 15.)

195 *Dhammapada* 1.

196 In his *Buddhist Dictionary* (Buddhist Publication Society, Kandy 1988), Nyanatiloka translates *ceto vimutti* (Pāli) as deliverance of mind, and *paññā vimutti* as deliverance through wisdom, stating that deliverance of mind, in the highest sense, is that kind of concentration (*samādhi*) which is bound up with the path of arhantship; and deliverance through wisdom is the knowledge (*ñāṇa*) bound up with the fruition of arhantship. These two deliverances are often paired, as in, for example, the *Mahāsīhanāda Sutta, Majjhima Nikāya* 12 (i.71), where they are jointly described as the tenth of the ten powers of a Tathāgata:

> Realizing for himself with direct knowledge the Tathāgata here and now enters upon and abides in the deliverance of mind and deliverance by wisdom that are taintless with the destruction of the taints.

See Bhikkhu Ñāṇamoli and Bhikkhu Bodhi (trans.), *The Middle Length Discourses of the Buddha,* Wisdom Publications, Boston 1995, p. 166; or I. B. Horner (trans.), *The Collection of the Middle*

Length Sayings, vol. i, Pali Text Society London 1976, p. 95.

197 For more about the two 'requisites' or 'accumulations', of merit and of wisdom, see p. 463 below.

198 Devadatta was a cousin of the Buddha, and initially one of his closest followers, but he later took against the Buddha and twice tried to kill him. On another occasion Devadatta sent a boulder rolling down a hill towards the Buddha, damaging his foot. These two incidents are described at Vinaya Piṭaka ii.193–5 (*Cullavagga* 7.3); see I. B. Horner (trans.), *The Book of the Discipline*, part 5, Pali Text Society, London 1975, pp. 271–4. See also Bhikkhu Ñāṇamoli, *The Life of the Buddha*, Buddhist Publication Society, Kandy 1984, pp. 261–3.

199 *Aṅguttara Nikāya* v.342. This is one of several *suttas* more commonly called the *Mettā Sutta*.

200 *Dhammapada* 137–40.

201 In other words, if you express negative opinions about the 'Great Vehicle', or Mahāyāna, there are those who will take what you are saying sufficiently seriously not to get involved with it at all. This can have a profound effect on their present and future lives, which is why Nāgārjuna takes those critics of the Mahāyāna so strictly to task.

202 For more about Acharya Vinoba Bhave and his land donation programme see Hallam Tennyson, *India's Walking Saint*, Doubleday, New York 1955.

203 The *Jātaka* stories are a collection of folk tales that describe the heroic acts of the Buddha-to-be in former lives. Some of them depict him in human form, others in the form of an animal or bird. See *The Eternal Legacy*, *Complete Works*, vol. 14, pp. 61ff. The Pāli tradition has preserved a vast collection of *Jātakas* now published in English translation by the Pali Text Society in three volumes, edited by Professor E. B. Cowell (London 1981). The Sanskrit tradition has its own series of *Jātaka* stories, the *Jātakamālas* or '*Garlands of Birth Stories*', the most famous of which is that by the poet Āryaśūra, who lived during the fourth century CE.

204 This teaching is echoed in another of Nāgārjuna's works, the *Mahāprajñāpāramitāśāstra*, in which he refers to the *trimaṇḍalapariśuddha*, the 'great generosity', in which there is no distinction between giver, gift, and recipient. See Étienne Lamotte, *Le traite de la grande vertu de sagesse de Nāgārjuna* (*Mahāprajñāpāramitāśāstra*), Publications de L'Institut Orientaliste de Louvain, Louvain-la-Neuve 1980, vol. 5,

p. 1834. Similarly in section four of the *Diamond Sūtra*:

> Subhūti, those who have set out in the bodhisattva-vehicle should give gifts without being supported by the notion of a sign.

Edward Conze, *Buddhist Wisdom Books*, Harper Torchbooks, New York 1972, p. 27.

205 From the sevenfold puja recited at centres run by the Triratna Buddhist Order. This verse is a rendition of *Bodhicaryāvatāra* 3.20–1.

206 Nan-in was a Japanese master during the Meiji era (1868–1912). The story is told in Paul Reps (ed.), *Zen Flesh, Zen Bones*, Penguin Books, Harmondsworth 1971, p. 17.

207 There is also the formulation of the 'three endurances in the Dharma', a teaching that echoes the three levels of wisdom. These are enumerated in the Chinese Mahāyāna *Infinite Life Sūtra,* of which a reliable English translation is not yet available. The three endurances are: endurance or patience in hearing (receiving the teachings through hearing them); endurance or patience in accord (aligning oneself with the teachings through reflecting upon them); endurance or patience in the realization of the non-arising of *dharmas* (realizing the truth that *dharmas* have neither birth nor death). See the *Sūtra of Contemplating the Buddha of Immeasurable Life as Told by the Buddha*, in Qu Yingguang et al., *Wúliàng Shòu Jīng*, Zhai Ming Temple, Taoyuan 1956, chapter 15. Sangharakshita gives an account of the three levels of wisdom in *What is the Dharma?*, *Complete Works*, vol. 3, pp. 302–3.

208 Cecil Frances Alexander, *Hymns for Little Children*, SPCK, London 1908, p. 24.

209 Romans 31:1.

210 See, for example, the Dalai Lama's teaching on 'Sexual Union and the Spiritual Path' in H. H. the Dalai Lama, *Mind of Clear Light*, Jeffrey Hopkins (ed.), Atria Books, New York 2003, pp. 176–9.

211 The *Therīgāthā*, or the stories of the *therīs* (female elders) is a text of the Pāli canon which tells the inspiring life stories of the Buddha's female disciples. There are various translations; for example, C. A. F. Rhys Davids and K. R. Norman (trans.), *Poems of Early Buddhist Nuns (Therīgāthā),* Pali Text Society, Oxford 1989; or Susan Murcott, *The First Buddhist Women*, Parallax Press, Berkeley 1991.

212 A Stream Entrant is someone who has developed a degree of insight sufficient to attain to the first stage of the transcendental path, thereby breaking the first three of the ten fetters, i.e. fixed self-view, doubt or lack of

commitment, and dependence on mere morality and religious observances as ends in themselves. Traditionally, once one has gained Stream Entry, progress towards the goal of full Enlightenment is irreversible. Among the many references to Stream Entry in the Pāli canon, the *Saṃyutta Nikāya* has a whole section devoted to the subject. See Bhikkhu Bodhi (trans.), *The Connected Discourses of the Buddha*, Wisdom Publications, Boston 2000, pp. 1788–837; or F. L. Woodward (trans.), *The Book of the Kindred Sayings*, part 5, Pali Text Society, London 1979, pp. 296–351. See also notes 21 and 296 in this volume.

213 *Ariyapariyesanā Sutta, Majjhima Nikāya* 26 (i.163); see Bhikkhu Ñāṇamoli and Bhikkhu Bodhi (trans.), *The Middle Length Discourses of the Buddha*, Wisdom Publications, Boston 1995, p. 256; or I. B. Horner (trans.), *The Collection of the Middle Length Sayings*, vol. i, Pali Text Society, London 1976, p. 207.

214 i.e. an ideal beauty that is in a sense more 'real' than worldly experience and gives meaning to it. Plotinus associates such beauty with the highest virtue:

> The Good, which lies beyond, is the Fountain at once and the Principle of Beauty: the Primal Good and the Primal Beauty have the one dwelling-place and, thus, always, Beauty's seat is There.

Plotinus, *First Ennead*, 6.9.

215 For an introduction to Schopenhauer's philosophy, see Michael Tanner, *Schopenhauer*, Routledge, New York 1999, and Bryan Magee, *The Philosophy of Schopenhauer*, Oxford and New York 1997.

216 In Jungian psychology, projection is a process by which one begins to be aware of certain qualities, such as beauty or hatred, that lie unrecognized in oneself. Initially, one is only able to attribute those qualities to an external person or group, being unaware of their presence within. Once those projected qualities are recognized as subjective, however, it becomes possible to get to know them in oneself and integrate them consciously into awareness. Projection is therefore seen as an essential means by which to discover those aspects of one's inner life that have hitherto remained hidden. To quote Jung,

> Projection is one of the commonest psychic phenomena.... Everything that is unconscious in ourselves we discover in our neighbour, and we treat him accordingly.

Carl Jung, *Archaic Man*, quoted in Judith R. Harris, Tony Woolfson (eds.), *The Quotable Jung*, Princeton University Press, Boston 2016, p. 25. For more on projection in sexual relationships, see Robert A. Johnson, *We: Understanding the Psychology of Romantic Love*, Harper & Row, San Francisco 1983.

217 The Ajanta caves, near Aurangabad, date from the second century BCE to about 480 CE. They are particularly noted for their wall paintings, which date from the fifth century CE. The film producer was Raj Kapoor, who had invited Sangharakshita to RK Studios in Bombay to advise him on a film he was planning to make. The film was to be called *Ajanta*, featuring a Buddhist monk (to be played by himself). See *Facing Mount Kanchenjunga*, *Complete Works*, vol. 21, pp. 399–413.

218 Bunnō Katō and W. E. Soothill (trans.), *The Threefold Lotus Sūtra*, Kosei Publishing, Tokyo, 1975, pp. 86–109.

219 The parable of the burning house is considered in more detail in *The Drama of Cosmic Enlightenment*, *Complete Works*, vol. 16, pp. 68–80.

220 For more on dishonesty (*śāṭhya*) as a negative mental event, see pp. 659–63 below.

221

> Fool: Prithee, nuncle, keep a schoolmaster that can teach thy fool to lie: I would fain learn to lie.
> King Lear: An you lie, sirrah, we'll have you whipped.

William Shakespeare, *King Lear*, Act I, Scene iv.

222 *Sāmaññaphala Sutta, Dīgha Nikāya* 2 (i.53–4). See M. Walshe (trans.), *The Long Discourses of the Buddha*, Wisdom Publications, Boston 1995, p. 95.

223 The astrological Age of Aquarius is a putative 2,000-year period of global harmony, scientific progress, and mystic revelation, said to have dawned towards the end of the twentieth century. New Age culture refers to a variety of 'alternative' approaches to traditional Western culture, all of which foreground spirituality, mysticism, holism, and environmentalism.

224 For more on Pure Land Buddhism see *A Survey of Buddhism*, *Complete Works*, vol. 1, pp. 336–48.

225 See *Apaṇṇaka Sutta*, *Majjhima Nikāya* 60 (especially i.403–4).

226 This is the second of the four noble truths, a teaching delivered by the Buddha not long after his Enlightenment.

> Now this, monks, is the noble truth of the cause of pain: the craving, which tends to rebirth, combined with pleasure and lust, finding pleasure here and there, namely the craving for passion, the craving for

existence, the craving for non-existence.

Saccasaṃyutta, *Saṃyutta Nikāya* v.421–2. Edward J. Thomas (trans.), *Early Buddhist Scriptures*, Kegan Paul, Trench, Trubner and Co. Ltd., London 1935, pp. 29–31. See also F. L. Woodward (trans.), *The Book of the Kindred Sayings*, part 5, Pali Text Society, London 1979, pp. 356–7; or Bhikkhu Bodhi (trans.), *The Connected Discourses of the Buddha*, Wisdom Publications, Boston 2000, pp. 1843–4.

227 For a detailed examination of the emptiness of cause and effect, see chapter 1 of Nāgārjuna's *Mūlamadhyamakakārikā*. Garfield offers a helpful commentary in Jay L. Garfield, *The Fundamental Wisdom of the Middle Way*, Oxford University Press, Oxford 1995, pp. 103–123.

228 See pp. 442ff below.

229 T. S. Eliot, *Four Quartets*, East Coker V.

230 The Buddha describes these four kinds of disciple in the *Vitthāra Sutta*, *Aṅguttara Nikāya* ii.149–50 (4.162). See Bhikkhu Bodhi (trans.), *The Numerical Discourses of the Buddha*, Wisdom Publications, Boston 2012, pp. 528–9; or F. L. Woodward (trans.), *The Book of the Gradual Sayings*, vol. ii, Pali Text Society, Oxford 1995, pp. 153–5.

231 See note 100 above.

232 *Lady Windermere's Fan*, Act 3.

233 See note 216.

234 For more on wrong view (*dṛṣṭi*) as a negative mental event, see pp. 617ff. below.

235 Psalms 37:35.

236 For more details, see Sangharakshita, *The Taste of Freedom*, Windhorse Publications, 1997 (*Complete Works*, vol. 11).

237 These are listed by Nāgārjuna in verses 403–33, but scholars disagree over how fifty-seven unskilful mental states can be enumerated. For a discussion see Jeffrey Hopkins, *Buddhist Advice for Living and Liberation*, Snow Lion, New York, 1998, p. 149.

238 Sangharakshita's *Know Your Mind* offers more discussion of anger or *pratigha* (pp. 598–9 below), resentment or *upanāha* (pp. 645–7 below) and belligerence or *krodha* (pp. 643–5 below), all considered as negative mental events.

239 From book 3, 'Of the Origin and Nature of the Affects', in Benedict de Spinoza, *Ethics*, Penguin Books, London, 1996, pp. 68–112.

240 Tennyson, 'Flower in the Crannied Wall', 1869.

241 For more on pride (*māna*) as a negative mental event, see pp. 603–7 below.

242 *Aṅgulimāla Sutta*, *Majjhima Nikāya* 86; the story is reproduced in Bhikkhu Ñāṇamoli's *The Life of the*

Buddha, Buddhist Publication Society, Ceylon 1978, pp. 134ff.

243 This is further indicated in Jeffrey Hopkins' translation of verse 425 (see p. 286 below), where the Sanskrit version of 'attachment to objects' appears as 'attachment to country', suggesting the pride of attachment to self on a larger scale. See Jeffrey Hopkins, *Buddhist Advice for Living and Liberation*, Snow Lion, New York 1998, p. 153, note a.

244 William Blake, *The Marriage of Heaven and Hell.*

245 'Reverence ... is only excitable in man towards ideal truths which are always mysteries to the understanding.' from 'Table Talk' in *The Complete Works of Samuel Taylor Coleridge*, Harper & Brothers, 1853, p. 454.

246 For more on concealment (*mrakṣa*) as a negative mental event, see pp. 647–50 below.

247 For a collection of Zen stories popular at the time, see for example, Paul Reps (comp.), *Zen Flesh, Zen Bones*, Penguin Books, Middlesex 1971.

248 For more on jealousy (*īrṣyā*) as a negative mental event, see pp. 653–6 below.

249 William Shakespeare, *Othello*, Act V, Scene i.

250 *Bodhicaryāvatāra* 6.81. See Kate Crosby and Andrew Skilton (trans.), *Bodhicaryāvatāra*, Windhorse Publications, Birmingham 2002, p. 77.

251 The mandala of the five Buddhas originated in Mahāyāna Buddhism, and became central to the practice of Tibetan Buddhism, in whose art it is frequently depicted. For more about the mandala of the five Buddhas, see chapter 8, 'The Five Buddhas, "Male and "Female"', in Sangharakshita, *Creative Symbols of Tantric Buddhism*, *Complete Works*, vol. 13, pp. 296ff.

252 For more on desire (*rāga*) as a negative mental event, see pp. 596–8 below.

253 *Dhammapada* 121.

254 For more on the Maha Bodhi monks' pragmatic approach to mealtimes, see *Facing Mount Kanchenjunga*, *Complete Works*, vol. 21, pp. 374–5.

255 For more on avarice (*mātsarya*) as a negative mental event, see Sangharakshita, *Know Your Mind* pp. 656–7 below.

256 Molière (1622–1673) was a French playwright at the court of Louis XIV. Tartuffe is a pious fraud who deceives his way into the heart of a wealthy yet gullible family. When first published in 1664, 'Tartuffe or the Impostor' hit its mark so expertly that the play was banned for several years by the church authorities.

257 The five *nivaraṇas* or hindrances. See pp. 118–22 above.

258 These are the core teachings of Buddhism. The four noble truths were expounded

by the Buddha in his first major pronouncement after his Enlightenment, the *Dhammacakkappavattana Sutta* (*Saṃyutta Nikāya* 56.11), and comprise (1) the truth of the existence of suffering, (2) the truth of the cause of suffering, which is egotistical desire and craving, (3) the truth of the cessation of suffering, which is the cessation of egotistical desire, and (4) the truth of the way to the cessation of suffering known as the Noble Eightfold Path. The Three Jewels are the main objects of devotion for Buddhists of all schools: the Buddha, the Dharma, and the Sangha.

259 For more on doubt (*vicikitsā*) as a negative mental event, see pp. 612–17 below.

260 The *Iliad* is an epic poem dating from the eighth century BCE and attributed to Homer. It focuses on a brief period in the conflict between the Bronze Age kingdoms of Troy and Greece known as the Trojan War. Characters include the warrior Achilles, King Agamemnon, and Hector, prince of Troy. Like the *Odyssey*, also attributed to Homer, the *Iliad* provides a powerful exploration of the heroic ideal, serving as the model for subsequent epics in the classical tradition.

261 Both these terms are used to describe the goal of the spiritual life, effecting complete liberation from cyclic existence. The word *nirvāṇa* literally means 'extinguished'. The word *śūnyatā* (Pāli *suññatā*) first occurs in what is probably the oldest section of any Buddhist text, the *Pārāyanavagga*, where the Buddha tells a layman, Mogharāja, to see the world as empty in order to escape Māra, the king of death (*Sutta-Nipāta* 5.15, verse 4). However, it is in the texts of the Mahāyāna schools that the doctrine of *śūnyatā* is fully developed, and it is the principal subject of the *Prajñāpāramitā* (Perfection of Wisdom) *sūtras* and the writings of the Madhyamaka school.

262 For an account of the various Pure Land *sūtras* see *The Eternal Legacy*, *Complete Works*, vol. 14, pp. 168–78. See also Ratnaguna and Śraddhāpa, *Great Faith, Great Wisdom*, Windhorse Publications, Cambridge 2016. For more on the Pure Land doctrine see *A Survey of Buddhism*, *Complete Works*, vol. 1, pp. 336–48.

263 Tennyson, *In Memoriam* lxxxiv.

WRATHFUL DEITIES

264 *Yamarāja*: the Lord of Death and King of Hell.

265 *Rākṣasa*: one of a class of demigods that possesses superhuman strength and can fly, or run like the wind during the hours of darkness. Its staple diet is human flesh.

266 *Vidyārāja*: lit. king of knowledge.

267 *Yakṣas*: a class of nature spirit, often guardians of the earth or trees. They are shape-shifters and possess the power to fly or disappear at will, which powers can be applied for the good or ill of beings.

LIVING WISELY

268 This story occurs in the Pāli canon at Vinaya Piṭaka i.6, and in the *Āyācana Sutta, Saṃyutta Nikāya* i.136 (6.1). A Mahāyāna source gives

> But how could liberation, which is so exquisite and profound, be expressed in words? It may be better not to give out my thoughts [he said to himself], and so he remained silent and at peace.

Aśvaghoṣa, *Buddhacarita*, translated in William Theodore de Bary, *The Buddhist Tradition in India*, China and Japan, New York 1972, p. 70.

269 The phrase 'but little dust on their eyes', is used to describe those whose vision might readily be cleared by the Buddha's teaching. It appears in the incident immediately following the Buddha's Enlightenment, when Brahmā Sahampati appeals to the Buddha to communicate the Dhamma for the benefit of 'beings with little dust on their eyes who are perishing through not hearing Dhamma'. See *Mahāpadāna Sutta, Dīgha Nikāya* 14 (ii.39); M. Walshe (trans.), *The Long Discourses of the Buddha*, Wisdom Publications, Boston 1995, p. 214. See also the *Āyācana Sutta*, *Saṃyutta Nikāya* i.137 (6.1); Bhikkhu Bodhi (trans.), *The Connected Discourses of the Buddha*, Wisdom Publications, Somerville 2000, p. 232; or C. A. F. Rhys Davids (trans.), *The Book of the Kindred Sayings*, part 1, Pali Text Society, London 1979, p. 173.

270 In many Buddhist traditions the *nāgas* are water deities who guard Buddhist scriptures that have been placed in their care until human beings are ready to receive them. See also note 169.

271 Asaṅga was born in the fourth century CE, of a Brahmin family from Peshawar. His half-brother was Vasubandhu. Asaṅga began his Buddhist career as a Sarvāstivādin, later embraced Nāgārjuna's view of emptiness, and eventually became known as the founder of the Yogācāra school. For more about Asaṅga, see Kulananda, *Teachers of Enlightenment,* Windhorse Publications, Birmingham, 2000, pp. 161–5.

272
> We have as the metaphysical background of Mahāyāna Buddhism the all-dominating conception of *śūnyatā*, or Voidness, the state

> wherefrom all conceptions, including that of Voidness itself, have been prescinded.

Sangharakshita, *A Survey of Buddhism*, *Complete Works*, vol. 1, p. 243.

273 Aristotle, *Nicomachean Ethics*, book 8.

274 Nigaṇṭha Nāthaputta's claimed omniscience is often discussed and disputed in the Pāli scriptures. For one of many examples, see the *Cūḷadukkhakkhandha Sutta, Majjhima Nikāya* 14 (i.93); Bhikkhu Ñāṇamoli and Bhikkhu Bodhi (trans.), *The Middle Length Discourses of the Buddha*, Wisdom Publications, Boston 1995, pp.187–8; or I. B. Horner (trans.), *The Collection of the Middle Length Sayings*, vol. i, Pali Text Society, London, Henley & Boston 1976, pp. 122–3.

275 See the Buddha's 'song of victory' in the *Dhammapada*:

> House-builder, (now) you are seen! Never again shall you build (me) a house. Your rafters are all broken, your ridgepole shattered. The (conditioned) mind too has gone to destruction: one has attained to the cessation of craving.

Dhammapada 154, trans. Sangharakshita (*Complete Works*, vol. 15).

276 According to some Mahāyāna Buddhists, including the Gelugpas, Buddhas in their *dharmakāya* aspect are indeed omniscient in the literal sense, being said to directly cognize all phenomena all the time. See, for example, J. Hopkins, *Meditation on Emptiness*, Wisdom Publications, London 1983, pp. 188ff., and Paul Williams, *Mahāyāna Buddhism*, Routledge, London and New York 1989, p. 180.

277 More information on ancient Indian Buddhist cosmology can be found in Randolph Kloetzli, *Buddhist Cosmology*, Motilal Banarsidass, Delhi 1983; see also Sangharakshita, *Creative Symbols of Tantric Buddhism*, *Complete Works*, vol. 13, pp. 261–2.

278 For an exploration of writing since the nineteenth century that alleges the compatibility of Buddhism and science, see Donald S. Lopez Jr, *Buddhism and Science*, University of Chicago Press, Chicago 2010. Lopez argues that by presenting Buddhism as having anticipated scientific discoveries, such writers from the nineteenth century onwards have ignored more basic debates on the role of religion in the modern world.

279 See for example, ibid., p. 3.

280 'East and West' is to be found in 'Lectures on Zen Buddhism', by Erich Fromm, D. T. Suzuki, and Richard de Martino, *Zen Buddhism and Psychoanalysis*, Harper & Row, New York 1960, pp. 1–5.

281 Tennyson, 'Flower in the Crannied Wall', 1869.

282 For more on the doctrine-follower and the faith-follower, see p. 35 above and note 39.

283 The five spiritual faculties (*pañca-indriya*) are faith (*śraddhā*, Pāli *saddhā*), vigour (*vīrya*, Pāli *viriya*), mindfulness (*smṛti*, Pāli *sati*), concentration (*samādhi*), and wisdom (*prajñā*, Pāli *paññā*). Sangharakshita explores these in detail in *The Way to Wisdom* in this volume, pp. 3ff.

284 Gerbert W. Guenther, for example, translates faith as 'confidence trust'. See H. W. Guenther, *Mind in Buddhist Psychology*, Dharma Publishing, Berkeley 1975, p. 38.

285 In the Abhidharma, faith (*śraddhā*) is the first of the eleven positive mental events. For more about faith as a mental event, see pp. 552ff below.

286 The four *brahma vihāras* or 'sublime abodes' are four meditation practices through which one cultivates four positive emotions: loving-kindness (*maitrī*), compassion (*karuṇā*), sympathetic joy (*muditā*), and equanimity (*upekṣā*). For more on the *brahma vihāras* see, for example, Kamalashila, *Buddhist Meditation*, Windhorse Publications, Cambridge 2012, and Sangharakshita's own teachings on meditation, *The Purpose and Practice of Buddhist Meditation*, in *Complete Works*, vol. 5.

287 John Middleton Murry, *Things to Come*, Ayer Publishing, 1928, p. 34.

288 For example, 'worship the Lord in the beauty of holiness.' (1 Chronicles 16:29) and the more equivocal 'O worship the Lord in the beauty of holiness: fear before him, all the earth.' (Psalm 96:9).

289 This is in the first chapter of the *Śūraṅgama Sūtra*:

> Then the Buddha spoke to Ānanda saying: 'You and I are from the same ancestral blood and we have always cherished a fraternal affection for each other. Let me ask you a few questions and you answer me spontaneously and freely. When you first began to be interested in Buddhism what was it that impressed you in our Buddhist way of life and most influenced you to forsake all worldly pleasures and enabled you to cut asunder your youthful sexual cravings?' Ānanda replied, 'Oh my Lord! The first thing that impressed me were the thirty-two marks of excellency in my Lord's personality. They appeared to me so fine, as tender and brilliant, and transparent as a crystal.'

Dwight Goddard (ed.), *A Buddhist Bible*, Beacon Press, Boston 1970, pp. 111–12.

290 The *Mahāvastu Avadāna* ... describes itself as a work of the Vinaya Piṭaka of the Lokottaravādins, a branch of the Mahāsāṅghikas.... The *Mahāvastu* is probably the sole surviving example of a primitive biography that has been made to incorporate ... legends in the form of *Jātakas* and *Avadānas*.

Sangharakshita, *The Eternal Legacy*, *Complete Works*, vol. 14, pp. 69–70. For an account of Sangharakshita's Wesak experience, see *Moving Against the Stream*, *Complete Works*, vol. 23, pp. 121–2.

291 This is the story of the encounter between Milarepa and Dharma Wonshu (later Repa Shiwa Aui or the Cotton Clad Light of Peace); see Garma C. C. Chang (trans.), *The Hundred Thousand Songs of Milarepa*, vol. 1, Shambhala Publications, Boston 1999, p. 179.

292 Nāropā (1016–1100), the *mahāsiddha* and transmitter of Mahāmudrā teachings, was the teacher of Marpa, who was in turn the teacher of Milarepa. His dream yoga

> can lead one to purify the habitual thoughts of Saṃsāra, to realize that all things are manifestations of the mind, and that mind is devoid of self-entity like dreams.

Garma C. C. Chang, *The Six Yogas of Nāropa*, Snow Lion, New York 1977, p. 94.

293 Advaita Vedānta teaches that all experience takes place in one of the following three states: waking (*jāgrat*), dreaming (*svapna*) and dreamless sleep (*suṣupti*). Regarding the latter, it is said that

> In this state a father is no father, a mother no mother, the worlds no worlds, the gods no gods, the Vedas no Vedas.... One is then beyond all the woes of the heart (mind).

Brihadāraṇyaka Upaniṣad 4.3.22.

294 This story is told in the *Meghiya Sutta* of the Pāli canon (*Udāna* 4.1). The Buddha's attendant Meghiya wants to meditate in a mango grove which seems to him especially suitable for meditation. The Buddha asks him to wait a 'until some other *bhikkhu* comes', but Meghiya is insistent, and the Buddha eventually says, 'Do what you think it is time for.' Meghiya duly goes to meditate in the 'pleasing and charming' mango grove, but to his dismay he is unable to concentrate. On his return, he tells the Buddha what happened, and the Buddha advises him that 'when

the heart's release is immature, five things conduce to its maturity' – the five things being spiritual friendship, ethics, steadfastness, Dharma-talk, and awareness of the arising and passing away of things.

295 The *mettā bhāvanā* is a traditional Buddhist meditation practice which involves the cultivation of feelings of *mettā* or loving-kindness towards all living beings. See Sangharakshita, *The Purpose and Practice of Buddhist Meditation*, in *Complete Works*, vol. 5.

296 Stream Entry (*srotāpanna*, Pāli *sotāpanna*).

> The Stream Entrant has developed insight sufficiently powerful to break, completely and finally, the three fetters of wrong belief concerning the nature of individuality (*satkāya-dṛṣṭi*, Pāli *sakkāya-diṭṭhi*); 'sceptical doubt' (*vicikitsā*, Pāli *vicikicchā*) in the sense of wilfully incomplete, or hesitant, acceptance of the Doctrine; and dependence upon mere morality and external ascetic observances (*śīlavrata-parāmarśa*, Pāli *sīlabbata-parāmāsa*) as though they were by themselves a sufficient means to Enlightenment. Such a disciple is exempt from rebirth in any of the lower worlds, and has not more than seven lives to pass through, all on the human and divine planes, before attaining the total emancipation of mind which is Nirvaṇa. His characteristics are unshakeable faith in the Buddha, the Dharma, and the Sangha, and absolutely unblemished morality.

Sangharakshita, *A Survey of Buddhism*, *Complete Works*, vol. 1, p. 177. See also note 212 in this volume.

297 Ānanda was one of the foremost disciples of the historical Buddha. He was the Buddha's cousin and entered the Buddhist order two years after its founding, later becoming the Buddha's personal attendant. Ānanda was renowned for his powers of memory, by virtue of which he was able to retain the Buddha's discourses, and was integral to the oral tradition by means of which the Buddha's teachings were preserved for several centuries. He is said to have attained arhantship only after the death of the Buddha. For more about Ānanda, see Kulananda, *Teachers of Enlightenment*, Windhorse Publications, Birmingham 2000, pp. 104–9.

298 The expression used everywhere in Buddhist texts referring to persons who realized Truth is 'The dustless and stainless Eye of

Truth (*dhamma-cakkhu*) has arisen.'

Walpola Rahula, *What the Buddha Taught*, Gordon Fraser, London 1967, p. 9.

299 The term *sthavira*, literally meaning 'elder', is also the name of one of the two earliest Buddhist schools, the other being the Mahāsāṃghika.

300 Only four views regarding the relation between cause and effect are possible [according to Nāgārjuna in the *Kārikās*]: that cause and effect are identical; that they are different; that they are both identical and different; that they are neither identical nor different. The first view ... was held at the time of Nāgārjuna by the Sāṃkhya school; some centuries later Śaṃkara incorporated it into his non-dualist Vedānta.

Sangharakshita, *A Survey of Buddhism*, *Complete Works*, vol. 1, p. 314.

301 For more on the significance of non-violence (*avihiṃsā*) considered as a positive mental event, see pp 582–7 below.

302 Quoted by C. C. Martindale in Martin D'Arcy (ed.), *Saint Augustine*, Meridian Books, New York 1957, p. 89.

303 This story also appears in Sangharakshita, *The Drama of Cosmic Enlightenment*, *Complete Works*, vol. 16, pp. 201–2.

304 A party of travellers is bound for a place called Ratnadvīpa (Place of Jewels), and has employed a guide to show them the way through the dense forest. It is a very difficult, dangerous road, and long before they have reached their destination the travellers become exhausted, and say to their guide, 'We can't go on another step. Let's all go back.' But the guide thinks 'That would be a pity. They've come so far already. What can I do to persuade them to keep going?' Well, apparently the guide has some sort of magic power, because what he does is conjure up a magic city. He says to the travellers, 'Look! There's a city right here in front of us. Let's rest there and have something to eat, and then we'll decide what to do next.' The travellers, of course, are only too pleased to stop and have a rest. They have a meal and spend the night in the magic city, and in the morning they feel much better, and decide that they will carry on with their journey after all. So the guide makes the magic city disappear and leads the travellers to their destination, the Place of Jewels.

The meaning of the parable is not hard to fathom in the context of the *sūtra*. The guide is of course the Buddha, the travellers are the disciples. The Place of Jewels is Supreme Enlightenment, and the magic city is the Hīnayāna Nirvāṇa – Nirvāṇa as the comparatively negative state of freedom from passions, without positive spiritual illumination. And, as the parable suggests, the Buddha first of all speaks of Nirvāṇa in the ordinary psychological sense. Only when this teaching has been assimilated – only when his disciples have rested in the magic city – does he lead them on to the higher spiritual goal of perfect Buddhahood, the Place of Jewels.

Ibid. pp. 42–3.

305 One of the few canonical references to the twelve positive *nidānas* is found in the *Saṃyutta Nikāya* ii.30–1, trans. C. A. F. Rhys Davids, *The Book of the Kindred Sayings*, part 2, Pali Text Society, Oxford 1997, p. 27 ; or Bhikkhu Bodhi (trans.), *The Connected Discourses of the Buddha*, Wisdom Publications, Boston 2000, pp. 554–5. See also Sangharakshita *A Survey of Buddhism*, *Complete Works*, vol. 1, p. 115. For more on the spiral path generally see *What is the Dharma?*, *Complete Works*, vol. 3, pp. 258–79.

306 Why do those cliffs of
 shadowy tint appear
More sweet than all the
 landscape smiling near? –
'Tis distance lends
 enchantment to the view,
And robes the mountain in
 its azure hue.

From 'The Pleasures of Hope' by Thomas Campbell in Lewis Campbell (ed), *Poems Of Thomas Campbell*, Macmillan, London, 1904, p. 58.

307 *Śūnyavāda* literally means the way (*vāda*) of emptiness (*śūnya*).

This conditionality or unreality of all phenomena the Mahāyānists indicate by the term *śūnyatā* or Emptiness. Doctrines such as the four truths and conditioned co-production, since they refer to unrealities, are themselves unreal in the ultimate sense, and whatever truth they possess is not absolute but only conventional. *Śūnyatā* or *tathatā* alone is the absolute truth.

Sangharakshita, *A Survey of Buddhism*, *Complete Works*, vol. 1, p. 265.

308 Lokāyata, literally 'belonging to the world of sense', is the broad name for the materialist doctrinal schools that flourished in India from the time of the Buddha until the twelfth century CE. From then on, all Lokāyata

records appear to have been lost, leaving only a handful of aphorisms and extracts from the commentaries. Sharma quotes the *Prabodha Chandrodaya*, a Sanskrit philosophical drama by Krishnapati Mishra from the eleventh or twelfth century CE:

> Lokāyata is the only Shāstra; perception is the only authority; earth, water, fire, and air are the only elements; enjoyment is the only end of human existence; mind is only a product of matter.

Chandradhar Sharma, *A Critical Survey of Indian Philosophy*, Motilal Banarsidass, Delhi, 2016, p. 41.

309 The Vaiśeṣika school is a non-Buddhist school founded by Kaṇāda (meaning 'atom eater') in around the second century CE. His cosmological system, set out in the *Vaiśeṣika Sūtra*, is one of the six classic systems of philosophy making up the orthodox tradition of Indian thought.

310 Mahāvīra, the founder of Jainism, was the twenty-fourth and last Jaina *tīrthaṅkara* ('maker of the river crossing') and a contemporary of the Buddha.

311 These are in fact the final words of Schopenhauer's *World as Will and Idea* (book 4).

312 Nāgārjuna's refutation of *nirvāṇa* occupies chapter 25 of the *Mūlamadhyamakakārikā*. Garfield offers a helpful commentary in Jay L. Garfield, *The Fundamental Wisdom of the Middle Way*, Oxford University Press, Oxford 1995, pp. 322–34.

313 As a washerman uses dirt
To wash clean a garment,
So, with impurity,
The wise man makes himself pure.

From a late seventh-century Indian Tantric text 'Disquisition on the Purification of the Intellect' (*Cittaviśuddhiprakaraṇa*) by Āryadeva, translated in William Theodore de Bary, *The Buddhist Tradition in India, China and Japan*, New York, 1972, p. 120.

314 The *kṣaṇikavāda* doctrine is mentioned in chapter 1.1 of Hemacandra's eleventh-century Jain text the *Triṣaṣṭiśalākāpuruṣacaritra*, a Sanskrit epic poem narrating the history and legends of sixty-three important persons in Jainism. Nāgārjuna's refutation of time is presented in greater detail in chapter 19 of the *Mūlamadhyamakakārikā*. He approaches the same idea in a slightly different way by refuting motion in chapter 2. Garfield offers a helpful commentary on both chapters in Jay L. Garfield,

The Fundamental Wisdom of the Middle Way, Oxford University Press, Oxford 1995, pp. 254–7 (on 'time') and pp. 124–35 (on 'motion').

315 The Abhidharma is the third of the three baskets (*tripiṭaka*) or collections of the Buddha's words. Abhidharma means 'about Dharma', though traditionally the term was often interpreted as 'higher Dharma' in the sense of a philosophically more exact exposition of the teaching. For a full discussion of *dharma* theory in the Abhidharma, see Sangharakshita, *A Survey of Buddhism*, *Complete Works*, vol. 1 pp. 97ff.

316 See note 312.

317 In other words the adjective 'baseless' is used here not in the pejorative sense of a teaching that is unreliable or untrue, but as what Conze calls 'not supported' in his translation of the *Diamond Sūtra*:

> Subhūti, a Bodhisattva who gives a gift should not be supported by a thing, nor should he be supported anywhere. When he gives gifts he should not be supported by sight-objects, nor by sounds, smells, tastes, touchables, or mind-objects. For, Subhūti, the Bodhisattva, the great being, should give gifts in such a way that he is not supported by the notion of a sign.

Edward Conze, *Buddhist Wisdom Books*, Harper Torchbooks, New York 1972, p. 27.

318 See note 317 above.

319 Śāntideva (c.685–763 CE) is the author of the *Śikṣā-samuccaya* and the *Bodhicaryāvatāra*. The arguments against anger occur in chapter 6 of the *Bodhicaryāvatāra*, the chapter on the perfection of forbearance. See Śāntideva, *Bodhicaryāvatāra*, trans. K. Crosby and A. Skilton, Windhorse Publications, Birmingham 2002.

320 The Zen teaching of great doubt is commonly attributed to Boshan (1575–1630) (Pinyin Bóshān), one of the leading Chinese masters of the Ming dynasty, also known as Wuyi Yuanlai (Pinyin Wúyì Yuánlái) or Dayi (Pinyin Dàyǐ). See Boshan, *Great Doubt*, trans. Jeff Shore, Wisdom Publications, Somerville, 2016. See also Walt Whitman, 'On the Terrible Doubt of Appearances', in book 5, 'Calamus', of *Leaves of Grass*.

321
> The victorious ones have said
> That emptiness is the relinquishing of all views.
> For whomever emptiness is a view
> That one has accomplished nothing.

Nāgārjuna, *Mūlamadhyamakakārikā* 27.8.

Quoted in Jay L. Garfield, *The Fundamental Wisdom of the Middle Way*, Oxford University Press, Oxford 1995, p. 354.

322 Although Sangharakshita refers to fourteen 'inexpressibles', in the Pāli canon, the 'inexpressibles' are always presented as a common list of ten. They appear in the *Cūḷamāluṅkya Sutta, Majjhima Nikāya* 63, for example, in the form of ten questions regarding whether (1) the universe is eternal, (2) the universe is not eternal, (3) the universe is finite, (4) the universe is infinite, (5) the soul and the body are identical, (6) the soul and the body are different, (7) a *tathāgata* exists after death, (8) a *tathāgata* does not exist after death, (9) a *tathāgata* both exists and does not exist after death, (10) a *tathāgata* neither exists nor does not exist after death. Nonetheless, a list of fourteen *avyākṛta* does indeed appear in the later Buddhist Sanskrit literature. A helpful discussion of the Buddha's noble silence, with particular regard to Nāgārjuna's doctrine of the Middle Way, is to be found in 'The Silence of the Buddha and its Madhyamic Interpretation' in Gadjin M. Nagao, *Mādhyamika and Yogācāra*, SUNY, New York 1991, pp. 35–50. See also p. 621 below.

323 The refutation of becoming and destruction occupies chapter 21 of Nāgārjuna's *Mūlamadhyamakakārikā*. See Garfield's commentary in Jay L. Garfield, *The Fundamental Wisdom of the Middle Way*, Oxford University Press, Oxford, 1995, pp. 267–74.

324 See Sangharakshita's commentary on p. 219 above.

325 For the appearance of Brahmā Sahampati, see note 269 above.

For the difficulty of grasping the truth of conditionality, see also the *Mahānidāna Sutta, Dīgha Nikāya* 15:

> [Ānanda:] How deep is this causal law, and how deep it seems! And yet do I regard it as quite plain to understand! [The Buddha:] Say not so, Ānanda! Say not so! Deep indeed is this causal law, and deep it appears to be. It is by not knowing, by not understanding, by not penetrating this doctrine, that this world of men has become entangled like a ball of twine, become covered with mildew, become like munja grass and rushes, and unable to pass beyond the doom of the Waste, the Way of Woe, the Fall, and the Ceaseless Round (of rebirth).

326 See note 307.

327 Sangharakshita has more to say on this particular form of literal-mindedness on p. 92 above. In the *Eternal Legacy*,

Sangharakshita refers to *The Lion's Roar of Queen Śrīmālā*, a *sūtra* in which the bodhisattva Queen Śrīmālā

> expounds the theory of the *tathāgatagarbha* or 'matrix' or 'embryo' of the Tathāgata, according to which there exists in sentient beings an intrinsically pure element capable of developing into Buddahood – a theory that may be seen as a reification of the principle of potentiality.

The Eternal Legacy, *Complete Works*, vol. 14, p. 175. The *sūtra* itself is available as Alex Wayman and Hideko Wayman (trans.), *The Lion's Roar of Queen Śrīmālā*, Columbia University Press, New York and London 1974. For a Tibetan Buddhist view of the *tathāgatagarbha* doctrine see S. K. Hookham, *The Buddha Within*, State University of New York Press, New York 1991, pp. 94ff.

328 The distinction between 'self-power' (*jiriki*) and 'other-power' (*tariki*) is attributed to the Japanese master Hōnen. See Andrew Skilton, *A Concise History of Buddhism*, Windhorse Publications, Birmingham 1997, p. 180.

329 Sydney Smith is quoted in Richard Brinsley Sheridan (ed), *Bon-mots of Sydney Smith and R. Brinsley Sheridan*, J. M. Dent, London 1893, p. 94.

330 *À Rebours*, published in English as J. K. Huysmans, *Against Nature*, Penguin Books, Harmondsworth 2003.

331 From *Time Regained* in Marcel Proust, *Remembrance of Things Past*, vol. iii, Penguin, Harmondsworth 1986, p. 1060. Proust (1871–1922) was a French novelist whose seven-volume masterpiece *À la Recherche du Temps Perdu* is widely regarded as a milestone in twentieth-century literature. Throughout this formidable work, time and consciousness are evoked as mutability and flow, transcended and made meaningful by the power of the creative mind.

332 See also Sangharakshita, *Living with Awareness* (*Complete Works*, vol. 15) chapter 13 'Sensing' for more information.

333 John Stuart Mill, *Examination of Sir William Hamilton's Philosophy*, vol. i, chapter 11.

334 Nāgārjuna's critique of the elements seen as discrete entities is set out in chapter 5 of the *Mūlamadhyamakakārikā*. See Jay L. Garfield, *The Fundamental Wisdom of the Middle Way*, Oxford University Press, Oxford 1995, pp. 149–52.

335 Chapter 3 of the *Mūlamadhyamakakārikā* is a detailed treatment of the senses and sense organs. See Garfield's commentary, ibid., pp. 136–41.

336 Chapter 10 of the *Mūlamadhyamakakārikā* is Nāgārjuna's more detailed analysis of the relations between fuel and fire. See Garfield's commentary, ibid., pp. 189–95.

337 Nāgārjuna deals more systematically with 'desire and the one who desires' in chapter 14 of the *Mūlamadhyamakakārikā*, ibid., pp. 216–19.

338 Sangharakshita's *Know Your Mind*, included in this volume (pp. 429ff), is entirely devoted to the topic of mind and mental events.

339 To paraphrase Sangharakshita's argument: Suppose we compare awareness to a light, such as a torch or a headlight. The illumination of that light is self evident. You do not need a second light in order to see it shining. In the same way, when an object is perceived, you do not need a 'second mind' in order to be aware of perception taking place. Awareness, too, is self-evident, and this is why awareness is sometimes said to be 'self-luminous'.

340 The bodhisattva, 'hovers benignly between being and nonbeing upon a plateau of pure thought'. Marion L. Matics, *Entering the Path to Enlightenment*, Macmillan, London 1970, p. 32.

341 The *bhūmis* are the ten stages or 'grounds' progressively attained by the bodhisattva. According to the *Daśabhūmika Sūtra*, the first *bhūmi* marks the beginning of the path of vision (*darśanamārga*) and the following nine stages comprise the path of transformation (*bhāvanāmargā*). In the eighth *bhūmi*, the immovable (*acalā*), the bodhisattva is said to dwell imperturbably in the truth. In the second *bhūmi*, the immaculate (*vimalā*), the bodhisattva is freed from all unskilful moral actions of body, speech, and mind. For more about the ten *bhūmis* in general, see *A Survey of Buddhism*, *Complete Works*, vol. 1, pp. 450–4. For a discussion of the eighth *bhūmi* in particular, see ibid., pp. 258–9. The classic Mahāyāna source for the Buddha's teaching on the *bhūmis* is the *Daśabhūmika Sūtra*, which appears as chapter 26 of Thomas Cleary (trans.), *The Flower Ornament Scripture (Avataṃsaka Sūtra)*, Shambhala Publications, Boston 1993, pp. 695–811.

THE THREE CHIEF PATHS

342 Geshe Wangyal, *Door of Liberation*, Wisdom Publications, Boston 1995, pp. 135–72.

343 An appellation meaning 'inhabitant of Tsongkha'. To translate it as 'Man from the Onion Country' as some do, is rather arbitrary, since the

meaning of *bTsong* (also in the sense of 'onion' spelled Tsong, as here) in this context is really too obscure for definitive rendition. Moreover, the 'translation' referred to leads to confusion with the 'Ts'ung-ling' or 'Onion Mountains' in Chinese Turkestan. Tsongkhapa's personal name is *Blo-bzan grags-pa* (Lobsang Trakpa) and he is at least equally well known thereby to Tibetans; *rJe rin-po-che* (Je Rimpoche) is a title of honour often used to refer to him. (S)

344 Not to be confused with the concise (three leaves) treatise 'Lam-rim chung-ngu' in volume 2. (S)

345 Lobsang Phuntsok Lhalungpa, 'Buddhism in Tibet' in Kenneth W. Morgan (ed.), *The Path of the Buddha*, Ronald Press, New York 1956, p. 250. (S)

346 The commentary by Phabongkhapa Rimpoche to which Sangharakshita refers is included in Tsongkhapa, *Principal Teachings of Buddhism*, Geshe Lobsang Tharchin and Michael Roach (trans.), Mahayana Sutra and Tantra Press, Howell, 1988. In addition, readers are directed to Geshe Wangyal, *Door of Liberation*, Wisdom Publications, Boston, 1995, pp. 135–7, which presents Tsongkhapa's text followed by a commentary by the Fourth Panchen Lama. Another translation can be found in Robert Thurman, *Life and Teachings of Tsong Khapa*, Library of Tibetan Works & Archives, Dharamsala 1982, pp. 57–8. Finally, an oral teaching by Geshe Sonam Rinchen is available in Ruth Sonam (trans.), *Three Principal Aspects of the Path*, Snow Lion Publications, Ithaca 1999, where Tsongkhapa's text is interspersed with Geshe Sonam Rinchen's commentary.

347 Lit. 'chief (best, most important) of [all the] paths'. Jetsun (*rje-btsun*) is a title applied to (e.g.) Milarepa, Tārā, etc. (S)

348 As opposed to exegesis. (S)

349 Lit. 'teachings of the *Jina*' i.e. the victorious one. (S)

350 Lit. '*Jina*-sons', i.e. bodhisattvas. (S)

351 Those of the civilized human condition. (S)

352 Lit. *Jina*-. (S)

353 Or relinquishment. Sanskrit *nirveda* (Pāli *nibbida*) = disgust with and repudiation of the world. (S)

354 The eight opportunities (*kṣaṇa*) are: not to be born in hell, as a *preta*, a beast, a long-lived god, a heathen, one of false views, in a universe where no Buddha appears, or as an idiot. The ten advantages (*sampad*) are: that a Buddha has arisen, preached the Dharma, the Doctrine survives, one has entered it, and been taken up by a spiritual teacher (five opportunities depending on others); to be a human being, of whole faculties, in a

'central' country (one where Buddhism is heard of), with a livelihood that is not wrongful, and with faith in the Doctrine (five opportunities acquired from oneself). (S)

355 Tibetan readers would be familiar with the four rivers that have their sources on Kailash, the sacred mountain. These are the four major rivers of Asia, namely the Brahmaputra, the Sutlej, the Indus, and the Karnali, which flows into the Ganges. Sangharakshita clarifies in his original endnote in the *Middle Way*, however, that the four rivers are 'here a metaphor for desire, existence, ignorance, and opinion (*dṛṣṭi*)'.

356 Lit. 'in the hollows of'. (S)

357 Lit. 'holding [to be] I [or mine]', the term also covers 'holding to be *itself*'. (S)

358 *Duḥkha*. (S) In the Tibetan tradition, suffering is said to be of three kinds: the suffering of suffering (painful feeling), the suffering of change (in that there is nothing to hold onto), and the all-pervasive suffering of conditioned existence (i.e. the *skandhas*).

359 In countless former existences; in other words, all conscious beings. (S)

> Like most Buddhists, the Tibetans believe in rebirth, and they take this to its logical conclusion.... They believe that we have each lived on this Earth thousands or even millions of times, and that therefore, if we look far enough back, it is practically certain that everybody we meet has at some time, ten or a hundred or a thousand lifetimes ago, been our mother or our father. It's as though we have not just one set of parents, but millions of them.

Tibetan Buddhism, *Complete Works*, vol. 13, p. 80.

360 Though the Tibetan *locāvas* translate *samutpāda* simply as *byung-ba*, 'origination', we have followed Dr E. Conze in rendering it, as if directly from the Sanskrit, by 'co-production'. (S)

361 *Prajñā*. (S)

362 *rten'brel*, lit. *pratītya*[-*samutpāda*] – apparently used in a special sense here. For a more detailed explanation of conditioned co-production see Sangharakshita, *A Survey of Buddhism*, *Complete Works*, vol. 1, pp. 105ff. (S)

363 Lit. '[of] the Round and Nirvāṇa'. (S)

364 Of which nothing can in the ultimate sense be affirmed or denied. (S)

365 Lit. *muni*. (S)

366 Lit. 'object-grasping modes'. (S)

KNOW YOUR MIND

367 Herbert V. Guenther and Leslie S. Kawamura (trans.), *Mind in Buddhist Psychology*, Dharma Publishing, Berkeley 1975,

p. xvi. That the translation is the work of both scholars should be understood whenever Guenther's name is mentioned.

368 The term is *maggam bhavati*. Nyanatiloka notes that many Pāli *suttas* offer similar descriptions of what he calls 'the gradual course of development in the progress of the disciple'. For more on this see Nyanatiloka, *Buddhist Dictionary*, Buddhist Publication Society, Kandy 1988, p. 169, 'The Progress of the Disciple'.

369 *Dhammapada* 183.

370 See Herbert V. Guenther and Leslie S. Kawamura (trans.), *Mind in Buddhist Psychology*, Dharma Publishing, Berkeley 1975, p. xxiv.

371 Although there are some very ancient Sāṃkhya *sūtras* (*sūtra* here meaning 'aphorism', not 'discourse', as it usually does in the Buddhist context) the teaching was probably not fully systematized until a long time after the Buddha, in a work called the *Sāṃkhyakārikā*, which is attributed to Īśvara Kṛṣṇa. (S) For the *Sāṃkhyakārikā*, see John Davies (trans.), *The Sankhya Karika of Iswara Krishna*: *An Exposition of the System of Kapila*, Susil Gupta (India) Ltd., Calcutta 1957.

372 See Bhikkhu Ñāṇamoli (trans.), *The Path of Purification*, Buddhist Publication Society, Kandy 1991, or Buddhaghosa, *The Path of Purity*, trans. Pe Maung Tin, Pali Text Society, London 1975.

373 Inevitably, the banished elements eventually reasserted themselves in what came to be called Mahāyāna Buddhism and Vajrayāna or Tantric Buddhism. (S)

374 For the historical background to the emergence of the Theravāda and the Sarvāstivāda, see Andrew Skilton, *A Concise History of Buddhism*, Windhorse Publications, Birmingham 1997, chapter 8.

375 The seven books of the Theravādin Abhidhamma are available in translation from the Pali Text Society. The books of the Sarvāstivādin Abhidharma are less accessible. The original Sanskrit texts are no longer extant, and while Chinese versions do exist, they have not yet been translated into any European language. The most accessible and most famous source for the Sarvāstivādin Abhidharma is the *Abhidharmakośa(bhāṣya)*, which has been translated in full into French and English. See Vasubandhu, *Abhidharmakośabhāṣyam*, trans. L. de La Vallée Poussin, Asian Humanities Press, Berkeley 1988, and Vasubandhu, *Abhidharmakośabhāṣya*, trans. L. de la Valleé Poussin, translated into English

by L. M. Pruden, Asian Humanities Press, Berkeley 1991.

376 This claim was vigorously contested by other early Buddhist schools, notably the Sautrāntikas. (S)

377 The Buddha first taught the five *skandhas* very soon after his Enlightenment, as part of his teaching to his first five disciples. See Vinaya Piṭaka i.13 in I. B. Horner (trans.), *The Book of the Discipline*, part 4, Pali Text Society, Oxford 1996, pp. 20–1; or Bhikkhu Ñāṇamoli, *The Life of the Buddha*, Buddhist Publication Society, Kandy 1978, pp. 45–7.

378 H. V. Guenther, *Philosophy and Psychology in the Abhidhamma*, Shambhala Publications, Berkeley and London 1976, p. 146.

379 This distinction is made clearly in the *Nyāyānusāra* of Saṃghabhadra, which is extant only in Chinese. For a partial English translation and analysis see C. Cox, *Disputed Dharmas: Early Buddhist Theories of Existence*, International Institute for Buddhist Studies, Tokyo 1995. For a discussion of the *prajñaptisat–dravyasat* distinction in Abhidharma texts, see Paul Williams, *Journal of Indian Philosophy* 9, 1981, pp. 227–57.

380 Vinaya Piṭaka ii.201 (*Cullavagga* 7.4.5) as translated in Bhikkhu Ñāṇamoli, *The Life of the Buddha*, Buddhist Publication Society, Kandy 1978, p. 271.

381 Asaṅga's *Abhidharmasamuccaya* is available in an English translation by Sara Boin-Webb (Asian Humanities Press, 2001).

382 See Vasubandhu, *Abhidharmakośabhāṣyam*, English translation by Leo M. Pruden of the French translation by Louis de la Vallee Poussin, Asian Humanities Press, Berkeley 1988–1990, four volumes.

383 See Plato's *Parmenides.* For the 'negative dialectic' of Parmenides and the 'positive dialectic' of Plato see *Proclus' Commentary on Plato's Parmenides*, trans. Glenn R. Morrow and John M. Dillon, Princeton University Press, 1987, pp. 40–7.

384 Published as Herbert V. Guenther and Leslie S. Kawamura (trans.), *Mind in Buddhist Psychology*, Dharma Publishing, Berkeley 1975.

385 Dharmapāla's commentary is known as the *Vijñaptimātratāsiddhi Śāstra*, or 'Treatise on the Establishment of the Doctrine of Consciousness-Only', and is based on Vasubandhu's ground-breaking Yogācāra work, the *Triṃśikā-vijñaptimātratā* ('Thirty Verses on Consciousness-only'). Xuanzang translated Dharmapāla's commentary

from the Sanskrit during the early Tang dynasty (around 600–650 CE). Xuanzang's disciple Wŏngch'ŭk, an expatriate from Korea, wrote a commentary on the *Saṃdhinirmocana Sūtra* which made its way to Tibet and may have influenced the work of Tsongkhapa. Xuanzang's *Cheng Weishi Lun* was also transmitted to Korea and thence to Japan. See Xuanzang, *Cheng Weishi Lun* (Pinyin *Chéng Wéishì Lùn*) published as Xuanzang, *Cheng Weishi Lun: Doctrine of Mere-Consciousness*, trans. Wei Tat, Cheng Weishi Lun Publication Committee, Hong Kong 1973.

386 The path of five stages, to which Guenther devotes the greater part of his introduction to *Mind in Buddhist Psychology*, is outlined in Vasubandhu's *Abhidharmakośa*. See also Edward Conze, *Buddhist Thought in India*, Ann Arbor Paperbacks, Michigan 1967, pp. 175–7.

387 The three *yānas* (vehicles) are the three historical phases of the development of Buddhism: the Hīnayāna (more neutrally referred to as early Buddhism), the Mahāyāna, and the Vajrayāna. In Tibetan Buddhism the three *yānas* came to be seen as constituting successive stages of the path. For more about this, see *Tibetan Buddhism*, *Complete Works*, vol. 13, p. 12 .

388 For more on the four right efforts, see *The Buddha's Noble Eightfold Path*, *Complete Works*, vol. 1, pp. 554–66. The four right efforts were taught by the Buddha as the sixth limb of his Noble Eightfold Path, as recorded in various contexts in the Pāli canon; see, for example, the *Mahāsatipaṭṭhāna Sutta, Dīgha Nikāya* 22 (ii.311); M. Walshe (trans.), *The Long Discourses of the Buddha*, Wisdom Publications, Boston 1995, p. 348; or T. W. and C. A. F. Rhys Davids, *Dialogues of the Buddha*, part 2, Pali Text Society, London 1971, p. 344.

389 Both these meditation practices were taught by the Buddha. For his teaching of the mindfulness of breathing, see *Majjhima Nikāya* 22. For the *mettā bhāvanā*, see the *Karaṇīya-mettā-sutta* or *Kālāma Sutta, Aṅguttara Nikāya* iii.65.

390 The four bases of psychic power or literally 'roads to power' have their origin in the Pāli canon (the Pāli is *iddhipādā*); see, for example, *Saṃyutta Nikāya* v.254 (51.2). The order in which they are listed varies.

391 According to the Pāli canon, the Buddha spoke of these five spiritual faculties just after his Enlightenment; see *Saṃyutta Nikāya* v.232 (48.57); or Bhikkhu Ñāṇamoli, *The Life of the Buddha*, Buddhist

Publication Society, Kandy 1978, p. 35. See also *The Way to Wisdom* above, and *A Survey of Buddhism*, *Complete Works*, vol. 1, pp. 279ff.

392 Paul Williams, *Mahāyāna Buddhism*, Routledge, London and New York 1989, p. 209.

393 Gampopa, *The Jewel Ornament of Liberation*, trans. H. V. Guenther, Rider, London 1959, chapter 21.

394 See Bhagavan Dhas, *Science of the Emotions*, Theosophical Publishing House, Adyar, Madras 1924, p. 218; or Sangharakshita, *The Religion of Art*, *Complete Works*, vol. 26, p. 174.

395 See note 276 above.

396 For traditional life stories of the 'six ornaments of India' see, for example, Lama Chimpa and Alaka Chattopadhyaya (trans.), *Taranatha's History of Buddhism in India*, Motilal Banarsidass, Delhi 1990.

397 Various translations of Nāgārjuna's *Mūlamadhyamakakārikā* are available. See for example K. K. Inada, *Nāgārjuna*, Hokuseido, Tokyo 1970; D. J. Kalupahana, *Nāgārjuna: The Philosophy of the Middle Way*, State University of New York Press, 1986; B. Bocking, *Nāgārjuna in China: A Translation of the Middle Treatise*, Edwin Mellen, Lewiston 1995; Jay L. Garfield, *The Fundamental Wisdom of the Middle Way*, Oxford University Press, Oxford 1995.

As Sangharakshita notes, the above verses' pithy mode of expression makes their arguments virtually impossible to understand without an explanation by a teacher. The commentary by Garfield is very useful in this respect. An audiobook of Garfield's translation and commentary on the *Mūlamadhyamakakārikā* is available, as well as an especially wholehearted reading of Śāntideva's *Bodhicaryāvatāra*. For the print version of the latter, see Śāntideva, *Bodhicaryāvatāra*, trans. Kate Crosby and Andrew Skilton, Windhorse Publications, Birmingham 2002.

For an English translation of Nāgārjuna's *Ratnāvalī* or Precious Garland, see J. Hopkins et al. (trans.), *The Precious Garland and the Song of the Four Mindfulnesses*, George Allen and Unwin, London 1975.

398 Sugata is another title of the Buddha. (S)

399 See D. T. Suzuki (trans.), *Laṅkāvatāra Sūtra*, Routledge, London 1932, p. 239.

400 For an account of Milarepa's life see Lobsang P. Llalungpa (trans), *The Life of Milarepa*, Shambhala Publications, Boston and London 1985.

401 This is a reference to Nāgārjuna's refutation of time as an ultimate truth.

Sangharakshita explores this doctrine in his commentary on verses 63–5 of Nāgārjuna's *Precious Garland* (p. 365 above). Nāgārjuna's refutation of time is presented in some detail in chapter 19 of the *Mūlamadhyamakakārikā*, to which Garfield offers a helpful commentary in Jay L. Garfield, *The Fundamental Wisdom of the Middle Way*, Oxford University Press, Oxford 1995, pp. 254–7.

402 Origen (c.185–c.253) is one of the best known Christian theologians of the early Greek Church. African by birth, Origen spent the first half of his life in Alexandria, after which he travelled widely throughout the Mediterranean. Whilst in Egypt he attended the lectures of the Neoplatonist Ammonius Saccas, whose philosophy is known through his other famous pupil, Plotinus (205–270 CE).

403 A fifth possibility might also be included, that of scepticism in the proper sense. We do not know whether we existed before birth, nor in what manner. Similarly, we do not know whether or in what way we will exist after death.

404 Henry Vaughan, *Silex Scintillans*, 'The Retreat'. Vaughan (1621–1695) was a British Metaphysical poet. His *Silex Scintillans* is a series of sacred poems in which rebirth appears as a major theme.

405 William Wordsworth, 'Ode: Intimations of Immortality'.

406 Thomas Traherne, *Centuries*, Harper, New York 1960, p. 110. Thomas Traherne (c.1636–1674) was an English poet, clergyman, theologian, and religious writer. *Centuries of Meditations*, from which this quotation is taken, was first published in 1908 having been discovered in manuscript ten years earlier.

407 According to Buddhist tradition a *kalpa* is the time taken for a world system to evolve and involve; a *kalpa* is divided into four *asaṃkhyeya-kalpas*. See Sangharakshita, *A Survey of Buddhism*, *Complete Works*, vol. 1, pp. 40–50.

408 See, for example, *Saṃyutta Nikāya* iv.230–1 (36.21); Bhikkhu Bodhi (trans.), *The Connected Discourses of the Buddha*, Wisdom Publications, Somerville 2000, p. 1279; or F. L. Woodward (trans.), *The Book of the Kindred Sayings*, part 4, Pali Text Society, London 1980, pp. 155–6.

409 *Dhammapada* 1–2.

410 For a fuller account of karma and rebirth see *Who is the Buddha?*, *Complete Works*, vol. 3, pp. 92–115.

411 A plan is an idea or conception of what one wishes to see happen. In the following two quotations, Yeshe Gyaltsen seeks to extend this line of thought.

412 We are reminded not to take this idea of twelve

'links' too literally by the fact that the Buddhist tradition also enumerates other combinations of links, sometimes five, sometimes ten, to describe the same process. The Abhidharmikas themselves, as we shall see, came up with a rather different – though related – picture, with their classifications of mind and mental events. However, the twelve links do give a clear and useful idea of the way life unfolds. (S)

413 See W. M. McGovern, *Manual of Buddhist Philosophy*, Kegan Paul, London 1923, p. 166.

414 See note 262 above.

415 H. V. Guenther, *Philosophy and Psychology in the Abhidhamma*, Shambhala Publications, Berkeley and London 1976, p. 146. See also p. 445 above.

416 There are a great many *Jātakas* – literally 'birth stories' – giving accounts of the Buddha's previous lives. See *The Eternal Legacy*, *Complete Works*, vol. 14, pp. 61–71.

417 See Sangharakshita, *The Meaning of Conversion in Buddhism*, *Complete Works*, vol. 2, pp. 275–6.

418 In consequence, the Yogācāra school is sometimes called the Vijñānavāda. (S)

419 See S. Foster Damon, *Blake Dictionary*, Thames and Hudson, London 1973, pp. 195, 341.

420 This is not, however, a traditional Yogācāra distinction; for Paramārtha (499–569 CE), for example, the distinction was between the *ālaya-vijñāna* (by which he meant what I am calling the relative *ālaya*) and a ninth consciousness, the 'immaculate consciousness' (*amala-vijñāna*). See D. Y. Paul, *Philosophy of Mind in Sixth Century China*, Stanford University Press, 1984. (S)

421 For more on the mandala of the five Buddhas see, for example, Vessantara, *Meeting the Buddhas*, Windhorse Publications, Glasgow 1993, pp. 67–126.

422 According to Maitreyanātha, Absolute Mind is the sole reality, but its radiance is obscured by its own dynamic, or potentially dynamic, principle, the *abhūtaparikalpa* or unreal imagination. This dynamic principle comprises two aspects: the relative or tainted *ālaya-vijñāna* or store consciousness, and the *paravṛtti-vijñāna* or evolving consciousness. (S) See also Bodhisattva Maitreya (attrib.), *Madhyānta-Vibhāṅga, Discourse on Discrimination between Middles and Extremes*, trans. T. Stcherbatsky, Motilal Banarsidass, Delhi 1992, chapter 2. See also Sangharakshita, *A Survey of Buddhism*, *Complete Works*, vol. 1, pp. 369–70; and *The Meaning of Conversion in*

Buddhism, *Complete Works*, vol. 2, pp. 275–85.

423 The distinction here is between those texts that have to be interpreted (*neyārtha*) and those that can be taken literally (*nītārtha*). (S)

424 See *Saṃdhinirmocana Sūtra*, published as Thomas Cleary (trans.), *Buddhist Yoga*, Shambhala Publications, Boston and London 1995.

425 For Yeshe Gyaltsen's account of this, see Herbert V. Guenther and Leslie S. Kawamura (trans.), *Mind in Buddhist Psychology*, Dharma Publishing, Berkeley 1975, pp. 15–16.

426 Ibid., p. 16.

427 For a detailed exposition of the *bodhyaṅgas* or factors of Enlightenment, see Sangharakshita, *Mind – Reactive and Creative*, in *Complete Works*, vol. 11. For a canonical reference see, for example, the *Mahāsatipaṭṭhāna Sutta*, *Dīgha Nikāya* 22 (ii.303).

428 See T. Stcherbatsky (trans.), *Madhyānta-Vibhānga: Discourse on Discrimination between Middle and Extremes*, Motilal Banarsidass, Delhi 1992, pp. 113–4.

429 To put it another way, mind is the perception of what Guenther calls the haecceity of a thing. Haecceity is a term derived from scholastic philosophy which means 'this-ness' in the sense of the specific character of a thing – that it is this particular thing – rather than the this-ness of any particular quality. (S) On facticity and haecceity, see Herbert V. Guenther and Leslie S. Kawamura (trans.), *Mind in Buddhist Psychology*, Dharma Publishing, Berkeley 1975, p. 9.

430 Sangharakshita himself notes that the subject of this section is 'very complex'. In the interest of further clarity, we offer an alternative rendering of his main argument, re-edited from the original seminar transcript:

> I have suggested that it is possible for there to be awareness of an object without mental events coming into play. This does not, however, appear to be the conclusion we are being offered here. These two statements can be reconciled by the introduction of a third term: 'mind-as-such'. This third term serves to overcome any simplistic notion of a single 'mind' that is sometimes associated with mental events and sometimes not. After all, it would be a grave mistake to understand mind as a sort of stable centre or ego around which mental events come and go. It's not that – first of all – there is mind in its pristine glory and then mental events come along. Mind – in the sense in which the term is being used here

– and mental events arise together. Generally speaking, in the instant one perceives an object the mental concomitants are there.

Nonetheless, mental events are not necessarily always present. It's as though when mental events cease, mind in the sense of the consciousness that accompanies mental events also ceases. What one is left with then is what we can call 'mind-as-such', which is a different mode of awareness. We might perhaps illustrate this with an image from the natural world. If 'mind-as-such' can be represented by the image of a lake without any ripples, the ripples that arise can be said to have two sides to them (mind and mental events) which necessarily arise and cease at the same time. But sometimes the wind drops and the lake returns to its original state, free from any waves at all, and that is 'mind-as-such'. And here is another example. We might think of mind and mental events as twins, born together at the same time. If one twin were to disappear, the remaining twin would no longer be a twin, but would be an only child. In the same way, if mental events cease to exist – or have not yet arisen – awareness is no longer the same; it 'becomes' or 'is replaced by' a different kind of awareness, and again, we call this 'mind-as-such'. In short, while there cannot be mental events without mind, there can still be mind without mental events. The mind without mental events, however, is different in character from the mind with them and this is why we need to refer to it using the third term, 'mind-as-such'.

Mind in Buddhist Psychology seminar transcript (Padmaloka, 1976), pp. 163–4.

431 The term 'mind-as-such', incidentally, is not an Abhidharma expression, but translates *sems-nyid*, a term coined by the Tibetan Nyingmapa philosophers who studied the Abhidharma and developed their own perspective on it. (S)

Sems-nyid ('mind-as-such') can be contrasted with the Tibetan *sems*, which refers to the mind that arises along with mental objects. Guenther variously refers to 'mind-as-such' by the alternative terms 'pure awareness' and even 'psychic energy'. See Herbert V. Guenther and Leslie S. Kawamura (trans.), *Mind in Buddhist Psychology*, Dharma Publishing, Berkeley 1975, p. xxvii.

432 Ibid., p. 10.

433 This is Sangharakshita's version of Guenther's 'remarks

of a general logical nature' at ibid., pp. xxv–xxvi. In modern philosophy, it would be said that the relationship of sons is reversible, while the relationship of father to son is non-reversible. This is more precise than talking of symmetry.

434 Guenther's 'pure fact' and 'described fact' are translations of the Tibetan *rig-pa* (mind as pure fact) and *ma-rig-pa* (mind as described fact). See ibid., p. xxvi–xvii. In the interest of further clarity, Sangharakshita's exposition of the relationship between them may be paraphrased as follows:

> The term 'mind-as-such' helps us get back to an idea of mind as undescribed and thus unfalsified. This is what Guenther calls 'mind as pure fact' and it prevents us from taking it too literally. As nothing may be said about 'mind as pure fact', what we talk about when we speak of mind is termed by Guenther 'described fact', where 'described fact' is no more than our falsifying attempt to describe 'mind as pure fact'. We could therefore regard 'mind-as-such'or 'mind as pure fact' as what Guenther calls an 'operational concept' that guards against our mistaking mind for some permanent and unchanging ego.

435 i.e. washing your clothes in a stream using mud to clean them. See note 313.

436 The mental concomitant of 'lack of pure awareness' is *avidyā,* the fourth of the six basic negative emotions. This corresponds to the Tibetan *ma-rigs-pa*, or Guenther's 'mind as described fact' with which mental events are associated. See Herbert V. Guenther and Leslie S. Kawamura (trans.), *Mind in Buddhist Psychology*, Dharma Publishing, Berkeley 1975, p. xxvi–xvii. *Avidyā* is described in more detail on pp. 607–11 below.

437 See ibid., p. xxvi.

438 These are the five ways in which mind and mental objects correspond in any given instance. (S) See also J. Hopkins, *Meditations on Emptiness*, Wisdom, Boston 1996, p. 236.

439 See Herbert V. Guenther and Leslie S. Kawamura (trans.), *Mind in Buddhist Psychology*, Dharma Publishing, Berkeley 1975, p. 11.

440 H. V. Guenther, *Philosophy and Psychology in the Abhidhamma*, Shambhala Publications, Berkeley and London 1976, p. 146.

441 Herbert V. Guenther and Leslie S. Kawamura (trans.), *Mind in Buddhist Psychology*, Dharma Publishing, Berkeley 1975, p. 12.

442 Milton, *Paradise Lost*, book 1, line 249.

443 This statement by rGyal-tshab (one of Tsongkhapa's disciples) corresponds to Yeshe Gyaltsen's own definition: 'To be aware of the mere facticity and haecceity of an object is mind.' (S)

444 See Anuruddha, *Abhidhammattasaṅgaha* (*Compendium of Philosophy*), trans. C. A. F. Rhys Davids, Pali Text Society, London 1910, p. 29.

445 Herbert V. Guenther and Leslie S. Kawamura (trans.), *Mind in Buddhist Psychology*, Dharma Publishing, Berkeley 1975, p. 18.

446 Ibid.

447 See illustration on p. 477.

448 See book 3, 'Of the Origin and Nature of the Affects', in Benedict de Spinoza, *Ethics*, Penguin Books, London 1996, pp. 68–112.

449 William Blake, *MS Note-Book*, p. 99, 'Several Questions Answered'.

450 See Epicurus, *Sovran Maximus*, quoted in Diogenes Laertius: *Lives of Eminent Philosophers*, trans. R. D. Hicks, Cambridge, Mass. and London 1979, vol. ii, p. 665:

> It is impossible to live a pleasant life without living wisely and well and justly, and it is impossible to live wise and well and justly without living pleasantly.

451 Lama Govinda terms it 'hedonic indifference'. (S) See also Lama Anagarika Govinda, *The Psychological Attitude of Early Buddhist Philosophy*, Rider, London 1961, p. 117.

452 The *mettā bhāvanā* meditation is described by Buddhaghosa at *Visuddhimagga* 295–307 in Bhikkhu Ñāṇamoli (trans.), *The Path of Purification*, Buddhist Publication Society, Kandy 1991, pp. 288–99, especially p. 290.

Sangharakshita describes the *mettā bhāvanā* as practised in the Triratna Buddhist Community in various places such as a talk given in India during his 1981–2 tour; see *Lecture Tour in India*, *Complete Works*, vol. 9, pp. 204–5. The *mettā bhāvanā* meditation practice is usually taught in five stages. In the first stage one cultivates a feeling of goodwill, of loving-kindness, towards oneself, then in the second, third, and fourth stages extends this warm feeling to a friend, a 'neutral person', and an 'enemy'. In the fifth and final stage referred to here, one further extends this feeling of *mettā* to include, progressively, the people and other beings around one, then throughout the world.

For a detailed elucidation of the practice and all its aspects by Sangharakshita see *The Purpose and Practice of Buddhist Meditation*, *Complete Works*, vol. 5, pp. 109ff.; see also Sangharakshita, *Living with*

Kindness, Complete *Works*, vol. 15.

453 Tennyson, 'In Memoriam' LXIII.

454 The defining characteristic of *vedanā* is the overall feeling-tone in any given experience. Nonetheless, since awareness is always awareness 'of' something, an object must also be present, and this requires *saṃjñā*, the second of the omnipresent mental events.

455 i.e. we only know about the object because it arises in awareness. This is very different from knowing an object 'as it really is'.

456 Herbert V. Guenther and Leslie S. Kawamura (trans.), *Mind in Buddhist Psychology*, Dharma Publishing, Berkeley 1975, p. 23.

457 Ibid., pp. 24–5.

458 See *Visuddhimagga* 88 (3.21) in Bhikkhu Ñāṇamoli (trans.), *The Path of Purification*, Buddhist Publication Society, Kandy 1991, p. 89.

459 See for example Pe Maung Tin (trans.), *The Expositor (Aṭṭhasālinī)*, Pali Text Society, London 1920, vol. i, p. 156.

460 See note 305 above.

461 For the Nyāya school's views on ontological absence, see B. K. Matilal, *The Navya-Nyāya Doctrine of Negation*, Harvard University Press, Cambridge Mass. 1968.

462 See *Aṅguttara Nikāya* iii.196 in E. M. Hare (trans.), *The Book of the Gradual Sayings*, Pali Text Society, Oxford 1995, vol. iii, p. 145. See also Narada Thera, *Manual of Abhidhamma*, Vajirarama Publications, Colombo 1956, p. 85; and Anuruddha, *Abhidhammattasaṅgaha (Compendium of Philosophy)*, trans. C. A. F. Rhys Davids, Pali Text Society, London 1910, pp. 43–5.

463 Herbert V. Guenther and Leslie S. Kawamura (trans.), *Mind in Buddhist Psychology*, Dharma Publishing, Berkeley 1975, p. 25.

464 For more about the three doors to Enlightenment, also known as the three 'entrances to liberation', see *The Three Jewels*, *Complete Works*, vol. 2, pp. 121–2.

465 See Anuruddha, *Abhidhammattasaṅgaha (Compendium of Philosophy)*, trans. C. A. F. Rhys Davids, Pali Text Society, London 1910, p. 30.

466 i.e. illness is not something we consciously choose. We encounter it as the result of various factors, internal and external, but it can be 'used', as it were, to one's advantage.

467 These are: to abstain from harming living beings, from taking what is not freely offered, and from sexual wrongdoing; to abstain from false, harsh, useless, and slanderous speech; and to abstain from covetousness, animosity, and false views. These ten precepts have numerous

canonical sources; see, for example, the *Kūṭadanta Sutta*, *Dīgha Nikāya* 5, and the *Sevitabbāsevitabba Sutta*, *Majjhima Nikāya* 114. See also *The Ten Pillars of Buddhism*, *Complete Works*, vol. 2. pp. 326–34. See also note 190 above.

468 *Dhammapada* 80.

469 'It is a determination' is a rather unhelpful choice of expression on Guenther's part. He is using the term determination in its philosophical sense of specific mode – so a determination of something is that thing existing in a certain mode. (S)

470 To maintain the coherence of Sangharakshita's main argument, the following section has been transferred here from the main text of the first edition: 'The *Vijñaptimātratāsiddhi-śāstra* (in the translation of which *manaskāra* appears as 'attention') deals with a couple of misleading explanations quite constructively:

> According to Sanghabhadra, attention causes the mind to turn towards another object; according to the Abhidharmasamuccaya, it holds the mind fixed on an object. Both explanations are contrary to reason because, in accepting the first, attention would not be 'universal', and the second explanation confuses attention and samādhi. (Xuanzang, *Cheng Weishi Lun: Doctrine of Mere-Consciousness*, trans. Wei Tat, Cheng Weishi Lun Publication Committee, Hong Kong 1973, p. 159.)

'Quite obviously, the mind does not always turn at once to another object; nor does it always remain fixed on the object.' (*Know Your Mind*, Windhorse Publications, Birmingham 2002, p. 99.)

471 Nyanatiloka, *Buddhist Dictionary*, Buddhist Publication Society, Kandy 1988, p. 112. One might still object, though, that rather than an omnipresent mental event something rather like *samādhi* – *samādhi* meaning 'meditative concentration' – seems to be referred to in the second part of the definition. (S)

472 *Chanda* is also the first of the *ṛddhipādas*, the 'bases of psychic power'. These are: *chanda, vīrya, citta*, and *mīmāṃsā*'. See page 457 above. (S)

473 Herbert V. Guenther and Leslie S. Kawamura (trans.), *Mind in Buddhist Psychology*, Dharma Publishing, Berkeley 1975, pp. 29–30.

474 See Gampopa, *The Jewel Ornament of Liberation*, trans. H. V. Guenther, Rider, London 1959, p. 183.

475 Sangharakshita has more to say on the three 'knowledges'

or 'wisdoms' in his discussion of non-deludedness (*amoha*). See pp. 566ff below. Sangharakshita's commentary on Edward Conze's account of the three wisdoms can be found at p. 127 above.

476 In his *Buddhist Dictionary*, Nyanatiloka notes that there are six *anussatis* often described in the *suttas* of the Pāli canon: recollection of the Buddha, the Dharma, the Sangha, morality, liberality, and heavenly beings. A further four are listed less frequently: mindfulness of death, of the body, of breathing, and of peace. See Nyanatiloka, *Buddhist Dictionary*, Buddhist Publication Society, Kandy 1988, pp. 20–2.

477 According to the Pāli Abhidhamma *cittass'ekaggatā* (the Pāli equivalent of *samādhi*) is an omnipresent mental event rather than an object-determining one; this is a key difference between the Theravādin Abhidhamma and the Sarvāstivādin Abhidharma. (S)

478 Herbert V. Guenther and Leslie S. Kawamura (trans.), *Mind in Buddhist Psychology*, Dharma Publishing, Berkeley 1975, p. 35.

479 Xuanzang, *Cheng Weishi Lun: Doctrine of Mere-Consciousness*, trans. Wei Tat, Cheng Weishi Lun Publication Committee, Hong Kong 1973, p. 379.

480 Herbert V. Guenther and Leslie S. Kawamura (trans.), *Mind in Buddhist Psychology*, Dharma Publishing, Berkeley 1975, p. 35.

481 i.e. by means of what Guenther terms 'categorical perception' (*mano-vijñāna*). (S)

482 F. L. Woodward (trans.), *Some Sayings of the Buddha*, Oxford University Press 1973, pp. 136–7.

483 *Prajñā*, which Guenther sometimes translates as 'analytical appreciative discrimination'. (S) See, for example, where Guenther quotes Buddhaghosa's *Aṭṭhasālinī*:

> In worldly matters an attitude is the chief, an attitude is the leader, an attitude is the forerunner; but in matters spiritual, analytical appreciative understanding is the leader, analytical appreciative understanding is the forerunner.

Pe Maung Tin (trans), *The Expositor (Aṭṭhasālinī),* Luzac & Co, London 1958. vol. iii, p. 44, as quoted in Herbert V. Guenther, *Philosophy and Psychology in the Abhidharma*, Buddha Vihara, Lucknow 1957, p. 21.

484 The *viparyāsas* are listed in *Aṅguttara Nikāya* viii.20. See also Sangharakshita, *What is the Dharma?*, *Complete Works*, vol. 3, pp. 280–1.

485 An oblique reference to Guenther's description of *vedanā* 'feeling-tone' (see page 502 below). Guenther's term 'appreciative discrimination' here suggests that, like *vedanā*, *prajñā* involves a felt awareness of what is known, its meaning and value. See also Herbert V. Guenther and Leslie S. Kawamura (trans.), *Mind in Buddhist Psychology*, Dharma Publishing, Berkeley 1975, p. xxvii.

486 Ibid. p. 37.

487 *Dhammapada* 183.

488 The seven *bodhyaṅgas* comprise recollection (*smṛti*), investigation of mental events (*dharma-vicaya*), energy (*vīrya*), rapture (*prīti*), tension release (*praśrabdhi*), concentration (*samādhi*), and tranquillity (*upekṣā*).

489 Though it would seem that people are often encouraged to take up [insight] practice with insufficient preparation in terms of *śamatha* meditation, so that they are attempting insight meditation on the basis of an inadequately concentrated and positive state of mind. (S) Buddhist meditation practices are broadly of two kinds: *śamatha*, calming meditation, and *vipaśyanā*, insight meditation. *Śamatha* practices such as the mindfulness of breathing and the *mettā bhāvanā* give one a positive and calm basis upon which to approach more reflective insight practices such as the one described here.

490 Xuanzang, *Cheng Weishi Lun: Doctrine of Mere-Consciousness*, trans. Wei Tat, Cheng Weishi Lun Publication Committee, Hong Kong 1973, p. 389.

491 Ibid., p. 388.

492 Herbert V. Guenther and Leslie S. Kawamura (trans.), *Mind in Buddhist Psychology*, Dharma Publishing, Berkeley 1975, p. 39.

493 Ibid., p. 40.

494 Psalm 146.

495 John Middleton Murry, *Things to Come*, Ayer Publishing, 1928, p. 34.

496 See *The Little Flowers of St Francis*, J. M. Dent, London 1976, p. 34.

497 William Wordsworth, 'Lines Composed a Few Miles above Tintern Abbey', lines 93–101.

498 Herbert V. Guenther and Leslie S. Kawamura (trans.), *Mind in Buddhist Psychology*, Dharma Publishing, Berkeley 1975, p. 42.

499 See *Aṅguttara Nikāya* ii.7.

500 Lama Anagarika Govinda, *Foundations of Tibetan Mysticism*, Century, London 1987, p. 230.

501 *Apatrāpya* is not really 'to refrain from evil action … because others will despise me'. 'Others' have all sorts of views of what is objectionable. The implication here is that one's teacher and other people deserving of respect simply stand at the centre

of an indeterminate locus of authority made up of 'others', but this is wrong. (S)

502 In his *Manual of Abhidhamma*, a translation of the Pāli *Abhidhammatthasaṅgaha*, Narada Thera describes *ottappa* (the Pāli equivalent of *apatrāpya*) as fear of consequences that arise from without, but this is no better because it fails to convey the fact that this is a positive mental event. (S) See Narada Thera, *Manual of Abhidhamma*, Vajirarama Publications, Colombo 1956, pp. 93–4.

503 See, for example, *What is the Sangha?*, *Complete Works*, vol. 3, pp. 457–8. See also note 44 above.

504 Nicholas Paxton (d.1744) was tasked with checking all new publications for any libel against the government or the monarch. He was eventually sent to Newgate Prison charged with election bribery. Alexander Pope, 'Epilogue to the Satires', in *Imitations of Horace*, Dialogue 2, line 208.

505 In the Pāli scriptures shame and fear of blame are sometimes classed alongside faith and energy as spiritual faculties. See, for example, *Aṅguttara Nikāya* iii.1–2 (5.1–2), which describes a set of five powers called the *pañca sekha-balāni* consisting of *saddhā* (faith), *hiri* (shame), *ottappa* (respect for wise opinion), *viriya* (energy), and *paññā* (wisdom). Considered in this positive light, embarrassment and shame are not so much feelings as moral capacities, powers even, that protect one against unskilful acts of body, speech, and mind.

506 Non-attachment (*alobha*), non-hatred (*adveṣa*), and non-deludedness (*amoha*), the three positive mental events that now follow, are the positive counterparts of the three poisons, namely greed, hatred, and delusion.

507 Xuanzang, *Cheng Weishi Lun: Doctrine of Mere-Consciousness*, trans. Wei Tat, Cheng Weishi Lun Publication Committee, Hong Kong 1973, p. 395.

508 For Sangharakshita's specific meaning of the term 'true individual', see *What is the Sangha?*, *Complete Works*, vol. 3, pp. 467–517.

509 Xuanzang, *Cheng Weishi Lun: Doctrine of Mere-Consciousness*, trans. Wei Tat, Cheng Weishi Lun Publication Committee, Hong Kong 1973, p. 395.

510 Ibid, p. 397.

511 i.e. terms that indicate a quality more by what it is not than by what it intrinsically is.

512 i.e. they do not have a simple one-to-one relationship.

513 See Śāntideva, *Bodhicaryāvatāra* 6.48–9, trans. Kate Crosby and Andrew Skilton, Windhorse Publications, Birmingham 2002, p. 73.

514 It may be noted that three of the above four origins of *amoha* involve the term '*prajñā*', which has already been considered as one of the object-defining mental events. The question of whether or not *prajñā* is to be understood in the same sense in both instances is one to which Xuanzang turns in the quotation that follows.

515 Xuanzang, *Cheng Weishi Lun: Doctrine of Mere-Consciousness*, trans. Wei Tat, Cheng Weishi Lun Publication Committee, Hong Kong 1973, p. 397.

516 It was above all the teaching of Dharmapāla, who was the abbot of the great monastery of Nālandā in northern India, that inspired the author of the *Vijñaptimātratāsiddhi-śāstra*, Xuanzang, to found the Faxiang school on his return to his native China. Not that Dharmapāla was Xuanzang's personal teacher – in fact the abbot had been dead for many years by the time of Xuanzang's arrival in India – but the legacy of Dharmapāla's interpretation of the Dharma was the Chinese pilgrim's inspiration. Generally, therefore, Xuanzang favours Dharmapāla's interpretation over those of the other nine commentators he consults. But on this occasion he does not offer an overt opinion of his own, which might suggest that he actually disagrees with Dharmapāla, but doesn't want to say so out of respect. (S)

517 i.e. both *prajñā* and *amoha* are conceptual designations, not inherent realities, and as such they have been developed with two distinct purposes in mind.

518 i.e. *prajñā* is a term applied to a mental event that helps us get close to a given object by clarifying what is in fact going on. *Amoha* is a view of that mental event as entirely positive, in that it makes possible practical distinctions between what is skilful and what is unskilful.

519 For more about the twelve classes of literature, see *The Eternal Legacy*, *Complete Works*, vol. 14, pp. 23–5.

520 This distinction between doctrine-followers (*dharmānusārins*), and faith-followers (*śraddhānusārins*) originates in the *Aṅguttara Nikāya* of the Pāli canon; see Nyanatiloka, *Buddhist Dictionary*, Buddhist Publication Society, Kandy 1988, pp. 25–6. See also note 39 above.

521 The term *apratiṣṭhita nirvāṇa* was probably introduced by the Yogācāra tradition. For an excellent account of this 'non-abiding *nirvāṇa*' see Paul Williams, *Mahāyāna Buddhism*, Routledge, London 1989, pp. 181–4. The *apratiṣṭhita nirvāṇa* appears in various Yogācāra texts. It is, for example,

the topic discussed in the ninth chapter of Asaṅga's *Mahāyānasaṃgraha*. See G. M. Nagao, *Mādhyamika and Yogācāra*, trans. L. S. Kawamura, State University of New York Press 1991, pp. 23–34.

522 William Blake, *Milton*, Preface, 'And did those feet in ancient time'.

523 i.e. understood in this initial sense, *vīrya* is a matter of one's readiness to engage wholeheartedly with a given situation.

524 See trans. Bunnō Katō et al. (trans.), *The Threefold Lotus Sūtra*, Weatherhill/Kosei, New York and Tokyo 1978, pp. 58–9.

525 See note 305 above.

526 See *Mahāparinibbāna Sutta, Dīgha Nikāya* 16 (ii.156).

527 S. Dasgupta, *An Ever-expanding Quest of Life and Consciousness*, Orient Longman, New Delhi 1971, pp. 189–92.

528 *Dhammapada* 21.

529 'Hedonic indifference' is a term coined by Lama Govinda to describe 'neutral feeling': an unresponsive, flat feeling-tone. *Upekṣā* in this sense is not a positive mental event, and is discussed instead as an aspect of the omnipresent mental event *vedanā* – see p. 508 above. See also Lama Anagarika Govinda, *The Psychological Attitude of Early Buddhist Philosophy*, Rider, London 1961, p. 117.

530 It is not that one-pointedness is a separate mental factor as such – it is a way of describing the integration itself. (S)

531 See, for example, the *Nidānakathā*, N. A. Jayawickrama (trans.), *The Story of Gotama Buddha*, Pali Text Society, Oxford 1990, p. 87.

532 *Jīvaka Sutta, Majjhima Nikāya* 55 (i.369). See Bhikkhu Ñāṇamoli and Bhikkhu Bodhi (trans.), *The Middle Length Discourses of the Buddha*, Wisdom Publications, Boston 1995, pp. 474ff; or I. B. Horner (trans.), *The Collection of the Middle Length Sayings*, vol. ii, Pali Text Society, Oxford 1994, p. 33.

533 D. T. Suzuki (trans.), *Laṅkāvatāra Sūtra*, Routledge, London 1932, p. 217.

534 This anecdote may be apocryphal, although a similar story appears at *Theragāthā* 1055–6. A leper's finger fell into a bowl of food as it was being offered to the *arhant* Mahākassapa. Such was Mahākassapa's indifference towards likes and dislikes that he continued to take nourishment as usual from the rice, although the finger, not being food in any meaningful sense, remained uneaten.

535 Bhikkhus are obliged to shave the head and, if present, 'the hairs that the women lack', i.e. the beard.

Ven. Dhamma Sāmi, *Manual of the Bhikkhu*, Dhammadāna, Paris 2002.

536 The foregoing list of positive mental events has been discussed as an aid to the analysis of one's mental states as they arise. In the following section, the eleven positive mental events are presented as equally valuable subjects for reflection in their own right.

537 Herbert V. Guenther and Leslie S. Kawamura (trans.), *Mind in Buddhist Psychology*, Dharma Publishing, Berkeley 1975, p. 58.

538 The above reflection on the qualities shared by all the eleven positive mental events now leads on to a more practical consideration of ways in which we can bring them into being.

539 Herbert V. Guenther and Leslie S. Kawamura (trans.), *Mind in Buddhist Psychology*, Dharma Publishing, Berkeley 1975, p. 59.

540 The four *saṃgraha-vastus* are mentioned several times in the Pāli canon (i.e. as the *saṅgaha-vatthus* in Pāli). See, for example, *Dīgha Nikāya* iii.152. They also occur in numerous Mahāyāna texts: see, for example, *The Holy Teaching of Vimalakīrti*, trans. Robert A. Thurman, Pennsylvania State University Press 1976, p. 150; see also Sangharakshita, *The Inconceivable Emancipation*, *Complete Works*, vol. 16, pp. 485–88. For an excellent account see also H. Dayal, *The Bodhisattva Doctrine in Buddhist Sanskrit Literature*, Motilal Banarsidass, Delhi 1978, pp. 251–9.

541 Herbert V. Guenther and Leslie S. Kawamura (trans.), *Mind in Buddhist Psychology*, Dharma Publishing, Berkeley 1975, p. 60.

542 The following sentence has been omitted here. Its provenance is obscure and the terms 'red merit' and 'white merit' are not in current usage among Chinese Buddhists:

> By this is meant actions producing what in Chinese Buddhism is described as 'red merit' – that is, mundane merit, as opposed to 'white merit' or merit leading to Enlightenment.

Know Your Mind, Windhorse Publications, Birmingham 2002, p. 155.

543 Herbert V. Guenther and Leslie S. Kawamura (trans.), *Mind in Buddhist Psychology*, Dharma Publishing, Berkeley 1975, p. 62.

544 See *Mahācattārīsaka Sutta*, *Majjhima Nikāya* 117 (iii.71–2); Bhikkhu Ñāṇamoli and Bhikkhu Bodhi (trans.), *The Middle Length Discourses of the Buddha*, Wisdom Publications, Boston 1995, pp. 934–40; or I. B. Horner (trans.), *The Collection of the Middle Length Sayings*, vol. iii,

Pali Text Society, Oxford 1993, p. 114.

545 The first five fetters are: belief in a separate and unchanging self, sceptical doubt with respect to the Buddha's teaching, dependence upon morality and observances, sensual desire, and ill will. For further explanation of the fetters that bind consciousness to conditioned existence see *The Taste of Freedom*, chapter 1, in *Complete Works*, vol. 11, for the first three fetters.

546 From Shelley's essay, 'A Defence of Poetry', quoted in *The Ten Pillars of Buddhism*, *Complete Works*, vol. 2, p. 360:

> The great secret of morals is love; or a going out of our own nature, and an identification of ourselves with the beautiful which exists in thought, action, or person, not our own. A man, to be greatly good, must imagine intensely and comprehensively; he must put himself in the place of another and of many others; the pains and pleasures of his species must become his own.

547 See *Visuddhimagga* 101–2 (3.74). See Bhikkhu Ñāṇamoli (trans.), *The Path of Purification*, Buddhist Publication Society, Kandy 1991, p. 101.

548 There is even a bodhisattva of intelligence, Akṣayamati, whose name means 'indestructible intelligence'. (S)

549 The complete verse reads:

> My name is George Nathaniel Curzon,
> I am a most superior person.
> My cheek is pink, my hair is sleek.
> I dine at Blenheim once a week.

Quoted in David Gilmour, *Curzon: Imperial Statesman*, Farrar, Straus and Giroux, New York 1994, p. 30.

550 H. C. Beeching, in W. G. Hiscock, *The Balliol Rhymes*, Shakespeare Head Press, Oxford 1939.

551 I would suggest that if we take Guenther's rendering of *prajñā* as 'analytical appreciative understanding', we should be able to take the step of interpreting his rendering of the related term *vidyā* as awareness to mean 'aesthetic appreciative understanding'. (S)

552 See Bryan Magee, *The Philosophy of Schopenhauer*, Oxford and New York 1997, pp. 170 et seq.

553 See Sangharakshita, *Wisdom Beyond Words*, *Complete Works*, vol. 14, pp. 518–24.

554 See Sangharakshita, *A Survey of Buddhism*, *Complete Works*, vol. 1, pp. 444–5.

555 An aphorism popularly attributed to Chan master Yúnmén Wényǎn (862–949 CE).

556 For more on 'the gravitational pull', see *What is the*

Dharma?, *Complete Works*, vol. 3, pp. 241ff.

557 See, for example, the *Aṭṭhakavagga* (Chapter of the Eights) in the *Sutta-Nipāta*. This chapter is one of the oldest sections of the Pāli canon. One of its main themes is that the wise man relinquishes all views. For a translation, see K. R. Norman (trans.), *The Rhinoceros Horn and Other Buddhist Poems*, Pali Text Society, London 1985, pp. 129–58.

558 Herbert V. Guenther and Leslie S. Kawamura (trans.), *Mind in Buddhist Psychology*, Dharma Publishing, Berkeley 1975, p. 76.

559 See note 322.

560 'The Marriage of Heaven and Hell' in Geoffrey Keynes, *Poetry and Prose of William Blake*, vol. i, Nonesuch Press, London 1927, p. 182.

561 The Pali Text Society's *Pāli–English Dictionary* (Oxford 1995, p. 521) states that a *manomayakāya* 'can be created by great holiness of knowledge; human beings or gods may be endowed with this power'. The *Dictionary* cites *Majjhima Nikāya* i.410; *Dīgha Nikāya* i.17, 77, 186; Vinaya Piṭaka ii.185; *Aṅguttara Nikāya* i.24, iii.122, iii.192, iv.235, v.60.

562 The Buddha teaches that freedom from either extreme is the goal of Buddhist practice. See, for example, *Udānavarga* 26.20:

> There is no agitation for one who has no dependence, and here one finds calming down. There is neither going nor passing away, called the end of suffering.

The conclusion of this *udāna*, 'neither here nor there nor in between exist. Just this is the end of suffering', also occurs at *Udāna* 1.10 (the discourse to Bāhiya) and in the *Māluṅkyaputta Sutta* at *Saṃyutta Nikāya* iv.73; see Bhikkhu Bodhi (trans.), *The Connected Discourses of the Buddha*, Wisdom Publications, Boston 2000, pp. 1176; or F. L. Woodward (trans.), *The Book of the Kindred Sayings*, part 4, Pali Text Society, London 1980, pp. 43–4.

The end of suffering is the subject of the four noble truths, which finds its definitive expression in the Buddha's first teaching after his Enlightenment. See Vinaya Piṭaka i.10–11 (*Mahāvagga* 1.6.19–23), or Bhikkhu Ñāṇamoli, *The Life of the Buddha*, Buddhist Publication Society, Kandy 1978, p. 42.

563 See Candrakirti's commentary on Nāgārjuna's *Mūlamadhyamakakārikā*, xiii.8. See also Sangharakshita, *What is the Dharma?*, *Complete Works*, vol. 3, p. 237.

564 The development of a strong personal basis for the arising of insight is covered by the first two stages of Sangharakshita's 'system of meditation', i.e. the cultivation of integration and positive emotion. For further details, see Kamalashila, *Buddhist Meditation*, Windhorse Publications, Cambridge 2012, pp. 7, 10, *passim*. For a discussion of a range of Pāli canonical references to the building up of a strong self, see Peter Harvey, 'Developing a Self without Boundaries', *Buddhist Studies Review* 1.2 (1983–4), pp. 115–26.

565 See Bhikshu Thich Thien Chan, *The Literature of the Personalists (Pudgalavādins) of Early Buddhism*, Motilal Banarsidass, Delhi 1999.

566 See Edward Conze, *Buddhist Thought in India*, George Allen & Unwin, London 1962, pp. 122–34.

567 The Venerable A. P. Buddhadatta (1887–1962) was a Theravādin monk and professor of Buddhist Philosophy at Vidyalankara University. A scholar and teacher of Pāli, he was author of a Pāli–English dictionary. See A. P. Buddhadatta et al., *Pāli–English Dictionary*, Bharatiya Kala Prakashan, Delhi, 1999. For more on the Pudgalavāda, see Paul Williams, *Altruism and Reality*, Curzon, London 1997, pp. 238–9.

568 The ten fetters are enumerated at, for example, *Saṃyutta Nikāya* v.61. See Bhikkhu Bodhi (trans.), *The Connected Discourses of the Buddha*, Wisdom Publications, Boston 2000, pp. 1565–6; or F. L. Woodward (trans.), *The Book of the Kindred Sayings*, part 5, Pali Text Society, London 1979, p. 49. See also *Saṅgīti Sutta, Dīgha Nikāya* 33 (ii.234) in M. Walshe (trans.), *The Long Discourses of the Buddha*, Wisdom Publications, Boston 1995, p. 495; or T. W. and C. A. F. Rhys Davids (trans.), *Dialogues of the Buddha*, part 3, Pali Text Society, London 1971, p. 225.

569 See Sangharakshita, *The Taste of Freedom*, Birmingham 1997, pp. 19–22 (*Complete Works*, vol. 11).

570 'Square' Zen being the other extreme of insisting on all the rules, paraphernalia, and rituals of traditional Zen Buddhism. (S)

571 i.e. the devotee of 'beat' Zen assumes that Enlightened beings have transcended good and evil, and one can therefore do whatever one likes without regard for the consequences.

572 The Sāṃkhya philosophers are generally identified as the *satkāryavādins*, in that they hold that the effect is pre-existent (*sat*) in the cause. The causal operation simply makes manifest the effect, which is already existing but latent in the cause. The

Nyāya-Vaiśeṣika philosophers are generally identified as the *asatkāryavādins*. For these thinkers, the effect is not pre-existent (*asat*) in the cause. The causal operation brings into being an effect which previously did not exist at all. Nāgārjuna explores these ideas in some detail in his *Mūlamadhyamakakārikā*, to which Garfield provides a worthwhile commentary. See Jay L. Garfield, *Fundamental Wisdom of the Middle Way*, Oxford University Press, Oxford 1995, pp. 102–23. A helpful audiobook version is available from audible.com. See also S. N. Dasgupta, *A History of Indian Philosophy*, Motilal Banarsidass, Delhi 1991, vol. 1, pp. 257–8, 320. See also D. J. Kalupahana, *Causality: The Central Philosophy of Buddhism*, University Press of Hawaii, Honolulu 1975.

573 This is not to say one cannot be both sexually liberated and thoroughly blocked emotionally – one can, very easily. (S)

574 Sangharakshita says more on the power of higher mental states to dissipate less skilful impulses in *The Way to Wisdom*. See p. 100 above.

575 Herbert V. Guenther and Leslie S. Kawamura (trans.), *Mind in Buddhist Psychology*, Dharma Publishing, Berkeley 1975, p. 80.

576 The sentence appears as follows in the first edition of *Know Your Mind* (Windhorse Publications, Birmingham 2002), p. 202:

> This is the first *sutta* of the collection known as the *Dīgha Nikāya*, which is the first *nikāya* of the Sutta Piṭaka (the whole body of *suttas*), which in turn is the first *piṭaka* of the Pāli canon.

577 See, for example, D. T. Suzuki (trans.), *Laṅkāvatāra Sūtra*, Routledge, London 1932, pp. 46–8.

578 i.e. one 'guards it jealously'.

579 William Shakespeare, *Othello*, Act V, Scene i, line 19.

580 See Nietzsche, *Beyond Good and Evil*, chapter 4, aphorism 116.

581 See note 216 above.

582 Herbert V. Guenther and Leslie S. Kawamura (trans.), *Mind in Buddhist Psychology*, Dharma Publishing, Berkeley 1975, p. 87.

583 For more on the four dimensions of awareness (awareness of self, of others, of things, and of reality) see *The Buddha's Noble Eightfold Path*, *Complete Works*, vol. 1, pp. 567–78. Sangharakshita sometimes refers to these as four 'levels' of awareness. These four levels, or dimensions, of awareness are not to be confused with the four 'foundations' of mindfulness: awareness of the body, feelings, consciousness, and mental objects – outlined in, for example, the

Mahāsatipaṭṭhāna Sutta, Dīgha Nikāya 22; see M. Walshe (trans.), *The Long Discourses of the Buddha*, Wisdom Publications, Boston 1995, pp. 335–50; or T. W. and C. A. F. Rhys Davids (trans.), *Dialogues of the Buddha*, part 2, Pali Text Society, London 1971, pp. 327–37.

584 By the same token, some people seem to have a stable quantum of positivity that remains more or less unaffected by the ups and downs of life. (S)

585 The parable of the raft originates in the Pāli canon. See, for example, the *Alagaddūpama Sutta, Majjhima Nikāya* 22 (i.134–5). Bhikkhu Ñāṇamoli and Bhikkhu Bodhi (trans.), *The Middle Length Discourses of the Buddha*, Wisdom Publications, Boston 1995, pp. 228–9; or I. B. Horner (trans.), *The Collection of the Middle Length Sayings*, vol. i, Pali Text Society, London 1976, pp. 173–4. See also Sangharakshita, *What is the Dharma?*, *Complete Works*, vol. 3, pp. 165ff.

586 Herbert V. Guenther and Leslie S. Kawamura (trans.), *Mind in Buddhist Psychology*, Dharma Publishing, Berkeley 1975, p. 97.

587 According to Yeshe Gyaltsen, not all the six varieties he lists are really variants of this *upakleśa* of *vikṣepa*; the first, he says, is indeterminate, and the last is actually positive, while of the other four it is really the second and third on the list that we should focus on as being of the essence of this particular negative mental event. (S)

588 The four *viparyāsas* (Pāli *vipallāsa*), the 'mental perversities' or 'topsy-turvy views', are listed in the *Vipallāsa Sutta, Aṅguttara Nikāya* ii.52. See Bhikkhu Bodhi (trans.), *The Numerical Discourses of the Buddha*, Wisdom Publications, Boston 2012, pp. 437–8; or F. L. Woodward (trans.), *The Book of the Gradual Sayings*, vol. ii, Pali Text Society, Oxford 1995, pp. 60–1. See also *The Three Jewels*, *Complete Works*, vol. 2, pp. 80ff.

589 Nonetheless in the Theravāda Abhidhamma, *thīna* (sloth/tiredness) and *middha* (sleepiness/torpor) are both listed as negative mental events. See, for example, Anuruddha, *Abhidhammattasaṅgaha (Compendium of Philosophy)*, trans. C. A. F. Rhys Davids, Pali Text Society, London 1910.

590 Whereas feeling split off from intellect he calls the Emanation. (S)

591 It would be better, *bhikkhus*, for the uninstructed worldling to take as self this body composed of the four great elements rather than the mind. For what reason?

> Because the body composed of the four great elements is seen standing for one year, for two years, for three, four, five, or ten years, for twenty, thirty, forty, or fifty years, for a hundred years, or even longer. But that which is called 'mind' and 'mentality' and 'consciousness' arises as one thing and ceases as another by day and by night.

Saṃyutta Nikāya ii.94 (12.61) in Bhikkhu Bodhi (trans.), *The Connected Discourses of the Buddha*, Wisdom Publications, Somerville 2000, p. 595.

592 See Buddhaghosa, *Visuddhimagga* 142–3 (4.90–1). See Bhikkhu Ñāṇamoli (trans.), *The Path of Purification*, Buddhist Publication Society, Kandy 1991, p. 140.

593 See Sister Nivedita and Ananda Coomaraswamy, *Myths of the Hindus and Buddhists*, Harrap, London 1914, p. 296.

594 In the Buddhist tradition this difficulty is recognized; there is, indeed, a sublimated form of Kāmadeva in the figure of Kurukullā, the bodhisattva representing the fascination aspect of Enlightenment, or Enlightenment as the beautiful. (S)

INDEX

Abhidharma (Pāli Abhidhamma) 435–6, 439–47, 546, 572, 703
- limitations of 441, 493–4, 686
- Mahāyāna and 248, 447–52, 494, 690; *see also under* Yogācāra
- Piṭaka 442, 572, 714n, 749n
- Sarvāstivādin 441–3, 446–7, 449, 451, 455, 479, 496, 500, 571, 755n, 767n
- tendency to atomism/reification 248–9, 367–8, 443, 447–9
- Theravādin 441–7, 450–1, 456, 496, 499–500, 571, 712n, 755n, 767n, 777n

Abhidharmakośa (*Abhidharmakośabhāṣya*) 447, 449, 451, 455, 491, 495, 499, 512, 528, 702, 725n, 726n, 755n, 756n, 757n

Abhidharmasamuccaya 449, 452, 496, 500, 512, 702, 756n

abhijñās, *see* superknowledges

Absolute
- Mind 760n
- the 470

accumulations (or requisites)
- of merit and wisdom 161, 187, 336, 415, 461, 463, 467
- path of 455–7, 459, 536

acquisitiveness (*mātsarya*) 294, 656–7, 700

actions, unskilful 170–3, 292–6; *see also* karma

activity, beneficial (*arthacaryā*) 175, 590

addiction xxiv, 255–7, 285, 512–13

adveṣa, *see* non-hatred

aesthetic
- appreciation 222, 226, 227, 271, 336, 337, 608–9, 694–5
- perspective 516–17; *see also* awareness, appreciative
- pleasure 226, 395–6, 513, 554

aggregates (*skandhas*) 87, 272, 343, 346–51, 353, 355, 358–9, 362, 373, 377, 444–6, 448, 474–5, 478, 482, 501–2, 604–5, 618–21, 623–6, 721n, 754n, 756n

Akṣayamati Sūtra 69, 717n

Akṣobhya 488, 729n

ālaya
- absolute 486, 488
- relative 486–8, 760n

ālaya-vijñāna 486–8, 760n

alienation 104, 509, 599, 644, 717n; *see also* awareness, alienated

alobha, *see* non-attachment

altruism 190–1, 287, 296–7, 306

Amitābha 147, 282, 298, 390, 488, 558

Amoghasiddhi 487

amoha, *see* non-deludedness

Ānanda 333, 337, 348–9, 480, 571, 743n, 745n, 750n

Ananda Bodhi 88, 728n

Anaṅga 691–2

ānāpānasati, *see* mindfulness of breathing

anapatrāpya 666–7, 700; *see also* *apatrāpya*

anātman (Pāli *anattā*) 219, 383, 448–9, 624–5, 629–30; *see also* self, no- or non-
anātmavāda 629–30
anger (*pratigha*) 99, 248, 268–71, 281, 496–7, 583, 598–603, 700, 738n, 749n; *see also* malice, rage, resentment, spite
'Great' (*mahā*) 314
Aṅgulimāla 274, 738–9n
Aṅguttara Nikāya 95, 189, 252, 456, 520, 545, 558, 573, 681, 722n, 734n, 738n, 757n, 765n, 767n, 768n, 769n, 770n, 774n, 777n
aniyata, *see* mental events, four variables
anxiety 120, 183, 254, 260, 290, 688–9; *see also* worry
apatrāpya (Pāli *ottappa*) 275–6, 557–61, 666–7, 669, 700, 768n, 769n; *see also* *anapatrāpya*, respect for wise opinion
apramāda, *see* non-heedlessness
apraṇihita samādhi 521–2, 765n
arhant ideal 268, 574, 616, 682
arhants 134, 277, 457, 511, 683, 727n, 771n
arhantship 733n, 745n
Aristotle 327, 722n, 742n
Ariyapariyesanā Sutta 167, 221, 731n, 736n
arrogance (*māna*) 271, 273, 279–80, 596, 603–7, 700; *see also* pride
arts 225–6, 271, 395–6, 536–7, 609, 685
arūpaloka or *arūpadhātu* 497–8, 597; *see also under dhyānas*; realms, god
Āryadeva 464, 475, 509–10, 705, 748n
Āryasaṅgha 40, 561, 650–1, 711n
asaṃprajanya, *see* inattentiveness
Asaṅga 325, 449, 452, 464–5, 489, 496, 498, 500, 702, 705, 741n, 756n, 771n
Asatkāryavādins 637, 776n; *see also* Nyāya-Vaiśeṣika school
asceticism 109, 253, 585
āśraddhya, *see* faith, lack of
āsravakṣayajñāna 519
āśravas 357, 519, 520
aśubha, *see* impurity
aśubha bhāvanā 220, 221, 222–3, 681; *see also* body, impurity of
asuras 144, 298, 497, 731n
Aśvaghoṣa 440, 573, 722n, 741n
Atīśa 423
ātman 220, 448, 630, 632
ātmavāda 95, 631, 722n
attachment 168, 250–1, 281–6, 371, 383, 396, 512–13, 564, 739n; *see also* desire, non-attachment
cupidity- *see rāga*
to ideologies 628–32
to observances (*śīlavrataparāmarśa*) 632–5, 745n, 773n
attainments (*siddhis*) 143, 318, 728n
attention, *see manaskāra*
Aṭṭhasālinī 130–1, 518, 545, 726n, 727n, 765n, 767n
auddhatya (Pāli *uddhacca*), *see* ebullience, restlessness
Avalokiteśvara (Lokeśvara) 143, 144, 729n
avarice (*mātsarya*) 256, 282, 284, 656–7, 700, 739n
Avataṃsaka Sūtra 731n, 752n
aversion xxii, 250, 252, 290, 543, 594, 600; *see also* hatred
avidyā, *see* ignorance
avihiṃsā, *see* non-violence
avyākṛtavastūni, *see* inexpressibles
awareness (*smṛti* (Pāli *sati*)) xviii, xxi–xxii, 260, 266, 340, 543, 608, 713n, 752n; *see also* mindfulness, recollection
alienated 88–9, 103–4; *see also* alienation
appreciative 608–9, 773n; *see also* aesthetic perspective
discriminating 484, 487, 567, 568, 679; *see also vijñāna*
four dimensions of 87, 536–9, 661, 721n, 776n
Guenther's translation of *jñāna* 610
intrinsic, *see vidyā*
non-dual 483–4
pure 227, 486–7, 490, 493, 729n, 762n; *see also* mind-as-such; mind, pure

bardo 47, 622, 678, 708n, 713n
baselessness 369–72, 377, 749n; *see also śūnyatā*
beauty (*śubha*) 221–3, 225, 271, 298, 337, 462, 545, 736n, 778n; *see also* purity
belligerence (*krodha*) 268, 700, 738n
bewilderment and confusion (*moha*) 47, 295, 597; *see also* ignorance
bhāvanā-mayī-prajñā 129–30, 567, 573, 611
bhavaṅga-sota, *see* life-stream
Bhave, Vinoba 199–200, 734n
bhūmis 143, 412, 729n, 752n
bhūtas 144, 729n
Bible, references to 20, 24–5, 172, 212, 263, 337, 552, 575, 708n, 709n, 732n, 735n, 738n, 743n, 768n
Blake, W. 117, 275, 470, 484, 506, 575, 622, 685, 739n, 764n, 771n, 774n

bleak things, four 659–62
bliss (*sukha*) 122, 262–3, 300, 303, 357, 364, 511, 518, 527, 528, 596, 725n; *see also* happiness
Blyth, R. H. 64–7, 716n
Bodhicaryāvatāra 7, 173, 204–5, 280, 322, 376, 417, 465, 476, 566, 659, 732n, 735n, 739n, 749n, 758n, 769n
bodhicitta 174, 186, 189–90, 192–3, 412, 421, 424, 732n
bodhicitta-utpāda 424, 427
bodhisattva
  attitude 653, 661, 694
  of fascination or the beautiful 778n
  gifts of 180, 182, 206, 749n
  ideal 165, 174, 183, 465, 682, 707n
  path 463
  and Pure Land 243
  vow 268
bodhisattvas 134–5, 153, 182, 187, 193, 277, 312, 412, 511, 609, 657
  and Buddhas, *see under* Buddhas
  and rebirth 411–12, 752n
  visualization of 542, 544–5
  wrathful, *see* deities, wrathful
bodhyaṅgas, *see* Enlightenment, seven factors of
bodies (*kāyas*), of the Buddha 546, 729n
body 118, 122, 384, 687, 777–8n; *see also* form (*rūpa*)
  awareness/mindfulness of 103–4, 456, 537–8, 721n, 767n
  dearness of 304, 306
  impurity of 217–20, 389, 543; *see also aśubha bhāvanā*
  made of mind (*manomayakāya*) 622, 774n
  and mind xviii, xxiii, 393, 621–3; *see also* mind, and matter
  mortifying 251–2
boredom xxii–xxiii, 398–400
Botticelli 222, 223
Brahmajāla Sutta 640–1
Brahmā Sahampati 167, 389, 741n
brahma vihāras 183, 262–3, 335, 415, 542, 743n
Buddha 109, 188, 191–2, 324, 326–9, 389, 402–3, 440, 442, 447, 709n, 724n, 743n, 745n; *see also* Śākyamuni, Tathāgata
  bodies (*kāyas*) of 146, 623, 729n, 742n
  confidence and faith in 27, 28–9, 33–5, 37–9, 45, 336–7, 553–4, 745n
  death or *parinirvāṇa* 384, 621, 750n
  as friend 326–7
  recollection of, *see buddhānusmṛti*
  revering 276–7
Buddhacarita 440, 741n
Buddhadatta, A. P 632, 775n
Buddhaghosa 43, 67, 68, 82, 115, 423, 441, 712n, 714n, 767n
Buddhahood 277, 390, 594, 625, 751n; *see also* Enlightenment
Buddha Land or Buddha-field (*buddhakṣetra*) 296–8, 472
Buddha-nature 92–5, 275, 558; *see also* potentiality, metaphysics of; *tathāgatagarbha*
buddhānusmṛti (Pāli *buddhānussati*) 89–90, 541, 721n
Buddhas, five, *see* mandala, of the five Buddhas
Buddhas and bodhisattvas 169, 299, 560–1, 659, 662–3
  confessing to 650–1
  denial of attainments of 639–40
Burns, R. 122, 124, 555, 645

Campbell, T. 358, 747n
Candragomin 141, 143–5, 728n
Candrakīrti 570, 630, 705, 728n, 774n
Carroll, Lewis 65, 717n
causality 46, 55, 350; *see also* conditionality
  wrong views about 635–7, 775–6n
cause and effect 33, 247–9, 352, 362, 635–7, 738n, 746n
celibacy 217, 219, 221, 364; *see also* chastity
cessation 246–7, 365, 368, 740n
cetanā, *see* mind, directionality of
cetasika, *see* mental events
ceto vimutti 186–7, 733n
chanda, *see* interest
chanting 75, 81, 119, 298, 417
chastity 216; *see also* celibacy
Chen, C. M. (Yogi Chen) 141, 728n
cintā-mayī-prajñā, *see* reflection
citta, *see* mind
citta-mātra, *see* Mind Only
cittas, eighty-nine 496
clarity 168, 172, 187, 256, 390–1, 551, 598, 613–15
cognition 323, 334, 514, 520; *see also* recognition, *samjñā*
Coleridge, S. T. 276, 739n
commitment 47, 287, 307–8, 328, 370, 435–6, 555, 571, 616, 647, 672, 711n
communication, four levels of 229–30
comparison 273–4, 279, 604
compassion (*karuṇā*) 134–5, 143, 174, 193, 248, 263, 304, 335, 424, 583, 603

compassion (*cont.*)
cultivation of, *see karuṇā bhāvanā*
and wisdom 153, 158, 174, 187, 411, 694
concealment, *see* slyness-concealment
conceit, *see* pride
concentration (*samādhi*) 82–3, 113–26, 130, 335, 357, 533–4, 544, 695, 699, 725n, 733n, 766n, 767n, 768n
higher or 'transic' 118, 120–1, 124, 127, 130; *see also dhyānas*
and integration, *see under* integration
intellectual 115–18
intense 542–4, 547, 699; *see also* one-pointedness
and mindfulness 114–15
and *prajñā* 611, 695
concern, *see* non-heedlessness
conditionality xx, 173, 246–8, 389, 446, 626, 636–7, 750n; *see also* causality; cause and effect; conditioned co-production; dependent-arising; *nidānas*
five levels or orders of 472–3; *see also niyamas*
the conditioned 626
gravitational pull of 612, 676, 773n
and the unconditioned (*saṃskṛta* and *asaṃskṛta*) 443
conditioned co-production (*pratītya-samutpāda*) 27, 33, 324, 357, 424, 427–8, 710n, 747n, 754n; *see also* conditionality
conditioning 475, 538
confession 270, 417, 648–52, 657
confidence-trust, *see* faith
consciousness xxi–xxii, 242, 340–1, 688; *see also vijñāna*
defiled mind, *see kliṣṭa-mano-vijñāna*
dream xxi, 340, 485, 686–7
Enlightened 343, 379, 389; *see also* Enlightenment
evolving (*paravṛtti-vijñāna*) 760n
expanded (*mahaggata*) 608
higher states of, *see dhyānas*
immaculate (*amala-vijñāna*) 760n
mind, *see mano-vijñāna*
reflexive xviii
sense, *see* sense consciousness
store, *see ālaya-vijñāna*
translated as 'perception' 484
'turning about' in (*āśraya-parāvṛtti*) 481, 486–7
contact (*spārśa*) 404, 478, 529–30, 699
contemplation 262, 336, 539, 573, 695–6
aesthetic, *see* aesthetic appreciation
of loathsomeness of the body, *see aśubha bhāvanā*
of six elements 382, 623
contentment 252, 271, 301, 335, 551
contrition 289, 290, 701; *see also* worry
conversion, four means of, *see saṃgraha-vastus*
Conze, E. xii, xvii, 5, 6, 137, 631, 707n, 708n, 710n, 716n, 717n
covetousness 175, 241, 257–8, 271, 561, 765n
craving (*lobha*) 50, 241, 357, 398, 512–13, 530, 596, 597, 677; *see also* desire, greed, *tṛṣṇā*
counteracting 169, 542–3, 590
for existence or non-existence 243, 426–7, 727n, 737–8n
sexual 218–21, 223, 226–7, 271
three cankers of (*āśravas*) 357
creation 641, 722n
cupidity-attachment, *see rāga*
Curzon, Lord 604, 773n
cynicism 160, 238, 276, 556

ḍākas and *ḍākinīs* 133, 727n
Dalai Lama 287, 422, 425, 704, 735n
'Dark Night of the Soul' 109, 673, 724n
Daśabhūmika Sūtra 157, 731n, 752n
Dasgupta, S. 580–1, 722n, 771n, 776n
death 15, 25, 56, 162, 189, 241–4, 286, 354, 357, 468–9, 708n, 767n
body and 622–3
Buddha and 384, 621, 750n
and karma 526; *see also* karma and rebirth
lord of, *see* Yamarāja
spiritual 354
deceit (*māyā*) 172, 657–9, 700
decorum, *see apatrāpya*
defensiveness (*pradāśa*) 261, 657, 700; *see also* spite
defilements (*kleśas*) 95, 131–3, 495, 610, 617, 637, 643, 722n, 726n, 727n, 729n; *see also* mental events, negative
definition 596
deities, wrathful 313–18
deluded type 603
delusion 256, 260, 344, 596; *see also* ignorance
demons 602, 643, 691, 732n
dependent-arising 374; *see also* conditionality
desire 271, 281–2, 290, 398, 752n, 754n; *see also* craving, greed, *rāga*
realm of, *see kāmaloka*
desultoriness (*vikṣepa*) 680–2, 701, 721n, 777n; *see also* distraction
Devadatta 188, 480, 734n

devotion 448, 553–5, 556, 719n, 727n, 740n
devotional practice 271, 333, 417, 526, 541, 554, 685; *see also* puja, worship
Dhammapada 186, 189, 283, 324, 328, 436, 473, 529, 549, 581, 733n, 734n, 739n, 742n, 755n, 759n, 766n, 768n, 771n
Dhammasaṅgaṇī 130, 714n
Dhardo Rimpoche xxvi–1, 7, 315, 318, 412, 707n
Dharma 158–9, 261, 324, 332, 334, 674; *see also* doctrine
  danger of misunderstanding 40, 87–8, 275, 388–90, 447, 454
  explicit and implicit teachings (*neyārtha* and *nītārtha*) 488, 761n
  eye of (*dharmacakṣu*) 348–9, 745–6n
  gift of (teaching) 180, 203, 205–7, 328, 465
  study 72, 156, 460, 535, 567, 571, 573, 589, 745n
  teachings, Abhidharma classifications of 441, 571–2
  use of negative terms 291, 295–6, 343, 355, 520, 549, 565–6
Dharmakīrti 464, 544
Dharmapāla 453, 568, 756n, 770n
dharmas (Pāli *dhammas*) 86, 87, 133, 443, 446–7, 720n
  atomism or reification of 248–9, 442–3, 445
  emptiness of (*sarvadharmāḥ-śūnyatā*) 97, 131–2, 135–6, 448–9
dhyāna (Pāli *jhāna*), or meditation factors, five 518, 578, 582, 725n
dhyānas (Pāli *jhānas*) 108, 124–6, 136, 436, 494–8, 525, 526, 527–8, 578, 597, 725n; *see also* concentration, higher
  as 'expanded consciousness' (*mahaggatacitta*) 608
  first 122, 125, 222, 682, 689
  second 125–6, 518, 624, 689
  third 125–6, 518, 582
  fourth 123, 508, 582, 713n
  four (*rūpa*, world of form) 121–3, 517, 725n; *see also rūpaloka*
  four (*arūpa*, formless or higher) 121, 123, 125, 263, 495, 517–18, 608, 682, 689, 690, 725n; *see also arūpaloka*
Diamond Sūtra (*Vajracchedikā Prajñāpāramitā*) 364, 731n, 735n, 749n
Dīgha Nikāya 714n, 721n, 726n, 732n, 737n, 741n, 750n, 757n, 761n, 766n, 771n, 772n, 774n, 775n, 776n, 777n
Dignāga 464, 705n
diligence, *see vīrya*
disciples 160, 208, 252, 337, 440, 650, 735n, 738n
discipline 105, 119, 169, 226, 267–8, 458–9, 635; *see also* self-discipline, spiritual training
discrimination 282, 380, 407, 699; *see also saṃjñā*
  appreciative 493, 699, 767n, 768n; *see also vidyā*
dishonesty (*śāṭhya*) 659–63, 700; *see also* precepts, speech
distraction (*vikṣepa*) 89–91, 98, 115, 260, 395, 397, 399–400, 678, 680–2, 701, 712n, 721n
doctrine 158–9, 324, 369–70, 391; *see also* Dharma
  'bearing' or 'enduring' the 205, 208, 735n
  followers (*dhammānusārins*) 35, 332–3, 573, 603, 614, 710n, 743n, 770n
  and method 218, 593–4
Doctrine of Mere-Consciousness (*Cheng Weishi Lun*) 453, 542, 551, 561, 563, 568, 757n, 766n, 767n, 768n, 769n, 770n
Dōgen 423, 732n
Don Quixote 5, 62–7, 715n, 716n
Door of Liberation 421, 704, 752n, 753n
doubt (*vicikitsā*) 23, 48, 50, 118, 119, 289, 290, 632, 633, 700, 740n, 745n, 773n; *see also* indecision
  Great 378, 749n
dreams 684, 686–7
dream yoga 340, 744n
drink 56–7, 255–7
Driver, J. xxvi, 141, 425, 728n
drowsiness (*middha*) 288, 674–5, 683–8, 701, 777n; *see also* sloth and torpor
dṛṣṭi, *see* opinionatedness
drugs 132–3, 255, 285, 341, 527
dualism xx, 251, 365–6, 368, 372, 481, 485, 521, 622; *see also* subject-object duality
duḥkha (Pāli *dukkha*) *see* suffering

eagerness, *see* interest
ebullience (*auddhatya*) 670–1, 701, 727n; *see also* excitement
effort xxi, 93, 98, 243, 435, 460, 525, 533, 550, 594, 676; *see also vīrya*
effortlessness 187–8

efforts, four right 456, 757n
ego xxiv, 193, 279–80, 339–45, 348, 351–4, 359, 364, 376, 391, 475, 625, 687; *see also* non-ego, self-view
ego-centric demanding, *see manaskāra*
ego-consciousness, *see kliṣṭa-mano-vijñāna*
egotism 37, 147, n600, 664, 668
Eightfold Path 86, 110, 720n, 721n, 740n, 757n, 776n
elements 373–4, 377–9, 382, 439
  four great (*mahābhūtas*) 445–6, 777–8n
  six 373, 377, 380, 407–8, 751n
    contemplation of 382, 623
  or spheres, eighteen (*dhātus*) 404
elephant, illusory 385–7
emotion(s)
  and feelings, distinguished 503–4, 537
  negative, *see under* mental events, negative
  positive 186, 297, 457, 508, 537, 543, 555, 775n; *see also brahma vihāras*; mental events, eleven positive; *mettā*
    effect of radiating 297–8
  and reason/intellect 685, 689
emptiness 33, 37, 38, 151, 153, 168, 249, 380, 488; *see also* baselessness, *śūnyatā*
energy 202, 248, 266, 400, 522, 529, 683
  and anger 599, 644
  centres (chakras) 228
  and faith 69–71, 78, 576
  integration of 459–60, 495, 546
  and laziness 675–6
  male and female 74–6
  neurotic 60–1
  psychic 521, 762n
  in pursuit of the good, *see vīrya*
  release of xxi, 345, 349, 579, 670
  stagnation of (*styāna*) 669; *see also* sloth and torpor
  and work 72–3, 194
Enlightenment 27, 92–3, 242, 353–4, 360, 380–1, 390, 459, 483, 520; *see also* Buddhahood, Nirvāṇa
  seven factors of (*bodhyaṅgas*) 87, 489, 508, 550, 582, 720n, 761n, 768n
  three doors to 521–2, 765n
  will to, *see bodhicitta*
envy (*īrṣyā*) 653–4, 700
Epicurus 507, 764n
equanimity (*upekṣā*) 183, 263, 335, 507–8, 581–2, 700, 768n, 771n
  cultivation of, *see upekṣā bhāvanā*
eternalism (*śāśvatavāda*) 241–5, 250–1, 286, 360, 449, 624–5
ethical
  absolutism 593
  identity 696–7
ethics (*śīla*) xxiv, 118, 119, 152, 153–4, 251, 254, 270, 323, 360, 542, 572, 745n; *see also* precepts
  attachment to codes of (*śīlavrata-parāmarśa*) 632–4, 745n
  fifty-seven faults 153, 291, 730n
  and imagination 598, 773n
  meditation, and wisdom, *see* threefold path
  and mental states 186, 644
  and *saṃprajanya* 679
  and wisdom 154, 158, 176, 323
  and worldly benefits or high status 160–1, 170–1, 323–4, 356–7
  wrong views of 636–8
evolution, spiritual 242–3, 640
excitement or excitedness 61–2, 79, 81–2, 100–1, 118–20, 288, 308, 701; *see also* ebullience, restlessness
exemplification (*samānārthatā*) 175, 590, 772n
existence
  conditioned 173, 180, 445, 754n; *see also saṃsāra*, wheel of life
    marks of (*lakṣaṇas*) 33, 161, 219, 350, 545, 612; fourth, *see* impurity
  relative plane of 343, 609, 626; *see also* truth, relative
experience
  direct or actual xxi, xxiv, 46, 135, 263, 341, 437–8, 451, 465, 544, 546, 578, 719n
  realms of, *see* realms, of experience

facticity, and haecceity 490, 761n, 764n
faith (*śraddhā* (Pāli *saddhā*)) 10, 17–57, 168, 290, 300, 334–8, 535, 550–7, 639, 671–4, 700, 712n, 745n; *see also* trust
  Conze's four factors of 17, 22, 35, 37, 39, 54–5
  and credulity or fantasy 43, 47, 62–4
  cultivation of 43–5, 71, 83, 90
  and devotion, *see* devotion
  and doctrine 22, 27–35
  emotional aspect 28, 34–5, 37–9, 55
  and energy 69–71, 78, 576
  and intellect 22–3, 34–5, 55
  lack of (*āśraddhya*) 671–4, 701
  Nāgārjuna and 326–7
  and pleasure 552–5, 672–3
  as 'seed' 17, 708n
  social aspect 39–42, 55, 559–60
  stage of spiral path 357
  three aspects of 551

and volition 35–7, 55
and wisdom 333–5
faith-followers (*saddhānusārins*) 35, 43, 332–3, 573, 603, 614, 710n, 743n, 770n
family 40, 111, 191, 279, 303, 342, 345, 363, 364, 638, 711n
Faxiang school 453, 770n
fear 180–1, 258, 278, 340, 559; *see also* terrors, five
and *apatrāpya* 558–61, 565, 769n
of fearlessness 352–3
feeling (*vedanā*) 357, 444, 478, 502–14, 527–8, 530, 699, 765n, 771n
and emotion distinguished 503–4, 537
indifferent, *see* indifference
mental and physical 509–10
pleasant and unpleasant, *see* pleasure and pain
transpersonal 510–12
fetters (*saṃyojana*)
first, *see* self-view
second, *see* doubt
third 632–5
first three 632–3, 735–6n, 745n
ten 597, 608, 632–3, 727n, 773n, 775n
firebrand 350, 406–8
food 11–12, 14, 16, 169, 283–4, 290, 585–6, 719n, 771n
forgetfulness (*muṣitasmṛtitā*) 677–8, 701; *see also* unmindfulness
form (*rūpa*) 384, 444–5, 479–80, 501, 523, 620–1
four noble truths 290, 457, 458, 551, 593, 607, 628, 737n, 739–40n, 747n, 774n
freedom 169, 245, 301, 328, 368, 409, 434–5, 519, 632; *see also ceto vimutti*, liberation
friendship, *see* spiritual, friendship
Friends of the Western Buddhist Order (FWBO) 61, 635, 709–10n; *see also* Triratna Buddhist Community

gambling 256–7, 393
Gampopa 459, 534, 758n, 766n
Gandhi, M. 199, 605
Gelugpa school 376, 423, 425, 451–2, 463, 466, 573, 707n, 731n, 742n
gender 77, 297
generosity or giving (*dāna*) 174, 180, 186, 251, 254, 297, 356, 562, 589, 590, 598, 657, 734–5n; *see also* precepts, second
gloominess (*styāna*) 669, 675, 701
God 19–20, 25, 275, 641, 662
gods 297, 774n; *see also* realms, god
Goethe, W. von 97, 397–8
Going for Refuge to the Three Jewels 287–8, 414, 589, 635, 672, 711n
going forth 110–12, 191–2, 711n
goodness, definite 160–1, 164–5, 323, 339, 357, 371, 391, 421; *see also* wisdom
frightening 323, 324, 339–40, 352–3, 369–70, 372
goose in the bottle 366
Govinda, Lama 558, 703, 764n, 768n, 771n
grasping (*upādāna*) 357, 370, 411, 478, 482
gratitude 185, 201–2, 274, 553
greed 42–3, 56, 121, 222, 596; *see also* craving, desire
-types 42, 602–3
group, the 52–4, 184–5, 279, 371, 672
and the spiritual community 40–1, 559, 562, 711n
growth 28, 94, 110, 343, 356–7, 435
Guenther, H. V. xvii, xix, 98, 431, 453, 464, 484, 494, 703, 723n, 724n, 755n, 757n, 758n
guilt 19, 95, 223, 253, 293, 302, 559, 638, 647–8; *see also* self-recrimination
as hindrance 118, 119, 120, 614, 615; *see also* worry-and-anxiety
Gyaltsen, Yeshe xii, 452

habit 474, 525, 526, 633
haecceity, and facticity 761n, 764n
happiness 158, 164–8, 170, 182, 210–11, 226–7, 270, 300, 335–6, 338, 360, 507; *see also* bliss, joy
harm, *see* malice
harmony 459
hate type 189, 602–3
hatred (*dveṣa*) 241, 258, 269, 295, 512–13, 597, 600–2, 677; *see also* anger, aversion, ill will, non-hatred
self- *see* self-hatred
heavens, *see* realms, god
heedlessness (*pramāda*) 580, 676–7, 701
hell
beings 170, 731n
realm 170, 259, 468, 472, 497, 525, 594, 688, 713n, 731n, 732n
Hīnayāna 154, 353, 360, 383, 448, 456, 546–7, 572, 757n; *see also* Sarvāstivāda, Theravāda
and Nirvāṇa 353, 574, 747n
hindrances (*nivaraṇas*), five 118, 119–22, 288, 335, 725n, 739n
Homer 294, 740n

Hopkins, J. 152, 332, 495, 699, 703, 704, 730n, 735n, 738n, 739n, 742n, 758n, 763n
hrī (Pāli *hiri*) 557–8, 561, 666, 700, 769n; *see also* shame
humility 273, 553, 605, 617
Humphreys, C. 31–2, 65, 412, 634, 709n, 716–17n
hungry ghosts (*pretas*) 170, 285, 294, 497, 729n, 731n
hypocrisy 277–8, 282, 285, 647, 659

ignorance (*avidyā*) 50, 132–4, 249, 313–14, 343, 357, 377, 408, 433–4, 476, 478, 493, 546, 596, 602, 607–11, 700, 727n, 763n; *see also* bewilderment and confusion, delusion, heedlessness, laziness
illness xiv, xxiii, 526, 714n, 765n; *see also* pain
ill will (*vyāpāda*) 118, 119, 120, 270, 293, 564, 660, 725n, 773n; *see also* hatred
imaginal faculty 674
imagination 303, 403, 412–13, 484, 485, 544, 597–8, 620, 684–5, 687
 unreal (*abhūtaparikalpa*) 760n
impermanence (*anitya*) 99–100, 129–30, 136, 162–3, 219, 331, 371, 378, 444, 516, 657
impurity (*aśubha*) 219–20, 389, 748n; *see also aśubha bhāvanā*
inattentiveness (*asaṃprajanya*) 678–80, 701
indecision (*vicikitsā*) 596, 612–16, 648, 700; *see also* doubt
indifference 183, 288, 508–9, 582, 771n
indignation (*krodha*) 643–4, 700, 738n
individual, the 21, 54, 86, 95, 111, 116–17, 697
 and spiritual, community 711–12n
 true 178–9, 185, 239, 562–3, 711n, 769n
individuality 549–50, 563, 631
 violation of 179, 198, 214
 wrong view of, *see* self-view
inexpressibles, ten or fourteen (*avyākṛtavastūni*) 152, 384–5, 621, 624, 641, 750n
insight 22, 70, 83, 129–33, 160, 164, 168–9, 187, 208, 262, 323, 421, 438, 463, 519, 775n
 and *dhyānas* 121, 126
 and faith and devotion 417, 555
 imaginative 117
 kṣānti (patience) and 566, 735n
 meditation, *see vipaśyanā* meditation
 reflection and, *see* reflection
 and scientific ignorance 329–31
 sharing 349
 and Stream Entry 437, 735n
 as third of 'five paths' 455, 458, 459, 542
 as third of 'three chief paths' 424
inspiration 71, 73, 162, 182–3, 460, 466, 554, 670, 770n
integration 59–60, 136, 194, 224, 290, 371, 457, 459–60, 549–50, 582, 682, 685, 696–7, 736n, 771n, 775n
 and concentration 116–19, 126, 495
 imaginal faculty and 674
 and making vows 169–70
 vertical 119–20, 123, 130
intellect 35–6, 118, 333, 484, 620, 673–4, 777n
intelligence 260, 304, 348, 415, 567, 595, 603, 773n
intention 200–1, 264, 292, 531, 563–4, 589, 590, 644, 679
interest (*chanda*) 457, 532–5, 675, 699, 766n
interest, intensified (*adhimokṣa*) 535, 699
intoxication 255–7
 self- (*mada*) 663–4, 700
investigation
 dharma-vicaya as xix, 131, 260–1, 265, 267, 428, 489, 550, 768n
 mīmāṃsā (4th *ṛddhipāda*) as 457
 vitarka as, *see* mind, initial application of
īrṣyā, *see* jealousy

Jains (Nirgranthas) 328, 362, 440, 584, 748n
Jamyang Khyentse Rimpoche 523, 728n
Jātakas 200, 480, 571, 734n, 744n, 760n
jealousy (*īrṣyā*) 653–4, 700, 739n
Jewel Ornament of Liberation 459, 534, 758n, 766n
jñāna, *see* knowledge, or understanding
jñāna, *prajñā* and *vidyā* distinguished 610–11
jñānas, five, *see* wisdoms, five
jñānasattva 544–5
John of the Cross, Saint 109, 673, 724n
Johnson, S. Dr 598, 675
Jowett, B. 605
joy 68, 80, 182, 252, 266, 302, 326–7, 336, 338, 357, 396, 553, 555; *see also* happiness
 sympathetic- (*muditā*) 183, 263, 335
  cultivation of, *see muditā bhāvanā*

Kagyu school 715n, 730n
Kāmadeva 691–2, 778n
kāmaloka or *kāmadhātu* 497–8, 513, 516–17, 527, 597; *see also* world, sensory
karma 14, 28–33, 37, 55–7, 163, 170–1, 263, 467, 476, 483, 439, 523–7, 662; *see also* actions, unskilful
'collective' or 'common' 297, 479, 483
fruits of (*karma vipāka*) 237, 244–5, 263, 476, 478–9, 497–8, 499, 520–1, 523–6, 545, 623, 636, 651
and feelings 502, 504, 525, 528
and intention 171, 200, 292
and rebirth 26–33, 160, 163, 170–3, 208–13, 279, 292, 294, 467–73, 480, 520, 524–7, 607, 679, 759n; *see also* wheel of life
not responsible for everything 293, 472–3; *see also niyamas*
weighty 526–7, 557
wrong views about 636
karma-cetanā, *see* mind, directionality of
karuṇā, *see* compassion
karuṇā bhāvanā 183, 263, 743n
Kashyap, J. 630
Kasibhāradvāja Sutta 17, 708n
kaukṛtya (Pāli *kukkucca*) *see* worry
kausīdya, *see* laziness
Kawamura, L. S. 432, 453, 704, 754n, 755n
killing, *see* precepts, first
kindness, *see mettā*
kleśas, *see* defilements
kliṣṭa-mano-vijñāna 329, 485–6, 488–9; *see also manas*
knowledge
spiritual and mundane 329–31
or understanding (*jñāna*) 143, 147, 483, 610–11
accumulation of (*jñāna-sambhāra*) 187, 415
of the destruction of the *āśravas* 357
five *jñānas*, *see* wisdoms, five
and merit (*puṇya*) 463; *see also* accumulations
vidyā and *prajñā* distinguished 610–11
and vision of things... 357, 519
krodha, *see* belligerence, indignation
kṣānti, *see* patience
Kurukullā 778n

lakṣaṇas, *see* existence, conditioned, marks of
language, limitations of 248–9, 295, 344, 352, 436
Laṅkāvatāra Sūtra 466, 585, 758n, 771n, 776n
laziness (*kausīdya*) 281, 288, 533–5, 576, 613, 671, 674–6, 686, 701
Lhalungpa, L. P. 423–4, 753n
liberation (*vimokṣa* (Pāli *vimutti*)) 160–1,
164, 251, 324, 355, 639, 729n; *see also* freedom
individual, *see arhant* ideal
two aspects of (*ceto vimutti/paññā vimutti*) 186–7, 733n
life-principle or life-force (*jīvitindriya*) 384, 522, 621–2
life-stream (*bhavaṅga-sota*) 523
The Lion's Roar of Queen Śrīmālā 751n
literalism 98, 232, 286, 371, 390, 479, 488, 493, 513, 750n
livelihood, *see also* work
right 193–7, 525
wrong 194–6
lobha, *see* craving
Locanā 146, 729n
Locke, J. 499, 685
logic 326, 375–6, 449, 451–3, 464–5, 519, 573, 642, 717n
Lokāyatas or Lokāyatikas 362, 747–8n
Lotus Sūtra 232, 356, 577, 722n, 737n, 771n
love 26, 314, 727n, 732n, 773n; *see also mettā*
mode and power mode 583–4
for oneself (*self-mettā*) 189, 667–9
romantic 655–6, 668, 737n
loving kindness, *see also mettā*

mada, *see* self-intoxication
Madhyamaka 112, 133, 321, 326, 360, 376, 449–52, 465–6, 488–9, 730n, 740n; *see also* Śūnyavāda
lineage 153, 375, 450–2, 463–4
origins 156, 325, 450
Madhyamakakārikā, *see Mūlamadhyamakakārikā*
Madhyānta-Vibhāga 489, 760n, 761n
Mahāsatipaṭṭhāna Sutta 85, 87, 107, 539, 721n, 757n, 761n, 777n
Mahāvastu Avadāna 337, 744n
Mahāvīra 328, 362, 584, 748n
Mahāyāna 151, 153, 155–7, 182, 206, 208, 254, 268, 456, 463, 546–7, 645, 741n, 757n
and Abhidharma 248, 447–52, 494, 690
effect of criticizing 190–1, 734n
and Nirvāṇa 355, 411, 574
philosophy, *see* Madhyamaka, Yogācāra

Mahāyāna (*cont.*)
sūtras 156–7, 187, 297–8, 329, 337, 466, 472, 735n, 740n, 751n; *see also* Perfection of Wisdom *sūtras*
Maitreya 325, 464, 760n
Five Books of 464, 489
Maitreyanātha 461, 463–4, 760n
Majjhima Nikāya 85, 167, 221, 243, 274, 456, 585, 594, 710n, 720n, 725n, 731n, 733n, 736n, 737n, 738n, 742n, 750n, 757n, 766n, 771n, 772n, 774n, 777n
malice (*vihiṃsā*) 269, 600, 664–6, 700
Māmakī 146, 729n
māna, *see* arrogance, pride
manas 484, 486; *see also kliṣṭa-mano-vijñāna*
manaskāra (Pāli *manasikāra*) 501, 502, 531, 699, 766n
mandala 277, 299
of the five Buddhas 487, 487, 488, 728n, 729n, 739n, 760n; *see also* wisdoms, five
greater/non-utilitarian 608–9
offering verse 1
Mañjughoṣa or Mañjuśrī 461–3
manomayakāya 622, 774n
mano-vijñāna 484–5, 487, 690, 767n
mantras 119, 299, 417–18, 525, 526, 686, 722n
materialism 362, 444, 469, 556, 656–7, 722n, 747n
spiritual 171, 211, 594
Matics, M. 411, 752n
mātsarya, *see* avarice
māyā, *see* deceit
meditation 262–4, 288, 341, 496–7, 525, 708n; *see also* contemplation
Abhidharma and 135, 438, 441–2, 447, 454, 532, 539, 550, 697
brahma vihāras, *see brahma vihāras*
breathing, *see* mindfulness of breathing
calming, *see śamatha*
on corpse 543, 681; *see also aśubha bhāvanā*
and distraction 680–1; *see also* hindrances
enjoyment and pleasure 226, 393, 396, 513–14
heat in (*tapas*) 457–8
hindrances, *see* hindrances
on impurities of the body 543; *see also aśubha bhāvanā*
insight, *see vipaśyanā* meditation
'just sitting' 62, 715n
and karma 526–8
mettā bhāvanā, *see mettā bhāvanā*
resistance to 533–4
and self-intoxication 664
six element practice 382, 623
system of 715n, 775n
and third level of wisdom 567; *see also bhāvanā-mayī-prajñā*
visualization 119, 542, 544–5, 728n
Visuddhimagga as reference for 712n
Yogācāra and 450, 451, 483
Meghiya 342, 744n
memory 536, 540–1, 745n; *see also* forgetfulness
mental, proliferation (*prapañca*) 147, 730n
mental events (*caitta* (Pāli *cetasika*)) 438, 446, 488, 490–3, 697
classification of 268, 446–7, 449, 500, 532, 738n, 767n
eleven positive (*kuśala*) 549–90, 700, 772n
arising of 589–90
characteristics 588
five object-determining (*viniyata*) 532–48, 568, 699
five omnipresent (*sarvatraga*) 491, 501–31, 699
four variables (*aniyata*) 683–90, 701
investigation of, *see* investigation
and mind, *see under* mind
negative or unskilful xx, 98–9, 180–1, 268, 289–90, 438
arising of 593–4
basic (*mūlakleśas*) 500, 591, 596–642, 700
characteristics 591–2
proximate (*upakleśas*) 643–82, 700–1
mental inflation (*mada*) *see* self-intoxication
mental objects xviii, 446, 484, 528, 690, 720n
four classes of 542–3
mental perversities, *see* views, 'topsy-turvy'
mental states, *see* mental events
merit (*puṇya*) 143, 147, 161, 306, 333, 471, 587, 590, 772n
accumulation of, *see* accumulations
rejoicing in 417, 654
transference or dedication of 415–17, 418, 694
mettā (Sanskrit *maitrī*) 172, 182–9, 222, 248, 295, 342, 511, 583, 668; *see also* love
benefits or virtues of 187–9, 263
lack of 583, 664–5
self- *see* love, for oneself

mettā bhāvanā 97, 183–4, 456, 504, 511, 542, 644, 645, 665, 693, 733n, 745n, 757n, 764n, 768n
Order 42, 712n
Mettānisaṃsa or *Mettā Sutta* 189, 734n
middha, *see* drowsiness
middle way 81, 157, 226, 244, 253, 325, 624, 626
Milarepa 155, 194, 302, 333, 338, 354, 376, 467–8, 553, 555, 574, 688, 730n, 744n, 758n
Milindapañha 70, 131, 717n, 726n
Mill, J. S. 404, 751n
Milton, J. 497, 763n
mind (*citta*) xx, 434, 436–8, 446, 457, 493, 498
mind
Absolute 760n
'-as-such' 491–3, 510, 607, 761n, 762n, 763n; *see also* awareness, pure
compared to a house 676–7
as conditioner of worlds 475–6, 479, 483–4
consciousness, *see mano-vijñāna*
creative 128–9, 260, 344, 357, 434, 550, 751n
directionality of (*cetanā*) 501, 502, 520–9, 530, 531, 584, 699, 723n
essential purity of 95, 98, 722n
and heart, liberation through (*ceto vimutti*) 186–7, 733n
initial application of (*vitarka*) 125, 518, 683, 689–90, 701, 725n
and matter 404, 482–3; *see also* body, and mind
and mental events or factors xviii, 410, 437–8, 531, 582
classification of 446, 449, 690, 760n
distinguished 489–94, 761–2n
functional co-relations 495–6, 498, 588
nature of 437, 481–99
patterns, *see* patterns
pure 95, 490, 496; *see also* awareness, pure
rational xxi–xxii, 18, 376, 391, 616–17; *see also* reason
and irrationality 65–6, 687
'self-luminous' 411, 752n
as sixth sense 13, 439, 478, 495, 516, 543; *see also mano-vijñāna*
sustained application of (*vicāra*) 125, 518, 683, 689–90, 701, 725n
-watching xvi–xvii, xix–xx, xxii, 282–3
Western idea of 436, 437, 450
mindfulness (*smṛti* (Pāli *sati*)) xviii, xxiii, 60, 79–112, 256, 265–7, 456–7, 489, 539, 543, 723n; *see also* awareness, recollection, unmindfulness
of the body 103–4, 456, 537–8, 721n, 767n
of breathing (*ānāpānasati*) 105, 114–15, 119, 186, 456, 541, 724n, 733n, 757n, 767n, 768n
effect of limiting 397
four dimensions of, *see under* awareness
four foundations of 87–8, 456, 536, 539, 721n, 776n
higher levels of 110–11
in Hīnayāna and Mahāyāna 456
and intoxication 255–7
of purpose (*saṃprajanya*) xviii, 540–1, 581, 679
and remembering 89–91, 114, 539–40
wrong sort of 88–9
mindfulness, *apramāda* as, *see* non-heedlessness
Mind in Buddhist Psychology 43, 108, 431–2, 434, 724n
Mind Only (*citta-matra*) 450, 481–8
mirage 251, 346, 357–9, 379–80, 384, 385, 386–7
moha, *see* bewilderment and confusion
Molière 285, 739n
momentariness, philosophy of (*kṣaṇikavāda*) 366–7
motivation 11, 190, 287, 292, 299, 303, 460, 467–8, 472, 475–6
mrakṣa, *see* slyness-concealment
muditā, *see* joy, sympathetic-
muditā bhāvanā 183, 263, 335, 743n
mūlakleśas, *see under* mental events, negative
Mūlamadhyamakakārikā 153, 321–2, 465–6, 475, 702, 714n, 723n, 731n, 738n, 748n, 749n, 751n, 752n, 758n, 759n, 774n, 776n
Murry, J. Middleton 336, 743n, 768n
muṣitasmṛtitā, *see* forgetfulness
myth 297, 686–7

Nāgārjuna xvi, 153, 156–8, 321, 323, 450, 464, 465, 466, 702–3, 704, 705, 714n, 730n, 731n, 734n, 741n, 746n, 758–9n
nāgas 7, 147, 325, 730n, 741n
Nāropā 340, 744n
nature
and culture 95–8, 332
or things, dimension of awareness of 87, 536, 776n

The Necklace of Clear Understanding xii, xvii, 452–3, 481
Neoplatonism 222, 736n, 759n
nidānas
twelve cyclic 357, 476, 502, 503, 530, 609–10, 759–60n; *see also* conditionality
twelve positive 357, 578, 706n, 747n; *see also* path, spiral
Nietzsche, F. 620, 655, 776n
nihilism (*ucchedavāda*) 175, 241–6, 249–51, 359–60, 371, 388, 411, 488, 624–5
Buddhism mistaken for 163, 360, 362–3, 389, 444
nirmāṇakāya 623, 729n
Nirvāṇa 160, 171, 187, 233, 242, 245, 296, 355–7, 362, 443, 446, 547–8, 582, 740n; *see also* Enlightenment
faith and doubt in 34, 612
non-abiding (*apratiṣṭhita nirvāṇa*) 574, 770n
and *saṃsāra* 365, 368, 380, 411, 424, 582, 593, 623
niyamas, five 55, 478–9, 714n; *see also* conditionality, levels of
non-attachment (*alobha*) 168, 205, 508–9, 561–3, 565–6, 574, 579, 581, 700, 769n; *see also* attachment
non-deludedness (*amoha*) 295, 546, 566–72, 574, 579, 581, 700, 767n, 769n, 770n
non-duality 424, 481, 623
non-ego 193, 344, 353, 411
non-harm, *see* precepts, first
non-hatred (*adveṣa*) 295, 563–6, 574, 579, 581, 700, 769n
non-heedlessness (*apramāda*) 579–81, 677, 700; *see also* senses, guarding
non-violence (*avihiṃsā*) 199, 353, 582–7, 594, 700; *see also* precepts, first
Nyāya-Vaiśeṣika school 440, 765n, 776n; *see also* Asatkāryavādins
Nyingma school 451–2, 494, 728n, 762n

object-determining mental events, *see under* mental events
omniscience 323, 328–9, 369, 461, 463, 742n
One Mind 133, 569, 570; *see also* *śūnyatā*
one-pointedness (*ekāgratā* (Pāli *ekaggatā*)) 113, 518, 542, 578, 582, 725n, 767n, 771n
operational concepts 98, 493–4, 631, 690, 723n, 763n
opinionatedness (*dṛṣṭi*) 596, 617–42, 700, 738n, 754n; *see also* views, wrong
Origen 468, 759n
Otto, R. 135, 727n

Padmasambhava 451, 574, 640, 708n
pain, *see also* illness, suffering
and pleasure 392–409, 503, 505–7
Pāṇḍaravāsinī 146, 729n
paññā vimutti 186–7, 733n
parables
burning house 232–3, 737n
magic city 356, 746–7n
raft 675, 777n
pāramitās, *see* perfections
parents 167, 637–8, 668, 696, 754n
Parmenides 450, 756n
path
of five stages or five paths (*mārgas*) 455–60, 757n
of accumulation (*saṃbhāra-mārga*) 455–7, 459, 536
of insight or vision (*darśana-mārga*) 455, 458, 495, 542, 752n
of no more learning (*niṣṭhā-mārga*) 455, 459–60
of practice (*prayoga-mārga*) 176, 335, 455, 457–8, 495, 620
of transformation or cultivation (*bhāvanā-mārga*) 455, 458–9, 752n
of irregular steps 83–4, 109
noble eightfold, *see* Eightfold Path
not 'out there' 435, 755n
of regular steps 83–4, 109, 268, 421, 459–60
spiral xxv, 357, 519, 706n; *see also* *nidānas*, twelve positive
stages of in Tibetan Buddhism 423–4, 703, 757n
The Path of Purity, *see* *Visuddhimagga*
paths
four (Hindu) 134, 727n
three, of Tsongkhapa, *see* *Three Chief Paths*
patience (*kṣānti*) 46, 251, 254, 270, 335, 566, 582, 602, 735n; *see also* tolerance
patterns, in one's experience xx, 350, 434, 470, 473, 475, 538, 541, 562
perception, *see also* *saṃjñā*
categorical or mental, *see* *mano-vijñāna*
objects of 482–5, 499, 690
sense 486, 496, 498, 510, 514, 516, 528, 543, 690; *see also* sense, consciousness
perceptual situation xviii–xx, 377, 404, 445, 479–80, 482–4, 501, 515, 756n

Perfection of Wisdom 247, 321; *see also* Prajñāpāramitā
origin 325, 730n
sūtras 153, 157, 323, 325, 488, 730n, 731n, 740n
perfections (*pāramitās*) 153, 254, 289, 415, 458, 463, 610
philosophy 619–20, 626, 685, 759n
Buddhist 433, 438, 448; *see also* Madhyamaka, Mind Only (Yogācāra)
schools of classical Indian 712n, 747n; *see also* Nyāya, Vaiśeṣika, Sāṃkhya
Plato 588, 756n
pleasure xxiv, 56, 166, 187–9, 221, 226, 253, 300–3, 513, 528
and faith 552–5, 672–3
and pain 392–409, 503, 505–7
poetry 117, 271, 331–2, 441, 620, 684–5, 686, 687, 716n
poisons, three 164, 512, 574, 596, 602, 769n; *see also* roots
Pope, A. 560–1, 769n
pot, four kinds of 160
potentiality, metaphysics of 92–5, 97, 722n, 751n
prajñā (Pāli *paññā*) 187, 463, 545–8, 581, 699, 767n, 768n, 770n, 773n; *see also* wisdom
connotations and definition of 130–2
liberation through (*paññā vimutti*) 186–7
and non-deludedness (*amoha*) 567–72, 770n
and *samādhi* 611, 695
vidyā and *jñāna*, distinguished 610–11
Prajñāpāramitā 39, 40, 715n, 730n; *see also* Perfection of Wisdom
pramāda, *see* heedlessness
praśrabdhi, *see* tranquillity
pratigha, *see* anger
precepts 106, 170, 176, 572–3; *see also* ethics
first 175, 178–97, 293–4, 644; *see also* non-violence
second 198–213, 294; *see also* generosity
third 214–17, 227, 294
five 228
ten 153, 174–7, 255, 293, 528–9, 730n, 732n, 765–6n
'mind' 228, 241–64, 528
positive counterparts 176–7
speech 228–40, 525, 651, 765n
harmonious 230, 237
harsh/kindly 229, 237, 240; *see also* speech, kindly
truthful/untruthful 229–36; *see also* dishonesty
useless/helpful 232–3, 237–8
Precious Garland of Advice for a King (*Rāja-parikathā-Ratnamālā* or *Ratnāvalī*) xi, xvi–xvii, 151, 153–5, 321–3, 465, 703, 758n
pretence (*māyā*) 657–9, 700, 732n
pride
Buddha-, or vajra- 275, 558
or conceit (*māna*) 271–4, 285, 604, 700, 727n, 739n; *see also* arrogance
positive, *see apatrāpya*
prīti, *see* rapture
projection 77, 224–5, 234, 258, 658, 661, 665, 736–7n
protection 561
Proust, M. 402, 751n
psychic power, four bases of, *see ṛddhipādas*
psychological, model of development 437, 454, 644–5, 670–1, 673, 679, 694–5, 747n
psychology 107, 433, 436, 440, 446, 449, 453, 649, 661
pudgala 248, 442, 448, 631–2
pudgalavāda 631–2, 775n
puja 183, 205, 317, 525; *see also* worship
sevenfold 204–5, 414–18, 735n
puṇya, *see* merit
Pure Land 174, 243, 296–9, 479
sūtras 740n
purification 121–2, 187, 314
purity (*śubha*) 85, 87, 220, 304, 561; *see also* beauty
purpose, mindfulness or recollection of (*saṃprajanya*) xviii, 540–1, 581, 679
purposelessness (*asaṃprajanya*) *see* inattentiveness
puruṣa 442

Radhakrishnan, S. 35–6, 444, 710n, 712n
rāga 596–8, 602, 700; *see also* desire
rage (*krodha*) *see* indignation
rākṣasas 146, 317, 740n
rapture (*prīti*) 357, 518, 579, 596, 768n
Ratnasambhava 488, 729n
ṛddhis or *ṛddhipādas* (Pāli *iddhipādās*), four 145, 147, 457, 729n, 757n, 766n
reality
body of (*dharmakāya*) 729n, 742n
ultimate or true 33, 34, 133, 368, 410, 456, 678, 694, 696; *see also* truth, ultimate

realms xxii, 24, 341, 497–8, 731n; *see also* worlds
animal 170, 497, 525, 731n
of anti-gods, *see asuras*
of *dharmas* 133
of experience 24, 297, 325, 496–8, 513, 686; *see also dhyānas*
god (*devalokas*) 116, 263, 325, 442, 464, 525, 527, 731n; *see also arūpaloka*; worlds, of Brahmā
hell, *see* hell, realm
human 160, 173, 497, 731n
hungry ghost, *see* hungry ghosts
reason, *see also* mind, rational
and emotions 685, 689
rebirth 28–33, 45–6, 49–50, 55, 242, 350, 357, 468–71, 475, 607–8, 754n, 759n; *see also* karma and rebirth
bodhisattvas and 411–12
eternalist/nihilist views and 241–5, 250–1
no further 351, 353, 411
integration and 522–3
opportune and inopportune (*kṣaṇa/akṣaṇa*) 168, 427, 731–2n, 753n
with other people 480
over-literal view of 286
in a Pure Land 298–9, 479
recollection of 46, 713n
in *saṃsāra* 14, 160, 168, 170, 173, 245, 263, 323
spiritual 118–19, 481
Stream Entry and 745n
wheel of life and 351, 478, 497
receptivity xxi, 76–7, 208, 234, 261, 607, 667
recognition xxii, xxv, 435, 690, 699; *see also* cognition, *saṃjñā*
recollection (*smṛti*) xviii, 535–41, 581, 699, 719n, 768n; *see also* awareness, mindfulness
of the Buddha, *see buddhānusmṛti*
recollections, six or ten (*anussatis*) 541, 767n
reflection (*cintā-mayī-prajñā*) xvi, 127–9, 247, 403, 535, 543, 567, 570, 573, 588, 607, 611
Refuges, Three, *see* Three Jewels
reification 248, 383, 408, 751n
rejoicing in merits 417, 654
omission of, as dishonesty 661–2
renunciation 41, 226, 338, 363–4, 381, 396, 421
resentment (*upanāha*) 160, 268–70, 564, 645–7, 651, 700, 738n
respect 260–1, 275–6, 462, 606
for wise opinion 305, 306; *see also apatrāpya*
responsibility 696
restlessness (*auddhatya*) 596, 670, 681, 727n; *see also* excitedness
retreats 284, 298, 381, 396, 401, 526
solitary 16, 42, 99, 112, 303
reverence 91, 261, 275–7, 281, 605, 739n
roots, three skilful and unskilful 550, 566, 568, 574, 727n; *see also* poisons
rūpa, *see* form
rūpaloka or *rūpadhātu* 497–8, 513–14, 597; *see also under dhyānas*; world of form

Śākyamuni 461, 463, 640; *see also* Buddha
samādhi, *see* concentration
śamatha (Pāli *samatha*) xvii, 186–7, 611, 729n, 768n
samayasattva 544–5
Saṃdhinirmocana Sūtra 488, 757n, 761n
saṃgraha-vastus 174–5, 590, 772n
saṃjñā (Pāli *saññā*) 444, 502, 514–20, 699, 765n; *see also* cognition, discrimination, perception, recognition
four bases for 516
six levels of 516–17
six sense bases 516
Sāṃkhya school 362, 439–40, 636, 712n, 746n, 755n; *see also* Satkāryavāda school
saṃsāra 232, 357, 475, 592, 610, 633; *see also* existence, conditioned
and *nirvāṇa* 365, 368, 380, 411, 424, 582, 593, 623
saṃskāras, *see* volitions
Saṃyutta Nikāya 85, 127, 243, 290, 324, 357, 458, 473, 632, 707n, 708n, 720n, 721n, 725n, 736n, 738n, 740n, 741n, 747n, 757n, 759n, 774n, 775n, 778n
Sangha 39, 169, 261, 363, 364, 370, 656; *see also* Āryasaṅgha, spiritual community
means of unification of, *see saṃgraha-vastus*
Sangharakshita, seminars xi–xiii, xvii, 5–6, 49, 151, 431
Śāntideva 204, 375–6, 417, 728n, 749n
Śāriputra 333, 442
Sarvāstivāda 155, 650, 741n, 755n; *see also under* Abhidharma
sarvatraga, *see* Mental events, five omnipresent
śāṭhya, *see* dishonesty

Satipaṭṭhāna Sutta, *see Mahāsatipaṭṭhāna Sutta*
Satkāryavāda school 636–7, 775n; *see also* Sāṃkhya school
Sautrāntika school 449, 756n
Schopenhauer, A. 222, 362, 608, 736n, 773n
science xviii, xxiii, 43–4, 329–31, 443, 444, 446, 637, 685, 742n
seeds (*bījas*) 486–7
self
  ālaya-vijñāna interpreted as 486
  -confidence 36–7
  -deception 134, 196, 215, 257
  -discipline 44–5, 253
  fixed, *see ātman*, *pudgala*, *puruṣa*
  -hatred 169, 185, 189, 191, 243, 250–4, 624–5, 629
  -indulgence 109, 624–5
  -intoxication (*mada*) 663–4, 700
  -love (self-*mettā*) 189, 667–9
  Nāgārjuna's central point about 249
  -nature (*svabhāva*) 448, 520, 730n
  no- or non- 37, 38, 339–45, 382–3, 511–12; *see also anātman*
    and five *skandhas* 347, 358–9, 444, 474–5, 721n; *see also* aggregates
  and others 192–3, 692–6, 698; *see also* subject-object
  -power, and other-power 751n
  -purification 121–2
  -recrimination 166, 176, 215, 270; *see also* guilt
  -respect, *see hrī*
  'strong' 631, 775n
  useful purpose of 630–1
  -view (*satkāyadṛṣṭi*) 383, 390–1, 493, 608, 618–23, 632, 633, 745n, 773n; *see also* ego
sems-nyid, *see* 'mind-as-such'
sense
  -based instincts and impulses 10–15
  bases, twelve (*āyatanas*) 404
  consciousness 377, 393, 484, 487, 529–30, 688; *see also* perception, sense; *vijñānas*, eight
  desire (*kāmachanda*) 118, 119–20, 725n, 773n
  objects 100, 119–20, 404, 405, 408, 529–30
senses
  five physical 13, 393–4, 445, 484, 516, 751n
  'guarding doors of' 96–102, 723n; *see also* non-heedlessness
  six (*ṣaḍāyatanas*) 404, 478, 496, 529–30
  sixth, *see* mind, as sixth sense
sex 12, 214–27, 255, 271, 284, 598, 638–9, 658, 668, 765n, 776n
sexual relationships 214–16, 224, 294, 506, 564–5, 600, 638–9, 668, 737n; *see also* precepts, third
Shakespeare, W. 185, 238, 280, 549, 654, 733n, 737n, 739n, 776n
shame 565, 669; *see also hrī*
shamelessness (*āhrīkya*) 666–7, 700
Shelley, P. B. 598, 773n
Śikṣā-samuccaya 69, 717n, 749n
śīla, *see* ethics
silence 80, 230, 387, 624, 741n, 750n
six ornaments of India 461, 464–6, 758n
skandhas (Pāli *khandas*) *see* aggregates
sleep 167, 189, 340–1, 518, 602, 683–4, 685, 686, 701
sleepiness (*middha*), *see* drowsiness
sloth (*styāna* (Pāli *thīna*)) 683, 777n
  and torpor (*styāna-middha*) 118, 119, 120, 683, 725n, 777n; *see also* drowsiness
slyness-concealment (*mrakṣa*) xxii, 268, 278, 647–9, 651, 653, 657, 659, 661, 700, 739n
smṛti (Pāli *sati*) *see* mindfulness, recollection
soberness 67–8, 79–81, 88
solitude 303, 428
space 367, 380, 384–5, 443, 446, 495
  and time 387, 402
spārśa, *see* contact
speech
  kindly (*priyavāditā*) 174–5, 229, 308, 590
  precepts, *see* precepts, speech
spheres of infinite space and consciousness 495, 517, 725n; *see also arūpa dhyānas*
Spinoza, B. 269, 503, 738n, 764n
spiral, *see* path, spiral; *nidānas*, twelve positive
spiritual
  community 40–2, 73, 111–12, 184–5, 239, 269, 307, 327, 559–60, 584, 673; *see also* sangha
    and arising of *bodhicitta* 186, 190
    concealment and lying 647, 660
    and confession 650
    and the group 40–1, 559, 562, 711n
    the individual and 711–12n
    means of unification, *see saṃgraha-vastus*
  faculties (or virtues), five (*pañca-indriya*) xvii, xxiv, 5, 10–11, 13, 60, 105–6, 135–7, 707n, 720n, 743n, 757n, 769n

spiritual (*cont.*)
balance of 59–60, 62, 64–5, 67, 70–1, 82–3, 134, 333–4
developed in sequence 83–4, 458
friends 559–61, 614, 647–8, 673
friendship 71, 183, 230, 255, 297, 307, 308–9, 327–8, 363–4, 541, 553, 745n
life 436–7
five stages of, *see* path, of five stages
settling down in 675–6
materialism 171, 211, 594, 656
progress 10–11, 13, 109–10, 161, 166, 267, 302, 306, 333, 633
rebirth 118–19, 481
teachers 156, 230, 277, 303, 304, 307–8, 329, 466, 558, 607, 650, 753n; *see also* the wise
lying to 660
temperament and 332
training or practice 103, 178, 253–4, 569–71; *see also* discipline
spite (*pradāśa*) 651–3, 700; *see also* defensiveness
spontaneity 83, 265–6, 268, 328, 399, 459–60
śraddhā, *see* faith
śruta-mayī-prajñā 128–9, 567, 573, 611
stagnation (*styāna*) *see* gloominess
status, 'high' 160–1, 170–1, 323–4, 356–7; *see also* rebirth, in *saṃsāra*
Stcherbatsky, T. 489–90, 760n, 761n
Stream Entry (*srotāpanna*) 11, 70, 131, 221, 345, 437, 676, 707–8n, 711n, 735–6n, 745n
styāna, *see* gloominess
styāna-middha, *see* sloth and torpor
subject-object duality 521–2, 693–6; *see also* dualism; self and others
suffering or unsatisfactoriness (*duḥkha*) 219, 252, 357, 368, 397, 434, 592–3, 774n; *see also* pain
in the course of spiritual practice 302–3
three kinds of 427, 563–4, 754n
sukha, *see* bliss
śūnyatā 133, 296, 314, 326, 346–61, 391, 404, 424, 450, 517, 546, 710n, 730n, 740n, 741–2n; *see also* baselessness, emptiness, One Mind
Śūnyavāda 362–3, 389, 747n; *see also* Madhyamaka
superficiality (*śīlavrataparāmarśa*) *see* attachment to observances
superknowledges (*abhijñās*) 46, 712–13n
Śūraṅgama Sūtra 337, 743n
Sūtra Piṭaka 442, 572
Sutta-Nipāta 17, 157, 547, 708n, 740n, 774n, 771n, 776n
Suzuki, D. T. 65, 331–2, 717n, 742n, 758n, 771n, 776n
svabhāva, *see* self-nature

Tantra 133, 314, 366, 423, 451, 494, 546, 595, 638, 685–6, 704, 730n; *see also* Vajrayāna
tantras 452, 461, 466, 573–4, 728n
Tārā 141, 142, 143–7, 715n
Tāranātha 705, 728n, 758n
Tathāgata 617–18, 733n, 750n, 751n; *see also* Buddha
tathāgatagarbha 390, 722n, 751n; *see also* Buddha-nature
temperament 43, 202, 244, 332–3, 573, 602–3, 684
Tennyson, A. Lord 304, 331–2, 511, 738n, 740n, 743n, 765n
termas xvii, 452, 706n
terrors, five 37
theosophy 31–2, 64, 709n
Theravāda 186, 191, 456, 473, 632–4, 724n; *see also under* Abhidharma
Therīgāthā 218, 735n
thinking, clear 383, 442, 614–15, 617
thought 479, 484–5, 607
applied (*vitarka*) *see* mind, initial application of
sustained (*vicāra*) *see* mind, sustained application of
Three Chief Paths (*lam gtso rnam gsum*) 421, 424–8, 704, 753n
threefold path (ethics, meditation and wisdom) xvii, 455, 542, 543, 572
Three Jewels 27, 34, 55, 71, 277, 535, 551, 672, 740n, 767n
Tibetan Book of the Dead (*Bardo Thödol*) 15, 354, 678, 708n, 713n
Tibetan Buddhism 155–6, 277, 340, 423, 451–2, 466, 526, 554, 728n, 730n, 751n; *see also* Tantra, Vajrayāna
stories 193, 338, 744n
time 357, 365, 385, 403, 405–6, 408, 468, 494, 497, 748–9n, 751n, 758–9n
and eternity 609, 611
and space 387, 402
Tiratana Vandanā 466, 631, 721n
tolerance 51–4; *see also* patience
torpor (*middha*) *see* drowsiness, sloth and torpor
Traherne, T. 470, 759n
tranquillity (*praśrabdhi*) 59–60, 263, 438, 533, 577–9, 582, 700, 768n
the transcendental 44, 437, 454, 457–8, 463, 570

transformation, path of (*bhāvanāmargā*) 455, 458–9, 752n
transmission, oral 154–6, 440
Trethong, Mr. xxvi, 422, 425
trikāya 546
Triratna Buddhist Community xi, xii, 710n, 717n, 718n, 719n, 764n; *see also* Friends of the Western Buddhist Order
  communication exercises 80, 719n
  Refuge Tree 716n
Triratna Buddhist Order xvi, 7, 718n; *see also* Western Buddhist Order
tṛṣṇā 478, 503; *see also* craving
trust 23–4, 33, 39, 50, 263, 552–3, 671; *see also* faith
  lack of, *see under* faith
truth 493
  ability and willingness to hear 239–40, 290–1
  relative or conventional 54, 249, 383, 546, 618, 713n, 747n; *see also* existence, relative
  ultimate or absolute 424, 758n
truthfulness, *see under* precepts, speech; dishonesty
Tsongkhapa 155, 333, 376, 421–5, 425, 452, 463, 466, 533–4, 595, 596, 695, 703–4, 730–1n, 752–3n, 757n, 764n

Udāna 157, 342, 402, 547, 571, 744n, 774n
uddhacca-kukkucca, *see* worry-and-anxiety
unconcern 663, 701; *see also* heedlessness
the Unconditioned 219–20, 223, 359
  gravitational pull of 612, 676, 773n
universalism 52–4, 713n
unmindfulness 100, 117, 282, 524, 701; *see also* forgetfulness
upakleśas, *see under* mental events, negative
upekṣā (Pāli *upekkhā*) *see* equanimity
upekṣā bhāvanā 183, 263, 743n

vagueness 633; *see also* doubt
Vairocana 488
Vaiśeṣika school 362, 440, 712n, 748n, 776n
Vajrapāṇi *316*
Vajrayāna 275, 299, 465, 546–7, 715n, 730n, 755n, 757n; *see also* Tibetan Buddhism
Vasubandhu 447, 449, 453, 464–5, 489–90, 704–5, 725n, 741n, 756n
Vaughan, H. 470, 759n
Vedānta 636, 712n, 744n, 746n
vegetarianism 285, 569, 584–6, 617
vicāra, *see* mind, sustained application of
vidyā 493, 607–11, 773n; *see also* discrimination, appreciative
  jñāna and *prajñā* distinguished 610–11
view, right (*samyag-dṛṣṭi*) xix–xx, 245, 259, 617–18, 631
views
  ethics of, *see* precepts, 'mind'
  fixed 238–9, 307, 428
  freedom from all, or 'no-view' 245, 617–18, 774n
  of modern scholarship 156–7
  of *prajñā* from three *yānas* 546–7
  'topsy-turvy' (*vipariyāsas*) 219–20, 545, 681, 767n, 777n
  wrong or false (*micchā-diṭṭhis*) xxi, xxiii, 21, 216, 241–3, 245, 251, 257, 259, 369, 465, 594, 602, 617–21, 629–31, 635–42, 765n; *see also* opinionatedness
    'extreme' 245, 247, 424, 428, 444, 623–9; *see also* eternalism, nihilism
    of 'self'; *see* self-view
    sixty-two 640–2
vigour 10, 57–79, 83, 457, 714n; *see also vīrya*
vihiṃsā, *see* malice
vijñāna 444, 478, 482–4, 502; *see also* consciousness; awareness, discriminating
vijñānas, eight 483–7, 729n; *see also* sense consciousness
Vijñaptimātratāsiddhi-śāstra 551, 561, 563–5, 567, 756n, 766n, 770n
Vijñaptimātratāsiddhi-triṃśikā 453, 725n, 756n
Vijñāvāda school, *see* Yogācāra
vikṣepa, *see* distraction
vinaya 572, 583, 587
Vinaya Piṭaka 324, 337, 442, 444, 447, 452, 572, 734n, 741n, 744n, 756n, 774n
viniyata, *see under* mental events
viparyāsas, *see* views, 'topsy-turvy'
vipaśyanā (Pāli *vipassanā*) 187; *see also* insight
  meditation xvii, 550, 611, 768n
    alienation and misapprehension in 88–9, 253
vīrya (Pāli *viriya*) 58, 335, 457-8, 574–7, 581, 670, 700, 768n, 771n; *see also* effort, energy, vigour

vision
or insight, path of (*darśana-mārga*) 455, 458, 542, 752n
or view, perfect (*samyag-dṛṣṭi*) 458, 571, 617–18, 676
Visuddhimagga 42, 59, 67, 85, 112, 127, 131, 135, 441, 447, 518, 531, 602, 689, 712n, 713n, 715n, 717n, 720n, 721n, 727n, 764n, 765n, 773n, 778n
vitarka, *see* mind, initial application of
volition, stage of (*javana*) 499–500
volitions (*saṃskāras*) 17, 434, 444, 473, 475, 476, 478–9, 502, 610
and *cetanā*, *see* mind, directionality of
vows 169–70, 268, 528, 561, 633
vyāpāda, *see* ill will

Wangyal, Geshe 421, 704, 752n, 753n
The Way of Wisdom: the Five Spiritual Faculties xii, xvii, 5, 10, 137, 707n, 712n, 717n
The Way to Wisdom xii–xiii, xvii, 5–6
Western Buddhist Order xvi, 7, 287, 672, 712n, 718n, 735n; *see also* Triratna Buddhist Order
wheel of life, Tibetan (*bhavacakra*) 11, 160, 170, 245, 263, 350–1, 476, 477, 478, 497, 503–4, 512, 609–10, 731n
White Lotus Sūtra, *see Lotus Sūtra*
Whitman, W. 378, 749n
Wilde, O. 258, 281
will ('*der Wille*') 222, 521, 608
Wilson, C. 66, 708n, 717n
wisdom xxv, 10, 99–100, 127–36, 245, 267, 306–7, 333, 421; *see also* goodness, definite; *prajñā*; *vidyā*
accumulation of, *see* accumulations
bodhisattva of 462
and compassion 153, 158, 174, 187, 411, 694
discriminating or distinguishing 282, 487–8
and ethics 154, 158, 176, 323
and faith 333–5
liberation by (*paññā vimutti*) 186–7, 733n
non-intellectual 134–5, 324, 331–3, 391
perfection of, *see* Perfection of Wisdom
three levels of xvi, 127–30, 516, 535, 567, 573, 611, 725–6n, 766–7n
type, *see* doctrine follower
wisdoms, five (*jñānas*) 143, 145–6, 282, 483, 487–8, 728–9n; *see also* mandala, of the five Buddhas
the wise 260–1, 304, 306–7, 324, 558–60; *see also* spiritual teachers
Wish-Fulfilling Gem 143, 595
withdrawal (*niḥsaraṇa*) 424, 426–7
withdrawal (*nirveda* (Pāli *nibbidā*)) 519, 753n
Wordsworth, W. 470, 557, 759n, 768n
work 72–3, 266, 399–400; *see also* livelihood
world
degeneration of 691–2
end or limit of 384–5, 387
of form 464, 597; *see also rūpaloka*
formless 597, 727n; *see also arūpaloka*
protectors of (*lokapālas*) 557–8, 561
sensory 44, 97–9, 121–2, 712n; *see also kāmaloka*
worldlings (*pṛthaflanas*) 10–12, 777n
worlds 297–9, 609; *see also* realms
of Brahmā 185, 187, 189; *see also brahma vihāras*; realms, god
conditioned by mind 475–6, 479, 483–4
of dreams 340, 686–7
three (*dhātus* or *lokas*) 144, 145, 497, 498, 561, 607
worry (*kaukṛtya*) (Pāli *kukkucca*)) 37–8, 683, 688, 688–9, 701; *see also* anxiety, contrition, guilt
-and-anxiety (*uddhacca-kukkucca*) 120, 260
worship 183, 275–6, 417, 593, 640, 743n; *see also* devotional practice, puja
writing 262, 402

Xuanzang 453, 542, 551, 756–7n, 766n, 767n, 768n, 769n, 770n

yakṣas 147, 318, 741n
Yamarāja 317, 740n
yānas, three 546–7, 757n
Yogācāra 133, 449–53, 481–9, 492, 704–5, 756n, 760n, 770–1n
Abhidharma 449, 500, 641
lineage 449, 451–3, 463–4, 741n
origins 156, 325, 464
philosophy, *see* Mind Only
Yogācārabhūmi 449

Zen 64–7, 253, 331, 378, 390, 594, 612, 636, 653, 675, 716n, 717n, 728n, 749n, 775n
stories 73, 208, 279, 352, 718–19n, 735n, 739n

A GUIDE TO THE COMPLETE WORKS OF SANGHARAKSHITA

Gathered together in these twenty-seven volumes are talks and stories, commentaries on the Buddhist scriptures, poems, memoirs, reviews, and other writings. The genres are many, and the subject matter covered is wide, but it all has – its whole purpose is to convey – that taste of freedom which the Buddha declared to be the hallmark of his Dharma. Another traditional description of the Buddha's Dharma is that it is *ehipassiko*, 'come and see'. Sangharakshita calls to us, his readers, to come and see how the Dharma can fundamentally change the way we see things, change the way we live for the better, and change the society we belong to, wherever in the world we live.

Sangharakshita's very first published piece, *The Unity of Buddhism* (found in volume 7 of this collection), appeared in 1944 when he was eighteen years old, and it introduced themes that continued to resound throughout his work: the basis of Buddhist ethics, the compassion of the bodhisattva, and the transcendental unity of Buddhism. Over the course of the following seven decades not only did numerous other works flow from his pen; he gave hundreds of talks (some now lost). In gathering all we could find of this vast output, we have sought to arrange it in a way that brings a sense of coherence, communicating something essential about Sangharakshita, his life and teaching. Recalling the three 'baskets' among which an early tradition divided the Buddha's teachings, we have divided Sangharakshita's creative output into six 'baskets' or groups: foundation texts; works originating in India; teachings originally given in the West; commentaries on the Buddhist scriptures; personal writings; and poetry, aphorisms, and works on the arts. The 27th volume, a concordance, brings together all the terms and themes of the whole collection. If you want to find a particular story or teaching, look at a traditional term from different points of view or in different contexts, or track down one of the thousands of canonical references to be found in these volumes, the concordance will be your guide.

1. FOUNDATION

What is the foundation of a Buddhist life? How do we understand and then follow the Buddha's path of Ethics, Meditation, and Wisdom? What is really meant by 'Going for Refuge to the Three Jewels', described by Sangharakshita as the essential act of a Buddhist life? And what is the Bodhisattva ideal, which he has called 'one of the sublimest ideals mankind has ever seen'? In the 'Foundation' group you will find teachings on all these themes. It includes the author's *magnum opus, A Survey of Buddhism*, a collection of teachings on *The Purpose and Practice of Buddhist Meditation*, and the anthology, *The Essential Sangharakshita*, an eminently helpful distillation of the entire corpus.

2. INDIA

From 1950 to 1964 Sangharakshita, based in Kalimpong in the eastern Himalayas, poured his energy into trying to revive Buddhism in the land of its birth and to revitalize and bring reform to the existing Asian Buddhist world. The articles and book reviews from this period are gathered in volumes 7 and 8, as well as his biographical sketch of the great Sinhalese Dharmaduta, Anagārika Dharmapala. In 1954 Sangharakshita took on the editing of the *Maha Bodhi*, a journal for which he wrote a monthly editorial, and which, under his editorship, published the work of many of the leading Buddhist writers of the time. It was also during these years in India that a vital connection was forged with Dr B. R. Ambedkar, renowned Indian statesman and leader of the Buddhist mass conversion of 1956. Sangharakshita became closely involved with the new Buddhists and, after Dr Ambedkar's untimely death, visited them regularly on extensive teaching tours.

From 1979, when an Indian wing of the Triratna Buddhist Community was founded (then known as TBMSG), Sangharakshita returned several times to undertake further teaching tours. The talks from these tours are collected in volumes 9 and 10 along with a unique work on Ambedkar and his life which draws out the significance of his conversion to Buddhism.

3. THE WEST

Sangharakshita founded the Triratna Buddhist Community (then called the Friends of the Western Buddhist Order) on 6 April 1967. On 7 April the following year he performed the first ordinations of men and women within the Triratna Buddhist Order (then the Western Buddhist Order). At that time Buddhism was not widely known in the West and for the following two decades or so he taught intensively, finding new ways to communicate the ancient truths of Buddhism, drawing on the whole Buddhist tradition to do so, as well as making connections with what was best in existing Western culture. Sometimes his sword flashed as he critiqued ideas and views inimical to the Dharma. It is these teachings and writings that are gathered together in this third group.

4. COMMENTARY

Throughout Sangharakshita's works are threaded references to the Buddhist canon of literature – Pāli, Mahāyāna, and Vajrayāna – from which he drew his inspiration. In the early days of the new movement he often taught by means of seminars in which, prompted by the questions of his students, he sought to pass on the inspiration and wisdom of the Buddhist tradition. Each seminar was based around a different text, the seminars were recorded and transcribed, and in due course many of the transcriptions were edited and turned into books, all carefully checked by Sangharakshita. The commentaries compiled in this way constitute the fourth group. In some ways this is the heart of the collection. Sangharakshita often told the story of how it was that, reading two *sūtras* at the age of sixteen or seventeen, he realized that he was a Buddhist, and he has never tired of showing others how they too could see and realize the value of the '*sūtra*-treasure'.

5. MEMOIRS

Who is Sangharakshita? What sort of life did he live? Whom did he meet? What did he feel? Why did he found a new Buddhist movement? In these volumes of memoirs and letters Sangharakshita shares with his readers much about himself and his life as he himself has experienced it, giving us a sense of its breadth and depth, humour and pathos.

6. POETRY, APHORISMS, AND THE ARTS

Sangharakshita describes reading *Paradise Lost* at the age of twelve as one of the greatest poetic experiences of his life. His realization of the value of the higher arts to spiritual development is one of his distinctive contributions to our understanding of what Buddhist life is, and he has expressed it in a number of essays and articles. Throughout his life he has written poetry which he says can be regarded as a kind of spiritual autobiography. It is here, perhaps, that we come closest to the heart of Sangharakshita. He has also written a few short stories and composed some startling aphorisms. Through book reviews he has engaged with the experiences, ideas, and opinions of modern writers. All these are collected in this sixth group.

In the preface to *A Survey of Buddhism* (volume 1 in this collection), Sangharakshita wrote of his approach to the Buddha's teachings:

> Why did the Buddha (or Nāgārjuna, or Buddhaghosa) teach this particular doctrine? What bearing does it have on the spiritual life? How does it help the individual Buddhist actually to follow the spiritual path?... I found myself asking such questions again and again, for only in this way, I found, could I make sense – spiritual sense – of Buddhism.

Although this collection contains so many words, they are all intent, directly or indirectly, on these same questions. And all these words are not in the end about their writer, but about his great subject, the Buddha and his teaching, and about you, the reader, for whose benefit they are solely intended. These pages are full of the reverence that Sangharakshita has always felt, which is expressed in an early poem, 'Taking Refuge in the Buddha', whose refrain is 'My place is at thy feet'. He has devoted his life to communicating the Buddha's Dharma in its depth and in its breadth, to men and women from all backgrounds and walks of life, from all countries, of all races, of all ages. These collected works are the fruit of that devotion.

We are very pleased to be able to include some previously unpublished work in this collection, but most of what appears in these volumes has been published before. We have made very few changes, though we have added extra notes where we thought they would be useful. We have had the pleasure of researching the notes in the Sangharakshita Library at 'Adhisthana', Triratna's centre in Herefordshire, UK, which houses his own collection of books. It has been of great value to be able to search among the very copies of the *suttas*, *sūtras* and commentaries that have provided the basis of his teachings over the last seventy years.

The publication of these volumes owes much to the work of transcribers, editors, indexers, designers, and publishers over many years – those who brought out the original editions of many of the works included here, and those who have contributed in all sorts of ways to this *Complete Works* project, including all those who contributed to funds given in celebration of Sangharakshita's ninetieth birthday in August 2015, and to a further outpouring of generosity after Sangharakshita's death in October 2018. All these donors have made the publication of this series possible, and we are very grateful. Many thanks to everyone who has helped; may the merit gained in our acting thus go to the alleviation of the suffering of all beings.

Vidyadevi and Kalyanaprabha
Editors

THE COMPLETE WORKS OF SANGHARAKSHITA

I FOUNDATION

VOLUME 1 A SURVEY OF BUDDHISM / THE BUDDHA'S NOBLE EIGHTFOLD PATH
A Survey of Buddhism
The Buddha's Noble Eightfold Path

2 THE THREE JEWELS I
The Three Jewels
The Meaning of Conversion in Buddhism
Going for Refuge
The Ten Pillars of Buddhism
The History of My Going for Refuge
My Relation to the Order
Extending the Hand of Fellowship
Forty-Three Years Ago
Was the Buddha a Bhikkhu?

3 THE THREE JEWELS II
Who is the Buddha?
What is the Dharma?
What is the Sangha?

4 THE BODHISATTVA IDEAL
The Bodhisattva Ideal
The Endlessly Fascinating Cry (seminar)
The Bodhisattva Principle

5 THE PURPOSE AND PRACTICE OF BUDDHIST MEDITATION
The Purpose and Practice of Buddhist Meditation

6 THE ESSENTIAL SANGHARAKSHITA
The Essential Sangharakshita

II INDIA

7 CROSSING THE STREAM: INDIA WRITINGS I
Early Writings 1944–1954
Crossing the Stream
A Sense of Direction

VOLUME 8 BEATING THE DHARMA DRUM: INDIA WRITINGS II
Anagarika Dharmapala and Other 'Maha Bodhi' Writings
Dharmapala: The Spiritual Dimension
Beating the Drum: 'Maha Bodhi' Editorials
Alternative Traditions

9 DR AMBEDKAR AND THE REVIVAL OF BUDDHISM I
Ambedkar and Buddhism
Lecture Tour in India, December 1981–March 1982

10 DR AMBEDKAR AND THE REVIVAL OF BUDDHISM II
Remembering Ambedkar
Buddha and the Future of His Religion
The Mass Conversion and the Years After, 1956–61
Lectures in India and England 1979, 1982–92
Wisdom before Words: The Udāna

III THE WEST

11 A NEW BUDDHIST MOVEMENT I
Ritual and Devotion in Buddhism
The Buddha's Victory
The Taste of Freedom
Buddha Mind
Human Enlightenment
New Currents in Western Buddhism
Buddhism for Today – and Tomorrow
Buddhism and the West
Aspects of Buddhist Morality
Dialogue between Buddhism and Christianity
Buddhism and Blasphemy
Articles and Interviews

12 A NEW BUDDHIST MOVEMENT II
Previously unpublished talks

13 EASTERN AND WESTERN TRADITIONS
Tibetan Buddhism
Creative Symbols of Tantric Buddhism
The Essence of Zen
The FWBO *and 'Protestant Buddhism'*
From Genesis to the Diamond Sūtra

IV COMMENTARY

VOLUME 14 THE ETERNAL LEGACY / WISDOM BEYOND WORDS
The Eternal Legacy
The Glory of the Literary World
Wisdom Beyond Words

15 PĀLI CANON TEACHINGS AND TRANSLATIONS
Dhammapada (translation)
Karaṇīyamettā Sutta (translation)
Living with Kindness
Living with Awareness
Maṅgala Sutta (translation)
Auspicious Signs (seminar)
Salutation to the Three Jewels (translation)
The Threefold Refuge (seminar)

16 MAHĀYĀNA MYTHS AND STORIES
The Drama of Cosmic Enlightenment
The Priceless Jewel (talk)
Transforming Self and World
The Inconceivable Emancipation

17 WISDOM TEACHINGS OF THE MAHĀYĀNA
Know Your Mind
Living Ethically
Living Wisely
The Way to Wisdom (seminar)

18 MILAREPA AND THE ART OF DISCIPLESHIP I
The Yogi's Joy
The Shepherd's Search for Mind
Rechungpa's Journey to Enlightenment

19 MILAREPA AND THE ART OF DISCIPLESHIP II
Rechungpa's Journey to Enlightenment, continued

V MEMOIRS

20 THE RAINBOW ROAD FROM TOOTING BROADWAY TO KALIMPONG
The Rainbow Road from Tooting Broadway to Kalimpong

VOLUME 21 FACING MOUNT KANCHENJUNGA
Facing Mount Kanchenjunga
Dear Dinoo: Letters to a Friend

22 IN THE SIGN OF THE GOLDEN WHEEL
In the Sign of the Golden Wheel
Precious Teachers
With Allen Ginsberg in Kalimpong (essay)

23 MOVING AGAINST THE STREAM
Moving Against the Stream
1970 – A Retrospect

24 THROUGH BUDDHIST EYES
Travel Letters
Through Buddhist Eyes

VI POETRY AND THE ARTS

25 POEMS AND SHORT STORIES
Complete Poems 1941–1994
Other Poems
Short Stories

26 APHORISMS, THE ARTS, AND LATE WRITINGS
Sayings, Poems, Reflections
Peace is a Fire
A Stream of Stars
The Religion of Art
In the Realm of the Lotus
The Journey to Il Convento
St Jerome Revisited
A Note on The Burial of Count Orgaz
Criticism East and West
Buddhism and William Blake
Urthona Interviews
Madhyamaloka Reflections
Adhisthana Writings

27 CONCORDANCE AND APPENDICES

WINDHORSE PUBLICATIONS

Windhorse Publications is a Buddhist charitable company based in the UK. We produce books of high quality that are accessible and relevant to all those interested in Buddhism, at whatever level of interest and commitment. We are the main publisher of Sangharakshita, the founder of the Triratna Buddhist Order and Community. Our books draw on the whole range of the Buddhist tradition, including translations of traditional texts, commentaries, books that make links with contemporary culture and ways of life, biographies of Buddhists, and works on meditation.

To subscribe to the *Complete Works of Sangharakshita,* please go to: windhorsepublications.com/sangharakshita-complete-works/

THE TRIRATNA BUDDHIST COMMUNITY

Windhorse Publications is a part of the Triratna Buddhist Community, an international movement with centres in Europe, India, North and South America and Australasia. At these centres, members of the Triratna Buddhist Order offer classes in meditation and Buddhism. Activities of the Triratna Community also include retreat centres, residential spiritual communities, ethical Right Livelihood businesses, and the Karuna Trust, a UK fundraising charity that supports social welfare projects in the slums and villages of India.

Through these and other activities, Triratna is developing a unique approach to Buddhism, not simply as a philosophy and a set of techniques, but as a creatively directed way of life for all people living in the conditions of the modern world.

For more information please visit thebuddhistcentre.com

SANGHARAKSHITA.ORG

You can find out more about Sangharakshita's life, teachings, and the Buddhist movement he founded on his official website: sangharakshita.org